Crime and Criminal Justice
in American Society

Crime and Criminal Justice in American Society

Randall G. Shelden
University of Nevada–Las Vegas

William B. Brown
Western Oregon University

Karen S. Miller
Glenville State College

Randal B. Fritzler
Western Oregon University

WAVELAND

PRESS, INC.

Long Grove, Illinois

For information about this book, contact:
Waveland Press, Inc.
4180 IL Route 83, Suite 101
Long Grove, IL 60047-9580
(847) 634-0081
info@waveland.com
www.waveland.com

10-digit ISBN 1-57766-478-7
13-digit ISBN 978-1-57766-478-9

Printed in the United States of America

7   6   5   4   3   2   1

This book is dedicated to Jim Russell
(a 1970 Kent State Survivor)
who died July 2007

Jim Russell was a wonderful friend, father, and husband. He survived the attack on dissent at Kent State in 1970 when the National Guard killed four students and wounded nine. I introduced him to his future wife Nelda and encouraged him to move to Oregon to take some time to heal. After coming to grips with the trauma, we began speaking to students in the spring of each year. Jim was always gentle but passionate when we told our story. He lived his life fully and was involved in many activities—some political, some personal, and some professional. He had an Easter brunch every year and organized lunch with his co-workers regularly. He was my blood brother and my closest friend. I will always remember his coy smile and his playful attitude.

Peace, Jim, and love.

Your friend,

Joe Lewis

About the Authors

Randall G. Shelden is Professor of Criminal Justice, University of Nevada–Las Vegas, where he has been a faculty member since 1977. He is also a senior research fellow with the Center on Juvenile and Criminal Justice in San Francisco. He received his master's degree in sociology at Memphis State University and PhD in sociology at Southern Illinois University. He is the author or co-author of the following books: *Criminal Justice in America: A Sociological Approach*; *Girls, Delinquency and Juvenile Justice* (third edition) with Meda Chesney-Lind (which received the *Hindelang Award* for outstanding contribution to Criminology in 1992); *Youth Gangs in American Society* (third edition) with Sharon Tracy and William B. Brown; *Controlling the Dangerous Classes: The History of Criminal Justice* (second edition); *Delinquency and Juvenile Justice in American Society* (Waveland Press); *Juvenile Justice in America: Problems and Prospects* (Waveland Press, co-edited with Daniel Macallair). He is currently in the middle stages of books about punishment and the crime control industry. He is also the author of more than 50 journal articles and book chapters on the subject of crime and justice. He has written more than 100 commentaries appearing in local and regional newspapers. His Web site is: www.sheldensays.com.

William B. Brown is an Associate Professor of Criminal Justice, Western Oregon University, where he has been a faculty member since 2002. He is also the research director for both the Pacific Policy and Research Institute and the Pacific Sentencing Initiative. He received a bachelor's degree in social work at the University of Nevada–Las Vegas, and a master's degree and PhD in sociology at the University of Nevada–Las Vegas. He is an author of *Youth Gangs in American Society* (third edition) and *The American Jail* (forthcoming, Waveland Press). He has authored or co-authored articles focusing on youth gangs, African-American families with gang-affiliated children, girls and gangs, jail overcrowding, recidivism, and the criminal justice industrial complex. He has also published articles that focus on parents in jail, generational criminogenics, methamphetamine abuse, mental illness, homelessness, re-entry, and veterans of the Iraq and Vietnam Wars. He has also conducted ethnographic research in Nicaragua, Cambodia, and Vietnam with a focus on U.S. interventions and human rights. He was an invited lecturer at the University of Warsaw (Poland) and Open University (Vietnam). His current research focuses on problems confronting veterans returning from the current Iraq War.

Karen S. Miller is an Assistant Professor of Criminal Justice at Glenville State College in West Virginia. She received a master's degree in criminal justice from Eastern Kentucky University and a PhD in sociology from the University of Kentucky. She is the author of *Wrongful Capital Convictions and the Legitimacy of the Death Penalty.* Her work has focused on innocence cases and the intersection of race and class as they relate to capital prosecutions, sentencing, and executions. She has also published in the areas of juvenile justice, white-collar crime, and reproductive privacy.

Randal B. Fritzler began a private litigation practice in 1974. He was elected to the Clark County, Washington, District Court bench in November 1986. In 1997, he began organizing the Clark County Domestic Violence Court and was honored as the "Outstanding Judge of 1998" by the Washington State Misdemeanant Corrections Association. He founded the Clark County Mental Health court; in 1999 he was selected to chair the American Judges Association Therapeutic Jurisprudence Committee and represented the AJA to the Council of Chief Justices. He has contributed to several books and published articles and commentaries on "problem-solving courts" in five countries. He is an advocate for court-adopted dynamic risk-management processes to increase public safety while reducing the use of prisons and jails. Fritzler has recently left the bench and has resumed private law practice. He is a founder and principal of Pacific Policy and Research Institute, Inc., teaches at Western Oregon University, and consults on court reform issues.

Contents

Preface

In this text we are offering an alternative interpretation of criminal justice that is rarely presented either in traditional textbooks or in the media. It is normal that whenever one focuses on any public issue there are many emotions and points of view involved. The problem of crime touches many lives and is the subject of many heated debates, especially around election time. When writing about crime and criminal justice, it is impossible to be purely objective. Even if we merely presented facts, some subjectivity and some values enter the picture; facts rarely speak for themselves. In a world filled with an endless variety of facts, not every one of these facts can be selected and placed into a text—or any piece of writing. Many facts are often conveniently omitted (sometimes by accident, sometimes through carelessness, sometimes on purpose).

We should make clear that what we are presenting in this book is not the only possible view of the subject. There is no rigidly defined correct way of interpreting anything in life. There is no right or wrong way of interpreting a poem, a painting, a photograph, a movie, or any work of art. In fact, there is no correct way to view or interpret an individual human being.

Our purpose in writing this book is to present an alternative interpretation of the criminal justice system. To present every possible interpretation would take literally several thousand pages (and no student would want that). We do offer a few interpretations that differ from our own. However, the overall thrust of the book is, as you will soon realize, very critical and quite at variance with what one normally receives in standard texts, in the media, from politicians, and from criminal justice officials. Whether each person who reads this agrees with our interpretation is irrelevant. All we expect from you, the reader, is that you try to understand this interpretation, then read the interpretations of others (and we give numerous references to other views), and then come to your own conclusion and act accordingly.

As an example, we refer to *Bury My Heart at Wounded Knee*. This book was written about thirty years ago by Dee Brown, a Native American.[1] In this book he made clear his bias. He said that traditional American history was written "looking westward." His book was written from the perspective of "looking eastward." Think about that for a moment. Most historical books were written from the point of view of those coming from a western direction, namely the Europeans who set out to conquer the west and in the process decimated most of the Native American population. But, Brown asked, what did this history look like from the point of view of those who already lived here? Obviously this view was quite different. But which interpretation is the correct one? Both are correct. They are different. Each is a view on the same events and covers the same period. It is just that each side sees things differently. We are certain that American history is also viewed differently by women and men, by African Americans and Mexican Americans and whites, by the rich and by the poor. Likewise, crime and criminal justice can be seen from different perspectives. For example, recall the different interpretations of the O. J. Simpson case.

Many will notice that we express a great deal of anger and passion throughout this book. We are angered about what we perceive to be gross injustices in this country and passionate about writing and talking about them and about wanting to do something. We cannot and will not hide our anger and passion behind the so-called objectivity of the social sciences. We are all humanists at heart and are proud of it. While all of us have a vested interest in the system of justice under which we live, it's easy to become complacent. We might think that as law-abiding citizens, we are far removed from the criminal justice system. Perhaps we don't feel any connection to people whose life circumstances differ radically from ours.

The chapters in the text emphasize that the poor and minority groups are the most likely to be caught in the net of criminal justice. For example, Angela Davis, a law professor at American University, previously worked as a public defender in Washington, DC. One client was a Jamaican immigrant accused of rape. He had no criminal record and declared he was innocent but was jailed because he could not afford bail. The case was weak, and the defender asked the prosecutor to release her client. He refused, saying he had nine months to get an indictment. At the end of the nine months, the case was dismissed for lack of evidence. The prosecutor's reaction? "I know he's guilty. At least he did nine months in jail."[2] Davis was outraged at the power and arrogance of the prosecutor and worked to expose that power through the media and in a book, *Arbitrary Justice.*[3] Her attempts to demonstrate the power prosecutors have and the potential for abuse were helped by another example of injustice.

In March 2006, three Duke University lacrosse team members were charged with rape. On April 11, 2007, all charges were dropped and the case dismissed—but not before the reputations of three young men had been destroyed by the national media. The case "offers a chilling portrait of how the criminal justice system can nail and punish the innocent."[4] The case inverted the much more frequent situation in which the innocent are poor people without any connections or resources to defend themselves. In this case, the racial and socioeconomic factors were reversed. The defendants were white male students at a prestigious private university accused by a poor black stripper. Clarence Page, a columnist for the *Chicago Tribune*, noted that the confluence of circumstances:

> excited passions in a different ideological direction. Left-progressive activists, pundits and intellectuals allied with the prosecutor to steamroll over any presumption of the boys' innocence. For some petitioners and op-ed writers, the young jocks provided too convenient a target as symbols of white male hegemony, runaway testosterone and every other agenda that could be hung on them like tree ornaments.[5]

To be reelected as prosecutor, Mike Nifong needed votes from a district in which 40% of the population was black. His prosecutorial misconduct was astounding for its flagrant procedural abuses, including withholding DNA evidence for nine months that proved the innocence of the defendants. Page faults the media and academia for not fulfilling their responsibilities.

> Think about it. If any institutions should be engaged in the critical reasoning that it takes to analyze situations like these, weighing claims and counterclaims, and sorting out facts from rumors, it is the media and college professors. The university, of all places, should teach not only good ideas but also the rational thinking that leads one to a lifetime of producing good ideas.

Reade Seligmann, one of the falsely accused, commented: "This entire experience has opened my eyes up to a tragic world of injustice I never knew existed." Page summarized the case and issued solid advice to avoid repeating the errors:

> He and his teammates were fortunate to have the resources to fight back. Most defendants don't. That's all the more reason for those of us who believe in justice to scrupulously avoid pursuing personal agendas at the expense of the truth, no matter how much it may satisfy our preconceived notions.

Perhaps you are wondering how one person can make a difference against years of tradition and power. Anna Quindlen wrote about the thirty-year anniversary of the National Women's Conference in Houston in 1977. It was the first meeting of its kind since the 1848 gathering in Seneca Falls, which discussed the social and civil rights of women. According to Quindlen, the Houston conference "obliterated the two walls that have always divided women and made them blame themselves for their own lack of status: isolation and silence." She also noted that at political conventions, the primary action takes place in the skyboxes where the big money and consultants work out deals and questioned whether the point of women's political leadership was to get to the skyboxes themselves—before reaching the opposite conclusion.

> But maybe the key to real leadership is no skyboxes at all. After Houston I found the political conventions artificial and disappointing, with most of the action taking place among the few at a remove from the many. It takes a special kind of confidence to do it the other way, to wrestle democracy to the ground out in the open, with all voices heard.[6]

We hope the discussions in the text prompt you to examine why you believe what you believe about crime and punishment—to discover new insights and to expand your perspective beyond the beliefs you have accepted to this point. We hope that those who read this text will also be angered and passionate and take some appropriate action to correct the problem. Regardless of whether you agree or disagree with some of the ideas presented in this text, we hope they will encourage you to think about the issues and discuss them. Potential solutions to difficult problems require awareness of multiple perspectives, careful analysis, and a willingness to take action.

Acknowledgements

Each of us owes a special thanks and gratitude to Carol and Neil Rowe at Waveland Press who gave us another chance to extend the life of this book. Carol was especially supportive along the way, inserting her own passion about the subject matter with helpful suggestions.

Finally, we all owe a special thanks to the people closest to us in our daily lives. Shelden sends his love and thanks to his wife, Virginia, and stepdaughter Marcie. Special thanks is extended to several fellow academics who have helped shape his view of the world and whose works are cited throughout this book, especially Richard Quinney, Noam Chomsky, and Meda Chesney-Lind. He also extends his gratitude to colleagues and graduate students (especially Magann Jordan, Michael Small, Jeff Groebner, and Violet Colavito) at UNLV.

Brown gives thanks and love to his wife Judy. Brown also extends a special thanks to Bernadette Olson, who provided a unique insight into the meaning of humanity; Raul Ramirez, former Sheriff of Marion County, Oregon, who demonstrates that understanding and compassion is a mandatory and crucial component of progressive law enforcement; and Brian Kauffman, who provides a realistic prescription for community policing. Finally, he is indebted to Joe Lewis and Jim Russell, who were both victims of the Kent State shootings in May 1970. Joe Lewis provides a unique approach and perception to the concepts of humanity and justice in chapter five. Jim consistently maintained a positive outlook on life and continued to participate in the struggle to further the ideals of peace and justice, which had always helped him to continue forward. Sadly, Jim Russell recently died of a heart attack at his Deer Island, Oregon, home. Jim Russell inspired all of Brown's contributions to this book.

Karen Miller gives her love and thanks to her partner Matthew Greene.

Fritzler would like to acknowledge his wife Barbara, who is always there no matter what happens in life, and Bruce Winick and David Wexler, who opened his eyes to the possibility of a new court system for the twenty-first century.

Notes

1 Brown, D. *Bury My Heart at Wounded Knee.* New York: Holt, Rinehart and Winston, 1971.

2 Holding, R. "Power Outrage." *Time* (August 6, 2007) p. 51.

3 Davis, A. *Arbitrary Justice: The Power of the American Prosecutor.* New York: Oxford University Press, 2007.

4 Page, C. "What the Duke Lacrosse Case Has Taught Us." *Chicago Tribune* (September 9, 2007) p. 7.

5 Ibid.

6 Quindlen, A. "Out of the Skyboxes." *Newsweek* (October 15, 2007) p. 90.

one

An Overview of the Criminal Justice System

On April 19, 1989, a group of approximately 40 boys gathered for an evening of "wilding" in New York's Central Park.[1] They harassed passersby, beat one man and doused him with beer, stomped and kicked another, and groped a female bicyclist. After seeing a police officer, the boys split into smaller groups. Five of the boys were eventually arrested and confessed to brutally beating and raping a 28-year-old jogger. The victim almost died, faced many months of rehabilitative therapy, and suffered amnesia. The case received national media attention. Within a year, the boys were tried, convicted, and sentenced to prison. Thirteen years later, DNA tests and the confession of a known rapist and murderer resulted in the convictions being overturned. They had not, in fact, committed or participated in the attack. The exonerations raised questions about the New York City Police Department's handling of the investigation, including the possibility of coerced confessions and the role of racism.[2]

The Central Park Jogger case illustrates many of the issues encountered in an exploration of the criminal justice system: crime, a victim, defendants, police, courts, and corrections. It also raises the issues of technology and evolving investigatory techniques, wrongful convictions, juvenile delinquency, the roles of race and poverty, and the public's fascination with violent crime. Most importantly, this case exemplifies the fact that cursory examinations can lead to faulty interpretations. To fully understand the U.S.

system of criminal justice, it is necessary to do more than scratch the surface.

Americans are fascinated by crime, especially violent crime. We are both fearful of and titillated by violence. We have watched in fascination as many "celebrated" cases unfold. For example, millions watched as O. J. Simpson was acquitted of double murder charges. The nation was shocked by the arrest of Dennis Rader, a local church leader, for the serial murders known as BTK (Bind–Torture–Kill). We were saddened by and collectively continue to hope for justice in the murder of six-year-old JonBenet Ramsey. The nation watched as Andrea Yates was arrested for the murders of her five young children. We continued to watch as she was convicted, retried, and found not guilty by reason of insanity.

Fictional accounts of crime and criminal trials are consistently on best-seller lists and are among the highest grossing movies. Millions of Americans watch television crime dramas regularly. *CSI, Cops, Law & Order,* and *Cold Case* are consistently very highly rated television shows. The popularity of books, movies, and television dramas about crime illustrate people's fascination with the subject, particularly violent crime.

The picture of the U.S. criminal justice system presented by both the news and entertainment media is grossly distorted. Celebrated cases are highly unusual and completely atypical examples of the daily operation of the criminal justice system. While gory headlines capture public atten-

1

tion, literally millions of routine cases are quickly processed rather unceremoniously through the various stages of the criminal justice system. Media overreporting of violent crimes increases the public's concern about and fear of crime.

The *criminal justice system* is a formal mechanism of social control. In theory, it is designed to prevent crime, enforce laws, and mete out justice. The three components of the system are: law enforcement, courts, and corrections. In the United States, the activities of the organizations within each component must perform duties that fit into the framework of laws and procedures that protect individual rights. It is something of a misnomer to refer to the criminal justice "system"; it could more accurately be called a "loosely articulated hierarchy of subsystems."[3]

You probably already have some ideas about the criminal justice system. You have seen police cars driving around; you may even have been stopped for speeding. Perhaps you visited a courthouse or toured a correctional facility. You may have helped a friend post bail or visited a juvenile court during your high school days. In all likelihood you probably have formed some impressions from your experiences and/or the experiences of your friends and family. Watching the fictional portrayals on television or movies could also have affected your perceptions. As you may suspect, there are many complex issues attached to each element of the system and its subsystems. Understanding the U.S. criminal justice system requires taking a journey, with many detours along the way. The point of departure is the Constitution.

THE CONSTITUTIONAL BASIS OF THE CRIMINAL JUSTICE SYSTEM

The ultimate source of authority for our criminal justice system is the United States Constitution, which provides the foundation for the creation of *laws*, or "formal statements of authority that are exercised by the state."[4]

The Constitution outlined three separate branches of government designed to operate independently. The separation of powers works as a source of checks and balances on governmental power and authority. The *legislative branch* is where laws are written, defining what behaviors are prohibited as well as the appropriate punishments. The bulk of criminal acts are violations of state and local laws. Without criminal law (discussed more thoroughly in chapter 3), there would be no purpose for a criminal justice system, which in the United States is more precisely described as a dual justice system. We have state and federal legislatures, state and federal law enforcement systems, state and federal courts, and state and federal prison systems.

The *judicial branch* includes the U.S. Supreme Court, state supreme courts, and various appellate courts. This branch interprets laws and determines whether or not they meet the requirements of the Constitution. The *executive branch* is comprised of public officials such as presidents, governors, mayors, etc. These officials determine and implement official responses to new laws. They determine the agencies and personnel who will be responsible for enforcing laws. The police fall under the administrative control of this branch.

Executive branch officials and the courts are given authority, through provisions in the Constitution, to enforce and/or interpret laws. Those provisions are founded on the principles of security for individuals and for the nation as a whole. The criminal justice system is the *instrument* designated by executive branch officials to enforce laws that pertain to criminal behavior. The criminal justice system is the apparatus used to enforce the standards of conduct, reflected in criminal law, established by a legislative body for a given society.

Thumbnail Sketch of the Criminal Justice System

The criminal justice system is very complex. It is much more than simply *making an arrest, taking the defendant to court, and sentencing her or him to prison or probation*. Each subsequent chapter will explore the components of the system in much more detail. For now, we will briefly explore the system's major components.

The Police

There are roughly 20,000 police departments, ranging from small town departments of one officer to large urban departments with 1,000 or more officers. As of March, 2003, there were more than 1 million law enforcement employees with a monthly payroll of more than $4 billion.[5] The federal law enforcement system includes such well-known agencies as the FBI, National Park Service, Border Patrol, U.S. Marshals Service, U.S. Postal Inspector, and many more. Law enforcement on the state level includes the state police or highway patrol, drug control agencies, fish and game control agencies, investigative bureaus (the state equivalent of the FBI), and others. County and municipal police agencies are by far the largest law enforcement group. These agencies include city police, county sheriff's offices, constables, and village police departments.

The police engage in a wide variety of duties, many of which do not relate directly to the control of crime. The essential role of the police officer is both *proactive* and *reactive*. Proactive duties include routine patrol in communities to identify potential criminal activities and to maintain order. Reactive duties take place after a crime has occurred. Typical activities include arriving at the scene of the incident, interviewing witnesses, collecting evidence, attempting to locate and/or identify a suspect, making the arrest, and transporting the suspect to the local jail. Police officers often testify at various pretrial hearings and trials.

The Courts

In the United States there are two major court systems: federal and state. Within each system there are two general types of courts: trial and appellate, which make up the *dual court system*. Trial courts hear cases and decide on guilt or innocence. Parties convicted at trial can appeal the decision to an appellate court. The primary function of the appellate court is to review the original trial to make sure it correctly interpreted applicable law.[6] In essence, the appellate courts police the behavior of the trial courts. The decision is made by a group of judges; there are no witnesses and no jury. Appellate judges generally provide a written opinion (unlike trial court judges), which can then become a precedent for future cases.

The bulk of criminal and civil cases in the United States come before the state court system. Most criminal cases are heard in *trial courts of limited jurisdiction,* or what are more commonly known as *lower* or *inferior* courts. These courts are variously known as municipal, justice of the peace, city, magistrate, or county courts. They are usually created by local governments, either at the city or county levels, and are not part of the larger state court system. These lower courts handle misdemeanor offenses, traffic cases, city ordinance cases, and minor civil disputes. They are also responsible for initial appearances and preliminary hearings in felony cases. They account for the largest number of courts, roughly 14,000, and collectively represent 84% of all state judicial bodies. Cases in *lower courts* are heard in a rather perfunctory manner and often take as little as one minute, leading to the metaphor "assembly line justice."

The Prison System

The prison system consists of a vast array of institutions designed to supervise and control convicted persons. Jails and prisons are two major institutions within the prison system. The primary difference is that jails house inmates for shorter periods of time. About half of jail inmates are awaiting a court appearance or trial, and the other half are serving sentences of less than one year. Prisons house those serving sentences of one year or more. In some instances, and generally for logistical or economic reasons, some convicted persons do much of their prison sentence in jails due to overcrowded prison facilities. There are now more than 1,700 prisons and more than 3,300 jails.[7] Prisons and jails are the most recognizable components of the correctional system, which also includes probation and parole.

Probation is the result of a court action. The court *suspends* the sentence to jail or prison for a certain period of time. During the court-prescribed time of probation, a probation officer supervises the defendant in the community. As long as the defendant complies with the rules set forth by the court, he or she will not be incarcerated.

Parole is a *post-prison* status, a prison administrative action that follows a period of incarceration. The paroled individual is released prior to the expiration of a sentence and serves the remaining time under the supervision of a *parole officer*. In some jurisdictions, probationers and parolees report to the same caseworker, who is responsible for supervising and controlling their behavior.

This very brief overview introduced some of the components of a very complicated system. Two models are frequently used to illustrate what takes place in the criminal justice system.

MODELS OF THE CRIMINAL JUSTICE SYSTEM

The President's Commission Model

More than thirty years ago the President's Commission on Law and Administration of Justice provided perhaps the most famous depiction of the criminal justice system. Figure 1.1 (on pp. 6–7) shows the sequential stages of the decision-making process. The steps below summarize the stages of the system.

1. **Investigation**. An investigation begins when a crime is reported to or discovered by police. Importantly, police do not witness most crimes; instead, they depend on members of the public to report infractions. Investigation involves collecting physical evidence as well as interviewing witnesses and possible suspects.

2. **Arrest**. When evidence indicates that a certain person was responsible for an offense the police take the suspect into custody.

3. **Booking (record of the arrest)**. The suspect is fingerprinted, photographed, and questioned.

4. **Charging**. This marks the entrance of the prosecutor, who determines there is probable cause for the arrest—if it is reasonable to believe that an offense was committed and that the defendant committed it.

5. **Initial Appearance**. Within a few hours of the defendant's arrest, he or she is taken before a judge. The judge advises the defendant of his/her rights, gives formal notice of charges, appoints counsel if necessary, and determines if the defendant is eligible for pretrial release. If so, bail is set.

6. **Preliminary Hearing/Grand Jury**. In about half the states, preliminary hearings are formal proceedings during which a judge determines whether or not there is probable cause that the defendant should be subject to a criminal trial. Other states use a grand jury system for the same purpose.

7. **Information/Indictment**. The formal charging document prepared by the prosecutor outlines the specific charges. Indictment is the term used when a grand jury charges a defendant with a specific crime.

8. **Arraignment**. An arraignment is a court proceeding during which the information or indictment is read to the defendant in open court. The defendant may enter a plea. Most defendants plead guilty and accept a prearranged plea bargain. It is very rare that a case proceeds to trial.

9. **Trial**. Less than 15% of cases reach this point. Trials are adversarial processes during which the prosecution and defense try to convince a judge or jury that their version of events is true. The state holds the burden of proof and must convince the judge or jury of the defendant's guilt beyond a reasonable doubt.

10. **Sentencing**. When a defendant pleads or is found guilty the judge hands down a formal sentence. Sentencing guidelines exist, but judges have some discretion depending on how the laws are written.

Sanctions can include: probation, incarceration, fines, and community service.

11. **Appeal**. This option is available to defendants who are found guilty. Appeals are filed before review courts and generally claim that the trial court did not follow proper procedure and/or that the defendant's constitutional rights were violated.

12. **Corrections**. The correctional system (probation, intermediate sanctions such as community service, jails, prisons) is charged with carrying out the sentence.

13. **Release**. When the defendant has completed the sentence, he or she is released. If released early (parole), the defendant continues under the supervision of the system and must comply with rules or risk being incarcerated for the remainder of the sentence.

The model provides a framework that identifies general patterns and implies interrelationships among the components as cases flow through the system. It suggests an efficient, single system in which all cases are processed in the same manner.[8] It is both a description of how the system is supposed to work and a prescription for how it can be improved. Often the system is fragmented—perhaps more nearly a nonsystem with little coordination among the different parts. Efficiency and cost-effectiveness often dictate outcomes rather than justice.

The social context of the system—how and why cases move through the system the way they do—is missing from the model. There are no depictions of the roles played by race, gender, and social class at the various stages. Most importantly, it ignores one very crucial stage that precedes all others: the legislation that defines what behaviors are regarded as criminal.

The "Wedding Cake" Model

Samuel Walker discusses the *wedding cake model* of criminal justice, originally developed in 1981 by Lawrence Friedman and Robert Percival in their book, *The Roots of Justice.*[9] The model emphasizes that the

system handles different kinds of cases differently; it depicts four layers or tiers of cases.

The top and smallest layer consists of the small number of celebrated cases. Two types of cases fall in this category. The first group includes rich and famous defendants or rich and famous victims. The trials of O. J. Simpson, Susan Smith, Jeffrey Dahmer, Timothy McVeigh, and the Menendez brothers fit into this category. Also included would be various examples of white collar or corporate crime such as the Martha Stewart, Enron, or Tyco cases. The second group includes defendants at the lowest end of the class system whose cases become landmark Supreme Court decisions, such as Dolree Mapp (*Mapp v. Ohio*), Ernesto Miranda (*Miranda v. Arizona*), and Gerald Gault (*In re Gault*). There are a very small number of cases at this level, but they capture public attention and have enormous impact on public perceptions of how the criminal justice system works. In reality, this layer could be described as the frosting on a very different cake.

The original model put all felony cases in one category. As Walker notes, Michael and Don Gottfredson refined the model in 1988 in their book *Decision Making in Criminal Justice* by dividing felonies into two tiers.[10] The second layer consists of "heavy-

Figure 1.1   The President's Commission Model of Criminal Justice

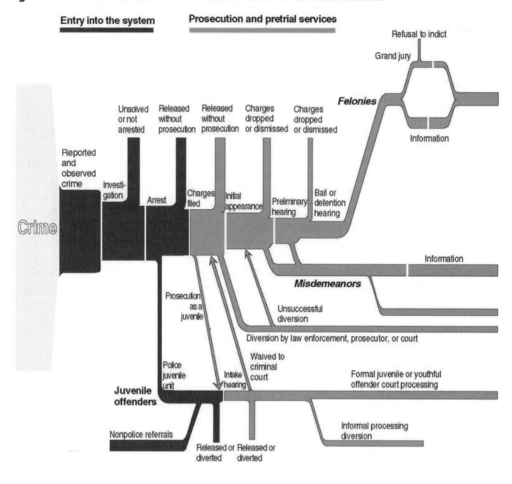

duty," serious felonies. These cases are violent crimes committed by defendants with long criminal histories. Most importantly, the victims are unknown to the defendant.

The third layer involves what many lawyers call "lightweight" felonies. Although the crimes may be identical to those in the second layer, the prosecutor decides they are less serious, often because the defendant has no prior convictions or because of the relationship between the victim and defendant. If a prosecutor believes that the particular crime was a dispute among acquaintances, the felony will be treated as more ordinary than "real" crime, where the perpetrator is a stranger to the victim. Many rape cases and serious cases of spousal abuse are deemed

third-layer felonies because the victims and offenders know one another.[11]

Walker describes the fourth layer as "a world unto itself."[12] These cases fill the lower courts. Millions of misdemeanor cases are handled by the criminal justice system each year. The bulk of the cases are public-order violations, such as drunkenness, disorderly conduct, or minor thefts like shoplifting. As mentioned earlier, the metaphor of "assembly-line justice" is frequently applied to the procedures of these courts. Many defendants are arraigned *en masse* without the assistance of a lawyer, and each case is disposed of in a manner of minutes. The usual sentence is a light fine; jail time is rare. Malcolm Feeley entitled his book about the

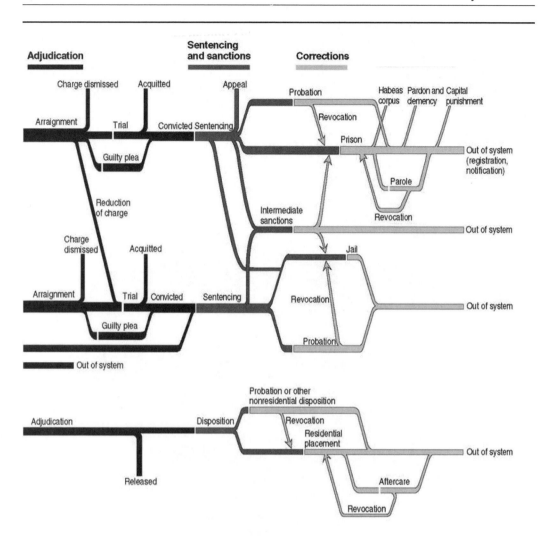

handling of cases in lower criminal courts *The Process Is the Punishment*.[13]

While the wedding cake model offers an accurate typology of cases processed through the system, its primary focus is on the decisions of prosecutors, defense attorneys, and judges. We glimpse the role of power and status in such decisions, but the factors of race, class, and gender are not explicit. Neither the ***President's Commission model*** nor the wedding cake model focuses on the lawmaking process and the social inequalities in the surrounding economic and political systems in which laws are forged. To explain why minority and poor defendants are disproportionately processed and incarcerated, we need another model.

The Criminalization Model

The ***criminalization model*** (see figure 1.2 on p. 8) explores the role of social class in the criminal justice system. It recognizes that the system is used to control certain groups of people—accomplished by criminalizing their behaviors and then focusing on them for arrest and incarceration. Social class is the first key component of the model. The higher one's status in the social hierarchy, the more power one wields. Power is the ability to get what you want. The greater amount of money and other resources at one's disposal, the greater the likelihood of getting one's way, in spite of opposition. This applies to being healthy, getting a good education, becoming wealthy, getting elected to office, and to thousands of other opportunities. Access to these opportunities depends largely on *social class*. As one writer puts it, *class counts*.[14]

Social class determines almost everything that matters in a capitalist society—including criminal justice. One's social class position primarily determines whether or not certain behaviors are considered crimi-

Figure 1.2   The Criminalization Model of Criminal Justice

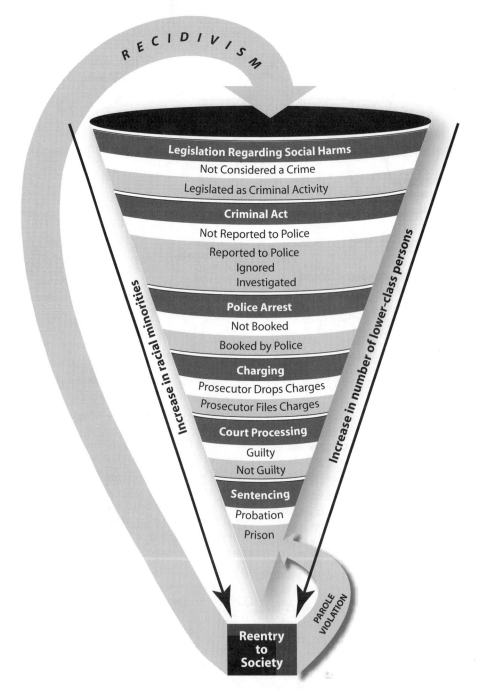

nal; whether or not one is arrested and charged with a crime; whether or not the defense lawyer prevails at trial. An inverse relationship exists between social class and the probability of contact with the system. Quite simply, the odds of being arrested, charged, convicted, and sentenced to prison are greater the lower one is in the social class hierarchy. This is particularly true for racial minorities.[15]

The criminalization model recognizes the major stages of the criminal justice process. It also considers the political process that defines certain behaviors as criminal. It recognizes the role of powerful interest groups in determining the administrative and legislative responses to those behaviors, and it explores the role of criminal justice officials who assume the responsibility for the interpretation and implementation of those policies.

In addition to the typical stages set forth in traditional models of criminal justice, this model examines the likelihood of reentry to the system following release. We argue that reentry is not necessarily because of new crimes committed or even because of increased attention by criminal justice officials. It is frequently because of diminished opportunities resulting from social stigmatization and alienation.[16]

Defining "Criminals"

Other models of the system begin with the discovery of a crime; the criminalization model begins with the political process. Certain behaviors and groups are defined as criminal; offenders are presented as being different from other members of society. Our society views criminals as social trash—rabble who have proven that they cannot live in a civil society.[17] Modern crime policies have effectively created a criminal/noncriminal dichotomy.

Despite the fact that an overwhelming majority of Americans have participated in behaviors that could have resulted in imprisonment, criminals are not viewed as those who were *caught* participating in deviant acts. Instead, criminals are viewed as law-breaking, norm violating, disruptive individ-

uals who threaten the moral order of society. "The appeal of an emphasis upon the pathologies of criminals and the utility of punishing them lies partly in what it negates: the tracing of crime to pathological social conditions."[18] Stuart Scheingold points out that the individualistic culture in the United States generates insecurities that prompt a search for scapegoats. For example, if the public school system is failing, drug dealers or gangs could be blamed and targeted rather than lack of funding, inadequate nutrition, poor living conditions, etc. The criminal justice system becomes a mechanism for controlling scapegoats—in particular members of the underclass or the "dangerous classes."

Various crime control policies established at both the national and local level ultimately determine the structure and operations of the entire criminal justice system as well as what laws will be enforced. It is by definition a very political process.[19] The identification of certain behaviors and groups as criminal has effectively been a *homogenization process*. The offenses and the offenders have become more and more homogeneous in terms of social class, race, and gender. The further one goes into the criminal justice system, the more marked these distinctions become.[20]

Three factors encourage and reinforce an ideology that is supportive of contemporary crime policies. First, lawmakers focus their attention on the crimes of the poor.[21] In doing so, Americans are presented with an inaccurate "reality" of crime. The most significant result of this focus is that it deflects attention from social inequalities and macro explanations for street-level criminality. Second, the criminalization process presents street crime as a public problem that threatens the moral order. Presenting crime as an omnipresent threat leads to a reality of fear.[22] Those who are fearful of fellow citizens are more trusting of crime policies. Finally, crime policies create and maintain dangerous classes.[23]

The poor, the young, ethnic minorities, and women have the least representation in both federal and state legislatures. These groups have a minimal political voice and the least amount of political influence. They become easy targets for those interested in creating scapegoats to shield their interests—whether corporations looking to increase profits, legislators seeking reelection, or criminal justice system functionaries protecting their turf.

Stages in the Criminalization Process

Stage 1 in the criminalization process is **legislation**. In U.S. society, numerous acts are considered to be *social harms*—harms done to individuals and society as a whole. Some of these are treated as criminal while others are not.[24] Crimes are defined by laws written by legislators. This process determines the behaviors that are deemed criminal and their corresponding punishments.

The process of writing legislation is impacted by public perceptions, the influence of powerful interest groups, lobbyists, and the interests of the legislators themselves. Interest groups are organized groups of individuals who try to influence public policy decisions. Most of these interest groups disproportionately include people of high social standing and represent powerful corporations, rather than average citizens. In most cases, these are the interests of white, upper- class males who together constitute what some believe to be a "ruling class" in U.S. society.[25] It is not by accident that many harmful acts engaged in by those of high social standing are considered either noncriminal or misdemeanors.

> The more likely that a crime is the type committed by middle- and upper-class people, the less likely it is that it will be treated as a criminal offense. When it comes to crime in the streets, where the perpetrator is apt to be poor, he or she is even more likely to be arrested and formally charged. When it comes to crime in the suites, where the offender is apt to be affluent, the system is most likely to deal with the crime non-criminally, that is, by civil litigation or informal settlement.[26]

Most lawmakers are individuals who occupy the highest social class position in society, a position that impacts both their ideology and their perceptions of social issues.[27] Lobbyists, interest groups, and corporations rarely act on behalf of poor and minority groups. They work to impact legislation in a way that will continue to protect their interests and profits. The linkage between powerful interest groups and political influence lies in the control of purse strings before, during, and after elections.

When a legislative body defines a certain behavior as criminal, it provides an agenda for those who work within the criminal justice system. Criminal law is the foundation of the criminal justice system; police, prosecutors, and judges are empowered to enforce *criminal law*. For the most part, the decisions that determine what constitutes a crime are based on narrow vested interests. Criminal laws "are formulated by those segments of society which have the power to shape public policy." Thus, lawmaking "represents the translation of specific interests into public policy."[28]

Stage 2 involves the commission of a **criminal act**. If the act is reported to or observed by police, they may investigate the incident or ignore it. If it is investigated, it may lead to stage 3.

Stage 3 is **arrest**. The suspect is physically taken into custody. As a general rule, the more serious the violation the more likely an arrest will occur. The arrested party is a highly probable suspect, which may be based on detailed information, social stereotypes, or administrative pressure to "clear the case." A case is considered cleared when an arrest is made.

Stage 4 is **charging**, which is actually two theoretically separate substages. The police are the first to charge a defendant through "booking," but this is followed by actions of the prosecutor who makes a decision to either accept the original charges, alter some or all of the charges, or dismiss the charges.

Stage 5 is **court processing**. This involves the initial appearance, arraignment, preliminary hearings, grand jury investigations, plea bargaining, pretrial motions, and the trial.

Stage 6 is **sentencing**. If at any point the defendant pleads or is found guilty in stage 5, he or she is subject to a sanction determined by legislation and judicial discretion. The sanction depends on the type of offense, the defendant's history, and extralegal factors such as race, gender, and social class. The sanctions can include probation, community service, restitution, drug treatment, or incarceration in a prison or jail. The criminal justice process is often viewed as terminated when the sentence has been served, although a convicted person often continues to encounter criminal justice agents. Those encounters may result in additional time in prison or the commission of a new crime, which starts the cycle anew.

All models present idealized versions of what is *supposed* to happen in the criminal justice process. What really happens varies depending on time and place.

At each progressive stage, the number of potential defendants becomes smaller. More importantly, *the kinds of people involved become more and more homogeneous.* For instance, they become more alike in terms of age (younger), sex (more are males), race (increasingly non-white), social class (increasing numbers of lower- and working-class people and the poor), offense (the kinds of offenses typically associated with the poor and the powerless), and previous experiences with the criminal justice system. When we arrive at the last stage—those who are incarcerated in the nation's prisons and jails—we have the *most homogenous* grouping. Quite simply, the vast majority of inmates are poor, unskilled, uneducated, and have had multiple contacts with the criminal and/or juvenile justice system. The sifting and sorting are often based on legal criteria such as seriousness of the offense and past record. However, extralegal variables such as class, race, and sex become "proxy variables" and play an important role in the criminal justice process.

Jeffrey Reiman argues "Not only is the main entry to the road to prison held wide open to the poor, the access routes for the wealthy are largely sealed off."[29] This is contrary to portrayals of the criminal justice system as a sieve in which the innocent are progressively sifted out from the guilty. Reiman notes that the sieve also works another way. It sifts the affluent out from the poor so that the guilty poor end up in prison:

The criminal justice system does not simply weed the peace-loving from the dangerous, the law-abiding from the criminal. At every stage, starting with the very definitions of crime and progressing through the stages of investigation, arrest, charging, conviction, and sentencing, the system *weeds out the wealthy.* It refuses to define as "crimes" or as serious crimes the dangerous and predatory acts of the well-to-do. . . . Instead, the system focuses its attention on those crimes likely to be committed by members of the lower classes. Thus, it is no surprise to find that so many of the people behind bars are from the lower classes. The people we see in our jails and prisons are no doubt dangerous to society, but they are not *the danger* to society, not *the gravest danger* to society.[30]

SOCIAL INEQUALITY AND CLASS STRUCTURE IN THE UNITED STATES

It is difficult to understand the role that extralegal factors play in the U.S. system of justice without understanding the class structure in our society. The share of the financial wealth of the top wealth-holders has increased in recent years, with 1% of the households getting 40% of all financial wealth in 2001, doubling from about 20% in 1976. The largest increase occurred during the 1980s.[31] Overall inequality, measured by the *Gini Index of Inequality* (a ratio between 0 denoting perfect income equality—everyone earns the same amount and 1 denoting perfect income inequality—one person earns everything) has gone up since the late 1960s. Whereas in 1970 the index for the United States was 0.396, in 2005 it was at 0.469, the largest of any industrialized nation.[32]

In 2005 the average chief executive officer earned 431 times the pay of the average worker, up from a ratio of 42 to one in 1980. Indeed, the rich are getting richer and practically everyone else is getting poorer.[33]

The proportion of Americans living in poverty has increased. As inequality has grown, the social conditions of the most disadvantaged sectors of society have worsened. Massive cutbacks on social spending for programs for the poor have been especially devastating to children. Indeed, one of the most striking facts is that more than 18% of all children, 35% of African-American children, and 28% of Latino children now live in poverty. The poverty line is set by the Social Security Administration; in 2006, the poverty threshold was $20,000 for a family of four.[34] The method of calculation remains the same as it was in the 1960s—multiplying the amount of money needed for a subsistence diet by three, adjusted for inflation. As many critics point out, food costs are currently a much smaller portion of family budgets; rent, transportation costs, child care, and health care now account for much larger shares of household expenditures. Most critics contend that the official poverty rate should be raised by at least 50%. Under that standard, the official poverty rate would increase to 22.5% and children living in poverty would jump to 31%.

There are many different definitions of social class. Sociologists who have studied this subject have never completely agreed on a uniform definition. It is important, however, to attempt a definition. Here we will combine the definitions given by two different sociologists, Robert Rothman and Martin Marger. *Social class* refers to *groups of individuals or families who have about the same income and occupation and have a similar position within the larger system of economic production in an industrial society.*[35]

The class structure of U.S. society can be seen as a system consisting of six major parts or subgroupings (see table 1.1). These social classes are differentiated mainly by the amount of income and wealth families or individuals have, the sources of such income and wealth (mostly their occupation but at the upper levels the assets they have, such as land, stocks and bonds, etc.), and the amount of education they have. Table 1.1 illustrates what this class system looks like.

There are direct and indirect consequences stemming from one's social class position—plus race and gender. Social class affects *life chances*, which include the prospect of a healthy and lengthy life, the possi-

Table 1.1   The American Class Structure

Class	Percent	Salary Range	Source of Income	Typical Occupation
Upper	1–2	> $1 million	Assets*	Investors, corp. exec.
Upper-middle	14–20	$80,000–$1,000,000	Salaries	Upper-level mgrs., professionals, small business owners
Lower-middle	25–30	$35,000–$75,000	Salaries & Wages	lower-level mgrs., semi-prof, small-bus. owners, craftspersons
Working	20–30	$25,000–$40,000	Wages	low-skilled workers, clerical, retail sales, some service workers
Working poor	10–15	$12,000–$25,000	Wages	lowest level skills, low level service workers, unskilled workers
Underclass	8–12	< $12,000	Public assistance; "underground economy"	unemployed

*Assets include mostly stock and bonds, and other investments, land, companies owned, etc. Many of the very rich inherited a substantial amount of money.

Sources: Rothman, R. A. *Inequality and Stratification* (3rd ed.). Upper Saddle River, NJ: Prentice-Hall, 1999, p. 7; Marger, M. N. *Social Inequality*. Mountain View, CA: Mayfield, 1999, p. 28; Gilbert, D. *The American Class Structure* (5th ed.). Belmont, CA: Wadsworth, 1998, p. 15.

bility of a college education, the potential for becoming a professional or finding a satisfying occupation, attaining income and wealth, plus, on the negative side, the risk of being a crime victim or an offender. Life chances affect the possibility of getting arrested, convicted, going to jail or prison, and especially receiving the death penalty.

While the United States does offer the possibility of *mobility* between classes, the bulk of any movement is from one layer to the layer immediately above it. Thus, using the class layers in table 1.1, most mobility would be between the lower-middle to the upper-middle, or from the working class to the lower-middle. It should also be pointed out that there has been a great deal of *downward mobility* in recent years. The majority of Americans, however, remain in the social class in which they were born. Movement that does occur, either upward or downward, stems mostly from a combination of structural changes in the economy beyond the control of the average person.[36]

In the context of crime and criminal justice, it is critically important to note that *power* and privilege primarily reside with the small percentage of upper-class Americans. To put it bluntly, the top 1–2% essentially run the country—they pass most of the laws, they create foreign and domestic social policies, they help themselves and fellow members of the upper class get elected, and they control the bulk of the assets of the country. For these reasons, this group is referred to as the "ruling class," "dominant class," "governing class," or simply "the powers that be."[37]

It is also important to understand that racial minorities are far more likely to be in the lower socioeconomic brackets. For example, African-American families are about three times more likely to live in poverty than whites.[38] Gender is also correlated with poverty. Women are, for instance, far more likely to be single parents. They earn far less than men due to the nature of their jobs, the wage gap, and the likelihood that they will work part-time.[39]

Conversely, the working poor and the underclass have virtually no power or resources, both of which are needed to resist receiving the label of "criminal." This point will become clearer and clearer in each subsequent chapter. These huge discrepancies in wealth and power make it virtually impossible to have a system that promotes equal justice. David Cole's book, *No Equal Justice*, posits two systems of justice in the United States, one for the privileged, another for the nonprivileged.[40]

THE CRIME CONTROL INDUSTRY

The U.S. criminal justice system is large and complex. It is also very expensive to operate. For example, the most recent figures reveal that federal, local, and state governments spent $196 billion on police, courts, and corrections in 2004 (see table 1.2) Expenditures increased 439% since 1982; expenditures on the correctional system soared 585%.[41] There are over 50,000 different governmental agencies employing over 2.3 million people in this system who share a payroll of more than $5 billion per month.[42] We suggest that this system is part of a much larger system known as the *crime control industry.*[43]

The *crime control industry* consists of more than the three components of the criminal justice system. It includes the businesses that profit from the existence of crime and/or attempts to control crime. Examples include private security firms, a prison industrial complex, drug testing firms, gun manufacturers, 3,000 colleges and universities that offer degrees in criminal justice, and media outlets that depend on stories about crime and criminals.

The war on crime has become a booming business, with literally hundreds of com-

Table 1.2	Criminal Justice Expenditures, Fiscal Years 1982 and 2004 (in billions)			
	1982	**1996**	**2004**	**% Increase**
Total	$36	$120	$194	439
Police	19	53	89	368
Judicial	8	26	43	438
Corrections	9	41	62	589

panies profiting from it and others seeking to share in the wealth. Employment in this industry offers careers for thousands. The criminal justice system provides a steady supply of career possibilities (police, correctional officers, probation and parole officers, and administrative staff, to name just a few) with good starting pay and benefits, along with job security.

In his book *Class, State and Crime,* Richard Quinney wrote that the criminal justice industrial complex is a part of the "social-industrial complex." He described this larger complex as "an involvement of industry in the planning, production, and operation of state programs. These state-financed programs like education, welfare, and criminal justice are social expenses necessary for maintaining social order and are furnished by monopolistic industries." Large corporations, Quinney suggested, have found a new source of profits in this industry, with the criminal justice industry leading the way. Private industry, in short, has found that there is much profit to be made as a result of the existence of crime.[44]

In 1967, the President's Crime Commission suggested that the solution to crime requires a combination of science and technology.

> More than 200,000 scientists and engineers have applied themselves to solving military problems and hundreds of thousands more to innovation in other areas of modern life, but only a handful are working to control the crimes that injure or frighten millions of Americans each year. Yet the two communities have much to offer each other: Science and technology is a valuable source of knowledge and techniques for combating crime; the criminal justice system represents a vast area of challenging problems.[45]

Policy makers embraced this technocratic solution to the crime problem. The crime control industry is so huge that it is almost impossible to estimate the amount of money spent and the profits made.

Employment within the crime control industry is growing rapidly, providing many career opportunities for both college students and high school graduates. As already noted, there are more than 2.3 million people employed within this system. The largest component is within the corrections category, with just over 1.4 million, representing an increase of over 90% from 1982. The U.S. Census reports that the hiring and training of correctional officers is the fastest-growing segment of government employment. There are more people working in corrections than all of the people employed in any Fortune 500 company except General Motors.[46]

Literally thousands of companies, large and small, are seeking profits in this booming industry. An advertisement placed in the July 2005 issue of *Corrections Today* by a distance-learning company included this headline: "Crime doesn't pay, but a degree in Criminal Justice does!" The same issue contained ads from four academic institutions that offer degrees, certificates, workshops, and other assorted programs.[47] Advertisers at an annual meeting of the American Jail Association used lines such as "Tap into the Sixty-Five Billion Local Jails Market" and "Jails are BIG BUSINESS" to attract customers.[48] Trade journals that serve the correction industry have seen their advertisements triple since the 1980s. Aramark, a food service company, advertised that while "your correctional officers are watching the food line, Aramark will be watching your budget." General Marine Leasing, a modular facility builder, asked and advised: "Overcrowded? Don't let overflow put them back on the street." Companies that sell health care, fences, tea, blankets, transport vehicles, security scanners—or anything else needed to house and feed inmates—have an expanding market for their products.

SUMMARY

In this chapter we began with the observation that the basis of the U.S. criminal justice system is found within the three branches of our government: legislative, executive, and judicial. The Constitution provides for the creation of laws by state legislatures and Congress; it grants executive branch officials and the courts the authority to enforce those laws. The criminal justice system is the *instrument* designated by executive branch officials to enforce laws that pertain to criminal behavior.

We reviewed the basic components of the criminal justice system: the police, the courts, and the prison system. Each component is involved in different stages of the criminal justice process. We then reviewed two traditional models of the criminal justice system, beginning with the President's Commission model of the late 1960s. We noted that such a depiction, however, does little more than outline the stages one may or may not pass through. The model suggests that the system is an efficient one where cases are processed in a more or less orderly manner from the beginning to various exit points. The wedding cake model depicts the criminal justice system as consisting of four major layers. Walker's assumption is that the system handles different kinds of cases differently, mainly in terms of the disparities between cases in different layers.

We presented a criminalization perspective, in which criminal justice is a process that is not always about responding to *crime per se* but rather the *processing* of certain kinds of defendants accused of committing certain kinds of crimes. Legislation determines what acts are criminal, and the criminal justice system is the apparatus for processing those who violate the laws. The further one goes into the system, the more the offenses and the offenders become homogeneous in terms of social class, race, gender and other characteristics.

Key variables in understanding this model are inequality and power. Social class affects life chances and the probability of having the power to protect one's interests. Differentials in power based on such criteria as race, sex, and social class largely determine what kinds of behaviors are deemed criminal and how or if one is processed through the system. The criminal justice system has grown to such an extent that numerous industries depend on it for their profits, adding another layer of interests served by the labeling of certain people and behavior as criminal.

Key Terms

- crime control industry
- criminal justice system
- criminalization model
- dual court system
- Gini Index of Inequality
- laws
- life chances
- lower courts
- power
- President's Commission model
- social class
- three branches of government (executive, legislative, judicial)
- wedding cake model

Notes

[1] No one is certain of the origin of the term "wilding," but the media repeatedly used it to express the violent, remorseless activities of the "pack" (another repeated description) of youths that evening. 6 February 2007 http://www.cjr.org/issues/2003/1/rapist-hancock.asp

[2] Haughney, C. "Central Park Rape Case Conviction in Question." *Washington Post* September 6, 2002, p. A3.

[3] Hagan, J. "Why Is There So Little Criminal Justice Theory?" *Journal of Research in Crime and Delinquency* 26: 116–135 (1989).

[4] Zalman, M. and L. Siegel. *Cases and Comments on Criminal Procedure.* St. Paul: West, 1994, p. 13.

[5] *Sourcebook on Criminal Justice Statistics.* [Online] http://www.albany.edu/sourcebook/pdf/t1172003.pdf

[6] Neubauer, D. W. *America's Courts and the Criminal Justice System* (8th ed.). Belmont, CA: Wadsworth, 2005, p. 53.

[7] Allen, H. E., E. J. Latessa, B. S. Ponder, and C. E. Simonsen. *Corrections in America* (11th ed.). Englewood Cliffs, NJ: Prentice-Hall, 2007, pp. 105, 167.

[8] Walker, S. *Sense and Nonsense about Crime and Drugs* (6th ed.). Belmont, CA: Wadsworth, 2006, pp. 33–34.

[9] Ibid., p. 34.

[10] Ibid., p. 38.

[11] Ibid., p. 41.

[12] Ibid., p. 43.

[13] Feeley, M. *The Process is the Punishment.* New York: Russell Sage Foundation, 1979.

[14] Wright, E. O. *Class Counts.* New York: Cambridge University Press, 2000.

[15] Documentation is provided in Shelden, R. G. *Controlling the Dangerous Classes: A Critical Introduction to the History of Criminal Justice.* Boston: Allyn & Bacon, 2001.

[16] Irwin, J. *The Felon.* Englewood Cliffs, NJ: Prentice-Hall, 1970. Terry, C. M. "Beyond Punishment: Perpetuating Differences From the Prison Experience."

Humanity and Society 24: 108–135 (2000); Richards, S. C. *Structure of Prison Release: An Extended Case Study of Prison Release, Work Release, and Parole.* New York: McGraw-Hill, 1995.

[17] Shelden, R. G. *Controlling the Dangerous Classes.* Boston: Allyn & Bacon, 2001; Irwin, J. *The Jail: Managing the Underclass in American Society.* Berkeley: University of California Press, 1985.

[18] Scheingold, S. A. *The Politics of Street Crime.* Philadelphia: Temple University Press, 1991, p. 173.

[19] Scheingold, S. A. *The Politics of Law and Order: Street Crime and Public Policy.* New York: Longman, 1984; and Scheingold, *The Politics of Street Crime.*

[20] Newton, C. H., R. G. Shelden, and S. W. Jenkins. "The Homogenization Process within the Juvenile Justice System." *International Journal of Criminology and Penology* 3: 213–227 (1975); Shelden, R. G. *Criminal Justice in America: A Sociological Approach.* Boston: Little Brown, 1982.

[21] Reiman, J. *The Rich Get Richer and the Poor Get Prison* (8th ed.). Boston: Allyn & Bacon, 2007.

[22] Altheide, D. L. *Creating Fear: News and the Construction of Crisis.* Hawthorne, NY: Aldine De Gruyter, 2002.

[23] Shelden, *Controlling the Dangerous Classes.*

[24] Michalowski, R. *Order, Law and Crime.* New York: Macmillan, 1985; and Reiman, *The Rich Get Richer and the Poor Get Prison.*

[25] For documentation of the existence of this "ruling class" see, e.g., Mills, C. W. *The Power Elite.* New York: Oxford University Press, 1956; Domhoff, W. *Who Rules America? Power and Politics in the Year 2000.* Mountain View, CA: Mayfield, 1998.

[26] Reiman, *The Rich Get Richer and the Poor Get Prison,* pp. 122–123.

[27] Domhoff, *Who Rules America?*; see also his *The Powers That Be.* New York: Random House, 1979; Quinney, R. *Critique of Legal Order: Crime Control in Capitalist Society.* New Brunswick, NJ: Transaction Books, 2002 [1974]; Chambliss, W. J. and M. S. Zatz (eds.). *Making Law: The State, the Law, and Structural Contradictions.* Bloomington: Indiana University Press, 1993.

[28] Quinney, R. *The Social Reality of Crime.* New Brunswick, NJ: Transaction Books, 2001 [1970], p. 43.

[29] Reiman, *The Rich Get Richer and the Poor Get Prison,* p. 123.

[30] Ibid., p. 155.

[31] Sklar, H. "Let Them Eat Cake." *Z Magazine* (November 1998); Collins, C., B. Leondar-Wright and H. Sklar. *Shifting Fortunes: The Perils of the Growing American Wealth Gap.* Boston: United for a Fair Economy, 1999, p. 10; see also Heintz, J., N. Folbre, and the Center for Popular Economics. *The Ultimate Field Guide to the U.S. Economy.* New York: The New Press, 2000; and Collins, C. and F. Yeskel. *Economic Apartheid in America.* New York: The New Press, 2000.

[32] U.S. Census Bureau. *Income, Poverty, and Health Insurance Coverage in the United States: 2005.* Table A3, pp. 40–41. March 27 2007. [Online] http://www.census.gov/prod/2006pubs/p60-231.pdf

[33] Sklar, H. "For CEOs, a Minimum Wage in the Millions." *Z Magazine* (July/August 1999); see also the following studies for further confirmation of the increase in inequality: Collins, C., B. Leondar-Wright and H. Sklar. *Shifting Fortunes: The Perils of the Growing American Wealth Gap.* Boston: United for a Fair Economy, 1999, pp. 11–13; Wolff, E. "Trends in Household Wealth in the United States, 1962–83 and 1983–98." *Review of Income and Wealth* 40(2) (June 1994); Wolff, E. *Top Heavy: A Study of Increasing Inequality of Wealth in America.* New York: The Twentieth Century Fund Press, 1995; Phillips, K. *The Politics of the Rich and the Poor.* New York: Random House,1990; Domhoff, *Who Rules America?*

[34] National Center for Child Poverty. *United States Demographics of Poor Children.* Columbia University, 2006.

[35] Rothman, R. A. *Inequality and Stratification* (3rd ed.). Upper Saddle River, NJ: Prentice-Hall, 1999, p. 5; Marger, M. N. *Social Inequality.* Mountain View, CA: Mayfield, 1999, p. 364. For a variation, see Gilbert, *The American Class Structure,* p. 15.

[36] Marger, *Social Inequality,* pp. 153–157.

[37] Numerous citations can be given here that documents these assertions. See previous notes above. See especially Parenti, M. *Democracy for the Few* (7th ed.). New York: Bedford/St. Martin's, 2002, chapter 2.

[38] Rothman, *Inequality and Stratification,* p. 91.

[39] Ibid., pp. 83–84.

[40] Cole, D. *No Equal Justice: Race and Class in the American Criminal Justice System.* New York: The New Press, 1999, p. 9.

[41] 2004 was the most recent year available when this book went to press. Visit http://www.ojp.usdoj.gov/bjs/eande.htm for the most recent information on expenditure and employment statistics. 30 March 2007 [Online] http://www.ojp.usdoj.gov/bjs/glance/tables/expgovtab.htm

[42] The latest figures can be found on the *Sourcebook on Criminal Justice Statistics.* [Online] http://www.albany.edu/sourcebook/toc_1.html

[43] Shelden, R. G. and W. B. Brown. "The Crime Control Industry and the Management of the Surplus Population." *Critical Criminology* 9: 39–62 (Spring

2001); Parenti, C. *Lockdown America: Police and Prisons in the Age of Crisis.* New York: Verso, 1999.

[44] Quinney, R. *Class, State and Crime* (2nd ed.). New York: Longman, 1980, p. 133.

[45] President's Commission on Law Enforcement and Administration of Justice. *The Challenge of Crime in a Free Society.* Washington, DC: U.S. Government Printing Office, 1967, p. 1.

[46] Shelden, *Controlling the Dangerous Classes,* chapter 7.

[47] *Corrections Today* (July 2005). These ads are found on pages 27, 90, and 100. This issue includes the annual "Buyers Guide," containing about 100 pages of ads for about 150 different companies.

[48] Donziger, S. *The Real War on Crime.* New York: Harper/Collins, 1996, p. 93.

two

The Problem of Crime in American Society

In some Nevada counties, it is legal to engage in prostitution. In the neighboring state of California, prostitution is illegal, but filming sexual activity to sell as pornography is not. In Kentucky, it is illegal to sell, display, or possess a living baby chick that has been dyed or colored.[1] In Indiana, it is legal to catch turtles by hand but illegal to catch fish with your bare hands. Virginia law forbids radar detectors, and the interstate speed limit tends to be 65 mph, while West Virginia allows radar detectors with a speed limit of 70 on the same interstate.

If we stop people on the street and ask them to give an example of "crime," it is unlikely that a person in Kentucky would mention painting a baby chicken. They would probably say murder, robbery, rape, burglary, or other similar offenses. These responses are normal considering that the media is most likely to report murder, robbery, drug trafficking, and rape, while someone caught fishing barehanded in Indiana is not likely to be a hot news item.

THE MEANING OF CRIME

Most Americans receive their crime knowledge from media sources, especially television.[2] Television crime shows and major motion pictures reinforce our perceptions of crime by focusing much of their attention on murder and other violent offenses. This focus on violent crime leads to a social reality of fear.[3] Studies have indicated that despite decreased victimization rates public fear of crime increases when media outlets increase the number of stories about violent crimes.[4]

Stereotypes of Crime

Since the late 1960s, politicians have recognized that certain portrayals of crime are more likely to win votes. During election years, politicians decry the breakdown in "law and order" and urge crackdowns on "street crimes." As discussed in chapter 1, politicians and the media present a distorted reality of crime. This directs the public's attention to specific crimes, which facilitates the establishment of those crimes as true social problems. The net effect of a social reality of fear is that it legitimates the government's responses to crime. A fearful public is more accepting of formal social control initiatives and more readily believes that those who violate societal norms are different.[5]

The reality of crime often directly contradicts media and political scenarios. For example, stranger child abductions, murders by serial killers, and stranger rapes are heavily reported, yet they are far less probable than similar crimes perpetrated by someone known to the victims.[6] Similarly, when we think of a "criminal," the first image that often comes to mind is a young black male who commits a murder, robbery, rape, or some other street crime.

It is important to understand that street crimes are not the only crimes. They are not the only behaviors that lead to injury, financial loss, and even death. Reiman explains that the fixation on the stereotypical criminal blocks a more expansive view of what constitutes criminal behavior and **indirect harm**—damages perhaps not intended but resulting nonetheless from criminal actions.

> It is important to identify this model of the Typical Crime because it functions like a set of blinders. It keeps us from calling a mine disaster a mass murder even if ten men are killed, even if someone is responsible for the unsafe conditions. . . . What keeps a mine disaster from being a mass murder in our eyes is that it is not a one-on-one harm. . . . If [a mine executive] cuts corners to save a buck, he is just doing his job. If ten men die because he cut corners on safety, we may think him crude or callous, but not a murderer. He is, at most, responsible for *indirect harm.* . . . Because we accept the belief—encouraged by our politicians' statements about crime and by the media's portrayal of crime—that the model for crime is one person specifically trying to harm another, we accept a legal system that leaves us unprotected against much greater danger to our lives and well-being than those threatened by the Typical Criminal.[7]

Common Definitions of Crime

Classic definitions of crime link it with criminal law. "The most precise and least ambiguous definition of crime is that which defines it as behavior which is prohibited by the criminal code."[8] Thus, *crime* is defined by the legal codes of a state. The "legalistic" definition of crime has been the subject of extensive criticism.

Some critics suggest that there are two concepts of crime—the legal concept and the social/popular concept. The **legal concept** refers to crime as a "legal category assigned to conduct by authorized agents of the state." Legislators are the authorized agents of the state who introduce and enact laws. The **social/popular concept** refers to "conduct that does not necessarily involve either the violation of a criminal law or the application of the legal category to the conduct."[9] Some have suggested that criminology should not be limited to the study of the violation of criminal laws but should instead examine the violation of "conduct norms."[10]

Edwin Sutherland once argued that criminologists should expand their focus to include illegal corporate behavior.[11] Still other criminologists have argued that there should be a human rights definition of crime. Such a definition would include many behaviors plus structural features of modern society that result in tremendous harm to people, such as sexism, racism, and imperialism. Additional violations include unsafe working conditions, inadequate opportunities for employment and education, substandard housing, and a lack of access to medical care.[12]

Although people disagree on a universal definition of crime, ultimately behaviors that violate criminal statutes are the behaviors that are subject to sanctions. Thus, crime is actually "created" through the passage of criminal laws. As discussed in chapter 1, the process that shapes criminal statutes is very important to understanding what behaviors will be labeled criminal.

CLASSIFICATIONS OF CRIME

Criminal behavior includes a wide variety of acts that are prohibited by legal codes. These acts range from the most serious, such as homicide and rape, to the most innocuous, such as loitering. There are several ways to classify crimes.

Felonies and Misdemeanors

One of the most common methods of classifying crimes is to distinguish between felonies and misdemeanors. A *felony* is a crime punishable by a year or more in prison, while a *capital felony* is a crime punishable by death. For example, homicide, rape, and robbery are felony offenses. Espionage, murder during the course of another felony, and kidnapping under certain circumstances are capital felonies in some jurisdictions. *Misdemeanors* are crimes punishable by a fine, forfeiture, or less than one year in a jail. For example, disorderly conduct, vandalism, simple assault, and prostitution are misdemeanors. Theoretically, these two categories reflect the extent of harm done and the degree of moral outrage by society about the behavior. Most offenders convicted of a felony serve a term of imprisonment in a state or federal prison. Offenders convicted of a misdemeanor are usually sentenced to a local jail.

Mala in Se and Mala Prohibita Crimes

Another method of classification is the common law distinction between *mala in se* and *mala prohibita* crimes. *Mala in se* crimes are acts that are considered wrong in and of themselves. In other words, these crimes assault the moral conscience of society. They include offenses like murder, rape, arson, burglary, and other similar crimes. Other offenses, however, are criminal for a different reason. Basically *mala prohibita* offenses are illegal because the law says so. They are prohibited acts or acts of omission that in and of themselves are not criminal. Certain behaviors have been criminalized through legislation. *Mala prohibita* crimes generally refer to "victimless crimes," such as prostitution, public drunkenness, drug offenses, and failure to file income tax returns. Theoretically, these two categories reflect the extent of harm done and the degree of moral outrage by society that such acts elicit.

Classification by Governmental Jurisdiction

Jurisdiction refers to the geographical area where the court has the power and authority to hear and determine judicial proceedings, as well as the power to render a particular judgment. There are three principal jurisdictions in the United States: federal, state, and local. Each jurisdiction has its own legal codes and procedures for enforcing its codes. *Federal offenses* are those either committed within federal territories (such as national parks), crimes that are carried on across the boundaries of two or more states (e.g., interstate transportation of stolen goods), and attempts to assassinate a government official, such as a president or senator. *State crimes* are those found in state penal codes, a generic term for the compilation of laws and corresponding punishments published by every state under such titles as

penal codes or revised statutes. *Local crimes* or ordinances are those that apply to cities, townships, and counties. Parking violations and traffic laws tend to be local ordinances.

This threefold classification is important because there are, correspondingly, three types of criminal justice systems. For instance, someone charged with a federal offense would be prosecuted by a federal prosecutor and, if convicted, would go to a federal prison. Those who are charged and prosecuted for a state crime would be processed through a state court system and, if found guilty, may be sentenced to a state prison. Failing to stop for a red light can draw the attention of a city police officer and result in a summons to appear at a city or municipal court. Ignoring that summons could result in a fine or jail time within that local jurisdiction.

TYPES OF CRIMES

While criminologists may not be able to agree on what behaviors should be crimes, at the most basic level, they do identify categories of crimes. There are nine major categories of crime.

Crimes of violence. Violent crime is that which involves the threat of or actual physical harm to the victim. While most crime does not involve violence, these offenses are the most feared. Interpersonal crimes of violence include: murder, robbery, assault, rape, domestic abuse and battering, state violence, and workplace violence.

Property crime. Crimes directed at property involve unlawfully damaging or taking the property of another. Property crimes are far more common than violent crimes. Major property crimes include: grand larceny (theft of money or property in excess of a certain dollar value, usually $400–$500), burglary, motor vehicle theft, and arson. Petty property crimes include: shoplifting and buying/receiving stolen property.

Public order offenses. These offenses tend to occur in public locations and are often referred to as victimless crimes because there is no complaining victim. They involve behaviors that are often considered misdemeanors, such as illegal gambling, prostitution, drug use, public drunkenness, disturbing the peace, and disorderly conduct.

State crime. Sometimes referred to as government or political crime, this category includes offenses committed by or against the government. For example, police corruption, violations of international human rights laws, treason, and conspiracy to overthrow the government.

Individual fraud. These are offenses that involve attempts by individuals to obtain money or property under false pretenses and usually involve face-to-face encounters with the victim but no physical force. Included are such crimes as confidence games (such as the "big con" or "sting"), swindles, insurance fraud, credit card fraud, and check fraud (passing bad checks).

Occupational crime. These are offenses that are directly related to one's occupation. Generally there are two types: (1) crimes committed by employees against their employers, commonly referred to as pilferage or embezzlement; (2) crimes committed during the course of normal occupational pursuits, such as maintenance and repair fraud, health care fraud, Medicare and Medicaid fraud, fee splitting, and unnecessary surgeries by doctors.

Corporate crime. These offenses are acts by large corporations that do physical or economic harm to the environment, their employees, or to customers. Such crimes "arise from the ownership or management of capital or from occupancy of positions of trust in institutions designed to facilitate the accumulation of capital."[13] Examples include creating occupational health hazards, price-fixing, manufacturing unsafe products, pollution, price gouging, false advertising, economic exploitation of employees, corporate stealing from employees, unfair labor practices, and many more.[14]

Organized crime. This category refers to those persons whose criminal behavior is viewed as a career or a profession. There are two major categories. First, there are those individuals who are persistently involved in criminal behavior, whether alone or in concert with others. A small number will special-ize in one major crime such as pick pocketing or safecracking. However, most will commit a wide variety of crimes, mostly major property offenses. Second, there are those who belong to organized criminal "syndicates" or "crime families," such as the "Mafia," "La Costra Nostra" or similar organizations who engage in such crimes as loan-sharking, drug smuggling, and racketeering.

Hate crime. These are crimes motivated by prejudice against particular groups due to differences in ethnicity, race, religion, physical or mental capacity, or sexual orientation. Examples include gay bashing, threatening, intimidation, and vandalism when the victim is chosen because they fall into one of the listed categories.[15]

There are many ways of categorizing crime. Measuring crime, however, is a more difficult task.

MEASURING CRIME

Measuring crime is difficult. In fact, the actual amount of crime committed in the United States is probably unknowable, despite the vast technology available. There are several reasons for this. First, there are literally hundreds of acts that are prohibited by law. Many of these acts lack precise definition, such as "disorderly conduct" and "disturbing the peace." Identical behavior could result in an arrest in one precinct and escape any notice whatsoever in another. Second, most crime is a private event known only to the offender and victim, sometimes just the offender. Most crime remains hidden from official agencies, making measurement difficult at best. Third, in order to know the true extent of crime each individual would have to be monitored 24 hours a day, an unsettling and unlikely state of affairs.

Despite the difficulties of determining the true amount of crime, there are four primary sources of crime statistics: (1) the FBI's annual Uniform Crime Report; (2) National Incidence-Based Reporting System; (3) victimization surveys; and (4) self-report surveys. Crime data can be official or unofficial. Official crime data consists of statistics compiled by governmental bodies. Unofficial data includes statistics gathered by qualitative and quantitative researchers.

Official Statistics

Uniform Crime Reports

The most commonly cited source of official crime statistics is the **Uniform Crime Report (UCR)**. The UCR is an annual publication of the Federal Bureau of Investigation (FBI). The data for the UCR are collected from more than 17,000 state and local police agencies in the United States. The FBI began collecting this data in 1930. Supplying data is voluntary, meaning that the FBI depends on cooperation from police departments to collect and report information.[16]

The UCR categorizes the data into Part I and Part II offenses. Part I offenses are also referred to as *index crimes.* There are eight index crimes: murder, forcible rape, robbery, aggravated assault, burglary, larceny-theft, motor vehicle theft, and arson. Part II offenses are less serious and include: fraud, embezzlement, vandalism, prostitution, gambling, disorderly conduct, liquor law violations, and weapon charges, among many others. The UCR tracks only crimes "known to the police"—meaning the police observed the crime taking place or a citizen reported the crime.

Included in the report is a section called clearances. It includes tables showing the percentage of crimes cleared by an arrest or exceptional means. A small portion of crimes committed are cleared by arrest. The percentage varies according to the type of crime. In 2005 about 62% of all reported homicides were cleared, while only 41% of all rapes were cleared (see figure 2.1). Property crimes were the least likely to be cleared: 25% of robberies, 18% of larcenies, and about 13% of burglaries and automobile thefts.[17]

The UCR provides more information for Part I than for Part II offenses. For index crimes, the UCR includes aggregates, or the total number of crimes reported to police. It also provides race, age, and gender characteristics of those arrested. The UCR provides information on the percent changes in the amount of crime between years. For example, the murder rate decreased 15% between 1996 and 2005.[18] The most commonly cited information, however, is the crime rate.

The crime rate provides the number of crimes committed per 100,000 people. For example, when the UCR reports that the murder rate was 5.6 in 2005, it means that about 5 people in every 100,000 fell victim to murder between January 1 and December 31, 2005. The crime rate is calculated by dividing the total U.S. population into the number of crimes reported multiplied by 100,000.

$$\frac{\text{Number of Crimes Reported}}{\text{Population}} \times 100,000 = \text{Crime Rate}$$

The UCR has several flaws that impact its usefulness for the study of crime.

Problem 1: The UCR underestimates the true amount of crime. Crime not known to the police is often referred to as the *dark figure of crime*. There are five primary factors that impact the underestimation of crime. First, most crime is not reported to authorities and very little crime is discovered by police. In fact, only about 40% of crime is reported to the police. Second, law enforcement agencies cooperate with the FBI on a voluntary basis, meaning that crime that is reported to nonparticipating departments is not included in the UCR. The FBI can refuse data from jurisdictions if they do not conform to UCR standards. For example, the 2005 data included only limited arrest data from Illinois and no arrest data for New York City or Florida.[19] Third, the UCR does not provide information on violations of federal law, which leads to inaccurate statistics on crimes like blackmail and kidnapping. Fourth, the UCR data is compiled using the "hierarchy rule," meaning that if multiple crimes are committed at the same time, only the most serious offense is reported in the UCR. Finally, only behaviors that have been labeled as "criminal" are included. For example, violations of constitutional and human rights such as police brutality are not reported.

Problem 2: The UCR focuses on Part I offenses. In focusing on index crimes, the

FBI gives the perception that these offenses are the most serious threats to society. While murder, rape, armed robbery, aggravated assault, and arson are easy to discern as serious crimes, the FBI includes larceny and burglary in this category. Basically, the theft of a bicycle (a larceny) is recorded as a serious crime but child abuse is not.[20] In addi-

---

Figure 2.1   Offenses Included in NIBRS

NIBRS collects extensive data on Group A offenses. Specific definitions of each offense category are included in the NIBRS codebook.

1. Arson
2. Assault Offenses
   - Aggravated Assault
   - Simple Assault
   - Intimidation
3. Bribery
4. Burglary/Breaking and Entering
5. Counterfeiting/Forgery
6. Destruction/Damage/Vandalism of Property
7. Drug/Narcotic Offenses
   - Drug/Narcotic Violations
   - Drug Equipment Violations
8. Embezzlement
9. Extortion/Blackmail
10. Fraud Offenses
    - False Pretenses/Swindle/Confidence Game
    - Credit Card/Automatic Teller Machine Fraud
    - Impersonation
    - Welfare Fraud
    - Wire Fraud
11. Gambling Offenses
    - Betting/Wagering
    - Operating/Promoting/Assisting Gambling
    - Gambling Equipment Violations
    - Sports Tampering
12. Homicide Offenses
    - Murder and Nonnegligent Manslaughter
    - Negligent Manslaughter
    - Justifiable Homicide
13. Kidnapping/Abduction
14. Larceny/Theft Offenses
    - Pocket-picking
    - Purse-snatching
    - Shoplifting
    - Theft from Building
    - Theft from Coin-Operated Machine or Device
    - Theft from Motor Vehicle
    - Theft of Motor Vehicle Parts or Accessories
    - All Other Larceny

15. Motor Vehicle Theft
16. Pornography/Obscene Material
17. Prostitution Offenses
    - Prostitution
    - Assisting or Promoting Prostitution
18. Robbery
19. Sex Offenses, Forcible
    - Forcible Rape
    - Forcible Sodomy
    - Sexual Assault with an Object
    - Forcible Fondling
20. Sex Offenses, Nonforcible
    - Incest
    - Statutory Rape
21. Stolen Property Offenses (Receiving, etc.)
22. Weapon Law Violations

NIBRS keeps only arrestee data on Group B offenses.

1. Bad Checks
2. Curfew/Loitering/Vagrancy Violations
3. Disorderly Conduct
4. Driving Under the Influence
5. Drunkenness
6. Family Offenses, Nonviolent
7. Liquor Law Violations
8. Peeping Tom
9. Runaway
10. Trespass of Real Property
11. All Other Offenses

Source: National Archive of Criminal Justice Data. *NIBRS Concepts*. (2006). Online http://www.icpsr.umich.edu/NACJD/NIBRS/concepts.html http://www.icpsr.umich.edu/NACJD/NIBRS/concepts.html#Group_B_Offenses

tion, corporate and political crimes are virtually ignored by the UCR, primarily because they are difficult to detect and are rarely reported. As a result, UCR data reports the crimes of the powerless, perpetuating the idea that criminals are poor minorities whose behavior threatens the social fabric of society.

The categorization of certain crimes as serious and the failure to include others is also problematic because it minimizes the threat to women and children from crimes that occur in the traditional family. Crimes by relatives, friends, and acquaintances are usually classified as less serious than crimes committed by strangers. Many domestic crimes are classified as wanton endangerment or misdemeanor assault.[21] This prevents them from appearing as Part I offenses and facilitates the notion that women and children are at greater risk of injury from strangers.

Problem 3: The UCR is a better indicator of police activity than of crime. Quite simply, the FBI reports who the police arrested and for what offenses. It fails to indicate the situations in which police officers declined to arrest and offers no context for the information provided. For example, if a police agency is compelled to crack down on prostitution, the number of charges for that offense will increase. This increase does not indicate an increase in the number of prostitution offenses in that jurisdiction for that period of time, it indicates increased police department activity.

Problem 4: Crime definitions are affected by individual interpretations. What one police officer would charge as a simple assault, another may charge as an aggravated assault. The decision to arrest and the determination of charges to file will impart UCR data. For example, one study determined that the rape rate in Boston and Los Angeles differed considerably in the late 1960s. Further investigation determined that Los Angeles police recorded any attempted sexual assault as rape, while the Boston police complied with the UCR's definition of rape.[22]

Problem 5: Police departments can intentionally or unintentionally manipulate data. Why would a police agency manipulate data? The primary reason is to justify a request to increase its budget. Additionally, it can show the necessity of hiring more officers, expanding existing units, adding new units, or even diverting public attention from internal problems within the police department.[23] Law enforcement agencies need to protect themselves—to project an image to the public that they are doing their job. One high profile example of political manipulation occurred during the Nixon presidency. Nixon implemented a crime control experiment in Washington, DC to illustrate the effectiveness of his national crime control proposals. In order for his crime initiative to be effective, crime in the District of Columbia had to decrease. While the crime rate did decrease, it was not the crime initiative that caused the reduction, it was a concerted effort among the police to list the value of stolen property as less than $50 regardless of the actual value, greatly reducing the number of property crimes in the District of Columbia.[24]

Unintentional manipulation affects UCR figures. For example, New York City reported 14,339 drug sales one year and only 4,317 the next, a decrease of 70%. This unlikely reduction was the result of unwritten policy shifts that changed how drug sales were counted. One change eliminated phone reports of drug sales from the data; the second changed how drug arrests were counted. Each site at which drug sales occurred was counted as one crime, no matter how many people were arrested.[25]

Problem 6: If someone is arrested and charged with more than one crime, only the most serious of the crimes is counted in the final tabulation of arrest data. In some cases multiple acts are counted as a single offense, and in others each act is counted as a separate offense. For example, if several people are robbed in a restaurant by the same offender, one robbery would be counted. However, if the same offender physically attacked four people, four assaults would be tallied.

Problem 7: The UCR offers no information about what eventually happened to each arrest. If the charges are dropped, they are still included in the arrest data. If the person is not convicted, it is still included in the data.

Some of these problems are methodological; others are conceptual. In response to criticism of the UCR, the FBI is creating the National Incident-Based Reporting System.

National Incident-Based Reporting System (NIBRS)

The *National Incident-Based Reporting System* is an attempt to revise the definitions of crime utilized by the UCR. It will be an additional form to be filled out by local police departments that will provide a much wider variety of data. All crimes will be reported, not just the index crimes, and attempted crimes will be distinguished from completed crimes. While some states already have such a system, it is still far from uniform.

NIBRS will utilize two categories of offenses. Group A includes the eight index crimes plus 14 other offenses. Group B offenses are similar to Part II offenses. The system is incident driven, asking police agencies to collect detailed information about an individual offense. Specifically, for Group A offenses NIBRS will collect information on the offense, the victim, the offender, damage to property, the presence of drugs or alcohol, witnesses, and the context of the incident. Multiple offenses will be treated as individual incidents in the reports.

This system is not yet operational, but it potentially offers a transformation of official crime data. If NIBRS develops according to plan, it will offer more information on crime known to the police. Non-reporting and police discretion will still affect the reliability of the data gathered through NIBRS. While it does seek to correct many of the problems with the UCR, it still depends on voluntary reporting from police agencies, a fundamental flaw with all official crime data.

National Crime Victimization Survey

The other main source of official crime data is the *National Crime Victimization Survey (NCVS)*. Since 1972, the Bureau of Justice Statistics (BJS) has conducted surveys of U.S. households to gather information on crime victimization. A random sampling procedure selects approximately 52,000 households to survey. More than 100,000 people 12 years of age and older are asked a series of questions about their experiences with crime. They are asked if they were victimized by rape or sexual assault, robbery, assault, personal theft, burglary, household larceny, and automobile theft. If victimized, they are asked if they reported it and if they did not report it, why not. They are also asked to describe the offender(s) in cases of personal crimes, about how they reacted (did they resist, etc.), and if weapons were used.

The NCVS was designed and implemented to glean information about the dark figure of crime, which is a strength of the instrument and resulting data. The NCVS measures both reported and unreported crime victimization. It is not affected by police discretion, changes in police department policy, or record keeping. The NCVS offers a more accurate representation of crime rates than the UCR, and the surveys have consistently shown some rather significant differences from the annual FBI report.

Another strength is that respondents are asked to provide information about the offender. Because the victim provides the demographic information about a specific incident, the information reflects actual offenses rather than the demographics of who was arrested. The accuracy regarding the offender's age, however, is subject to the perceptions of the victim. This can affect the reliability of NCVS reports on juveniles.

The third strength of the NCVS is its longitudinal design. Because respondents are interviewed every six months for three years, information can be collected that reflects changes in victimization over time. First, it allows analysis of what, if any, role respondent geographic mobility plays in repeated victimization. This is especially useful for analyzing regional differences in victimization. Second, researchers can achieve a better understanding of the health and economic consequences of crime victimization.[26] This is significant because not all injuries and problems related to victimization are immediately apparent. Third, it enables the examination of victim contact with the criminal justice system over time. Fourth, it allows researchers to examine and make comparisons between the characteristics of onetime versus repeat victims. These areas of inquiry are fruitful and have facilitated a better understanding of crime victims in recent decades.

While the NCVS is a useful source of crime data, it does have weaknesses. The first is that it underestimates the amount of crime, primarily from respondent underreporting. Forgetfulness, lying, intentionally not reporting rape and domestic violence, and even not being aware of victimization all contribute to underreporting. When it comes to crimes committed by family members, individuals are less likely to answer honestly—or even to recognize the behavior as criminal, particularly when the victims are children. Women who are victims of spousal abuse often rationalize or minimize such behavior, or it may occur so often that they consider it normal. Women who have been raped are often reluctant to report the crime.

Underreporting is also affected by the way the populations respond to the survey. Mobility affects who will be surveyed. Someone who moves frequently, is homeless, or is a runaway is at risk for victimization but is unlikely to be included in the surveys. Some argue that underreporting is an issue of social class, with whites more likely to report victimization than blacks and college-educated respondents more likely to report victimization than the less educated.[27]

The second major problem with the NCVS is the choice of crimes it explores with respondents. Like the UCR, the NCVS focuses on street crime. It does not ask about commercial, white-collar, and political crimes. Because it is concerned with crimes that are more interpersonal in nature, it gives the impression that these victimizations are more serious. It is doubtful, however, that the employees of Enron who lost their pensions would view an act of vandalism or petty theft as more serious than the corporate fraud. The NCVS also does not attempt to glean information about child abuse. While children under twelve are not interviewed, likely for ethical reasons, the lack of information in this area is a weakness of the instrument. Despite the problems with the NCVS, it is a valuable research tool that is widely analyzed.

Unofficial Data

Self-Report Surveys

One of the most popular methods of determining the extent of crime is the *self-report survey.* These surveys are designed to gather information from individuals about their own criminality. Since the 1940s there have been a rather large number of such studies, and the studies have taken several different forms: anonymous questionnaires; questionnaires signed by the person who confesses his or her offenses confirmed by police records; questionnaires plus follow-up interviews; or "interviews" confirmed by police records.

Self-report surveys have a long history and have consistently indicated that criminal behavior is a universal activity. Nearly everyone has committed some act that could be designated as criminal or delinquent, but few people have been caught. Most people have not committed serious forms of criminal or delinquent behavior, or they have not committed these acts on a regular basis. Self-report studies show that crime and delinquency are distributed throughout the social class structure and that blacks and whites have similar rates of deviance. Unfortunately, with few exceptions, the majority of self-report surveys are taken by school-age children. Some national self-report surveys of adults focus specifically on drug usage and the abuse of wives by their husbands.

Survey Strengths and Weaknesses

Self-report surveys have four major strengths. First, they provide information on prevalence rates, or the proportion of offenders who committed a particular offense at least once in a specific time period. Second, they provide incidence rates, or the average number of offenses per respondent. Third, self-report surveys allow researchers to determine biases in the criminal justice system and differences in offending based on race and social class. Beginning with a 1946 study of delinquency, self-report surveys have revealed that rates of offending are far more evenly distributed in terms of race and social class than official arrest statistics and prison inmate information indicate. Recent studies, however, have indicated that class-based differences exist in the seriousness of offenses as well as the incidence of offense. Fourth, self-report surveys can be as broad or as narrowly defined as the researcher desires. This facilitates the gathering of detailed information and allows researchers to address selected issues in depth.

There are weaknesses with self-report surveys. Historically, these instruments were criticized for focusing on minor offenses and male respondents. Researchers have, however, improved the instruments to address these issues. There are three primary problems with self-report surveys. First, there are respondent issues inherent in all surveys. Some respondents lie; others exaggerate; and some forget. The wording of questions affects responses, and different people interpret questions differently. What one person considers a serious violent crime will not necessarily match the interpretation of another respondent. Although these issues affect the data, many researchers argue that these problems are minimal.

Second, many self-report surveys do not utilize representative samples. Instead, a convenient group is targeted, such as high school students or prisoners. This weakness makes it difficult to generalize the survey results to a population.

Third, as with the other forms of crime data, self-report surveys ignore elite deviance. Essentially, what is regarded as criminal and what is regarded as a serious offense

is not a constant. Is stealing a car more serious than manufacturing thousands of unsafe cars that cause serious injuries or even deaths? There have been no self-report surveys that focus on the undetected deviant activities of corporate executives or other high-status people. Instead, self-report studies focus almost exclusively on conventional criminal and delinquent behavior.

THE EXTENT OF CRIME

Despite the methods of measurement and changes to address problems in the collection of official and unofficial statistics, we cannot accurately report the extent of crime in the United States. We cannot say with certainty how many crimes occur. What we can say with certainty is that many different types of harms are committed against a lot of people. As we explore the extent of crime, keep in mind that data is collected about certain types of crimes. Just as we fail to count the number of baby chickens dyed blue in Kentucky, we also fail to keep track of very damaging offenses committed by powerful corporations. The next section uses the UCR and the NCVS to describe what is known about street crime.

Crimes Known to Police

In 2006, 1,417,745 violent crimes and 9,983,568 property crimes were reported to police.[28] Table 2.1 lists the rate of *crimes known to police* at 10-year intervals from 1976

Table 2.1   Rate (per 100,000) of Crimes Known to the Police, 1976–2006*

	1976	1986	1996	2006
Murder	8.8	8.6	7.4	5.7
Rape	26.6	38.1	36.3	30.9
Robbery	199.3	226.0	201.9	149.4
Aggravated Assault	233.2	347.4	391.0	287.5
Burglary	1448.2	1349.8	945.0	729.4
Larceny-Theft	2921.3	3022.1	2980.3	2206.8
Motor Vehicle Theft	450.0	509.8	525.7	398.4
Total Crime Index	5287.3	5501.9	5087.6	3808.1
Total Violent Crime	467.8	620.1	636.6	473.5
Total Property Crime	4819.5	4881.8	4451.0	3334.5

* Arson was omitted because there was insufficient data to estimate totals, according to the FBI.
Sources: *Sourcebook on Criminal Justice Statistics.* http://www.albany.edu/sourcebook/pdf/t31062005.pdf; *Crime in the United States, 2006,* Table 1. http://www.fbi.gov/ucr/cius2006/data/table_01.html

to 2006. Again, this crime data represents the primary source of the popular image of crime in U.S. society; when the media and politicians discuss crime, they focus on street crime, as reflected in these numbers. Information on crimes known to police, however, is not a measure of criminal behavior. It is a measure of the extent to which certain crimes come to the attention of local police departments. As shown in table 2.1, property crimes are far more common than violent crimes. In fact, the vast majority of crimes known to police are property crimes, with the category "larceny-theft" being the most frequent.

The amount of traditional street crime rose from the late 1960s until 1991 and has declined since then. In fact, the overall crime rate in 1971 was 4165, and in 2001 it was 4163 (after 2001, UCR stopped publishing the overall crime rate).[29] This is quite remarkable since the U.S. population increased by almost 80 million during that time (reaching 300 million in 2006).[30] During roughly the same time period (1980 through 2001), criminal justice expenditures increased 366% and the number of adults under correctional supervision increased 357%.[31]

Table 2.2 offers a comparison between crimes known to the police (UCR data) and the number of victimizations per type of crime (NCVS data). The comparison provides a statistical portrait of the discrepancy between crimes known to the police and crimes identified by victims. While UCR data is not an accurate measure of crime in the United States, it is not without value. It is an important indicator of police activity and sheds light on the demographics of those arrested and for what types of offenses.

Arrests

Perhaps the most revealing figures from the FBI reports are those pertaining to arrest categories. Arrest does not mean guilt; it simply means that an individual was taken into police custody. The vast majority of arrests involve Part II crimes (see table 2.3). This trend has remained constant for the past 50 years or so. The offense category that is responsible for most arrests is "all other offenses," which consists primarily of violations of local ordinances, failure to appear, and violation of probation and parole regulations. The only index crime in the five most frequently committed categories is larceny-theft. We can summarize UCR arrests data as follows: (1) The majority of arrests are for relatively minor offenses; (2) Most arrests involve either property crimes or public-order and victimless crimes; (3) At least half may be drug or alcohol related.

Arrest figures do not tell very much about the real extent of law violations. For example, they do not reveal the number of people who drove a car after drinking and escaped detection even though they would have been guilty of driving under the influence if caught. Similarly, arrests for possession of illegal drugs is more of a measure of police activity—and the visibility of particular groups of people—than a measure of the actual number of people who use illegal drugs. As William Chambliss notes:

> The transgressions of lower-class persons are much more visible than are the transgressions of middle-class persons. Crowded living conditions create an environment in which most behavior, even that which occurs in one's own home, is susceptible to screening by the neighbors and by law enforcement officials. Domestic disputes, drinking to excess and other quasi-illegal acts are much more likely to be seen in the lower classes than in the middle classes.[32]

Table 2.2	Comparing FBI and (NCVS) Data 2005	
	Total Crime Known to Police	Total Victimizations
Rape	93,934	191,670
Robbery	417,122	624,850
Aggravated Assault	862,947	1,052,260
Burglary	2,154,126	3,456,220
Larceny-Theft	6,776,807	13,605,590
Motor Vehicle Theft	1,235,226	978,120

Sources: FBI, *Crime in the United States 2005*. Online: http://www.fbi.gov/ucr/05cius/data/table_01.html; Catalano, S. *Criminal Victimization, 2005*. Online: http://www.ojp.usdoj.gov/bjs/pub/pdf/cv05.pdf

Police officers are under enormous pressure to make arrests. They look for situations that make an arrest highly likely. Most Part II offenses, especially drug dealing and public disturbances, are highly visible in lower-class and minority communities, where the greatest amount of police patrol occurs.

Table 2.3   Persons Arrested 2006

Total[a]	**14,380,370**
Murder and nonnegligent manslaughter	13,435
Forcible rape	24,535
Robbery	125,605
Aggravated assault	447,948
Burglary	304,801
Larceny-theft	1,081,157
Motor vehicle theft	137,757
Arson	16,582
Violent crime[b]	611,523
Property crime[b]	1,540,297
Other assaults	1,305,757
Forgery and counterfeiting	108,823
Fraud	280,693
Embezzlement	20,012
Stolen property; buying, receiving, possessing	122,722
Vandalism	300,679
Weapons; carrying, possessing, etc.	200,782
Prostitution and commercialized vice	79,673
Sex offenses (except forcible rape and prostitution)	87,252
Drug abuse violations	1,889,810
Gambling	12,307
Offenses against the family and children	131,491
Driving under the influence	1,460,498
Liquor laws	645,734
Drunkenness	553,188
Disorderly conduct	703,504
Vagrancy	36,471
All other offenses	4,022,068
Suspicion	2,482
Curfew and loitering law violations	152,907
Runaways	114,179

[a] Does not include suspicion.

[b] Violent crimes are offenses of murder, forcible rape, robbery, and aggravated assault. Property crimes are offenses of burglary, larceny-theft, motor vehicle theft, and arson.

Source: Federal Bureau of Investigation. *Crime in the United States 2006*. Washington, DC: Author. Online: http://www.fbi.gov/ucr/cius2006/data/table_29.html.

Racial Distribution of Arrests

African Americans, while constituting around 12% of the U.S. population, account for 28% of all arrests, 39.3% of violent crime arrests, and 29.4% of property crime arrests. They account for 50.9% of homicide arrests and 56.3% of robbery arrests.[33] Once again, it is important to remember that arrest data reflect police behavior; they do not indicate guilt or innocence.

There are two possible explanations for this disproportionate representation of African Americans in arrest data. The first is that they commit more crime than other racial groups. This is simply not the case. Self-report and victimization surveys indicate that crime rates for blacks and whites are similar. Second, the data reflect bias in police practices. Police use of racial profiling to stop individuals without probable cause and the concentration of police efforts in low-income, minority neighborhoods explains some of the disproportionate arrests of blacks.[34]

Women account for about 24% of all arrests. Women are more likely to be arrested for crimes such as fraud, forgery and counterfeiting, embezzlement, and larceny-theft. They have always led their male counterparts in both runaway and prostitution arrests. See chapter 17 for a more comprehensive discussion of women and crime.

Age Distribution of Arrests

Arrests vary by age and by offense. In 2006, those under 18 accounted for 15.5% of all arrests.[35] The popular conception of juvenile crime being out of control is inaccurate. The majority of those arrested are, and always have been, adults. Adults are far more likely than juveniles to be arrested for index crimes, with the exception of arson. Juvenile crime is discussed in chapter 16.

THE OTHER SIDE OF THE CRIME PICTURE: CORPORATE AND STATE CRIME

As mentioned previously, there are a variety of behaviors that are illegal in the United States. Some, like the examples in the first paragraph of this chapter, seem a little silly. Others, however, are very damaging to society. Not all behaviors that threaten the well-being of U.S. citizens are treated as criminal. Even some that are illegal are not widely investigated, nor are they counted by the measures of crime reviewed earlier. There is a great deal more to crime than what is described by the UCR and NCVS. An alternative view of crime and the extent of crime presents a radically different picture than that provided by the media and official statistics.

Who are the "dangerous" people in society? Who threatens us with death and serious bodily injury? Who puts our money or property at risk? There is no question that we would be frightened if a robber confronted us on the street or if we came home and discovered that a stranger had broken into our house. We do not want to downplay the significance of traditional crimes of violence. These are, however, only part of the total crime picture.

Statistically speaking, the gravest threats to us are not from robbers, burglars, rapists, or others threatening one-on-one harm. According to FBI figures about two people will be murdered within the next hour, most often by a gun or knife.[36] However, more than seven will die in the next hour from an occupational injury or from diseases they contracted through their employment. Another source reports 4.4 million nonfatal workplace injuries and illnesses per year.[37] Occupational diseases, death, and injuries cost us around $155 billion each year, dwarfing the crimes shown on television.[38] Importantly, about half of these workplace harms are preventable. They could be avoided if employers complied with various state, federal, and local laws and regulations. *White-collar crime* is a violation of the criminal law committed by someone in the course of his or her occupation.

Categories of Corporate Crime

Corporate crime involves two primary categories: corporate violence and corporate abuse of power, fraud, or economic exploitation.[39]

Corporate violence: Violence committed by corporations usually does not involve direct harm. Instead, it exposes people to harmful conditions, products, or substances over time. For example, manufacture of faulty tires is not immediately apparent, but the eventual deterioration will cause injury. Corporate violence tends to involve many people working collectively rather than a single offender. Corporate practices, policies, and procedures can and often do have life-threatening consequences. For example, corporate environmental practices can cause various forms of cancer and other life-threatening diseases. Each year, the manufacture of unsafe foods, products, and medicine injures millions of Americans, kill tens of thousands, and costs more than $100 billion in property damages, lost wages, and other expenses.[40]

It is important to note that we are not arguing that all work accidents and deaths are deliberate. Some are truly accidental. Others, however, were allowed to occur with malice aforethought and recklessly endangered employees or consumers. Consider these examples:

McWane Inc.: Ten employees have been killed on the job since 1995 at McWane Inc. facilities. Three of the deaths resulted from deliberate safety standard violations. In five others, safety lapses were contributing factors. One man died when he was directed to use an industrial oven to incinerate highly combustible paint. The oven exploded. Investigators determined that the explosion was the result of reckless criminal actions by McWane. The company was forced to pay a fine but has not been held accountable for any employee deaths.[41]

Current and former managers said McWane viewed regulatory fines as far less costly than complying with safety and environmental rules. For example, after an employee was run over by a forklift that had known safety defects and brakes that were not working properly, McWane paid $10,500 to settle OSHA violations for operating unsafe forklifts and failing to train drivers.[42]

BP Oil: In March 2005, fifteen workers died in an explosion at BP's refinery in Texas City, Texas. It was the third fatal accident at that facility in four years. BP admitted "mistakes" and took responsibility for the explosion. Under Texas law, executives could be charged with reckless homicide or involuntary manslaughter. This leading death penalty state, however, declined to file any charges.[43]

Merck: The pharmaceutical company Merck manufactured Vioxx, a drug designed to treat arthritis. The company's early clinical trials revealed high risks of heart attack and stroke in patients using the drug. The company ignored the risks, and the drug was widely marketed and prescribed to patients. The FDA estimates that between 88,000 and 139,000 people suffered heart attacks or stroke after taking the drug, and 60,000 died.[44]

Table 2.4 provides a small sampling of the deaths and injuries caused by corporate violence. Crimes of violence are not limited to the interpersonal. We will highlight several examples. Pharmaceutical products such as Thalidomide did extensive damage to women and their unborn children in the 1960s. Unsafe consumer products have contributed to the violence. For example, General Motors produced pickup trucks with defective gas tanks that led to 150 unnecessary deaths. Ford knew that its Pinto of the 1970s could explode after rear impact. They ignored the threat in favor of larger profits and allowed many to die. In 1998, a Tampa, Florida, company and the company's plant manager were found guilty of violating a federal hazardous waste law.[45] Those illegal acts resulted in the deaths of two nine-year-old boys who were playing in a dumpster at the company's facility. A 1989 explosion at a Kentucky mine operated by Costain Coal killed 10 workers. The company pled guilty to a pattern of misconduct; it was charged with 23 felony counts and 9 misdemeanors. The fine was $3.75 million. Odwalla, Inc., the beverage company, pled guilty in 1996 to violating federal food safety laws and selling contaminated apple juice that killed a 16-month old girl and injured at least 70 others. The company paid a $1.5 million fine, the largest criminal fine for a food injury case in the history of the Food and Drug Administration and the first such criminal conviction. In 1993, the manufacturer of a heart catheter, C.R. Bard Inc., pled guilty to a 391-count criminal charge for marketing an unapproved medical device. One patient died, and 10 underwent emergency heart surgery. The company paid $60.1 million in fines and penalties, including a $30.9 million criminal fine.

Deaths from occupational diseases, such as black lung and asbestosis, and deaths from pollution, contaminated foods, hazardous consumer products, and hospital malpractice do violence to thousands of Americans each year and are often the result of criminal recklessness. The workers who have died in preventable accidents, the children who have died from cancer due to dumping of toxic waste, and the people who died because they trusted that their cars were safe are just as dead (and their deaths just as painful to loved

Table 2.4   Death and Injury from Selected Corporate Crimes

Corporation/Industry	Problem	Extent of Death and Injury
Union Carbide	Chemical gas leak in Bhopal, India	500 deaths and 200,000 injuries
Miscellaneous	Asbestos	Estimated 100,000 workers may eventually die
Pharmaceutical	Oraflex (arthritis drug)	Killed at least 49 elderly
Firestone	Firestone 500 Tires	Loss of tread believed to have resulted in 41 deaths
General Motors	Faulty brakes	Estimated 13 people killed
Ford Pinto and Mercury Bobcat	Exploding fuel tanks	Estimated more than 50 killed
Pharmaceutical	Dalkon Shield	Estimated to have killed 17 women and injured as many as 200,000

Source: T. Miethe and R. McCorkle. *Crime Profiles*. Los Angeles: Roxbury Press, 1998, chapter 7.

ones) as if they had died at the hands of a street criminal.

Corporate theft: Many of the crimes of corporations have an economic impact rather than violent consequences. The property crimes reported to the FBI cost the American people an estimated $3 to $4 billion per year. In direct contrast, the most recent estimate of the costs of corporate and "white collar" crime is in excess of $200 billion, or 500 times the estimated cost of property crimes, each year.[46] Table 2.5 explores some of the financial costs of corporate crime.

In many cases the number and costs of corporate crimes are based on estimates, since hard data are difficult to come by. By the same token, much of what is reported by the FBI in its annual report is based on estimates. The fines paid by corporations, while repre-

senting only those who have been caught, do provide hard data. The Corporate Crime Reporter compiled a list of the top 100 corporate criminals of the 1990s. They listed only the corporations that pled guilty or no contest to crimes and were fined for the criminal behavior.[47] There were 14 categories of crime committed by the 100 corporations: environmental (38), antitrust (20), fraud (13), campaign finance (7), food and drug (6), financial crimes (4), false statements (3), illegal exports (3), illegal boycott (1), worker death (1), bribery (1), obstruction of justice (1), public corruption (1), and tax evasion (1). The fines ranged from $150,000 to $500 million. Six of the corporations—Exxon, Royal Caribbean, Rockwell International, Warner-Lambert, Teledyne, and United Technologies were each guilty of two crimes that made the list.

The report listed several caveats, beginning with a caution that companies on the list represent "only the tip of a very large iceberg of corporate wrongdoing." The other caveats were that corporations have the power and resources to define the laws that regulate them (by influencing legislation) and to defend themselves both in court and in the court of public opinion.[48] For example, Royal Caribbean Cruise Lines hired defense attorneys who had previously headed the Justice Department's Environmental Crimes Section. They also hired two former attorneys general, a former prosecutor, a University of Virginia law professor, two former State Department officials, and four retired senior admirals.

As the case proceeded to trial, Royal Caribbean engaged in a massive public relations campaign, taking out ads during the Super Bowl, putting former Environmental Protection Agency (EPA) administrators on its board of directors, and donating thousands of dollars to environmental groups.[49]

Although federal prosecutors won two cases against them ($18 million in 1999 and $9 million in 1998, both for dumping waste in the ocean and lying to the Coast Guard), the details indicate the resources available to corporations to try to avoid conviction.

The list of corporate crimes includes bribery of government officials, defense contract fraud, health care provider fraud, corporate

Table 2.5	The Costs of White-Collar and Corporate Crime (in billions of dollars)
Offense	**Estimated Cost**
Corporate crime (fraud, antitrust violations, bribery, corruption, price-fixing, illegal mergers, etc.)	$700+
Embezzlement (employee theft)	$6–435
Tax fraud	$100–300
Money laundering	$100–300
Computer-related, "high-tech" crime	$.1–200
Consumer/personal fraud (telemarketing)	$40–100
Health care fraud (Medicare, Medicaid)	$10–100
Insurance fraud	$18–31
Savings and loan scandal bailout	$8–15
Check fraud	$10
Phone and cellular fraud	$.5–9
Credit/debit/charge/ bank card fraud	$.75–1.5
Total Estimated Costs	**$993.35–$1,491.5**

Sources: Coleman, J. W. *The Criminal Elite* (3rd ed.). New York: St. Martin's Press, 1994; Friedrichs, D. O. *Trusted Criminals: White Collar Crime in Contemporary Society* (3rd ed.). Belmont, CA: Wadsworth, 2007; Green, G. S. *Occupational Crime*. Chicago: Nelson-Hall, 1990; T. Miethe and R. McCorkle. *Crime Profiles*. Los Angeles: Roxbury Press, 1998.

tax evasion, price-fixing, false advertising, product misrepresentation, cheating workers out of overtime pay, violations of minimum wage laws, unfair labor practices, surveillance of employees, theft of trade secrets, monopolistic practices, and defrauding investors.[50] While the list of crimes increases, the corporate share of the tax burden has been declining from around 25% in the 1950s to less than 10% today.[51]

Corporate crime is not new. Edwin Sutherland discussed the extent of corporate crime in 1949. He focused on law violations by 70 corporations and found a total of 980 specific violations, about one-third of which were restraint of trade.[52] About 20 years later another study found that over a two-year period more than 60% of the 582 largest corporations had at least one violation. Automobile, oil refining, and drug companies accounted for about one-half of all violations.[53] At about the same time a very detailed case study of a mining company discovered that for several years it had used a nearby stream to dump waste material, which eventually piled up to produce a large dam with a lake behind it. The dam eventually collapsed during a rainstorm, resulting in the deaths of 125 people and, almost literally, wiping out an entire community. Most of the people who died had worked for the company.[54]

State Crime

The final category of crime involves the state as the offender. Examples include the officials we elect or appoint, the institutions that govern us, and their representatives. State crime involves harmful behaviors committed by the government, sometimes in collusion with private corporations. It can occur at the national, state, or local level. Crimes of the state can take various forms, but the behaviors have two commonalities: they are generally committed against powerless people and they are rarely, if ever, called crimes.

The primary categories of state crime are terrorism, torture, war crimes, genocide, military invasion, colonization, and environmental crimes. The U.S. government could be labeled recidivist for its long criminal history. There are numerous examples of intervening

in the affairs of Third World countries in support of dictatorships and the overthrow of democratically elected governments—often in support of private corporate interests: Guatemala (1950s), Zaire (1960s), Dominican Republic (1961–62), Indonesia (including East Timor, 1960s–1970s), Greece (1967), Chile (1973), Angola (1975), Libya (1980), Grenada (1980s), El Salvador (1980s), Nicaragua (1980s), Haiti (late 1980s, early 1990s), and Iraq (1990s, 2004).[55]

One particularly gruesome example—and one almost completely ignored by the mainstream press—was what amounted to genocide in East Timor. East Timor, a portion of Indonesia just north of Australia, was a country of around 600,000. This country, rich in oil and other resources, became a pawn of the Indonesian dictator Suharto, who, with the help of the CIA, had overthrown the democratically elected President Sukarto. The United States provided arms for the coup. This event killed around 200,000 innocent citizens in what has been described as the worst example of genocide since the Holocaust.[56]

All of the above cases are examples of criminal offenses or at least violations of international human rights laws committed by offenders who came from the highest echelons of society. In the minds of most people, however, their behavior was not criminal. They were not perceived as dangerous. Yet these offenses cost thousands of lives and several hundred billion dollars. The atrocities committed by corporate and state criminals far outweigh the costs of street crimes. Yet, the actions of the criminal justice system overwhelmingly target street crimes, and these offenders—often minorities—fill our jails and prisons. It is a rare occurrence when a perpetrator of a corporate or state crime goes to prison.

State and corporate crimes are not part of the popular image of "crime" and "criminals." Until we consciously expand the definition of criminal behavior, the probability is that we will be at risk from harms we don't currently acknowledge as crimes. One-on-one harm is terrifying, but indirect harm can damage millions.

SUMMARY

This chapter focused on the meaning of crime in the United States. Crime has many dimensions, ranging from the street crimes reported by the FBI in their annual report to crimes rarely reported or prosecuted—corporate and state crime. We reviewed the classifications of crime (felonies and misdemeanors), and the governmental jurisdictions that determine where crimes will be prosecuted (federal, state, local), and the various types of crime. The difficulties with measuring crime were discussed. Official statistics include the annual FBI report, victimization surveys, and self-report studies.

"Crimes known to the police" is the first category of data compiled by the FBI. Its usefulness is limited because it measures only reported crime. "Persons arrested" is the second major category. The limitation here is that it is a more accurate reflection of police activity than of guilt. Victimization surveys are a means of measuring crime that has not been reported to local police departments. Self-report studies, although focusing mostly on the behavior of school-aged children, are another source that reveals criminal behavior that would otherwise not be reported.

In the section on the extent of crime, we compared conventional statistics and socioeconomic data with the other side of the crime picture: corporate and state crime. Crimes committed by those of high social standing range from price-fixing and various forms of fraud to murder and genocide. While the toll from these offenses is great, they do not represent interpersonal crimes, ("one-on-one harms") so they are treated differently in our society.

Key Terms

- capital felony
- corporate crime
- crime
- crimes known to police
- dark figure of crime
- federal offenses
- felony
- index crimes
- indirect harm
- legal concept of crime
- local crimes
- *mala in se* and *mala prohibita* crimes
- misdemeanors
- National Incident-Based Reporting System (NIBRS)
- National Crime Victimization Survey (NCVS)
- self-report survey
- social/popular concept of crime
- state crimes
- Uniform Crime Report (UCR)
- white-collar crime

Notes

[1] Amended 1972 Ky. Acts ch. 374, sec. 1. Created 1966 Ky. Acts ch. 215, sec. 5.

[2] Bourdieu, P. *On Television.* New York: The New Press, 1998, p. 18.

[3] Altheide, D. L. *Creating Fear: News and the Construction of Crisis.* Hawthorne, NY: Aldine De Gruyter, 2002.

[4] Kivivuori, J., S. Kemppi, and M. Smolej. *Front-page Violence: Reporting on the Front Pages of the Finnish Tabloid Press 1980–2000.* National Research Institute of Legal Policy Helsinki, Publication no. 196 (2002). Lane, J. and J. W. Meeker. "Ethnicity, Information Sources, and Fear of Crime." *Deviant Behavior.* 24(1): 1–26 (2003).

[5] Shelden, R. G. *Controlling the Dangerous Classes: A Critical Introduction to the History of Criminal Justice.* Boston: Allyn & Bacon, 2001; Miller, K. S. *Wrongful Capital Convictions and the Legitimacy of the Death Penalty.* New York: LFB Scholarly Publishing, 2006.

[6] Best, J. *Random Violence: How We Talk about New Crimes and New Victims.* Los Angeles: University of California Press, 1999; Kappeler, V. E. and G. W. Potter. *The Mythology of Crime and Criminal Justice* (4th ed.). Long Grove, IL: Waveland Press, 2005.

[7] Reiman, J. *The Rich Get Richer and the Poor Get Prison* (8th ed.). Boston: Allyn & Bacon, 2007, pp. 72–73.

[8] Michael, J. and M. J. Adler. *Crime, Law and Social Science.* New York: Harcourt, Brace, 1933, p. 5.

[9] Quinney, R. and J. Wildeman. *The Problem of Crime: A Peace and Social Justice Perspective* (3rd ed.). Mountain View, CA: Mayfield, 1991, p. 4.

[10] Sellin, J. T. *Culture, Conflict and Crime.* New York: Social Science Research Council, 1938.

[11] Sutherland, E. *White Collar Crime.* Chicago: University of Chicago Press, 1949.

[12] Schwendinger, H. and J. Schwendinger. "Defenders of Order or Guardians of Human Rights." *Issues in Criminology* 5: 113–146 (1970).

[13] Michalowski, R. *Order, Law and Power.* New York: Macmillan, 1985, p. 314.

[14] Friedrichs, D. O. *Trusted Criminals: White Collar Crime in Contemporary Society* (3rd ed.). Belmont, CA: Wadsworth, 2007.

[15] A great deal has been written on the subject of "hate crimes." See, for example: Ferber, A. *Home-Grown Hate.* New York: Routledge, 2003.

[16] The annual reports are available online: http://www.fbi.gov/ucr/ucr.htm

[17] Table 26. [Online] http://www.fbi.gov/ucr/05cius/data/table_26.html

[18] Percent Change in Volume and Rate, FBI. [Online] http://www.fbi.gov/ucr/05cius/data/table_01a.html

[19] Ibid.

[20] Beirne, P. and Messerschmidt, J. *Criminology* (3rd ed.). Boulder, CO: Westview, 2000, p. 38.

[21] Eigenberg, H. M. *Women Battering in the United States: Till Death Do Us Part.* Long Grove, IL: Waveland Press, 2001, p. 198.

[22] Chappell, D., G. Geis, S. Schafer, and L. Siegel. "Forcible Rape: A Comparative Study of Offenses Known to the Police in Boston and Los Angeles." In J. M. Henslin (ed.), *Studies in the Sociology of Sex.* New York: Appleton Century Crofts, 1971.

[23] This assertion is based upon personal observations of the authors, confidential conversations with members of police departments in two different cities and internal memos we have obtained. Documentation about using "gangs" to divert attention away from internal problems is found in Miethe, T. and R. McCorkle, "The Political and Organizational Response to Gangs: An Examination of a 'Moral Panic' in Nevada." *Justice Quarterly* 15: 41–64 (March, 1998).

[24] Seidman, D. and M. Couzens. "Getting the Crime Rate Down: Political Pressure and Crime Reporting." *Law & Society Review* 8: 457–493 (1974).

[25] Brownstein, H. H. *The Rise and Fall of a Violent Crime Wave: Crack Cocaine and the Social Construction of a Crime Problem.* Guilderland, NY: Harrow and Heston, 1996, p. 22.

[26] Beirne and Messerschmidt, *Criminology.*

[27] Ibid.

[28] Federal Bureau of Investigation. *Crime in the United States.* http://www.fbi.gov/ucr/05cius/data/table_01.html

[29] *Sourcebook of Criminal Justice Statistics.* [Online] http://www.albany.edu/sourcebook/pdf/t31062004.pdf

[30] U.S. Census Bureau. [Online] http://www.census.gov/popest/archives/

[31] *Justice Expenditure and Employment in the United States, 2001.* [Online] http://www.ojp.gov/bjs/pub/pdf/jeeus01.pdf; *Adults on Probation, in Jail or Prison, and on Parole.* [Online] http://www.albany.edu/sourcebook/pdf/t612005.pdf

[32] Chambliss, W. J. (ed.). *Criminal Law in Action.* New York: McGraw-Hill, 1984, p. 201.

[33] *Crime in the United States 2005*, table 43. [Online] http://www.fbi.gov/ucr/05cius/data/table_43.html

[34] Trojanowicz, R., V. E. Kappeler, and L. K. Gaines. *Community Policing: A Contemporary Perspective* (3rd ed.). Cincinnati, OH: Anderson, 2002.

[35] *Crime in the United States 2005*, table 41. [Online] http://www.fbi.gov/ucr/05cius/data/table_41.html

[36] *Crime in the United States 2005.* [Online] http://www.fbi.gov/ucr/05cius/about/crime_clock.html; Cullen, L. *A Job to Die For.* Monroe, ME: Common Courage Press, 2002.

[37] Reiman, *The Rich Get Richer and the Poor Get Prison,* p. 82.

[38] Cullen, *A Job to Die For.*

[39] Friedrichs, *Trusted Criminals: White Collar Crime in Contemporary Society,* p. 59.

[40] Ibid., p. 63.

[41] Barstow, D. "Officials at Foundry Face Health and Safety Charges." *The New York Times* (August 30, 2003), p. 28.

[42] Kappeler and Potter, *The Mythology of Crime and Criminal Justice,* p. 154.

[43] Associated Press. "BP's Own Experts Knew of Risks at Plant in Texas City Where Blast Killed 15, Report Says." *Sioux City Journal,* 2006.

[44] Herper, M. "David Graham on the Vioxx Verdict." *Forbes* (August 19 2005). [Online] http://www.forbes.com/home/sciencesandmedicine/2005/08/19/merck-vioxx-graham_cx_mh_0819graham.html

[45] Mokhiber, R. "Top 100 Corporate Criminals of the Decade." *Corporate Crime Reporter.* [Online] http://www.corporatecrimereporter.com/top100.html

[46] Mokhiber, R. "Corporate Crime: Underworld U.S.A." In K. Danaher (ed.), *Corporations are Gonna Get Your Mama: Globalization and the Downsizing of the American Dream.* Monroe, ME: Common Courage Press, 1996, p. 61; Clinard, M. B., Quinney, R., and Wildeman, J. *Criminal Behavior Systems* (3rd ed.). Cincinnati: Anderson, 1994, p. 192.

[47] Mokhiber, *Top 100 Corporate Criminals.*

[48] It is interesting to note that virtually all of the tobacco companies have significantly increased the marketing of their product overseas and toward the young in our country. Given that tobacco is directly related to around 300,000–400,000 deaths each year, one could reasonably argue that these companies are among the biggest drug traffickers in the world! The same can be said for the liquor industry. However, largely because of their collective power, such behaviors are not labeled as "crimes," while the mere *possession* of marijuana is a felony in some states (such as Nevada).

[49] Mokhiber, "Top 100 Corporate Criminals of the Decade."

[50] Friedrichs, *Trusted Criminals: White Collar Crime in Contemporary Society,* pp. 74–84.

[51] Friedman, J. "The Decline of Corporate Income Tax Revenues." Center on Budget and Policy Priorities, October 24, 2003. [Online] http://www.cbpp.org/10-16-03tax.htm

[52] Sutherland, E. *White Collar Crime.* Chicago: University of Chicago Press, 1949.

[53] Clinard, M. B. and P. C. Yeager. *Corporate Crime.* New York: The Free Press, 1980.

[54] Erickson, K. T. *Everything in Its Path: Destruction of Community in the Buffalo Creek Flood.* New York: Simon & Schuster, 1976.

55 Detailed discussions of these and other state crimes fill entire books. See, for example: Parenti, M. *Against Empire*. San Francisco: City Lights Press, 1995; Chomsky, N. *Year 501: The Conquest Continues*. Boston: South End Press, 1993; Zepezauer, M. *The CIA's Greatest Hits*. Tucson, AZ: Odonian Press, 1994; Barak, G. (ed.), *Crimes by the Capitalist State*. Albany: SUNY Press, 1991. U.S. foreign policies leading to various crimes are concisely summarized in Chomsky, N. *What Uncle Sam Really Wants*. Tucson, AZ: Odonian Press, 1992. See also his latest books: *Hegemony or Survival?* New York: Metropolitan Books, 2004; *Failed States*. New York: Metropolitan Books, 2006.

56 Extensively documented in Chomsky, N. *Powers and Prospects*. Boston: South End Press, 1996, chapter 7; Parenti, *Against Empire*, pp. 26–27; Zepezauer, pp. 30–31.

three

Perspectives on Criminal Justice and Law

Why do we have a criminal justice system? What is its purpose? What does it really do? Should it impose sanctions only after the fact? Should it try to prevent crime before it occurs? Is the system truly egalitarian, or does it dispense biased justice? Whose interests does the system serve—all of the people or only some of the people? These are a few of the questions people routinely ask about the U.S. system of criminal justice.

Two schools of thought have attempted to address such questions.[1] After reviewing the *classical* and *positivist* schools we will offer our own perspective on crime and criminal justice, which differs significantly from each of them.

THE CLASSICAL SCHOOL

The core ideas of classical thinking about human nature and society emerged during the Enlightenment with the work of John Locke (1632–1704), Jean-Jacques Rousseau (1712–1778), Charles Louis Montesquieu (1689–1755), and Thomas Hobbes (1588–1679). The Renaissance (1300–1600) had swept away feudal customs and institutions and fostered intellectual development. According to the classical school, an unwritten social contract emerged that allowed humans to move from a state of nature to a modern, civil society. The solitary, uncomplicated existence where nature could fill basic needs disappeared as population increased. Humans could use reason to lift the veil of ignorance and enter into a social

contract in which they grant authority to another in exchange for social order and security. This perspective stressed that humans have free will; theoretically, there was no limit to what they could accomplish. It was also asserted that humans are essentially hedonistic—that humans, by their very nature, freely choose actions that maximize pleasure and minimize pain. Social contract thinkers claimed that the main instrument for the control of human behavior is fear, especially fear of pain. Punishment, as a principal method of operating to create fear, is seen as necessary to influence human will and thus to control behavior. Also, society has a right to punish an individual and to transfer this right to the state. Finally, some code of criminal law, or some system of punishment, was deemed necessary to respond to crime.[2]

The *classical school* of thought about crime and criminal justice derives mainly from the work of Cesare Beccaria (1738–1794), whose influential book *On Crimes and Punishment* was first published in 1764.[3] Beccaria and other liberal thinkers believed that the major principle that should govern legislation was "the greatest happiness for the greatest numbers" (this supports the view that government should be "of the people, by the people, for the people"). This philosophical doctrine is known as *utilitarianism,* the idea that punishment ought to be based on its *usefulness* or *utility* or *practicality.* In his book, Beccaria noted, "For a punishment to attain its end, the evil which it inflicts has only to exceed the advantages derivable from the crime." In other words, punishment should not be excessive; *it should fit the crime.*

Beccaria was the first to provide a basic outline of what turned out to be the modern system of criminal justice. "In order for punishment not to be, in every instance, an act of violence of one or of many against a private citizen, it must be essentially public, prompt, necessary, the least possible in the given circumstances, proportionate to the crimes, dictated by the laws."[4] Beccaria also argued that punishment should be "swift and certain"—it should immediately follow the commission of a crime and there should be a common understanding that the penalty would be applied. The classical school emphasized that the purpose of the criminal justice system was to prevent criminal behavior through deterrence—a potential criminal would decide against committing a crime because the punishment would be too costly. Jeremy Bentham (1748–1832), one of Beccaria's contemporaries, believed that criminal behavior (like all human behavior) is a rational choice, born of free will. To prevent crime, punishment should be greater than any potential gain from the criminal act.

The classical school makes the following assumptions: (1) All people are self-interested by nature; therefore they are liable to commit crime for personal gain; (2) In order to live in harmony and avoid a "war of all against all" (as Hobbes stressed), people agree to give up certain freedoms in order to be protected by a strong central state; (3) Punishment is necessary to deter crime, and the state has the prerogative (which has been granted to it by the people through a social contract) to administer it; (4) Punishment should fit the crime and not be used to rehabilitate the offender; (5) Use of the law should be limited, and due process rights should be observed; (6) All people are equal and each individual is responsible for his or her actions; mitigating circumstances or excuses are inadmissible.[5]

The classical school of thought has generally given rise to two contrasting models of the criminal justice system that are roughly the equivalent of two differing political ideol-

ogies—namely, conservatism and liberalism.[6] From the conservative ideology comes the *crime control model.* It is based on the assumption that the fundamental goal of the criminal justice system is the repression of crime through aggressive law enforcement and harsh punishments, including the death penalty. From this point of view, protecting citizens from crime is more important than protecting the civil liberties of citizens. The primary concern of the crime control model is public safety.

From the liberal ideology comes the *due process model.* If the crime control model resembles an "assembly line," the due process model resembles an "obstacle course." The due process model stresses the importance of individual rights and supports the general belief that it is better to let several criminals go free than to falsely imprison an innocent person. This model is based on the assumption that the criminal justice process is plagued by human error and that at each stage individual rights need to be safeguarded. The accused should be accorded legal counsel and equitable treatment. The discretion of criminal justice personnel, especially the police, should be limited.

The classical school and its modern derivatives are subject to several criticisms. First, the assumptions that people always act rationally and that all people are hedonists and self-serving can be challenged. In fact, over one hundred years of social science research has demonstrated that this is clearly not the case; humans are much more complex than such a simplistic view implies.[7] Second, the assumption that people are equal or are equally likely to commit a crime can also be challenged. In point of fact, people in society (especially when the classical school emerged) are hardly equal by any method of measurement. The French philosopher Anatole France once praised the "majestic equality of the law" because it "forbids rich and poor alike to sleep under bridges, to beg in the streets and to steal bread."[8]

This point leads us directly to the third objection—the classical school does little to address the causes of crime. Classical writers avoided any discussion of the relationship between inequality and crime and instead focused on problems associated with the control of crime.[9] Criminology became "administrative and legal criminology" during which justice became "an exact scale of punishments for equal acts without reference to the nature of the individual involved and with no attention to the question of special circumstances under which the act came about."[10]

The problems associated with the classical approach as proposed by Beccaria were felt as soon as legislatures began to adopt it. The French Code of 1791 tried to adopt, almost literally, Beccaria's proposals. Legislation tried to fix an exact amount of penalty to every crime and left nothing for the courts to do except to determine guilt. No attempt was made to allow for extenuating circumstances. It was nearly impossible to ignore the various social determinants of human behavior "and to proceed as if punishment and incarceration could be easily measured on some kind of universal calculus."[11] What eventually occurred was the rise of what criminologists have called the neoclassical school. Lawyers and jurists, mostly in Europe, attempted to revise the classical approach to account for the practical problems in the administration of justice. Certain reformers attacked the French Code as unjust because of its rigidity and recognized the "need for individualization and for discriminating judgment to fit individual circumstances," including past record of behavior, the degree of incompetence or the mental state of the offender, and the impact of age on criminal responsibility.[12] In short, there was recognition that all offenders did not possess the same degree of "free will," and not every offender was suitable for imprisonment.

It is important to note, however, that the basic thrust of the classical school's view of human nature and the proper response to crime was, for all practical purposes, left unchanged.

> The doctrine continued to be that humans are creatures guided by reason, who have free will, and who therefore are responsible for their acts and can be controlled by fear of punishment. Hence the pain from punishment must exceed the pleasure obtained from the criminal act; then free will deter-

mines the desirability of noncriminal conduct. The neoclassical school therefore represented primarily the modifications necessary for the administration of the criminal law based on classical theory that resulted from practical experience.[13]

The beliefs of the classical school were challenged almost from the time that Beccaria's proposals were being debated. The challenge came from the positivist school.

THE POSITIVIST SCHOOL

The *positivist school* of thought about crime and criminal justice originated in the nineteenth century. The scientific revolution, especially the discoveries of Charles Darwin, represented a sharp break from the past. Answers to fundamental questions about human beings and the universe began to be presented through the means of an "objective" science instead of religious beliefs or armchair philosophy. In *On the Origin of Species* (1859), Darwin presented evidence that "humans were the same general kind of creatures as the rest of the animals, except that they were more highly evolved or developed." Humans were beginning to be "understood as creatures whose conduct was influenced, if not determined, by biological and cultural antecedents rather than as self-determining beings who were free to do what they wanted."[14] It was at this time that the first "scientific" studies of crime and criminal behavior began.

Positivism is a method of inquiry that attempts to answer questions through the scientific method. The researcher examines the real world of empirical facts through the testing of hypotheses. The main goal is to arrive at the ultimate "truth" and to derive "laws" (e.g., the law of gravity or the law of relativity). The positivist mode of inquiry gained respectability in the social sciences largely through the work of Auguste Comte (1798–1857), often credited as being the founder of positivism and the founder of the discipline known as sociology. According to Comte, knowledge passes through three stages: theological, metaphysical, and positive or scientific. The positive or scientific is the highest or final stage of knowledge. At this stage human beings are able to discover regularities among social phenomena and thus to predict and control outcomes.[15]

The positivist school of criminology argues that humans do not have free will and that human behavior is determined by various biological, psychological, and sociological factors. Thus, responsibility for one's actions is diminished. The solution to the problem of crime, from this perspective, is to eliminate the various factors that are thought to be the most likely causes of it. Such a task might include, but certainly is not limited to, psychiatric and/or psychological testing and treatment, dietary monitoring and supplements or adjustments, and the reduction of poverty or greater emphasis on education. The criminal justice system has attempted to accomplish the goal of reducing crime by making the punishment *fit the offender* (rather than fit the crime, as the classical school proposes), through the wide exercise of discretion by criminal justice officials. The goal is to rehabilitate the offender.

Adolphe Quételet (1796–1874), a Belgian mathematician, laid the foundation for positivist criminology through his work in statistics.[16] His quest for identifying lawlike regularities in society, using traditional scientific methods, resulted in an interest in studying crime by studying rates of crime. Quételet looked at official crime data for France and found striking regularities within the French criminal justice apparatus. For example, there were consistencies in the number of defendants who failed to appear in court; certain courts were more likely to impose particular sanctions for particular offenses. Looking at different types of crimes committed in France between 1826 and 1829, he concluded, "one passes from one year to the other with the sad perspective of seeing the same crimes reproduced in the same order and bring with them the same penalties in the same proportions."[17]

Identifying a correlation between crime and the ability to read and write, Quételet found that as reading and writing proficiency increased, the frequency of criminal acts decreased. Looking at the years 1828 and 1829, he was able to identify over 2,000 crimes against the person committed by people who could not read or write. He noted that during the same period only 80 similar offenses were committed by people who received academic instruction. He found that those with education were much less likely to be involved in property crimes than their uneducated counterparts. He identified 206 property offenses committed by the well-educated and 6,617 property offenses committed by illiterate offenders during the same time period.

> It is possible, in fact, that individuals of the knowledgeable class of society, while committing fewer manslaughters, murders, and other serious crimes than those individuals who have not received any instruction, nevertheless commit even fewer crimes against property.... This conjecture likewise becomes probable if one considers that the knowledgeable class implies more affluence and, consequently, less need to resort to the different varieties of theft which make up a great part of crimes against property; while affluence and knowledge do not succeed as easily in restraining the fire of the passions and sentiments of hate and vengeance.[18]

Later, Quételet turned his attention to propensities for crime and found striking correlations between crime and independent variables such as climate and the age, sex, and socioeconomic status of offenders. Young males between the ages of 21 and 25 were found to have the highest propensity for crime; women had the lowest. When Quételet compared female and male offenders, he discovered that males committed nearly four times as many property offenses as women and were involved in over six times more violent offenses. He also noted that violent offenses were most likely to occur in the summer months, and property offenses during the winter. The poor and the unemployed were found to have a higher propensity for crime than members of the working and upper classes. Quételet also discovered that economic changes were related to crime rates, and he surmised that society itself, through its economic and social attributes, was responsible for crime. Although people may have free will, there nevertheless were scientific laws to which criminal behavior corresponded.

Recognizing that all people had the "capacity" to commit crime (an idea that would later be adopted by neo-Freudians), Quételet argued that the average person rarely transformed that option into action. He eventually turned away from the social influences of criminal behavior (as most contemporary criminologists have done) and focused on the correlation between crime and morality, suggesting that certain "types" of people (e.g., vagabonds, Gypsies, and others with supposedly "inferior moral stock") were more prone to criminal behavior than others.

The big breakthrough as far as positivist criminology is concerned was made by an Italian doctor named **Cesare Lombroso** (1836–1909). In 1876 he published *Criminal Man,* which earned him the title "father of criminology." In this work Lombroso emphasized the *biological* basis of criminal behavior. He argued that criminals are born biologically inferior and can be distinguished from noncriminal persons by the presence of certain physical characteristics or stigmata—characteristics that are throwbacks to primitive people.

Chapter 4 discusses Lombroso's theories in more detail. Since Lombroso's time, positivist criminology has branched out into psychological and sociological approaches. *Biological* positivism (which began with Lombroso) locates the causes of crime within an individual's physical makeup; *psychological* positivism suggests the causes are faulty personality development; *sociological* positivism stresses social factors within one's environment or the surrounding culture and social structure.[19]

The positivist approach suffers from several problems. First, it assumes that pure objectivity is possible. The German sociologist Max Weber strongly cautioned researchers about the assumption of objective or value-free research. Second, positivism takes for granted the existing social and economic order—that is, it generally accepts the status quo and the official definition of reality. Because the state's definition of crime is part of the accepted reality, positivists have

focused their research on people who violate criminal law, rather than on the law itself; positivists' efforts are aimed at controlling or changing the lawbreaker, not changing the law or the social order of which it is a part. Third, positivists assume that the scientific method offers the only way of achieving knowledge—of arriving at the truth. Fourth, positivism provides no assistance in the search for alternatives to the present social and economic order and hence to the present method of responding to crime.[20]

There is also a more frightening implication of the positivist orientation. Two of Lombroso's followers, Enrico Ferri (1856–1928) and Raffaele Garofalo (1852–1934), became supporters of fascism. For Ferri especially, the positivist orientation justified elevating the authority of the state over the "excesses of individualism."

> It is centered on the core idea of the superior knowledge and wisdom of the scientific expert who, on the basis of scientific knowledge, decides what kind of human beings commit crimes, and prescribes treatment without concern for public opinion and without consent from the person so diagnosed (i.e., the criminal). There is an obvious similarity between the control of power in society advocated in positivism and the political reality of centralized control of the life of the citizen by a governmental bureaucracy indifferent to public opinion.[21]

Like the classical school, positivism is primarily concerned with the *control* of crime, rather than with the amelioration of the social conditions that foster crime. Although positivism does pay lip service to the causes of crime, positivists have been most interested in the offender and how he or she can be controlled or changed. What is needed is a method of thinking and inquiry that allows us to question the taken-for-granted assumptions of both the positivist and the classical schools of thought. We need a method that allows us to conceive of something other than the status quo and to seek alternatives to the business-as-usual approach of the modern criminal justice system.

A CRITICAL PERSPECTIVE ON CRIMINAL JUSTICE

At the heart of our approach to the criminal justice system is *critical thinking* about the current social order and institutional arrangements. Rather than automatically accepting what is, we attempt to visualize what could be. To paraphrase the late senator Robert Kennedy, some may think about what is and ask "why" while others think about what could be and ask "why not." Our *critical perspective* encourages us to *question* what is often taken for granted.

Many of the beliefs that you hold reflect the views of people in authority—parents, teachers, political leaders, academics, or experts. But how do you know they are right? The best thing to do is to look deeper. What is the foundation for the positions?[22] The historian Howard Zinn once suggested it isn't enough to check out what people in authority say; it is also necessary to check out what they are *not* saying. Are they omitting certain facts? Are they hiding or covering up information?

A critical perspective utilizes what C. Wright Mills called the *sociological imagination.*[23] The sociological imagination is a mindset that connects the most basic individual experiences to seemingly impersonal historical forces—the capacity to shift from one perspective to another and to see connections between the two. To fully understand one's own experiences, it is necessary to understand what kind of people inhabit a particular society (which Mills called biography) and how institutions in that society operate (the social structure). Private problems must be understood within the context of public issues—connecting individual experiences with the workings of society. A focus limited to one's personal situation can create feelings of being trapped by circumstances beyond one's control.

Using the sociological imagination lets us distinguish between what Mills called "personal troubles of milieu" and "public issues of social structure." By "personal troubles" Mills meant those very personal, private matters that "occur within the character

of the individual and within the range of his immediate relations with others." A problem becomes a "public issue of social structure" when the issue has to do with "matters that transcend those local environments of the individual" and when "some value cherished by publics is felt to be threatened."

Social structure includes the basic institutions of society, such as the economy, family, education, law, and government. We all work and live every day of our lives within these institutions and often are constrained by roles created for us. Individual police officers, for instance, may be sensitive to the issues of racism and the racist nature of the drug laws, but they are nevertheless required to enforce the law. Police officers are products of a police subculture that helps shape their attitudes, values, and views of the world. In short, they are constrained by "the system."

Viewed from this perspective, humans are products of the larger social environment in which they live and work, but they have the power and ability to make significant changes even while working within the system. Karl Marx once wrote that human beings "make their own history" but "do not make it just as they please; they do not make it under circumstances chosen by themselves, but under circumstances directly encountered, given and transmitted from the past. The tradition of all the dead generations weighs like a nightmare on the brain of the living."[24] Students who hope to work within the criminal justice system need to keep this perspective in mind so they can expand the focus beyond currently accepted understandings and situate issues within their historical context and potential for change in societal relations and public institutions.

Key Assumptions of the Critical Perspective

Our critical approach to the criminal justice system rests on several key assumptions.

1. The current *social order and the nature of this order* help determine the nature of the law and therefore the definitions of crime. Thus, for instance, in a feudal system, law concerns mostly issues of land tenure and

inheritance; in a capitalist system, the law is concerned mostly with private property.[25]

2. The *legal institution* (including lawmaking bodies and agencies that enforce the law, such as police, courts, and penal systems) and other social institutions (e.g., education, politics) support and perpetuate the existing social order. In modern U.S. society the legal institution supports a capitalist order. Because modern capitalist societies are based on the private ownership of capital by a relatively small class of people—a "ruling" or "upper" class, which has created a great amount of structured social inequality (based on social class, race, and gender)—it follows that the legal institution helps to perpetuate such inequality, at least indirectly.[26]

3. Inequalities in a capitalist system such as U.S. society result from an unequal distribution of resources (e.g., wealth, education), which in turn creates an unequal distribution of power (and with it the ability to control others).

4. In general, the legal institution favors those with the most resources and power.[27]

From these general assumptions we offer three propositions that together constitute our operating theory of the criminal justice system:

1. *Role of the State.* The state (which includes legal institutions), while representing the long-term interests of the ruling class and the capitalist system, does not always act as a mere instrument of the ruling class. The state often acts as an autonomous unit and against the interests of the ruling class. Thus, state definitions of crime do not always reflect the interests of the ruling class.[28]

2. *Definition of Crime.* The defining of behaviors as criminal by the state and the application of such definitions are exercises in power; the ability to define behaviors as criminal and to resist such definitions varies with the degree of power one has. Crime describes behaviors that are most likely to correspond to behaviors committed by groups with the least amount of power in society. Similar behaviors committed by those with the most power are the least likely to be defined as a crime.[29]

3. *Application of Criminal Definitions.* At each stage of the criminal justice process, key decisions are made by agents of the state to either dismiss the case or process it further. *As the degree of powerlessness of defendants increases, so does the probability of advancing further into the system.* At each stage, those who remain become more and more homogeneous in social class, race, and other social demographic characteristics. By the time a case reaches the final stage (sentencing), the group that has the least amount of power is the most likely to receive a prison sentence or the sentence of death.

Is the Criminal Justice System Designed to Fail?

Our critical perspective challenges conventional wisdom about the criminal justice system by arguing that the system not only fails to provide protection from crime and make people feel safe, but it is *designed to fail.* In making this argument, we are borrowing the ideas of Jeffrey Reiman, who calls this view of criminal justice the *Pyrrhic defeat theory.* In military terminology, a Pyrrhic victory is a victory won at such a great loss of life that it amounts to a defeat. Reiman suggests that "the failure of the criminal justice system yields such benefits to those in positions of power that it amounts to success."[30] Such "success" manifests itself in the following ways:

1. By focusing primarily on the crimes of the poor and racial minorities, the criminal justice system distorts the crime picture. It deflects the discontent and anger of middle-class Americans toward the poor and racial minorities, rather than toward those in positions of power who maintain the system.

2. The U.S. criminal justice system, in its "war on crime," makes it look as if the most serious threat comes from the crimes of the poor and racial minorities. The greatest harms, in terms of both life and property, come from the crimes of the very rich.

3. By focusing on crime control and the punishment of *individual offenders,* the system fails to address some of the major causes of crime. Focusing exclusively on the individual offender diverts attention away from institutions, away from consideration of whether institutions themselves are wrong or unjust or indeed "criminal." It diverts attention from the evils of the social order.[31]

Debra Seagal looked at the implications of a prime-time television show based on videotapes of real police arrests. She discusses how focusing on individual criminals diverts attention away from the social context of crime and, indeed, communicates the idea that these offenders exist in a social vacuum.

> By the time our 9 million viewers flip on their tubes, we've reduced fifty or sixty hours of mundane and compromising video into short, action-packed segments of tantalizing, crack-filled, dope-dealing, junkie-busting, cop culture. How easily we downplay the pathos of the suspect; how cleverly we breeze past the complexities that cast doubt on the very system that has produced the criminal activity in the first place.[32]

It should be emphasized that there is an important difference between *understanding* or *explaining* certain behaviors (like crime) and *justifying* or *excusing* such behaviors. It is important to develop an understanding of *why* rape, murder, or corporate crimes occur, not to excuse the behavior but to search for possible solutions. Similarly, we condemn the terrorist attacks of September 11, 2001, but we need to understand why they happened in order to prevent anything similar from occurring again. If a police officer faces someone wielding a gun in a threatening manner, he or she will not at that point try to understand the behavior. But later reflection on why someone might resort to such behavior could help save a life if it leads to preventive measures.

Critical thinking and sociological imagination help to keep us informed.

> To look only at individual criminality is to close one's eyes to social injustice and to close one's ears to the question of whether

our social institutions have exploited or violated the individual. *Justice is a two-way street—but criminal justice is a one-way street.* Individuals owe obligations to their fellow citizens because their fellow citizens owe obligations to them. Criminal justice focuses on the first and looks away from the second. *Thus, by focusing on individual responsibility for crime, the criminal justice system literally acquits the existing social order of any charge of injustice.*[33]

Reiman is not suggesting (and neither are we) that the crimes of the poor and racial minorities do not constitute a major problem. Indeed, those who are the most likely to be victimized come from the ranks of the urban poor and racial minorities. We cannot ignore the human wreckage that occurs every day in urban areas in the form of violence and predatory crime, including crimes against women and children (usually falling within the category "domestic violence"), not to mention the devastating effects of drugs and alcohol. However, we agree with Reiman when he writes, "On the other hand, there are enough benefits to the wealthy from the identification of crime with the poor and the system's failure to reduce crime that those with the power to make profound changes in the system feel no compulsion nor see any incentive to make them."[34]

It should also be noted that we are not claiming that many who work within the criminal justice system do not try their best to deal with people fairly and equitably. We have met many who do. Our point is that *the system itself* and most of the people who ultimately control it (and control the major institutions in society, especially economic and political institutions) have become part of the problem and help perpetuate the crime problem.[35]

Throughout this book you will view the criminal justice system from a variety of perspectives. Try to identify the relationship between the various facets of the system; evaluate the assumptions underlying each perspective; and weigh the evidence presented. The various perspectives are analogous to viewing a panorama through different colored lenses. The insights gained become a foundation for examining many topical areas surrounding the criminal justice system, questioning the current approach, and considering alternatives to the existing system of criminal justice in America. We begin expanding our "criminal justice imagination" with the basic foundation of the criminal justice system, the criminal law. Without the criminal law there is, technically, no "crime."

PERSPECTIVES ON CRIMINAL LAW

Why does the law prohibit some behaviors but not others? Some very harmful behaviors are perfectly legal—such as the possession and consumption of cigarettes, alcohol, and addictive prescription drugs. Laws prohibit the killing ("homicide" or "murder") of another human being, but in some contexts the taking of a human life can be perfectly legal, such as a police officer killing a citizen who threatens his life, the application of the death penalty, or killing in time of war. Behaviors that do tremendous harm to women—namely, rape and battering—are illegal. Yet numerous studies document how men accused of rape or battering may escape arrest, prosecution, and/or conviction if certain key actors in the criminal justice system decide that "she deserved it," or "she led him on," and so on.[36]

The law is more than the words on paper; it has a dynamic quality of its own. It is a reflection of a particular society at a particular time. As Quinney writes, the law "is also a method or *process* of doing something. As a process, law is a dynamic force that is continually being *created and interpreted.* Thus, law in action involves the making of specialized (legal) decisions by various *authorized agents.*"[37] Law is a creation of specific people holding positions of authority; it is not the creation of a divine authority, as people once believed.

The law, because it is a *social* product, must be viewed *sociologically,* for the law is first and foremost a social institution complete with a system of roles and status positions (lawyers, judges, legislators, police officers). It contains an ideology, a set of values supportive of the legal system and the existing social order.[38] The law, moreover, is a *social process*—many different people interpret and apply the law in various social contexts. How the law is interpreted and applied depends on many extralegal factors, such as class and race.

A question that has concerned scholars for many years is that of the origins and functions of criminal law. Through the years scholars have offered a variety of perspectives: consensus, societal needs, pluralist, interactionist, interest group, conflict, elite theory, ruling class theory, and Marxist. For purposes of simplification, we will look at three main categories: (1) consensus/pluralist, (2) interest-group/conflict, and (3) critical.[39]

Consensus/Pluralist Model

Perhaps the oldest and most articulated perspective on criminal law, the *consensus/pluralist model*, holds that legal norms are a reflection of the values held in common by the majority of the population; they reflect the will of the people. A variation of this view is that criminal law merely makes official what are common norms or rules of everyday behavior. In other words, what was customary behavior (e.g., rules followed because everybody has always followed them) eventually becomes the law. From this perspective the criminal law reflects the social consciousness of a society and the kind of behavior a community universally condemns. Thus, the criminal law (and law in general) represents a synthesis of the most deeply held moral values and beliefs of a people or society. The violation of such laws establishes the "moral boundaries" of a community or society, according to nineteenth-century sociologist Émile Durkheim.[40]

Another variation of this view is that the law functions to achieve social equilibrium or to maintain order. The law is an instrument used to resolve conflicting interests in a society. The legal philosopher Roscoe Pound believed that the law is a specialized organization of social control as well as a form of social engineering in a civilized society. Without organized social control, said Pound, people's aggressive self-assertions would prevail over their cooperative social tendencies, and civilization would come to an end. Hence, criminal law serves as a social glue. Pound also suggested that the law adjusts social relationships in order to meet prevailing ideas of fair play.[41]

Another way of expressing the consensus view is the common phrase "there ought to be a law," meaning that people "rise up" and demand that a certain form of behavior be outlawed. This model is based on the assumption that there is a common consensus by the majority of the people in a society on what is good and proper conduct—an assumption that is highly suspect.

There are three main points in the consensus/pluralist model. First, law helps to maintain social order, and it is the best way to do so. The only way to maintain order in society is through the law or, as commonly phrased, the *rule of law.* Second, law reflects a more or less universal consensus on what is or is not "proper" behavior. Third, law and the criminal justice system protect public, not private, interests. The law is neutral and helps to resolve conflicts between competing interest groups. Those who uphold and interpret the law—police, courts, and so on—are neutral as well.

According to this perspective, society needs not only law but also a strong, centralized state to prevent people from becoming barbarians and engaging in what seventeenth-century philosopher Thomas Hobbes described as a "war of all against all." The assumption is that prior to the evolution of nation states, human nature created constant strife and war because of selfish interests. This view is contradicted by years of anthropological and historical research, which has substantiated thousands of human societies existing in small, economically cooperative groups prior to our modern era. State-created law is not the only way to maintain order and peace. Modern capitalist societies based on competitive social relations support the view of human nature as self-centered and in need of control and the idea that we need law in order to restrain people's "naturally wicked" ways.[42]

Interest-Group/Conflict Model

The consensus/pluralist model assumes that law is a reflection of societal needs. This assumption leads us to ask, "Whose needs?" The answer "society" is far too general and vague—it assumes that what is good for one group or segment is good for all segments. The *interest-group/conflict model* begins with the fact that modern industrialized societies are highly stratified and unequal in the distribution of power and in life chances. Using this base, conflict theorists contend that the law reflects the interests of some groups at the expense of others. Quinney states that society is characterized by diversity, coercion, change, and conflict. Law is a *result* of the operation of *interests.* More specifically, "law incorporates the interests of specific persons and groups. . . . Law is made by men, representing special interests, who have the power to translate their interests into public policy."[43]

Quinney's model is based on a conception of society as segmental rather than singular. In a singular society there is a common value system to which all persons conform. The law reflects these common values (as claimed by consensus/pluralist theorists). In a segmental society there are numerous segments, each having its own values and interests. Thus, "some values of a segment may be incorporated into some of the criminal laws." Moreover, some segments have values and interests that conflict with other segments. The passage of laws is primarily the outgrowth of conflicting interests—the products of interest groups organized to promote their interests. Modern U.S. society is characterized by an unequal distribution of *power and economic resources,* and those who have the greatest amount of power are best equipped to have their interests represented by the law. Indeed, those groups that have little or no power will have few opportunities to have their interests represented by the law and public policies in general. Powerless groups such as women, minorities, youth, and poor people are rarely represented.[44] Quite often, laws are passed after vigorous campaigning by various interest groups (or perhaps even one group) or by what one writer has called "moral entrepreneurs." These groups lobby Congress, write letters to newspapers, and engage in other activities in order to get a piece of legislation written into law. Such groups do not necessarily represent "the people"; more often than not, they represent themselves or some other small but powerful group.[45]

A Critical Model

Our *critical model* derives from the theories of Karl Marx and modern-day Marxist writings. It resembles the interest-group/conflict model in its focus on group conflict and power as important variables, but it differs in many important ways. This theory challenges us to view the law and the legal order in a specific social and historical context. Such a view argues that the law—and in fact the entire legal system—is one of many institutions that are part of what Marx called the *superstructure* of society and therefore operates to help support and perpetuate the *substructure* or economic base—namely a capitalist economic and social system.[46] Variations of the critical perspective can be categorized as: (1) instrumentalist and (2) structuralist.

Marx himself set forth the *instrumentalist perspective* when he asserted that law and the legal order (in fact the state itself) serves mostly as a tool through which the ruling class (the relatively small group that owns and controls most of the wealth in society— or what Marx called the "means of production") dominates society.[47]

Quinney further illuminated the instrumentalist position. "Criminal law is used by the state and the ruling class to secure the survival of the capitalist system, and, as capitalist society is further threatened by its own contradictions, criminal law will be increasingly used in the attempt to maintain domestic order."[48] The legal order keeps the ruling class in power and keeps subordinate classes "in their place" (perpetuating a social class system) by defining some of their behaviors as criminal while ignoring similar behaviors by powerful individuals.

Critics of this position maintain that it exaggerates the cohesiveness of the ruling class and its use of the legal order. Not every law is passed to preserve the current social order, nor is every law passed solely to represent the interests of the ruling class. Clearly some legislation favors groups other than the dominant class; some subordinate classes are represented in legislation, although such legislation does not threaten the basic social order and the ruling class. Critics also note that the instrumentalist position ignores the many occasions when members within the ruling class have conflicting interests—meaning that not all of their interests will be reflected in law. It may be true that the instrumentalist position is most helpful for analyzing the relationship between social class and law in earlier periods of development in the United States and that the law does not always support economic interests alone.[49]

The *structuralist perspective* suggests that law is the result of contradictions inherent in the capitalist system, which in turn create problems that even the ruling class cannot easily manipulate. Thus, the nature of the capitalist economic system is that law might sometimes operate against the short-term interests of the ruling class but in favor of the long-term interests of the capitalist system as a whole. A classic example is the passage of antitrust laws in the early 1900s and laws against discrimination in employment, minimum-wage laws, consumer protection laws, and laws supporting labor unions.[50] The ruling class does not always get its way.

Those supporting this position also maintain that the state often acts independently of the ruling class, rather than being a mere "instrument" of that class. To be sure, the law can and will be used when the capitalist system appears to be threatened. However, in day-to-day affairs, the various parts of the "superstructure" (e.g., law, ideology, politics, education, and media) have a lot of autonomy. Thus, not every political decision, not everything that is taught in school, and not every law is a reflection of the narrow interests of capitalists.

Too often, the law is regarded as a cure-all for societal ills. Our position is that the law is not some mystical force beyond human comprehension and control. The "rule of law" implies that society is ruled by an unassailable abstraction, not by men. As we have seen, people decided society's laws, and people interpret and enforce these laws. Moreover, it has been commonly believed that the law serves as a protective device that shields the victim and punishes the offender, that it is capable of righting wrongs, and that it is impartial, incorruptible, and equitably applied, providing equal justice for all. In the review that follows, however, we cite instances in which this has not been the case, and we show that this view is largely a fiction.

As noted previously, U.S. society is characterized by a tremendous amount of inequality. In the final analysis, the legal order is controlled by the small proportion of the population with the power to influence legislation.

It really doesn't matter that the law does not always side with those in power. It doesn't have to, as long as profits can be made and the capitalist system survives. Many people benefit from capitalism. Howard Zinn notes that the Constitution and the Bill of Rights were primarily passed to protect private property. Because so many people at that time owned property, it was in the interests of a lot of people to have property protected. But although a lot of people owned property, most owned only a little property and only a small group owned a lot (as they still do today).

> The Constitution, then, illustrates the complexity of the American system: that it serves the interests of a wealthy elite, but also does enough for small property owners, for middle-income mechanics and farmers, to build a broad base of support. The slightly prosperous people who make up this base of support are buffers against the blacks, the Indians, the very poor whites. They enable the elite to keep control with a minimum of coercion, a maximum of law—all made palatable by the fanfare of patriotism and unity.[51]

While the law and the legal order favor enough of the population to appear to be equal, it has never done a good job supporting the most marginalized sectors of the population: the poor in general and African Americans, Native Americans, and other minorities.

THE NATURE OF CRIMINAL LAW

Law: What Is It?

Law is a concept that most people think they understand, but legal scholars have found that providing a definition of law is not a simple task. Law, in its generic sense, can be defined as rules of action or conduct prescribed by a controlling authority with enforcement power. Oliver Wendell Holmes argued that law is that which judges make: "The prophecies of what the courts will do in fact, and nothing more pretentious, is what I mean by law."[52] Benjamin Cardozo, who succeeded Holmes on the Supreme Court, described law as: "A principle or rule of conduct so established as to justify a prediction with reasonable certainty that it will be enforced by the courts if its authority is challenged."[53] Donald Black, a leading law and society scholar, argues that, "Law is the normative life of a state and its citizens, such as legislation, litigation, and adjudication."[54] Thus, according to Black, law is government social control.

From this brief sampling, we might conclude that there are as many definitions as there are legal scholars.[55] Law can be viewed as an abstract concept, which takes on different meanings for different audiences. Someone in the legal profession could view the law in terms of right or wrong; behavior either complies with the law or it does not. To the sociologist, law may be a topic of inquiry that leads researchers into the domain of power, influence, and the relativity of law to the real world. Sociologists ask, who benefits from law, and does law reflect the desires and needs of the majority? To criminal justice practitioners, law might represent a foundation from which political and tactical decisions are constructed and implemented, or law may simply serve as legitimation for engaging in daily routines (e.g., police officers arresting homeless people or "shaking down" young black males in the inner city). We support the notion that law is a formal institution that continuously reifies itself and its importance while it simultaneously engages in legitimating state social control.

Thus, law controls the lives of individuals who live under the jurisdiction of law.

Law often seems estranged from other parts of life, yet everyone is affected by law in nearly all aspects of life—beginning at birth. Parents are required by law to file documentation for a birth certificate and to secure a Social Security number for their newborn child. Law dictates the age at which the child begins compulsory education. Law prescribes the minimum number of years the child must attend school. The law establishes age and knowledge requirements for the issuance of a driver's license. The law prescribes the age requirements, medical tests, and licensing procedures for marriage. Law governs contracts that a person may enter into as he or she goes through life (financing a car or a home, regulations for licensing a new business, etc.). Near the end of one's life journey, in many cases, law specifies whether a person can die quickly or must linger in pain and suffering (regulation of life-support apparatuses, physician-assisted suicide, etc.). Law even follows the individual after death; the administration of estates and wills is regulated by law. Like it or not, law is an integral part of life.

If you now find yourself somewhat overwhelmed by the law, you are not alone. Many people are intimidated by the complexity and the apparent mystique of law. Although many would rather distance themselves from any personal involvement in law, they cannot divorce their lives from legal oversight. Most people agree with the assumption that in order for society to exist we must have an institution of law. To support this claim, they often rely on an explanation such as, "We cannot exist as a society without formal written laws." This claim is debatable. Earlier societies managed to flourish without formal written laws.

Throughout world history, human behavior has been subject to a variety of social control mechanisms other than formal law. There is nothing inevitable about the need for people to be controlled by a formal legal system. For example, if we take a close look at the history of Native Americans, predating European intervention, we find no evidence of written laws or of an elaborate legal system. This does not mean that Native Americans did not have rules. They had rules, and everyone knew those rules. They generally were based on religious beliefs rather than on secular principles (to regulate commerce, contracts, etc.) and were strictly enforced. Despite the absence of written laws and elaborate legal systems, Native Americans developed and maintained diversified cultures, formed communities, developed personal relationships, and raised families.

Law and Social Norms

Today, most human behavior is regulated by rules that are unwritten or otherwise informally expressed. These rules are called *social norms*, and they can be defined as the expectations, both spoken and universally understood, that direct human behavior in a society. There are two basic categories of social norms: folkways and mores. *Folkways* are society's conventional rules that we deal with every day. In many ways our compliance with folkways (rules of etiquette, dress, language, etc.) seems almost automatic. This conformity generally results from informal methods of social control (gossip, ridicule, ostracism, etc.). Folkways are not believed to be essential to the survival of the group. Although we may get upset at someone for violating a folkway, we probably would not express disgust or indignation for such a violation.

Mores, in contrast, are stronger norms that reflect the moral judgments of society. Violations of mores are subject to stronger sanctions because they are believed to threaten group survival. The violation of mores prohibiting murder, rape, incest, and assault usually calls forth moral indignation and can result in severe punishment. Mores are frequently codified into laws; folkways are not.[56]

To illustrate possible responses to the violation of a folkway or of mores, imagine that you are dining out with a business client at a restaurant. After reviewing the menu, you decide to order spaghetti with tomato sauce. When the waiter serves your meal, you set your fork and spoon aside and begin to eat with your hands. Other diners, who direct their attention to you, shake their heads at such unacceptable behavior; your client quickly decides never to accept another dinner invitation from you. Now imagine another scenario. You become irritated at the service you and your guest receive in the restaurant. To express your irritation, you stand up and turn over the table; dishes and glasses break as they hit the floor. The other diners again shake their heads in dismay at your behavior, but this time you could be arrested for "disturbing the peace" or "destruction of private property." There is a distinction in the seriousness of these two forms of behavior. In the first scenario (bad manners), you are violating a folkway. In the second, you are violating mores. Such a violation might be sufficient to launch formal social control measures; the owner of the restaurant could call the police.

Formal Social Control

Formal social control measures (summoning the criminal justice system into action) are often adopted when informal social control measures (e.g., being ridiculed or ostracized) are inadequate for maintaining conformity. The adoption of formal social control measures is most likely to occur when societies become more diverse and social class distinctions become more prevalent. Hallmarks of formal social control include systems of specialized agencies (e.g., law enforcement agencies), the application of standardized techniques (e.g., court procedures), and the general predictability of universal sanctions (e.g., probation or prison). Thus, *formal social control* consists, ideally, of (1) explicit rules of conduct, (2) planned use of sanctions, and (3) designated officials to interpret and enforce the rules.[57]

There are two types of formal social control: political and nonpolitical. *Political social control* is most relevant to the study of criminal justice. It is characterized by the state's authority to use force, if the state deems it necessary, to ensure conformity to established rules. Black identifies four styles of political social control.

1. *Penal* social control views the offender as a violator of a prohibition and subjects her or him to condemnation and punishment.

2. *Compensatory* social control occurs when the offender is considered to have contractual obligations and is expected to pay restitution to the victim.

3. *Therapeutic* social control occurs when the offender's behavior is perceived to be abnormal, requiring psychiatric treatment.

4. *Conciliatory* social control may be applied to restore social relationships without consideration of who is right or who is wrong.[58]

Nonpolitical social control is used by institutions that are not a direct part of the state's political social control apparatus (e.g., the church or the university). This type of social control employs either rewards or punishments to elicit conformity to the institution's rules, because these kinds of institutions do not have the authority to use force. For example, a university may have a policy that places students on the dean's list when they achieve a designated grade point average in a given semester. The university may also place a student on academic probation if the student's grades fall below a prescribed level. In the first situation, students are rewarded for their compliance with university academic standards; in the second instance, students are punished for failing to meet university standards. The university, however, cannot place a student with a lower-than-required grade point average in prison for noncompliance with its academic standards.

TYPES OF LAW

There are many types of law in U.S. society—for example, administrative law, absolute law, canon law, constitutional law, civil law, criminal law, general law, foreign law, international law, case law, maritime law, organic law, military law, municipal law, and statutory law. A person might reasonably arrive at the conclusion that the United States is a society with an endless set of laws. Because the list is so extensive, we limit our discussion to the types that have the greatest impact on the U.S. criminal justice system.

Civil Law

Civil law consists of the rules and procedures that regulate relationships between individuals. Violations of civil law are usually referred to as *civil wrongs*, and a civil suit is initiated by a *plaintiff* who claims a harm.

Suppose you invite a guest to your house for dinner and he trips over your son's tricycle on the front porch and breaks his leg. Your guest gets angry, calls his lawyer, and sues you for damages. The purpose of this civil suit is to seek restitution (e.g., payment of medical bills) from the defendant (you or your insurance company) due to negligence.

Civil law consists of several different subtypes, such as tort law, corporate law, contract law, and divorce law. Of particular importance to the study of crime is the law of torts. *Torts* are acts "that cause injury to the financial, physical, emotional, or psychological well-being of some individual."[59] A tort can also be defined as "a wrongful act that does not violate any enforceable agreement but that nevertheless violates a legal right of the injured party."[60] Common examples of torts include wrongful death, intentional or negligent personal injury, destruction of property, trespassing, and defaming someone's character. The injured party seeks compensation or restitution, but no one is sent to jail or prison.

The distinction between *criminal law* (and thus *crime*) and *civil law,* especially torts (and thus *wrongs*), is rather curious. Under criminal law, the "state," which theoretically is synonymous with "the people," assumes the role of the victim, and prohibited acts are those that supposedly threaten society as a whole (the social order). In contrast, torts constitute a general class of harms done to *individuals* rather than to society. Convictions under tort law do not carry the stigma associated with the criminal law—the perpetrator is not viewed as part of some dangerous or criminal class. Nevertheless, the harm done by many persons who violate tort law (especially corporate, occupational, and political crimes) clearly exceeds the harm done by those who violate criminal law.

As one writer notes:

Socially recognized harms in America have been divided into civil and criminal wrongs in a way that generally protects middle-class and elite Americans from being stigmatized as "criminals" for the harms they are most likely to cause. In contrast, nearly all those forms of harm that the working class and the underclass can commit bear the full weight of criminal stigma.[61]

Civil law and criminal law often overlap. A person may stand trial for the criminal charges of murder and also be held accountable for civil damages resulting from the same act (e.g., the wrongful taking of life). O. J. Simpson was tried and found not guilty of murdering Nicole Simpson and Dan Goldman. He was tried and convicted of wrongful death in a civil suit. A successful conviction for a criminal offense results in criminal sanctions (e.g., prison); a conviction in a civil case results in a monetary settlement.

Criminal Law

Suppose someone stops you on the street and, at gunpoint, demands your wallet. After the ordeal, you probably will call the police, who will use the information you give them (e.g., a description of the suspect) to try to locate the offender and make an arrest. The holdup man violated a *criminal* law and committed a *crime.*

Criminal law defines specific, prohibited behaviors and prescribes sanctions for committing the forbidden behaviors. As mentioned above, when someone violates a criminal law, he or she has harmed the "state" or "the people." From a strictly legal standpoint, crime is considered a harm to the *public* rather than a harm to an *individual* (as in a civil suit), even though an individual is harmed in both instances. Thus, instead of the plaintiff taking action against a defendant (as in a civil suit), the state (specifically, representatives of the state, such as police and prosecutors) takes action against an *offender.* Instead of the victim taking personal action against the offender and seeking compensation (civil suit for the money lost) or revenge (you and your friends go out and beat up the holdup man), the offender is *punished* by the state. The agents of the state are acting as your representatives in the arrest and prosecution of offenders. Often it is said that the "state" is the victim, and the criminal case may be described as "The State of Michigan v. Jones."

Criminal law outlines proper procedures for the state to follow if an offense comes to the attention of the authorities. Thus, criminal law is divided into two subsets: substantive law and procedural law. *Substantive law* is a written body of rules specifying the *elements of a crime*, which is a legal way of describing in some detail offenses such as homicide and robbery and sanctions for committing those offenses. *Procedural law* consists of a body of rules specifying the conditions required before, and the manner in which, the state may proceed against an alleged offender. Procedural laws include laws on search and seizure, rules of evidence, and laws concerning proper arrest procedures. Included within procedural laws are the fundamental rights of the accused guaranteed by the U.S. Constitution.

A *constitution* is the fundamental law of a state or a nation that establishes the character and conception of government. For example, assume that a state or nation claims to promote equality, freedom of speech, and freedom of movement for all citizens within its boundaries. Ideally, each of these concepts must be stipulated in that state's or nation's constitution to ensure that all citizens can practice free speech, move about freely, and be treated equally. A constitution regulates the organization, powers, and framework of government, as well as the relationship between the government and citizens. The constitution must also specify procedures for subsequent amendments to its own text.

Constitutional law ensures that all amendments and subsequent laws (enacted after the adoption of a constitution) comply with that state's or nation's fundamental law (constitution). Suppose that a legislative body (e.g., the U.S. Congress) passes a particular law. That law is subject to a constitutional test or interpretation by the court (e.g., the Supreme Court) to ensure that it conforms to the fundamental law contained within the U.S. Constitution. If it fails that test, the law is considered unconstitutional and not binding on or applicable to the citizens bound by the Constitution. Constitutional law also applies to the *Bill of Rights*, the first ten amendments to the U.S. Constitution, which safeguards individual rights and freedoms and offers protection from governmental abuse of power.

In theory, individuals sworn to uphold the law are required to follow certain rules. Procedural law in general and the Bill of Rights in particular must be placed within a larger social and historical context. The Bill of Rights made the U.S. Constitution acceptable to the general public. It appeared to guarantee that the government would be the guardian of *all* the people and of their basic rights—to bear arms, to petition, to worship, to assemble, to speak, to be tried fairly by a "jury of their peers," and so on. What was never made clear, notes Zinn, "was the shakiness of everyone's liberty when entrusted to a government of the rich and the powerful."[62]

The men in power at the time of the writing of the Constitution and the Bill of Rights (we really are talking here about *white men*—women and African slaves and Native Americans were totally excluded) wanted a system of laws that would enable them to pursue their own interests. They needed the "consent of the governed." The myths of "equal justice for all" and "a government of laws, not men" became a very convenient ideology of class (not to mention race and gender) control.

Key Constitutional Amendments that Apply to Criminal Justice

Several amendments directly apply to the criminal justice system. Let's consider the Fourth, Fifth, Sixth, Eighth, and Fourteenth Amendments in turn.

The Fourth Amendment

> The right of the people to be secure in their persons, houses, papers, and effects, against unreasonable searches and seizures, shall not be violated, and no warrants shall issue, but upon the probable cause, supported by oath or affirmation, and particularly

describing the place to be searched, and the persons or things to be seized.

The writers of this amendment were heavily influenced by the fact that there had been little freedom under British rule. Little did these writers realize that this amendment would become the subject of great controversy two centuries later when the police engaged in systematic violations, especially when it came to the behaviors of minority citizens. The police complain that they are "handcuffed" by an overly broad interpretation of the Fourth Amendment. It is curious that a guarantee of one of the ultimate freedoms—the right to privacy—should be called a "technicality."

The Fifth Amendment

No person shall be held to answer for a capital, or otherwise infamous crime, unless on a presentment or indictment of a Grand Jury, except in cases arising in the land or naval forces, or in the militia, when in actual service in time of war or public danger; nor shall any person be subject for the same offense to be twice put in jeopardy of life or limb; nor shall be compelled in any criminal case to be a witness against himself; nor be deprived of life, liberty, or property, without due process of law; nor shall private property be taken for public use, without just compensation.

If a charge is very serious (especially an offense punishable by death), there must be a "presentment or indictment of a grand jury."[63] The Fifth Amendment is also the source of the "double jeopardy" clause (which is why O. J. Simpson cannot ever be brought to trial again in a *criminal* case for killing Nicole Brown and Ron Goldman, even if additional incriminating evidence is discovered). You do not have to take the witness stand in your own trial; the Fifth Amendment protects you from being a witness against yourself. You cannot be deprived of life, liberty, or property without due process. The due process clause is crucial; the state (especially the police) cannot arrest you, charge you, hold you in jail, or bring you to court unless they abide by all the applicable rules of procedure, including

all of the relevant Bill of Rights. This is the concept of *due process of law*. Related to this amendment is *Miranda v. Arizona* (1966)—the case which requires police to inform suspects that they have the right to remain silent so that they do not incriminate themselves (see chapter 5 for a more detailed discussion).

The Sixth Amendment

In all criminal prosecutions, the accused shall enjoy the right to a speedy and public trial, by an impartial jury of the state and district wherein the crime shall have been committed, which district shall have been previously ascertained by law, and to be informed of the nature and cause of the accusations; to be confronted with the witnesses against him; to have compulsory process for obtaining witnesses in his favor, and to have the assistance of counsel for his defense.

The Sixth Amendment also provides a number of safeguards. A person has the right to a "speedy" as well as a "public" trial. This requirement has been subject to a lot of interpretation over the years. What exactly is a *speedy* trial? Is it 30, 60, 90, or 180 days? Also, what is meant by *public?* Does everyone have the right to be a spectator? If everyone cannot attend, should the proceedings be televised (as was done in the Simpson criminal trial)? Also important are the issues of "impartial jury" and venue. Does the trial always have to be where the crime occurred? Finally, there's the critical issue of the right to counsel, which has been extended to earlier stages of the process (including immediately after the arrest). Does this mean that everyone is entitled to an F. Lee Bailey or a Johnnie Cochran? Should such high-powered attorneys provide cut-rate prices for indigent defendants? (See chapters 8 and 9.)

The Eighth Amendment

Excessive bail shall not be required, nor excessive fines imposed, nor cruel and unusual punishments inflicted.

The term *bail* refers to a bond the accused puts up so that he or she can be released from jail while awaiting trial. The bond is intended to ensure that the accused shows up and does not skip town, but the issue is complex, as we discuss in chapter 9. Notice that this amendment does not guarantee that a person receives bail; it only protects against "excessive" bail. But what constitutes "excessive"? This is largely a *class* issue. Five hundred dollars may not be a lot to you, but for a homeless or otherwise poor person, it very well may be too much. The mere existence of a bail system guarantees that jails become poorhouses.

Another critical issue contained within this amendment is the phrase "cruel and unusual punishment." Whnishments are "cruel" and "unusual"? This issue has yet to be settled. Although the Supreme Court has ruled that capital punishment is neither cruel nor unusual, the United States is the only industrialized nation that sanctions the death penalty (see chapter 10).

The Fourteenth Amendment

All persons born or naturalized in the United States, and subject to the jurisdiction thereof, are citizens of the United States and of the state wherein they reside. No state shall make or enforce any law which shall abridge the privileges or immunities of citizens of the United States; nor shall any state deprive any person of life, liberty, or property, without due process of the law; nor deny to any person within its jurisdiction the equal protection of the laws.

This amendment was adopted in 1868, following the Thirteenth Amendment (which abolished slavery), so it figures prominently in the battle for civil rights. The key phrase here is that no state can "deprive any person of life, liberty, or property, without due process of the law"; every state must act in accordance with the Bill of Rights. The civil suit filed by Rodney King charged that he had been deprived of his rights by the police officers who beat him—a violation of the Fourteenth Amendment.

The Bill of Rights is stated in relatively straightforward wording and attempts to guarantee a number of liberties. The raw facts of what occurs in the real world sometimes differs starkly from the idealism in the words. It is true that if your rights are violated you can seek redress. If you are poor, however, your "freedom" to do so will be restricted by your class background, unless (as in the case of Rodney King) you become a sort of celebrity and attract the attention of lawyers willing to take your case for free. The real question is: For every Rodney King, how many others are similarly abused but never gain celebrity status and never have their cases heard in a civil court?

Other Forms of Law

Laws govern just about every imaginable human behavior. What is not covered under civil or criminal law is covered under other forms of law. One of the most important is **administrative law** (*regulatory law*)—rules, regulations, orders, and decisions issued by executive branch agencies granted rulemaking authority by legislation. The relationship between administrative law and criminal justice is often ignored. However, regulatory law includes criminal penalties if citizens or organizations violate certain rules. Thus, administrative agencies have the authority to "create" crimes without direct legislative action. Administrative law also can impact the personnel configuration of organizations and agencies (e.g., criminal justice agencies). Regulations govern hiring practices and procedures. For example, the U.S. Equal Employment Opportunity Commission (EEOC) enforces regulations that prevent job discrimination based on sex, race, religion, age, disability, or national origin.

There are several regulatory agencies set up to oversee the activities of corporations and, especially, to protect consumers. The Interstate Commerce Commission regulates various types of transportation businesses and intervenes on behalf of consumers when complaints occur. Other regulatory agencies include the Federal Communications Commission, the Securities and Exchange Commission, and the National Labor Relations Board. Only on rare occasions is the criminal justice system involved in the processing of corporate offenders.[64]

Legislatures at all governmental levels write statutory law. The laws are called *statutes* if passed on the state or federal level and *ordinances* if passed on the local level. Elected officials, such as state legislators or congressional representatives, pass most of the laws (and decide corresponding punishments). Statutory law is most important for the criminal justice system because it polices, prosecutes, and punishes violations of state and federal laws passed by legislative bodies. At the state level such laws (both substantive and procedural) are published in state penal codes (e.g., the California Penal Code, the Nevada Revised Statutes).

While written statutory law (legislative branch) and rulemaking by administrative agencies (executive branch) form the bulk of the laws that govern us, there is one other type of law with substantial influence. *Case law* is identified with the judicial branch of government. Historically it was referred to as *common law*—the common customs (general law) of an entire realm versus the traditions of a single community (special law). The courts decided common law. Most of the criminal and procedural laws before the twentieth century were common law; even today the law of torts and rules of evidence (see section on *mens rea*) are based on common law. *Stare decisis* is the principle on which case law rests. In Latin it means "to stand by that which is decided." A trial court is bound by appellate court decisions (precedents) on questions of law. While the rationale is that reliance on precedents insures certainty, consistency, and stability in the administration of justice, Jonathan Swift offered a distinctly different perspective in *Gulliver's Travels.*

> [*Stare decisis*] is a maxim among . . . lawyers, that whatever has been done before may legally be done again: and therefore they take special care to record all the decisions formerly made against common justice and the general reason of mankind.[65]

Before moving to a discussion of the essential elements in the legal definition of crime, we want to emphasize again that law, like all the elements in the criminal justice system, is socially constructed. It is not an abstract, concrete entity. Oliver Wendell Holmes stated a similar point in 1880.

> The life of the law has not been logic; it has been experience. The felt necessities of the time, the prevalent moral and political theories, institutions of public policy, avowed or unconscious, even the prejudices which judges share with their fellow men, have had a good deal more to do than the syllogism in determining the rules by which men should be governed. The law embodies the story of a nation's development through many centuries, and it cannot be dealt with as if it contained only the axioms and corollaries of a book of mathematics.[66]

ESSENTIAL ELEMENTS OF CRIME

A crime has been committed if an actor satisfies all of the elements stipulated in the definition of the crime. The debate over what elements are essential is ongoing and too extensive for this introduction. We have distilled the three most important elements: (1) a voluntary act (*actus reus*), (2) omission, and (3) culpable intent (*mens rea*).

A Voluntary Act: *Actus Reus*

A crime begins with a *voluntary* act— any bodily movement that qualifies for criminal liability. There are, however, exceptions. If the act is not of the actor's own volition, if the act is reflexive or convulsive, or if the act is performed while the actor is asleep or otherwise unconscious, criminal liability is not established.

Suppose you are standing behind someone on the curb waiting for a bus. Someone behind you shoves you, causing you to push the person in front of you under the front wheel of the bus, resulting in that person's injury. Is your act criminally liable? No, it was not a result of your own volition. Now consider an individual who experiences an epileptic seizure and during this episode injures another person. Again, there is no criminal liability. Finally, suppose that you are sound asleep at home. You get up and begin sleepwalking. Remaining asleep, you walk into the guest room and begin to strangle an overnight visitor. Again, criminal liability does not attach. But suppose you become very sleepy during a lecture at school and then, on your way home, you fall asleep at the wheel and your car crashes into another car, injuring the driver of the other vehicle. In this instance, you satisfy the criminal liability requirement.

People cannot be arrested, charged, and convicted for merely talking about violating a law; the law requires the voluntary bodily movement toward the furtherance of a crime. In theory, this rule places a check on the arbitrary power of the state. In reality, this principle is violated on numerous occasions. For instance, people (especially those who fit the stereotype of the "criminal," such as young black males) are often arrested on "suspicion" or for "disorderly conduct" or "trespassing."

For an act to be considered a crime, it must be *specifically* prohibited by law—that is, the act must be specified in such a way that the average person will know that it is illegal. The legal term for this act is ***actus reus,*** "guilty act." A closely related concept is expressed by the Latin phrase *nullum crimen, nulla poena, sine lege,* which means "there is no crime, there is no punishment, without law." This is one of the unique features of Western legal systems, for there is an emphasis on the elimination of vaguely worded statutes. Under such a system individuals are to "be given the maximum legal protection to conduct their lives as they see fit."[67] Such an emphasis is not without its problems, however.

From a critical perspective, an emphasis on such legal specificity tends to separate moral obligations from legal obligations. "No legal system can specifically enumerate every possible violation of a general moral standard. As a result, where the law emphasizes specificity a proportion of moral violations will always fall beyond the law's reach."[68] Indeed, people involved in legislative actions are not likely to define their own morally questionable actions as illegal (e.g., a legislator who has business interests would be unlikely to support legislation that would restrict the aggressive practices of the business).

Legal specificity also limits the power of community and social groups to influence and control the behavior of their members. There is a tendency to rely only on authorized agents of the state (police, courts, etc.) to solve problems that may more easily be solved by citizens. If only authorized agents of the state (e.g., police, courts) can pursue violators of the legally prohibited behavior, the victim may be at the mercy of the reluctance of the agents or limited by resources from seeking judicial reprieve. One example is the reluctance of the police and the courts to take seriously the crime of battering. The police may not arrest, and the courts may refuse to issue a restraining order. In such cases, the woman may have to resort to civil law and hire her own attorney to take some action against the offender. In many cases the victim has neither the time nor the resources to take the perpetrator to court. Even if they do, they may find the experience frustrating. For example the senior author, while working at a juvenile court, was told by a woman whose ex-husband was behind in his child support payments that the court was "like a lion with no teeth!"

Legal specificity helps perpetuate the cultural emphasis on self-oriented rather than altruistic behavior because individuals tend to "identify their obligations toward others as legal and specific rather than moral and general." It then "becomes difficult to motivate people to engage in altruistic acts that may benefit others or society as a whole."[69] People may believe that as long as they are obeying the "letter of the law" that is all that is necessary to be a good citizen.

Omission: Failure to Comply with the Legal Duty to Act

Because a voluntary action (*actus reus*) is required before behavior can be considered a crime, in most cases failure to act—*omission*—will not be grounds for criminal liability. Criminal law in the United States has no provisions that stipulate a legal duty to rescue. In certain circumstances, however, there may be a *legal duty to act*. There are five circumstances in which a person has a legal duty to act.

The first circumstance is *statutory*. For example, there are statutes (federal, state, or city) that stipulate that people must file income-tax returns and pay income tax. The second circumstance is *contractual:* there is an obligation to act when there is a distinct relationship between one's "profession" and certain circumstances. For example, a licensed paramedic with certified training in CPR has a legal obligation to act in many emergency situations. The failure to act in such situations may be grounds for criminal liability.

The third circumstance in which there is a legal requirement to act arises when the legal obligation is based on the *relationship between parties*. For example, parents have a legal obligation to protect their children. The fourth circumstance arises when someone *voluntarily assumes a duty of care toward another person*. Suppose you are at the beach with several friends. All of a sudden you hear someone in the water yell for help. You tell your friends that you are going to swim out and assist the person who yelled. You enter the water and begin swimming. Just as you are about to reach the person, you recognize him. You don't like him, and you say to yourself, "I don't like that person, and I'm not going to save him." You turn around and swim back to shore. The person drowns, and you are criminally responsible because you "voluntarily" assumed the legal duty of care of another individual.

The fifth circumstance requiring you to act arises if your *conduct created the peril*. Although you have no legal obligation to rescue, you may be criminally liable if, after creating a peril, you fail to act or respond. Suppose you are near a pool at a party and you bump into someone and she falls into the water. Neither you nor the person whom you knocked into the water can swim. You are not required by law to jump into the water, but you are required to go and seek help.

Culpable Intent: *Mens Rea*

When criminal law developed in England, it emerged as common law (judge-made law or case law). Although the roots of U.S. criminal law were propagated in common law, most jurisdictions in the United States have codified their original common-law crimes into statutes. However, we continue to cling to one of the most important artifacts of common law—the doctrine that most crimes require a true **mens rea,** a "guilty mind." In other words, before someone can be convicted of a criminal act, there must be proof, in most cases, that the accused "had in mind" (mental state) causing harm or violating the law. Under common-law standards, there are four mental state requirements: (1) general intent, (2) specific intent, (3) malice, and (4) strict liability.

For most crimes under common law, the offender's **intent** is inferred from the act itself. These acts are known as *general intent crimes*. *General intent* means intent to do that which the law prohibits. Nearly all crimes in today's state criminal codes are general intent crimes. A general intent crime "refers to an actor's physical conduct in the sense that the actor intends the consequences of his or her voluntary actions."[70] In contrast, *specific intent crimes* require proof that the accused desired to do something to further the basic criminal act *(actus reus)*. For example, to substantiate common-law burglary (a specific intent crime), the state must show that the offender not only intended to break into and enter a residence but also intended to steal something once inside the residence. Specific intent crimes are crimes in which the defendant "intends a particular result."[71] General intent means that the offender intended to commit a specific act (i.e., crime); specific intent means that the offender intended to accomplish a particular result.

Malice is the commission of an intentional wrongful act and the intention to inflict an injury—an act that by its very nature implies evil intent. Malice in law does not necessarily assume hatred or ill will against a particular individual by the offender; rather, it is the offender's state of mind that is viewed as reckless of law itself or of the legal rights of individuals. Under common law, there are only two malice crimes: murder and arson.

The final common-law mental state is *strict liability*. Strict liability offenses are generally crimes that endanger the public welfare. These crimes are typically in the administrative, regulatory, or morality area of law; their elements do not require criminal intent or *mens rea*. Suppose that X, an adult, purchases alcohol for Y, who is a minor. The intention of X, who provided the alcohol, is not a legal consideration; the law does not care what X's intention was. The law is concerned only that X purchased alcohol for Y. Other examples of strict liability crimes include statutory rape (an adult having intercourse with a minor), illegal dumping of toxic wastes (pollution), and concealing a weapon while boarding an aircraft. As in the case of X purchasing alcohol for Y, the state is not required to prove the intent of the defendant charged with statutory rape, polluting the water, or having a concealed weapon at the terminal gate. The state needs to prove only that the offender committed the acts with which he or she has been charged.

Today, many jurisdictions have moved away from the ambiguities of general and specific intent. These jurisdictions reject the common-law terms of intent and instead stipulate four mental states: (1) purposely, (2) knowingly, (3) recklessly, and (4) negligently. *Purposely* and *knowingly* are equal to specific intent at common law; *recklessly* and *negligently* are not equal to specific intent at common law.

When an individual *consciously desires* to engage in an illegal act, and is *aware* of the *probable consequences,* it is argued that he or she acted *purposely.* Suppose you are provided with evidence that shows A was extremely angry at B and had a conscious desire to kill B. After purchasing a gun and ammunition, A loaded the gun, drove to B's house, pointed the loaded gun at B's head, and pulled the trigger. Instantly, B died. It can be argued that A consciously desired to kill B. Furthermore, A was aware of the probable consequences—death—associated with shooting B in the head. Thus, you can, with some degree of certainty, successfully argue that A acted purposely.

Closely related to *purposely* is the mental state *knowingly.* The principal difference between them rests with the *consciously desired* result of the act. For example, A wants to kill B so that he can collect insurance money. A places a bomb on an airplane where B is a passenger. Shortly after takeoff, the bomb explodes. B is killed, along with the other passengers. Did A purposely kill the other passengers? It can be argued that A *purposely* killed B, because that was his conscious desire. It can be argued that A *knowingly* killed the other passengers. Although he lacked the conscious desire to kill them, he was aware that it was practically certain that they would die in the explosion.

A person is said to act *recklessly* if he or she consciously ignores a substantial risk. For example, assume that L is late for work one morning. As she drives down the very familiar street to work, she seems to be "hitting" every possible red light. Looking at her watch, L realizes that she has only ten minutes left to drive twenty blocks. All of a sudden she finds herself stopped behind a school bus with blinking red lights. L looks carefully and decides that she cannot afford to wait any longer. With the red lights still flashing she passes the school bus. Out of nowhere a child steps in front of L's car. She slams on the breaks, but it is too late; the impact kills the child. Clearly, L's behavior grossly deviated from the norm; she made a conscious decision to disregard a substantial and unjustifiable risk. It is assumed that law-abiding people understand that small children are likely to be present when a school bus has its red lights flashing. Thus, L is criminally liable for the child's death. The law applies an objective standard to the mental state *negligently.* A person is negligent

> when he [or she] should be aware of a substantial and unjustifiable risk. . . . The risk must be of such a nature and degree that the actor's failure to perceive it, considering the nature and purpose of his [or her] conduct and the circumstances known to him [or her], involves a gross deviation from the standard of care that a reasonable person would observe in the actor's situation.[72]

Recall our previous example, in which you become sleepy during a lecture, leave the lecture hall, get into your car, and begin to drive home. You fall asleep while driving and hit another vehicle. The act is negligent: you should have pulled off the road and taken a nap.

Most courts require a greater degree of culpability for criminal negligence (typically gross negligence) than for civil negligence. The law clearly defines each category of culpability, in contrast to common-law interpretations of specific intent and general intent, which have caused much confusion across legal jurisdictions.

CRIMINAL DEFENSES

A defendant who has been formally charged has three legal options.

1. The defendant can plead guilty to the formal charges or plead guilty to a lesser charge after plea-bargain negotiations. In such cases, defense is a nonissue; most criminal defendants choose this option.

2. The defendant can plead *nolo contendere* ("I will not contest the charge(s)"). The defendant is neither admitting to nor denying the charges. The court must give its consent before a defendant can plead *nolo contendere*. The legal effect of a *nolo contendere* plea is similar to that of a guilty plea. Once the plea is entered, the defendant proceeds to the sentencing phase of the court process.

3. The defendant can plead not guilty to the formal charges. In such cases, the defendant must present a defense to the charges.

The two principal categories of criminal defense are: *denial of the charges,* in which the defendant purports that factual allegations presented by the state (prosecutor) are wrong; and the *affirmative defense,* in which the defendant introduces new factual allegations that may constitute a defense to the criminal charges. In an affirmative defense, the defendant does not necessarily dispute all or most of the facts presented by the prosecutor but provides an explanation (sometimes referred to as *excuse*) in the form of evidence. In essence, the defendant is saying, "Yes, I did it, *but. . . .*" When using an affirmative defense, the defendant has the burden to prove extenuating circumstances that will allow him or her to escape conviction, even though the prosecution is able to prove all of the elements of the crime.

In the remainder of this section we discuss several affirmative defenses: infancy;

duress; intoxication; entrapment; use of force in defense of self, others, and property; insanity; and the battered-person syndrome. This collection of defenses is by no means exhaustive, but it does lay the groundwork for a general understanding of criminal defenses and their applications.

Infancy

One of the most important assumptions in Western law is that an individual has free will and is capable of knowing right from wrong. We may assume that in the absence of the ability to distinguish between right and wrong, the *mens rea* element of a crime cannot be satisfied. The belief that persons under a certain age do not have the capacity to know the difference between right and wrong is one of the oldest traditions in Western law. Roman law and then common law operated on the assumption that an individual cannot tell right from wrong before reaching the "age of reason"—age 7 (age 7 is still considered the minimum).[73] According to common law, children between the ages of 7 and 14 were presumed not to have the capacity to commit crimes. Western law ruled that between the ages of 7 and 14 a child's capacity to know right from wrong needed to be proved, and prosecutors were given the opportunity to rebut the infancy defense and introduce evidence demonstrating that a child did possess the mental capacity to fulfill the necessary culpable intent element of a crime.

During the nineteenth century, the number of offenders between ages 7 and 14 increased, and more and more attention was directed to the issue of capacity. With the creation of the first juvenile court in 1899 in Chicago, it was determined, through the passage of the Juvenile Court Act, that children below the age of 16 could not be convicted of a criminal act, regardless of whether they knew right from wrong.[74] The intent of the legislation was to protect the juvenile from entering into a life of crime; the juvenile court system sought to rehabilitate rather than punish (see chapter 16).

Duress

Duress is an unlawful threat or coercion used by someone to induce another person to act in a way in which he or she would not normally act. In the case of crimes of omission, an unlawful threat or coercion used to induce a person *not* to act as he or she normally would act is also considered duress. A defendant must establish five elements of the duress defense:

1. There was a *threat* by a third party.
2. The threat produced a reasonable *fear* in the defendant.
3. The defendant was in *imminent danger* at the time of the alleged duress.
4. Failure to comply would have resulted in *serious bodily injury or death.*
5. There was *no opportunity to escape* the duress without committing the crime.

In order for this defense to be successful, the defendant must show that the harm that he or she was likely to experience was greater than the harm the defendant caused the victim(s) of the crime. Duress would not be a successful defense in the case of intentional murder.

Suppose that E pulls out a gun and threatens F, saying, "If you don't go into this store and help me rob the clerk, I'm going to kill you." F then accompanies E into the store and holds open a paper bag as the clerk fills it with money. After they leave the store, E looks at F, says, "Thanks, stupid," and runs away. Several minutes later the police arrive and arrest F for robbery. Duress is a viable defense in this case.

Intoxication

Two types of intoxication may be used as a defense: voluntary and involuntary. *Voluntary* (self-induced) intoxication was rarely considered a viable defense under common law. Today, most jurisdictions recognize voluntary intoxication as an acceptable defense if it negates an element of the offense, but this only applies to specific intent crimes (robbery, burglary, larceny, etc.). No jurisdictions allow voluntary intoxication as a defense for general intent crimes.

The *involuntary* intoxication defense is rarely used. It is viable only when the defendant became intoxicated through coercion or deception. Some courts have allowed the involuntary intoxication defense in cases in which the defendant mistakenly became intoxicated or was ignorant about the pharmacological properties of the intoxicating substance. The latter option is limited to prescription drugs.[75]

Intoxication cannot be a defense for the crime of drunk driving, because alcohol is obviously an element of the crime. The language of the law places full responsibility for becoming intoxicated, and for the effects resulting from intoxication, on the individual. It might be argued, however, that people with physical dependencies on alcohol or drugs cannot help themselves. Given that the justification for liquor laws is the inability of minors to handle alcohol responsibly, one could also argue against the language of the law for minors.

Entrapment

The entrapment defense is very narrow and almost never available to the defendant. The police view one of their principal roles as catching people who want to break the law. The only defendant who is going to benefit from this defense is someone who can prove he or she had absolutely no predisposition or desire to commit the offense until trapped into doing so. *Entrapment* became a household word during the ABSCAM investigations in the late 1970s. These investigations, conducted by the FBI, were directed against elected officials in the U.S. Congress, who claimed that the FBI had entrapped them—meaning that were it not for the FBI's tactics, the defendants would have committed no crimes.[76]

Generally speaking, entrapment can occur in only two ways. Entrapment occurs when law enforcement or informants induce a person to engage in criminal activities by (1) making knowingly false statements that the conduct they are encouraging is not illegal or (2) using inducements that create a substantial risk that people other than those who are ready to commit an offense will be persuaded to do so. The defense can be successful only if the defendant can prove by a preponderance of evidence that his or her behavior was the result of entrapment. A major reason why this defense is rarely successful is that determining the validity or truthfulness of testimony of witnesses often boils down to the question of "Who is telling the truth, the police or the defendant?" There is an overwhelming tendency for juries and judges to take the word of police officers over defendants.

Use of Force in Defense of Self, Others, and Property

Under certain conditions, the law allows individuals to protect themselves, other people, and property against unlawful threats or force. There are, however, limitations, which are contingent on the severity of the unlawful threat. Individuals may use *nondeadly* force in self-defense whenever they believe force will be used against them and that the use of force is necessary for protection. Most jurisdictions allow individuals to employ *deadly* force in self-defense when they believe that deadly force is about to be used against them. Some jurisdictions, however, stipulate that in certain conditions the defender must *retreat to the wall*—break contact with the threat if such a movement can be accomplished with complete safety. In three situations, however, the retreat rule does not apply: (1) inside one's own home, (2) if one is the victim of a rape or robbery, and (3) if one is a police officer—police officers have no duty to retreat.

Essentially, the same rules apply in situations in which one is compelled to use force in order to protect others. Under common law, a special relationship must exist between the parties in question before protective force could be used, and a person may use force to protect another person if the situation is such that the defender would be justified to use force if it were he or she who was subjected to the threat. Finally, the defender must believe that her or his intervention is necessary for the protection of the other person. The retreat requirements for self-defense also apply to the use of force for the protection of another person.

Although many people believe that they have a legal right and moral duty to kill someone who violates their property, deadly force may never be used to defend property only. Most jurisdictions allow the use of reasonable force to protect property from immediate criminal acts. However, if verbal instructions are sufficient to protect property, no force is permitted.

Certain devices may be used to protect one's property. First, the device cannot be designed to create a significant risk of death or substantial bodily injury. Second, the actor's use of a device to protect her or his property from entry or trespass must be reasonable under the circumstances. Finally, the device must be one that is customarily used for the specified purpose. Reasonable care must be taken to alert potential intruders that such a device will be employed.

Insanity

The insanity defense is perhaps one of the most controversial issues of affirmative defense. The courts have generally attempted to measure a person's mental capacity through one of five major tests: (1) the M'Naghten rule, (2) the "irresistible impulse" test, (3) the Durham rule, (4) the Model Penal Code rule, and (5) the Insanity Defense Reform Act passed by Congress in 1984.[77]

The *M'Naghten rule* was established in England in 1843. Daniel McNaghten shot and killed Edward Drummond, the private secretary of the prime minister of England. The defense claimed McNaghten suffered from delusions so pronounced that he did not know what he was doing at the time of the crime. He was found not guilty by reason of insanity. The judges who ruled in the case said a defendant was insane at the time of the crime only if he was

> laboring under such a defect of reason, from disease of the mind, as not to know the nature and quality of the act he was doing; or, if he did know it, that he did not know he was doing what was wrong.[78]

Under the M'Naghten rule (also known as the right-or-wrong test), the defense must show that the defendant lacks awareness of the wrongfulness of his or her act(s) or fails to understand the nature and quality of the act(s). In the United States this rule is used in thirty states; however, many added the concept of "*irresistible impulse,*" sometimes called the "wild beast test," which considers a person's emotions and self-control. "The idea was that certain conditions had the power to affect human emotions without necessarily destroying cognitive functions. The person is in the helpless grip of a force outside himself, borne away by a tornado of instinct or drive."[79] An accused cannot be held criminally liable if it can be proved that he or she was suffering from such illnesses that "rendered them incapable of controlling their actions."[80]

The **Durham rule** arose from a case in 1954.[81] David Bazelon, a federal judge, ruled that "an accused person is not criminally responsible if his [or her] unlawful act was the product of mental disease or mental defect."[82] This ruling opened the door for the consideration of all sorts of mental and emotional problems as they relate to criminal behavior.

The test of insanity proposed by the American Law Institute in the "Model Penal Code" has been increasingly used by some courts.[83] The *Model Penal Code rule,* often referred to as the *"substantial capacity" test,* states: "A person is not responsible for criminal conduct if at the time of such conduct as a result of mental disease or defect, a person lacks substantial capacity either to appreciate the wrongfulness of his conduct or to conform his conduct to the requirements of the law."[84]

The most recent federal standard is the *Insanity Defense Reform Act of 1984.*

> It is an affirmative defense to a prosecution under any Federal statute that, at the time of the commission of the acts constituting the offense, the defendant, as a result of a severe mental disease or defect, was unable to appreciate the nature and quality or the wrongfulness of his acts. Mental disease or defect does not otherwise constitute a defense.[85]

It should be noted that the courts continue to struggle with this problem, and one of the latest methods is to use the verdict "guilty but mentally ill" when the defendant's insanity has been established but the person nevertheless will be subject to some form of incarceration and treatment.

Battered-Person Syndrome

Domestic violence is a relatively new legal concept, similar to *child abuse* that did not become a recognized term until the 1960s. Historically, women and children were treated legally as the property of males, who had the right to do with their property as they saw fit. Although laws were enacted to dispel the woman-and-children-as-property tradition, Congress did not pass the Violence against Women Act, which provides civil rights relief for women who are victimized by males, until 1994.

The **battered-person syndrome** is a relatively new legal defense tool. Originally referred to as the *battered-wife syndrome,* the term was changed to *battered-person syndrome* to accommodate children who, after years of abusive treatment at home, assault or kill their parent(s). This term is employed in all cases where evidence of long-term battering is presented in defense of a criminal act, or as mitigating circumstances in the negotiation of a sentence or a plea for clemency following a conviction.[86] The battered-person syndrome is often used by defendants to shore up a self-defense strategy.

SUMMARY

In this chapter we described two traditional perspectives on crime and criminal justice and presented our alternative, critical perspective. The classical approach assumes that people have free will and that most offenders act rationally. It focuses on the crime itself and argues that punishments must be "proportionate to the offense" in order to reduce crime. In contrast, the positivist approach stresses various biological, psychological, and sociological factors determining human behavior. It argues that crime is not necessarily rational behavior; it is caused by factors external to the individual. Instead of punishment, positivists generally favor social reform or rehabilitation. The classical and positivist approaches generally take the existing social and economic order for granted. Our critical approach challenges this view. Our focus is on the inherently unequal distribution of resources within a capitalist society and on the relationship between this inequality and crime and criminal justice.

We discussed three perspectives on criminal law: the consensus/pluralist model, the interest-group/conflict model, and our critical model of law. We pointed out that the criminal justice system exists primarily to enforce the *criminal* law, not other forms of law. Thus, under normal circumstances when a corporation dumps toxic chemicals into a river or engages in price-fixing or other harmful acts, the criminal justice system is rarely involved. You are not likely to see the police handcuff the CEO of a corporation on the evening news. A rather obvious class bias is built into the legal system. There is one system of justice for the rich and powerful (civil law, administrative law, etc.) and another system (criminal law and the criminal justice system) for the rest of the population.

Legal definitions of crime include *actus reus* and *mens rea*. We looked at the specific instances where the failure to act—versus a purposeful behavior and intention—is considered criminal. After being charged with a crime, defendants have three options. If they plead not guilty, they can deny the charges or assert an affirmative defense.

Key Terms

- *actus reus*
- administrative law
- Adolphe Quételet
- battered-person syndrome
- Bill of Rights
- case law/common law
- Cesare Lombroso
- civil law
- classical school
- consensus/pluralist model
- constitutional law
- crime control model
- criminal law
- critical model
- due process model
- Durham rule
- Eighth Amendment
- elements of a crime
- Fifth Amendment
- folkways
- formal social control
- Fourteenth Amendment
- Fourth Amendment
- instrumentalist perspective
- intent
- interest-group/conflict model
- M'Naghten rule
- *mens rea*
- mores
- ordinances
- political social control
- positivist school
- procedural law
- Pyrrhic defeat theory
- rule of law
- Sixth Amendment
- social norms
- sociological imagination
- statutes
- structuralist perspective
- substantive law
- torts

Notes

[1] Cullen, E. and K. Gilbert. *Reaffirming Rehabilitation.* Cincinnati: Anderson, 1982, p. 27.

[2] Social contract theory became a convenient ideology to justify a strong central government or state, which is ultimately concerned with protecting the interests of private property and profits. The theory also justified the build-up of police forces and other formal methods of handling conflicts and disputes—in short, a formal criminal justice system. Crime was defined as a harm to the state and the people—the terms were often used interchangeably.) Rousseau wrote that the ultimate source of inequality was man taking a plot of ground and claiming it as his own, which was exactly what happened during the *enclosure movements* in England during the sixteenth century. Powerful landlords built fences around common ground (land formally used by all and not legally owned) and claimed it as their own or charged rent. This resulted in thousands of vagrants

invading European cities in search of work and eventually being labeled the *dangerous classes* (or worse) by the privileged. The prevailing view of crime—that it was a voluntary violation of the social contract—became an essential idea in much of the subsequent thinking about crime, especially classical views.

3 This classic book is available in many bookstores and libraries. See Beccaria, C. *On Crimes and Punishment.* New York: Bobbs-Merrill, 1963 [1764].

4 Ibid., p. 99.

5 Taylor, I., P. Walton, and J. Young. *The New Criminology.* London: Routledge & Kegan Paul, 1973, p. 2.

6 Packer, H. L. *The Limits of the Criminal Sanction.* Palo Alto, CA: Stanford University Press, 1968.

7 For a good discussion of human nature and the fact that humans are not inherently hedonistic see Michalowski, R. *Order, Law, and Crime.* New York: Macmillan, 1985, ch. 3. See Taylor, Walton, and Young, *The New Criminology,* for a critique of the classical school of thought. For an excellent discussion of deterrence (a central feature of the classical school) see Zimring, F. and G. J. Hawkins. *Deterrence: The Legal Threat in Crime Control.* Chicago: University of Chicago Press, 1973.

8 Quoted in Burtch, B. *The Sociology of Law.* Toronto: Harcourt Brace Jovanovich, 1992, p. 6.

9 Taylor, Walton, and Young, *The New Criminology,* p. 5.

10 Vold, G. and T. J. Bernard. *Theoretical Criminology* (3rd ed.). New York: Oxford University Press, 1986, p. 25.

11 Taylor, Walton, and Young, *The New Criminology,* p. 7.

12 Vold and Bernard, *Theoretical Criminology,* p. 26.

13 Ibid., p. 27.

14 Ibid., p. 36.

15 Bottomore, T., L. Harris, V. G. Kiernan, and R. Miliband (eds.). *A Dictionary of Marxist Thought.* Cambridge, MA: Harvard University Press, 1983, p. 382.

16 For a more detailed discussion of the work of Guerry and Quételet, see Lanier, M. M. and S. Henry. *Essential Criminology.* Boulder, CO: Westview Press, 1998, pp. 183–192.

17 Quételet, A. *Research on the Propensity for Crime at Different Ages.* Cincinnati: Anderson, 1984 [1831], p. 69.

18 Ibid.

19 Cullen, E. and K. Gilbert. *Reaffirming Rehabilitation.* Cincinnati: Anderson, 1982, p. 33.

20 Quinney, R. and Wildeman, J. *The Problem of Crime* (3rd ed.). Mountain View, CA: Mayfield, 1991, pp. 32–33.

21 Vold and Bernard, *Theoretical Criminology,* p. 42.

22 We encourage readers to challenge us, the authors of this text. Check our sources; question other people about what they believe and why.

23 Mills, C. W. *The Sociological Imagination.* New York: Oxford University Press, 1959, pp. 5–8.

24 Marx, K. *The 18th Brumaire of Louis Bonaparte.* New York: International Publishers, 1963 [1852], p. 15.

25 Michalowski, *Order, Law, and Crime,* pp. 14, 22–23.

26 See the discussion on social class and social inequality in chapter 1. Also see chapter 2 in Parenti, M. *Democracy for the Few* (7th ed.). New York: Bedford/St. Martin's, 2002.

27 We elaborate on this theme throughout the text. For supporting evidence see: Chambliss, W. and R. Seidman. *Law, Order, and Power* (2nd ed.). Reading, MA: Addison-Wesley, 1982; Chambliss, W. and M. S. Zatz (eds.). *Making Law: The State, the Law, and Structural Contradictions.* Bloomington: Indiana University Press, 1993; Reiman, J. *The Rich Get Richer and the Poor Get Prison* (8th ed.). Boston: Allyn & Bacon, 2007.

28 Lynch, M. and R. Michalowski. *A New Primer in Radical Criminology* (3rd ed.). New York: Harrow and Heston, 2000.

29 Quinney, R. *The Social Reality of Crime.* Boston: Little, Brown, 1970.

30 Reiman, *The Rich Get Richer,* p. 5.

31 Ibid., p. 175.

32 Seagal, D. "Tales from the Cutting-Room Floor: The Reality of 'Reality-Based' Television." *Harper's Magazine* (November 1993), p. 157.

33 Reiman, *The Rich Get Richer,* p. 176.

34 Ibid., p. 6.

35 Reiman (pp. 23–27) lists three "excuses that don't wash" for why we don't reduce crime. These excuses are (1) we are too soft on crime; (2) crime is inevitable in a complex society such as ours; (3) crime is the fault of young people.

36 For a good summary of the available research see Belknap, J. *The Invisible Woman: Gender Crime, and Justice* (3rd ed.) Belmont, CA: Wadsworth, 2007, chapters 7 and 8; and Eigenberg, H. *Woman Battering in the United States: Till Death Do Us Part.* Long Grove, IL: Waveland Press.

37 Quinney, *The Social Reality of Crime,* p. 37.

38 Quinney, R. *Critique of Legal Order: Crime Control in Capitalist Society.* Boston: Little, Brown, 1974.

39 See: Chambliss, W. J. "On Lawmaking" and "The Creation of American Law and Crime Control in Britain and America," in Chambliss and Zatz, *Making Law;* Quinney, *The Social Reality of Crime* and *Class, State and Crime;* Michalowski, *Order, Law, and Crime;* Lynch and Michalowski, *A New Primer on Radical Criminology;* J. A. Whitt, "Toward a Class-Dialectical Model of Power: An Empirical Assessment of Three Competing Models of Political Power," in Chambliss and Zatz, *Making Law.*

40 Durkheim, E. *The Division of Labor in Society.* Glencoe, IL: Free Press, 1947 [1893].

41 Pound, R. *An Introduction to the Philosophy of Law.* New Haven: Yale University Press, 1922; Pound, R. *Social Control through Law.* New Haven, CT: Yale University Press, 1942; Geis, G. "Sociology and Jurisprudence: Admixture of Lore and Law." *Kentucky Law Journal* 52: 267–293 (Winter 1964); Quinney, *The Social Reality of Crime,* p. 33.

42 Michalowski, *Order, Law, and Crime,* pp. 47–48.

43 Quinney, *The Social Reality of Crime,* p. 35.

44 Ibid., pp. 39–41.

45 Becker, H. S. *Outsiders: Studies in the Sociology of Deviance.* New York: Free Press, 1963.

46 See Domhoff, G. W. *Who Really Rules: New Haven and Community Power Re-Examined.* New Brunswick, NJ: Transaction Books, 1978; and *The Powers That Be.* New York: Random House, 1979.

47 There are literally hundreds of books and articles by and about Karl Marx. See for instance Giddens, A. *Capitalism and Modern Social Theory.* New York: Cambridge University Press, 1971 (reprinted in 1994). For an informal and enjoyable summary of Marx's thinking see Ruis, *Marx for Beginners.* New York: Pantheon Books, 1989.

48 Quinney, *Critique of Legal Order,* p. 16.

49 Lynch and Michalowski, *A New Primer in Radical Criminology,* pp. 44–58.

50 Chambliss and Seidman, *Law, Order, and Power;* Greenberg, D. (ed.). *Crime and Capitalism* (rev. ed.). Philadelphia: Temple University Press, 1993; O'Connor, J. *The Fiscal Crisis of the State.* New York: St. Martin's Press, 1973.

51 Zinn, H. *A People's History of the United States* (2nd ed.). New York: Harper, 1995, pp. 98–99.

52 Holmes, O. W. "The Path of the Law." *Harvard Law Review* 10: 461 (March 1897).

53 Cardoza, B. N. *The Growth of the Law.* New Haven, CT: Yale University Press, 1924, p. 52.

54 Black, D. *The Behavior of Law.* New York: Academic Press, 1976, p. 2.

55 McIntyre, L. *The Public Defender: The Practice of Law in the Shadows of Repute.* Chicago: University of Chicago Press, 1994.

56 Sumner, W. G. *Folkways.* Lexington, MA: Ginn, 1906.

57 Quinney, *The Social Reality of Crime,* p. 36. See also Sutherland, E. and D. Cressey. *Criminology* (10th ed.). Philadelphia: Lippincott, 1978, pp. 5–7.

58 Black, *The Behavior of Law.*

59 Michalowski, *Order, Law, and Crime,* p. 139.

60 Scheb, J. M. and J. M. Scheb II. *Criminal Law and Procedure* (4th ed.). St. Paul: West, 2000, p. 7.

61 Michalowski, *Order, Law, and Crime,* p. 141.

62 Zinn, *A People's History of the United States,* p. 99.

63 The Supreme Court has ruled that states are not bound to provide grand juries. Thus, only federal cases now require grand jury indictments to proceed with prosecution.

64 See Chambliss and Seidman, *Law, Order, and Power;* and Reiman, *The Rich Get Richer.* For a perfect example of how corporate offenders are dealt with we need only cite the savings and loan scandal, for which taxpayers will have to pay most of the estimated $500 bil-

lion by the year 2021 to bail out insolvent savings and loan institutions. See Calavita, K. and H. N. Pontell. "'Other People's Money' Revisited: Collective Embezzlement in the Savings and Loan and Insurance Industries." In Chambliss and Zatz, *Making Law.*

65 Jon Roland. [Online] http://www.constitution.org/col/0610staredrift.htm

66 From the first of twelve Lowell Lectures delivered by Oliver Wendell Holmes, Jr. on November 23, 1880, which were the basis for *The Common Law.* [Online] http://www.law.harvard.edu/library/collections/special/online-collections/common_law/index.php

67 Scheb and Scheb, *Criminal Law and Procedure.*

68 Michalowski, *Order, Law, and Crime,* p. 155.

69 Ibid., p. 156.

70 Scheb and Scheb, *Criminal Law and Procedure.*

71 Ibid.

72 Ibid.

73 Ibid., ch. 14.

74 Ill. Laws 131 1899.

75 Scheb and Scheb, *Criminal Law and Procedure.*

76 Ibid.

77 Michalowski, *Order, Law, and Crime,* pp. 161–163; Scheb and Scheb, *Criminal Law and Procedure,* pp. 339–342.

78 Friedman, L. M. *Crime and Punishment in American History.* New York: Basic Books, 1993, p. 143.

79 Friedman, p. 144.

80 Michalowski, *Order, Law, and Crime,* p. 162; Scheb and Scheb, p. 273.

81 *Durham v. United States.* 214 F.2d 862,876 (D.C. Cir. 1954).

82 Friedman, p. 403.

83 The "Model Penal Code" was a proposal put together in 1962 by the American Law Institute, an organization of distinguished judges, lawyers, and academics. It consisted of several provisions concerning criminal liability, sentencing, defenses to crime, and several other important criminal law matters. It is not a law per se but rather a model that has been adopted by most states.

84 Scheb and Scheb, *Criminal Law and Procedure,* p. 273.

85 Ibid., pp. 273–274.

86 Ibid., ch. 14.

four

Theories of Crime

Theory is an important part of any academic discipline, including criminal justice. In chapter 3 we examined the classical and positivist perspectives of crime and criminal justice. The classical perspective has dominated theories of the criminal justice system; the positivist paradigm has dominated theories of criminal behavior. In this chapter we review three categories of theories within the positivist paradigm. Three factors have been used to explain criminal behavior: the offender's body (biological), mind (psychological), or environment (sociological). We'll also look at rational choice theory, an extension of the classical approach.

BIOLOGICAL THEORIES

The central thesis of biological theories is that criminals are biologically different from noncriminals. Linked with this theory is the assumption that criminals are inferior to noncriminals. The quest for a biological explanation for criminality began with the work of Franz Joseph Gall (1758–1828).

Joseph Gall

Gall wondered why some people commit crime and others do not. He anticipated finding the answer by studying the physiological characteristics of humans and searching for differentiating traits between criminals and noncriminals. Gall's primary endeavor was the study of *phrenology*. He hypothesized that the pattern of bumps found on an individual's head would indicate criminal tendencies. Gall recognized the significance of the brain as the center of

thought and believed that the skull was an indicator of the brain within. Based on this assumption, Gall set about measuring and comparing the skulls of incarcerated and noninstitutionalized people. While Gall's theory made no lasting contribution to the understanding of crime, his ideas marked the beginning of the scientific study of deviance. The most famous early representative of this perspective was Cesare Lombroso.

Lombroso's Views

Lombroso (1836–1909), along with two of his followers, Enrico Ferri (1856–1928) and Raffaele Garofalo (1852–1934), are often referred to as the "Italian School." They posited that criminals were atavistic or biological throwbacks to an earlier evolutionary stage—primitive individuals with very particular features.

Lombroso's theory included five propositions: (1) Criminals are, at birth, a distinct type of human being. (2) They can be recognized by certain stigmata, such as high cheekbones, large jaws, deformed or oddly shaped ears, and excessive body hair. Lombroso arrived at these and other conclusions as a result of performing autopsies on the bodies of hundreds of Italian prisoners who had died in confinement. It never dawned on him that the physical conditions of these prisoners could have been the *result of their confinement* rather than the *cause* of their criminal behavior, an especially appropriate explanation given the horrible conditions in Italian prisons and jails of the time. (3) Five or more of these stigmata indicate criminal tendencies. Lombroso believed that women

69

offenders were worse in many ways than their male counterparts; they had "fallen from grace" and were inferior even to male criminals. (4) Stigmata do not so much cause criminal behavior as they indicate that someone is *predisposed* to becoming a criminal. (5) Because of their natures these distinct types of human beings cannot help but become criminals, unless they grow up under extremely favorable conditions.[1]

Prior to his death, Lombroso de-emphasized the importance of atavism in accounting for the range of criminality.[2] He conceded that biology explained only about one-third of crime and modified his theory. In a later analysis, Lombroso identified four classifications of criminals: born criminal, insane criminal, epileptic criminal, and occasional criminal. Lombroso's ideas inspired several notable researchers.

Variations of Lombroso's Views

One famous variation of Lombroso's views is the general theory of *body types,* sometimes referred to as *physiognomy*, which gained popularity during the first half of the twentieth century. According to this view, humans can be divided into three basic **soma-totypes**. These body types correspond to certain inmate *temperaments*. The first type is the **endomorph**, characterized by excessive body weight and described as being "soft" and having an extroverted personality. The second type is the **mesomorph**, who is athletically built and muscular. These are active individuals who behave aggressively. They are believed to be the most likely to be involved in serious criminal activity and to join gangs. The third type is the **ectomorph.** They tend to be delicate and introverted; as loners, they are unlikely to engage in crime.[3]

One of the most popular variations of biological theories claims criminal behavior is genetically transmitted from one generation to another. Throughout the twentieth century various researchers reported findings to support this view, primarily from studies of twins. While correlations in the behaviors of identical twins raised in different geographical locations have been found, there are many problems with these studies. The samples have been much too small to be generalizable, and the studies have not agreed on definitions and indicators of crime.

Another view holds that the genetic abnormality of an extra "Y" chromosome makes individuals with the trait "super-males" who exhibit more aggressive behavior than other individuals. The extra Y chromosome is found in about one male out of every 1,000. The vast majority of male offenders, including most violent offenders, do not have the trait.[4]

Still another variation of these views focuses on women offenders and the *premenstrual syndrome* (PMS). Although popular in explaining women's crime, there is virtually no research that proves PMS is a factor. Part of the problem is the lack of precise definition of the term itself.[5] Despite the shortcomings, PMS has been used as a form of insanity defense in France and as a defense in both England and the United States.

One final variation focuses on the functioning of the central nervous system, which encompasses conscious thought and voluntary motor activities. Abnormal brain wave patterns, measured through electroencephalographs (EEGs), have been associated with various abnormal behavioral patterns in individuals. Some studies have found that the brain wave activity of offenders is excessively slow, while other studies have found just the opposite. Still other studies have examined the role of epilepsy and certain forms of brain damage, all with mixed or inconclusive results.[6]

The evidence is not sufficient "to conclude that biological differences can be found in the majority of criminals, and where those differences are found, the causal linkages to criminal behavior are still weak."[7] Instead, biological factors should be viewed as one of many factors influencing behavior. Biological factors have zero influence on whether or not *society defines certain behaviors as criminal.* Most importantly, these types of theories, based on notions of biological inferiority, have consistently been used to describe people of certain races and ethnic groups.

RATIONAL CHOICE THEORY

A theory that became popular in the 1970s and 1980s takes the position that crime is a product of "rational" choices and decisions that people make in their daily lives.[8] The perspective learned from the mistakes of the original classical school, which erroneously assumed that all humans behave rationally all the time. There are constraints on our choices because of lack of information, various moral values, the social context of the situation, and other situational factors. In short, not everyone acts logically and rationally all the time, which may be especially true for young offenders.[9] Modern *rational choice theory* is based on the **hedonistic calculus**. It assumes that people freely choose to commit crime because they are goal oriented and seek to maximize their pleasure and minimize their pain. In short, they are acting mostly out of self-interest.

One variation of rational choice theory is *routine activities theory*. This version states three circumstances must converge for a crime to occur: suitable targets, a lack of capable guardians, and motivated offenders. According to the theory, criminals plan and commit crimes by carefully selecting specific targets based on vulnerability. Certain "routine activities" during a day—such as leaving a house empty during regular working hours, or not locking your doors, leaving keys in your car, or being out in high crime areas at night—provide opportunities for victimization. Active criminals select the most likely targets, after weighing the odds of getting caught. The theory is linked to situational crime prevention, which sometimes suggests staying home is one solution to avoid being victimized. However, some groups, especially women and children, are much more vulnerable to victimization at home than anywhere else.[10]

Rational choice theory is overly simplistic and fails to consider many other factors that influence decision making. Our choices are determined by various social and cultural factors. The senior author always illustrates this by asking his students to explain why they chose to attend UNLV and not Har-

vard. Think about this and apply it to whatever college or university you are attending (if you happen to be at Harvard, ask yourself why you did not choose UNLV).

PSYCHOLOGICAL THEORIES

Psychological theories of criminal behavior try to find a connection between crime and such factors as intelligence, personality, and various abnormalities of the brain. Biological views portrayed criminals as biologically inferior; psychological views portray them as psychologically or mentally inferior.

Feeblemindedness and Crime

Early in the twentieth century psychologist Henry Goddard began to study intelligence and argued that there was a correlation between low intelligence and crime. He was one of the first to use the term *feeblemindedness* and associated this with a certain intelligence level as measured by tests that would result in an IQ score, which theoretically measures one's "mental age." Goddard administered an IQ test to inmates at the New Jersey Training School for the Feebleminded. He found that none of the inmates scored higher than a mental age of 13. Since these inmates were in a "school" for the "feebleminded" he came to the conclusion that an IQ score of 13 demarcated the level of "feeblemindedness." This view has been totally discredited because of poor measurement tools and the linkage of such testing and attempts to control, or even eliminate, certain "undesirables." The early twentieth century was marked by claims that various racial and ethnic minorities were inferior and "dangerous," requiring control or even elimination. The eugenics movement was based on the notion that some people could not escape their biologically determined fates because they were predisposed to deviance and criminal behavior. A scientific cause of crime called for a scientific "cure." During the first two decades of the twentieth century, the eugenics movement was responsible for the sterilization of a number of people, often European immigrants. Science was used to sanction class and racial control.[11]

Psychoanalytic Theories

Sigmund Freud did not concentrate on criminal behavior per se, but many of his analytic theories have been used by others to link crime and personality. Essentially, crime is seen as a symptom of deep-seated mental problems stemming from defects in one's personality. Freud identified the following problems, which are often said to cause criminal behavior: (1) difficulties during one of the psychosexual stages of development (e.g., anal, phallic, oedipal); (2) an inability to sublimate (or redirect) sexual and aggressive "drives" or "instincts"; (3) an inability to successfully resolve the *oedipal* (in men) or *Electra* (in women) complex; and (4) an unconscious desire for punishment.[12]

Often researchers claim that specific crimes are associated with certain stages of development. For example, problems during the *phallic* stage, in which a child begins to understand the pleasure associated with his or her sexual organs, can be related to such crimes as sexual assault, rape, or prostitution. Problems during the *oral* stage may result in crimes associated with alcoholism or drug addiction. Other aspects of personality related to criminal behavior that derived from Freud's work include studies of such personality types as sociopaths, psychopaths, and people with antisocial tendencies. The primary focus is the lack of a sense of guilt and no sense of right and wrong.

Personality Trait Theories

Researchers have devised various standardized tests for the study of personality traits, the most famous of which is the *Minnesota Multiphasic Personality Inventory*. The first version was developed at the University of Minnesota in the 1930s. It was formulated by administering sample questions to people with identified psychological disorders and comparing the responses to a control group. Questions that clearly distinguished different types of pathological respondents from "normal" respondents were retained. Despite its widespread use, there were numerous problems, including an inadequate statistical basis for scoring. For example, questions supposedly identifying homosexual tendencies were based on the responses of 13 gay men compared to the "normal" responses of 724 Minnesota farmers.[13]

The test was revised in 1989. MMPI-2 consists of 567 true and false questions. Ten clinical scales are used to assess the responses; because the scales are not pure measures of psychiatric diagnoses, they are usually referred to by their numbers. For example, scale 4 measures social deviation, lack of acceptance of authority, and amorality. This is the scale often associated with criminal behavior. The California Psychological Inventory (CPI) was developed by Harrison Gough, who received his doctorate in 1949 from the University of Minnesota. CPI was designed to assess personality traits such as dominance, sociability, etc., among normal individuals. Test responses in the benchmark group were correlated with personal assessments by trained observers, family, coworkers, and so on. The problem with personality tests is that they are often invalid, unreliable, culture-bound, and unfair. They tend to overpathologize certain groups, particularly teenagers and nonwhites.[14]

Personality theories assume that we can easily distinguish between criminals and noncriminals. If we were to try to devise a test to identify criminality by questioning a group of prison inmates and comparing the responses to a group of college or high school students, would we be certain we had fairly determined the extent of involvement in crime by the college or high school students? As self-report studies have shown, most high school and college students have done something that could have landed them in jail. Yet they are viewed, during these kinds of research projects, as the "nonoffender" control group. Ronald Akers notes that: "The research using personality inventories and other methods of measuring personality characteristics have not been able to produce findings to support personality variables as major causes of criminal and delinquent behavior."[15]

Antisocial Personality

The concept of antisocial personality (sometimes referred to as psychopathy or sociopathy) often surfaces when attempting to explain why some people commit violent crime. Individuals who suffer from this disorder often have above-average intelligence, are risk takers, egocentric, manipulative, and show little emotion; they suffer from an inability to be remorseful or empathetic.[16] Psychopaths are hedonistic, but they do not respond to punishment. A variety of factors may contribute to the development of psychopathy, including neurological disorders, brain abnormality, and traumatic socialization. Many researchers believe that sociopaths are chronic offenders, meaning that they engage in criminality throughout their lives.

Jeffrey Dahmer, Theodore Kaczynski (the Unabomber), David Berkowitz, and Ted Bundy suffered from serious psychological problems. They may even have met the definition of a sociopath. Offenders that meet these criteria, however, shed little real light on the problem of crime because they are so rare. Can these theories explain all crime? No. Does everyone who catches fish barehanded in Indiana suffer from a flawed psyche? It is highly unlikely.

Policy Implications

Attempts to find an explanation for crime in biology or psychology has a long, continuing history. Many questions remain unanswered. One problem is that cross-cultural research has failed to reach findings similar to those in the United States. For instance, since crime tends to be concentrated in the inner cities of the United States and in areas of concentrated poverty and heavily populated by racial minorities, why don't the same biological and psychological traits turn up in the inner cities of other countries? Why is the risk of being a crime victim higher in the United States than in most other countries? Is there an "American crime gene" or "American personality trait"?

Even more important than whether a particular theory is reliable are the policy implications of these explanations. Nazi

Germany during World War II is the most infamous example of promoting one set of characteristics by eliminating those who did not meet the criterion, but there are other examples. Between 1907 and 1937 in the United States, 31 states enacted laws permitting sterilization or castration of epileptics, the mentally deficient, and the mentally ill without their consent. Almost 70,000 people were involuntarily sterilized and many more were institutionalized.[17] Since the advent of positivism, body appendages, fluids, and emotions have been measured, probed, scrutinized, and interpreted. The results of these endeavors have led to lobotomies, the removal of organs, involuntary castration, and even the injection of chemicals. What we must remember is that crime is a social construction. It varies by culture, geographic location, and it evolves over time. How can predisposition to criminality possibly be biologically innate?

SOCIOLOGICAL THEORIES

Elliott Currie refers to the "fallacy of autonomy," or the idea that people act totally on their own, without the influence of others and totally unaffected by their surrounding culture and social institutions.[18] If crime were caused by some inferior gene, or a certain personality trait, then how do we explain the high rate of corporate and white-collar crime by supposedly "normal" upper-class, white males? Why is it that the crime rates have remained the highest in certain parts of large urban areas, regardless of the kinds of people who live there, over about a 100-year period? Why are crime rates higher in urban than in rural areas and why do males have a crime rate about four times the rate of females? For these and other questions, we need to turn to sociological theories of crime.

Sociological theories can be grouped into seven general categories: (1) social disorganization/social ecology, (2) strain/anomie, (3) cultural deviance, (4) control/social bond, (5) social learning, (6) labeling, and (7) critical/Marxist. Figure 4.1 summarizes these perspectives.

Figure 4.1   Sociological Perspectives on Crime

Theory	Major Points/Key Factors
Social Disorganization/ Social Ecology	Crime stems from certain community or neighborhood characteristics, such as poverty, dilapidated housing, high density, high mobility, and high rates of unemployment. *Concentric zone theory* is a variation that argues that crime increases toward the inner-city area.
Strain/Anomie	Cultural norms of "success" emphasize goals such as money, status, and power, but the means to obtain such success are not equally distributed. As a result of blocked opportunities, many among the disadvantaged resort to illegal means, which are more readily available.
Cultural Deviance	Certain subcultures, including a gang subculture, exist within poor communities and foster values, attitudes, beliefs, and norms that run counter to the prevailing middle-class culture. An important feature of this subculture is the absence of fathers, resulting in female-headed households, which tend to be poorer than traditional two-parent families. Youths are exposed to this subculture early in life and become *embedded* in it.
Control/Social Bond	Delinquency persists when a youth's bonds or ties to society are weak or broken, especially bonds with family, school, and other institutions. When this occurs, a youth is likely to seek bonds with other groups, including gangs, in order to fulfill his or her needs.
Social Learning	Delinquency is *learned* over time through association with others, especially gang members. Delinquency results from a process that includes the acquisition of attitudes and values, the instigation of a criminal act based on certain stimuli, and the maintenance or perpetuation of such behavior.
Labeling	Definitions of delinquency and crime stem from differences in power and status in the larger society. Youths without power are most likely to have their behaviors labeled as "delinquency." Delinquency may be generated, and perpetuated, through negative labeling by significant others and by the judicial system. A person may associate with others similarly labeled, such as gangs.
Critical/Marxist	Crime is an inevitable product of social (and racial) inequality brought about by capitalism itself; power is unequally distributed and those without power often resort to "criminal" means to survive.

Social Disorganization/ Social Ecology Theory

Social disorganization theory has been one of the most popular and enduring sociological theories of crime and delinquency. *Social ecology* is one variation and offers a perspective on the *spatial or geographical distribution* of crime, delinquency, and gangs.[19] Modern versions of this perspective began with the work of several sociologists at the University of Chicago during the first three decades of the twentieth century. The original idea behind the spatial distribution of crime began with Adolphe Quételet and Michel Guerry. As discussed in chapter 3, these two were the first two scientists to col-

lect and analyze various crime data and the residences of offenders, matching them with various socioeconomic variables, such as poverty, infant mortality, unemployment, and other social indicators. Their work initiated the **Cartographic School** of criminology, which involved plotting the location of criminals and various social indicators on a city map. Many police departments use colored pins or dots to mark the locations of certain crimes or the locations of a series of muggings, auto thefts, etc.

"Mapmaking" and the more general notion that crime is *spatially* distributed within a geographical area became one of the hallmarks of the **Chicago School** of sociology. During the twentieth century, many researchers from the sociology department at the University of Chicago noticed that crime and delinquency rates varied by areas of the city of Chicago and in other major cities. They found the highest rates of crime and delinquency in areas that also had high rates of other social problems, such as single-parent families, unemployment, multiple-family dwellings, welfare cases, and low levels of education.

Social ecology views people as being in a relationship with one another and their physical environment. Just as plant and animal species tend to *colonize* their environment, humans colonize their "geographical space."[20] One of the key findings of the social ecology of crime perspective was that high rates of crime and other problems persist within the same neighborhoods over long periods of time, *regardless of who lives there*. Something about the *places* themselves, rather than the people living there, seemed to produce and perpetuate high crime rates.[21]

Clifford R. Shaw and Henry McKay sought to explain crime within the context of the changing urban ecology. They recognized that Chicago had developed distinct neighborhoods with differing problems, residents, and levels of income. They utilized the *concentric zone* model of city life, developed by Ernest Burgess and Robert Park.[22] This model identified five zones (see figure 4.2). Shaw and McKay used extensive official data gathered from the courts and police to examine different rates of crime in the five zones.

- **Zone 1, the "Loop,"** was the Central Business District, the seat of financial and political power. The decisions made in zone 1 affect all residents; in essence, zone 1 propels social change in other zones.

- **Zone 2** is the transitional zone. Marked by high poverty rates, high unemployment, and poor schools, the neighborhood was inhabited by recent immigrants. It also suffered from the highest delinquency rates in

Figure 4.2   Concentric Zones

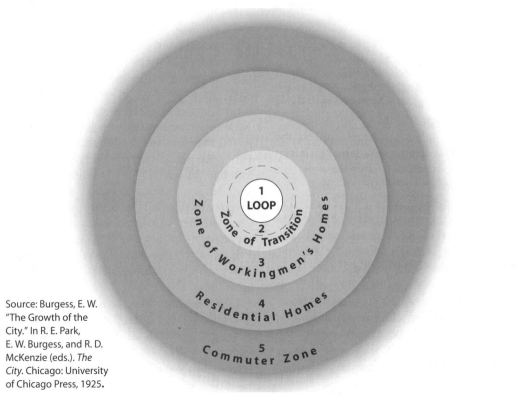

Source: Burgess, E. W. "The Growth of the City." In R. E. Park, E. W. Burgess, and R. D. McKenzie (eds.). *The City*. Chicago: University of Chicago Press, 1925.

the city. Importantly, Shaw and McKay found that the delinquency rates remained the highest over time, regardless of the ethnic group living in that area.

- **Zone 3** was the working-class zone, with a more stable population of skilled laborers living in multifamily dwellings. The residents were primarily second-generation immigrants who moved out of zone 2 over time but were not affluent enough to move beyond.

- **Zone 4** was the residential zone characterized by single-family homes inhabited by the middle class.

- **Zone 5** was the commuter zone. Home to the very wealthy, it consisted of large, single-family dwellings.

Shaw and McKay noted the movement of residents from zone 2 into zone 3 or possibly even 4. Each time this shift occurred the delinquency rates for that group decreased with the movement to a new zone. The new inhabitants of zone 2, regardless of ethnicity, exhibited the highest delinquency rates in the city. Shaw and McKay argued that delinquency was the product of the social disorganization in the decaying transitional neighborhood.

The concentration of human and social problems within these zones is not the inevitable result of some abstract laws of nature. The actions or inactions of powerful groups in a city (e.g., politicians, wealthy business leaders, and urban planners) affect the schools in a neighborhood, whether hospitals or other medical facilities are nearby, and the availability of affordable homes and jobs paying a living wage. If the resources necessary to improve neighborhood conditions are not allocated, the residents will suffer. Shaw and McKay's use of official crime data was both a flaw and a contribution. Their research revealed that the police targeted a specific area and population for law enforcement efforts. The populations that moved from zone 2 did not necessarily stop committing crime and delinquency. More likely, they were not policed the same way after the shift.

Frederic Thrasher's classic work, *The Gang,* utilized the social disorganization perspective. His insight into gangs is as relevant today as when it was published in 1927. He found that gangs originate from

> the spontaneous effort of boys to create a society for themselves where none adequate to their needs exists. What boys get out of such associations that they do not get otherwise under the conditions that adult society imposes is the thrill and zest of participation in common interests, more especially in corporate action, in hunting, capture, conflict, flight, and escape. Conflict with other gangs and the world about them furnishes the occasion for many of their exciting group activities.[23]

Thrasher noted that gangs flourish in what he called *interstitial areas*—"a region characterized by the deteriorating neighborhoods, shifting populations, and the mobility and disorganization of the slum. . . . Gangland represents a geographically and socially interstitial area in the city."[24] Names such as slum, ghetto, and barrio are now used to denote the impoverished areas identified by Thrasher as the most likely places for gangs to surface.

Subsequent studies have also focused on the community or neighborhood as the primary unit of analysis. The studies begin with the assumption that crime and gang activities vary according to neighborhood or community characteristics. In a study called *Racketville, Slumtown and Haulberg,* Irving Spergel found that the three neighborhoods he studied varied according to a number of criteria and had different kinds of traditions, including delinquent and criminal norms. For instance, Racketville, a mostly Italian neighborhood, had a long tradition of organized racketeering. Gangs in this neighborhood were mostly involved in the rackets because this was where the criminal opportunities were found.[25]

In contrast, the area Spergel called "Slumtown" was primarily a Puerto Rican neighborhood with a history of conflict and aggression. The gangs in this area were mostly involved in various conflict situations with rival gangs, usually over turf. Haulberg was a mixed ethnic neighborhood (Irish, German, Italian, and others) with a tradition of mostly property crimes; hence, a theft subculture flourished.

Mercer Sullivan studied three neighborhoods in Brooklyn. His ethnographic fieldwork provides important information about the relationship between social, cultural, and economic factors and gangs. The three neighborhoods varied in several socioeconomic indicators and had significantly different patterns of crime. The two neighborhoods with the highest crime rates had: (1) the highest poverty level (more than half the families received public assistance); (2) the highest percentage of single-parent families; (3) the highest rate of renter-occupied housing; (4) the highest rate of school dropouts; and (5) the highest levels of unemployment.[26] Sullivan noted that the primary source of income for teenagers in the two poorest neighborhoods was high risk, low-return theft.

> The primary causes for their greater willingness to engage in desperate, highly exposed crimes for uncertain and meager monetary returns were the greater poverty of their households, the specific and severe lack of employment opportunities during these same mid-teen years, and the weakened local social control environment, itself a product of general poverty and joblessness among neighborhood residents.[27]

Strain Theories

Strain theories posit that most people share similar values and goals, but the ability to satisfy those needs and aspirations depends on socioeconomic class. Crime and delinquency result from the frustration and anger people experience over their inability to achieve legitimate social and financial success. Strain theory can be summarized in three propositions. (1) Americans share the same goals and values. We all want a good income, a nice home, and two cars. (2) Those who do not have access to legitimate means of achieving financial success become frustrated. (3) The frustration leads some to substitute a deviant value system and to seek alternate means of achieving financial suc-

cess. To fully understand these theories, it is important to explore what is meant by "goals" and the "means" of achieving them in U.S. society.

Crime and the American Dream

The ethos of the "American Dream" is deeply embedded in our culture. Material success is generally assumed to be a universal desire. Capitalist societies are also individualistic. The assumption is that if everyone works to achieve material success, the individual pursuits in a free market system will interact with the individual pursuits of others and everyone will benefit.

The *American Dream* is marked by four core beliefs: achievement, individualism, universalism, and reverence for money (see figure 4.3). There is, however, a "dark side" to the American Dream, which stems from a contradiction in American capitalism: the same forces that promote "progress" and "ambition" also produce a lot of crime because of the pressure to succeed "at any cost."

The emphasis on competition and achievement promotes selfishness and drives people apart, weakening a collective sense of community. Because monetary rewards are such a high priority, tasks that are noneconomic receive little cultural support. For example, housewives and child-care workers are important to the well-being of society, but the financial rewards are very low. Those who fail are looked down upon, and their failure is viewed as *individual failure*, rather than a failure affected by institutional and cultural factors.

To understand how crime links to the American Dream, we need to understand the means humans have invented to satisfy three needs: (1) adaptation to the environment, (2) mobilization of resources to achieve collective goals and (3) socialization of members to accept fundamental normative patterns. *Social institutions* are a persistent set of organized *methods* of meeting these needs. The most important of these institutions include the (1) economy, (2) family, (3) education, and (4) politics. Other important institutions include health care, media, religion, and the legal system.[28]

Figure 4.3   Core Values of U.S. Culture

1. ***Achievement***—One's *personal worth* is typically evaluated in terms of monetary success and/or celebrity. U.S. culture emphasizes "doing" and "having" rather than "being." Failure to achieve is equated with the failure to make a contribution to society. This value is highly conducive to the attitude "it's not how you play the game; it's whether you win or lose" or "winning isn't everything; it's the *only* thing."

2. ***Individualism***—People are encouraged to "make it on your own." This value discourages other approaches that could (and has proven to do so) reduce crime, namely cooperation and collective action. The "rugged individualist" is perhaps the most famous representation of this cultural value. A corollary to this value is "I don't need any help." Intense individual competition pressures people to ignore or suppress about how their actions might affect others if the altruistic behavior would interfere with the realization of personal goals.

3. ***Universalism***—Everyone shares the same desire for the "American Dream," and everyone has an equal opportunity to succeed if they work hard (Protestant Work Ethic.)

4. ***Reverence for Money***—Money is so important in our culture that it often overrides almost everything else. It is the *currency* for measuring just about everything. People are a *consumerist culture* socialized from the day they are born to be a *consumer*. In a consumerist culture there does not seem to be an amount of acquisitions—including money—that is recognized as enough.

Source: Messner, S. F. and R. Rosenfeld. *Crime and the American Dream* (3rd ed.). Belmont, CA: Wadsworth, 2001, pp. 62–64.

It is important to understand that when institutions fail to satisfy the needs of at least a sizeable proportion of the population then alternative forms or methods of meeting needs will begin to develop. For example, if the prevailing economic system is failing, then more and more people will engage in alternative means of earning a living; if organized religion is not providing answers to fundamental questions about the meaning of life, then people will seek out unorthodox religious forms; if the legal institution is not perceived as providing "justice," then people may "take the law into their own hands"; or if the mainstream media provide too much disinformation and do not allow dissenting views, then we will see alternative media emerge.

Steven Messner and Richard Rosenfeld note that U.S. society is unique in that the economic institution almost completely dominates all other institutions. Unlike capitalism in other countries, there were no existing institutions that could tame or offset the economic imperatives. The goal is to make a *profit*, and everything else becomes secondary. Over time this has become a "market society" in contrast to a "market economy." Unequal access to legitimate means of pursuing the American Dream is the basis for the next sociological theory of crime.

Anomie

Strain theory originated with Robert Merton, who borrowed the term *anomie* from the nineteenth-century French sociologist Émile Durkheim and applied it to the problem of crime in the United States.[29] The concept of ***anomie*** refers to a condition of relative normlessness. When social regulations break down, individuals pursue their goals without social controls. "Anomie does not refer to a state of mind, but to a property of the social structure. It characterizes a condition in which individual desires are no longer regulated by common norms."[30] Anomie weakens the normative order of society if approved means of success are not available. Susceptibility to anomie depends on the social process—the relations between individuals—rather than individual tendencies. Merton noted: "Social structures exert a definite pressure upon certain persons in the society to engage in nonconforming rather than conforming conduct."[31]

Merton argued that two elements of U.S. culture converge to produce potentially anomic conditions. The legitimate means of achieving culturally defined goals of wealth, success, and power are hard work and education. Anomie describes the gap between the desire to achieve those goals and the means of achieving them. According to Merton, this gap creates *strain* for certain groups and individuals, who respond with various forms of deviance. Thus, people who find themselves at a disadvantage relative to legitimate economic activities are motivated to engage in illegitimate activities. Within a capitalist society like the United States, the main emphasis is on the "success" goals, while less emphasis is on the legitimate *means* to achieve these goals. Moreover, these goals have become *institutionalized* in that they are deeply embedded in the psyches of everyone via a very powerful system of corporate propaganda.[32] At the same time, the legitimate means are not as well defined nor as strongly ingrained. In other words, there is a lot of discretion and a lot of tolerance for deviance from the means, but not the goals. One result of such a system is high levels of crime.

Our culture contributes to crime because the opportunities to achieve success goals are not equally distributed. *Culture promises what the social structure cannot deliver.* This contradiction creates pressures or "strains" to seek alternatives. Merton identified five **modes of adaptation** to the strain caused by limited access to approved means of pursuing success.

1. **Conformity**—accepting both the legitimate means and the success goals. This category involves seeking financial success through hard work and education.

2. **Ritualism**—accepting the means but rejecting the goals. Someone in this category will work hard without striving for financial reward.

3. **Innovation**—accepting the goals of success but rejecting the legitimate means to obtain them. This mode of adaptation is the most relevant to criminal activity. The goal of pursuing financial reward is accepted but legitimate means are rejected.

4. **Retreatism**—rejecting both the goals *and* the means. This person basically drops out of society. Drug addicts and vagrants fall in this mode.

5. **Rebellion**—rejecting both the goals and the means and substituting an alternative set of goals and means. Those who seek radical social change, sometimes through revolutions, pursue this mode of adaptation.

Messner and Rosenfeld note that strain explains high rates of crime among both the disadvantaged and the privileged. The impulse to make more money becomes a strain to use any means necessary. This point helps explain the large amount of "corporate crime" and emphasizes the importance of the relationship of *social institutions* to the American Dream.[33]

Differential Opportunity Structures

Richard Cloward and Lloyd Ohlin expanded on Merton's idea of unequal access to legitimate means of goal achievement.[34] They argued that (1) blocked opportunity causes poor self-concepts and feelings of frustration and (2) these frustrations lead to delinquency, especially within a gang context. The key concept in their theory is *differential opportunity structure*—an uneven distribution of both legal and illegal means of achieving economic success.

Cloward and Ohlin believed that many members of the lower class seek middle-class status while others are driven purely by financial reward. They developed a four-part typology to describe the different orientations.

Type 1: Oriented toward class status and economic success.

Type 2: Oriented toward middle-class status, but less concerned with economic success.

Type 3: Unconcerned with middle-class status, but very concerned with economic success.

Type 4: Not concerned with middle-class status or economic success.

Type 3 are the most likely to be involved in serious delinquency. They are not concerned with middle-class values, but they seek the material rewards associated with that status. Because type 3 youth do not have access to legitimate opportunities to improve their position, they engage in illegitimate opportunities if they arise. Cloward and Ohlin argued that three different types of gangs emerge in lower-class communities based on the characteristics of the neighborhoods.

1. **Criminal gangs** are organized mainly around the commission of property crimes and exist in areas where adult criminal activity is relatively organized. The youths in these neighborhoods see adult criminals as successful role models.

2. **Conflict gangs** engage mostly in violent behavior, such as gang fights over turf. These gangs exist in neighborhoods where living conditions are unstable and transient, resulting in the lack of any adult role models, whether conventional or criminal.

3. **Retreatist gangs** engage in mostly illegal drug use and exist in neighborhoods dominated by a great deal of illegal drug activity. These youths are described as double failures by Cloward and Ohlin.

Among the specific assumptions of this theory is that blocked opportunities or aspirations create feelings of frustration and low self-esteem, which in turn often leads to delinquency and gang behavior.

Social Embeddedness

One of the most interesting variations of strain theory comes from John Hagan, who uses the term *social embeddedness* to describe a developmental view of involvement in delinquency.[35] Hagan notes that instead of unemployment precipitating involvement in criminal behavior, the process begins at a much earlier age. One needs to be socialized into the labor market. This means, among other things, that a youth begins to earn money by doing odd jobs such as mowing lawns, babysitting, washing windows, shoveling snow, delivering papers, and so on long before the age of sixteen. Through such activities a youth begins a process of social embeddedness early in life.

Just as one can become socially embedded in the world of regular job contacts and the world of work, so too can one become embedded in a network of crime and deviance. In most of the high-crime, inner-city neighborhoods, the jobs noted above do not exist in large numbers. For example, there are no lawns to be mowed in most public housing projects. For youths who do poorly in school and/or drop out, contacts with

people who could offer jobs or serve as models for the labor market become difficult to establish. Hagan notes that parental involvement in crime will integrate youths into networks of criminal opportunities. Likewise, association with delinquent peers or contacts with drug dealers can also integrate youths into criminal networks. Delinquent acts isolate youths from networks of employment. A snowballing effect takes place; each delinquent act and/or contact with the world of crime further distances a youth from the legitimate world of work. Thus, the perspective of social embeddedness identifies "a process of separation and isolation from conventional employment networks" that has a time sequence with a "lagged accumulation of effect that should build over time."[36]

Cultural-Deviance Theories

Cultural-deviance theory proposes that delinquency results from a desire to conform to cultural values that conflict to some extent with those of conventional society. This perspective is an offshoot of social disorganization theory. Criminal values and traditions emerge within communities most affected by social disorganization.

Cohen's Delinquent Subculture Theory

Albert Cohen wrote *Delinquent Boys: The Culture of the Gang*[37] more than 50 years ago, but much of what he had to say is still relevant. Cohen's cultural-deviance theory incorporates the following assumptions: (1) a high proportion of lower-class youths (especially males) do poorly in school; (2) poor school performance relates to delinquency; (3) poor school performance stems from a conflict between the middle-class values of the school system and the values of lower-class youths; and (4) most lower-class male delinquency is committed in a gang context, partly as a means of meeting some basic human needs, such as self-esteem and belonging.

There are two key concepts in Cohen's theory. *Reaction formation* involves rejecting the values endorsed by mainstream society and replacing them with alternatives that strike back at the system that excludes the lower class. *Middle-class measuring rod* refers to the fact that children are evaluated by middle-class standards even when they have not been socialized into them. Evaluations of school performance and behavior within the school are based on norms and values associated with the middle class. Cohen argues that delinquents often develop a culture that is at odds with the norms and values of the middle class. The primary thesis of Cohen's theory is that school failure leads to status frustration, which leads to reaction formation, which leads to gang involvement. Gang affiliation provides lower-class youth with a different measuring rod. It enables the child to obtain status based on a different value system.

Lower-Class Focal Concerns

Still another variation of this perspective comes from the work of Walter B. Miller. His theory includes an examination of what he calls the *focal concerns* of a distinctive lower-class culture. Miller argues that members of the lower class have their own value system that differs from that of the middle class.[38] Focal concerns include:

1. *Trouble:* preoccupied with getting into and staying out of trouble; higher social status sometimes awarded for being in trouble.
2. *Toughness:* seeking recognition of physical toughness; fighting skills; demonstrating masculinity.
3. *Smartness:* maintaining an image of being able to outwit and outsmart others; street-smart.
4. *Excitement:* a desire to be involved in risk taking; searching for fun.
5. *Fate:* destiny ruled by forces beyond the individual's control.
6. *Autonomy:* being independent; rebel against authorities; don't let others control you.

Miller also argued that *female-dominated households,* commonplace in lower-class communities, are a primary reason for the emergence of street-corner male adolescent groups. The age-graded, one-sex peer unit constitutes the major psychic focus and reference group for young people. For boys reared in female-headed households, the street-corner group provides the first real opportunity to learn essential aspects of the male role by learning from other boys in the group with similar sex-role identification problems. The adolescent street-corner group is one variant of the lower-class structure, and the gang is a subtype distinguished by law-violating activities. Gangs present male members opportunities to prove their masculinity.

Echoing Thrasher's work, Miller states that the two central concerns of the adolescent street-corner group are belonging and status. One achieves belonging by adhering to the group's standards and values. When there is conflict with other norms—for example, middle-class norms—the norms of the group are far more compelling because failure to conform means expulsion from the group. Status is achieved by demonstrating qualities valued by lower-class culture (smartness, toughness, and autonomy).

There is also a pecking order among different groups, defined by one's reputation. Each group believes its safety depends on maintaining a reputation for toughness compared with other groups. Reputation involves both law-abiding and law-violating behavior. The dominant behavior depends on a complex set of factors, such as which community reference groups (criminals or police) are admired or respected or the individual needs of the gang members. Status is the crucial factor and is far more important than the means selected to achieve it.

Control/Social Bond Theory

The essence of *control/social bond theory* is that the weakening, breakdown, or absence of effective social control accounts for delinquency. A unique feature of this perspective is that instead of asking "Why do they do it?" it asks "Why *don't* they do it?" Control theory wrestles with trying to identify what prevents people from committing crime.

The basic assumption of control theory is that proper social behavior requires proper socialization. Proper socialization leads to conformity; improper socialization leads to nonconformity. Criminality is one consequence of improper socialization. According to control theory, delinquent behavior occurs because steps were not taken to prevent it.

There are several versions of this theory. One view asserts that the delinquent lacks either strong *inner* controls (i.e. a positive self-image or strong ego) or strong *outer* controls (i.e. strong family controls, community controls, legal controls, and so on).[39] According to another version of the theory, many youths commit delinquent acts because they rationalize deviance before it occurs—that is, they neutralize the normal moral beliefs they have learned while growing up. For instance, they deny that there is a victim by saying things like, "He had it coming," or they deny that there was any real harm by saying something like, "No one was really hurt" or "They won't miss it."[40]

Travis Hirschi devised the most popular version. According to his perspective, all humans are basically antisocial, and all are capable of committing a crime. What prevents most of us from deviating is what he calls the social bond to society, especially the norms of society that we have internalized. Hirschi identifies the four elements of this bond: attachment, commitment, involvement, and belief (see figure 4.4).[41]

Most people accept these traditional values about what is and is not appropriate role behavior for young people. Juvenile justice workers endorse this perspective every day as they try to *reattach* delinquents to family, school, and so on; to get them to *commit* themselves to the demands of childhood; to *involve* them in conventional activities; and to help them acquire a *belief* and respect for the law. This theory becomes an important starting point for the social development model and the risk-focused approach of delinquency prevention.

Social Learning Theory

According to *social learning theory,* people learn to be delinquent or criminal through the same kind of process by which they learn anything else. Individuals learn behavior as well as values, beliefs, and attitudes through association with other human beings. Edwin Sutherland developed one of the earliest variations of social learning theory as it applies to crime and delinquency—*differential association.*[42] According to Sutherland's theory, a person becomes a delinquent or criminal through contact with others who are delinquent, by learning values, beliefs, and attitudes supportive of criminal or delinquent behavior, and through exposure to the various techniques used to commit such acts. One of the central points of this theory is that one becomes a delinquent or criminal "because of an excess of definitions favorable to violation of law over definitions unfavorable [to violation] of law."[43] In other words, a young person becomes delinquent through his or her association with delinquent youths. Together these delinquents reinforce beliefs, values, and attitudes that lead to, and perpetuate, delinquency.

Figure 4.4   The Elements of the Social Bond

1. ***Attachment.*** Hirschi uses this term to refer to ties of affection and respect between kids and parents, teachers, and friends. Attachment to parents is most important because kids learn the norms of society. Attachment is similar to Freud's concept of superego but is a more conscious recognition.

2. ***Commitment.*** Similar to Freud's concept of ego, commitment describes the extent to which kids accept the ideal requirements of childhood, such as getting an education, postponing participation in adult activities (working full time, living on their own, getting married, etc.), and dedication to long-term goals. If kids develop a stake in conformity, engaging in delinquent behavior would endanger their future.

3. ***Involvement.*** Large amounts of unstructured time may weaken the social bond. Kids who are busy doing conventional things (chores at home, homework, sports, camping, working, and dating) do not have time for delinquency. The concept mirrors the "idle hands are the devil's workshop" belief.

4. ***Belief.*** Hirschi uses this term to reflect belief in the law, especially the morality of the law (stealing is just plain wrong).

Source: Adapted from Hirschi, T. *Causes of Delinquency* (3rd ed.). Berkeley: University of California Press, 1969.

Social learning theory suggests that there are three related processes that lead a person to become a delinquent or criminal: (1) acquisition, (2) instigation, and (3) maintenance.[44] *Acquisition* refers to the original learning of behavior. The key to this process is reinforcement through the modeling influences of one's family and the immediate subculture (especially the peer subculture) and symbolic modeling (for example, via television). A child who witnesses violence within the home is likely to engage in violence later in life, especially if violence within the home is rewarded or no sanctions are applied. Children tend to acquire behaviors they observe in others and behaviors that they see rewarded.

Instigation refers to the process whereby once a person acquires a behavior, certain factors work to cause or instigate a specific event—in this case, an act of delinquency. Learning theory suggests five factors as major instigators:

1. *Aversive events*—frustration, relative deprivation, and, of particular importance in gang violence, verbal insults and actual assaults. Threats to the reputation and status of an individual, who is especially violent, especially threats occurring in public, are very important instigators of violent acts.

2. *Modeling influences*—observing delinquent or criminal behavior by someone who serves as a role model.

3. *Incentive inducements*—anticipated rewards. A person can be motivated to commit a crime by some perceived reward, usually monetary.

4. *Instructional control*—following orders from someone in authority. A gang member, for instance, may obey a direct order from a leader within the gang.

5. *Environmental control*—factors in one's immediate environment, such as crowded conditions (including traffic), extreme heat, pollution, and noise. Each of these can cause someone to "lose it" and act out, sometimes in a violent manner.

In order for delinquent or criminal behavior to persist, there needs to be consistent *maintenance,* or reinforcement. Social learning theory suggests four kinds of reinforcement: (1) direct reinforcement, (2) vicarious reinforcement, (3) self-reinforcement, and (4) neutralization of self-punishment. *Direct reinforcement* refers to extrinsic rewards like money or recognition that correspond with an act. *Vicarious reinforcement* occurs from seeing others get rewards or escape punishment for delinquent or criminal acts. For example, a youth sees someone carrying a lot of money obtained by selling drugs. *Self-reinforcement* means that a person derives his or her self-worth or sense of pride as a result of criminal acts. *Neutralization* is the process whereby one justifies or rationalizes delinquent acts.

A long-standing sociological theory is commonly referred to as *techniques of neutralization.*[45] The authors of this perspective suggest that delinquents often come up with rationalizations or excuses that absolve them of guilt. A youth may say that no one was harmed or that the victim deserved it ("he had it coming"). Or a youth may condemn persons who condemn him or her ("adults do these things, too"). Other techniques are to appeal to higher loyalties ("I'm doing it for the 'hood'"), or to blame external factors. Techniques of neutralization dehumanize the victim, and there is a gradual desensitization regarding the use of violence or other means of force to get one's way.

The sociological theories summarized so far do not seriously question the existing social order, although social disorganization and strain theories provide at least an indirect critique. The next two sociological perspectives question the social order of advanced capitalism. Instead of focusing on how offenders and potential offenders or at-risk youths can be made to accommodate to the existing social order, the labeling and critical/Marxist perspectives call for changing the social order so that fewer people will be drawn into criminal behavior.

Labeling Theory

Labeling theory, also known as the *social reaction perspective*, does not address the causes of criminal or deviant behavior. Instead, it focuses on three interrelated processes: (1) how and why certain behaviors are defined as criminal or deviant; (2) the response to crime or deviance by authorities; and (3) the effects of such definitions and official reactions on the person or persons so labeled.[46] The key to this perspective is: "Social groups create deviance by making the rules whose infraction constitutes deviance, and by applying those rules to particular people and labeling them as outsiders."[47] Advocates of labeling theory insist that the criminal justice system itself, including the legislation that creates and defines crime and criminals, helps to perpetuate crime and deviance.

Labeling theory is concerned less with what causes the onset of deviance and more with the effects of official processing by police, the courts, and correctional agencies. Importantly, labeling theory argues that what is defined as deviant is determined by those with the power to force their perspectives on others. Labeling theorists argue that deviance is not inherent in any act or attribute; rather, it is something crafted and defined through social and political processes.

Labeling theory identifies primary and secondary deviance. *Primary deviance* includes acts that the perpetrator or others consider alien to, or at odds with, a person's true identity or character. In other words, an act is "out of character." *Secondary deviance,* in contrast, refers to a process whereby the deviance takes on self-identifying features. Essentially, significant others or agents of social control label the person as a result of the deviance. It comes to reflect the person's true self. Deviance becomes secondary "when a person begins to employ his deviant behavior as a means of defense, attack, or adjustment to the overt and covert problems created by the consequent societal reaction to him."[48]

Important to the labeling process is the concept of *dramatization of evil*. Essentially, this is shifting the focus from the act to the actor. First, the political process describes a particular behavior as bad or wrong. When someone is caught participating in that behavior, the person is then labeled as bad.[49] When this negative label by significant others and/or agents of social control is given, the label may be internalized. The notion of *looking glass self* implies that our view of self is influenced by the way we believe others perceive us. Therefore, when a negative label is applied, the labeled person may engage in a *self-fulfilling prophecy* and view the negative label as accurate. The internalization of the negative label leads to more deviance.

Labeling theory argues that extralegal factors impact who is formally labeled. These factors include race, social class, and gender. These factors also impact what behaviors are declared to be deviant. Quinney made this point when he organized his theory around six interrelated propositions:[50]

1. Crime is a definition of human conduct that is created by authorized agents in a politically organized society.

2. Criminal definitions describe behaviors that conflict with the interests of the segments of society that have the power to shape public policy.

3. Criminal definitions are applied by the segments of society that have the power to shape the enforcement and administration of criminal law.

4. Behavior patterns are structured in a segmentally organized society in relation to criminal definitions, and within this context persons engage in actions that have relative probabilities of being defined as criminal.

5. Conceptions of crime are constructed and diffused in the segments of society by various means of communication.

6. The social reality of crime is constructed by the formulation and application of

criminal definitions, the development of behavior patterns related to criminal definitions, and the construction of criminal conceptions.

Labeling theory led some scholars to begin to question not only the criminal justice system but also the social structure and institutions of society as a whole. In particular, some research in the labeling tradition directed attention to such factors as class, race, and sex not only in the formulation of criminal definitions but also as major causes of crime itself. This in turn led to a critical examination of existing institutions of U.S. society and to a critique of the capitalist system itself.

Critical/Marxist Perspectives

Richard Quinney and John Wildeman place the development of a *critical/Marxist theory* in the historical and social context of the late 1960s and early 1970s:

> It is not by chance that the 1970s saw the birth of critical thought in the ranks of American criminologists. Not only did critical criminology challenge old ideas, but it went on to introduce new and liberating ideas and interpretations of America and of what America could become. If social justice is not for all in a democratic society—and it was clear that it was not—then there must be something radically wrong with the way our basic institutions are structured.[51]

In *Class, State and Crime* Quinney outlined his own version of a critical or Marxist theory of crime. He linked crime and the reaction to crime to the modern capitalist political and economic system. This viewpoint suggests that the capitalist system itself produces a number of problems that are linked to various attempts by the capitalist class to maintain the basic institutions of the capitalist order. These attempts lead to various forms of accommodation and resistance by people who are oppressed by the system, especially the working class, the poor, and racial and ethnic minorities. In

attempting to maintain the existing order, the powerful commit various crimes, which Quinney classified as crimes of control, crimes of economic domination, and crimes of government. At the same time, oppressed people engage in various kinds of crimes related to accommodation and resistance, including predatory crimes, personal crimes, and crimes of resistance.[52]

Much of what is known as gang behavior, including gang-related crime, can be understood as an attempt by oppressed people to accommodate and resist the problems created by capitalist institutions. Many modern gang members adapt to their disadvantaged positions by engaging in predatory criminal behavior. Much of their behavior, moreover, is in many ways identical to normal capitalist entrepreneurial activity. For instance, drug gangs engage in buying and selling drugs—a commodity. They seek "market share" on certain street corners and in certain parks and alleys, not unlike typical legitimate businesses. The law of supply and demand operates as well: drugs (or other illegal commodities, such as stolen goods) are in high demand; someone will always find a way to provide the goods desired.[53]

A critical/Marxist perspective goes even further by focusing on:

> those social structures and forces that produce both the greed of the inside trader as well as the brutality of the rapist or the murderer. And it places those structures in their proper context: the material conditions of class struggle under a capitalist mode of production.[54]

The material conditions include the class and racial inequalities produced by the contradictions of capitalism.

Mark Lanier and Stewart Henry identify six ideas common to critical/Marxist theories of crime and criminal justice (see figure 4.5).[55] The importance of the capitalist system in producing inequality and hence crime is apparent when we examine recent economic changes in U.S. society and the effects

Figure 4.5   Crime and Capitalism

1. *Capitalism shapes social institutions, social identities, and social action.* The actual "mode of production" in any given society tends to determine many other areas of social life, including divisions based on race, class, and gender, plus the manner in which people behave and act toward one another.

2. *Capitalism creates class conflict and contradictions.* Because a relatively small group (about 1–2% of the population) owns or controls the "means of production," conflict between classes over control of resources is inevitable. The contradiction is that workers need to consume the products of the capitalist system, but in order to do this, they need to have enough income to do so and thus increase growth in the economy. However, too much growth may cut into profits. One result is the creation of a *surplus population*—a more or less steady supply of able workers who are permanently unemployed or underemployed.

3. *Crime is a response to capitalism and its contradictions.* The surplus population may commit crimes to survive. These can be described as crimes of *accommodation*. Crimes among the more affluent can also result (see next point), in addition to crimes of *resistance* (e.g., sabotage and political violence).

4. *Capitalist law facilitates and conceals crimes of domination and repression.* The law can be repressive toward certain groups (*crimes of control and repression*). Crimes of *domination* also occur with great frequency as corporations and their representatives violate numerous laws (fraud, price-fixing, pollution, etc.) that cause great social harms but are virtually ignored by the criminal justice system.

5. *Crime is functional to capitalism.* There is a viable and fast-growing *crime control industry* that provides a "Keynesian stimulus" to the economy by creating jobs and profits for corporations (e.g., building prisons or providing various products and services to prisons, jails, police departments, and courthouses).

6. *Capitalism shapes society's response to crime by shaping law.* Those in power (especially legislators) define what is a crime and what constitutes a threat to social order and, perhaps more important, *who* constitutes such a threat (usually members of the underclass). As a result, various "problems" that threaten the dominant mode of production become "criminalized" (e.g., the use of certain drugs used by minorities rather than drugs produced by corporations, such as cigarettes, prescription drugs, and alcohol).

of these changes. In particular, many scholars have tried to explain crime by examining changes in the economic structure of society and how those changes contribute problems for populations that lack the skills and resources to adapt. In many ways, this perspective is an extension of some of the basic assumptions and key concepts of the social disorganization/ecology, strain, and cultural deviance theories.

SUMMARY

This chapter reviewed three major perspectives on crime. Biological perspectives stress physical features of human beings (such as Lombroso's stigmata) and defects in the central nervous system or genetic mutations (extra Y chromosomes) as causal factors in crime. There is little empirical support for this perspective.

Psychological theories stress various abnormalities in the mental makeup of human beings that appear to cause criminal behavior. Starting with Freud's views of unresolved childhood issues and continuing with low intelligence and defective personalities, these theories, like their biological counterparts, largely ignore social and cultural factors. Again, little empirical support exists for most of these theories.

Several themes emerged from our review of sociological theories. First, the external socioeconomic environment is of major significance. Social disorganization/social ecology theory (especially the early work of Thrasher) links crime to such environmental factors as poverty, social inequality, lack of community integration, lack of meaningful employment and educational opportunities, as well as to the larger economic picture of a changing labor market and the corresponding emergence of an underclass mired in segregated communities.

A second theme is that adolescents who grow up in such environments are faced with constant struggles for self-esteem, a sense of belonging, and protection from outside threats. These and other basic human needs are not being met by social institutions such as the family, the school, the church, and the community.

A third theme is that becoming a "delinquent" or "criminal" is a social process that involves learning various roles and social expectations within a given community. It involves the reinforcement of expectations through various rationalizations or "techniques of neutralization." The lifestyles, attitudes, and behaviors of significant others in the lives of these youths perpetuate certain behaviors. Over time (beginning at a very early age) a youth becomes "embedded" in his or her surrounding environment and cultural norms, and it becomes increasingly difficult to leave the world of crime.

A fourth theme is that crime and delinquency are shaped to a large degree by the societal reaction to such behavior and to the kinds of individuals who engage in such behavior. The negative responses reinforce the very behavior of which society disapproves.

A fifth theme is that one cannot possibly explain crime without considering the economic context of capitalism. Most criminal activity is consistent with basic capitalist values, such as the law of supply and demand, the need to make money, and the desire to accumulate consumer goods. As the economy continues to pass over the most disadvantaged segments of the population, crime will continue to be an alternate lifestyle.

Key Terms

- "American dream"
- anomie
- Cartographic School
- Chicago School
- concentric zone
- control/social bond theory
- critical/Marxist theory
- cultural deviance theory
- differential association
- ectomorph
- endomorph
- feeblemindedness
- hedonistic calculus
- labeling theory
- mesomorph
- Minnesota Multiphasic Personality Inventory (MMPI)
- modes of adaptation
- phrenology
- primary deviance
- secondary deviance
- social ecology theory
- social institutions
- social learning theory
- somatotypes
- strain theories

Notes

[1] Bohm, R. M. *A Primer on Crime and Delinquency.* Belmont, CA: Wadsworth, 1997, p. 35. See also Vold, G. and T. J. Bernard. *Theoretical Criminology* (3rd ed.). New York: Oxford University Press, 1986.

[2] McCaghy, C. H. (1985). *Deviant Behavior: Crime, Conflict, and Interest Groups.* New York: Macmillan.

[3] Glueck, S. and E. Glueck. *Physique and Delinquency.* New York: Harper and Row, 1956; Sheldon, W. *Varieties of Delinquent Youth.* New York: Harper, 1949; Hooton, E. A. *The American Criminal: An Anthropological Study.* Cambridge: Harvard University Press, 1939. These scholars were all on the faculty of Harvard University at one time, and their work received a great deal of attention.

[4] DeKeseredy, W. S. and M. D. Schwartz. *Contemporary Criminology.* Belmont, CA: Wadsworth, 1996, p. 180.

[5] Ibid.

[6] Ibid.

[7] Vold and Bernard, *Theoretical Criminology,* p. 107.

[8] Some of the derivations of rational choice theory include criminal opportunity theory and routine activities theory. See, for example, Cook, P. J. "The Demand and Supply of Criminal Opportunities." In M. Tonry and N. Morris (eds.), *Crime and Justice,* Vol. 7. Chicago: University of Chicago Press, 1986; Cohen, L. and M. Felson. "Social Change and Crime Rate Trends: A 'Routine Activities' Approach." *American Sociological Review* 44: 588–608 (1979).

[9] Shelden, R. G. *Delinquency and Juvenile Justice in American Society.* Long Grove, IL: Waveland Press, 2006, pp. 187–188.

[10] Messner, S. and K. Tardiff. "The Social Ecology of Urban Homicide: An Application of the Routine Activities Approach." *Criminology* 23: 241–267 (1985); Maxfield, M. "Household Composition, Routine Activities, and Victimization: A Comparative Analysis." *Journal of Quantitative Criminology* 3: 301–320 (1987).

[11] Rafter, N. H. (ed.). *White Trash: The Eugenic Family Studies, 1899–1919.* Boston: Northeastern University Press, 1988.

[12] DeKeseredy and Schwartz, *Contemporary Criminology,* pp. 182–183.

[13] Adams, C. "What Does Alice in Wonderland Have to Do with Psychological Testing?" December 23 2005. [Online] http://www.straightdope.com/columns/051223.html

[14] Adams; [Online] http://en.wikipedia.org/wiki/Minnesota_ Multiphasic_Personality_Inventory

[15] Akers, R. L. *Criminological Theories: Introduction and Evaluation.* Los Angeles: Roxbury Press, 1994, p. 88.

[16] Samenow, S. *Inside the Criminal Mind.* New York: Random House, 2004.

[17] McCaghy, *Deviant Behavior.*

[18] Currie, E. *Confronting Crime.* New York: Pantheon, 1985.

[19] Lanier, M. M. and S. Henry. *Essential Criminology.* Boulder, CO: Westview Press, 1998, ch. 9; Stark, R. "Deviant Places: A Theory of the Ecology of Crime." *Criminology* 25: 893–909. (1987).

[20] Lanier and Henry, p. 182. Lanier and Henry also note that the term "social" or "human" ecology comes from the Greek word *oikos* which translates roughly into "household" or "living space."

[21] Stark, "Deviant Places."

[22] Burgess, E. W. "The Growth of the City." In R. E. Park, E. W. Burgess, and R. D. McKenzie (eds.), *The City.* Chicago: University of Chicago Press, 1925.

[23] Thrasher, F. *The Gang.* Chicago: University of Chicago Press, 1927, pp. 32–33.

[24] Ibid., pp. 20–21.

[25] Spergel, I. A. *Racketville, Slumtown and Haulberg.* Chicago: University of Chicago Press, 1964.

[26] Sullivan, M. L. *Getting Paid: Youth Crime and Work in the Inner City.* Ithaca, NY: Cornell University Press, 1989, pp. 21–27, 98.

[27] Ibid., p. 203.

[28] Ibid., pp. 65–66.

[29] Merton, R. K. *Social Theory and Social Structure.* New York: Free Press, 1968.

[30] Coser, L. A. *Masters of Sociological Thought: Ideas in Historical and Social Context.* Long Grove, IL: Waveland Press, 1977, p. 133.

[31] Ibid., p. 133.

[32] For an excellent discussion of the role of corporate propaganda see the following: Herman, E. and N. Chomsky. *Manufacturing Consent: The Political Economy of the Mass Media* (2nd ed.). New York: Pantheon, 2002; Chomsky, N. *Necessary Illusions: Thought Control in Democratic Societies.* Boston: South End Press, 1989; Fones-Wolf, E. *Selling Free Enterprise.* Indianapolis: University of Indiana Press, 1994; Carey, A. *Taking the Risk Out of Democracy.* Chicago: University of Illinois Press, 1995.

[33] Messner and Rosenfeld, *Crime and the American Dream.*

[34] Cloward, R. and L. Ohlin. *Delinquency and Opportunity.* New York: Free Press, 1960.

[35] Hagan, J. "The Social Embeddedness of Crime and Unemployment." *Criminology* 31: 465–491 (1993).

[36] Hagan, p. 469.

[37] Cohen, A. *Delinquent Boys: The Culture of the Gang.* New York: Free Press, 1955.

[38] Miller, W. B. "Lower Class Culture as a Generating Milieu of Gang Delinquency." *Journal of Social Issues* 14: 5–19 (1958).

[39] Reckless, W. *The Crime Problem* (3rd ed.). New York: Appleton-Century-Crofts, 1961.

[40] Sykes, G. and D. Matza. "Techniques of Neutralization." *American Journal of Sociology* 22: 664–670 (1957).

[41] Hirschi, T. *Causes of Delinquency.* Berkeley: University of California Press, 1969.

42 Sutherland, E. H. and D. R. Cressey. *Criminology* (8th ed.). Philadelphia: Lippincott, 1970.

43 Shoemaker, D. J. *Theories of Delinquency* (3rd ed.). New York: Oxford University Press, 1996, pp. 152–153.

44 Goldstein, A. P. *Delinquent Gangs: A Psychological Perspective.* Champaign, IL: Research Press, 1991, pp. 55–61.

45 Sykes and Matza, "Techniques of Neutralization."

46 Schur, E. *Labeling Deviant Behavior.* New York: Harper & Row, 1971.

47 Becker, H. *Outsiders.* New York: Free Press, 1963, pp. 8–9.

48 Lemert, E. *Social Pathology.* New York: McGraw-Hill, 1951.

49 Tannenbaum, F. *Crime and the Community.* New York and London: Columbia University Press, 1938.

50 Quinney, *Social Reality of Crime, pp. 15-23.*

51 Quinney and Wildeman, *The Problem of Crime,* p. 72.

52 Quinney, *Class, State and Crime,* pp. 33–62.

53 Shelden, R. G., S. Tracy, and W. Brown. 2004. *Youth Gangs in American Society* (3rd ed.). Belmont, CA: Thompson/Wadsworth, ch. 4.

54 Quinney and Wildeman, *The Problem of Crime,* p. 77.

55 Lanier and Henry, *Essential Criminology,* pp. 256–258.

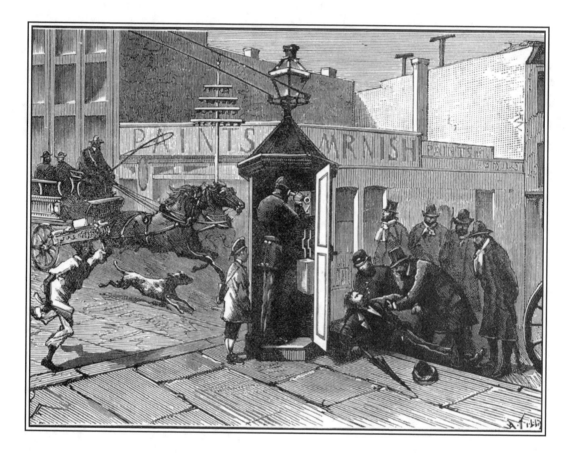

five

A Historical Overview of American Policing

With the red and blue lights fully engaged and flashing brightly, the scout car executed an abrupt U-turn and sped after the light blue Caprice. The driver of the Caprice pulled over to the side of the road and stopped. Both officers approached the car. One officer moved close to the driver's side of the Caprice and instructed the driver to provide his driver's license, registration, and proof of insurance. The other officer stood at the passenger side of the vehicle; his right hand rested on his service weapon. The driver of the Caprice asked the officer why he stopped him. The officer did not provide an answer. The officer instructed the driver to get out of his vehicle and move to the back of the car. The officer then told the driver to place both hands on the trunk of the Caprice, spread his legs, and remain in that position. After patting-down the driver, presumably for weapons, both officers then returned to the patrol car, opened their respective doors, and got in.

It was raining very hard. One officer used the unit's mobile computer to seek information about the driver and the vehicle he was driving. Within several minutes, the information sought arrived from the central computer. The suspect had no warrants. His driver's license was current, and the vehicle registration reflected the driver was the registered owner. Both officers remained in the car for more than 30 minutes after the information about the driver and the vehicle arrived. They were engaged in a discussion about their favorite basketball team. Finally, one officer got out of the car, walked toward the Caprice, and "flipped" the driver's license, registration, and insurance card toward the driver, and said, "Have a nice evening." All three documents landed in the pool of water the driver had been standing in. Completely soaked, the driver of the Caprice looked pathetic in the glare of the patrol car's headlights as he reached into the water to retrieve his documents. Later in the shift, I asked the officers why they had stopped the Caprice. One officer stated, in a quite matter-of-fact manner, "He knew he wasn't supposed to be here this time of night." The answer was spontaneous and offered in such a way that no need of further explanation occurred to either officer. The driver was a black male, it was late at night, and he was in an all-white suburb of Detroit.[1]

This scenario raises issues of legality/illegality, ethics, and violation of civil rights. People could take positions on either side of the debate over any or all of the issues. The driver of the Caprice, however, suffered the consequences of the officer's behavior, regardless of how their acts were characterized. The issues of authority, power, vulnerability, and race will reoccur throughout the chapters on law enforcement.

Policing is "the use of state power by delegated authorities for the purposes of law enforcement and the maintenance of order."[2] This definition raises two essential questions: What is law enforcement? What is the maintenance of order? Law enforcement is the enforcement of enacted laws designed to accommodate the majority of the people. Maintenance of order is the preservation of the status quo by keeping so-called problem components of the population under control. The status quo includes those in whose interest it is to keep social, economic, and political arrangements as they are. Problem components include ethnic/racial minorities, people who are homeless, young people, people who simply seem to be "out of place," or those who resist the status quo. Problem components also include civil rights advocates (e.g., Martin Luther King, Jr.), labor leaders (e.g., Eugene Debs, a labor movement activist during the early twentieth century), antiwar protesters, university students, workers on strike, and any others who dare to question or contest the status quo. Many are jailed, beaten, or killed by police and other social control agents of the state (see figure 1.1 for a description of the events at Kent State University in 1970).

The familiar phrase, *law and order,* implies order maintenance within the framework of law. Political figures often weave law and order into slogans, promising that more police will result in more protection (a position unsupported by most criminological research). This sound-bite strategy constructs an artificial creation of people's needs (in need of protection from constant danger) and proposed solutions to those needs.

The media also package and sell myths of crime to the public, whether through reports about actual crime or fictional television or movie plots. Often, these myths become entertainment for the targeted audience, the American consumer. Largely, the public has been willing to purchase these mythical products.[3]

Politicians have been successful in their sales of crime-fighting methods that, under scrutiny, are social and fiscal failures. The constant message is that more and more police is the answer to people's fear of crime. Crime, however, is a symptom of larger social problems that have been carefully compacted into this conceptual illusion called crime.[4]

In May 2001, President Bush unveiled *"Project Safe Neighborhoods"* to an audience in Philadelphia. The program transfers prosecution of many weapons violations from state to federal jurisdiction and subsidizes state prosecution of the remaining offenses. "Project Safe Neighborhoods" resonates with the public; it has a reassuring protective spin. However, it makes a significant transfer of authority—limiting or reducing the power and authority of the state while increasing that of the federal government.[8]

Crime emerges as a political product—carefully crafted, marketed, and sold by a media that consist of a shrinking number of corporate conglomerates.[5] In essence, police have become commodity products to solve

---

Figure 1.1

As a freshman at Kent State, I was a sponge for every kind of learning. I was quick to appreciate the freedom that I found and eager to become involved in the working of our democracy. I participated in several antiwar demonstrations [against the Vietnam War] and listened to speakers from the SDS (Students for a Democratic Society) and other political points of view. I was watching as the ROTC building burned, and I believe that government agents were involved. I saw the National Guard come to town and occupy our campus with school scheduled to continue as usual. I came to resent the newly imposed curfew and was determined to protest the National Guard presence on Monday. The demonstration was peaceful, if occasionally a little raucous. The National Guard had several opportunities to halt their campus sweep but they continued to escalate and inflame the student demonstrators by increasing the level of intimidation. Then the Guard suddenly turned and aimed as if they heard an order. I happened to be very near to them. They leveled their guns and aimed at me. I knew they were not loaded and they would not fire. I was wrong and though we did not engage in wrong or illegal behavior by any stretch of the imagination, the National Guard shot 13 of us and killed four of our fellow students. Subsequent investigations called the shootings unnecessary, unwarranted, and unjustified. In spite of that, not one Guardsman was held accountable for his actions.

The freedoms of speech and assembly were called into question and I believe we remained always within our rights.

In retrospect, I believe there was a conspiracy to stop dissent in America and that the Nixon administration was behind it.

Joe Lewis, December 2006[7]

the crime problem. The media and political figures have, through the successful sales of their products, managed to create a public addiction for stronger social control measures. The public is increasingly apathetic over issues related to individual rights, resulting in a reduction of individual liberties for all.[6]

American policing is vital to the operation of the criminal justice system. It is reasonable to suggest that the police are to criminal justice what procurers of raw materials such as steel and plastic are to the automobile industry. Corporations cannot sustain an industry without raw materials, and the criminal justice system cannot operate its industry without criminal defendants. From this perspective, prosecutors, judges, and wardens need police to procure products for their respective criminal processing roles within the criminal justice system. Policing faces a dilemma. Confronted with two conflicting roles, the police must decide on an image to offer to the public. As agents of the state, the police must perform their principal role as social control agents. To a large degree, this role requires a widespread, visible police presence, often reinforced through a vast assortment of paramilitary gear.[9] This attire projects the image of combat soldiers or occupation forces ready for a major enemy attack—consistent with a declaration of "war on crime," "war on drugs," "war on gangs," and the need to protect against constant "enemies."

As social control agents, police are authorized to intervene, without invitation, in disputes between citizens. They also can deprive citizens of their freedom through detainment or arrest (as vividly shown in the story that began this chapter). Committing a crime is not a prerequisite for anyone to experience intervention, detainment, or arrest.

In contrast to the role of social control agents, the police must also present a positive image of their institution and of the state. People, as a rule, tend to respond more favorably to information presented as in their interest. The police institution controls the flow of information about crime and its own performance as guardians of public safety. Allowing police to keep track of crime and of

their responses to that social problem is problematic. As demonstrated in Philadelphia, Boca Raton, and elsewhere, police often underreport crime to make communities appear safe—often for the benefit of the tourist and recreation industries.[10] Other jurisdictions engage in the practice of *arrest-overkill,* the arrest of many suspects for an individual crime. For example, there typically is one arrest for each murder, but the Detroit police in 1999 arrested about three suspects for each murder (1,152 murder arrests for 415 killings).[11]

The mass media have enhanced the image of police. The typical image presented of the institution of policing is that law enforcement exists to *serve* and *protect* the public (and they always "get their man"). The mainstream presentation of police is that of the crime-fighter, but maintaining order has always been the primary goal of the police institution.[12] The state often portrays itself as a just entity that, though imperfect, can and must be trusted. The police often define themselves as the "thin blue line" between "civilization" and "anarchy." Unfortunately, there are too many examples of uncivilized police behavior. The increasing availability of video cameras has captured such moments, beginning with the beating of Rodney King in Los Angeles. In 2007, a bar surveillance videotape recorded an off-duty police officer beating a female bartender who had refused to serve him additional drinks. A police captain ordered squad cars to block parking lots in the area where the officer's hearing was scheduled and to issue parking tickets to reporters and photographers who tried to cover the hearing. The scandal over an initial misdemeanor charge precipitated the resignation of the police superintendent.

To develop an understanding[13] of policing as an institution of social control and as an occupational subculture, we will first trace the historical development of this unique institution. Policing did not emerge from a vacuum. The practice of governments policing citizens is not a new activity, but policing as an institution is a relatively recent creation that is unique to industrialized societies.[14]

EARLY POLICE SYSTEMS

In the early seventeenth century, the verb *policier* meant "to order, govern, rule advisedly," and the term *police* meant "civil government" (derived from the Greek term *politeia*). During ancient times patriarchal rule sustained social control. Some argue today that policing continues to be an extension of social control through patriarchal rule.[15] Contemporary policing is an artifact of nineteenth century empires and nation-states.[16]

Organized police systems were not germane to all societies—certainly not in the context that we think of policing today. "As a general rule, the more stratified a society, the greater will be the reliance on formal methods of social control."[17] As a corollary to this general principle, police forces in stratified societies have tended to help preserve class differences. The preservation of class differences serves the interests of dominant groups.[18]

During ancient times, clan and tribal members served as the police forces of their respective groups. Those members of the community with enforcement power did not compose an organized police force. One of the earliest known police systems existed in Babylonia at the time when the Code of Hammurabi was instituted (2181–2123 BC). During this period, the ruling class maintained control of the police. Later, some societies, usually ruled by kings and monarchs, had strong, efficient central governments that maintained order with a totalitarian police force as well as standing armies.[19]

The Roman Empire adopted forms of policing that relied on a police force and a standing army. Rome had many of the characteristics of stratified societies elsewhere. The inequalities that existed within the Roman Empire created wars, internal strife, and riotous behavior among the masses. Following years of strife, Augustus (63 BC–AD 14) took control and maintained order with *vigiles,* an imperial force of police and firemen (also referred to as *Vigiles Urbani*—watchmen of the city). Augustus had a police force of 10,000 in a city with a population of about three-quarters of a million, or one policeman for every 75 citizens.[20] By comparison, today we have one police officer for every 400 or 500 citizens.[21] Given the degree of inequality that existed in Rome during this period, one of the principal functions of the police was to protect the property and the powerful positions of the rulers.[22]

A POLICE INSTITUTION EMERGES IN ENGLAND

Prior to the Norman invasion by William the Conqueror, policing in England was a community responsibility. England divided villages into *tythings*—units of ten families. A *tythingman* within these units was responsible for keeping order in his section of the village. These sections are comparable to police beats or police sectors in contemporary U.S. policing. A system known as the *mutual pledge system* emerged whereby citizens who reported crimes to the tythingman or responded to the tythingman's *hue and cry* (an announcement that a crime had occurred) would receive small monetary awards. In addition to catching thieves, the tythingman also reimbursed individuals who lost property.[23] The mutual pledge system and other forms of citizen participation in crime control were forerunners of the vigilantes and bounty hunters that would eventually play significant roles in U.S. culture and history. The practice of reimbursing lost property reaches back to the Code of Hammurabi. One section of that code stipulated that if they could not catch a robber, and if the victim swore to the amount lost while under oath, the community was obliged to compensate the victim.

As villages grew, tythings were combined into *hundreds* (each hundred consisted of ten tythings) policed by *constables*. The creation of *shires* (similar to present-day counties) resulted by combining hundreds. A *shire-reeve* (sheriff) policed each shire. The tythingman later became the *chief pledge*. The chief pledges came under the authority of the knights of the shire, later known as *justices of the peace*, who were under the direct authority of the king. By the fourteenth century, the chief pledge became the petty constable and later the parish constable.

The *constabulary system* was the dominant form of policing in England until early in the nineteenth century and was influential in America. "The constable did not use his power to discover and punish deviation from the established laws. Rather, he assisted complaining citizens if and when they sought his help."[24] The constable performed his duties during the day while citizen volunteers took turns performing their duties at night, during what was known as the *night-watch*. Policing remained a community responsibility and was under the control of the community members. The constable was not concerned with crime prevention as we know it today. He did not spend his time looking for potential criminals. Then, in the face of rapid population growth, more pronounced class divisions, and emerging capitalism, the *voluntary observance* of law no longer seemed able to hold the social order together, and community-responsibility policing changed.

> The advent of community prosperity . . . inevitably [brings] differences in wealth and social status, and creates . . . classes and parties and factions with or without wealth and power and privileges. In the presence of these divisions, community unanimity in voluntary law observance disappears, and some other means of securing law observance and the maintenance of authority and order must be found.[25]

Those in power define authority and order. To keep the masses under control, the powerful in England created definitions of behavior that they considered deviant or criminal. The broader the gap between the rich and the poor, the less likely that the poor will be satisfied with their place in society. As the poor seek to remedy their position, those in power often resort to formal social control approaches—the police—to protect their interests.

The Metropolitan Police of London

From 1674 to 1834, policing in London changed from the responsibility of the community to semi-official thief-takers to salaried constables and eventually to a professional police force. In the late seventeenth century, the government began offering substantial rewards for apprehending those who committed serious crimes, such as highway robbery. In the eighteenth century, individual victims offered rewards for the return of their stolen goods. Daily newspapers advertised such rewards, which substantially altered the character of criminal justice in London.[26]

"Thief-takers" were paid fees for finding the people responsible for stealing property or committing other crimes. They were often corrupt individuals who would play victims against thieves to see who would offer the largest reward, or they would induce someone to steal goods and then apprehend the "thief" for the reward.

The Bow Street Runners: Managing Class Struggle

To encourage victims to report crimes, magistrates established offices in London. Sir Thomas De Veil established one office on Bow Street in 1739, which was next to St. Giles Parish, where 30,000 people lived in crowded, unsanitary conditions.[27] Henry Fielding (the novelist, who eventually became a magistrate) took over the office in 1748. He employed thief-takers to apprehend the suspect after a crime was reported, thinking that the certainty of capture and prosecution would deter others from pirating, highway robbery, and stealing. He also collected and distributed information about crimes and suspected criminals. In 1749 he hired six constables, who became known as the *Bow Street Runners*.

When Henry Fielding retired, his blind half-brother, John Fielding (who had assisted him for four years), took over Bow Street Court. He formed the Bow Street Horse Patrol. The men were armed and wore leather hats, blue coats with brass buttons, blue trousers, and boots. The Bow Street Runners and Horse Patrol were the forerunners of increased state control over street life.

By 1770, prices were rising much faster than wages. People who worked could not support their families. The Gordon Riots began as a protest by Protestants against the lessening of restrictions on Catholics. Sixty thousand people marched to the House of Commons on June 2, 1780. The demonstration quickly turned to violence and looting.[28] The civil unrest over extreme poverty, high taxes, repressive laws, and conscription into the army that had seethed below the surface erupted into riots. The Bank of England and prisons, including Newgate and Fleet, were damaged substantially, releasing prisoners. Alarmed by the mobs in the streets and the mounting damages, members of parliament and property owners (often indistinguishable) called for military intervention on June 7.[29] The military fired on the crowds, killing 285.[30]

Economic conditions remained unsettled in England. In 1807, England blockaded French ports. The result was increasing unemployment and an increase in hunger and poverty among English workers and their families. The severe winter of 1810 and the harvest failure of 1812 compounded the problems confronting the working class and the poor. Men, women, and children worked up to 18 hours per day under grueling conditions in factories, and they worked for wages insufficient to support themselves and their families. Not surprisingly, the workers began to protest. One of the most famous revolts was the Luddite Riots of late 1811 and early 1812. Textile workers attacked the machines that were displacing them, and they generally disrupted the oppressive factory system. The British government's response was to make the destruction of machines punishable by death.

The War of 1812 with the United States increased demand for factory goods, temporarily reducing the tension between workers and owners as unemployment decreased. However, hard times for the poor returned between 1815 and 1822. An economic depression once again brought widespread unemployment and worker unrest. In 1815, Parliament enacted the Corn Laws, and the price of bread, a staple food of the poor, increased. The result was more poverty and rioting in the streets. Once again, the British government responded with a series of repressive measures. The Six Acts (known also as the Riot Acts) authorized the seizure of "seditious and blasphemous literature." Similar laws had been passed to control the American colonists shortly before the American Revolution.[31] Although the depression temporarily ended around 1822, a financial panic occurred in 1825, which sparked a new wave of riots and protests by displaced workers.[32]

Robert Peel and Preventive Policing

Until the Gordon Riots, there had been strong resistance to the creation of an organized police force. "By the late 1820s the fear of crime and disorder overshadowed the potential threats to liberty inherent in an organized police, at least for the politically dominant upper classes."[33] Concern about mob action was not unique; many police forces have been established for this reason.

> The paramilitary form of early police bureaucracy was a response not only, or even primarily, to crime per se, but to the possibility of riotous disorder. Not crime and danger but the "dangerous classes" as part of the urban social structure led to the formation of uniformed and military organized police. Such organizations intervened between the propertied elites and the propertyless masses who were regarded as politically dangerous as a class.[34]

Sir Robert Peel became the Home Secretary of England in 1822. For several years, he and his supporters advocated the creation of a new police force. The ***Metropolitan Police Act*** passed in 1829. It established a centralized police force of 3,000 men under the control of the Home Secretary. Uniformed and carrying truncheons, the new "Bobbies" (named after Peel) were expected to patrol the streets on prescribed beats.

Peel took his case for a centralized police force to the people, and he argued that the police would serve the interests of all the people. He stressed that the new role of the police would be the prevention of crime through increased patrols. This claim rested on the premise that more police would automatically result in less crime.

The police would have a civilian character because members would be recruited from the ranks of the working class.[35] The beat policeman came from the working or peasant classes in the nineteenth century, and although he aspired to respectable status, his job was, by and large, unskilled. The pay was less than a respectable working-class level, but it was regular. There were additional benefits as well. For instance, the uniform saved on clothing, and some officers received housing allowances. Although there was talk about a pension, it did not materialize until the twentieth century.[36]

Alan Silver offers another explanation for the passage of the Metropolitan Police Act: shielding rulers from the masses.

> If the power structure armed itself and fought a riot or a rebellious people, this [would create] more trouble and tension than the original problem. But, if one can have an independent police which fights the mob, then antagonism is directed toward the police, and not the power structure. A paid professional police force seems to separate "constitutional" authority from social and economic dominance.[37]

The recruitment of police from the lower classes shielded the ruling class. Police brutality became the brutalization of the lower classes by other members of the lower classes—the police. This strategy remains in practice today in England and in the United States.

The enactment of the Metropolitan Police Act shifted control by the community (i.e., the constabulary system) to control by the state, which was under the control of the ruling class. The idea that the presence of the police in the streets would prevent crime paved the way for the police practice later called selective enforcement. The police could now serve more direct class functions, as well as more routine functions, by patrolling communities where the poorest and most oppressed people resided, thus reducing the potential for organizational activities associated with riots, rallies, and demonstrations. The police were now able to keep the rabble in line.[38]

Most of the crime prior to the establishment of the police force was of a petty nature and emerged out of class conflicts. For example, the rate of males going to trial increased from 170 per 100,000 in 1824 to 250 by 1830. The proportion committed for vagrancy increased by 34% between 1826 and 1829

and rose by 65% between 1829 and 1832. Over half of the prisoners during this period were persons convicted of vagrancy, poaching, petty theft, disorderly conduct, and public drunkenness.[39] Only 25% of those awaiting trial in local jails or serving actual sentences were being held for indictable crimes; deserters and debtors constituted the remainder.[40] The new police force increased the attention to minor offenses. During the 1830s about 85%of all arrests were for drunkenness, disorderly conduct, and similar minor offenses.[41] The emphasis on minor offenses committed primarily by the poor and the working classes reflected the trend toward the regulation and control (i.e., repression) of the laboring population, often referred to as the "dangerous classes."[42] They *were* dangerous, because they had the capacity to disrupt business and production and thus cut into the profits of the owners.

There is much evidence that the wealthy classes had different views of the police than the working classes and the poor. A committee of Parliament in 1834 reported the possibility of abuses of power by the Metropolitan police, but it also observed that the centralized police were a valuable modern institution for maintaining peace and order. In contrast, the poor and the working classes

> considered the police more as an element of control than as a group of protectors. In a sense the police monitored the behavior of the dangerous classes so that the comfortable and satisfied could sleep more soundly at night or not be annoyed by the sight of public drunkenness.[43]

Several characteristics of the London Metropolitan Police stand out. First, there was a striking attempt to make policing strong enough to maintain order but restrained in its response to political conflict. To accomplish this goal, the London police was founded on military principles, observed strict rules of conduct, and used management practices that were well-defined.[44] Second, police in London tended to refrain from personalization in their functions of policing. One method employed to accomplish this goal was to recruit officers from outside

London—officers who had no personal ties to those whom they would be policing. Finally, police in London implemented the legal system, although the ruling class remained in control of defining criminal behavior through legislation.

AMERICAN POLICING EMERGES

We divide the emergence of American policing into four periods. The *colonial pre/post revolutionary period* encompasses the earliest forms of American policing, which was largely a community affair, and extends into the first couple of decades of the nineteenth century. The second period, the *political era*, began about 1840 and extended into the early decades of the twentieth century. Policing took the initial steps toward becoming an institution during this period, and the link between politics and police was quite overt. The *professional model era* lasted from about 1920 into the 1970s. This period is characterized by progressive training and educational programs for police officers and by innovative technology. The final period, *actuarial policing,* began in the early 1970s and continues to the present, characterized by increased surveillance and control over U.S. citizens.

The Colonial and Pre/Post Revolution Period

English customs and traditions—including those related to policing— accompanied the early colonists to America. Early colonial policing consisted primarily of public punishment. The ducking stool for people who gossiped, the stocks for petty thieves, the branding iron for thieves, and the gallows for murderers were shaming devices employed both to punish the offender and to deter others from committing the same offenses. Jails, often a social control tool associated with police, provided temporary detention of suspects between arrest and trial, or those convicted between trials and sentencing. Jails were not places where punishment or rehabilitation occurred. Before the emergence of large cities and the mass immigration of the

nineteenth century, policing largely depended on community consensus and citizens who were willing to assist in capturing criminals or report deviant behavior. Sin and crime were interchangeable concepts in Puritan New England.[45]

Policing in the South was somewhat different. The middle and southern colonies adopted policing methods quite similar to those found in the countryside of England where many of these early settlers originated. The county court was the dominant institution and was controlled by local elites, but people in the southern colonies, who often lived in the countryside, preferred resolving disputes themselves rather than relying on the court.[46] African slaves in the South had no rights, were viewed as property, and were under constant surveillance by slave patrols and local militia.[47]

Constables were the first form of law enforcement in the American colonies. They were not professional police, nor were they always volunteers. They were elected or often drafted into service.[48] Policing was largely viewed as a community obligation. The night-watch system was used in the colonies and remained a component of American policing until the mid-1800s.

The first night-watch was organized in Boston in 1631. Citizens were expected to serve on the night-watch, although many prosperous citizens paid others to take their place. Failure to serve or to pay a surrogate could result in a stiff penalty. In some cases, defendants were sentenced to night-watch as a punishment.[49] New Amsterdam (New York), under Dutch control until 1664, instituted a paid night-watch in 1658. This night-watch was known as the *rattle watch* because of the wooden rattles shaken by its members to make their presence known. By 1700, Philadelphia had created its own night-watch, and in 1712 Boston adopted a paid (50 cents per night), full-time night-watch. Other cities followed these early examples (e.g., Cincinnati in 1803, New Orleans in 1804).[50] The silence of darkness was broken by night-watchmen calling out the hour and sometimes giving weather reports as they performed the task of watching for suspicious characters.

The role of the early American colonial constable centered on assisting citizens in resolving disputes, bringing alleged offenders to court, tax collection, collecting fines, and, in some instances, dispensing corporal punishment to the convicted. Private police became popular in the later colonial years, and from time to time, the wealthy would "hire out" their private police to the community. Periodically, the militia was called upon to suppress disorders, which were common during the late eighteenth century. For the most part, however, policing in early America was at the community level, with some form of constabulary system dominant. During the colonial period, constables were citizen police. They had no formal training; any training was limited to on-the-job training.[51]

Whereas the northeastern part of America relied on the constable/night-watch approach to law enforcement, the South relied on county sheriffs and slave patrols. The first sheriff appeared in Virginia in 1634. It is quite possible that this early reliance on the sheriff accounts for the power enjoyed by that office throughout the South today. Performing night-watch services and serving on the slave patrol were considered community obligations. Slave patrols had a dual purpose: to apprehend runaway slaves and to ensure that slaves did not revolt.

Regardless of the geographic region, early American policing was community centered, and participation in law enforcement was considered an obligation for citizens. Certainly policing, in both North and South, was of particular benefit to wealthy landowners, businessmen, and others who had the most to lose from angry citizenry.

Politics and Police: The Political Era of Policing (1840–1920)

Between the 1830s and 1850s, many cities began to consider the constable/nightwatch system inadequate in both organization and personnel. The population of New York City quintupled between 1790 and 1830, primarily from the arrival of immigrants. Many had little choice but to seek residence in New York's slum district known as "Five Points." New York's rapid urbanization was generated by economic and industrial developments that greatly benefited the owners. Rioting was the viable means of protest available to poor and lower-class laborers. In 1834, later called the "year of riots," New York sustained a succession of uprisings (the Stonecutter's Riot, the Five Points Riot, the Chantham Street Riots, etc.).[52] By 1845, New York had one hundred marshals and a part-time watch of nearly a thousand men known as constables. These police officers were not paid a salary, but they received fees for recovering stolen property and for providing other police duties.[53]

Between 1830 and 1845 in New York, there was "rapid population growth with sharp increases in immigration, heightened distinctions between class, ethnic, and religious groups with consequent social strain, and a dizzy economic cycle of boom and bust."[54] Boston was plagued with some of the same changes: "Riot, one of the first problems recognized as beyond control, dramatized the need for force. The leaders of government were firmly set against popular violence as a means of political and social protest."[55] Although the leaders of the American Revolution had supported popular violence as a means of political and social protest, the leaders some fifty years later did not sanction that method of protest by other oppressed groups.

Business and political leaders in large cities in the North promoted the organization of a full-time organized police force. They felt threatened by the specter of urban disorder, the presence of "mobs," and the "dangerous classes." Their attitude toward these groups, and toward the working class in general, was similar to white attitudes toward blacks in the South: they feared that these powerless groups would somehow seize power. Studies of the police in Buffalo and Milwaukee present evidence that (1) the size of the police force increased more rapidly than both the rise in population and the increase in crime, (2) "crime" was primarily of the public-order variety (disorderly conduct, vagrancy, etc.), and (3) the police were created by and under the strict control of business and political leaders.[56] Similarly, the rise in police personnel in Boston did not correspond to a rise in crime.[57]

Throughout the nineteenth century, there was widespread political turmoil and resistance as workers sought to gain some control of their lives, especially in the workplace. In many instances, the police were simply tools used by the owners to break up strikes and arrest workers on vague charges such as disorderly conduct. Such arrests increased during periods of rioting and declined sharply after the turmoil ceased.

In many large cities during the mid-1800s, party politics played a significant role in policing. The Republican Party supported state control over police; the Democratic Party preferred local control. In New York, Cleveland, Detroit, and several other large cities during the mid-1800s, the state took control of the police. When the Democrats regained power, the police were once again under local control.[58] Regardless of the ruling party, the common people rarely played an active role in the control of police (in this respect, not much has changed).

Before the close of the nineteenth century, nearly every large city in the United States had a police force. Rural areas had a sheriff as the chief law enforcement official. Federal marshals were the mainstays of law enforcement in the territories in the West. The discovery of gold in California prompted more than 100,000 people to migrate to California by 1850, and the number exceeded 300,000 by 1851. As the population of the West expanded, there was a demand for supplies from the East and security to guarantee delivery of the goods to the purchaser. Private police began to flourish in the mid-1800s. Wells Fargo became one of the largest private security companies. With the western migration also came the railroad, which solicited the services of private police organizations like the Pinkerton detective agency.[59] *Pinkertons*—employees of the agency—were also used for strikebreaking during the late 1800s. Contracted by mine owners in Pennsylvania, the Pinkertons infiltrated the Molly Maguires, an organization of coal miners said by the mine owners

to have committed a number of "terrorist activities." The testimony of an undercover Pinkerton agent resulted in the hanging of nineteen men who were later found to be innocent. Their "crime" was successful union organizing—not "terrorism."[60]

Some private security firms were actually innovative in their efforts to prevent crime. Edwin Holmes was responsible for the first burglar alarm in 1858, and Washington Perry Brink began a package-delivery service by truck in Chicago in 1859. Brink eventually expanded his business to provide security for payroll deliveries. Following an episode where two employees were gunned down in 1917, Brink developed the armored car.[61] By the close of the nineteenth century, private security firms—or private police—had carved out a formidable niche for themselves politically, socially, and, of course, economically.

For the police, the early years of the twentieth century proved disastrous for public relations. Race riots raged out of control. In 1908, several thousand whites assaulted African-American neighborhoods in Springfield, Illinois. Homes were burned, stores were looted, and two elderly African Americans were mutilated and lynched. The police did nothing. In 1917, after African Americans had been hired in a factory holding government contracts, several thousand whites stabbed, clubbed, and hanged dozens of African Americans in East Saint Louis. More than 6,000 African Americans were driven from their homes. The police did nothing. In 1918, sixty-four lynchings were attributed to Ku Klux Klan activities. That number increased to eighty-three in 1919, and there were race riots in Washington, DC, Arkansas, Tennessee, and Texas.

The year 1919 was also the year of the Chicago race riot. Rapid population increases in South Chicago (the African-American population increased from 44,000 in 1910 to nearly 110,000 in 1920), coupled with discriminatory hiring practices, unemployment, and horrible poverty, set the stage. The murder of a young African American swimming in a "whites only" area of Lake Michigan and the refusal of police to arrest the killers sparked the riot. Chicago was under siege for thirteen days, in spite of efforts by the state militia to control the angry mobs. At the end of the thirteen-day ordeal twenty-three African Americans and fifteen whites were dead, over five hundred people were injured, and more than a thousand African-American families were homeless. U.S. president Woodrow Wilson pointed the finger at whites and accused them of being the aggressors. Again, the police did nothing. Some believed that it was time to rethink American policing.

The Professional Model Era (1920 to the 1970s)

Shortly after the turn of the twentieth century, the institution of policing sought professional status. Changes in the administrative and operational functions of police were the hallmarks of professionalism—recruitment, training, and the adoption and implementation of scientific crime-detection and crime-fighting technology. Recruitment practices placed more emphasis on education and psychological evaluations. Training was instituted in most police departments, and national training academies were established (e.g., the FBI National Academy). Scientific technology was integrated into U.S. policing: mobile methods of patrolling, radio communications, modernized fingerprint identification methodologies, and modern methods of record-keeping. Policing charted a course that continued through the acquisition and use of high-tech equipment today.

Three individuals are notable for their influence and impact on modern U.S. policing: August Vollmer, Orlando Winfield Wilson, and J. Edgar Hoover. Although their personalities, philosophies, and approaches differed, their fingerprints are present on many aspects of U.S. policing today.

August Vollmer has been called the father of modern U.S. policing. Most of the changes that occurred in policing during the political era were influenced by the activities of special-interest groups and politicians. Vollmer was among the first to initiate change from within the institution of policing. The changes that he launched occurred

during a period when policing was mired in external politics and strongly affiliated with political figures.

Vollmer was the chief of police in Berkeley, California, from 1905 through 1932. Following the policing model established by Sir Robert Peel in London, Vollmer instituted the first U.S. police training school in 1909. He developed the police call box and one of the first fingerprinting bureaus in the United States. His officers patrolled first on bicycles, then on motorcycles in 1911, and then in cruisers with radios by 1913. The Berkeley police force was completely mobile by 1920.

Central to Vollmer's philosophy on policing was the idea that the police should be the vanguard for the socialization of America's youth. Police officers, he argued, should also take a more active part in casework for social agencies. He was adamantly opposed to unorthodox behavior by police officers. Vollmer helped author the 1931 Wickersham Commission (formally known as the National Commission on Law Observance and Enforcement) report, which exposed brutality and other unconstitutional practices in which police officers had engaged.[62] One of the most influential reports was titled Report on Lawlessness in Law Enforcement. Vollmer promoted higher education for his own officers in Berkeley, and he organized the first college-level police course at the University of California at Berkeley. Vollmer's influence on policing produced a reform agenda for professionalizing in policing that included:

1. Elimination of political influence

2. Appointment of qualified chief executives

3. Establishment of a mission of nonpartisan public service

4. Raising personnel standards

5. Introduction of the principles of scientific management

6. Emphasis on military-style discipline

7. Development of specialized units[63]

Critics of Vollmer viewed many of these goals as overly idealistic and impractical. Many of Vollmer's students, however, eventually became chiefs of police and worked to reform their departments.[64] This new generation of police executives demonstrated willingness to confront issues associated with citizen abuse by police officers, and they instituted formal internal affairs units to investigate citizen reports of police abuse.[65]

Orlando Winfield Wilson was a police officer under Vollmer's command for almost four years and received his degree from the University of California at Berkeley. His first position as chief of police was in Fullerton, California. Community leaders there, however, believed that his reform methods were too "radical," and he was fired after one year. Wilson then became chief of police in Wichita, Kansas. Wilson's ideas about accountability and ethics were indeed radical. After several years of implementing progressive policing ideas in Wichita, he was again fired. Wilson returned to California and took a position teaching in the School of Criminology at the University of California at Berkeley.

Wilson was especially interested in the efficiency of police management. He worked to reduce response time (the time between the report of a crime and the time of arrival by law enforcement) and to maximize police coverage—to place police officers in vehicles and offer more geographic coverage based on a formula taking into account, among other factors, crime reports in each sector beat (designated area of operation).[66] Wilson also was an advocate for police accountability, particularly as it applied to the abuse of power.[67] In 1960, Wilson left the University of California and accepted a position as police commissioner of Chicago. He remained in that position until his retirement in 1967. One year later, the Chicago police made international headlines with their brutal performance at the 1968 Democratic National Convention.

John Edgar Hoover was born in Washington, DC, on January 1, 1895. While working as a messenger boy at the Library of Congress, he studied law at George Washington University. In many ways, Hoover was strikingly different from Vollmer and Wilson. Although their views on the importance of law enforcement efficiency and professionalism were parallel, Hoover's methods and objectives were sharply different.

Alexander Palmer, the U.S. attorney general, recruited Hoover to the Department of Justice in 1917. Working as Palmer's special assistant, Hoover gathered evidence on suspected subversives and communists. Under the pretense of enforcing the Espionage Act (1917) and the Sedition Act (1918), the two men initiated campaigns against anyone they considered sympathetic to left-wing ideas—anyone who supported organized labor, women's suffrage, or other progressive causes. Hoover created extensive card files on those who had leftist views; in a few years he had indexed more than 450,000 names and compiled detailed biographies on nearly 60,000 of the individuals whom he considered the most dangerous.

Many lawyers found themselves listed in Hoover's file because they were willing to represent radicals such as Eugene Debs, an organized-labor activist, and Emma Goldman, who promoted women's rights and birth control.[68] Clarence Darrow, a famous defense attorney, was placed in Hoover's file because of an article he wrote for the May 1936 issue of *Esquire* magazine. In this article, Darrow criticized the jury selection process and mentioned the futility of the state fighting crime while ignoring social and economic issues related to crime and criminal defendants. Hoover added Darrow to his list of unscrupulous criminal lawyers who "stimulate disrespect for law and influence crime conditions."[69]

Hoover was rewarded for his efforts by being appointed assistant director of the Bureau of Investigation. The function of the Bureau was to investigate violations of federal law and assist other law enforcement agencies throughout the United States. The Bureau's power, however, was limited—agents were not allowed to carry weapons or authorized to arrest suspects. After he was appointed director in 1924, Hoover regularly lobbied Congress to extend the Bureau's power. In 1935, Congress established the Federal Bureau of Investigation (FBI), and Hoover's agents were permitted to carry weapons and to arrest citizens.

Hoover created and implemented the FBI National Academy.[70]

Hoover impacted law enforcement through control and manipulation of politics/politicians and media/journalists. He also skillfully manipulated public opinion. He portrayed the FBI as protecting the American people from insidious subversives and at no taxpayer expense. He argued that the value of the stolen property recovered by the FBI was greater than the agency's entire budget. Hoover would often point to the FBI's role in the recovery of stolen vehicles. He conveniently neglected to mention that local police recover the vast majority of stolen vehicles and that most stolen vehicles are used for joyriding and eventually are returned to their owners. (The FBI would be able to draw a valid comparison between its budget and the value of recovered stolen vehicles only if all of the recovered stolen vehicles became property of the federal government.)[71]

Many people in government feared Hoover. They knew that he collected information that he would use against anyone whose political and moral views differed from his own. The list of people on whom Hoover kept files was extensive (i.e., Albert Einstein, W. E. B. Du Bois, Amelia Earhart, George Orwell, John Steinbeck, Jackie Robinson, Mickey Mantle, Eleanor Roosevelt, Jacqueline Kennedy, and John Lennon). Anyone with connections to the Black Panther Party, Students for a Democratic Society (SDS), or the civil rights movement were targets, regardless of whether they had ever engaged in criminal behavior.

FBI agents paid informants to infiltrate organizations deemed subversive. Hoover ordered his agents to keep Martin Luther King, Jr. under surveillance. The FBI tapped his telephone conversations, threatened his life, blackmailed individuals to discredit him, and even sent him a letter suggesting that he commit suicide. A Senate report in 1976 stated that the FBI intended to destroy King.[72] The agency engaged in burglary, illegal wiretapping, illegal mail tampering, and conspiracy to commit murder against the Black Panther Party.[73] In a 1976 subcommittee hearing, the FBI admitted to more than

ninety false allegations against the Black Panthers. The FBI used blackmail, illegal surveillance tactics, arson, perjury, smear campaigns, and allegations of assassination against SDS members and other antiwar or civil rights demonstrators.[74] Although the Civil Rights Act of 1967 (prompted by inner-city riots) provided for stronger penalties for the violation of people's civil rights, it failed to address the violence committed by social control agents like the FBI and the police.

The small unit that was created in 1908 and had no name until George W. Wickersham (of the Wickersham Commission), then attorney general, named it the Bureau of Investigation in 1909, became the largest federal police agency under Hoover's 48 years of direction. Today the FBI has 30,600 employees in 56 field offices and a budget of $5.7 billion.[75] It has jurisdiction over all federal crime. As discussed in previous chapters, the FBI also publishes the annual Uniform Crime Reports (UCR). It began collecting, publishing, and archiving those statistics in 1930. The Wickersham Commission report in 1931 included a discussion of criminal statistics, and several members criticized the system and its control by the FBI, but the system remained in place.[76]

Violations of the civil rights of citizens were by no means limited to the FBI. In the waning years of the professional era, the Supreme Court became the principal instrument for reforming police misconduct (see next section). There were, however, multiple examples of the misuse of power. The summer of 1968 was one of the most reported examples. Demonstrators gathered in Chicago where the Democratic Party was holding its national convention. Civil rights activists, antiwar demonstrators, and university students held rallies in the parks and marched in the streets to protest racial segregation and discrimination, the Vietnam War, and other social injustices. After several days of demonstrations, Mayor Richard Daly authorized the police to take action. Chicago police officers kicked and clubbed unarmed demonstrators lying on the ground trying to protect themselves from the blows. Tear gas was used frequently. Televised images of these events were projected around the world. Viewers watched in horror as citizens exercising their constitutional right to assemble peacefully and voice their objections to government policies and practices were assaulted by the police. Contrary to official accounts, the demonstrations had been peaceful; the Chicago Police Department initiated the violence. The era of police professionalism ended with scenes far too reminiscent of the worst cases of police brutality during the political era that the reforms were intended to prevent. Before discussing the fourth period in the evolution of policing, we will take a brief look at some Supreme Court decisions made at the end of the professional era that helped shape police procedures.

The Supreme Court: Policing the Police

In 1961 the Supreme Court dealt with the exclusionary rule and the Fourth Amendment's protection from unreasonable *search* and *seizure* in **Mapp v. Ohio**. Three Cleveland police officers knocked on the door of Dollree Mapp's home on May 23, 1957. They asked to search the premises for a person wanted in connection with a recent bombing; they also claimed they were seeking evidence of an illegal gambling operation. Ms. Mapp called her attorney, who instructed her to ask the police for a search warrant. The police did not have a search warrant, and the officers withdrew. Several hours later, they returned with additional officers. When Mapp failed to respond immediately to another knock on the door, the police forcibly entered the residence. Mapp again asked to see a warrant. One officer held up a piece of paper, stating that it was a warrant. She grabbed the paper to look at it, but officers snatched it away and placed her in handcuffs. In court, a search warrant was never produced, nor was any explanation offered as to why a search warrant was not entered as prosecutorial evidence.

Shortly after the police entered the premises, Mapp's attorney arrived. He was barred from entering the house, and he was not allowed to see his client. In the basement of the two-story dwelling, the police found a trunk of pornographic material, which Mapp said had belonged to a former tenant. The police failed to find anyone hiding in the house or any illegal betting material. Mapp was convicted for possession of obscene material.

The Fourth Amendment states individuals should be free from unreasonable searches and seizures, but it does not indicate how to treat evidence from a warrantless search. The Supreme Court, in two previous cases, had established an exclusionary rule that makes evidence gathered illegally inadmissible in court. The rulings applied to the federal government but not to state courts. In fact, the Supreme Court had previously ruled that the exclusionary rule did not apply to states. The Supreme Court agreed to hear Mapp's case and decided in her favor, overturning the previous decision. The ruling was controversial because it was perceived as allowing a guilty person to escape punishment because of mistakes made by law enforcement. Justice Benjamin Cardozo recognized the impact of the ruling but also noted that if the guilty are set free, it is the law that sets them free. In addition, he contended, nothing can destroy a government more quickly than its failure to observe its own laws. Therefore, and at the heart of the exclusionary rule, illegally obtained evidence cannot be used against a defendant.[77]

In 1963 in **Gideon v. Wainwright**, the Supreme Court ruled that a defendant charged with a crime has a fundamental right to an attorney.[78] The following year, the Court extended the principle in the *Gideon* decision with **Escobedo v. Illinois,** which held that suspects have the right to have an attorney present during police interrogation. In writing his opinion, Justice Arthur Goldberg anticipated potential criticism from law enforcement.

> No system of criminal justice can, or should, survive if it comes to depend for its continued effectiveness on the citizens' abdication through unawareness of their constitutional rights. No system worth preserving should have to fear that, if an accused is permitted to consult with a lawyer, he will become aware of, and exercise,

these rights. If the exercise of constitutional rights will thwart the effectiveness of a system of law enforcement, then there is something very wrong with that system.[79]

The third ruling guaranteeing a suspect's right to counsel was made in 1966. The Court argued in *Miranda v. Arizona* that suspects held in custody could not be interrogated before they are warned of their rights to remain silent and to have an attorney present during questioning.[80]

The police strenuously objected to *Mapp v. Ohio*, *Escobedo v. Illinois*, and *Miranda v. Arizona*. The decisions limited police searches for evidence and police interrogations. Law enforcement took the position that these rulings would seriously compromise their battle against crime. Hollywood's fictional representations supported law enforcement's dissatisfaction with the system hamstringing their efforts. Police officers and detectives were portrayed as heroes having to battle evil while the system protected criminals. In *Dirty Harry* and its sequels, Clint Eastwood portrayed a San Francisco detective confronting savage, ruthless killers. In general, the films implied that the only way to protect innocent victims was to violate the constitutional rights of guilty suspects. The films were box-office hits.

In reality, the Supreme Court decisions in the 1960s did more to advance the professionalism of policing than the policies and practices introduced by law enforcement agencies themselves. Police were required to substantiate information and to be specific about what they were looking for when requesting a search warrant. Deceit and unconstitutional law enforcement practices of earlier years risked setting the suspect free.

Actuarial Policing

The Knapp Commission's investigation of police corruption in New York City found widespread abuses. The Commission's report issued in 1972 raised serious questions about the course charted by the police in the struggle for professional status. The public alarm over the corrupt state of policing offered an opportunity to reshape law enforcement.

Efforts coalesced on several fronts. First, external funding was necessary for education and specialized training. Second, police operations needed legitimacy through the support of scientific research. Third, departments would acquire the most technologically advanced equipment. Fourth, the public would need to accept this new direction. Concerns over corruption would need to be countered by convincing people that law enforcement would police itself. Police accountability would be the new emphasis.[81]

Concurrent with the new focal points was another development. Law enforcement officers felt they needed protection. "Police officers were angry and alienated over Supreme Court rulings, criticism by civil rights groups, poor salaries and benefits, and inept management practices."[82] Police unions became prevalent in the 1970s. They offered promises of higher pay and representation in disciplinary hearings.[83]

Police accountability is an interesting, multidimensional concept. A police officer who shoots and kills an unarmed person has to explain why. The police officer may face department charges, criminal charges, and civil charges. On the surface, this seems to meet the necessary criteria for police accountability. The problem is that juries and judges tend to give the testimony of police officers greater credibility than the testimony of the complainant. Thus, the police seem to have a built-in advantage in the courts.[84]

Another dimension of law enforcement accountability is fiscal accountability. Are taxpayer dollars for police services spent effectively? In most instances, the public seems willing to accept the "executive summaries" provided by management. This differs significantly from the management–stockholder arrangement common to the corporate world. Law enforcement has received gargantuan funding increases while demonstrating little, if any, *production gains*.

The benefits of high-tech equipment appear endless for police.[85] The polygraph machine, introduced in the 1930s, was one of the first "scientific" developments to attract law enforcement attention. Today, there are a myriad of technologically advanced pieces of equipment available to police: microwave surveillance equipment, Bradley military vehicles, armored personnel carries, helicopters equipped with night-vision technology, state-of-the-art wiretapping devices, radar, automatic weapons, the latest computers—the list goes on. It is sometimes hard to understand why law enforcement claims that it is outgunned by the "bad guys." Ironically, despite all this new technology, the percentage of crimes "cleared by an arrest" has gradually declined over the past forty years. The new technology has not improved the chances of catching criminals. Nor has it made citizens feel any safer from crime.

Summary

Policing is the use of state power to enforce the law and to maintain order. As we have seen, the law is shaped by those with the power and resources to pass legislation that favors their interests. Maintaining order is a subjective goal—who defines the order to be maintained? In general, the police maintain the status quo. The media aid the police in presenting an image of safeguarding the pubic. Wars on crime, drug, and gangs project the image of police as crime fighters, but the general goal and purpose of police has always been social control.

Since ancient times, authorities—whether emperors, kings, nobles, or politicians—have granted power to their representatives for the purpose of social control. As civilization moved away from agrarian society and population increased, people were no longer interested in policing themselves. As people moved from farms to the cities, the new mobility required new techniques of control.

We divided the evolution of policing into four historical periods: colonial, political, professional, and actuarial. Efforts to shape particular functions varied during the periods, often as a result of new technologies. The radio and telephone changed the nature of police work; foot patrol was replaced with the squad car and then later revisited. In all eras, the police borrowed from the military: uniforms, weapons, and tactics.

The history of policing has been plagued with episodes of graphic brutality, extensive corruption, and blatant disregard for the rights of citizens, often the result of the class consciousness that pervades police control efforts. As Lawrence Friedman writes, "A strain of suppression runs through the whole of our story. The sufferers—burnt witches, whipped and brutalized slaves, helpless drunks thrown into fetid county jails, victims of lynch mobs—cry out to us across the centuries."[86] These episodes have been interrupted by reform movements, political and judicial activism, and other attempts to control the image of police. Throughout the changes in functions and technologies, the primary goal and purpose of the police has remained social control.

Key Terms

- arrest-overkill
- August Vollmer
- Bow Street Runners
- constables
- constabulary system
- *Escobedo v. Illinois*
- *Gideon v. Wainwright*
- hue and cry
- hundreds
- J. Edgar Hoover
- justices of the peace
- *Mapp v. Ohio*
- Metropolitan Police Act
- *Miranda v. Arizona*
- mutual pledge system
- Orlando Winfield Wilson
- Pinkertons
- shires
- shire-reeve
- tythings
- tythingman
- vigiles

Notes

[1] This story was generated from the field notes of W. B. Brown taken during numerous "ride-alongs" throughout the Detroit Metropolitan region from 1992 to 1998.

[2] Michalowski, R. *Order, Law and Crime*. New York: Macmillan, 1985, p. 170.

[3] Fromm, E. *Escape from Freedom*. New York: Henry Holt, 1994.

[4] Numerous studies can be cited, but see especially Currie, E. *Crime and Punishment in America*. New York: Metropolitan Books, 1998; Greenberg, D. (ed.). *Crime and Capitalism* (rev. ed.). Philadelphia: Temple University Press, 1993; Chambliss, W. J. *Power, Politics and Crime*. Boulder, CO: Westview Press, 1999.

[5] Bagdikian, B. H. *The New Media Monopoly*. Boston: Beacon Press. 2004.

[6] Staples, W. G. *The Culture of Surveillance: Discipline and Social Control in the United States*. New York: St. Martin's Press, 1997. If the reader is interested in the extent of the decline of individual rights, go to www.supremecourtus.gov/ where you will find thousands of pages of recent U.S. Supreme Court decisions related to criminal justice topics that affect individual rights.

[7] Written by Joe Lewis, one of the first Kent State students shot by the National Guard in 1970. Joe Lewis has been very active in antiwar and antiviolence movements since he was shot twice by the Ohio National Guard in 1970.

[8] Healy, G. "There Goes the Neighborhood: The Bush Ashcroft Plan to 'Help' Localities Fight Gun Crime." [Online] http://www.cato.org/pubs/pas/pa440.pdf

[9] Perhaps our ancestors in seventeenth-century Boston anticipated such excess when they expressed their concern about police wearing police uniforms as that institution emerged in their city. See Friedman, L. M. *Crime and Punishment in American History*. New York: Basic Books, 1993.

[10] McCorkle, R. and T. Miethe. "The Political and Organizational Response to Gangs: An Examination of a Moral Panic." *Justice Quarterly* 15: 41–64 (March 1998); Brownstein, H. H. *The Rise and Fall of a Violent Crime Wave: Crack Cocaine and the Social Construction of a Crime Problem*. Guilderland, NY: Harrow and Heston, 1996, p. 22; Butterfield, F. "Possible Manipulation of Crime Data Worries Top Police." *New York Times*, August 3, 1998. [Online] http://select.nytimes.com/gst/abstract.html?res=F00C13F8345C0C708CDDA10894D0494D81

[11] "Detroit's Crime Totals Still a Mystery." *Detroit Free Press*, March 9, 2001. "Detroit Cops Accused of Wholesale Arrests For Every Homicide Investigated, 3 People Are Tossed Into Lockup." ID: 0103090407.

[12] Friedman, *Crime and Punishment in American History*.

[13] Zorn, E. "Favoritism for Cops Assaults the Public Trust." *Chicago Tribune*, March 29, 2007, sec. 2, p. 1; "Scandal Topples Windy City Top Cop." *U.S. News & World Report* 142(11): 22 (April 16, 2007).

[14] Some of the following is an updated version of Shelden, *Controlling the Dangerous Classes*, ch. 2.

[15] Parenti, C. *Lockdown America: Police and Prisons in the Age of Crisis*. New York: Verso, 1999; Cole, D. *No Equal Justice: Race and Class in the American Criminal Justice System*. New York: The New Press, 1999; Shelden, R. G. and W. B. Brown. "The Crime Control Industry and the Management of the Surplus Population." *Critical Criminology* 8 (Autumn 2000).

[16] Emsley, C. *Policing and Its Context: 1750–1870: Themes in Comparative History*. London: Macmillan, 1983; Emsley, C. *Crime and Society in England: 1750–1900*. Essex: Longman, 1990; Emsley, C. *The English Police: A Political and Social History* (2nd ed.). London: Longman, 1996.

[17] Chambliss, W. J. and R. Seidman. *Law, Order and Power* (2nd ed.). Reading, MA: Addison-Wesley, 1982, p. 34.

[18] Bacon, S. "The Early Development of American Municipal Police." Unpublished Ph.D. diss., Yale University, 1939.

[19] Reith, C. *The Blind Eye of History: A Study of the Origins of the Present Police Era*. Montclair, NJ: Patterson Smith, 1975 [1952], p. 179.

[20] Kelly, R. M. "Increasing Community Influence over the Police." In A. W. Cohn and E. C. Viano (eds.), *Police Community Relations*. Philadelphia: Lippincott, 1975, p. 9.

[21] Bayley, *Police for the Future*.

[22] Wolff, H. J. *Roman Law: An Historical Introduction*. Norman: University of Oklahoma Press, 1951.

[23] Reith, *The Blind Eye of History*, p. 26.

[24] Parks, E. L. "From Constabulary to Police Society: Implications for Social Control." In J. F. Galliher and J. L. McCartney (eds.), *Criminology: Power, Crime and Criminal Law*. Homewood, IL: Dorsey Press, 1977, p. 196.

[25] Reith, *The Blind Eye of History*, p. 210.

[26] [Online] http://www.oldbaileyonline.org/history/crime/policing.html

[27] [Online] http://www.litencyc.com/php/stopics.php?rec=true&UID=1403

[28] [Online] http://www.nationalarchives.gov.uk/pathways/blackhistory/rights/gordon.htm

[29] Lyman, "The Metropolitan Police Act of 1829"; Critchley, T. A. "The New Police in London, 1750–1830." Both in J. Skolnick and T. Gray (eds.), *Police in America*. Boston: Little, Brown, 1975; Emsley, *The English Police*; Emsley, *Gendarmes and the State in Nineteenth-Century Europe*. Oxford: Oxford University Press, 1929.

[30] [Online] http://en.wikipedia.org/wiki/Gordon_Riots

[31] Shelden, R. G. *Criminal Justice in America: A Sociological Approach*. Boston: Little Brown, 1982, pp. 91–92.

[32] Lyman, "The Metropolitan Police Act of 1829," pp. 21–28; Emsley, *The English Police*.

[33] Richardson, J. F. *Urban Police in the United States*. Port Washington, NY: Kennikat Press, 1974, p. 11.

[34] David Bordura and Albert Reiss, quoted in Parks, "From Constabulary to Police Society," p. 199.

[35] Lyman, "The Metropolitan Police Act of 1829," pp. 33–36.

[36] Emsley, *Gendarmes and the State in Nineteenth-Century Europe.*

[37] Silver, A. "The Demand for Order in Civil Society." In D. Bordura (ed.), *The Police: Six Sociological Essays.* New York: Wiley, 1967, pp. 11–12.

[38] Chomsky, N. *Keeping the Rabble in Line.* Monroe, ME: Common Courage Press, 1994.

[39] Recent research has documented the fact that the vast majority of those incarcerated in prisons and jails today were convicted of relatively minor offenses. This is not surprising, for the majority of those arrested are charged with minor offenses, including disturbing the peace and similar public-order crimes. See, for instance, Austin, J. and J. Irwin. *It's about Time: America's Incarceration Binge* (3rd ed.). Belmont, CA: Wadsworth, 2001; and Irwin, J. *The Jail: Managing the Underclass in American Society.* Berkeley: University of California Press, 1985.

[40] Ignatieff, M. *A Just Measure of Pain.* New York: Pantheon, 1978, p. 179.

[41] Ibid., p. 185.

[42] Emsley, *The English Police;* Emsley, *Gendarmes and the State in Nineteenth-Century Europe.*

[43] Richardson, *Urban Police in the United States,* p. 14.

[44] Roberg, R. R. and J. Kuykendall. *Police and Society.* Belmont, CA: Wadsworth, 1993.

[45] Friedman, *Crime and Punishment in American History.*

[46] Berg, *Law Enforcement.*

[47] Friedman, *Crime and Punishment in American History.*

[48] Michalowski, *Order, Law and Crime;* Friedman, *Crime and Punishment in American History.*

[49] Berg, *Law Enforcement.*

[50] Ibid.

[51] Parks, "From Constabulary to Police Society"; Center for Research on Criminal Justice. *The Iron Fist and the Velvet Glove* (2nd ed.). Berkeley: Center for Research on Criminal Justice, 1977.

[52] Costello, A. E. *Our Police Protectors: A History of New York Police.* Montclair, NJ: Patterson Smith, 1972 [1885].

[53] Richardson, *Urban Police in the United States.*

[54] Richardson, J. F. "The Early Years of the New York Police Department." In J. Skolnick and T. Gray (eds.), *Police in America.* Boston: Little, Brown, 1975, p. 16.

[55] Lane, R. *Policing the City: Boston, 1822–1885.* Cambridge, MA: Harvard University Press, 1967, pp. 24–25.

[56] Harring, S. and L. McMullen. "The Buffalo Police: Labor Unrest, Political Power and the Creation of the Police Institution." *Crime and Social Justice* 4: 5–14 (1975); Harring, S. "The 'Most Orderly City in America': Class Conflict and the Development of the Police Institution in Milwaukee, 1880–1914." Paper presented at the annual meeting of the American Sociological Association, September 1978.

[57] Ferdinand, T. N. "The Criminal Patterns of Boston Since 1849." *American Journal of Sociology* 73: 84–99 (1967).

[58] Ibid.

[59] Berg, *Law Enforcement.*

[60] Zinn, H. *A People's History of the United States* (20th Anniversary Edition). New York: Harper Collins, 1999.

[61] Berg, *Law Enforcement.*

[62] Walker, S. *Popular Justice: A History of American Criminal Justice* (2nd ed.). New York: Oxford University Press, 1997.

[63] Walker, S. *The Police in America.* (3rd ed.). New York: McGraw-Hill, 1999.

[64] Fogelson, R. *Big City Police.* Cambridge, MA: Harvard University Press, 1977.

[65] President's Commission on Law Enforcement and Administration of Justice. *Task Force Report: The Police.* Washington, DC: Government Printing Office, 1967.

[66] Wilson, O. W. *Police Administration.* New York: McGraw-Hill, 1950.

[67] President's Commission, *Task Force Report: The Police.*

[68] Gentry, C. *J. Edgar Hoover: The Man and the Secrets.* New York: Norton, 1991. Also see Powers, R. G. *Secrecy and Power: The Life of J. Edgar Hoover.* New York: Free Press, 1987.

[69] Hoover memorandum dated June 24, 1936, which initiated the FBI file of Clarence Seward Darrow. Released via Freedom of Information Act.

[70] Keen, M. F. *Stalking the Sociological Imagination: J. Edgar Hoover's FBI Surveillance of American Sociology.* Westport, CT: Greenwood Press, 1999; Gentry, *J. Edgar Hoover;* Powers, *Secrecy and Power.*

[71] Chambliss, W. J. *Power, Politics, and Crime.* Boulder, CO: Westview.

[72] Zinn, *A People's History of the United States.*

[73] Newton, H. P. *To Die for the People.* New York: Writers and Readers, 1999 [1973], p. 200; Zinn, *A People's History of the United States;* Wilkins, R. and R. Clark. *Search and Destroy: A Report by the Commission of Inquiry into the Black Panthers and the Police.* New York: Metropolitan Applied Research Center, 1973; Kennebeck, E. *Juror Number Four: The Trial of Thirteen Panthers as Seen from the Jury Box.* New York: Norton, 1973.

[74] Powers, *Secrecy and Power;* Theoharis, A. *From the Secret Files of J. Edgar Hoover.* Chicago: Ivan R. Dee,

1991; Newton, *To Die for the People*; Newton, H. P. *War against the Panthers: A Study of Repression in America*. New York: Harlem River Press, 1996.

[75] [Online] http://www.fbi.gov/quickfacts.htm

[76] Walker, Samuel. *Records of the Committee on Official Lawlessness*. [Online] http://www.lexisnexis.com/academic/guides/jurisprudence/wickersham.asp

[77] Supreme Court of the United States, 1961. 367 U.S. 643, 81 S.Ct. 1684, 6 L.Ed.2d 1081.

[78] Supreme Court of the United States, 1963. 372 U.S. 335, 344, S.Ct. 792, 796 9 L.Ed.2d 799, 805.

[79] Supreme Court of the United States, 1964. 378 U.S. 478, 84 S.Ct. 1758, 12 L.Ed.2d 977; [Online] http://www.law.cornell.edu/supct/html/historics/USSC_CR_0378_0478_ZO.html

[80] Supreme Court of the United States, 1966. 384 U.S. 436, 86 S.Ct. 1602, 16 L.Ed.2d 694.

[81] Fanon, F. *The Wretched of the Earth*. New York: Grove Press, 1963; Robertson, G. *Crimes against Humanity: The Struggle for Global Justice*. New York: New Press, 2000.

[82] Walker, *The Police in America*.

[83] Juris, H. A. and P. Feuille. *Police Unions*. Lexington, MA: Lexington Books, 1973.

[84] Barker, T. and D. L. Carter. *Police Deviance*. Cincinnati: Anderson, 1991.

[85] Shelden and Brown, "The Crime Control Industry and the Management of the Surplus Population."

[86] Friedman, *Crime and Punishment in American History*, p. 462.

six

American Law Enforcement in the Twenty-First Century

Two city police officers repeatedly punched a 64-year-old man accused of public intoxication and a third officer hit a television news producer. . . . The three officers were arrested Sunday after questioning and charged with battery. . . . They were released and ordered to appear in court at a later date.[1]

A federal appeals court ruled Friday that the Los Angeles Police Department cannot arrest people for sitting, lying or sleeping on public sidewalks on skid row, saying such enforcement amounts to cruel and unusual punishment because there are not enough shelter beds for the city's huge homeless population. The long-awaited decision effectively kills Los Angeles Police Chief William J. Bratton's original blueprint for cleaning up skid row by removing homeless encampments that rise each evening throughout the 50-block downtown district . . . the ruling also has implications for police agencies around the nation that have grappled with how to deal with the homeless. Other communities have tried milder variations of the same approach. Las Vegas and Portland, Oregon . . . bar sleeping or standing on a sidewalk or other public space only if it obstructs pedestrians or cars, and Seattle, Tucson, and Houston limit the hours of enforcement.[2]

The Chronicle *began an investigation of how often San Francisco police use force . . . by doing what the police department itself has never done. It obtained through public records requests the department's handwritten use-of-force logs from 1996–2004 and created a computerized database that makes it possible to determine which officers reported using force and how often. That data showed the city has a core group of violent-prone officers—fewer than 100 in a force of 2,200. . . . The department recognizes that frequent use of force can be an indication of a dangerous officer, yet it has failed to address the problem presented by this group of officers. As a result: (1) Officers with questionable records are promoted to supervisory positions or assigned to train rookies, putting them into a position to carry forward a culture that tolerates or rewards the use of force. (2) In the years 2001–2004, San Francisco officers were the subject of more force allegations than officers in San Jose, Oakland, San Diego, and Seattle combined. (3) Taxpayers are exposed to high legal costs in defending lawsuits against officers involving force. From 1996–2005 the city paid more than $5 million in judgments and legal settlements. For that sum, it could have put 60 new officers on the streets this year.*[3]

The excerpts above provide a brief glimpse into a few topical issues relevant to law enforcement in the twenty-first century. Stories appear in newspapers and television news reports about police beating a suspect, harassing homeless people, killing a mentally ill suspect in Portland, Oregon, or killing a groom leaving a bachelor party in New York City, corruption on a large scale such as the Rampart Division "episodes" in Los Angeles, or abusing prostitutes, gays and lesbians, and people of color. We are not suggesting that these incidents define law enforcement in the United States, but we are noting that they are a part of the panorama that comprises the institution of policing in the twenty-first century.

Our goal in this chapter is to encourage an enriched inquiry into the politics and methodologies pertinent to policing in the

United States. As you read the various examples, reflect on whether Americans will continue to relinquish Constitutional rights (privacy, search and seizure protection under the Fourth Amendment, etc.). Under what circumstances, if any, will the public accept more intrusive oversight (e.g., civil forfeiture of property without due process, telephone and e-mail surveillance practices, etc.). Will the trend for police to become more militaristic (e.g., SWAT units dressed in G.I. Joe costumes) continue? In the aftermath of the tragedy in New York City on September 11, 2001, the need for answers to these questions is crucial.

There is a tendency to mythologize policing in America. The most popular myth about policing is that it is an institution composed of crime-fighters.[4] Research reveals that many police officers perpetuate this myth. They believe that crime fighting is what they do, and many select policing as an occupation because of a desire to become crime-fighters.[5] This myth encompasses the belief that police spend most of their time enforcing criminal law and waging war against various types of crime (the drug war, the war against gangs, etc.). This perception of policing is a myth. Police spend about one-third of their time enforcing criminal laws. Most police officers never fire a weapon in the line of duty, and few officers make more than an occasional felony arrest.[6]

Another prevailing myth is that police protect and serve the public. While certain segments of the public benefit from police presence, other segments receive relatively few services, even less protection, and often find themselves the targets of police activities. This is particularly the case in inner-city neighborhoods that fall in the lower socioeconomic ranks. In these neighborhoods, the police tend to be viewed as occupational forces.[7]

During the 1990s, New York City police embraced the **broken windows theory**.[8] According to this theory, broken or boarded-up windows suggest that residents do not care about their neighborhood and the neglect is a signal to criminals that no one is vigilant about protecting their property. Law-abiding people move away. In time, the entire neighborhood becomes a slum; the petty theft escalates to major crimes. The theory suggests that police need to intervene at the earliest stages of the deterioration process to ensure the safety of residents.

The problem is there is no empirical support for the theory.[9] Moreover, there is no explanation for why such neighborhoods begin to deteriorate in the first place.

In Los Angeles, the order of the day in the 1980s was police sweeps of alleged gang members. During Operation Hammer in 1988 more than fourteen hundred youths were rounded up; over 90% were released without charges. Although there were few arrests, the police used the sweep to initiate records on inner-city youths in South Central Los Angeles.[10]

PROMOTING FEAR AND SELLING THE ILLUSION OF PROTECTION

Scholars have argued that economic power facilitates control in capitalist societies.[11] Much of their research shows that an effective means of maintaining power there is retaining influence over the institutions that control information.[12] For example, the state subsidizes the companies that distribute information. They grant major broadcasting corporations the rights to the airwaves, often without charge.[13] The state also provides a substantial amount of information to media outlets.[14]

Richard Miller points out that President Richard Nixon met with almost fifty television producers to convince them to promote his version of the drug war. Several were production representatives of *Dragnet, Hawaii Five-O, Storefront Lawyers, I Spy, Felony Squad, The FBI, Mod Squad, Marcus Welby, M.D.*, and other television shows. Jack Webb, producer of *Dragnet,* obliged by dramatizing federal drug squads.[15] When the president of the United States turns to Hollywood to promote a political agenda, the state clearly wields influence in the *construction* of information delivered through mass media.

Media Accommodation

Many police departments go out of their way to accommodate journalists, and some major media outlets have facilities inside police headquarters.[16] Crime stories are easy stories. Typically, reporters only have to pay proper homage to local law enforcement, and the whole idea of investigative journalism becomes obsolete. A reporter only needs to practice proper etiquette: Get the information from a police contact person, or in certain cases from the police information officer, and make law enforcement look good. A crime reporter who practices good *support-the-police* etiquette need never worry about missing deadlines.

In most instances, law enforcement reaps benefits from the mass media. There have been numerous television programs from *Dragnet* to *Mod Squad* to *Kojak* to *Cagney and Lacey* to *Hill Street Blues* to *Miami Vice* to *NYPD Blue* to *Law & Order* to *CSI* that capture the attention of audiences across the country. Portraying police as the thin blue line standing between the public and hardened criminals is a much-peddled media fantasy. The excerpt below, written by a senior executive of the *New York Times*, expresses his views in support of the drug war. It illustrates both the media support of government policies and the question of what the public will accept under what circumstances.

> Inevitably, the time will come when the people of the country will no longer stand for it. They will seek the solution in death penalties and martial force. They will stop caring how many prisoners are crowded into a cell or how they are treated, just as long as they are off the streets. They will support judges, legislators, and politicians who understand their sense of hopelessness against drugs and who will support repression as a national policy. Repression will satisfy a totally understandable and justifiable public sense of fury and frustration.[17]

From most accounts, it appears that the writer was correct. People are afraid. They might not acknowledge being willing to succumb to the type of repression described above, but they might assume that since they are law-abiding citizens they won't be sacrificing their own freedoms. They might not make the connection to essentially a police state. Public perceptions of U.S. law enforcement may explain, at least in part, the unwillingness to recognize warning signs of an emerging police state.

Public Opinion

A considerable amount of literature addresses the tendency of police officers to believe that they do not receive proper respect from citizens. Returning to the media, there are occasional stories about police misconduct, but the preponderance of portrayals is positive. There is no hard evidence to support the idea that the public does not give policing substantial respect. To the contrary, data show that police officers have been held in high esteem for decades by those whom the police subculture refers to as *civilians who do not understand us.* Gallup polls between 1983 and 2006 show that police officers have been highly ranked by respondents in honesty and ethical standards (see table 6.1). The policing profession gained even more esteem after the terrorist strikes on September 11, 2001. A Gallup poll taken two months after the tragic event rated policing as the fourth most respected occupation for honesty and ethics (see table 6.2). Although the ranking dropped to ninth in 2006 police officers remained in the top 10 rated occupations (see table 6.3).

Respondents in 2001 indicated that they believed police officers were more honest and had higher ethical standards than doctors, dentists, and clergy. This is a lofty position for members of an occupation with the violent history described in chapter 5.

It is important to note that the rankings vary depending on individual characteristics. Race and age influence views of police honesty and ethical standards. Among whites in 2005 (the Department of Justice fails to indicate whether this category also includes Hispanics) there is a strong tendency to rank police officers high in the area of honesty and ethical standards (52%); blacks are more reluctant to offer a high rating (33%). Younger respondents (18–29

Table 6.1   Gallup Poll Results of Selected Occupation Ratings of Very High/High for Honesty and Ethical Standards by Respondents (selected years between 1977 and 2006)

	1983 (%)	1988 (%)	1993 (%)	1998 (%)	2000 %	2006 (%)
Druggists/pharmacists	61	66	65	64	67	73
Medical doctors	52	53	51	57	63	69
Clergy	64	60	53	59	60	58
College teachers	47	54	52	53	59	58
Dentists	51	51	50	53	58	62
Engineers	45	48	49	50	56	61
Policemen	41	47	50	49	55	54
Bankers	38	26	28	30	37	37

Source: Gallup Poll [Online]. http://www.gallup.com/poll/releases/pr001127asp [January 21, 2002].

Table 6.2   Top 10 Rated Occupations Rated Very High/High for Honesty and Ethics by Respondents, November 26–27, 2001

1. Firefighters	90%	6. Medical doctors	66%
2. Nurses	84%	7. Clergy	64%
3. U.S. military	81%	8. Engineers	60%
4. Policemen	68%	9. College Teachers	58%
5. Pharmacists	68%	10. Dentists	56%

Source: Gallup Poll [Online]. http://www.gallup.com/poll/releases/pr001127asp [January 21, 2002].

Table 6.3   Top 10 Rated Occupations Rated Very High/High for Honesty and Ethics by Respondents, December 14, 2006

1. Nurses	84%	6. Engineers	61%
2. Pharmacists	73%	7. College Teachers	58%
3. Veterinarians	71%	8. Clergy	58%
4. Medical Doctors	69%	9. Policemen	54%
5. Dentists	62%	10. Psychiatrists	38%

Source: Gallup Poll [Online]. http://www.galluppoll.com/content/default.aspx?ci=25888 January 6, 2007].

years of age) tend to rate police honesty and ethics somewhat lower than older respondents do.[18] There are also variations over time regarding the level of respect people have for police in their own area. In 1965, 70% of respondents indicated they had a great deal of respect for police. By 1991, that percentage had declined to 60% and remained at that level in 2000.[19] While the Gallup polls do not provide evidence that police are not supported by the public there is also enough variation to allow room for varying opinions—an important facet of almost any statistical question.

AMERICAN POLICING: THE FIFTH ARMED FORCE?

Over the years, law enforcement in the United States could be characterized as a quasi-military, multidimensional organization structured in such a way that each dimension is often an independent entity under the authority of an assigned or claimed jurisdiction.[20] In the twenty-first century, it has emerged as the *fifth armed force* (after the Army, Navy, Marines, Air Force, and Coast Guard) of the United States. Militarization of criminal justice and crime control has accelerated since 1981. The acceleration has included crossing international boundaries. For many years, U.S. law enforcement agents have crossed international boundaries to expand the war against drugs (DEA activity in Bolivia, Colombia, Panama, etc.).[21] More recently, many argue that the war against terrorism requires deployment of domestic law enforcers abroad (e.g., FBI in Afghanistan). Although it is quite likely that some of these incursions across sovereign international boundaries are violations of international law,[22] it is unlikely that the governments of these countries will protest loudly. The United States remains in firm control of institutions such as the International Monetary Fund (IMF), the World Bank (WB), and the World Trade Organization (WTO).[23] Protests by the governments of violated countries would result in one or more of these institutions exerting pressure to silence the objection.[24]

Nearly all law enforcement agencies in the United States have embraced and adopted, to varying degrees, characteristics that are common to the military. These characteristics include, but are by no means limited to, clothing/uniforms, divisions of labor based on job classifications and personnel location within a hierarchy of command, the authorization and use of high-tech equipment, operations/strategies, and the distribution and differentiation of policing areas/jurisdictions. *Jurisdiction* in law enforcement is similar to the military's *areas of operation* or *theaters of operation* (sectors, zones, regions, continents, etc.).

Law enforcement employees wear uniforms that highlight distinctions among the various police organizations (e.g., state police, sheriff's deputies, and city police), just as the U.S. military distinguishes individual branches with uniforms (e.g., Air Force, Army, Navy, Marines, and Coast Guard). In addition, uniforms and insignia identify unique units within individual law enforcement agencies (e.g., SWAT and typical patrol officers) in the same way that they identify individual units within a particular branch of the military service (e.g., U.S. Army Rangers, Special Forces; U.S. Navy SEALS; U.S. Marines Recon). Distinctive uniforms for individual units authorized by the various branches of the U.S. military often amplify the special nature of those units and promote esprit de corps. Many law enforcement organizations use military-style ranks (captain, lieutenant, sergeant, etc.) and insignia (stripes, bars, oak leaves, stars, etc.) to differentiate their hierarchal command structures. American law enforcement deploys the same assault weaponry found in the U.S. military arsenal (AR-15 assault rifles, helicopters, armored personnel carriers, etc.). These weapons are now mainstays of both military and police operations.[25]

JURISDICTIONAL CONSIDERATIONS

Many argue that U.S. policing is a complex, fragmented assortment of agencies without central control.[26] This is not particularly true in the twenty-first century. There is a hierarchy of jurisdictional control or responsibility. We argue that there is more centralized control of policing than meets the eye. Our position on this issue stems from jurisdictional responsibility, authority, and autonomy.

Law enforcement agencies are subject to specific jurisdictions.[27] The term *jurisdiction* refers to a legal or judicial area or boundary of authority (e.g., townships, cities, counties, states, nations, and territories).[28] The concept *jurisdiction* also has political and funding implications. Funding for the drug war depends on intelligence reports pertaining to the illegal drug trade, interdiction performances of one agency or another, and so on. These reports are often matters of jurisdictional control (federal jurisdictional control/authority, state or local jurisdictional control/authority, etc.). Substantial evidence supports the contention that each dimension of law enforcement may complement or compete with other dimensions.[29] The competition is often linked to funding and jurisdictional "rewards" given to those who successfully complete the specified task (e.g., federal funding for youth gang interdiction).[30]

Although local law enforcement agencies (municipal police, township police, etc.) are usually confined to their respective jurisdictions, there are times and situations in which they enter the jurisdiction of another agency. One such encroachment might occur in urgent situations (e.g., a high-speed chase involving an armed robbery suspect), or by invitation from an agency with jurisdictional control (e.g., to assist in an emergency). When these jurisdictional crossings occur, they are usually based on a formally agreed-upon arrangement. Law enforcement procedures or methods generally fall under the rules set forth by the jurisdiction's controlling agency. Returning to the high-speed chase example, some jurisdictions place significant limitations on high-speed chases by law enforcement because of the potential danger to innocent citizens. Other jurisdictions have fewer restrictions. If a patrol car from one jurisdiction chases a suspect across a jurisdictional boundary, the officers in the chase car must comply with high-speed chase rules of the jurisdictional area they entered.

Each agency sets and controls its standard operating procedures. This example supports the fragmented, decentralized structure characterization of American law enforcement. The local jurisdiction's high-speed chase procedures may not apply to a state police officer engaged in a high-speed chase. The state police officer may choose not to follow the local jurisdiction's procedures. The fact that the state police can choose to follow or disregard local procedures supports the idea that a hierarchy of law enforcement exists and that police power is indeed more centralized.

One perceptual advantage of promoting the decentralized perspective is that it allows agencies to distance themselves from responsibility if a lower agency violates citizens' rights, harbors discriminatory practices, engages in acts of brutality or corruption, and so on. For example, most state police agencies have the power, often under the authority of the governor, to intervene in the affairs of local law enforcement. If local law enforcement gets "caught," state agencies back away and claim no knowledge or no responsibility. There are specific examples of the federal government prescribing local policies. The 1994 Violent Crime Control and Law Enforcement Act authorizes the U.S. Justice Department to investigate local law enforcement agencies and to take control of agencies that abuse their authority; the U.S. Justice Department becomes the central authority. For example, the Justice Department launched an investigation of the Detroit Police Department in 2000. The investigation focused on the use of force, arrest and witness detention, and conditions of confinement. On June 12, 2003, the Justice Department filed consent decrees in the U.S. District Court that require the Detroit Police Department to:

- implement revisions to the use of force policy and training, with an emphasis on de-escalation techniques;
- require written supervisory review of arrests for probable cause, as well as prohibit the detention or conveyance of an individual without reasonable suspicion, probable cause or consent from the individual;
- analyze trends in uses of force, searches, seizures, and other law enforcement activities that create a risk of officer misconduct;
- improve the procedures for investigating allegations of misconduct and for completing investigations in a thorough, fair, and timely manner;
- develop a comprehensive medical and mental health screening program approved by qualified medical and mental health professionals; and
- implement a comprehensive fire detection, suppression and evacuation program in consultation with the Detroit Fire Department.[31]

LAW ENFORCEMENT: STRUCTURE, COMPOSITION, AND PERSONNEL

What do we know about the structure and organization of U.S. law enforcement?

We have chosen several vantage points: (1) jurisdiction—the geographic area of operation; (2) composition—configuration of internal components; and (3) personnel—demographic characteristics such as race, sex, educational training.

Imagine driving south on Interstate 75 near Detroit, Michigan (or on any other freeway near an urban setting in America). You are likely to witness or experience one or more of the following scenes: A state police vehicle, lights flashing, is parked behind a vehicle, and an officer is standing beside the driver's side of the stopped vehicle. One mile farther south on the side of the road, a Troy police vehicle is parked, and an officer is aiming a speed-detecting device toward oncoming traffic. A couple miles farther south, a Detroit police officer is peering into the window of an apparently abandoned vehicle. One-half mile farther south, a Wayne County deputy sheriff is handing a speeding ticket to a disgruntled motorist. If you follow Interstate 94 north through Chicago, you are likely to see similar scenes orchestrated by the Illinois State Police, Chicago police, Lynwood police, South Holland police, Dolton police, Lincolnwood police, Skokie police, Morton Grove police, Glencoe police, Highland Park police, Northbrook police, and a host of other law enforcement agencies. Each of these agencies is operating in its own jurisdiction. Assuming that each agency is handing out tickets to motorists, you can safely say that each is making money for its respective government body. You might consider that each police agency is, in and of itself, unique.

Interestingly, it is very difficult today to find consistent data to compare the number of police officers within various law enforcement agencies from one year to the next. We are not certain if government agencies such as the Bureau of Justice Statistics do not have access to such data or if agencies elect to be less than transparent regarding the number of law enforcement officers. In 2006, the United States had more than 683,000 sworn law enforcement officers working in more than 14,300 agencies. In addition, more than 303,700 civilian employees worked for law enforcement agencies.[32] The distinction between sworn officers and other police employees is that only sworn officers are authorized to carry firearms and make arrests. From 1987 (the first year agency-specific data was collected for the Law Enforcement Management and Administrative Statistics [LEMAS] survey) to 2003 local police employment increased by approximately 135,000 (27%), including an increase of 96,400 (30%) full-time sworn officers. In 2003, New York City had 35,973 full-time officers and was the largest police department in the United States. The second largest department was Chicago, with 13,469 officers.[33] In 1993, 69,000 federal officers were authorized to carry firearms and make arrests; in 2003, the number was approximately 105,000—an increase of 52%.[34] The number of police officers in the United States increased dramatically.[35]

We can look at the structure of law enforcement from the context of levels of government authority or jurisdiction. There are five levels of government-authorized law enforcement agencies: (1) townships and special districts; (2) municipal or metropolitan police; (3) county law enforcement; (4) state police; and (5) federal police. The demographic characteristics of law enforcement personnel, the operations and strategies employed by various levels of law enforcement, and the politics associated with law enforcement become more obscure as one moves up the hierarchical scale. In other words, there appears to be a great deal of information available to the public about law enforcement at local levels of jurisdiction (city police, sheriff's departments, etc.). This may be attributed to visibility and the fact that many local law enforcement personnel are drawn from local labor pools. For example, it is certainly not uncommon for deputy sheriffs to have attended schools in the jurisdictions they now police. Conversely, state and federal law enforcement officials are more likely to be transplants into the communities they police.

It is common to find more than one agency competing with another agency over the same turf, or jurisdiction, or embroiled in disputes over the same crime or offense. Specialized police often add to the confusion. Washington, DC, offers the premier example of a city with numerous types of police officers. While the average number of federal officers per 100,000 residents in the United States is 36, the number in the District of Columbia is 1,662. In addition to the almost 3,800 sworn officers in the DC police department, there are almost 1,600 uniformed Secret Service officers, more than 1,500 U.S. Capitol police officers, 1,500 FBI agents, almost 600 Immigration and Customs Enforcement (ICE) officers, 416 National Park Service Personnel, more than 200 Marshals Service Officers, 150 agents from the Bureau of Alcohol, Tobacco, Firearms and Explosives (ATF), 125 Supreme Court officers, over 100 Library of Congress police officers, more than 100 U.S. Postal Service inspectors, 100 IRS agents, more than 370 Metro Transit police officers, and 23 National Zoological Park Officers.[36] Imagine what a criminal investigation of a murder at the National Zoo might look like, particularly if the perpetrator escaped through the Smithsonian Institution and continued his escape using the subway and tried to hide behind some bushes near the White House. Who would have control over the investigation?

Jurisdiction has an interesting history in the five surveys of local police departments published by the Bureau of Justice Statistics and illustrates our earlier comment about attempts to compare statistics from various years. The report on local police departments in 1993 described "special police agencies" as those with limited jurisdictions such as parks, transit systems, airports, or schools. A table in the report said there were approximately 41,670 full-time sworn officers in 1,600 agencies. The next report contained 1997 data; the agencies decreased to about 1,300 and the officers increased slightly to 44,500. The category disappeared from table 1 in the 1999 data. It reappeared in 2000 as "special jurisdiction," listing almost 1,376 agencies with 43,413 sworn officers. In 2003, the category was missing again.[37]

Jurisdiction is an issue in policing that should receive more attention from researchers. The question of who has authority in a particular district is very complicated. Even media portrayals underline the difficulty of jurisdiction. Jack McCoy, the assistant district attorney on *Law & Order,* has battled the FBI, the military, and other federal agencies for jurisdiction and information. While a television program is a fictional example, the problem of sharing information and determining who has the authority to investigate and prosecute is a real problem. In a study of Clark County, Nevada, researchers found evidence that even local agencies (prosecution, law enforcement, etc.) had difficulty sharing information within a single jurisdiction.[38]

Local Law Enforcement

We include townships and special district police, municipal or metropolitan police, and county law enforcement in the category of *local law enforcement.* Each of these groups has shared tax bases and their jurisdictions overlap. For example, municipal or metropolitan police agencies and township police are located in counties that also have a sheriff's department. Ideally, these entities would collaborate to provide collective services, eliminating duplicated resources. Sheriff's offices could provide detainment facilities, allowing other local agencies to focus their resources on patrol. In reality, local agencies compete for scarce community resources, and there is not always a friendly relationship among them. The sheriff wants a new jail furnished with the most technologically advanced surveillance equipment and also wants a very expensive oak desk for his or her office. The chief of police wants new patrol cars and new uniforms for his or her officers. Taxpayers, however, have limited resources, so agencies compete with one another for resources.

Local Police Departments

Local police departments include township and special district police, constables, and municipal or metropolitan police departments. Some areas have local marshals who serve as bailiffs and perform other court duties such as serving subpoenas and writs and transporting prisoners to and from court. Local marshals are appointed or elected. These agencies can be viewed as local police department agencies because they operate in restricted jurisdictions and are under the control of some form of local government (mayor, township supervisors, city council, etc.). As of June 2003, 12,656 local police departments employed 580,749 full-time employees, including 451,737 sworn personnel. Slightly more than 3,000 sheriffs' offices employed 330,274 full-time employees, which includes 174,251 sworn personnel.[39] In addition, there are more than 75,165 part-time employees in local law enforcement, including 35,112 sworn officers. State and local law enforcement agencies employed 993,442 full- and part-time civilian employees. Fifty local police departments employed 1,000 or more officers. These large departments account for more than one-third of all local police officers.[40] The total operating budget of local police departments in the United States in 2003 was approximately $43.3 billion, on average, about $200 per resident. The average cost of a sworn officer was an estimated $93,300.[41] Local policing costs have increased significantly. In 1980, local law enforcement cost taxpayers almost $11.4 billion; by 19992 the expenditure reached 29.6 billion; in 2004 the total was increased to $60.3 billion.[42]

There are nearly 19,000 townships across the United States. Most of these townships, particularly those in rural areas, offer limited police services. Townships that border large metropolitan areas typically offer a broader range of policing services. Small communities often run into problems as they enter the law enforcement arena. Generally, funding shortages create hardships, and coordination is problematic. Many townships have only one officer, who is on call twenty-four hours a day. In 2003, 561 departments employed only one officer.[43]

Municipal or metropolitan police agencies range in size from organizations having fewer than ten officers and providing limited services to organizations having thousands of officers and offering a wide range of services. Small municipal agencies often have problems finding resources to provide emergency-oriented services. In many instances, the qualifications of officers in small municipal agencies are lacking compared to their counterparts in larger metropolitan police agencies. Some small municipal officers have no academy training, and the supervision in these small communities is questionable. In contrast, many metropolitan police agencies have large pools of applicants from which they can select candidates, and many have their own training academies. Because many large urban police departments serve diverse populations, they provide a wide range of policing services. Large urban police agencies also confront a wider range and amount of criminal behavior. Six of the largest police departments (New York, Chicago, Los Angeles, Philadelphia, Houston, and Detroit) serve approximately 6.4% of the U.S. population, but 13% of all reported violent crimes occur in these cities.[44]

Local Police Departments and Women

Eleven percent of all sworn local law enforcement officers are women. Local law enforcement agencies that serve larger populations tend to hire a larger proportion of women officers. In 2003, women accounted for 17.3% of all sworn officers in local law enforcement agencies serving populations of a million or more. In local law enforcement agencies serving populations between 10,000 and 24,999, women accounted for 6.7% of sworn officers. In agencies serving fewer than 2,500 citizens, only 5.7% of the officers were women.[45] Women account for more than 50% of the general population; the number of women in local law enforcement is a much smaller percentage. The 1972 Equal Employment Opportunity Act, which extended coverage of Title VII of the 1964 Civil Rights Act to include state and local governments, applies to local law enforcement agencies. There should be concern that agencies given the responsibility to enforce laws seem to violate, or at least circumvent, federal employment laws. We will return to gender discrimination later in the chapter.

Race and Ethnicity in
Local Police Departments

The racial/ethnic composition of local law enforcement agencies varies depending on the size of the agency. Larger police departments have more minority sworn-officers than smaller departments. Almost 39% of sworn officers in departments that serve populations of a million are minorities. Departments that serve populations of less than 10,000 average about 10%. African American and Hispanic sworn officers in local agencies represent 11.7% and 9.1%, respectively, of the total sworn-officer population. In departments that serve fewer than 50,000 citizens, the average percentage of African American and Hispanic officers is about 9.[46]

Educational Requirements
and Local Police Departments

The education requirements for new recruits in local law enforcement vary with the size of the agency, although the variations are minimal. In 2003, 82% of local law enforcement agencies serving less than 25,000 citizens required high school diplomas, compared with 72% of the agencies that served populations of half a million or more citizens. Only 1% of local law enforcement agencies serving a million or more citizens require a college degree, while 5% of agencies in the next category (500,000–999,999 population served) require a 4-year degree.[47] Some critics argue that requiring college degrees limits the pool of applicants and discriminates against minorities who have been victims of inferior schooling.[48] We find such an argument quite weak; the better solution is to strengthen the education system to end the disadvantage.

Local Police Department Training

Local law enforcement agencies often establish their own training requirements, sometimes based on state guidelines. Nearly all large metropolitan police departments (population greater than 250,000) operate their own training academies; 45% of all officers were employed by departments that had their own academies.[49] Smaller agencies rely on state-operated academies.[50] Police training consists of classroom and field instruction. Smaller police departments generally require the fewest hours of combined classroom and field training for recruits. For example, local law enforcement agencies serving fewer than 10,000 citizens required less than 950 hours of training, compared with 1,350 hours in jurisdictions with 50,000–100,000 residents, and 1500 hours for the largest departments (over 500,000).[51] The police academy serves a number of functions. It provides formal training for recruits. Today, this training is likely to include fundamental aspects of law enforcement along with other skills that introduce the recruit to areas such as domestic violence, ethics, and constitutional law. In addition, the academy socializes the recruit into the police subculture. We discuss the subculture of law enforcement in chapter 7.

County Law Enforcement

The county sheriff personifies *county law enforcement*. There are a minimal number of county police departments, but they compose less than 1% of county law enforcement. Many state constitutions designate the sheriff as the chief law enforcement official of the counties under their jurisdiction. Except in counties in Rhode Island and Hawaii, the chief officer is an *elected* sheriff.

> The office of sheriff is probably the most obvious example of mixing police and politics. This office was integrated into the American police system with little change from what it was in England. Today the office of sheriff is subject to popular election in almost all counties throughout the United States. . . . [W]hen a new sheriff is elected he will repay political debts by appointing new deputies and promoting others already employed. . . . This constant change of leadership and manipulation of the hierarchy has not been conducive to the provision of efficient police services.[52]

The sheriff, as an elected official, often must work to keep supporters happy—particularly if he or she wants to be reelected and to secure necessary funding. This can open the door to questionable law enforcement practices. However, an elected official enjoys more autonomy than an appointed official.

County sheriffs perform a number of functions, many of which are influenced by state legislation. The sheriff appoints deputies to assist in carrying out the responsibilities of the office. In small county sheriff's offices, deputies are often selected because of their political support, as well as state-defined attributes (education, training, etc.). An obvious responsibility is keeping the peace. In some jurisdictions the sheriff is principally an officer of the court. Some sheriff's offices are involved in criminal investigations and traffic duties. Often, the geographic location of a sheriff's office determines the types of duties and responsibilities expected of that office. In the northern United States, sheriff's offices do little criminal investigation. Instead, they perform mostly courtroom and processing duties. In the southern and the southwest sections of the United States, the sheriff may be the primary criminal investigator. In unincorporated sections of a county, the sheriff works closely with municipal police departments, as well as with state law enforcement agencies.

There are more than 3,000 sheriff's offices across the United States.[53] The cost of county law enforcement has increased significantly. In 1993, county law enforcement cost $10.7 billion ($45 per resident for the year).[54] In 2003, the cost was 22.3 billion ($82 per resident).[55] One of the principal functions of the sheriff's office is maintaining and managing county jails.[56]

County Police and Women

Women make up about 13% of all sworn officers in sheriff's departments across the United States. As in local law enforcement, the percentage of women who are sworn officers in sheriff's departments is greater in departments serving larger populations. In 2003, women accounted for at least 14% of sworn officers in sheriff's offices serving populations of 250,000 or more, compared with around 9% in offices that served populations with fewer than 25,000 (5% if under 10,000).[57] The representation of women in sheriff's departments is somewhat better than in local law enforcement but remains well below the level of women's representation in the general society.

Race and Ethnicity in County Policing

Department of Justice data indicate that the racial/ethnic composition of sworn employees in sheriff's departments is very similar to minority representation in local law enforcement agencies. Larger sheriff's departments tend to have more minority sworn officers than smaller departments. In departments that serve populations of a million or more, almost one-third of all sworn officers are minorities. In departments that serve populations of fewer than 10,000, about 6% of all sworn officers are minorities. The highest percentage (14.2%) of African American officers in 2003 was in departments serving a population of 500,000 to 999,999; the lowest (2.9) was in jurisdictions with fewer than 10,000 residents. The largest number of Hispanic officers (15.8%) worked in jurisdictions of 1 million or more; two populations, 50,000–99,999 and 10,000–24,999, had only 1.8% and 1.9% Hispanic officers respectively.[58]

Educational Requirements and County Policing

The educational requirements for new recruits in sheriff's departments vary from department to department. The highest percentage of departments requiring a minimum education level of a high school diploma are departments serving less than 10,000 residents (93%). Only 74% of departments serving 500,000 to 999,000 residents have that requirement. No sheriff's departments that serve a million or more citizens require a college degree.[59] Notice again the sad state of affairs concerning educational requirements. If law enforcement is becoming more complex, as many suggest, minimum educational requirements should be increased to meet the needs of law enforcement.

County Police Training

In general, the states mandate about three-fourths of the hours required for new recruits. Individual agencies decide the remaining requirements. As in local law enforcement training, sheriffs' department training consists of both classroom and field instruction. Small departments, as a general rule, require the fewest hours of combined classroom and field training for recruits. Departments serving fewer than 25,000 citizens require between 761 and 786 hours of combined classroom and field training. Departments that serve more than 500,000 citizens require between 1,194 and 1,288 combined hours of training.[60] Police academies that service sheriffs' departments perform a number of functions, ranging from teaching technical skills to familiarizing recruits with constitutional restraints and other procedural law requirements. Just as with training of local law enforcement, the academy socializes sheriffs' office recruits into the law enforcement subculture.

State Law Enforcement

State law enforcement emerged under a cloud of apprehension and contempt. Several reasons have been offered for the creation of state police: (1) to assist local law enforcement, which lacked satisfactory training and resources; (2) to bridge jurisdictions if criminal behavior crossed boundaries between agencies; and (3) to provide services to rural areas lacking local law enforcement services.[61] Despite these reasons, many people were apprehensive that state governors would have too much power if they had a state police force and that a state law enforcement agency would encroach on local law enforcement jurisdictions. Many local law enforcement agencies adamantly opposed the organization of state law enforcement agencies. Sheriffs—powerful political figures within their own jurisdictions who often had different political views than reigning governors—viewed state police agencies as extensions of control from the governor's office.[62]

In spite of the resistance raised by local law enforcement agencies, state law enforcement did emerge and spread across the United States. The earliest state law enforcement agency was the Texas Rangers in 1836. The Massachusetts legislature created a state police force with general law enforcement responsibilities in 1865. Its primary mission was to enforce vice laws. The agency was disbanded in 1875 as a result of controversy about its operations in cities. In Colorado, the state police was disbanded because of its support of industrial interests with brutal strikebreaking. In 1905, Pennsylvania created the first state police agency with general law enforcement capabilities. The agency emerged in the aftermath of a brutal coal miners strike in 1902, during which the Army was ordered to seize and operate the coal mines until the owners were willing to arbitrate the conflict with mine workers.[63] By the 1960s, all states, with the exception of Hawaii, had adopted and instituted some form of state-level law enforcement.[64]

State law enforcement in the United States is partitioned into two structural types: (1) state police and (2) highway patrol. State police typically have more general policing powers reflecting many of the duties of local law enforcement, but the jurisdictional boundaries are the entire state. Twenty-three states have state police organizations. Twenty-six states have highway patrol organizations, which focus their attention on the operation of motor vehicles on public highways and interstate freeways. Many states have created additional law enforcement capabilities. Some states have their own Bureau of Investigation and Bureau of Narcotics and Dangerous Drugs (e.g., Oklahoma); other states have created agencies like Gaming Control (e.g., Michigan and Nevada) to police the gaming industry within the state.

In total numbers of sworn officers, state law enforcement has the lowest growth rate of all law enforcement agencies. In 1980, there were 50,672 sworn state law enforcement officers; in 2003, the number was 57,611—an increase of less than 14%.[65] However, between 1982 and 2003, the expenditure for state police protection increased 293.4%.[66] Today, on average, there are about 21 sworn state police officers per 100,000 residents. Delaware has 81 state police officers per 100,000 residents; Wisconsin has 9 per 100,000.

The representation of women in the ranks of sworn officers in state police agencies across the United States is lower than in local law enforcement, where the numbers are already limited (see table 6.4). In 2003,

Table 6.4   Women in the State Police, 2000–2005[67]

Agency	Total Sworn Officers		Total Women Sworn Officers		Percentage of Women Sworn Officers	
	2000	2005	2000	2005	2000	2005
Alabama Dept of Public Safety	636	X	18	X	2.8	X
Alaska State Troopers	331	338	24	16	7.3	4.7
Arizona Dept of Public Safety	1,047	1,135	80	73	7.6	6.4
Arkansas State Police	559	X	31	X	5.5	X
California Highway Patrol	6,564	6,953	571	657	8.7	9.4
Colorado State Patrol	696	705	32	49	4.6	6.9
Connecticut State Police	689	1,190	43	78	6.2	6.6
Florida Highway Patrol	1,748	1,663	170	188	9.7	11.3
Idaho State Police	268	256	14	11	5.2	4.3
Illinois State Police	2,047	1,983	191	195	5.4	9.8
Indiana State Police	1,285	1,225	70	63	9.3	5.1
Iowa Dept of Public Safety	451	571	15	36	3.3	6.3
Kansas Highway Patrol	457	533	15	18	3.3	3.4
Kentucky State Police	937	927	32	30	3.4	3.2
Louisiana State Police	1,037	1,143	26	44	2.5	3.8
Maine State Police	344	298	14	21	4.1	7.0
Maryland State Police	1,611	1,496	159	123	9.9	8.2
Massachusetts State Police	2,228	2,259	218	193	9.8	8.5
Michigan State Police	2,102	1,797	259	218	12.3	12.1
Minnesota State Patrol	553	557	47	47	8.5	8.4
Missouri State Highway Patrol	1,083	921	41	35	3.8	3.8
Montana Highway Patrol	235	206	21	9	8.9	4.7
Nebraska State Patrol	356	478	16	26	4.5	5.4
Nevada Highway Patrol	429	503	24	75	5.6	14.9
New Hampshire State Police	313	288	26	27	8.3	9.4
New Mexico State Police	483	605	14	23	2.9	3.8
New York State Police	4,105	4,620	320	389	7.8	8.4
North Carolina Highway Patrol	1,336	1,662	24	44	1.8	2.6
North Dakota Highway Patrol	125	136	6	5	4.8	3.7
Ohio State Highway Patrol	1,408	1,547	130	143	9.2	9.2
Oregon State Police	798	610	72	61	9.0	10.0
Pennsylvania State Police	4,134	4,320	166	185	4.0	4.3
Rhode Island State Police	219	222	19	22	8.7	9.5
South Carolina Highway Patrol	1,109	833	52	26	4.4	3.1
South Dakota Highway Patrol	157	157	2	2	1.3	1.3
Tennessee Dept of Public Safety	899	935	45	44	5.1	4.7
Texas Dept of Public Safety	3,121	3,496	163	211	5.2	6.0
Utah Highway Patrol	406	431	14	17	3.4	3.9
Vermont State Police	292	316	21	24	7.2	7.6
Virginia State Police	1,821	1,903	74	97	4.1	5.1
Washington State Patrol	989	1,157	66	94	6.7	8.1
West Virginia State Police	682	634	17	18	2.5	2.8
Wisconsin State Patrol	508	492	71	60	14.0	12.2
Wyoming Highway Patrol	147	182	4	7	2.7	3.8

women made up approximately 11.3% of sworn officers in local police departments, 12.9% of sworn officers in sheriffs' departments, and only 5.8% of sworn officers in state police agencies.[68] Many in the dominant male majority in law enforcement have long argued that policing is too dangerous for women or that women are not capable of performing police duties as well as men. Research has disproved both arguments.[69] Women officers do, however, trail their male counterparts in the areas of police brutality and other forms of misconduct.[70]

Table 6.4 shows a very small increase in the number of women state police officers throughout the United States. In 2005, the state of Nevada had the highest percentage of women serving as sworn state police officers; South Dakota had the lowest percentage. Unless the rate of increase changes significantly, it will be 100 years before women can claim equality in the ranks of state police officers. Any excuse offered by law enforcement to continue blocking women from pursuing careers as sworn law enforcement officers is a clear civil rights violation.

Federal Law Enforcement

Section 8:1 of the U.S. Constitution gave Congress the power to provide for the common defense and general welfare of the United States. Section 8:6 gave Congress the power to "provide for the punishment of counterfeiting the securities and current coin of the United States." *Federal law enforcement* emerged from these congressional powers. Under the banner of common defense and general welfare, the federal law enforcement apparatus has expanded and flourished as a lucrative component of the criminal justice industrial complex. In 2004, there were 105,000 full-time federal law enforcement officers authorized to make arrests and carry firearms in nearly 65 federal law enforcement agencies. The number of federal officers increased by 36,000 since 1993—a 52% increase.[71] Federal agencies also employed a number of support personnel and operated on a budget of approximately $19 billion.[72] Federal law enforcement agencies with 500 or more officers employed 94% (98,500) of all federal officers.[73] Our discussion will focus on those agencies.

About 38% of federal officers are involved in criminal investigation. Police response and patrol account for 21%; corrections, 16%. Another 16% performed inspections related to immigration or customs laws.[74] Since 2003, in the aftermath of 9/11 and the adoption of the Patriot Act, the structure of federal law enforcement has changed. Today, several federal agencies have moved from the Department of Justice and Department of the Treasury to the newly formed Department of Homeland Security. We limit our discussion to the largest agencies within these three principal federal law enforcement employers.

Department of Justice

The **Department of Justice** was created in 1870 and was given the responsibility of enforcing federal laws. The Department of Justice houses five federal law enforcement agencies: The Federal Bureau of Prisons, the FBI, the DEA, the U.S. Marshals Service, and ATF.[75] The attorney general, a presidential appointee requiring confirmation by the Senate, heads the Department of Justice. Protection, law enforcement, and punishment are included in the mission statement of the Department of Justice:

> To enforce the law and defend the interests of the United States according to the law, to provide Federal leadership in preventing and controlling crime, to seek just punishment for those guilty of unlawful behavior, to administer and enforce the Nation's immigration laws fairly and effectively, and to ensure fair and impartial administration of justice for all Americans.[76]

Historically, agencies throughout the federal law enforcement apparatus—including the Department of Justice—have failed to comply with the mission statement. Forfeiture laws, "snitch programs," and illegal surveillance programs are a few examples. As noted in chapter 4, J. Edgar Hoover's activities at the FBI compromised the civil rights of a number of citizens. The Department of Justice is a complex apparatus with a direct link to the president of the United States.

As discussed in the previous chapter, the *Federal Bureau of Investigation (FBI)* became the first full-time federal investigative agency in 1935. The FBI is not a police agency; it is an investigative agency with broad jurisdiction extending to all areas and concerns relevant to U.S. interests. The FBI is particularly active in investigations pertaining to sabotage, treason, civil rights violations, robbery (federally insured banks), and other violations of federal law.

Until recently, there was no uniform definition of domestic terrorism and no specific legislative provisions that addressed domestic terrorism. The FBI had been responsible for the investigation of domestic terrorism and created its own definition grounded on the premise that domestic terrorism is the unlawful or threatened use of violence by individuals or groups within the boundaries of the United States or Puerto Rico, against individuals or property, for the purpose of coercing individuals, groups, or the government for political or social objectives.[77] Since the events of September 11, 2001, the existence of terrorism has been painfully clear. In past decades, however, the definition formulated by the FBI was employed, at least in part, against a variety of Americans in World Wars I and II, throughout the 1950s in the communist witch hunts, and during the 1960s and 1970s against civil rights advocates and anti-Vietnam War protesters.

The Federal Bureau of Investigation is the third largest Department of Justice employer. In 2006, with a budget of $5.7 billion, the FBI had 12,575 special agents with authorization to carry a firearm and make arrests.[78] We visited the Federal Bureau of Investigation Employment Web site and found an array of four photos.[79] At the top right of the page was a photograph of six employees—a mix of males and females. Below it was a picture of a female employee, and to the side were two pictures of male, ethnic employees. The photos, however, do not reflect the demographics of the FBI. In 2004, 81.5% of special agents were men, and 82.8% were white.[80]

After the Harrison Act was passed in 1914, the Miscellaneous Division of the Internal Revenue Service enforced the drug laws generated by that act. The responsibility for federal drug enforcement was transferred to the Federal Bureau of Narcotics (FBN) in 1930. In the late 1960s, the FBN was shifted from the Treasury Department to the Department of Justice and combined with the Bureau of Drug Abuse Control to form the Bureau of Narcotics and Dangerous Drugs. The *Drug Enforcement Administration (DEA)* was created in 1973.[81] The agency was glorified in the colorful television cop show, *Miami Vice*. Others have portrayed the DEA in less flattering ways. A retired federal drug agent claims that the DEA is "more about politics than drug interdiction," and one writer suggests the agency is another link in the attempt to create a police state in the United States.[82] While these opinions can be debated, there are data that call into question the legitimacy of the DEA, whose mission statement reads:

> The mission of the Drug Enforcement Administration (DEA) is to enforce the controlled substances laws and regulations of the United States and bring to the criminal and civil justice system of the United States, or any other competent jurisdiction, those organizations and principal members of organizations, involved in the growing, manufacture, or distribution of controlled substances appearing in or destined for illicit traffic in the United States; and to recommend and support non-enforcement programs aimed at reducing the availability of illicit controlled substances on the domestic and international markets.[83]

The DEA assists in the investigation and prosecution of major drug-law violators within the United States and in other countries. It has more than 21 domestic division offices throughout the United States (including Washington, DC) and 227 branch offices. The agency also has 86 foreign offices in 62 countries around the world. The DEA is also responsible for the collection and management of illegal drug trafficking intelligence, seizure and forfeiture of assets linked to the illegal drug trade, coordination of drug enforcement with local and international law enforcement agencies, and a laundry list of other drug-related duties.[84]

In 2006 there were 5,320 DEA special agent officers authorized to carry a firearm and make arrests; the budget was 2.4 billion dollars.[85] About 19% of special agents are minorities, and less than 95 are women (the lowest percentage in large federal agencies except for the Veterans Health Administration and the U.S. Fish and Wildlife Service).[86]

The *U.S. Marshals Service* was the first federal law enforcement agency. It was established by the Judiciary Act of 1789 but did not receive agency status until 1969. It was recognized as a federal bureau in 1984.[87] Early accounts of U.S. marshals focused on colorful, legendary characters such as Bat Masterson and Wyatt Earp, who have been the subjects of numerous movies, television programs, and books. Generally, U.S. marshals were portrayed as principled upholders of the law in the west.[88] Over the course of history the U.S. Marshals Service has been assigned to the presidency, the Treasury Department, the War Department, the Department of State, and the Department of Interior before finding its present home in the Department of Justice. U.S. marshals were deployed to provide security for James Meredith at the University of Mississippi. Ironically, U.S. marshals were directed to protect Dr. Martin Luther King through much of the civil rights movement, while J. Edgar Hoover simultaneously authorized the FBI to violate King's constitutional rights.[89]

The U.S. Marshals Service has 94 U.S. marshals, appointed by the president, and more than 3,200 officers authorized to carry a firearm and make arrests. Twenty percent of the officers are ethnic minorities, and only 12% are women. The budget for 2007 was approximately $813 million.[90]

The duties of the U.S. Marshals Service include providing security for federal courts. This security assignment extends to federal judges, court officials, witnesses, and jury members. With more than 2,000 federal judicial officers operating in more than 700 locations, this is a complex assignment. Following the enactment of the 1984 Comprehensive Crime Control Act, which contained provisions for forfeiture of assets, the U.S. Marshals Service was given the responsibil-ity for the maintenance, inventory, and disposal of property that the federal courts ordered seized.

U.S. marshals are responsible for the transportation of prisoners to federal courts. With assistance from the Federal Bureau of Prisons (BOP) they transport federal prisoners between BOP institutions. The U.S. Marshals Service handles the custody of approximately 27,000 detainees who are confined in local, state, and federal facilities across the United States. The U.S. Marshals Service contracts with nearly 1,200 state and local governments for the custody of federal prisoners. The Witness Security Program is operated by the U.S. Marshals Service. Following authorization from the attorney general, witnesses receive identity changes, relocation, job training, medical coverage, and so on. The U.S. Marshals Service also provides 24-hour protection for witnesses in what is determined to be a "threat" area. Marshals execute federal fugitive warrants, making approximately 55% of all arrests of federal fugitives. Fugitive investigations conducted by the U.S. Marshals Service are conducted within the United States and abroad and are assisted by surveillance and analytical support units within this agency.

The U.S. Marshals Service engages in special operations assignments, responding to emergency situations around the world. One of these special operations duties is the Missile Escort Program, which entails providing security for the movement of nuclear warheads by the Department of Defense and the U.S. Air Force.[91] This assignment raises a number of issues. Is it possible that the Department of Defense and the U.S. military are no longer capable of providing security for their own operations? Is U.S. law enforcement now in the business of providing security for the U.S. military? Does this shift in responsibility enhance or detract from the public image of law enforcement?

The *Bureau of Alcohol, Tobacco, Firearms and Explosives (ATF)* is an enforcement and regulatory agency. The Volstead Act (Prohibition) in 1919 was the initial impetus for the eventual implementation of the bureau. The National Firearms Act (1934) and the Federal Firearms Act (1938), in response to the proliferation of weaponry used by organized crime during Prohibition, also played a role in the shaping of the future ATF. Created in 1972 as a Treasury Department agency, ATF was moved to the DOJ in 2003.[92]

The vision statement of ATF reads:

> The Bureau of Alcohol, Tobacco, Firearms and Explosives must protect the public against crime, violence, and other threats to public safety. Our vision will help us chart the course to improve the way we serve and protect the public, provide leadership and expertise, and achieve new levels of effectiveness and teamwork.[93]

Despite the emphasis on protection, ATF was the agency responsible for the raid on the Branch Davidian compound in Waco, Texas, in 1993, during which 76 people, including 27 children, died.

The Bureau of Alcohol, Tobacco, and Firearms currently has 23 field division offices throughout the United States and operates several programs, including *alcohol/ tobacco programs*. The ATF alcohol and tobacco diversion program "seeks to reduce alcohol diversion and contraband cigarette trafficking activity, divest criminal and terrorist organizations of monies derived from this illicit activity and significantly reduce tax revenue losses to the States." Its mission is "to disrupt and eliminate criminal and terrorist organizations by identifying, investigating, and arresting offenders who traffic in contraband cigarettes and illegal liquor."[94] The agency also ensures the collection of excise taxes on alcohol and tobacco. The *arson and explosives program* provides resources to communities for the investigation of incidents involving explosives and/or arson-for-profit. The ATF maintains a computerized collection of data on national explosives, the Explosive Incident System. The *firearms program* brings ATF agents into the realm of violent offenders, career criminals, and narcotics traffickers. To monitor and control the illegal use of firearms, the ATF enforces federal firearms laws, issues firearms licenses, and conducts compliance inspections.[95]

In 2004, there were 2,398 officers with arrest power and authority to carry firearms.

Of these officers, 13.3% were female, and 19.9% were ethnic minorities.[96]

Department of Homeland Security

The federal law enforcement apparatus underwent significant changes with the enactment of the Homeland Security Act in November 2002. The newly created Department of Homeland Security (DHS) became the new home of several previous agencies that employed federal officers.

TITLE I–DEPARTMENT OF HOMELAND SECURITY

SEC. 101. EXECUTIVE DEPARTMENT; MISSION. (a) There is established a Department of Homeland Security, as an executive department of the United States within the meaning of title 5, United States Code. (b)**(1) The primary mission of the Department is to (A) prevent terrorist attacks within the United States; (B) reduce the vulnerability of the United States to terrorism; and (C) minimize the damage, and assist in the recovery, from terrorist attacks that do occur within the United States.** (2) In carrying out the mission described in paragraph (1), and as further described in this Act, the Department's primary responsibilities shall include (A) information analysis and infrastructure protection; (B) chemical, biological, radiological, nuclear, and related countermeasures; (C) border and transportation security; (D) emergency preparedness and response; and (E) coordination (including the provision of training and equipment) with other executive agencies, with State and local government personnel, agencies, and authorities, with the private sector, and with other entities. (3) The Department shall also be responsible for carrying out other functions of entities transferred to the Department as provided by law.

U.S. Customs and Border Protection (CBP) combined the inspectional arms of the former U.S. Customs Service (previously under the Treasury Department), the former Immigration and Naturalization Service (previously a DOJ department), and Animal and Plant Health Inspection Service with the former U.S. Border Patrol.[97] CBP's mission statement reads:

> We are the guardians of our Nation's borders. We are America's frontline. We safeguard the American homeland at and beyond our borders. We protect the American public against terrorists and the instruments of terror. We steadfastly enforce the laws of the United States while fostering our Nation's economic security through lawful international trade and travel. We serve the American public with vigilance, integrity and professionalism.[98]

CBP was the largest employer of Federal law enforcement officers with 27,705 officers in 2004; 15.3% were women, and 46.8% were ethnic minorities. Thirty-nine percent (10,895) of the officers worked border patrol. The United States has about 8,000 miles of boundaries—approximately 2,000 with Mexico—and 324 ports of entry; 89% of border control officers were stationed in the four States bordering Mexico. CBP employed nearly 17,000 officers who had been INS or U.S. Customs Inspectors before the creation of DHS.[99] The CBP budget was 7.8 billion in 2007.[100]

The law enforcement arms of the former Immigration and Naturalization Service and the former U.S. Customs Service were combined with the Federal Protective Service (transferred from GSA) to form *Immigration and Customs Enforcement (ICE)* in 2003. The new agency is the largest investigative branch of the DHS. It is charged with enforcing immigration and customs laws and providing protection against terrorist attacks. It targets illegal immigrants and the money and materials that support terrorism and other criminal activities.[101] The budget in 2007 was $4.7 billion.[102] In 2004, there were 10,399 ICE officers with arrest and firearms authority; 13.7% were women, and 33.9% were minorities. About 76% of the officers worked on criminal investigations and enforcement; 1,119 Federal Protective Service (FPS) officers performed security, patrol, and investigative duties related to Federal buildings and property and the employees and visitors using them.[103] In 2006, ICE removed 195,000

aliens—a record for the agency and a 13% increase over the previous year.[104]

The combined employment numbers of CBP and ICE totaled 38,104 in 2004—21% more than the comparable combined totals of the INS, U.S. Customs Service, and Federal Protective Service in 2002.

The U.S. Secret Service was also transferred to DHS in 2003 (previously the agency was in the Treasury Department).[105] The *U.S. Secret Service* was established as a law enforcement agency in 1865 to curtail the counterfeiting operations that emerged with the introduction of paper currency during the Civil War.[106] After the assassination of President William McKinley in 1901, the Secret Service was assigned the duties of protecting the president, vice president, their families, and foreign dignitaries. The Secret Service was transferred to the DHS in 2003; previously it was an agency in the Treasury Department. In addition to counterfeiting and protection services, the agency investigates financial crimes and computer fraud plus provides security for the White House, other presidential offices, and the main treasury building.[107] In 2004, there were 4,769 agents authorized to carry firearms and make arrests; 10.5% were women, and 19.6% were minorities.

Internal Revenue Service

The *Internal Revenue Service (IRS)* was established in 1862. Today it has three principal divisions: (1) the Investigative Intelligence Division, responsible for investigating tax-law violations and various automatic weapons registration laws, (2) the Audit Division, which is often a component of federally coordinated drug interdiction programs, and (3) the Collections Division, which has the responsibility to act on court orders to collect revenues due to the U.S. government.

The Internal Revenue Service had a budget of almost $767 million for investigation in 2006. The Criminal Investigation Division employed 2,777 special agents who have authorization to carry firearms and make arrests. Women accounted for 30% of the agents; 21% were ethnic minorities.[108]

SUMMARY

Policing has experienced significant changes in the past few decades. In the aftermath of legislation following the events of September 11, 2001, policing is likely to continue undergoing significant changes. In the midst of all these changes the police institution has been engaged in promoting the fear of crime (by greatly exaggerating the extent of crime), while at the same time "selling" the illusion that the public needs the police to protect them and that the police can fulfill that goal.

Perhaps the most dramatic change in social institutions has been the expansion of police powers. The fears created after the terrorist attack lessened resistance to encroachment on civil liberties. Urban police increasingly resemble the military—from the use of technology to the rhetoric used to describe activities to the structure of the institution. A wide variety of police agencies operate at every level of government, from the federal to the local. The employment of women and minorities within the police institution has increased somewhat but still constitutes a very small segment of the traditionally white male institution. The discussion of federal agencies, the DEA in particular, highlights the extent to which law enforcement has become more global. The justification, again, is the protection of the people—whether the threat is terrorists, illegal drugs, or people entering the country illegally.

Key Terms

- broken windows theory
- Bureau of Alcohol, Tobacco, Firearms, and Explosives (ATF)
- county law enforcement
- Department of Justice
- Drug Enforcement Administration (DEA)
- Federal Bureau of Investigation (FBI)
- federal law enforcement
- fifth armed force
- Immigration and Customs Enforcement (ICE)
- Internal Revenue Service (IRS)
- jurisdiction
- local law enforcement
- state law enforcement
- U.S. Customs and Border Protection (CBP)
- U.S. Marshals Service
- U.S. Secret Service

Notes

1 *Associated Press*, October 10, 2005.
2 *Los Angeles Times*, April 15, 2006.
3 *San Francisco Chronicle*, February 5, 2006.
4 Walker, S. and C. M. Katz. *The Police in America: An Introduction* (4th ed.). New York: McGraw-Hill, 2002.
5 Manning, P. "The Police: Mandate, Strategies, and Appearances." In V. Kappeler (ed.), *The Police and Society*. Long Grove, IL: Waveland, 2006, pp. 95–122.
6 Bercal, T. "Calls for Police Assistance." *American Behavioral Scientist* 13: 681–691 (1970); Myer, J. and W. Taylor. "Analyzing the Nature of Police Involvement: A Research Note Concerning the Effects of Forms of Police Mobilization." *Journal of Criminal Justice* 3: 141–146 (1975); Mastrofski, S. "Community Policing as Reform: A Cautionary Tale." In J. Greene and S. Mastrofski (eds.), *Community Policing*. New York: Praeger, 1988; Walker and Katz, *The Police in America*.
7 Nelsen, J. (ed.). *Police Brutality: An Anthology*. New York: Norton, 2000.
8 Duneier, M. *Sidewalk*. New York: Farrar, Straus and Giroux, 1999; Wilson, J. Q. and G. Kelling. "Broken Windows." *Atlantic Monthly* (March 1982), pp. 29–38.
9 A study of foot patrol by the Police Foundation (*The Newark Foot Patrol Experiment*. Washington, DC: The Police Foundation, 1981) found little evidence in support of this theory, although it did conclude that the police could reduce citizen fears of crime. For a thorough critique of broken windows, see Karmen, A. "Smarter Policing and Stepped-Up Imprisonment as the Primary Causes of Falling Crime Rates in New York City: The Emergence of an Urban Legend?" *The Justice Policy Journal* (2001). [Online] http://www.cjcj.org/journal/volnol/karmen/; and Karmen, A. *New York Murder Mystery: The Story Behind the Crime Crash of the 1990s*. New York: New York University Press, 2000.
10 Miller, J. G. *Search and Destroy: African American Males in the Criminal Justice System*. Cambridge: Cambridge University Press, 1996.
11 Giddens, A. and D. Held (eds.). *Classes, Power, and Conflict: Classical and Contemporary Debates*. Berkeley: University of California Press, 1982; Giddens, A. *The Global Third Way Debate*. Cambridge: Polity Press, 2001; Domhoff, W. G. *The Powers That Be*. New York: Vintage, 1979; Domhoff, W. G. *Who Rules America Now? Power and Politics in the Year 2000*. Mountain View, CA: Mayfield, 1998; Chomsky, N. *World Orders Old and New*. New York: Columbia University Press, 1996; Chomsky, N. *Class Warfare*. Monroe, ME: Common Courage Press, 1996; Chomsky, N. *Secrets, Lies and Democracy*. Tucson, AZ: Odonian Press, 1994.

[12] Chomsky, *Secrets, Lies and Democracy*; Schlesinger, P. and H. Tumber. *Reporting Crime: The Media Politics of Criminal Justice*. Oxford: Clarendon Press, 1994; Parenti, C. *Lockdown America: Police and Prisons in the Age of Crisis*. New York: Verso, 1999.

[13] Bagdikian, B. H. *The New Media Monopoly*. Boston: Beacon Press, 2004.

[14] Schlesinger and Tumber, *Reporting Crime*; Chomsky, *Secrets, Lies and Democracy*.

[15] Miller, R. L. *Drug Warriors and Their Prey: From Police Power to Police State*. Westport, CT: Praeger, 1996.

[16] Schlesinger and Tumber, *Reporting Crime*.

[17] Cited in Miller, *Drug Warriors and Their Prey*, p. 29.

[18] *Sourcebook of Criminal Justice Statistics*. [Online] http://www.albany.edu/sourcebook/pdf/t2212005.pdf

[19] *Sourcebook of Criminal Justice Statistics, 2000*, table 2.27, p. 117, 2001.

[20] Samaha, J. *Criminal Justice* (5th ed.). Belmont, CA: Wadsworth, 2000; Miller, L. S. and K. M. Hess. *The Police in the Community: Strategies for the 21st Century* (2nd ed.). Belmont, CA: Wadsworth, 1998; LaGrange, R. L. *Policing American Society* (2nd ed.). Chicago: Nelson-Hall, 1998; Roberg, R. R. and J. Kuykendall. *Police in Society*. Belmont, CA: Wadsworth, 1993; Walker, S. *The Police in America: An Introduction* (2nd ed.). New York: McGraw-Hill, 1992.

[21] Levine, M. *Deep Cover*. New York: Delacorte, 1990; Levine, M. *Big White Lie: The CIA and the Cocaine Crack Epidemic*. New York: Thunder's Mouth, 1994; Scott, P. D. and J. Marshall. *Cocaine Politics: Drugs, Armies and the CIA in Central America*. Berkeley: University of California Press, 1998.

[22] Chomsky, N. *Failed States: The Abuse of Power and the Assault on Democracy*. New York: Metropolitan Books, 2006.

[23] Tabb, W. *The Amoral Elephant: Globalization and the Struggle for Social Justice in the Twenty-First Century*. New York: Monthly Review Press, 2001.

[24] Chomsky, N. *Profit over People: Neoliberalism and Global Order*. New York: Seven Stories Press, 1999.

[25] Parenti, *Lockdown America*.

[26] Walker and Katz, *The Police in America*.

[27] Samaha, *Criminal Justice*; Miller and Hess, *The Police in the Community*; LaGrange, *Policing American Society*; Roberg and Kuykendall, *Police in Society*; Walker, *The Police in America*.

[28] Scheb, J. M. and J. M. Scheb II. *Criminal Law and Procedure* (4th ed.). Belmont, CA: Wadsworth, 2002.

[29] Shelden, R. G. and W. B. Brown. "Correlates of Jail Overcrowding: A Case Study of a County Detention Center." *Crime and Delinquency* 37(3): 347–362 (1991); Walker, *The Police in America*.

[30] Shelden, R. G., S. Tracy, and W. B. Brown. *Youth Gangs in American Society* (3rd ed.). Belmont, CA: Wadsworth, 2001.

[31] Department of Justice. "Justice Department Files Consent Decrees Concluding Investigation of Detroit Police Department," June 12, 2003. [Online] http://www.usdoj.gov/opa/pr/2003/June/03_crt_352.htm

[32] Federal Bureau of Investigation, *Crime in the United States, 2006*. [Online] http://www.fbi.gov/ucr/cius2006/data/table_74.html

[33] Hickman, M. J. and B. A. Reaves. *Local Police Departments, 2003* (NCJ 210118). Washington, DC: Bureau of Justice Statistics, May 2006, p. 2. [Online] http://www.ojp.usdoj.gov/bjs/pub/pdf/lpd03.pdf

[34] Bureau of Justice Statistics, *Federal Law Enforcement Officers, 2000*.

[35] Reaves, B. A. *Federal Law Enforcement Officers, 1993* (NCJ 151166). Washington, DC: Bureau of Justice Statistics, December 1994, p. 1. [Online] http://www.ojp.usdoj.gov/bjs/pub/pdf/fedlaw.pdf; Reaves, B. A. *Federal Law Enforcement Officers, 2004* (NCJ 212750). Washington, DC: Bureau of Justice Statistics, July 2006. [Online] http://www.ojp.usdoj.gov/bjs/pub/pdf/fleo04.pdf

[36] Reaves, *Federal Law Enforcement Officers, 2004*, p. 1, table 8; FBI, *Crime in the United States, 2006*, tables 78 and 81.

[37] Reaves, B. A. *Local Police Departments, 1993*. Washington, DC: Bureau of Justice Statistics, April 1996, p. 1; Reaves, B. A. and A. Goldberg. *Local Police Departments, 1997*. Washington, DC: Bureau of Justice Statistics, February 2000, p. 1; Hickman, M. and B. A. Reaves. *Local Police Departments, 1999*. Washington, DC: Bureau of Justice Statistics, May 2001, p. 1; Hickman, M. and B. A. Reaves. *Local Police Departments, 2000*. Washington, DC: Bureau of Justice Statistics, January 2003, p. 1; Hickman, M. and B. A. Reaves. *Local Police Departments, 2003*. Washington, DC: Bureau of Justice Statistics, May 2006, p. 1.

[38] Shelden and Brown, "Correlates of Jail Overcrowding."

[39] Hickman and Reaves, *Local Police Departments, 2003*, p. 1.

[40] Ibid., p. 2.

[41] Ibid., p. 10.

[42] *Sourcebook of Criminal Justice Statistics*. [Online] http://www.albany.edu/sourcebook/pdf/t122003.pdf; *Justice Expenditure and Employment Extracts 2004* (NCJ 215648). November 2006. [Online] http://www.ojp.usdoj.gov/bjs/eande.htm#selected

[43] Hickman and Reaves, *Local Police Departments, 2003*, p. 2.

[44] FBI, *Crime in the United States, 2006*, tables 1, 8.

[45] Hickman and Reaves, *Local Police Departments, 2003*, p. 7.

[46] Ibid.

[47] Ibid., p. 9.

[48] Walker and Katz, *The Police in America*.

[49] Hickman and Reaves, *Local Police Departments, 2003*, p. 9.

[50] Walker and Katz, *The Police in America*.

[51] Hickman and Reaves, *Local Police Departments, 2003*, p. 9.

[52] Folley, V. I. *American Law Enforcement*. Boston: Allyn & Bacon, 1980, p. 228.

[53] Hickman, M. J. and B. A. Reaves. *Sheriff's Offices, 2003*. Washington, DC: Bureau of Justice Statistics, May 2006, p. 2.

[54] Reaves, A. A. and P. Z. Smith, *Sheriffs' Departments 1993* (NCJ 148823). Washington, DC: Bureau of Justice Statistics, June 1996, table 10, p. 7.

[55] Hickman and Reaves, *Sheriff's Offices, 2003*, p. iii.

[56] Thompson, J. A. and G. L. Mays. *American Jails: Public Policy Issues*. Chicago: Nelson-Hall, 1998.

[57] Hickman and Reaves, *Sheriff's Offices, 2003*, p. 7.

[58] Ibid.

[59] Ibid., p. 9.

[60] Ibid.

[61] Gaines, L. K. and V. E. Kappeler. *Policing in America* (5th ed.). Cincinnati: Anderson, 2005.

[62] Berg, B. L. *Law Enforcement: An Introduction to Police in Society*. Boston: Allyn & Bacon, 1992; LaGrange, *Policing American Society*.

[63] Wiebe, R. H. "The Anthracite Strike of 1902: A Record of Confusion." *The Mississippi Valley Historical Review* 48(2): 229–251 (September 1961).

[64] Johnson, D. R. *American Law Enforcement: A History*. St. Louis: Forum Press, 1981; Berg, *Law Enforcement*; Roberg and Kuykendall, *Police and Society*; LaGrange, *Policing American Society*.

[65] Hickman and Reaves, *Sheriff's Offices, 2003*, p. 1.

[66] Hughes, K. A. *Justice Expenditure and Employment in the United States, 2003*. Washington, DC: Bureau of Justice Statistics, April 2006, pp. 3, 8.

[67] *Equality Denied: The Status of Women in Policing: 2000*, Penny E. Harrington, director, National Center for Women and Policing, a division of the Feminist Majority Foundation (April 2001); FBI, *Crime in the United States, 2006*. Full-Time State Law Enforcement by State, 2006. [Online] http://www.fbi.gov/ucr/cius2006/data/table_76.html

[68] Hickman and Reaves, *Local Police Departments, 2003*, table 13; Hickman and Reaves, *Sheriffs' Offices, 2003*, table 13; FBI, *Crime in the United States, 2003*, table 76. [Online] http://www.fbi.gov/ucr/cius_03/pdf/03sec6.pdf

[69] Balkin, J. "Why Policemen Don't Like Police Women." *Journal of Police Science and Administration*. 30: 16 (1988).

[70] Grennan, S. A. "Findings on the Role of Officer Gender in Violent Encounters with Citizens." *Journal of Police Science and Administration* 15(1): 78–85 (1987).

[71] Reaves, B. A. *Federal Law Enforcement Officers, 1993* (NCJ 151166). Washington, DC: U.S. Department of Justice, December 1994, p. 1.

[72] Reaves, B. A. *Federal Law Enforcement Officers, 2004* (NCJ212750). Washington, DC: Bureau of Justice Statistics, July 2006, p. 1; *Justice Expenditure and Employment Extracts, Direct Expenditure by Level of Government 1982–2004*. [Online] http://www.ojp.usdoj.gov/bjs/glance/tables/exptyptab.htm

[73] Reaves, *Federal Law Enforcement Officers, 2004*, p. 7.

[74] Ibid., p. 2.

[75] Ibid., p. 3.

[76] Ibid., p. 3.

[77] Federal Bureau of Investigation. *Terrorism in the United States, 1998*. Washington, DC: Federal Bureau of Investigation, 1999.

[78] Federal Bureau of Investigation. May 2007. [Online] http://www.fbi.gov/quickfacts.htm

[79] [Online] http://www.fbi.gov/employment/employ.htm

[80] Reaves, *Federal Law Enforcement Officers, 2004*, table 4.

[81] Berg, *Law Enforcement*; Gaines and Kappeler, *Policing in America*.

[82] Levine, *Deep Cover and Big White Lie*; Miller, *Drug Warriors and Their Prey*.

[83] U.S. Drug Enforcement Administration. *DEA Mission Statement*. May 2007. [Online] http://www.usdoj.gov/dea/agency/mission

[84] U.S. Drug Enforcement Administration. May 2007. [Online] http://www.usdoj.gov/dea/agency/domestic.htm

[85] U.S. Drug Enforcement Administration. May 2007. [Online] http://www.usdoj.gov/dea/agency/staffing.htm.

[86] Reaves, *Federal Law Enforcement Officers, 2004*, table 4.

[87] Gaines and Kappeler, *Policing in America*.

[88] Berg, *Law Enforcement*.

[89] Friedman, L. M. *Crime and Punishment in American History*. New York: Basic Books, 1993; Zinn, *A People's History of the United States*.

[90] Reaves, *Federal Law Enforcement Officers, 2004*, table 4; [Online] http://www.usmarshals.gov/duties/factsheets/facts.pdf.

[91] U.S. Marshals Service. May 2007. [Online] http://www.usdoj.gov/marshals/duties/factsheets/opssup.pdf.

[92] Bureau of Alcohol, Tobacco, and Firearms. May 2007. [Online] http://www.atf.gov/about/atfhistory.htm

[93] Bureau of Alcohol, Tobacco, and Firearms. [Online] http://www.atf.gov/about/mission.htm

[94] Bureau of Alcohol, Tobacco, and Firearms. [Online] http://www.atf.gov/antdiversion.htm

[95] Bureau of Alcohol, Tobacco, and Firearms. [Online] http://www.atf.gov/about/programs/proal.htm; http://www.atf.gov/about/programs/proex.htm; http://www.atf.gov/about/programs/profire.htm

[96] Reaves, *Federal Law Enforcement Officers, 2004*, table 4.

[97] U.S. Customs and Border Protection. [Online] http://www.cbp.gov/xp/cgov/toolbox/about/mission/cbp.xml

[98] U.S. Customs and Border Protection. [Online] http://www.cbp.gov/xp/cgov/toolbox/about/mission/guardians.xml

[99] Reaves, *Federal Law Enforcement Officers, 2004*, p. 2.

[100] U.S. Customs and Border Protection. [Online] http://www.cbp.gov/xp/cgov/newsroom/fact_sheets/budget/bush_2007_budget.xml

[101] Immigration and Customs Enforcement. [Online] http://www.ice.gov/about/index.htm

[102] Immigration and Customs Enforcement. [Online] http://www.ice.gov/doclib/pi/news/factsheets/FactSheet2007Budget020507a.pdf

[103] Reaves, *Federal Law Enforcement Officers, 2004*, p. 2.

[104] Immigration and Customs Enforcement. http://www.ice.gov/pi/news/factsheets/2006accomplishments.htm

[105] Department of Homeland Security. [Online] http://www.dhs.gov/xabout/history/editorial_0133.shtm.

[106] U.S. Secret Service. May 2007. [Online] http://www.secretservice.gov/history.shtml

[107] Reaves, *Federal Law Enforcement Officers, 2004*, p. 2.

[108] United States Government Accountability Office. May 2007. [Online] http://www.gao.gov/new.items/d05566.pdf, table 2.; Reaves, *Federal Law Enforcement Officers, 2004*, table 4.

seven

Police Functions and Problems

Expectations about what duties the police should perform depend on interests. The state wants police to maintain social control through law enforcement or order maintenance methods. Powerful interest groups want the police to protect their property and enforce laws that favor businesses and corporations. The public wants the police to provide security, prevent crimes, and respond to their calls and complaints on demand.

As noted in the previous chapter, the events of September 11, 2001, have altered some public expectations about personal liberties and constitutional rights. Protests over weakening Fourth Amendment restrictions on search and seizure have been minimal. People have seemingly been willing to ignore the loss of some rights in the hope that sacrificing some safeguards will prevent potential criminal behavior. The focus today is increasingly on *proactive policing*. Many believe this strategy helps prevent crime—perhaps it does have such an impact—but it also intrudes on the lives of Americans. *Reactive policing*, in contrast, responds to criminal behavior after it has occurred.

ENFORCING THE LAW OR MAINTAINING ORDER?

Police operations typically consist of patrol, investigation, traffic control, and special unit activities. As a rule, there are two principal rationales behind police operations: (1) law enforcement and (2) service. The guiding principles adopted by police administrators and carried out by police officers determine how police operations are organized and conducted.

Law enforcement means exactly what it says—enforcing the laws that apply to a given jurisdiction, whether county, state, and/or federal laws. The enforcement of laws is contingent on priorities and resources available to a law enforcement agency. For example, a local law enforcement agency may have to readjust its priorities for making arrests if the county jail is operating above capacity.[1]

The war on crime is a rhetorical device to emphasize the danger confronting the public and police officers, who serve as the thin blue line standing between ruthless criminals and their innocent public prey. The war has a number of fronts: the war against *drugs,* the war against *gangs,* the war against *drunk drivers,* the war against *child abuse, and* the war against *terrorism.* No one has proclaimed a war against corporate crime or a war against state crime, even though many laws are also broken by participants in corporate and state leadership positions.

Order maintenance is a police function based on keeping things under control and orderly. Police who practice order maintenance might ignore questionable or illegal behavior if it is discreet and does not disturb the normal routine of an area or community. If, however, that behavior threatens to expand beyond its geographical confines and extend to the general population, the police will generally take action.

Policing Styles

Law enforcement in the United States has embraced three *policing styles* to fulfill the

133

expectations of the interest groups they choose to serve: legalistic, watchman, and service.[2]

The *legalistic style* of policing emphasizes law enforcement. Instead of relying on informal methods of social control, the police strictly enforce the laws on the books without weighing the seriousness of the offense. This style of policing is often associated with agencies that pride themselves on being professional, but it thrives only during periods of prosperity and plentiful resources. Jails tend to fill rather quickly in geographic areas where law enforcement emphasizes the legalistic style of policing. If there is no additional money for jail construction or expansion of the court system, law enforcement administrators must ratchet down the legalistic methods practiced by their officers.

The *watchman style* of policing gives highest priority to order maintenance, based on the belief that it is important to allow society to operate smoothly, and police intervention is necessary only when order is clearly threatened. This approach allows behavior, legal or illegal, to go unchecked until that behavior threatens to contaminate larger portions of society. Such behavior may also draw police intervention if it poses political embarrassment to political leaders in power. This style of policing works most efficiently with small police agencies in areas where people live in relatively homogeneous communities.

The *service style* of policing is germane to departments that take all situations seriously but acknowledge that all situations do not require or necessitate arrest. Problem solving takes precedence over catching criminals. This style extracts the positive elements from the legalistic and watchman styles while providing services and protection to communities. It is most common in small or affluent communities.

In most instances, police departments utilize aspects of all three styles, although one style may receive more emphasis.[3] The personality of an individual officer may also dictate the style of policing practiced on a day-to-day basis. Some officers consider themselves crime-fighters. These officers may lean toward the legalistic style. Officers who are looking forward to retirement may subscribe to the "watchman" style of policing—stay back unless something very serious presents itself. Certain officers see their role as helping citizens, and these officers are likely to prefer service-oriented policing.

Common Functions

Most police officers perform patrol duty.[4] Automobiles, motorcycles, bicycles, boats, fixed-wing aircraft, and helicopters are all patrol vehicles. There also are foot patrols and patrols that require officers to develop equestrian skills—horse patrol. Automobile patrol seems to be the preferred method of maintaining order and enforcing laws in nearly all jurisdictions. Police drive through their assigned sectors looking for the usual and the unusual. The unusual may not be a criminal act, but any behavior that is out of the ordinary can draw the attention of police officers. Automobile patrol, because officers are confined in a vehicle, polices only behavior that occurs in plain view Some people, generally economically disadvantaged people, spend more time in open view than people who are not economically disadvantaged.[5]

Officers assigned to patrols are typically responsible for maintaining order or preserving the peace, enforcing laws, traffic control, investigating crimes, and answering calls from citizens. Administrators or supervisors prioritize these responsibilities. For example, it is common for a shift supervisor to announce, "Officers A and B have not written very many tickets this month. Is there a problem, officers?" Thus, Officers A and B might spend their entire shift writing tickets, perhaps even issuing a ticket to a driver whose front bumper extends two inches over the white line at a crosswalk. Often, however, patrolling responsibilities and prioritizing have a more profound impact on communities and in some instances on entire cities.

In 1994, Mayor Rudolf Giuliani appointed William Bratton as the new commissioner of the New York Police Department. Bratton focused attention on the subways and reinvigorated the subway police. He acquired new equipment and weapons for officers working below the streets. He authorized sweeps to stop fare evasion (turnstile jumpers) and to evict the homeless people from the New York subway tunnels, eventually "reclaiming" the subway. Commissioner Bratton received extensive public credit for "cleaning up the subways."

The justification for the sweeps was the *broken-windows theory*. As discussed in chapter 6, the theory proposes that crimes that are more serious evolve from minor infractions.[6] The Giuliani–Bratton team moved the war on crime from the subways to the streets. War was declared on "squeegee men" (unemployed individuals who washed the windshields of cars stuck in traffic), prostitutes, truant children (many of whom were truant because they had problems coping with inner-city school violence), and the homeless. Many people were relieved at not having to see or contend with people whose behavior was annoying or unsettling.[7]

Few gave much thought to where the displaced population had gone. Did the homeless and the unemployed simply vanish? Should this concern us? From another viewpoint, the sweeps could be characterized as a war against the poor. While the streets were more comfortable to negotiate, insider-trading violations, fraud, and other white-collar crimes continued unabated. Police patrol operations of the variety just discussed demonstrate *selective law enforcement*, whereby administrative policies prioritize the types of laws to be enforced. Selective law enforcement, closely linked to police discretionary power and practices, dictates who will be subject to arrest and who will receive a warning or be undetected.

Special Units

Some special units have been components of law enforcement for many years. Vice and narcotics units/squads combat offenses such as pickpocket activities, prostitution, and illegal drug activities. Some special units created over the past few years include SWAT (special weapons and tactics) teams—"Ninja Turtle units" that sport the latest in high-tech military attire. It is difficult to determine what impact special units have on the war against crime. Their performances, generally evaluated by police admin-

istrators or by the media, provide police with good press as previously noted. It is difficult to evaluate units like SWAT because there is no way to compare these units with the proficiency levels of line officers. There are also gang units. The creation of SWAT and gang units was thought to be necessary for responding to special situations that patrol officers were not equipped to handle for a variety of reasons—training, physical and psychological conditions, and so on. In addition, law enforcement agencies have specialized investigative units. Often these units employ detectives, generally selected based on experience, expertise, and in some cases political connections with administrators.

Policing agencies generally support the existence of their special-unit programs. For the record, crime rates have been consistent over the past several decades. Beyond large prison populations, there seems to be little evidence indicating that any special unit has made a major impact on its particular area of expertise. Youngsters today seem to be using illegal substances at a similar rate to youngsters who used drugs at the start of the war on drugs. Homicide detectives can do little to stop homicide; they are usually brought into a case when someone is reported missing or there is a body. Vice-squad detectives try in vain to control the world's "oldest profession," which is prostitution. Gang activities do seem to have declined in recent years, and we are certain that gang units around the country are taking credit. However, we contend that any decline is more likely a result of increases in employment and age/demographic changes rather than the result of gang-squad activity.[8]

THE POLICE SUBCULTURE

Subcultures are "groups within the society who share elements of the basic culture but who also possess some distinctive folkways and mores."[9] Peter Manning and John Van Maanen have described the *police subculture* as follows:

> The occupational culture [subculture] constructed by the police consists of long-

standing rules of thumb, a somewhat special language and ideology that help edit a member's everyday experiences, shared standards of relevance, matter-of-fact prejudices, models for street-level etiquette and demeanor, certain customs and rituals suggestive of how members are to relate not only to each other but to outsiders, and a sort of residual category consisting of the assorted miscellany of some rather plain police horse sense. All of these cultural modes of thinking, knowing, and doing are, of course, so rooted in the recurrent problems and common experiences of the police that they are regarded by insiders as perfectly natural responses to the world they inhabit. Indeed, cultures arise as a way of coping with, and making sense of, a given environment. That this occupational culture has displayed such remarkable stability through time is itself testimony to the persistence of the problematic habitat within which police work takes place.[10]

Like every subculture, the police subculture nestles within the broader social culture. Subcultures are small composites of a larger society; the members of a subculture have a stake in the subculture's interests, concerns, and values. For example, members of a sorority or fraternity are often most comfortable with members of their own house. Similarly, military personnel are more comfortable with other military personnel than they are with civilians unfamiliar with military life. Police officers, too, are most comfortable with other members of their profession.

Socialization

Socialization into the police subculture generally occurs in three stages. The police academy is the introductory stage. A civilian applicant is transformed into a police officer recruit and then into a bona fide police officer and member of the police subculture. The application process and oral examination weed out individuals who will not fit into the police subculture. One of our former students confided that he had "blown" the oral exam in his application to become a police officer:

> I was asked what I would do if I saw a fellow police officer being attacked by some-

one in the street. My response was that first I would sort out the situation in my mind, and then call for backup and then proceed to help the officer. The answer they wanted was to not think about the situation—just go and help the officer immediately. I guess that means that because I would think first then I wouldn't be a good cop. Maybe they are right, but I do not believe that thinking first should disqualify me—but it did.

University professors have contributed significantly to the oral exam process, and the furtherance of police culture.[11] Applicants typically come from working-class families; the attraction of working on the police force is generally economic rather than the desire to be in a position of authority. More often than not, applicants are seeking employment, and most have an idealistic notion that as police officers they will be able to help people.[12] The police academy stresses technical training—firearms training, arrest procedures, legal statutes, and survival skills—and subscription to values embraced by the occupation. Survival-skills training emphasizes the necessity for police officers to be able to rely on other police officers.

The second stage of the socialization process occurs after graduation from the academy. The recruit is now a rookie police officer. Recent graduates usually go to a field-training officer (FTO) for "street" training. The FTO is often a seasoned veteran who has the responsibility to familiarize the recruit with life on the streets. The FTO might be a *progressive* police officer who stresses protection of civil liberties, or he or she may subscribe to the *civilians-as-scumbags* view, which stresses the notion that it is "us against them." The recruit has very little if anything to do with the selection of an FTO. Relationships developed during the academy experience and early field experiences with the FTO gradually replace former friends and relationships.[13]

The third stage, which solidifies the commitment to policing, occurs when the individual makes the transition from rookie to police officer—becoming one of the "guys" (whether the individual is female or male). Assigned to a seasoned partner, and completing the probationary period, new police officers embrace the title *officer*. Of course, more seasoned officers may continue to view the new officers as rookies. The relationships developed in the academy and during the rookie period have matured and solidified. The new officer may still cling to previous relationships, but the commitment to those relationships often diminishes.

Officer Styles

The search for a style or niche in policing is not an easy task.

> I maintain that the work group molds the officer's personality. I call it street survival. Rookies find themselves under tremendous pressure and tend to gravitate from one end of the pendulum to the other in their search to find a comfortable style of policing. Every rookie knows his or her reputation needs to be established before fully being accepted as a fellow officer. Hence, rookies tend to be impetuous, aggressive, and very rough around the edges. They need to learn when and how to bullshit in the street, how to finesse the person they are confronting, and how to read the interactional cues and body language that dictate appropriate courses of action and impending danger.[14]

John Broderick developed a typology of four officer styles.

1. The *enforcer* focuses on clearing the streets of criminals. Individual rights or constitutional safeguards are not high priorities for officers subscribing to this style.

2. The *idealist* is the opposite of the enforcer. Officers subscribing to this style have faith in the law and procedures intended to protect citizens' rights.

3. The *realist* is a cynic. Officers subscribing to this style have little faith in the criminal justice system. Often they become alienated from other officers, in part because of their belief that cleaning the streets or preserving individual rights is not going to make much of a difference.

4. The *optimist* embraces the notion that police can make a significant difference in society. Rather than placing crime fighting at the top of their list of priorities, these officers see their role as being service providers.[15]

In their efforts to enforce the law and especially to maintain order, the police continuously create many problems for themselves. In the name of enforcing the law, they actively participate in the violation of the law. Cases of police *corruption* have been a mainstay of U.S. policing since the nineteenth century.

POLICE CORRUPTION

One of the difficulties limiting any discussion of police corruption is that of obtaining accurate data. The fact that the police are highly secretive about their activities no doubt contributes to this problem. More often than not, investigations of police corruption are in-house investigations conducted by the internal affairs division. A related problem is that a citizen's complaint can become entangled in bureaucratic red tape, and most citizens give up or bring no charges at all. When police corruption is exposed, it is usually when an individual police officer or a small number of officers blow the whistle or when investigative reporters dig a little deeper than usual, uncover, and then expose police corruption. One common source of exposure over the years has been the work of special crime commissions.

Knapp Commission

Since the Wickersham Commission in 1931, a number of governmental commissions have found corruption within police departments.[16] As mentioned in chapter 5, the ***Knapp Commission*** in New York City in 1973 was a comprehensive investigation into the problem of police corruption. A plainclothes police officer, Frank Serpico, provided the impetus for the Knapp investigation. Serpico became a celebrity; his story was told in a book, a movie, and a TV series.

The commission found that plainclothesmen were involved in a "pad," the collection of payments (up to $3,000 per month), from several gambling establishments. The share per month per officer ranged from $300 to

$400 in midtown Manhattan, and up to $1,500 in Harlem. Officer Serpico charged that nineteen Bronx plainclothesmen received an average monthly share (called the "nut" by the police) of $800. The commission found that Brooklyn plainclothesmen brought in an average "nut" of $1,200.[17]

Payoffs in narcotics enforcement (known as "scores") were common. The Commission found a pattern "whereby corrupt officers customarily collected scores in substantial amounts from narcotics violators. Some officers shared their scores with a partner or with a superior officer. They ranged from minor shakedowns to payments of many thousands of dollars." The largest payoff discovered was $80,000.[18]

The commission found that there were regular payoffs from construction sites, bars, grocery stores, and other business establishments. Many payoffs were as low as $20, but these payoffs were so numerous they added substantially to an officer's take-home pay. After-hours bars, prostitutes, and individuals wanting their court cases fixed also paid officers on a regular basis. Even superior officers were not immune. Often patrol officers served as "bagmen" who collected "fees" (bribes) for their superiors in return for a percentage of the "take."

The commission distinguished between two categories of corrupt police officers: meat-eaters and grass-eaters. *Meat-eaters* were those heavily involved in receiving payoffs. *Grass-eaters* accepted payoffs only if they happened to come their way. The commission believed that the grass-eaters were the heart of the problem:

> Their great numbers tend to make *corruption* "respectable." They also tend to encourage the code of silence that brands anyone who exposes corruption a traitor. At the time our investigation began, any policeman violating the code did so at his peril. The result was described in our interim report: "The rookie who comes into the department is faced with the situation where it is easier for him to become corrupt than to remain honest."[19]

As the Knapp Commission suggested, a police subculture that supports various forms of deviant behavior often contributes to the socialization of police officers. The commission distinguished between the *bad-apple theory* and the *group support theory* of police corruption.

Stoddard found widespread support for certain forms of deviance among officers. Specifically, Stoddard found an informal code that supported deviancy. Rookies, often pressured to go along with this code, were subject to group ostracism. "Lack of acceptance not only bars the neophyte from the inner secrets of the profession, but may isolate him socially and professionally from his colleagues and even his superiors."[20] The bad-apple theory suggests that police corruption stems only from a few bad apples in an otherwise clean barrel. The group support theory suggests that the barrel is not so clean after all, and most officers condone deviancy even if not everyone in the department participates in deviant behavior.

Both the bad-apple and the group support theories fail to adequately explain police corruption as a persistent phenomenon. Both imply that a new kind of police officer (perhaps of the Serpico variety) is the solution. Nevertheless, the persistence of corruption and the social, political, economic, and legal contexts of it suggest that this type of reform would not solve the problem. One reason is the fact that so much money is involved and there are very powerful interests (usually on the part of "respectable" people) enmeshed in police corruption. In other words, evidence suggests that police corruption is not the problem; the problem appears to be that the economic and political structure of U.S. society breeds corruption.

Police Corruption in Seattle

William Chambliss found corruption to be widespread in Seattle. The corruption involved not only police officers but also members of organized crime, key political and business figures, and high-ranking police officials. Chambliss discovered that all of these individuals participated in illegal activities such as gambling, prostitution, and loan-sharking. Individual police officers accepted substantial bribes. Most of the activities were restricted to the fringes of slum communities, where "respectable" citizens could participate in questionable behavior out-of-sight from their fellow citizens. The police made a few token arrests and even some "well publicized raids" but avoided involving influential citizens. .

Chambliss suggests that a symbiotic relationship exists between the law enforcement bureaucracy and the major suppliers of vice in Seattle:

> The gambling, prostitution, drug distribution, pornography, and usury which flourish in the lower-class center of the city do so with the compliance, encouragement, and cooperation of the major political and law enforcement officials in the city. There is in fact a symbiotic relationship between the law enforcement–political organizations of the city and a group of *local,* as distinct from national, men who control the distribution of vices.[21]

In fact, Chambliss points to the overemphasis on the *criminal* in the study of organized crime and a "corresponding de-emphasis on *corruption* as an institutional component of America's legal–political system. Concomitantly, it has obscured perception of the degree to which the structure of America's law and politics creates and perpetuates syndicates that supply the vices in our major cities."[22] Chambliss concludes:

> Organized crime becomes not something that exists outside law and government but is instead a creation of them, or perhaps more accurately a hidden but nonetheless integral part of the governmental structure. The people most likely to be exposed by public inquiries (whether conducted by the FBI, a grand jury, or the Internal Revenue Service) may officially be outside of government, but the cabal of which they are a part is organized around, run by, and created in the interests of economic, legal, and political elites.[23]

Another implication of Chambliss' study is that law enforcement is a form of class domination, especially in the case of vice laws. Most of the people arrested were from the lower class. The well-to-do who actively participated in vices were rarely if ever arrested. Seattle is only one of several cities across the nation that has experienced this type of corruption. The law enforcement bureaucracy was, in each case, deeply enmeshed in the corruption.[24]

Public Servants or Public Thugs? The Rampart Scandal in Los Angeles

Police corruption is not limited to the past. The city of Los Angeles was home to widespread corruption that began in a special anti-gang unit called *CRASH* (Community Resources against Street Hoodlums). The original name had been TRASH (the "T" stood for Total), but it was changed for obvious reasons. Under this program, the police engaged in "surveillance and harassment." Their explicit purpose was, to use one officer's words, to "jam" suspected gang members—to harass and then move on, making no arrest in most cases. Officers, due to unit rotation after two or three years, never had a real opportunity to develop detailed knowledge about the communities.[25]

During one five-week period in 1995, gang-squad officers brutalized two families in their homes. These cases eventually cost taxpayers about $1 million in civil suits. In one case, a police officer struck a 15-year-old boy in the mouth with a shotgun butt and suffocated his father, who passed out and required hospitalization. According to police records, there was no internal investigation of these incidents; the department ignored the claims of the family. In other incidents, at least twelve officers were relieved of duty for illegally shooting suspects, planting evidence, beating one man, falsifying evidence, and many other crimes.

By late October 1999, the Los Angeles Police Department (LAPD) recognized that the problem was more than a few "bad apples"[26]—it appeared to be systemic throughout "the barrel." One LAPD lieutenant revealed that a sergeant in the anti-gang unit had given officers instructions to plant guns on suspects, and that officers stole drugs from dealers and used prostitutes to sell the drugs for the officers. As the investigation continued, it became clear that the sergeant had done more than simply give orders to plant weapons on suspects. He also helped to create fictitious crime scenes such as the one in 1996, where 19-year-old Francisco Ovando was shot, framed, and falsely imprisoned. One officer indicated that the CRASH unit officers behaved like the gangs they were policing.[27]

In mid-November, evidence showed that Rampart police officers conducted random stops and were involved in confrontations where citizens were beaten and detained. Forty percent of the Rampart officers were Latinos, and residents indicated that those officers were among the worst. Some people indicated that even the Latino officers would refer to them as "wetbacks" and often asked them why they did not go back to Mexico. Some people indicated that Rampart officers set them up so they could not acquire legal residency. Al Pina, who moved to the area to take a job as vice president of the local community development corporation, stated that he was surprised to see the number of random stops conducted by Rampart police. In fact, Pina had been stopped by three officers, restrained, and searched while another officer held a gun on him. After the officers released him, he asked why he had been subjected to the search. Officer David Solis told him he "fit the profile of a drug dealer." Pina, a 36-year-old, clean-cut former Air Force sergeant, said he had never felt so humiliated in his life. In another case, Juan Jimenez, a United Parcel Service stock clerk, was handcuffed and detained by police at least twelve times in 1999 while en route to night school or to his volunteer job where he tutored children. On one occasion, Jimenez called police following a mugging. When the police responded, they handcuffed and searched him. In poor neighborhoods, everyone becomes a target for police abuse of power.[28]

In 1998, Officer Michael Buchanan arrested and framed Walter Rivas. Buchanan asked Rivas, "Who do you think they are going to believe, are they going to believe you or me?" Buchanan was relieved of duty in October 1999 in connection with another case, in which he and Officer Perez had framed a suspect.[29] Buchanan's illegal behavior placed the arrest and conviction of hundreds of people into question; cases could be reopened to determine if the evidence and/or testimony in those cases was also tainted.

POLICE ABUSE OF POWER

The police are granted powers reserved for a select few in any society: the power to deprive a person of liberty (via arrest) and even the power to take someone's life under certain circumstances. One of the most controversial issues in policing has been the use of violence against citizens. Compounding the controversy is the fact that the largest number of incidents involves minority citizens, especially African Americans.

In 2002, there were more than 26,500 citizen complaints about police use of force. The majority of the complaints (84%) were against officers in large municipal police departments. The number of complaints per officer in those departments was 9.5 per 100 officers and 15.4 per 100 for officers responding to calls for service. The national rates were 6.6 per 100 full-time sworn officers and 10.9 for officers responding to calls for service.[30] In 2005, 43.5 million people had at least one contact with the police; force was used or threatened in 1.6% of those contacts, and 83% of the victims of use of force felt it was excessive. Blacks and Hispanics experienced police use of force at higher rates than whites.[31]

The tragedy of Amadou Diallo illustrates the controversial issue of lethal force perhaps better than any other. Diallo, a 22-year-old man from Guinea living in New York City, was shot 19 times (police fired 41 times) on February 4, 1999, by four white New York City police officers who were involved in "aggressive patrol." The four officers were part of an elite, 380-member street crime unit whose assignment was to "get tough" on crime.[32] The officers claimed that Diallo acted suspiciously while starting to enter his apartment building. When told to "freeze," he reached for his wallet to show his ID. He was apparently confused about what the police wanted him to do, having received contradictory orders to show some ID yet not move. The officers said they thought his wallet was a gun. The four police officers were acquitted at trial.[33]

Another immigrant, Abner Louima, was brutalized by several NYPD officers. On August 9, 1997, he was beaten severely and sodomized with a toilet plunger while in police custody.[34] He spent more than two months in a hospital because of the injuries caused by the officers. The civil suit settlement of $8.75 million was the largest ever against the city of New York. The city paid $7.125 million, and the Patrolmen's Benevolent Association paid $1.625 million.[35]

Mayor Giuliani and law enforcement officials claimed that their "zero tolerance" policy toward crime was responsible for a 50% drop in index crimes in New York City from 1990 to 1996 (the corollary was a 45% increase in police misconduct charges between 1993 and 1997). The crime rate, however, had already begun to drop long before the introduction of the zero tolerance, "quality-of-life policing." In fact, crime rates had dropped all over the country, with or without a change in police tactics.[36] Examples of tough police tactics abound, ranging from normal everyday methods of harassment in minority communities—a long tradition documented in numerous studies—to physical brutality and murder.[37]

The Rodney King beating—documented when a citizen with a camcorder happened to be near the scene and taped almost the entire incident—resulted in nationwide publicity and a highly emotional trial. All the officers involved were acquitted, although three were subsequently convicted on federal civil rights violations. To most minority citizens—especially those living in the inner city—the beating reflected "business as usual" for the police. In 1994, the Mollen Commission on police corruption in New York City noted widespread police brutality in the Bronx. One officer was known as "the Mechanic" for his tendency to "tune people up"—police jargon for a beating. In Los Angeles, whenever most African Americans encounter a police officer, "They don't know whether justice will be meted out or whether

judge, jury and executioner are pulling up behind them."[38]

There is abundant evidence that police brutality and police killings disproportionately affect racial minorities. Until recent years, the ratio of African Americans shot and killed by the police compared to whites was as high as 8 to 1. After a multitude of complaints resulted in police departments changing their policies, the ratio has declined to a still unacceptable 3 to 1.[39]

Profiling

Police abuse of power extends to the highways. The most common reason for police-citizen contact is a traffic stop, accounting for about 4 out of 10 contacts with the police. In 2005, 17.8 million persons were pulled over in a traffic stop.[40] If race is the primary factor in an officer's decision to stop a motorist, *racial profiling* has occurred. The number of incidents where African-American motorists have been stopped and searched caused critics to label the suspicions supposedly justifying the traffic stop "*driving while black*" *(DWB)*.

Chambliss reports that a special unit of the Washington, DC, police known as the Rapid Deployment Unit (RDU) patrols certain areas in the inner city "continuously looking for cars with young black men in them." Vehicular stops for DWB, says Congressman John Conyers (D-Michigan), are "well-known to African-American males across the country." [41]A recent study found that between 1995 and 1997, 70% of the drivers stopped on Interstate 95 in Maryland were black, even though black and Hispanic motorists constituted only about 17.5% of drivers who were speeding.[42]

In 1993, the State of New Jersey agreed to pay more than $775,000 to motorists who were victims of racial profiling to settle lawsuits brought by the American Civil Liberties Union. Dr. Elmo Randolph, a dentist who drove a luxury car, was one of the motorists. He had been stopped approximately 100 times without ever receiving a ticket; his car was searched; and he was questioned about his profession and how and where he bought his car. After the settlement, he stated: "Police have harassed African Americans and other minorities on New Jersey's highways for years and it has created a climate where innocent people are afraid of police."[43]

Culture of Segregation

Profiling is an extension of beliefs about policing the poorer areas of large cities. Most inner cities in the United States are separated from the rest of society (both literally and figuratively speaking). The separation is evident in the amount of unemployment and underemployment, substandard housing, inadequate social services, high crime rates, and high rates of alcohol and drug abuse. These areas are almost like colonies where society sends those who do not meet certain standards. Essentially, these communities are segregated from the rest of society.

> Residential segregation has been instrumental in creating a structural niche within which a deleterious set of attitudes and behaviors—a culture of segregation—has arisen and flourished. Segregation created the structural conditions for the emergence of an oppositional culture that devalues work, schooling, and marriage and that stresses attitudes and behaviors that are antithetical and often hostile to success in the larger economy. [44]

Because of segregation (especially within the housing market), African Americans have been far less able than other minorities (e.g., Mexican Americans, Jews, Italians, Poles) to escape. Until about 1900 most African Americans lived in areas that were largely white. In 1930, the percentage of African Americans who lived in neighborhoods dominated by African Americans (isolation index) stood at 31.7 in northern cities (data for southern cities are unavailable); by 1970 this percentage had increased to 73.5.[45]

Douglas Massey and Nancy Denton note that about one-third of all African Americans live in areas that are *highly segregated* in at least four of five dimensions of segregation: unevenness, isolation, clustering, concentration, and centralization. *Unevenness* indicates that within an urban area, African Americans may be overrepresented in some

areas and underrepresented in others. *Isolation* refers to African Americans and whites rarely living in the same neighborhoods. *Clustering* occurs when African American neighborhoods constitute a continuous enclave occupying a large area of land instead of being scattered about the city. *Concentration* occurs when African Americans are concentrated in one small area. *Centralization* is high when most African Americans live in the central core of a city.

> A high score on any single dimension is serious because it removes blacks from full participation in urban society and limits their access to its benefits. . . . [B]lacks . . . are more segregated than other groups on any single dimension of segregation, but they are also more segregated on all dimensions simultaneously; and in an important subset of U.S. metropolitan areas, they are very highly segregated on at least four of the five dimensions at once, a pattern we call hyper segregation.[46]

Segregation has social control advantages for the police. Segregation may reduce the pressure on authorities to police minority populations, since segregation reduces interracial crime, the phenomenon most likely to result in pressure on crime control authorities. . . . Fear of crime, coupled with fear of loss of dominance, provides fertile ground for a mobilization of policing resources.[47]

The police in segregated neighborhoods often perceive themselves (and are perceived by the residents) as an "an alien force" in "enemy" territory. Several surveys on police attitudes toward inner-city residents and comparisons between the socioeconomic characteristics of the police and the residents in these areas point to the divide between the two groups.[48] Despite the divide, policing the inner city benefits the police bureaucracy, as noted above. In addition, arrests of urban, lower-class minorities are much easier to make because these citizens are so powerless. In contrast, arrests of "white middle-class offenders (on college campuses, for example, or in the law offices of Wall Street) are guaranteed to cause the organization and the arresting officers strain because people with political influence or money hire attorneys to defend them." Thus, in a class-stratified society "the powerless, the poor, and those who fit the public stereotype of 'the criminal' are the human resources needed by law enforcement agencies to maximize gains and minimize strains."[49]

One of the most persistent problems facing the police, which help to create social contexts where corruption and the abuse of power can take place, is the enforcement of laws that have no complaining victim, otherwise known as *victimless crimes.* Almost every case of police corruption and most cases of police abuse of power occur within the context of victimless crimes. Prostitution, gambling, and drugs are the most common contexts in which corruption and/or abuse of power occurs.

THE POLICE AND
THE WAR ON DRUGS

Most people have engaged in unlawful behavior at some time in their lives. Most were lucky enough not to be detected by the police. Drug violations are one of many categories of behavior where the number of violators is much higher than the number of arrests. People sometimes assert that over-representation is the result of more people in that group committing a particular crime.

> Contrary to public belief, the higher arrest rates of black drug offenders do not reflect higher rates of drug law violations. Whites, in fact, commit more drug crimes than blacks. . . . Statistical as well as anecdotal evidence indicate drug possession and drug selling cut across all racial, socioeconomic and geographic lines. Yet because drug law enforcement resources have been concentrated in low-income, predominantly minority urban areas, drug offending whites have been disproportionately free from arrest compared to blacks.[50]

A number of factors affect selective law enforcement, particularly in the case of juveniles:

> differential police policies and practices (targeting patrols in certain low-income neighborhoods, policies requiring immedi-

ate release to biological parents, group arrest procedures); location of offenses (African American youth using or selling drugs on street corners, White youth using or selling drugs in homes); different behavior by youth of color (whether they commit more crimes than White youth); different reactions of victims to offenses committed by White and youth of color (whether White victims of crimes disproportionately perceive the offenders to be youth of color); or racial bias within the justice system.[51]

Young African-American males have often been the target of law enforcement efforts to "crack down on drugs." In 1980 the national rate of all drug arrests was about the same for black and white juveniles. During the 1980s, the arrest rate for whites dropped by 32%, while the rate for blacks increased 249%. By 1989, the arrest rate for blacks was five times the rate for whites.[52] In 2005, 32% of the people under the age of 18 arrested for drug abuse violations were black.[53] We will revisit the topic of juveniles and drugs in chapter 16.

There is abundant evidence that the war on drugs has been essentially a war on African Americans. Drug law enforcement was concentrated in large urban areas, which have larger populations of African Americans, proportionally, than whites. Black drug offenders were thus at greater risk of arrest than were white offenders. Within those metropolitan areas, politics and law enforcement priorities determined how drug arrests would be distributed.

The major fronts in the drug wars were low income, minority neighborhoods. The spread of crack cocaine in the early 1980s contributed to the distribution of law enforcement efforts. Neighborhood residents appalled by the crime and violence that accompanied the sale of crack sought police protection.

Crack cocaine in black neighborhoods became a lightning rod for a complicated and deep-rooted set of racial, class, political, social, and moral dynamics. To the extent that the white majority in the U.S. identified both crime and drugs with the "dangerous classes"—i.e., poor urban blacks—it was eas-

ier to endorse, or at least acquiesce in, punitive penal policies that might have been
rejected if members of their own families and
communities were being sent to prison at
comparable rates.[54]

The war on drugs continues to adversely
affect African Americans. In 1992, about 3
in 5 defendants charged with drug sales were
black. In 2002, 53% of defendants charged
with drug trafficking were black.[55] The race-
specific arrest rates for blacks over the age of
18 were approximately 3.5 times higher than
for whites from 1993 to 1998. They declined
slightly the next two years and were about 3
times higher in 2001.[56]

The war on drugs has adversely affected
women as well. In 1986, there were less than
92,000 arrests for drug violations; in 2005,
the number of arrests was more than
202,000, an increase of 220%. The increase
in the number of arrests for men during those
two decades was 53%.[57] The police, following directives to stop drug violations, have
significantly increased the numbers of
arrests. The increased numbers have disproportionately affected minorities.

THE POLICE AND
THE WAR ON GANGS

As shown in table 2.1, the violent crime
rate in 2005 (469.2) was lower than the violent crime rate in 1975. The rate had
increased very slightly—a little over 1%—
compared to 2004 (463.2).[58] When the
increase was announced, articles failed to
discuss the size of the increase but didn't hes-
itate to assign blame to gangs. "In Minneap-
olis, Milwaukee, Washington, Boston and
elsewhere, police are reporting spikes in juvenile crime as a surge in violence involving
gangs and weapons has raised crime rates
from historical lows early this decade."
James Fox, a professor of criminal justice at
Northeastern University, offered this explanation: "There is an 'echo boom,' with an
increasing number of late adolescents, particularly blacks and Latinos. Also, more people
incarcerated in the '80s are now being
released to their neighborhoods, and some

are back to their old ways and old gangs."[59]
The Justice Department released a study in
May 2007 that showed a second year of
increased violent crime in 18 cities and suburban regions—and indicated youth violence, gangs, and gun crime were largely to
blame for the increasing rates.[60]

Controlling gangs has become one of the
major roles of the police institution and, in
fact, the entire criminal justice system.[61]
Police, viewed often as society's "first line of
defense" against crime, are the first segment
of the criminal justice system that responds
to the youth gang dilemma. Some of the
responses have been proactive, targeting
schools and neighborhoods with programs
that teach self-esteem, decision making, and
dealing with peer-group pressure.[62] Other
proactive approaches include D.A.R.E.
(Drug Awareness Resistance Education),
S.A.N.E. (Substance Abuse Narcotics Education), and the DEA's Demand Reduction,
Street Smart Prevention. Other programs
hire former gang members to try to persuade
potential recruits to reject gang life.

Many police officers pursue a dual-strat-
egy approach. The immediate response is an
interdiction (intervention or arrest) to preserve the peace and save lives. The follow-up
response is implementation of long-range
preventive measures such as recreation facilities that provide supervised activities for
youth, job training, and working with the
community to create jobs, etc.). One officer
who had worked with gang members for
nearly eight years stated, "Many of these
kids have zero options. They live in a shit
hole. I can arrest them. They may, in rare
instances, actually do some time. When they
get out, they are dumped back into the same
shit hole." Another officer commented
"These kids have no place to play. They find
some structure (e.g., a streetlight pole) to nail
a backboard and hoop, and play basketball in
the middle of the street. They disrupt traffic
and make drivers mad. Pretty soon the kids
just say fuck it and go find something else to
do—they go banging."[63] The references to
"kids" is an acknowledgment that these
youths are not necessarily gangsters or criminals; rather, many of them are children. This

language is qualitatively different from the rhetoric at the beginning of this section where "gang" is shorthand for violent, sociopathic individuals. The officers' comments draw attention to the crux of the problem: structural issues germane to many neighborhoods in the inner cities.

The interdiction dimension of law enforcement's response to youth gangs is a reflection of the tremendous pressure placed on police to produce results. Many law enforcement agencies rely on special units. With a nearly impossible mandate (to eradicate or at least control youth gangs), many law enforcement administrators and local governments often find themselves financially driven to replenish insufficient resources. Many have had to tap into funding sources that might help improve conditions and services in a community, giving youths an alternative to gangs.

During the past few years, the federal government has provided funding assistance through block grants for youth-gang interdiction. Most often, these grants create and support social control strategies rather than solution-oriented approaches. We found one law enforcement agency that formed a special "gang unit" in order to compete for a piece of the block-grant "pie." This particular jurisdiction did not have a youth gang problem at the time of application, nor does this jurisdiction have a gang problem now. During an interview, the detective in charge of the newly formed "gang unit" revealed that "The mayor wanted a gang unit because he had heard that federal grant money was available for police departments that had adopted this sort of special unit." When asked what his gang unit did, he responded, "Nothing. We do not have any gangs in this community. We have some kids who play with spray paint. At best, we have a few gang 'wanna-bees.'"[64]

One major Midwestern urban police department has a gang squad consisting of more than sixty officers and five units: administrative, enforcement, investigation, intelligence, and surveillance.[65] The general responsibilities of the squad include:

- Identification and patrol of high youth-group activity, and "shooting scenes" that do not result in death and are not dealt with by other special units
- Identification of active criminal youth and their leaders
- Collection, analysis, and dissemination of all information related to youth-group problems
- Investigation, enforcement, and intelligence gathering related to all youth-group criminal activities
- Deploying both uniformed and plainclothes officers as required to respond to scenes of youth-group criminal problems. This includes planned youth events that have the potential for youth criminal problems and violence (e.g., rock concerts, rap concerts, high school sporting events, and ethnic festival events)
- Surveillance of youth-oriented activities
- Handling, investigating, and securing warrants in probate and recorder's court for all arrests and detentions stemming from firearms offenses occurring in and around public and private schools in the city

Specific enforcement unit duties include "aggressive enforcement" that targets areas that have a *potential* for youth-crime activity (e.g., schools, gatherings of youth for social functions, and neighborhoods experiencing high incidents of street shootings and gang activity) and the use of aggressive techniques (traffic stops, stop-and-frisk, etc.). The duties of the investigative unit include conducting live "show-ups" and preparing warrant requests for the prosecution of gang members and their associates. The surveillance unit targets individuals, vehicles, groups, or locations based on information provided by the investigation and intelligence units.

The intelligence unit is responsible for such things as preparing profiles on perpetrators of criminal acts who are involved with various gangs and maintaining files with information relevant to gangs (nickname file, vehicle file, gang membership, affiliation with other gangs, etc.). This special unit uses the following criteria (similar to those used by many other jurisdictions) to identify gang members:

- An individual admits membership in a gang
- A reliable informant identifies an individual as a gang member
- A reliable informant identifies an individual as a gang member, and this information is corroborated by independent information
- An individual resides in or frequents a particular gang area, adopts a gang's style of dress, use of hand signs, symbols, and tattoos, and associates with known gang members
- An individual has been arrested several times in the company of identified gang members for offenses consistent with usual gang activity

If an individual has a "close relationship" (the factors determining this are not specified) with a gang but does not fit the above criteria, he or she is identified as a "gang associate."

An obvious paradox exists for this gang squad when one considers the specific duties of each unit in the context of what the squad calls its underlying philosophy. The squad is essentially a *proactive* group that curtails the activity of youthful offenders through *proactive enforcement in areas that are heavily concentrated with gang members.* What should also be obvious is that such a philosophy results in concerted efforts to maintain control and surveillance in mostly minority and lower class communities, because individuals living there have the greatest probability of "gang member" identification.[66]

On any given day, rarely are more than four or five officers actually working on gang-specific cases within their jurisdiction. Typically, "working gangs" for this squad is limited to conducting investigations when alleged gang members are "possible" suspects in a crime. Moreover, it is common knowledge in the department that assignment to the gang squad provides strong credentials for promotion; thus, membership in the gang squad in this jurisdiction is a political position. One officer commented: "Members of the gang unit profile around and play cowboy. When they do make contact with

gang members they do little more than harass them." According to another officer, "We (patrol officers) are the ones who work the gangs. We deal with them on a daily basis. The gang squad is too busy dealing with the media, and kissing the Chief's ass." The remarks of a San Jose police veteran of twenty-two years suggest that the midwestern jurisdiction is not unique: "Gang units are like every other special unit in policing— full of bullshit and totally political."[67]

One of the authors (WBB) interviewed a law enforcement official in Oregon. The topic of the interview was youth gangs. The officer explained that his chief did not tolerate racism in his department. As the interview continued, the officer reflected back to the neighborhood where he grew up. "It was a very nice neighborhood back then. Now it is full of 'greasers' and 'niggers' all trying to do each other in."[68] Geography and time may change, but some things seem to remain constant.

Conducting "sweeps" or "rousts" of targeted areas is another strategy employed by police; multiple officers converge on a target area to eradicate (or relocate) specific forms of criminal or undesirable behavior. In the case of youth-gang interdiction, this tactic is analogous to attempting to put out a forest fire with a water bucket. It is legally and morally questionable to remove youth-gang members from their neighborhoods, homes, and families. Often this tactic does more harm than good and is frequently perceived as racist.

Operation Hammer was a police response to gangs in a ten-square-mile area of South Central Los Angeles under the administration of Police Chief Daryl Gates. The crackdown began in April 1988; about 200 police officers participated.[69] Operation Hammer produced 1,453 arrests, mostly for minor offenses like curfew violation or disturbing the peace. The names and addresses of hundreds more were registered in an "electronic gang roster" for "future intelligence."[70] To aid in this repressive activity, the police used a special "mobile booking" operation next to the Los Angeles Coliseum. The overall purpose was social control (of African American youth) rather than a serious attempt at reducing crime. Proof of this is the fact that out of the 1,453 arrests, 1,350 persons (93%) were released without any charges filed. Interestingly, half of those arrested turned out *not* to be gang members. Only 60 felony arrests were made, and charges were filed on only 32 of these. Operation Hammer and other suppressive efforts resulted in the arrests of an estimated fifty thousand African American youth; about 10% were charged with an offense.[71]

CAN THE POLICE PREVENT CRIME?

David Bayley states very clearly that the police do not prevent crime.

> This seems to be one of the best-kept secrets of modern life. Experts know it, the police know it, but the public either does not know it or elects to ignore it. Yet the police seem to portray the image that they are society's best defense against crime and continually argue that if they are given more resources, especially personnel, they will be able to protect communities against crime.[72]

Hiring more officers and creating special units within police departments for the war on drugs and the war on gangs has not solved either of these social problems. The results are no different for the problem of crime in general. As dozens of studies have demonstrated, adding more cops bears little or no relationship to actual levels of crime. Yet the constant mantra of police departments is "we need more police officers" in order to keep citizens safe. In general, cities with the highest crime rates have the most police per capita.[73] This ratio varies considerably, from a high 6.3 officers per 1,000 citizens in Washington, DC (which has consistently had one of the highest crime rates in the country), to a low 1.6 officers per 1,000 citizens in San Jose.[74]

Adding more police typically results in more reported crime, although in some instances there is little or no change in overall crime rates. If we look at crimes known to police and cleared by arrest between 1971 and 2005, we see very little difference (see figure 7.1).

Some argue that it is not the number of officers in a department that matters but how they are used that affects crime rates. Increasing the number of police officers can

Figure 7.1   Percentage of Crimes Known to Police and Cleared by Arrest (1971–2005)

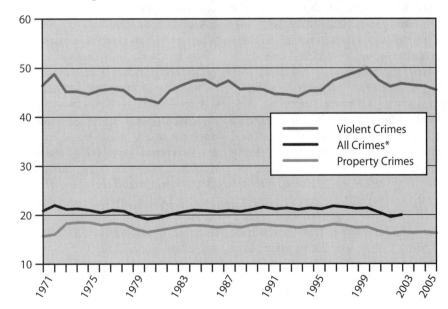

*UCR discontinued the Total Crime Index in 2003

Source: *Sourcebook of Criminal Justice Statistics*. Online, http://www.albany.edu/sourcebook/pdf/t4202005.pdf

produce modest reductions in crime, but it is not cost-effective. Faster response time will not have an appreciable effect on crime rates.[75] The vast majority of crimes are "cold" by the time the police are notified (i.e., well before the police know about a crime, the offender is gone). If the police arrive within one minute of a crime being committed, they are more likely to make an arrest; as the time increases, the chances become correspondingly remote. Similarly, expert investigations by detectives do little to solve crimes unless there is a specifically named suspect. When there is a named suspect, there is about an 86% chance of clearing the crime by an arrest; without a named suspect, clearance rates fall to 12%.[76] The majority of cases have no named suspect.

Altering the level of police patrols in an attempt to lower crime has been the subject of a number of empirical investigations. It was always assumed—without question and without supporting evidence—that adding more cops, especially in high-crime areas, would result in a lower crime rate, mostly because a greater police presence would deter potential criminals. In 1972, the Kansas City police department decided to test this idea. In the southern part of the city (a high-crime area), fifteen police beats were divided into five groups of three matched beats each. Each group had similar beats in terms of population characteristics, crime levels, and calls for police service. Three different patrol strategies were used for a period of one year. One beat (chosen at random), patrolled in the normal manner, the second beat increased patrol levels (often called *saturation patrol*), and the police in the third beat came to the area only when there was a complaint.[77]

Before and after the experiment, people in each beat were asked how they felt about police services, if they had been victimized by a crime, and to what extent they were fearful of crime. To the surprise of many, by the end of the year there had been no significant differences among the three beats in terms of criminal activity, the amount of reported crime, and victimization rates. Interestingly, citizens in the areas where

patrols were increased felt more apprehensive about the likelihood of being the victim of a crime, and respect for the police had actually decreased.

The results do not suggest that police have absolutely no effect on crime. They do suggest, however, that adding police patrols does not reduce crime. In any given area, the number of police patrols is rather small. Thus, additions still leave few officers patrolling an area. In addition, many offenders or potential offenders are not concerned about the level of police patrol. In fact, because most crimes lack planning, whether police are around is irrelevant. In the case of violent crimes, most are committed between people who are at least casually acquainted and most are committed indoors (robbery excepted).

Another study of foot patrol in Newark arrived at similar results. In this case, there was no effect on the crime rate, but increases in foot patrols reduced citizens' fear of crime.[78]

POLICING AND MENTAL ILLNESS

College students who aspire to a career in law enforcement rarely consider mental illness as a relevant topic, but people with mental illness pose significant challenges for law enforcement.[79] Police officers frequently encounter people with mental illness. About 5% of U.S. residents have a serious mental illness; the percentages increase to between 10 and 15% for those in jail.[80] Nearly 7% of police contacts in jurisdictions with 100,000 or more people involve the mentally ill.[81] In a three-city study, 92% of patrol officers had at least one encounter in a 30-day period with a mentally ill person in crisis, and officers averaged six such encounters per month.[82] The Lincoln (Nebraska) Police Department found that it handled over 1,500 mental health investigation cases in 2002, and that it spent more time on these cases than on injury traffic accidents, burglaries, or felony assaults.[83] The New York City Police Department responds to about 150,000 "emotionally disturbed persons" calls per year.[84]

Mental illness is not, by itself, a police problem—it is a medical and social services problem. Nevertheless, many problems caused by or associated with people with mental illness do become police problems. Traditional police responses to people with mental illness have often been ineffective. Sometimes they are tragic.

Police officers have encounters with people who have mental illness in many different types of situations. Often, these situations include criminal offenders, disorderly persons, missing persons, complainants, victims, and persons in need of care. According to one study, the five most frequent scenarios are:

- A family member, friend, or other concerned person calls the police for help during a psychiatric emergency.
- A person with a mental illness feels suicidal and calls the police as a cry for help.
- Police officers encounter a person with a mental illness behaving inappropriately in public.
- Citizens call the police because they feel threatened by the unusual behavior or the mere presence of a person with a mental illness.
- A person with a mental illness calls the police for help because of imagined threats.[85]

Situations involving the threat of suicide are considered the most difficult to handle, and the remaining situations are considered somewhat difficult to handle. The two most problematic behaviors are suicide threats and inappropriate public behaviors. When called to investigate shoplifting or disorderly conduct, for example, police officers are not always aware that mental illness is a factor. When police officers follow their normal routines for handling these cases, they may fail to get the cooperation or compliance expected. Often, this makes the situation more tense and escalation is likely. For these reasons, training is essential to learn crisis management techniques.[86]

The dominant perception is that people with a mental illness are quite likely to engage in violent behavior. In reality, a small portion of the mentally ill is more violent when compared to other people. This violent behavior is most common among those persons who experience serious psychotic symptoms. Second, individuals who have a mental illness may indeed harm others by committing personal or property crimes. On the other hand, a person with a mental illness can be a victim at the hands of family members or caretakers.[88]

Another problem that compounds the relationship between police and the mentally ill is the fact that homelessness and substance abuse often accompany mental illness. The

---

Figure 7.2   Death of a Mentally Ill Man

James P. Chasse, 42, died Sept. 17, 2006, after an encounter with police in the heart of Portland's swank Pearl District. The schizophrenic man was known to friends as "Jim." According to one officer's testimony, Jim was "doing something suspicious or acting just, um, odd." When Multnomah County Sheriff's Deputy Brad Burton and Portland Police Officer Christopher Humphreys approached Chasse, he ran and the officers ran after him. Portland Police Sgt. Kyle Nice was also nearby and responded.

Police estimated that initial contact took place at 5:18 PM. Chasse was pronounced dead by Providence Hospital staff at 7:04 PM. The events of that one hour and 46 minutes (the length of the movie *The Usual Suspects*) was the subject of much debate in the city and will probably be subject to litigation. Police Chief Rosie Sizer denounced those who posted fliers with the officers' pictures and "Stop me before I kill again!" on telephone poles in Northeast Portland, widening the rift between Portlanders and their police department.

But she was only half right when she urged in *The Oregonian*: "What would be productive at this point is a focus on the larger picture. Although this death is a tremendous tragedy, the real debate should focus on how our society is fulfilling its caretaker role for people who suffer from mental illness."

Portland Mayor Tom Potter took an important step in that direction when he announced his intention to spend $500,000 to train patrol officers in crisis management.

But a review by *Willamette Week* of transcripts, reports, and data from the police and medical examiner clearly indicated that this case demanded scrutiny. And answers.[87]

deinstitutionalization of people with mental illness from state and psychiatric hospitals placed this population in the streets. Lacking desperately needed social services, many of these people engaged in petty crimes and were processed through the criminal justice system. Medication is, in many cases, a viable approach to treating mental illness. However, the depletion of resources for the mentally ill forces many into self-medication—relying on illegal substances for relief. Finally, because much of the mental illness treatment apparatus has been privatized, many low income or impoverished people with mental illness do not receive services because they can't afford the services.[89] The "solution" is often jail or prison. Nationwide, 56% of jail inmates and 64% of prison inmates reported mental health problems during the past year.[90] This is clearly a major problem for policing in America.

COMMUNITY POLICING

The aftermath of 9/11, adoption of the Patriot Act, the implementation of the Department of Homeland Security, and a critical economic period (confronting one of the largest national debts in U.S. history) places law enforcement in a precarious situation. Federal monies focus primarily on national security. Law enforcement is required to accomplish more with less. People want the bad people locked up. Police, at least those officials who think long-range, understand that locking people up is a costly enterprise. Law enforcement, standing alone, is rather limited. The solution to safe communities may rest with community policing.

Community policing is a complex arrangement between law enforcement, citizens, community organizations, and public agencies. Community policing begins with the philosophy that police officers should be part of the community where they work. Western Community Policing Institute expands this philosophy. "Community Policing is a philosophy wherein the police and the community share resources and responsibility for solving recurring problems that directly or indirectly threaten community safety or livability."[91] Communities that subscribe to this philosophy tend to accomplish more community work compared to communities that have traditional police departments.[92] This often includes having more police officers who "walk the beat," rather than driving around in a squad car. Face-to-face contact creates bonds of trust and reliance between police and the public and requires police officers to be open minded, unbiased, and sensitive to the concerns and problems of all community members. Even if officers do not agree with a complainant's viewpoint, they must listen and understand the problem. Police officers should display empathy and compassion with sincerity.[93]

Methamphetamine Abuse Intervention and Prevention across Tribal Boundaries is an example of community policing.[94] It is an ongoing project funded by Community Oriented Policing Services (C.O.P.S.), a component of the U.S. Department of Justice. This program illustrates the complexities, philosophy, and rigors of successful community policing.

Methamphetamine abuse is a growing problem in many jurisdictions, particularly in many tribal areas across the United States. Multiple factors contribute to the problem. Tribal territories are predominately in rural areas, and extensive poverty and high unemployment rates are common. Jurisdictional boundaries complicate law enforcement in tribal territories. Education, employment, housing, mental illness, and generational criminogenics all affect methamphetamine abuse. Each factor needs to be considered individually and collectively to facilitate prevention.

Overcoming the obstacles requires cooperation, understanding, and active participation by agencies, commissions, organizations, and individuals who have a stake in the success of methamphetamine education and preventive programs. These individuals include members of the community from all socioeconomic levels and backgrounds. Successful intervention requires partnership and collaboration construction with multiple community participants on both sides of tribal boundaries. Local law enforcement and

Figure 7.3

345 North Monmouth Ave., Monmouth, OR 9736
1-877-601-6866
http://www.westernrcpi.com/

What We Do

The Western Community Policing Institute (WCPI) was established in 1996 as one of the national network of Regional Community Policing Institutes (RCPI) funded by the United States Department of Justice Office of Community Oriented Policing (COPS).

As a member of the RCPI network, the WCPI provides the latest and most advanced training and technical assistance on community policing issues vital to community safety to our six-state region: Alaska, Hawaii, Nevada, New Mexico, Oregon, Utah, and Indian Country.

As threats of terrorism increase and evolve and significant natural and man-made disasters continue to threaten our communities, the need to approach homeland security by improving the capabilities and collaboration of public safety personnel, governmental and non-governmental organizations, school and post-secondary education officials, medical professionals, tribal leaders, and community members, becomes increasingly evident. To respond to this need, in 2004, the Western Community Policing Institute was awarded a grant from the Department of Homeland Security Office of Grants and Training to develop a community-outreach approach to homeland security training that focuses on collaboration and the best efforts of the whole community, including the public and private sector.

Mission Statement

The mission of the Western Community Policing Institute is to improve the interaction and cooperation between police, community, and government to promote the development of community-based partnerships and problem solving to prevent crime, reduce the fear of crime, and enhance the quality of life throughout the region.

tribal police, judiciary (tribal and non-tribal), tribal councils, county commissions, and city councils are crucial stakeholders in this project. The primary goal of this program is to assist communities in the development of sustainable networks of methamphetamine educational and preventive programs.

Intervention/prevention strategy begins with a comprehensive community (tribal and non-tribal) situational assessment, which includes the extent of methamphetamine abuse and an inventory of available and potential community-based resources. Although communities frequently have resources, they often lack the necessary communication,

coordination, and resource-distribution networks to utilize them efficiently. The intervention program helps communities develop these connections. Many communities do not have a scientific starting point from which to address eco-social problems.

Data collection and analysis for the program began with a survey of inmates in all county, local, and tribal land jails that were most likely to detain and/or hold arrested methamphetamine abusers. The next step was to survey treatment agencies, programs, and facilities, law enforcement agencies, and judicial bodies likely to have contact with methamphetamine abusers. The third step was to conduct a survey of local education institutions to identify and measure substance abuse prevention programs. The final stage was data analysis, which was then used to develop the curriculum.

The goals of the training curriculum include developing community awareness, community-based partnerships, and collaborative problem-solving strategies to promote methamphetamine abuse prevention. Emphasizing cultural traditions provides background for police officers and other participants in the program. The curriculum provides training that creates a level of understanding and respect for tribal culture. Highlighted below are three aspects emphasized in the training.

- Native American Traditions: An overview of traditions presented as they relate to how tribal communities govern and how infractions against tribal members were handled. Topics will include the role of matriarchal societies, the role of the chiefs and council, elders, children, and the importance of various ceremonies.

- Spiritual Beliefs: An overview of spiritual values and beliefs, the role of the "Creator," the Grandfathers, and the spirits of nature, relative to tribal communities interaction within their communities, one on one, and with their environment.

- Cultural Aspects: An overview of the different cultural aspects making up a tribal community, which include the clan, colonies, bands, and the role of specific community members.

The program emphasizes the coordination and distribution of community resources; training all participants and recruiting individuals and agencies to help, plus adequate monitoring and evaluation; and education/prevention.

Community policing, as previously noted, depends on the ability of law enforcement to pursue and develop collaborations within their communities. Law enforcement efforts to provide public safety require community collaborations to be successful. Organizations such as Western Community Policing Institute provide training and evaluation for agencies and communities who are open to progressive changes.

Before concluding this chapter, it is important to note that community policing is now a viable component of the Department of Homeland Security training program, entitled *Creating Vigilant, Prepared and Resilient Communities for Homeland Security.* This is a new conceptualization for policing and for the Department of Homeland Security. Western Community Policing Institute provides this training to communities across the country. Below is a statement by the Executive Director of Western Community Policing Institute, who contributed significantly to this community policing-homeland security conceptualization.

Community Policing in an Era of Homeland Security

Now more than ever, the philosophy and tenets of community policing are needed to keep our communities vigilant, prepared, and resilient for homeland security. With the tragic events of September 11, 2001, and more recently, the implications of hurricane Katrina in Louisiana, it has become increasingly evident that community policing remains one of the most needed and effective strategies in addressing homeland security and all-hazards events.

Since the early 1980s, the philosophy and tenets of community policing have primarily been used for solving reoccurring problems that directly or indirectly threaten community safety or livability. The philosophy of community policing, which promotes shared resources and responsibilities, and the tenets, which include organizational change, partnerships, and problem solving, have had tremendous and long-lasting impacts in helping communities remain safe and secure. It is these proven successes that have demonstrated the continued need to apply community policing, not only to crime and livability issues, but to new and emerging issues such as homeland security.

As we enter a new era of protecting our nation, law enforcement and public safety providers will be required to look differently at how they protect, serve, and provide critical services. This is where community policing and homeland security come together to play a vital role in protecting our nation. Community policing provides public safety with the well-established foundational basis needed to support state, local, and federal efforts. This includes effective problem-solving strategies, enhanced partnerships, strong organizational structure, visionary leadership, and coordinated communication channels to build the vigilant, prepared, and resilient communities needed for homeland security.

Community policing remains one of the most important strategies and tools that public safety and the community can use in protecting our nation. While there has been discussion on the continued relevance and importance of community policing and even the suggestion that community policing has "died," the fact remains that community policing provides both the strategies and tools needed in protecting our communities and nation. These have been the long practiced, tried, tested, and successful strategies and tools used to successfully combat, prevent, and reduce crime and to improve community livability issues across our nation.

It will be incumbent on the leaders of today and on future leaders to recognize and continue to find the best, most effective, and innovative ways to use community policing strategies and tools to protect our communities and our nation. It will be through those ways that leaders will be able to continue to effectively address crime, support community livability efforts, and keep our nation safe and secure in a time of increased homeland security efforts. Community policing is, and will remain, *"not just a strategy to build homeland security, but* THE *strategy—the only one that will work."*

Brian Kauffman
Executive Director
Western Community Policing Institute
January 2007

SUMMARY

For years, the police in the United States focused primarily on order maintenance. This function all too often leads to significant problems, not the least of which occurs when the police violate the laws they are supposed to enforce. The socialization process into a special subculture often leads the police to abuse their awesome power. Whether through harassment ("driving while black"), the enforcement of drug laws, or the war on gangs, the police too often abuse and sometimes kill citizens, especially the poor and racial minorities. The police institution can be viewed as an "army of occupation" in inner-city areas, which are isolated from mainstream society. On the other hand, police have the option to become partner citizens with the communities in which they live and work. This strategy, which parallels community-policing principles, has the best chance to develop safe communities. It is also the responsibility of students and citizens to become involved in making their own communities safe through partnership development and active participation.

Key Terms

- bad-apple theory
- community policing
- CRASH
- driving while black (DWB)
- grass-eaters
- group support theory
- Knapp Commission
- meat-eaters
- Operation Hammer
- order maintenance
- police subculture
- policing styles
- proactive policing
- racial profiling
- reactive policing
- tribal police

Notes

1 "Solutions Scarce for Jail Too Small for County Needs." *Flint Journal* (February 13, 2002).

2 Wilson, J. Q. *Varieties of Police Behavior.* Cambridge, MA: Harvard University Press, 1968.

3 Senna, J. J. and L. J. Siegel. *Introduction to Criminal Justice* (9th ed.). Belmont, CA: Wadsworth, 2002.

4 Bayley, D. H. *Police for the Future.* New York: Oxford University Press, 1994.

5 Klockars, C. B. *The Idea of Police.* Newbury Park, CA: Sage, 1985.

6 Wilson, J. Q. and G. Kelling. "Broken Windows." *Atlantic Monthly* (March 1982).

7 Parenti, C. *Lockdown America: Police and Prisons in an Age of Crisis.* New York: Verso, 1999; Duneier, M. *Sidewalk.* New York: Farrar, Straus and Giroux, 1999.

8 Shelden, R. G., S. Tracy, and W. B. Brown. *Youth Gangs in American Society* (3rd ed.). Belmont, CA: Wadsworth, 2004.

9 Weston, L. *The Study of Society* (2nd ed.). Guilford, CT: Dushkin, 1977, p. 562.

10 Manning, P. K. and J. Van Maanen (eds.). *Policing: A View from the Streets.* Santa Monica, CA: Goodyear, 1978, p. 267.

11 Wilson, *Varieties of Police Behavior.*

12 Van Maanen, J. *Tales of the Field: On Writing Ethnography.* Chicago: University of Chicago Press, 1988.

13 Scheingold, S. A. *The Politics of Law and Order: Street Crime and Public Policy.* New York: Longman, 1984.

14 Doerner, W. C. "I'm Not the Man I Used to Be: Reflections on the Transition from Professor to Cop." In A. S. Blumberg and E. Niederhoffer (eds.), *The Ambivalent Force.* New York: Holt, Rinehart and Winston, 1985, pp. 394–399.

15 Broderick, J. *Police in a Time of Change* (2nd ed.). Long Grove, IL: Waveland Press, 1987.

16 U.S. National Commission on Law Observance and Enforcement (Wickersham Commission). *Reports.* Washington, DC: U.S. Government Printing Office, 1931.

17 Maas, P. "Serpico: The Cop Who Defied the System." In J. Skolnick and T. C. Gray (eds.), *Police in America.* Boston: Little, Brown, 1975.

18 Knapp Commission. "Police Corruption in New York." In Skolnick and Gray (eds.), *Police in America,* p. 235.

19 Ibid., p. 237.

20 Stoddard, E. R. "The Informal 'Code' of Police Deviancy." In Skolnick and Gray, *Police in America,* p. 262.

21 Chambliss, W. J. "Vice, Corruption, Bureaucracy and Power." In V. Kappeler (ed.), *The Police and Society.* Long Grove, IL: Waveland, 2006, p. 204.

22 Ibid., p. 144.

23 Ibid.

24 For another example, see Gardiner, J. "Wincanton: The Politics of Corruption." In W. J. Chambliss (ed.), *Crime and the Legal Process.* New York: McGraw-Hill, 1969.

25 Klein, M. *The American Street Gang.* New York: Oxford University Press, 1995, pp. 164–165.

26 "Rampart Probe May Now Affect over 3,000 Cases." *Los Angeles Times* (December 15, 1999).

27 "LAPD Corruption Probe Grows to 7 Shootings." *Los Angeles Times* (October 22, 1999.)

28 "Crime, Poverty Test Rampart Officers' Skill." *Los Angeles Times* (November 10, 1999).

29 "Latest Rampart Case Focuses on Third Officer." *Los Angeles Times* (December 2, 1999.)

30 Hickman, M. J. *Citizen Complaints about Police Use of Force* (NCJ 210296). Washington, DC: Bureau of Justice Statistics, June 2006, p. 2.

31 Durose, M. R., E. L. Smith, and P. A. Langan. *Contacts between Police and the Public, 2005* (NCJ 215243). Washington, DC: U.S. Department of Justice, April 2007, p. 1.

32 "Police Shooting Deepens Racial Tension." *Los Angeles Times* (February 15, 1999).

33 Ibid; see also Love, D. A. "Justice Department Must Take Over NYPD." *Las Vegas Review-Journal* (February 19, 1999). "The Message of the Diallo Protests." *New York Times* (February 29, 2000).

34 Beals, G. and M. Bai. "The Thin Blue Line." *Newsweek* (September 1, 1997).

35 "New York Pays for Police Brutality." British Broadcasting Company, July 13, 2001. [Online] http://news.bbc.co.uk/2/hi/americas/1436538.stm

36 Cole, D. *No Equal Justice: Race and Class in the Criminal Justice System.* New York: New Press, 1999, pp. 45–46.

37 Cole's book for a summary. Numerous studies dating back to the 1930s report similarly chilling results: The Wickersham Commission reports; the Kerner Commission report (U.S. Riot Commission. *Report of the National Advisory Commission on Civil Disorders.* New York: Bantam Books, 1967); the Christopher Commission report on the Rodney King incident (Christopher Commission. *Report of the Independent Commission on the Los Angeles Police Department.* Los Angeles: Author, 1991).

38 Cole, *No Equal Justice,* p. 23, quoting California Assemblyman Curtis Tucker.

39 Walker, S. and C. M. Katz. *Police in America: an Introduction* (4th ed.). New York: McGraw-Hill, 2002, p. 290.

40 Durose, Smith, and Langan. *Contacts between Police and the Public, 2005,* p. 3.

41 Chambliss, W. J. *Power, Politics and Crime,* pp. 64–68.

42 Cole, D. "Take the Unnecessary Force out of Law Enforcement." *Las Vegas Review-Journal,* May 21, 1999.

43 ACLU-NJ Wins $775,000 for Victims of Racial Profiling by State Troopers. January 13, 2003. [Online] http://www.aclu-nj.org/pressroom/aclunjwins775000forvictims.htm

44 Massey, D. S. and N. A. Denton. *American Apartheid: Segregation and the Making of the Underclass.* Cambridge, MA: Harvard University Press, 1993, p. 8.

45 Ibid., p. 48.

46 Ibid., p. 74.

47 Jackson, P. "Minority Group Threat, Social Context, and Policing." In A. E. Liska (ed.), *Social Threat and Social Control.* Albany: State University of New York Press, 1992, p. 90.

48 For a review of this evidence from surveys from the 1960s and 1970s, see Shelden, R. G. *Criminal Justice in America: A Sociological Approach.* Boston: Little, Brown, 1982, chapter 5; more recent evidence is reviewed in Lynch, M. and R. Michalowski. *The New*

Primer in Radical Criminology. Monsey, NY: Criminal Justice Press, 2000, pp. 160–162.

49 Chambliss, *Power, Politics and Crime.* Boulder, CO: Westview Press, 1999, p. 77.

50 Human Rights Watch. *Punishment and Prejudice: Racial Disparities in the War on Drugs.* May 2000. Vol. 12 No. 2 (G). [Online] http://www.hrw.org/reports/2000/usa/Rcedrg00-05.htm

51 National Council on Crime and Delinquency. *And Justice for Some: Differential Treatment of Youth of Color in the Justice System.* January 2007, p. 1. [Online] http://www.nccd-crc.org/nccd/pubs/2007jan_justice_for_some.pdf

52 Snyder, H. N. *Law Enforcement and Juvenile Crime.* National Report Series Bulletin. December 2001. [Online] http://www.fbi.gov/ucr/adducr/age_race_specific.pdf

53 *Sourcebook of Criminal Justice Statistics.* Table 4.12.2005. [Online] http://www.albany.edu/sourcebook/pdf/t4122005.pdf

54 Human Rights Watch, *Punishment and Prejudice.*

55 Reaves, A. A. and P. Z. Smith. *Felony Defendants in Large Urban Counties 1992 (*NCJ 148826). Washington, DC: Bureau of Justice Statistics, July 1995; Cohen, T. H. and B. A. Reaves. *Felony Defendants in Large Urban Counties 2002* (NCJ 210818). Washington, DC: Bureau of Justice Statistics, February 2006.

56 Race-specific Drug Abuse Violations. [Online] http://www.fbi.gov/ucr/adducr/age_race_specific.pdf

57 FBI, *Uniform Crime Reports 1995,* table 33. [Online] http://www.fbi.gov/ucr/Cius_97/95CRIME/95crime4.pdf; *Uniform Crime Reports 2005,* table 33. [Online] http://www.fbi.gov/ucr/05cius/data/table_33.html

58 FBI, *Uniform Crime Reports, 2005,* table 1. [Online] http://www.fbi.gov/ucr/05cius/data/table_01.html

59 Johnson, K. "Police Tie Jump in Crime to Juveniles." *USA Today* (July 13, 2006); Frieden, T. "Violent Crime Takes First Big Jump Since '91." CNN (June 12, 2006). [Online] http://www.cnn.com/2006/LAW/06/12/crime.rate/

60 Jordan, L. J. *Study to Show Violent Crime Rates Surge for Second Straight Year.* May 30, 2007. [Online] http://www.signonsandiego.com/news/nation/20070530-1510-fbi-crime.html

61 For more detail on the subject of gangs, see Shelden, Tracy, and Brown, *Youth Gangs in American Society.*

62 Boyle, J. and A. Gonzales. "Using Proactive Programs to Impact Gangs and Drugs." *Law and Order* 37: 62–64 (1989).

63 Shelden, Tracy, and Brown, *Youth Gangs in American Society,* p. 209.

64 Ibid.

65 Ibid., pp. 210–211.

66 Ibid., p. 211.

67 Ibid., p. 212.

68 Interview conducted in the summer of 2005 in Oregon.

69 Klein, M. *The American Street Gang,* p. 162.

70 Davis, M. *City of Quartz.* New York: Vintage Books, 1992, p. 268.

71 Ibid., p. 277.

72 Bayley, *Police for the Future,* p. 3.

73 Ibid., pp. 4–5.

74 Walker, S. *Sense and Nonsense about Crime and Drugs* (6th ed.). Belmont, CA: Wadsworth, 2007, p. 86.

75 Bayley, *Police for the Future,* pp. 5–7; Walker, *Sense and Nonsense,* pp. 87–93.

76 Walker, *Sense and Nonsense,* p. 96.

77 Kelling, G. L., T. Pate, D. Diekman, and C. E. Brown. *The Kansas City Preventive Patrol Experiment: A Summary Report.* Washington, DC: The Police Foundation, 1974.

78 The Police Foundation. *The Newark Foot Patrol Experiment.* Washington, DC: The Police Foundation, 1981.

79 Texas Law Enforcement Management and Administrative Statistics Program. *Law Enforcement Interactions with Persons with Mental Illness* 10 (January/February 2003).

80 Lamb, H. R., L. E. Weinberger, and B. H. Gross. "Mentally Ill Persons in the Criminal Justice System: Some Perspectives." *Psychiatric Quarterly* 75: 107–126 (June 2004).

81 Williams, M. W., H. J. Steadman, R. Borum, B. M. Veysey, and J. P. Morrissey. "Emerging Partnerships Between Mental Health and Law Enforcement." *Psychiatric Services* 50: 99–101 (1999).

82 Borum, R., M. W. Deane, H. J. Steadman, J. Morrissey. "Police Perspectives on Responding to Mentally Ill People in Crisis: Perceptions of Program Effectiveness." *Behavioral Sciences & the Law* 16: 393–405 (1998).

83 Lincoln, Nebraska Police Department, 2004.

84 Waldman, A. "Police Struggle with Approach to the Mentally Ill." *Christian Science Monitor* (March 17, 2004).

85 Texas Law Enforcement Management and Administrative Statistics Program, *Law Enforcement Interactions with Persons with Mental Illness.*

86 Cordner, G. *People with Mental Illness* (Guide No. 40). Washington, DC: U.S. Department of Justice, Office of Community Oriented Policing Services, 2006. [Online] http://www.cops.usdoj.gov/mime/open.pdf?Item=1731

87 *Willamette Week* (January 17, 2007). [Online] http://www.wweek.com/editorial/3252/8148/

88 Ibid.

89 Ibid.

90 Harcourt, B. E. "The Mentally Ill, Behind Bars." *New York Times* (January 15, 2007).

91 Western Community Policing Institute. "Creating Vigilant, Prepared, and Resilient Communities for Homeland Security," 2006. [Online] http://www.westernrcpi.com/training_homeland_security.php

92 Hughes, G. and A. Edwards. *Crime Control and Community: The New Politics of Public Safety.* Portland, OR: Willan Publishing, 2002.

93 Peak, K. J. and R. W. Glensor. *Community Policing and Problem Solving: Strategies and Practices* (4th ed.). Upper Saddle River, NJ: Prentice Hall, 2004.

94 One of the authors, William Brown, and Brian Kauffman, Western Community Policing Institute's Executive Director, designed and implemented this project.

eight

The Criminal Courts
The System and Participants

In countless criminal courtrooms across the United States, the same scene is enacted repeatedly. A young African-American male is on trial for burglary. Sitting behind the young man during the trial are two relatives: an older woman who often weeps and an older man who looks helpless and bewildered. The judge sentences the young man to prison and solemnly intones "justice has been served." The judge exits the courtroom, and two officers walk over to the young man. The white defense attorney pats the young man's shoulder, turns, and walks away. The woman reaches out to her son, but the officers won't allow the young man to take her hand. He is quickly ushered out of the courtroom. The older man put his arm around the woman, who is crying profusely. He tries to comfort her, and then they leave. They get into a very old vehicle and drive off. Some form of "justice" may have been served in this courtroom episode, but it was not social justice.

Images of the Courts

The U.S. criminal courts are a major component of the criminal justice system—the intervening step between the police and the prison system. The judicial system is a major institution in U.S. society. Drive through a town of any size in this country, and the local courthouse will be one of the most prominent buildings. In fact, in many towns the courthouse stands literally in the center of town, often with many other government offices in close proximity (local police or sheriff's department, jail, city hall, post office, etc.). The courthouse grounds are often neatly landscaped, with park benches and picnic tables. The phrase "Justice For All" is often inscribed over the entrance; there may be a statue of the "blind lady of justice" on the grounds nearby American and state flags.

The courts differ from most other institutions in at least two important ways.[1] First, the courts are (with some exceptions, to be sure) places where citizens most directly interact with government on an individual basis rather than in groups. Second, the courts are where people "have their day in court" (in the case of a small claims or traffic cases) or as victims in a criminal case, and where the guilty "get their due." The general image of the courts is often limited to phrases such as these and the symbols described above.

The courts are actually one of the least understood institutions—at least as far as the general public is concerned. Opinion polls consistently find that the public has less knowledge about the court system than about any other institution. The National Center for State Courts studied the issue and found that the public generally lacks confidence in the courts.[2] Other surveys consistently show that the public often feels mistreated and disrespected by the courts. The public comes to the court system wanting some resolution, either protection or punishment. Too often they get neither, and their claims are treated as trivial or frivolous.[3] Ordinary, working-class citizens most frequently share this opinion.[4]

The court has been defined as "an agency or unit of the judicial branch of government . . . which has the authority to decide cases, controversies in law, and disputed matters of fact brought before it."[5] The definition is usually associated with connotative meanings such as "justice," "fairness," "impartiality," and "objectivity." The court, however, is not an agency, nor a component of any agency; rather, it is an independent branch of government "stipulated in both the Constitution of the United States and in state constitutions."[6] On the surface, this statement suggests that the court is autonomous, free from the influence of other branches of government and other institutions. As we will see, however, the court can have an agenda far removed from any notions of justice and impartiality.

Criminal courts have been described as "marketplaces in which the only commodity traded seriously is time."[7] Civil courts can be viewed in a similar vein, with the exception that the commodities traded are power and privilege. With sufficient quantities of those commodities, corporations can do pretty much as they will; agencies can remove people from their homes (relocation of Native Americans); one parent can take custody of children in divorce cases; groups dictate what women can do with their bodies (abortion issues); the stronger party decides who can work and who cannot (labor issues); and state agencies decide the poverty level (welfare issues). Power and privilege control and impact many other social issues in contemporary society. If power and privilege can prevail in court, then the court is not justice oriented, objective, or impartial. "Justice" goes to the highest bidder, and fairness is replaced by the whims of power. Sometimes the function of the court is limited to efficiency. When these conditions prevail, the court is not very different from other institutions in a capitalist society.

Most people do not think of the court as a self-serving institution that conceals its true identity behind a cloak of justice, fairness, and impartiality. Rather, most people choose to view the court as a guardian of justice. Of course, justice is whatever we want it to be at a given point in time. Typically, we believe "justice" is served if the

court's decision favors us or our ideas about a particular case. When the court's decision goes against us, or against what we think the court should have done, we charge the court with "injustice."

SOCIAL JUSTICE

Few of us consider another form of justice that is relevant to most criminal cases—social justice, as noted in the opening paragraph. Social justice involves consideration of concepts such as race/ethnicity, sex/gender, and social class. The topic of social justice is often dismissed as an example of liberal thought unrelated to the reality that all poor or disadvantaged people do not commit crimes, so why make exceptions for the few who do.

Almost by definition, the U.S. criminal court system is class biased. Why? Because what is defined as "criminal" usually applies to behaviors that are typically committed by those of lower social standing, while various administrative and civil laws (or in some cases no law at all) are used to process cases involving those of higher social standing.

> Consider a poor woman prosecuted for selling crack, and a rich doctor administratively sanctioned for illegally prescribing Viagra to men who have no medical problem. Even if both were prosecuted according to legal procedures that were absolutely flawless, the difference in the systems that would judge them, and the resources each could muster in their defense, guarantee that the outcomes will be far removed from any standard of equality before the law. However, in a male- and white-centered society such as America, the legal system finds little reason to concern itself with a product that is promoted by white, male drug company executives and distributed by affluent white, male doctors to a clientele consisting primarily of white men who want to increase their sexual pleasure. In contrast, when poor people, particularly poor people of color, sell or use "illegal" drugs as part of a street-level system of self-medication, political leaders react with outrage, the legal system responds with drug wars and the courts lock up thou-

sands of poor drug dealers and users behind bars. In the American way of doing justice, the sexual pleasure of white men is far more important than the lives of poor people of color.[8]

Rush Limbaugh, a conservative talk show host, provides another example of differential treatment. Limbaugh was a strong proponent of harsh treatment for nonviolent drug offenders. After a 3-year investigation into "doctor shopping," Limbaugh was formally charged in April 2006—but not arrested or jailed—for illegally obtaining and using thousands of prescription pain killers. Limbaugh avoided jail time by agreeing to an 18-month diversion program.[9] The terms of the program were that he not commit additional violations, submit to random drug tests, and complete a drug treatment program. The criminal charges would be dismissed if he met the terms of the agreement. At the end of June 2006, Limbaugh's private plane landed at Palm Beach International Airport. He was returning from vacation in the Dominican Republic, and authorities found a bottle of Viagra in his bag. The prescription for the controlled medication was not in his name.[10] An impoverished defendant without connections (including a celebrated lawyer) would have been arrested and the diversion agreement voided. Instead, the agreement stayed in place, and the criminal charges were later dismissed. Limbaugh joked about the incident on his radio show, saying officials didn't believe him when he said he got the pills at the Clinton Library and he was told they were blue M&Ms. He later chuckled: "I had a great time in the Dominican Republic. Wish I could tell you about it."[11]

Social class plays a key role in public opinion. Are the courts really the "people's courts," or are they just another arm of the rich and the powerful, a system of class domination where one class stands in judgment of another? The "problem-solving court" movement recognizes that the public expects the courts to address society's ills and produce positive outcomes.

PROBLEM-SOLVING STATE COURTS

Today there are literally thousands of "problem-solving courts" testing new approaches to difficult cases where social, human, and legal problems intersect. These courts attempt to apply concepts of preventive law, risk management, restorative justice, and therapeutic jurisprudence. In spite of the encouraging growth of these new courts, they remain out of the mainstream of the criminal justice system. Despite the lack of universally accepted models for these new courts and the diversity of approaches, problem-solving courts share underlying principles in their attempts to depart from historical case processing principles.[12] We will revisit the topic of alternative case processing in chapter 9.

While problem-solving courts attempt to introduce concepts of social justice into the court system, these new courts may encounter the same type of approval/disapproval as traditional courts. If the courts solve problems and produce the results one expects, public opinion will be positive. But, of course, there is not universal agreement on problems and solutions. In addition, some of the public might fear activist judges who support social and economic policies that are controversial or unpopular. In this chapter, we explore these and other issues.

We begin with a brief historical overview of the development of the American court system, which reveals that the problems of social justice can be traced back to colonial times. We will then present a broad overview of the criminal court system comparing the federal and state systems. Next we will consider in some detail the major actors who play the most important roles in the court system: prosecutors, defense attorneys, and judges.

A BRIEF HISTORY

Our modern courts have their roots in colonial society, which for the most part copied the court system in England. The original charter of the Massachusetts Bay Colony created two types of courts: a general court and a court of assistants. The former acted as both a legislative body and a court, while the latter (which consisted of the governor, deputy governor, and magistrates) was in charge of appeals from the lower courts, which came to be known as county courts. These county courts were the heart of the local system of criminal justice—the same kinds of courts found in most cities and towns today. What is perhaps most interesting about these courts was the fact that they performed so many different functions: probate, spending money on road and bridge repairs, various forms of licensing, levying and collecting taxes, providing for the maintenance of the local ministry, regulation of wages, and of course all matter of criminal cases.[13]

"Ordinary people used the courts to get justice for themselves, vindication, and restitution; in criminal as well as civil matters."[14] The courts were also used as places to vent frustrations and anger, thus assisting in the stability of colonial society.[15] They provided residents with socializing opportunities, a place to conduct business, and the opportunity to engage in lively political discussions.[16]

The justice of the peace performed most of the day-to-day duties in the county courts. The position was appointed by the governor (who was himself an appointee of the English king). For all practical purposes, the position was controlled by the local elites. The legal profession became more and more specialized as the numbers of lawyers grew. Most lawyers, including some of the most famous who participated in the writing of the Constitution, learned the trade through apprenticeships with older lawyers. Among these notables were Thomas Jefferson and James Wilson (both signed the Declaration of Independence). The legal profession, then as now, was soon dominated by the wealthy and powerful.

The bulk of the cases brought before the justice of the peace were minor offenses; "breach of peace" was the most common. Three other offenses constituted a large proportion of the cases and illustrated the strength of religious influences: "profane swearing, profane cursing" (it is not clear what the difference was) and "profaning the Sabbath."[17] Religion was woven into codes throughout the colonies, but it was most evident in the northern colonies. "In one part of the Laws and Liberties of Massachusetts . . . The code contained a list of 'capital laws.' Each one came equipped with citations from the Bible."[18] The repressive features of colonial law based on Puritan ethics has been famously illustrated by the witch trials in Salem, Massachusetts.[19]

After the American Revolution, a federal court system emerged, complete with various appellate courts and the United States Supreme Court. This was an important development in the history of criminal justice. There had been much debate between those who believed that there should be a federal court system and those who did not; the debate was an extension of differences over whether there should be a strong central government. The federalists eventually won the debate, although with some compromises, such as establishing district courts. The *Judiciary Act of 1789* and the *Reorganization Act of 1801* empowered district courts (which were structured along state lines, and the judges had to be residents of that state) to enforce federal laws. By the end of the eighteenth century there was very little distinction between trial and appellate courts. In many instances, "high-court judges often doubled as trial or circuit judges."[20]

Senator Oliver Ellsworth was the author of The Judiciary Act of 1789, which established the Supreme Court. He later became the third Chief Justice. Throughout the history of the Supreme Court, its members have been drawn overwhelmingly from the upper crust of society. This was especially the case in the nineteenth century, when almost all of the justices came from the "landed gentry" and were schooled at Ivy League universities. The very first Court, 1790–1801, reflects this class bias, as did the second. The Marshall Court (1801–1836) was one of the most influential in the early years.[21]

The biggest changes in the court system came after the Civil War, largely because of the huge growth in population and particularly the growth in large cities. The old agrarian court system of small-town America was no longer sufficient to handle the changes. New courts emerged, including small claims courts, municipal courts (which handle misdemeanors and traffic citations), felony courts, and juvenile courts (1899).

AN OVERVIEW OF THE CRIMINAL COURT SYSTEM

When we examine the criminal court system, we once again find that social class, race, and sex play a major role. The bulk of cases coming before these courts, in sharp contrast to those coming before the civil courts, involve defendants from relatively poor and low-income backgrounds. The American bar system, like the society in which it operates, is highly stratified. The majority of criminal lawyers occupy the lowest position within the hierarchy of the legal profession. Thus, the less advantaged in society are defended by those with lower status in the field of law. At every stage, those who process, prosecute, or judge criminal defendants are generally from higher-status backgrounds (whether measured by income, education, or connections).

In the United States there are two major court systems: federal and state. Each system is a *dual court system* with two general types of courts: trial and appellate. U.S. District Courts are the trial courts that hear cases, find facts, and apply the substantive law to decide on guilt or innocence. U.S. Courts of Appeals hear cases that are appealing the verdicts handed down by the U.S. District Courts.[22] Appellate courts affirm or reverse the trial court's verdict based on the application of law to the facts found by the trial court. That is, they do not review the evidence or facts of the case; they rule on whether or not the laws were applied correctly.

Federal Courts

The federal court system consists of the following: (1) district courts, which are the trial courts for violations of federal laws (there are 89 districts in 50 states, plus one in the District of Columbia and four in U.S. ter-

ritories, such as Puerto Rico); (2) administrative courts or agencies, which include such regulatory agencies as the Federal Trade Commission, Security and Exchange Commission, and National Labor Relations Board; (3) U.S. Circuit Courts of Appeals (there are thirteen); and (4) the U.S. Supreme Court, the court of last resort on the appeals route.

There is at least one *U.S. District Court* in each state (California, New York, and Texas have four each). In 2005, there were 678 district court judges. District courts have jurisdiction over both criminal and civil matters. There are about 500 U.S. magistrates who hear minor offenses and conduct preliminary hearings. Between 1982 and 2005, the total number of criminal cases handled by U.S. District Courts rose by 113%. While the number of judges during this period of time increased by almost 32%, the average number of cases per judgeship went up by 62%. Drug cases accounted for most of the increase, going from just over 4,000 cases to more than 18,000; drug cases went from 13% of the total number of cases in 1982 to 26% in 2005.[23]

The *U.S. Courts of Appeals* were created in 1891 to relieve the Supreme Court from the growing number of appeals. These courts are the intermediate appellate courts of the federal system. The 94 U.S. judicial districts are organized into 12 regional circuits.[24] The thirteenth is the Court of Appeals for the Federal Circuit, which has jurisdiction over appeals in specialized cases such as patent law (see figure 8.1).

The total number of appeals has increased significantly in recent years, going up by 145% between 1982 and 2005; the number of judgeships increased 26.5%. Cases are heard by a 3-judge panel.[25] Most appeals (67%) are for civil cases. Private persons filed 48% of the total cases, while prisoner petitions in criminal cases accounted for 23% of the total cases in 2005.[26]

Federal appeals court judges are appointed by the president and serve for life after the appointment is confirmed by the Senate. These judges are drawn from a privileged segment of society. Consider the

Figure 8.1   U.S. Courts of Appeals

Circuit 1	Maine, Massachusetts, New Hampshire, Puerto Rico, Rhode Island
Circuit 2	Connecticut, New York, Vermont
Circuit 3	Delaware, New Jersey, Pennsylvania, U.S. Virgin Islands
Circuit 4	Maryland, North Carolina, South Carolina, Virginia, West Virginia
Circuit 5	Louisiana, Mississippi, Texas
Circuit 6	Kentucky, Michigan, Ohio, Tennessee
Circuit 7	Illinois, Indiana, Wisconsin
Circuit 8	Arkansas, Iowa, Minnesota, Missouri, Nebraska, North Dakota, South Dakota
Circuit 9	Alaska, Arizona, California, Guam, Hawaii, Idaho, Montana, Nevada, Northern Mariana Islands, Oregon, Washington
Circuit 10	Colorado, Kansas, New Mexico, Oklahoma, Utah, Wyoming
Circuit 11	Alabama, Florida, Georgia
Circuit 12	District of Columbia, Federal Circuit
Circuit 13	Court of Appeals for the Federal Circuit

appointments made between 1963 and 2005. The majority of appointees received both their undergraduate and law degrees from private universities. Most were already serving in the judiciary when appointed; the others were working in the government, at law firms, or at a university. The number of minority appointments began to improve in 1993. From 1993 to 2005, there were 95 appointments, and 23 were minorities (24%). Between 1963 and 1992, there were 268 appointments and only 21 were minorities (7.8%). Very few women (who represent more than half the population) have received appellate court appointments. The numbers began improving slightly in 1989. From 1989 to 2005, there were 132 appointments, and 34 were women (26%). From 1963 to 1988, only 16 of the 231 appointments were women (less than 7%).[27]

The *U.S. Supreme Court* is the highest court in the country. It consists of nine justices: eight associate justices and a chief justice, who are nominated by the president, confirmed by the Senate, and serve for life.

Through a *writ of certiorari* a lower court is ordered to produce the records of a trial for the Supreme Court to review, and the final appeal begins. In some cases, the Supreme Court may receive an *in forma pauperis* request from a prisoner—a request to file an appeal with the Supreme Court for the payment of legal fees.[28] In contrast to the U.S. District Courts and the U.S. Courts of Appeals, the number of cases heard by the U.S. Supreme Court has decreased from 183 cases argued 1982 to 68 decisions in the 2006–2007 term (the lowest since 1953).[29]

A president can influence judicial proceedings for decades through the nomination of Supreme Court justices. Nominees for the U.S. Supreme Court are typically selected on the basis of their political views, which are generally determined by their previous judicial views and decisions. Voters may vote a president out of office, but they are not able to rid themselves of U.S. Supreme Court justices at the polls. Supreme Court justices often continue to propagate the views of their nominating administration well into the tenure of another administration.[30]

State Courts

Most criminal and civil cases in the United States come before the state court system. Most criminal cases are heard in *trial courts of limited jurisdiction*, known collectively as lower or inferior courts. These courts have different names in different places—such as municipal, justice of the peace, city, magistrate, and county courts. They are usually created by local governments (cities or counties). These courts hear misdemeanor, traffic, and city ordinance cases plus minor civil disputes. They are also responsible for initial appearances and preliminary hearings for felony cases. There are more than 13,500 lower courts, representing 84% of all state judicial bodies, staffed by 18,000 judicial officers, who address about 61 million cases each year.[31]

Trial courts of limited jurisdiction are the courts most citizens come in contact with if they violate a law. Such courts can also be viewed as "poor people's courts," because the vast majority who parade through them are drawn from the ranks of the poor and the working classes.[32] (See section on public defenders below.)

Appeals from lower courts are heard in *trial courts of general jurisdiction*. These are the major state trial courts and are known as district, circuit, superior, and common pleas courts (in New York they are called supreme courts and county courts). These courts adjudicate primarily felony cases (and some serious misdemeanors).

Appeals from these courts go either to intermediate courts of appeals or to state supreme courts. Intermediate courts are found in thirty-nine states (primarily the most populous states) and are known by a number of names: appeals court, appellate court, commonwealth court, court of appeals, court of civil appeals, court of criminal appeals, court of special appeals, district court of appeals, intermediate court of appeals, and superior court. The number of judges within each appellate court varies from only three in Alaska and Iowa to eighty-eight in California.[33]

Each state court system has a "court of last resort," which is the state-level equivalent of the U.S. Supreme Court. In most states, the name of the court is Supreme Court. In a few others, the court is called Court of Appeals (Maryland and New York), Supreme Judicial Court (Maine and Massachusetts), and Supreme Court of Appeals (West Virginia). Oklahoma and Texas have two courts of last resort—a Supreme Court and a Court of Criminal Appeals.[34] The state supreme courts are the final interpreters of state law; the only possible appeal after their decision is to the U.S. Supreme Court, which is extremely rare.

PARTICIPANTS IN THE COURT SYSTEM

The criminal court system is a bureaucracy. As with all bureaucracies, there are a number of actors fulfilling certain roles in the daily functioning of the system. The important point is that key participants engage in daily interaction with each other. The popular image of the courts as adversarial places where the two major combatants—the prosecutor and the defense—"duke it out" while the judge sits above the fray as a neutral observer is inaccurate. There is a great deal of cooperation among all of the principal courtroom participants. It should be noted that their salaries come out of the same general fund (unless the defendant can afford a private attorney) and the same signature appears on their paychecks.

Many judges are elected officials and are accountable to the general public. Prosecuting attorneys generally work under another publicly elected official, the district attorney. *Public defenders* are either direct government employees or are salaried staff attorneys of public or private nonprofit organizations. Bailiffs may work for the local police department or sheriff, and court clerks work for the county or city. Ideally, private defense attorneys work for their clients; however, one might make the argument that they actually work for themselves and their own interests.

The Courtroom Workgroup

The *courtroom workgroup* consists of all the personnel you are likely to see on any given day in a courthouse anywhere in the country.[35] Officials include the three major actors—judges, prosecutors, and defense attorneys—along with a number of other important players, such as the court clerk, court reporter, bailiff, police officers, probation officers, and interpreters. These "courthouse regulars" interact with each other inside and outside the courtroom. They may be seen with one another at lunch and sometimes after hours (if you are curious, check out bars and restaurants in close proximity to courthouses between roughly 5 and 7 PM on any given day and see how many of these individuals are socializing together). You might observe a judge playing a round of golf with a prosecutor or a defense attorney.

Members of the courtroom workgroup interact with one another each working day, creating personal ties or bonds. They develop cooperative relationships and share a mutual interdependence in the disposition of cases. The solidarity within a workgroup can be affected by the amount of turnover. In stable offices, agreement is the norm. In offices where employees change frequently, there may be more conflict.[36] As we saw in chapter one, decisions are made at each stage of the criminal justice process. The decisions made in the courtroom are much more visible than those made by, for example, police officers. If an officer decides not to make an arrest, few people witness the decision. In a courtroom, however, a number of actors witness the decisions. The public nature of the decisions can contribute to workgroup solidarity.

Interactions in the courtroom workgroup determine the ebb and flow of court cases. The informal norms developed in the workgroup guide decision making. For example, there is rarely disagreement over the amount of bail to set. Contrary to the scene in every episode of *Law & Order* where the prosecuting attorney and the defense attorney argue about the amount of bail, members of the courtroom workgroup have developed a shared understanding of what each case is worth.[37] Probation officers prepare presentence investigation reports, which are theoretically independent assessments of offenders. However, one study found that the probation officers regularly discussed cases with prosecutors and essentially tailored the reports to match those discussions. The solidarity can foster a tendency to be more concerned with the maintenance of a smoothly running court system than with seeing that "justice" is done (although "justice" may sometimes be served by efficiency).

The Prosecutor: Gatekeeper of the Court System

The *prosecutor* is most commonly referred to as the district attorney (other job titles include county attorney, state's attorney, and prosecuting attorney). This person occupies one of the most powerful positions in the entire criminal justice system, because he or she is the gatekeeper for the court system. As William Chambliss and Robert Seidman remark:

> The prosecutor stands astride the criminal process, controlling the gates that lead to the trial court. . . . [T]he prosecutor's deci-

sion to initiate a prosecution, and the degree to be charged, lies entirely in his discretion. That discretion is, for all practical purposes, unreviewable.[38]

In colonial times the victim had a much larger role in the justice system process. Usually, the victim hired a private prosecutor (usually a privately retained lawyer) for the case. Judges and juries also had a more influential role during this period. Trials were the order of the day, and they took place immediately after the discovery of a crime. Following conviction the convicted person was "hanged, banished, lashed, or given in servitude to the victim until he made good his debt."[39] There were no prisons, no officially authorized police force, and no public prosecutor; the state had not yet stepped in to dominate the criminal justice process. In a small, relatively homogeneous, and agriculturally based society, there was little need for a centralized state apparatus.

American colonists borrowed the concept of the grand jury inquest from Great Britain. Groups of citizens would determine if charges were to be brought and would protect citizens from unjust prosecution. The first grand jury was established by the Massachusetts Bay Colony in September, 1635. As colonial towns grew, the grand jury provided a means for participation in municipal government and community problems.[40] Grand jurors inspected bridges, public buildings, and jails—and resisted the British. After the Revolution, the centralized government was created without a federal grand jury. In 1791, the Fifth Amendment was adopted as part of the Bill of Rights, and stated "No person shall be held to answer for a capital, or otherwise infamous crime, unless on a presentment or indictment of a Grand Jury.[41] The Amendment was designed to protect the people against malicious and oppressive prosecution. Grand jury proceedings were to be secret to guarantee that protection.

In the nineteenth century the entire criminal justice system underwent some noteworthy changes. States began to enact legislation creating "public" prosecutors and state prisons. The result was that the "domain of the victim of crime in the criminal justice system was greatly reduced. He no longer played a correctional role; and his role in the investigation and apprehension of criminals was minimized."[42]

The use of the grand jury began to diminish as the states, in their constitutions, "either did not provide for a grand jury system or provided for one but also allowed for the option of proceeding by way of information filed by the prosecutor." Years later, Justice Douglas observed: "It is, indeed, common knowledge that the Grand Jury, having been conceived as a bulwark between the citizen and the Government, is now a tool of the Executive."[43] The grand jury had lost its ability to reach an independent determination of probable cause. Composed of ordinary citizens, the most readily available guidance on legal questions came from the prosecutor.

An *information* is an instrument filed with the court by the prosecutor that provides relevant demographic data, charges, and the name(s) of victims.

> The prosecutor's domain expanded considerably. The victim of a crime was beginning to be largely ignored, while the criminal justice process was placed into the hands of "experts," a group of trained "professionals" who ostensibly would have the knowledge and motivation to "serve the public."[44]

Police participation in the charging decision also increased in the nineteenth century. In fact, until the present century the police had almost total control of this crucial decision. Today, however, the functions of the police, the prosecutor, judges, and juries, as well as the penal system, are fairly distinct, at least in theory.

The office of the prosecutor or district attorney now has extremely broad discretion in the handling of cases. The prosecutor is part of the executive branch of government and thus separate from the judiciary. The personnel in the offices of federal prosecutors totaled 11,142 in 2005 (an increase of 29% over 1992); the budget for U.S. attorneys' offices was $3.2 billion. The chief legal officer in each state is the state attorney general, who has limited authority over criminal matters. The chief law enforcement officer in a community is known as the chief prosecutor, district attorney, or prosecuting attorney. The staff in the nation's 2,344 state prosecutor's offices grew from 57,000 in 1992 to 78,000 in 2005, an increase of 37%. The budget for state prosecutors totaled 4.9 billion in 2005.[45] Local prosecutors are known as city attorneys or solicitors. They process the preliminary stages of felony cases and handle misdemeanors, drunkenness, petty theft, and disorderly conduct.[46] There are more than eight thousand state, county, city, and township district attorney offices in the country, and they are often huge bureaucracies, ranging from staffs of one or two in small towns to more than five hundred (in Los Angeles, for instance).

The prosecutor has enormous discretion and decisions are essentially unsupervised. Most district attorneys are elected by the voters. While this would seem to exert control over the exercise of power by the local district attorney, the problem is that few voters have any real knowledge of this particular branch of local government. In counties where the district attorney is elected by the public, the office of prosecutor is inherently political. This is not the case in Alaska, Connecticut, Delaware, the District of Columbia, New Jersey, and Rhode Island, where the chief prosecutors are appointed or are members of the state attorney general's office. As noted earlier in the section on federal courts, all U.S. attorneys are appointed by the president and confirmed by the Senate.

Much of the work within the prosecutor's office is done by assistant district attorneys (also known as deputy district attorneys), who are usually hired immediately after law school or after a brief period as solo practitioners. Not surprisingly, the turnover is quite high. The job is not very glamorous, and the caseload can be excessive (as many as a hundred cases). Given the kinds of cases that are handled, "the criminal courthouse can become a depressing place to work. Moreover, regular trial work creates numerous physical and psychological pressures."[47]

Prosecutors, like most criminal lawyers, tend to come from middle-class backgrounds. In contrast to their counterparts in civil and corporate law, prosecutors tend to be products of less prestigious law schools, and they typically graduated in the middle of their class.[48] There is an interesting stratification system within the legal profession. As one writer puts it: "The legal profession, like other occupations, is rigidly stratified. Entry into the profession, mobility within it and the status level in the profession which a lawyer eventually achieves are all strongly influenced by class origins, education, and job experience."[49] The prosecutor's office can be a launching pad for a political career.[50] Many judges, legislators, governors, congressional representatives, and senators began their careers in the prosecutor's office.

Prosecutors are typically reelected or promoted on the basis of conviction rates. "Successful convictions," however, are more a measure of successful negotiations than an accurate measure of justice. Indeed, the conviction rate is not based on the percentage of the total number of cases referred to the prosecutor's office; rather, it is based on the number of cases "accepted for prosecution." Thus, the conviction rate does not include all of the cases that are "denied." As cases proceed through the judicial system, between one-third and one-half are screened out by the prosecutor's office. This discretionary power has existed for almost a century. Several state crime surveys noted that almost half of all police cases presented to the prosecutor's office were rejected.[51] A study in Washington, D.C., in the mid-1970s found that out of every 100 felony cases submitted to the prosecutor, 50 were either rejected at an initial screening stage or dropped at a later stage, another 19 were reduced to misdemeanors, several more were dismissed by the judge, and some were acquitted by juries. There were only 16 guilty pleas or verdicts.[52]

An ACLU report on the aftermath of Hurricane Katrina on prisoners in New Orleans shines an interesting light on the office of the prosecutor. After receiving little cooperation from the district attorney's office when she and her students tried to locate and aid indigent defendants in the system, Tulane law professor Pamela Metzger remarked, "We need to have prosecutors who understand their obligations to the community. Their job is not simply to get convictions but to do justice, and what that means will vary according to the individual facts and circumstances."[53]

The prosecutor occupies a central position in the criminal justice system. He or she decides which cases to prosecute and is expected to advocate assertively for a guilty verdict on behalf of the people. A substantial portion of a prosecutor's time is spent drafting documents such as search warrants, preparing motions, filing information, charging defendants with crimes, filing briefs, setting trial dates, and other bureaucratic chores. The large numbers of cases mean doing a lot of routine administrative work, such as hiring new assistants and preparing budgets.

Since very few cases go to trial, the prosecutor spends a significant amount of time negotiating with the defense attorneys. The prosecutor is also responsible for counseling the "clients" of the court system—the victims of crimes. This includes coaching witnesses prior to their testimony or arranging restitution. The prosecutor has also been described as the chief law enforcement officer in the district. In some districts, this means the prosecutor is responsible for the supervision of a vast bureaucracy employing hundreds of people. As mentioned earlier, in most districts, the prosecutor, as an elected official, is also a politician.[54]

Most prosecutorial decisions are hidden from public view. Only rarely, in a high-profile or celebrity case, are such decisions made public. But even then many of the day-to-day decisions are kept away from public view. Even in the O. J. Simpson case, Marcia Clark, Christopher Darden, and the rest of the prosecution team made many decisions of which the public was never aware.

The Defense Attorney

Although the Sixth Amendment guarantees that accused persons have the right to the assistance of counsel in defending themselves, the issue of providing defense counsel for people who could not afford to hire an attorney was not addressed until 1932. In *Powell v. Alabama,* the U.S. Supreme Court ruled that indigent defendants (those with insufficient income or resources to hire an attorney) in state courts had a right to counsel in cases in which the death penalty might be imposed.[55] The decision did not address providing counsel in noncapital cases. In 1938, the court ruled that indigent defendants in federal court were entitled to court-appointed counsel.[56] In 1942 in *Betts v. Brady* the Court ruled that there is no such guarantee in state courts unless the defendant could show that to be deprived of counsel would result in a denial of due process.[57] This decision was overturned in *Gideon v. Wainwright*, a landmark 1963 decision in which the Court ruled that a defendant accused of a felony even in a noncapital case should be provided counsel.[58]

In *Gideon* the Court faced an ideological challenge to the myth of "equal justice for all." Clarence Earl Gideon had asked for counsel, but his request was denied. He acted as his own lawyer, but he was no match for the experienced prosecutor. It was found that any lawyer would have been able to prove Gideon innocent (as happened in a subsequent trial). This was a clear case in which the fact of being poor led to a denial of due process.[59]

> Reason and reflection require us to recognize that in our adversary system of criminal justice, any person hauled into court who is too poor to hire a lawyer, cannot be assured a fair trial unless counsel is provided for him. This seems to us to be an obvious truth. Governments, both state and federal, quite properly spend vast sums of money to establish machinery to try defendants accused of crime. Lawyers to prosecute are everywhere deemed essential to protect the public's interest in an orderly society. Similarly, there are few defendants charged with crime, few indeed, who fail to hire the best lawyers they can get to prepare and present their defenses. That government hires lawyers to prosecute and defendants who have the money hire lawyers to defend are the strongest indications of the widespread belief that lawyers in criminal

> courts are necessities, not luxuries. . . . From the very beginning, our state and national constitutions and laws have laid great emphasis on procedural and substantive safeguards designed to assure fair trials before impartial tribunals in which every defendant stands equal before the law. This noble ideal cannot be realized if the poor man charged with crime has to face his accusers without a lawyer to assist him.[60]

The Court gradually extended the right to counsel to earlier stages in the criminal justice process. *Miranda v. Arizona* in 1966 stated defendants were entitled to representation during the custodial interrogation.[61] In 1970 in *Coleman v. Alabama*[62] the court extended the right to counsel to the preliminary hearing; in 1972 in *United States v. Wade*[63] the court included police lineups. Also in 1972, the Supreme Court extended the right of an indigent defendant in a criminal prosecution to the assistance of counsel regardless of the classification of the offense or whether a jury trial took place. *Argersinger v. Hamlin* stated that no one could be deprived of liberty as the result of any criminal prosecution—whether felony or misdemeanor—in which the accused was denied the assistance of counsel.[64]

The case law establishes when the government should provide counsel for defendants, but the issue of quality of counsel remains. Can a bureaucratic court system provide the average defendant excellent counsel? Do public defenders and other lawyers for the poor provide the same kind of defense that a lawyer retained by a rich client provides? The majority of those in prison came from poor backgrounds, had public defenders, and had to await their trial in jail. Given the degree of inequality existing in our society, can justice be served if representation is unequal?

Today there are generally four types of defense attorneys: (1) privately retained, (2) court-appointed or assigned counsel, (3) the contract attorney, and (4) public defenders. In some areas legal aid services (storefront law offices) provide representation and advice in poor communities.

Retained Counsel

If a defendant can afford the fees, retained counsel generally provides more service. Private attorneys can hire investigators and spend more time collecting evidence, finding witnesses, and taking other measures to ensure an adequate defense. In addition, if a defendant can afford bail, he or she can assist in the defense. It is important to note that the average defendant—whether using retained counsel or the service provided for indigent defendants—has only one lawyer. Rare is the case where an entire legal team defends a client and employs dozens of investigators, expert witnesses, and so on.

Criminal defense lawyers have been portrayed in many television shows and motion pictures. Perry Mason is the iconic defense lawyer, and numerous other television series have followed, the most recent being *Boston Legal*; Movies as diverse as *And Justice for All* and *My Cousin Vinny* have depicted defense lawyers, as have movies based on John Grisham books, such as *The Firm* and *The Rainmaker.* Defense attorneys are generally portrayed as aggressive, knowledgeable, witty, and smooth-talking. They are no friends to the prosecutors; they vigorously defend each client and own expensive cars, private jets, designer clothes, and beautiful homes. In reality, there are few Perry Masons (or real-life counterparts such as Edward Bennett Williams, Roy Black, Johnnie Cochran, F. Lee Bailey, and Robert Bennett).

Criminal lawyers constitute a minority in the legal profession, and defense attorneys are a minority within that small group. Out of approximately 800,000 lawyers in the United States, only 10,000 to 20,000 focus on criminal matters (no more than 2.5% of the total), and the majority of these are public defenders.[65] The number of defense lawyers has remained relatively stable since 1973 when there were about 20,000 criminal lawyers out of about 350,000 practicing attorneys (6%), and only about 6,000 (2%) confined their practice to criminal law on a full-time basis.[66]

The lawyer-client relationship with retained counsel begins with the collection of fees. Most lawyers ask for some or all of the money before working on the case.[67] In setting the amount, the seriousness of the offense is the most important factor, followed by the length of time it will take to handle the case, and the client's ability to pay. An important factor is whether the case goes to trial. Lawyers charge more if a case goes to trial, so most clients are willing to plea bargain to save money.

Abraham Blumberg argues that the practice of criminal law is in many respects a "confidence game."[68] He suggests that in order to collect fees, lawyers have to convince the client that a service will be provided. Because most clients plead guilty and much of the legal work is done behind the scenes (negotiation over the telephone, letters typed, forms filled out, conversations with colleagues), there are often few visible results (compared with, for instance, the work of a plumber, shoe repairer, roofer, etc.). Thus, much of the behavior of the lawyer consists of reassuring the client that service will be forthcoming as soon as the fee payment is settled.

Assigned Counsel System

Even though defense counsel is a right at each stage of the criminal justice process, most defendants do not have attorneys to call immediately following arrest. In many cases, counsel is assigned by the court during the initial court appearance.[69] Under the assigned-counsel system a court appoints a specific attorney to handle a case. This is common throughout the United States, especially in large urban courts, where 82% of felony defendants were indigents.[70] The judge usually has a list of lawyers in private practice in a particular county or a list of those who have volunteered to serve as counsel for indigents. Often, these lawyers are inexperienced and many take cases simply because they need the money, the experience, or both. And the money won't make them rich, as their hourly fees generally range from $25 to $40.[71]

Contract Attorney System

Another means of providing defense counsel for indigent clients is the contract system. About 29% of state prosecutors reported that cases in their jurisdiction used a contract system (versus 68% using public defenders and 63% assigned counsel).[72] As the term implies, local governments sign contracts with local attorneys to handle indigent cases. This represents a sort of "privatization" of due process, as one study concluded.[73] The process involves competitive bidding. The lowest, not necessarily the best, bidder usually wins the contract. It should come as no surprise that several states have filed suits against this practice. In Arizona, the practice was ruled unconstitutional. The state supreme court held that the Mohave County contract system used the lowest bidder in violation of the Fifth and Sixth Amendments.[74]

Public Defender System

The public defender system has existed for centuries—in ancient Rome, fifteenth-century Spain, and many other European countries prior to the twentieth century. The first public defender program in the United States was instituted in Los Angeles in 1913. It replaced the assigned-counsel system that had been common in the nineteenth century in large U.S. cities.

There were ideological reasons for adopting the public defender system. This system emerged in the United States during a period of large-scale immigration. Many believed that it was necessary to provide defense counsel for the poor so that our system of justice would not engender a sense of injustice. Chief Justice Charles Evans Hughes said in 1920: "There is no more serious menace than the discontent fostered by a belief that one cannot enforce his legal rights because of poverty. To spread that notion is to open a broad road to Bolshevism."[75] The establishment of public defender systems would at least give the outward appearance that justice was equal in the United States.

The move away from assigned counsel and toward public defenders was part of a broader attempt to make the criminal justice system more efficient. Under the assigned-counsel system, an adversarial system prevailed, and there were more trials.

The public defender system was intended to reduce delays and promote "a situation conducive to cooperation" between defense and prosecution:

> The design and organization of the public defender system was to be consistent with and reflective of the modern system emphasizing a division of labor; through specialization and cooperation, the public defender and the district attorney were to omit the cumbersome technicalities, safeguards, and loopholes employed by private counsel on behalf of rich defendants.[76]

A public defender from Portland, Oregon, wrote in 1914:

> As the work was new here there was some question as to how far the public defender should go, how energetic he should be in defense of those he represents. For that reason it was thought best . . . that the public defender should limit his defense to assisting court in bringing out the prisoner's side of the case, rather than making a vigorous fight on technical grounds necessary to secure an acquittal.[77]

In other words, retained counsel would present a vigorous defense using any loopholes, delays, technicalities, and other available legal maneuvers for clients who could afford the fees, but the public defender would be limited to "assisting the court" rather than protesting vigorously for the indigent client.

The public defender is encouraged to cooperate and to take the perspective of the prosecutor. There are few rewards for noncooperation, so public defenders learn to adopt a bureaucratic (or magisterial) model of defense. If the public defender were to choose to adopt an adversarial stance, he or she would interrupt the normal bureaucratic processes.

> Instead of pleading practically everybody guilty (as his predecessor had done), he [a young public defender who took his position seriously] began to try a relatively high proportion of his cases. The docket in the local trial court immediately slowed up. Out of three judges assigned to that particular bench, one began to spend all his time on criminal trials instead of a third of that time. . . . After some six months, this

young public defender received a peremptory order to come to the state capitol to see the Chief Justice. The Chief Justice read him the riot act in terms of the need to avoid "frivolous" trials and the like, warning him of the necessity of "cooperating" with the prosecution and the judges. The Chief Justice was successful; the public defender resigned.[78]

There is really little comparison between the private counsel system and the public defender system. Public defenders become very closely tied to the court bureaucracy and, like other criminal justice workers, depend on the court system for their livelihoods. Whereas the average defendant confronts the court system only once or twice, the public defender comes in contact with it daily. Thus, cooperating with prosecutors and judges becomes an absolute necessity if one is to continue working in the field.

Some public defenders are assigned to certain courtrooms and handle all the cases within those courtrooms instead of handling one particular case from beginning to end. Thus, one defender handles the preliminary hearing, another handles the arraignment, and another the trial if there is one—an assembly-line approach to defending a client. The usual outcome in cases handled by a public defender is a guilty plea. Public defenders often have extremely large caseloads—350 cases or more.

The ACLU study looked at what happened to defendants held in local jails pending a court appearance when hurricane Katrina struck. It found that between 3,000 and 6,000 (no one could provide an exact number) people were denied both a trial and the right to counsel.[79] The vast majority were too poor to afford an attorney. Thousands of prisoners had never seen an attorney, never been arraigned, and never appeared before a judge. Metzger, who heads the Tulane Law School Criminal Law Clinic, said, "When we ask the district attorney's office to assist us with this, just so people can get lawyers, they say it's not their job."

The indigent defense system in Louisiana had serious problems long before Katrina, including chronic under-funding. After

the hurricane, authorities quickly reestablished law enforcement. The criminal courts began operation nine months after the storm, but the public defenders' office suffered an almost total collapse. Almost three-quarters of the public defenders left.[80] Approximately 85% of criminal defendants had no representation, and many had been jailed for minor crimes (disturbing the peace, trespassing, and spitting on the sidewalk). A U.S. Department of Justice report concluded:

> People wait in jail with no charges, and trials cannot take place; even defendants who wish to plead guilty must have counsel for a judge to accept the plea. Without indigent defense lawyers, New Orleans today lacks a true adversarial process, the process to ensure that even the poorest arrested person will get a fair deal, that the government cannot simply lock suspects up and forget about them.

Public defenders face the difficulty of balancing strong advocacy versus processing their many cases expeditiously with very limited funds. The conviction rates in large state courts were similar for defendants represented by publicly financed and private attorneys; 75% of defendants with court-appointed attorneys were convicted, and 77% of those with private counsel were convicted. Almost 25% of defendants with publicly financed or private attorneys were acquitted or their cases were dismissed.[81] However, of those found guilty, higher percentages of defendants with publicly financed counsel (71%) were sentenced to incarceration versus those who hired private counsel (54%). When defendants were sentenced to prison or jail, defendants with publicly financed attorneys received shorter sentences (average 2.5 years) than those with private counsel (average 3 years). About half of the defendants using a public defender or assigned counsel were released from jail prior to trial; 75% of defendants using a private attorney were released.

The court rulings mandating defense counsel for indigent defendants do not specify the type of system (public defender, assigned counsel, or contract) or how the system is to be funded. Of the three major components of the criminal justice system, the "judicial and legal" component receives the least amount of annual expenditures. In 2004, the total direct expenditures on the judicial system by state and local governments was $33 billion compared to $69.8 billion for police and $56.4 billion for corrections.[82] Expenditures on counsel for the indigent in state and local courts in 2005 were approximately $3.5 billion (10.6% of the total judicial expenditures).[83] Remember that about 82% of defendants in the system are indigent. In states and large cities all over the country, many public defenders' offices have been experiencing severe cutbacks. If they do receive an increase in funding, it barely enables them to make ends meet because of increasing caseloads.[84]

The Judge

Americans often equate the guarantees of due process of law and equal protection under the law with the judge, the symbol of fairness and impartiality. The symbolic representation is reinforced by the honorific "all rise" when the judge enters the courtroom, the black robes, the position on a bench elevated above the rough and tumble exchange between prosecutors and defense attorneys, and the gavel that signals order.[85]

There are several myths associated with judges, some of them previously mentioned. Judges are supposed to be neutral arbitrators and committed to the ideals of equal justice for all, and they are supposed to interpret existing laws. In fact, judges may be highly prejudiced and committed to the maintenance of the status quo.

While judges are constrained by the actions of other members of the courtroom work group, they are also the most prestigious members of the group and can bring pressure on prosecutors, defense attorneys, and probation officers.[86] Judges authorize search warrants, arrest warrants, and wiretaps. They determine whether there is probable cause to hold defendants; they set or revoke bail. They rule on pretrial motions, usually in writing. These rulings can set new precedents, which effectively translates to creating new laws if unchallenged. They

accept negotiated pleas of guilt (see chapter 9). If there is a trial, they serve as umpires or referees (the role most frequently portrayed by the media). Judges are also administrators; they spend a great deal of time keeping court dockets (a calendar showing court cases) current.

Judicial Selection

There are generally three ways of selecting judges. The first is by election, which may be either partisan (judges sponsored by a political party) or nonpartisan. The second method is merit selection (commonly referred to as the Missouri Plan). The third method of selecting judges is by appointment (either legislative or gubernatorial).

There is usually very little controversy in popular elections. Most of the time, the incumbent wins. The average citizen knows little or nothing about the judges running for office. One author (RGS) recalls that in Memphis, Tennessee, in 1970 a judge who had died a few months earlier won an election. Because of some bureaucratic rule, his name appeared on the ballot. Whether the voters simply did not know that the judge had died or they felt that, even dead, he was better than any of the other candidates is not known. Three significant features define judicial elections: (1) the only individuals who can run for judicial office (except for a few small, limited jurisdiction courts) are lawyers who have passed the state bar, have law practice experience, and are in good standing; (2) it is practically impossible for the ordinary voter to know if the judicial candidate truly possesses the technical skills and qualities to be a good judge; and (3) judicial candidates, while often deemed "nonpartisan," are financed and supported by corporations and certain business interest groups. These features result in a very conventional judiciary that is reluctant to take an independent or maverick position on issues. It also results in judicial candidates and judges focusing mainly on pleasing their attorney constituents because generally it is only disgruntled lawyers who can defeat the candidate or unseat the incumbent judge. It is the "good old boy system" raised to a new level.

The Missouri Plan of merit selection was established in 1940 in Missouri in order to remove politics from the courthouse; fifteen states and the District of Columbia now use this method.[87] When a vacancy occurs, a special committee of citizens and lawyers sends a list of recommendations to the governor. The governor then makes an appointment from this list. One year later there is a special election in which the voters are asked whether this judge should remain in office. If the voters say yes, then the judge serves a full term of office. Few judges have been defeated.

The Missouri Plan doesn't remove all vestiges of politics. In general, judges are selected who are essentially similar in class, political affiliation, and legal experience to those already in power in a given state. Most judges are and have been white, male, Protestant, and upper-middle class.[88]

Judicial Careers

Judges do, of course, vary in their training and status in the legal profession. The status of judges reflects the duties they perform and the level of the court in which they preside. The most famous, highest status judges are U.S. Supreme Court justices, and include people such as Oliver Wendell Holmes (1902–1932), Louis Brandeis (1916–1939), Benjamin N. Cardozo (1932–1938), Felix Frankfurter, (1939–1962), William O. Douglas (1939–1975), and Earl Warren (1953–1969). The chief justice attains the highest status of all, and the Court is known by the last name of the chief. So for example, the Court from 1953 to 1969 was known as the Warren Court. State supreme court justices and other appellate judges are next in status, followed by trial court judges.

The appellate system (including the Supreme Court) ultimately determines the entire criminal court system. As noted earlier in the chapter, judges in the appellate system are drawn almost solely from the ranks of the upper class.[89] These judges are not "instruments of ruling class domination" as some Marxists assert; they do have some degree of autonomy and do occasionally make rulings in favor of disadvantaged

groups, but they are not revolutionaries intent on creating lasting and radical social changes. Thus, the criminal court system, like the entire criminal justice system, remains largely a system of class justice. It reinforces and perpetuates the system of class inequality that surrounds it.[90]

Lower court judges earn the lowest salary and are the least qualified. In some states a law degree is not a requirement for justices of the peace and other kinds of lower court judges. One municipal court judge in North Las Vegas did not even have an undergraduate degree; he served several years as the only judge of that court before being driven out by the state ethics commission. The low status of lower court judges parallels the low status of lawyers practicing in the lower courts and the low status of most of the defendants.

The careers of judges also vary according to level of legal education and social class background. Federal judges, appellate judges, and many trial court judges serve for life; most lower court judges serve for only a few years. However, many lower court judges do move on to higher posts, but rarely higher than trial courts. Some judges are political appointees and leave their posts when there is a change in administration. As indicated by the terms served by the Supreme Court Justices named above, some judges have very long and fruitful careers.

CHANGING AND REFORMING THE COURT SYSTEM

In recent times, frustration with perceived ineffectiveness of the criminal court system has increased, and a range of new kinds of problems have been brought to the courts. Along with the public's growing dissatisfaction with the performance of the court system came a "tripartite crisis" in the legal profession consisting of a decline in professional standards for attorneys, low public opinion of attorneys, and lawyer dissatisfaction and distress. It had become evident by the turn of the century that the U.S. legal system was not entirely satisfactory to clients, to society, or even to lawyers and judges themselves.[91] As a result of dissatisfaction and the perceived shortcomings of the criminal justice system, there was renewed interest in court reform and applications of preventive law, risk management, restorative justice, and therapeutic jurisprudence. Much of the early experimentation and initial attempts at the reform of criminal procedure centered on new, specialized, "problem-solving courts." The drug court was the first of the new outcome-focused criminal courts to gain widespread acceptance. Soon other diversionary and therapeutic courts began to appear in rapid succession. Most of these courts were guided by the concepts of "therapeutic jurisprudence." In the words of Susan Daicoff, "The rapid rise of therapeutic jurisprudence in the last decade of the twentieth century heralds the emergence of a new era in the legal profession—one in which law and legal practice may be more humane, therapeutic, beneficial, humanistic, healing, restorative, curative, collaborative and comprehensive."[92]

Summary

The majority of all criminal cases in the United States are processed through the lower courts. These courts handle virtually all of the misdemeanors, initial appearances, and preliminary hearings. These courts of "limited jurisdiction" may or may not provide for jury trials. General jurisdiction trial courts, the next most dominant type of court, handle primarily felony cases and conduct trials. Appellate courts, such as the state supreme courts and the U.S. Supreme Court, focus solely on appeals.

Attorneys practicing criminal law are a small minority in the field of law. Both prosecutors and defense lawyers stand at the bottom of the status hierarchy of their professions, as do most of the judges they face. Because they all depend on one another (forming a courtroom workgroup) and owe their livelihoods to the court bureaucracy, a true adversarial relationship rarely exists. Instead, justice—quality defense for all and the protection of the pub-

lic—often becomes secondary to organizational goals and personal careers. Many who practice law at this level eventually move on to private practice, judgeships, politics, or some other legal career.

Providing counsel for indigents has a long tradition, but the right to counsel at every stage of the criminal justice process is a recent development. If defendants have the means to hire an attorney, there are a number of advantages, including increased probability of pre-trial release. Court decisions have defined when right to counsel applies to indigent defendants, but they have not defined the method. The method and the funding for indigent counsel is decided by each jurisdiction. Three methods of criminal defense are common: the public defender system, the assigned-counsel system, and the contract system. The reality is that plea bargains are routine, regardless of the type of representation available to the defendant.

The next chapter will discuss the process of the criminal courts. In this chapter, we briefly mentioned alternatives to the traditional criminal court system. Problem-solving courts may provide the means for incorporating social justice into the criminal court system.

Key Terms

- *Betts v. Brady*
- courtroom workgroup
- dual court system
- *in forma pauperis* request
- Judiciary Act of 1789
- *Powell v. Alabama*
- prosecutor
- public defenders
- Reorganization Act of 1801
- trial courts of general jurisdiction
- trial courts of limited jurisdiction
- U.S. Courts of Appeals
- U.S. District Courts
- U.S. Supreme Court
- *writ of certiorari*

Notes

[1] Zemans, F. K. "In the Eye of the Beholder: The Relationship between the Public and the Courts." In G. L. Mays and P. R. Gregware (eds.), *Courts and Justice: A Reader* (3rd ed.). Long Grove, IL: Waveland Press, 2004, p. 9.

[2] In early 1999, 1,826 Americans were asked to express their opinions about the courts in their communities. This survey, "How the Public Views State Courts," was conducted by the National Center for State Courts and funded by The Hearst Corporation. The survey revealed that only 23% of the respondents had a "great deal" of trust in the courts in their communities, and an additional 52% had "some trust." A quarter of the respondents had virtually no confidence in the courts at all. This view was reflected in survey responses on a number of issues. Only 10% of the respondents felt that the courts in their communities handled cases in an "excellent" manner. See http://www.ncsconline.org/WC/Publications/Res_Amt PTC_NatlActionPlanPub.pdf

[3] Zemans, "In the Eye of the Beholder," p. 15–16.

[4] Merry, S. E. *Getting Justice and Getting Even: Legal Consciousness among Working-Class Americans.* Chicago: University of Chicago Press, 1990.

[5] Rush, G. E. *Dictionary of Criminal Justice.* Boston: Holbrook Press, 1977, p. 78.

[6] Turkel, G. *Law and Society: Critical Approaches.* Boston: Allyn & Bacon, 1996, p. 139.

[7] Jackson, B. (ed.). *Law and Order: Criminal Justice in America.* Chicago: University of Illinois Press, 1984, p. 77.

[8] Lynch, M. J. and R. Michalowski. *The New Primer in Radical Criminology: Critical Perspectives on Crime, Power and Identity* (3rd ed.). Monsey, NY: Criminal Justice Press, 2000, p. 169.

[9] Drug Policy Alliance. "After Three-year Investigation, Rush Limbaugh Charged with Doctor Shopping for Prescription Painkillers." May 1, 2006. [Online] http://www.drugpolicy.org/news/pr050106a.cfm

[10] Skoloff, B. "Rush Limbaugh Under New Investigation." *Washington Post* (June 27, 2006). [Online] http://www.washingtonpost.com/wp-dyn/content/article/2006/06/27/AR2006062700194.html

[11] Skoloff, B. "Rush Limbaugh Jokes about Viagra Find." *ABC News* (June 23, 2006). [Online] http://abcnews.go.com/Entertainment/wireStory?id=2125598

[12] See The Center for Court Innovation. "Problem-Solving Justice." [Online] http://www.courtinnovation.org/index.cfm?fuseaction=page.viewPage&pageID=505&documentTopicID=31; and the International Network on Therapeutic Jurisprudence. [Online] http://www.law.arizona.edu/depts/upr-intj/

[13] Friedman, L. M. *A History of American Law.* New York: Simon and Schuster, 1973, p. 35.

[14] Friedman, L. M. *Crime and Punishment in American History.* New York: Basic Books, 1993, p. 31.

[15] Chapin, B. *Criminal Justice in Colonial America: 1600–1660.* Athens: University of Georgia Press, 1983, and *Provincial America: 1600–1763.* New York: Free Press, 1996.

[16] Knappman, E. W. *Great American Trials: From Salem Witchcraft to Rodney King.* Detroit, MI: Visible Ink Press, 1994.

[17] Shelden, R. G. *Controlling the Dangerous Classes.* Boston: Allyn & Bacon, 2001.

[18] Friedman, *Crime and Punishment in American History,* p. 34.

[19] For a more complete treatment of this topic, see Shelden, *Controlling the Dangerous Classes,* chapter 3. See also Knappman, *Great American Trials.*

[20] Friedman, *A History of American Law,* p. 140.

[21] Shelden, *Controlling the Dangerous Classes,* chapter 3.

[22] For a fascinating look at the work of the U.S. Court of Appeals in a book of fiction see Patterson, R. N. *Protect and Defend.* New York: Ballantine Books, 2000.

[23] *Sourcebook of Criminal Justice Statistics.* [Online] http://www.albany.edu/sourcebook/pdf/t582005.pdf

[24] The Federal Judiciary. [Online] http://www.uscourts.gov/courtsofappeals.html

[25] *Sourcebook of Criminal Justice Statistics.* [Online] http://www.albany.edu/sourcebook/pdf/t5662005.pdf

[26] *Sourcebook of Criminal Justice Statistics.* [Online] http://www.albany.edu/sourcebook/pdf/t5672005.pdf

[27] *Sourcebook of Criminal Justice Statistics.* [Online] http://www.albany.edu/sourcebook/pdf/t1812005.pdf

[28] Rush, *Dictionary of Criminal Justice,* p.184.

[29] *Sourcebook of Criminal Justice Statistics.* [Online] http://www.albany.edu/sourcebook/pdf/t5682004.pdf; Von

Drehle, P. "Inside the Incredibly Shrinking Role of the Supreme Court." *Time* (170)17: 46 (October 22, 2007).

[30] Dean, J. *The Rehnquist Choice*. New York: Free Press, 2001.

[31] Neubauer, D. W. *America's Courts and the Criminal Justice System* (8th ed.). Belmont, CA: Wadsworth, 2005, p. 82.

[32] Reiman, J. *The Rich Get Richer and the Poor Get Prison* (8th ed.). Boston: Allyn & Bacon, 2007; Chiricos, T. G. and W. Bales. "Unemployment and Punishment: An Empirical Analysis." *Criminology* 29 (November 1991).

[33] Rottman, D. B. and S. M. Strickland. *State Court Organization* (NCJ 212351). Washington, DC: Bureau of Justice Statistics, August 2006, pp. 9, 13.

[34] Ibid., table 2.

[35] Walker, S. *Sense and Nonsense about Crime and Drugs* (6th ed.). Belmont, CA: Wadsworth, 2006, pp. 38, 57–58.

[36] Ibid., pp. 59–60.

[37] Ibid., pp. 57–63.

[38] Chambliss, W. J. and R. Seidman. *Law, Order and Power* (2nd ed.). Reading, MA: Addison-Wesley, 1982, pp. 396–397. The wide discretion granted to the prosecutor has been recognized by many experts for years. For instance, the American Bar Association's Standards Relating to the Prosecution and Defense Function merely "admonishes" prosecutors not to be unduly influenced by personal or political motivations and not to charge more than can be "reasonably supported at trial" (Scheb, J. M. and J. M. Scheb II. *Criminal Law and Procedure*. St. Paul: West, 1989, p. 437). Gottfredson and Gottfredson, in their comprehensive review of decision making in the criminal justice system, observe that "the decision whether or not to charge is the single most unreviewed exercise of the power of criminal law available to an individual in the American system of justice" (Gottfredson, M. R. and D. M. Gottfredson. *Decision Making in Criminal Justice: Toward the Rational Exercise of Discretion*. New York: Plenum Press, 1988, p. 114).

[39] McDonald, W. F. (ed.). *The Prosecutor*. Beverly Hills, CA: Sage, 1979, p. 22.

[40] http://63.200.101.44/grandjury/gj9798/grand_jury_history.html

[41] http://www.law.fsu.edu/journals/lawreview/frames/241/kaditxt.html

[42] McDonald, *The Prosecutor*, p. 24.

[43] http://web72345.ntx.net/article/grand.shtml

[44] McDonald, *The Prosecutor*.

[45] Perry, S. W. *Prosecutors in State Courts, 2005* (NCJ 213799). Washington, DC: Bureau of Justice Statistics, July 2006, pp. 1, 4; http://www.albany.edu/sourcebook/pdf/t1792005.pdf; http://www.albany.edu/ sourcebook/pdf/t112.pdf

[46] Neubauer, *America's Courts and the Criminal Justice System* pp. 131–132.

[47] Ibid., p. 134.

[48] Schur, E. *Law and Society: A Sociological View*. New York: Random House, 1968; Neubauer, *America's Courts and the Criminal Justice System*, p. 134.

[49] Fishman, J. J. "The Social and Occupational Mobility of Prosecutors: New York City," in McDonald, *The Prosecutor*, p. 239.

[50] Flemming, R., P. Nardulli, and J. Eisenstein. *The Craft of Justice: Politics and Work in Criminal Court Communities*. Philadelphia: University of Pennsylvania Press, 1992.

[51] McDonald, *The Prosecutor*, p. 33.

[52] Gottfredson and Gottfredson, *Decision Making in Criminal Justice*, p. 116.

[53] *Drug War Chronicle*, "Living on Katrina Time: Lost in Louisiana's Gumbo Gulag." Issue #451, September 1, 2006. [Online] http://stopthedrugwar.org/chronicle/451/new_orleans_jail_scandal_post_katrina

[54] Jacoby, J. E. "Pushing the Envelope: Leadership in Prosecution." *Justice System Journal* 17: 291–307 (1995).

[55] *Powell v. Alabama*, 287 U.S. 45, 1932.

[56] *Johnson v. Zerbst*, 304 U.S. 458, 1938.

[57] *Betts v. Brady*, 316 U.S. 455, 1942.

[58] *Gideon v. Wainwright*, 372 U.S. 335, 1963.

[59] For a fuller treatment of this case see Lewis, A. *Gideon's Trumpet*. New York: Harper & Row, 1964.

[60] *Gideon v. Wainwright*. [Online] http://caselaw.lp.findlaw.com/scripts/getcase.pl?court=US&vol=372&invol=335

[61] *Miranda v. Arizona*, 384 U.S. 436, 1966.

[62] *Coleman v. Alabama*, 399 U.S. 1, 1970.

[63] *United States v. Wade*, 406 U.S. 25, 1972.

[64] *Argersinger v. Hamlin*, 407 U.S. 25, 1972. [Online] http://caselaw.lp.findlaw.com/scripts/getcase.pl?court=US&vol=407&invol=25

[65] Cole, G. E. and C. E. Smith. *The American System of Criminal Justice* (8th ed.). Belmont, CA: Wadsworth, 1998, p. 134.

[66] Shelden, R. G. *Criminal Justice in America: A Sociological Approach.* Boston: Little, Brown, 1982, p. 219.

[67] Wice, P. B. "The Private Practice of Criminal Law: Life in the Real World." *Criminal Law Bulletin* 14(5): 391 (1978); Lushing, P. "The Fall and Rise of the Criminal Contingent Fee." *Journal of Criminal Law and Criminology* 82: 498–568 (1992).

[68] Blumberg, A. "The Practice of Law as a Confidence Game." In W. J. Chambliss (ed.), *Criminal Law in Action.* New York: Wiley, 1975.

[69] Benner, L. A., B. Neary, and R. M. Gutman. *The Other Face of Justice: A Report of the National Defender Survey.* Chicago: National Legal Aid and Defender Association, 1973; Neubauer, *America's Courts*, pp. 159–162.

[70] Harlow, C. W. *Defense Counsel in Criminal Cases* (NCJ 179023). Washington, DC: Bureau of Justice Statistics, November 2000, p. 1.

[71] Cole and Smith, *The American System of Criminal Justice*, p. 319.

[72] Harlow, *Defense Counsel in Criminal Cases*, p. 4.

[73] Worden, A. P. "Privatizing Due Process: Issues in the Comparison of Assigned Counsel, Public Defender, and Contracted Indigent Defense System." *Justice System Journal* 14: 390–419 (1991), and "Counsel for the Poor: An Evaluation of Contracting for Indigent Criminal Defense." *Justice Quarterly* 10: 613–637 (1993); Spangenberg Group. *Contracting for Indigent Defense Services: A Special Report.* Washington, DC: Bureau of Justice Statistics, 2000.

[74] *Smith v. State*, 140 Arizona 355, 1984.

[75] Barak, G. "In Defense of the Rich: The Emergency of the Public Defender." *Crime and Social Justice* 3: 8 (1975).

[76] Ibid., p. 8.

[77] Ibid., p. 10.

[78] Chambliss and Seidman, *Law, Order and Power*, p. 402.

[79] American Civil Liberties Union. "Abandoned and Abused: Orleans Parish Prisoners in the Wake of Hurricane Katrina." Washington, DC: ACLU, August 2006.

[80] Parker, L. "Lack of Public Defenders May Free Accused Felons." *USA Today* (February 14, 2006).

[81] Harlow, *Defense Counsel in Criminal Cases*, p. 6.

[82] *Direct Expenditures by Criminal Justice Function, 1982–2005.* [Online] http://www.ojp.usdoj.gov/bjs/glance/tables/exptyptab.htm; Table #1: Percent Distribution of Expenditure for the Justice System by Type of Government, Fiscal 2004. *Justice Expenditure & Employment Extracts Series* (NCJ 215648). December 2006. [Online] http://www.ojp.usdoj.gov/bjs/eande.htm#selected

[83] The Spangenberg Group. *State and County Expenditures for Indigent Defense Services in Fiscal Year 2005.*

American Bar Association, December 2006. [Online] http://www.abanet.org/legalservices/sclaid/defender/downloads/FINAL_REPORT_FY_2005_Expenditure_ Report.pdf

[84] Budig, T. W. "Budget Cuts, Lack of Funding Puts Public Defender Effectiveness in Jeopardy." *Capitol Roundup*. [Online]
http://www.hometownsource.com/capitol/2004/june/22publicdefense.html;
Ferguson, M. J. "Improving Public Defense: Working Together to Fulfill Gideon's Promise." February, 2006. [Online] http://www.wsba.org/media/publications/barnews/publicdefup-2-06.htm);
Adams, M. "Senate Kills Public Defender Funding Bill." *The Roanoke Times* (September 2, 2006); ACLU. "Grant County's Public Defense on Trial." October 20, 2005. [Online]
http://www.aclu-wa.org/detail. cfm?id=295

[85] Kappeler, V. and G. Potter. *The Mythology of Crime and Criminal Justice* (4th ed). Long Grove, IL: Waveland, 2005, pp. 264.

[86] Neubauer, *America's Courts,* p. 174.

[87] Ibid., p. 176.

[88] Ibid., p. 181.

[89] Beard, C. *An Economic Interpretation of the Constitution*. New York: Macmillan, 1935; Domhoff, G. W. *Who Rules America? Power and Politics in the Year 2000*. Mountain View, CA: Mayfield, 1998; Chambliss and Seidman, *Law, Order and Power.*

[90] Lynch, M. J. and W. B. Groves. *A Primer in Radical Criminology* (2nd ed.). New York: Harrow and Heston, 1989, p. 105; this theme is discussed in more detail in Shelden, *Controlling the Dangerous Classes.*

[91] Daicoff, S. "Lawyer, Know Thyself: A Review of Empirical Research on Attorney Attributes Bearing on Professionalism." *American University Law Review* 46 (1997), pp. 1337, 1342–48; see also Daicoff, S. "Asking Leopards to Change Their Spots: Should Lawyers Change? A Critique of Solutions to Problems with Professionalism by Reference to Attorney Personality Attributes." *Geo. J. Legal Ethics* 11: 547, pp. 549–557.

[92] Daicoff, S. "The Role of Therapeutic Jurisprudence within the Comprehensive Law Movement." In D. P. Stolle, D. B. Wexler and B. J. Winick (eds.), *Practicing Therapeutic Jurisprudence: Law as a Helping Profession*. Charlotte, NC: Carolina Academic Press, 2000, p. 465.

nine

Criminal Courts
The Process

If I have done my homework, which I always do, I have a good idea if someone deserves to be allowed bail. The crime they are charged with is the first consideration, and then, well of course, their criminal record has revealing qualities also. . . . Yes, I consider the whole criminal record, all arrests and convictions. . . . You have to understand these people; just because they evade conviction does not, by any stretch of the imagination, mean they were innocent.[1]

PRETRIAL COURT PROCESSES

The prosecutor is the gatekeeper to the court system; he or she decides whether the person arrested will be formally charged with a crime. Given the obvious impact on the lives of people who go through any court process, the decisions made by the prosecutor in the screening process have a profound impact on the lives of both victims and defendants. As Paul Robinson and Michael Cahill note, both legal experts and ordinary citizens think that the fundamental reason for our legal system is "to help give people what they deserve when life has not." If a person harms someone, the law makes the wrongdoer pay. If someone has done nothing wrong, we expect the law to leave that person alone.[2] After commenting that probably no criminal justice system can punish every wrongdoer—and only wrongdoers—they mention factors that contribute to a lack of justice in the system:

limitations on resources for investigating crimes and prosecuting offenders, inevita-ble human error due to participants' imperfect knowledge and talents, the systems necessary reliance on the fallible observation and memory of witnesses, and the potential influence of bias and corruption.[3]

Deciding Whether to Prosecute

As many as half of all cases submitted to the prosecutor's office are not accepted for prosecution. In court jargon, the case is "nol-lied," "nolled," or "nol-prossed"—the allusion is to *nolle prosequi,* a Latin expression meaning "unwilling to prosecute."

Prosecutors have enormous discretion in when and how and against whom they bring charges. They can overcharge and pressure the defendant to plea bargain. They can undercharge if they feel there are mitigating circumstances associated with the crime. Or they can determine that despite the fact that a crime has been committed, in the interest of justice, charges ought not be brought at all.[4]

Overcharging adds counts to the crime. For example, in addition to a charge of drug possession, a defendant can be charged with possession of drug paraphernalia, resisting arrest, and, perhaps, multiple charges if more than one drug was present at the time of arrest. The inflated charges often extend beyond the boundary of what the prosecutor actually believes the defendant can be convicted of (e.g., charging possession of drugs with the intent to sell when simple possession would be the most realistic charge). Overcharging is a forceful attempt to convince the defendant to plead guilty to one of the counts. The prosecutor then "denies" all but one of the charges.[5]

The decision to accept or deny a case is typically based on two interrelated factors. Evidence is a primary consideration. If the prosecution determines there is insufficient evidence, the case will be denied. The second major factor is quality of witnesses (witnesses are usually a determining factor in personal crimes, such as assault and rape). Together, evidence problems and witness problems account for the vast majority of denials. These factors can influence the prosecutor to drop the case prior to a formal charge, or they can lead to dismissal after the filing of an information or an indictment. Prosecutors can also decide to drop charges to a misdemeanor and refer the case to a lower court.

Class and Racial Bias in Charging Decisions

As noted in earlier chapters, police decisions to arrest more frequently affect racial minorities and lower-class citizens. This bias extends, at least indirectly, to the prosecutor's office. Recall from the previous chapter that most people charged with crimes are indigent. The race of the victim and the race of the defendant play a key role in the decision to prosecute. When the defendant is African American and the victim is white or when both the offender and the victim are white, chances are greater for the case to be accepted for prosecution. Chances for denial are greater if both the victim and the offender are African American. In situations where the victims are white and employed, the cases are far more likely to be accepted and processed into the judicial system.[6]

A study in Los Angeles County found clear evidence of racial bias in prosecutors' charging decisions. After controlling for current offense, prior record, presence of a weapon, and other variables, researchers found that African Americans and Hispanics were the least likely to have their cases rejected by the prosecutor. Another study found evidence that in the instance of murder, those cases involving a white victim were far more likely to be fully prosecuted than were cases with African American victims.[7] Social class differences in prosecutors' charging decisions are especially evident in comparisons of ordinary street crimes with white-collar and corporate crimes.[8]

The Initial Appearance

The Sixth Amendment states that a defendant cannot be held for an indefinite period of time without a court appearance. In 1957 in *Mallory v. United States* the Supreme Court ruled that a suspect must come before a judge "as soon as possible" following an arrest.[9] In practice this usually means the next working day (or if the arrest was made on the weekend, the following Monday morning). This first appearance in court is usually known as the *initial appearance.* The main purpose of this hearing is to arrange for some form of *pretrial release,* usually through *bail.* Bail is a form of security (monetary or personal guarantee) that a defendant will appear in court when scheduled. During this hearing the judge has three important duties to perform. First, the judge informs the defendant of the charge(s) against him or her (often the defendant is given a copy of the information or complaint). Second, the defendant is informed of his or her constitutional rights, including the right to counsel and the right to remain silent. Third, there is a determination of whether to release the defendant pending subsequent hearings, including a trial, and the amount of bail if the individual is to be set free.[10]

Social class and race are obvious factors affecting defendants' prospects for pretrial release. First, people with little or no money frequently have a difficult time paying bail. Second, race becomes a proxy indicator of social class; this is particularly true in the case of African Americans and Latinos, who are disproportionately overrepresented among the social class that has little or no money to pay bail. The quality of defense counsel is another variable that must be factored into the pretrial release process. Indigent defendants or defendants without the means to pay bail also cannot afford to pay an attorney to represent them in the initial appearance.

Pretrial Detention

The Fifth Amendment stipulates that no person can be held, "nor deprived of life, liberty or property, without due process of law." According to the ideal, a person is presumed innocent until proved guilty "beyond a reasonable doubt" and there can be no punishment without conviction. However, the reality of criminal justice often does not match the ideal. On any given day, tens of thousands of people are held in jail awaiting court appearances (sometimes for many months). They have not been proved guilty; many are there simply because they cannot afford bail.

Bail

While the Eighth Amendment guarantees no excessive bail will be required, it does not codify which crimes are subject to bail or the powers of justice officials in setting bail. The Judiciary Act of 1789 specified the crimes eligible for bail and limited the discretion of judges in setting bail. All noncapital offenses were eligible for bail. In capital offenses, the decision to detain a suspect before trial was left up to the judge. Not until 1946 was a distinction made between bail before and bail after conviction during appeal. The Federal Rules of Criminal Procedure made the language in The Judiciary Act of 1789 the standard for pretrial release, but release after conviction pending an appeal was at the discretion of the judge. There were no changes in laws regarding bail until 1966.[11]

The Bail Reform Act of 1966 provided that noncapital defendants be released pending trial on personal recognizance or personal bond, unless a judicial officer determined that those assurances would not be sufficient to insure appearance at trial (i.e. risk of flight). Essentially, the 1966 Act created a presumption for releasing a suspect with as little burden as possible; appearance at trial was the sole standard in noncapital cases. The Supreme Court sustained the con-stitutionality of detention if it could be argued successfully that the defendant was a flight risk.[12] In capital cases, defendants were to be released unless the judicial officer had reason to believe that no conditions would assure that the person would not flee or if the person posed a danger. The Bail Reform Act of 1966 did not permit a judge to consider a defendant's danger to the community in noncapital cases. Some jurisdictions, and particularly the District of Columbia, criticized the restrictions. The Judicial Council committee recommended that a person's dangerousness should be considered in determining conditions for release even in noncapital cases. The District of Columbia Court Reform and Criminal Procedure Act of 1970 allowed judges to consider dangerousness and risk of flight when setting bail in noncapital cases. Increasing fear of crime in the 1980s pushed Congress to enact The Bail Reform Act of 1984. Perceived dangerousness was introduced as a consideration in granting release.[13] In 1987 the Supreme Court ruled in *United States v. Salerno* that the Eighth Amendment addresses pretrial release by providing only that excessive bail shall not be required—it does not address whether bail should be available at all. It further stated:

> Legislative history clearly indicates that Congress formulated the detention provisions not as punishment for dangerous individuals, but as a potential solution to the pressing societal problem of crimes committed by persons on release. Preventing danger to the community is a legitimate regulatory goal. . . . The Court of Appeals assumed that pretrial detention under the Bail Reform Act is regulatory, not penal, and we agree that it is.[14]

For most crimes there is a presumption that a defendant is eligible for release on "reasonable bail." Reasonable bail is the lowest bail that a judge, in his or her opinion, believes will ensure that the subject will return to court for all scheduled appearances. In spite of the expectation that reasonable bail will be established, a judge may exercise judicial discretion to deny pretrial release. Several legally prescribed factors affect the decision to deny pretrial release. The Seventh Circuit Court ruled that the trial court judge must consider all of these factors.[15] First, the nature of the offense charged is considered, including whether the offense is of a violent nature or involves narcotics. Second, the strength of the evidence against the defendant is considered. The Ninth Circuit Court ruled that the strength of evidence against the defendant is the *least* important of the factors.[16] Third, the defendant's character, physical and mental condition, employment status and history, family and community ties, drug and alcohol abuse history, and criminal record are examined. The legal status (e.g., probation, parole, release on bail) of the defendant at the time the alleged offense occurred is another element considered during the scrutiny of the defendant's history and characteristics. Finally, the potential danger that the release of the defendant would present to the community is considered.[17] Several other considerations take into account the situation in which pretrial release is sought—for example, release pending trial, release pending sentencing or appeal, release of a material witness, or release following a violation of conditions of a previous pretrial release.[18]

In theory, the court rules and case law are created to insure a fair and level playing field. In actual practice the rules and guidelines favor certain categories of individuals.

> One can only be troubled by the numerous and well-publicized recent cases involving convicted criminals, including some who were sentenced to death, who were later proved to be innocent. Less well-publicized, but perhaps more pervasive, are problems involving indigent defendants' lack of access to effective representation.[19]

In the vast majority of criminal cases the prosecution has significantly greater essential resources for legal research, investigation, fact gathering, witness availability, and control. It is essential that the defendant be able to work closely with the defense attorney and assist in his or her defense. It is extremely difficult for a defendant in custody to play the necessary role.

Even if released, the defendant may find that bail has depleted the few financial resources available for the defense. Criminal defense attorneys often learn that clients agreed to a previous guilty plea just to get out of jail within a reasonable period of time. The guilty plea becomes part of a permanent record, and judges give great weight to the defendant's criminal record, employment history, family ties, length of time in the community, residence, and factors indicating a stable history. Obviously, a person who is homeless, relatively transient, or unemployed is unlikely to be a candidate for release on his or her own recognizance. In spite of the Americans with Disabilities Act (ADA), individuals with a history of mental illness are often considered unstable and usually are not considered for release without bail.

The issue of dangerousness has been visited extensively by the U.S. circuit courts. For instance, the Third Circuit Court upheld pretrial detentions on the grounds that a defendant is *likely* to commit one of a number of previously designated offenses that are considered dangerous to the community.[20] The Second Circuit Court concurred with that ruling but rejected the premise that evidence must demonstrate the relationship between future dangerousness and the present offense.[21] The Ninth Circuit Court added potential economic danger to the community as grounds to support pretrial detention.[22]

If no other court remedy will reasonably ensure both the defendant's appearance in court and the safety of the community, the judge must remand the defendant to detention to await trial.[23] Most courts subscribe to the assumption that if a defendant is a flight risk, or the defendant poses a danger to society, then the defendant must be detained[24] however, all reasonable, less restrictive alternatives to detention must be explored.[25] The Eighth Circuit Court pointed out that reasonable assurance does not mean guarantee.[26]

Because bail secures release, the defendant, in effect, *buys* his or her freedom. In most jurisdictions, a police official (usually a desk sergeant at the station house where the defendant was booked) sets bail on misdemeanor charges according to a predetermined *bail schedule,* which specifies a monetary amount needed to secure release. The individual is usually released immediately after posting bail at the police station. For a felony charge, the accused stands before a judge during the initial appearance. Usually, the judge sets bail according to the bail schedule. Legislative bodies often establish minimum and maximum parameters from which judges can assign bail (e.g., not less than $5,000 or more than $15,000 for robbery). In more serious cases, the defendant along with his or her attorney and the prosecutor argue whether the individual should be released on bail.

There are four ways to secure one's release following an arrest:

1. Posting a cash bond. The defendant posts the full amount of the bond with the court.

2. Posting a property bond. A piece of property (e.g., a home) is used as collateral.

3. Being released on personal recognizance without having to post bond. This is usually reserved for persons charged with minor crimes or for prominent citizens of a community.

4. Using the services of a bail bondsman. The defendant pays the bondsman a certain percentage (typically 10%) of the bond (which is usually not refundable) and is allowed to go free.

Most defendants use bail bondsmen because cash bonds and property bonds require a sizable amount of cash or property, which most defendants do not have.

Legal factors are not the only determining factors in decisions about who is released and who is detained prior to a trial. Numerous studies, covering more than fifty years, consistently demonstrate two major points.[27] First, class and race affect pretrial release; minorities and the poor are far more likely to remain in jail. Second, those who are released are less likely to be convicted or if convicted less likely to be sentenced to a term of imprisonment.

One study examined whether the amount of bail required was below, above, or within the amount in the schedule. There were significant differences based on both race and gender. Whites and females were more likely than minorities and males to receive bail that was below the schedule amount.[28] The lower bail for whites and females was granted regardless of other factors, such as the seriousness of the offense and prior criminal record. In a study of violent felonies in Detroit, 71% of African Americans, but only 53% of whites, were detained. Of those detained, 88% were sent to prison, compared to only 45% of those not detained.[29] In another study, African Americans who were unemployed were the most likely to be detained.[30] Similarly, a prior felony conviction more adversely affected African Americans than whites, while having more education and a higher income had a more positive effect for whites than for African Americans.[31]

The *New York Times* reported a case that illustrates the injustice suffered by the poor when they cannot afford bail. A Hispanic man was charged with sexually assaulting a quadriplegic man for whom he worked. He was unable to raise the $5,000 for his bail. He refused to plead guilty and spent 19 months in jail awaiting his trial. He was found not guilty; ironically, he spent more time in jail awaiting his day in court than he would have spent had he pled guilty to a lesser charge. Investigation later revealed that the alleged victim had made similar unsubstantiated complaints to an agency that placed home-health-care employees.[32]

Freedom for Sale: The Bail Bondsman

The vicinity around many courthouses and jails is often home to a number of storefront offices with signs proclaiming "Bail Bonds, 24-Hour Service" or some catchy phrase like "Freedom for Sale." The sign displayed by a bail bondsman in southern California promised "I'll Get You Out If It Takes 20 Years" (it is no longer there—maybe people stopped doing business there after realizing the sign could be predicting a very lengthy stay). The bail bondsman is a shrewd businessperson—one of many who profit from crime.

Bail bondsmen have developed a close working relationship with others in the criminal justice system. Bondsmen help the courts by screening defendants, posting the bonds for those they consider to be good risks—reducing the congestion in jails. This relationship appears to be reciprocal since judges routinely do not pressure bondsmen to make good on bonds that are forfeited because the defendant did not show up for court. (The entire bond is forfeited and owed to the court if a defendant fails to appear for trial or other court appearance.) Bondsmen also have become part of the "courtroom workgroup" and are on a first-name basis with many of the court actors. They are sometimes financial contributors to judges' reelection campaigns.[33]

Many critics over the years have complained about the often shady practices of bail bondsmen, especially when they hire "bounty hunters" to track down those who skip town (there have been many cases of bounty hunters breaking into homes of suspected bail-jumpers, only to discover that they had the wrong address—in some notorious cases the occupants of the house have been killed). Bail bondsmen have been linked to many corrupt practices, such as paying "under-the-table" referral fees to lawyers, police, and sometimes even judges who in turn send them business (offenders or their families and friends). Such practices have resulted in at least five states abolishing bail bonding for profit (Kentucky, Oregon, Wisconsin, Nebraska, and Illinois).[34]

An article in the *Los Angeles Times* described what is known as "Bail Row," a "trash-blown block of downtown where the competition for freedom-buyers is as cutthroat as it gets." On this block there are "about a dozen bond offices" that are "lined shoulder to shoulder in a mustard-colored, carnival-lighted mini-mall and a stretch of neighboring storefronts in need of Windex." They are across the street from the Los Angeles County jail complex (two huge jails that hold more than 20,000 prisoners on any given day). The story notes that the jail complex is "a 24-hour-a-day gold mine for the bail sellers. And while it might appear that there is plenty of get-out-of-jail lucre to go around, the enterprises engage in a kind of urban combat for every dollar." This is also where two truck companies do a very lucrative business—towing cars owned by people trying to bail out friends and family, who are illegally parked in an area where parking is at a premium.[35] During the past decade the number of bail bondsmen in California has doubled (to about 2,200), while the average bond in Los Angeles County has quadrupled from $5,000 to $20,000. Since a defendant pays 10% of the amount of the bond, this means they have to come up with between $500 and $2,000—a financial impossibility for the majority of those arrested. Since only a small percentage of defendants fail to show up for court, bondsmen can make a lot of money. Companies advertise on radio and on billboards. A company called "Bad Boys" owns "a fleet of vehicles tattooed with images of a beefy man in women's clothing," along with the slogan, "Because Your Mama Wants You Home." Bad Boys earns $300 million annually. Maybe crime doesn't pay, but responding to crime does.

Preventive Detention

Pretrial preventive detention is the confinement in a secure facility of defendants who have not been found guilty but have been declared a danger to the community. As discussed earlier, some jurisdictions were unhappy with the Bail Reform Act of 1966. The first states to enact statutes allowing preventive detention were Alaska, Delaware, and Vermont in 1967, Maryland and South Carolina in 1969, followed by the District of Columbia action in 1970.[36] The Bail Reform Act of 1984 codified the use of danger as a consideration in all bail decisions. The concept is based on the unproved assumption that there is a way to predict who will commit a crime if released. The most controversial part of this practice is determining who is dangerous. In one of the earliest critiques of preventive detention, the American Friends Service Committee asserted in the early 1970s that *dangerous* has historically been reserved for those who in some way challenge existing power relationships. In *Struggle for Justice* the committee wrote:

> Those persons or groups that threaten the existing power structure are dangerous. In any historical period, to identify an individual whose status is that of a member of the "dangerous classes," the label "criminal" has been handy. The construct, criminal, is not used to classify the performers of all legally defined delicts [offenses against the law], only those whose position in the social structure qualifies them for membership in the dangerous classes.[37]

Are those currently locked up in jail awaiting trial "dangerous"? How many, when released, commit new offenses, and how many fail to appear in court? During the first six months after the enactment of The District of Columbia Court Reform and Criminal Procedure Act of 1970, only 20 of 6,000 felony defendants had bail revoked, and only 4 of the 20 were eventually detained.[38] Numerous studies over the years have examined various aspects of preventive detention.

One survey examined 1972 data on jail inmates across the nation. Of those charged with personal crimes (murder, rape, and robbery), 67% were granted bail but could not afford to pay it. If these "serious" offenders constituted a threat to the community, why was bail set in the majority of cases?[39] Subsequent surveys reported similar results.

A study of jail inmates in Las Vegas, Nevada, found that the majority were awaiting the final disposition of their cases and were eligible for some form of bail *but could not afford to pay it.*[40] Relatively few could be characterized as "dangerous." The most common charges pending were probation/parole violations (24%, by statute these individuals were not eligible for bail), drugs (15%), "all other offenses" (13%), larceny (8%), burglary (8%), fraud or forgery (7%), and traffic violations (6%). Most of these cases—81% of pretrial detainees—would not qualify as "dangerous."

John Irwin's study of the San Francisco jail found that 30% were charged with drug offenses, 14% were charged with burglary, and another 12% were charged with assault.[41] Most of the assault cases did not involve any injuries to the victims and were subsequently reduced to misdemeanors—a common occurrence all over the country. Jerome Miller found that of the more than 13,000 charges during a two-month period in Jacksonville, Florida, the most common were: "all other offenses" (18%), traffic (16%), shoplifting (9%), simple assault (7%), drugs (6%), aggravated assault (5%), disorderly intoxication (3%), worthless checks (3%), and burglary (3%). Together these accounted for 70% of the cases.[42] As in Irwin's study, most of the aggravated assaults did not involve an injury and were reduced to a misdemeanor.

National data on felony defendants from 1994 and 2002 (keep in mind that a significant proportion, sometimes as many as half, of jail inmates are charged with misdemeanors) provide additional support for the view that most jail inmates are not truly dangerous. In both years more than one-third were charged with drug offenses, while about 30% were charged with property offenses. As shown in table 9.1, among the roughly one-fourth who were charged with violent offenses, most were charged with assault or some other violent offense (other than murder and rape). It should be noted that these were the defendants' "most serious" charges and that most (58%) had other charges.[43] What is perhaps most interesting about these two studies is the fact that *the majority were released before the final disposition of their cases.* This includes just over half of all violent offenders (55%), two-thirds of those charged with assault, and almost two-thirds (64%) of those charged with property crimes and roughly the same percentage of those charged with drug offenses (66%) and public-order offenses (64%). It is interesting to note that the percentage distribution of the charges was almost identical for both years.

Table 9.1   A Profile of Felony Defendants in Large Urban Counties, 1992 and 2002

Most serious charge	Number		Percent	
	1992	2002	1992	2002
All Offenses	52,610	56,146	100%	100%
Violent offenses total	13,512	13,682	25.7	24.4
Murder	521	474	1.0	0.8
Rape	543	1,002	1.0	1.8
Robbery	4,081	3,036	7.8	5.4
Assault	6,128	7,122	11.6	12.7
Other violent	2,239	2,049	4.3	3.6
Property offenses total	16,346	17,021	31.1	30.3
Burglary	4,629	4,544	8.8	8.1
Larceny/theft	5,893	4,929	11.2	8.8
Other property	5,824	7,548	11.1	13.5
Drug offenses total	18,182	20,073	34.6	35.8
Trafficking	7,672	9,618	14.6	17.1
Other drug	10,510	10,455	20.0	18.6
Public Order offenses total	4,570	5,370	8.7	9.6

Sources: Reaves, B. A. *Felony Defendants in Large Urban Counties, 1994.* Washington, DC: U.S. Department of Justice, Bureau of Justice Statistics, January 1998, p. 2; Cohen, T. and B. A. Reaves. *Felony Defendants in Large Urban Counties, 2002.* Washington, DC: U.S. Department of Justice, Bureau of Justice Statistics, February 2006, p. 2.

Pretrial Release

What happens to individuals who are released? Numerous studies conducted during the past thirty or forty years have shown that most of those released on their own recognizance show up for court. Defendants with "roots in the community" (are employed, have family or relatives living in the area, lived there for several years, etc.) are not considered dangerous. Of the felony defendants in large urban counties who were released pending their court hearing, 78% made all court appearances. Those charged with violent offenses had the highest percentage (88%), and those charged with drug offenses the lowest (71%). Eighteen percent of released defendants were rearrested for a new offense (12% for felonies and 6% for misdemeanors). Violent offenders were the least likely to reoffend.[44]

Some Effects of Awaiting Trial in Jail

There are numerous disadvantages for defendants who do not obtain pretrial release. Defendants cannot spend time on the defense of their cases; attorneys are lim-ited in the amount of time they can spend with their clients; and defendants are separated from their families and their jobs (if they have jobs, they may lose them). In addition, the inability to make bail is in itself a type of sentence—punishment without conviction. There is no guarantee that the time spent in jail will be counted as time served toward an eventual sentence. There is also the problematic image presented by a defendant in court. Forty years ago, Jerome Skolnick made an observation that is equally relevant today:

> The man in jail enters the courtroom under guard, from the jail entrance. His hair has been cut by the jail barber, he often wears the clothes he was arrested in. By contrast, the civilian defendant usually makes a neat appearance, and enters the courtroom from the spectators' seats, emerging from the ranks of the public.[45]

Studies spanning four decades have shown that those awaiting trial in jail receive longer sentences than those out on bail.[46] (Remember, making bail has little relationship to the seriousness of the offense. It depends almost entirely on the defendant's economic resources and race.) In 2002, 81% of detained defendants were convicted, compared to 60% of those released.[47] Although the Supreme Court ruled that pretrial detention is regulatory rather than punishment, we argue that confinement in a jail is a form of punishment.

It should be obvious that the "blind lady of justice" that graces most courthouses is not so blind after all, for class and race enter into the picture quite frequently. By the time we arrive at the next critical stage of the criminal justice process, we are left with mostly lower-class and minority defendants, most of whom will spend a considerable amount of time behind bars awaiting their fate in court. In the remainder of this chapter we explore what happens during the preliminary hearing, plea bargaining, and that rare occurrence, the criminal trial.

As mentioned earlier, the initial appearance is technically the first stage in the criminal justice process following an arrest. It is the defendant's first exposure to the court system. However, the case may not yet have been reviewed in any detail by the district attorney's office (in fact, a prosecuting attorney may not have been assigned to the case), and the defendant may not yet have an attorney. The full weight of court procedures kicks in with the preliminary hearing, which can be viewed as a minitrial.

The Preliminary Hearing

The *preliminary hearing* is often referred to as the *probable-cause hearing*. For purposes of this hearing "probable cause" may be defined as establishing more likely than not that a crime was committed and that the defendant committed it. The state does not have to prove its case "beyond a reasonable doubt." Rather, the state has to present a *prima facie* case (Latin for "at first sight" or "on the face of it") that the defendant committed the crime. It should be noted that, legally speaking, there may in fact be "reasonable doubt" about the defendant's guilt, but this factor is not a consideration at this stage.

The preliminary hearing is usually required when a felony is charged by an *information* (a formal complaint filed by the prosecutor's office). In jurisdictions where the charge is filed with a grand jury, the preliminary hearing is often not used. In federal courts it is rarely used at all. It is currently used in about half of the states.[48]

The hearing process begins with the defendant presenting himself or herself before the court. The defendant is brought in by the bailiff (if held in jail) or emerges from the spectator's section (if at liberty through bail). Also appearing are the arresting or investigating officer, witnesses (if any), the prosecuting attorney, and defense counsel (if the defendant has one).

The hearing formally begins when the prosecuting attorney asks the arresting or investigating officer to give his or her account of the case. Other witnesses, usually victims, are then asked to do the same. The defense attorney, if assigned or present, calls witnesses (if any) and may ask the defendant to give his or her version. Both sides may cross-examine witnesses. Most of what takes place is routine and takes no more than ten minutes. The defendant does not have to enter a plea at this stage.

During the preliminary hearing, the judge often considers the social context of the offense to see whether prosecution is really justified or whether the defendant is a genuine threat to the community. For instance, the conduct in question may be normal in a particular community (e.g., in accordance with subcultural norms), or the complainant and the defendant know one another and have resolved the problems that produced the offense by the time the preliminary hearing is held. Some cases are dismissed because the complainants fail to show up.

There are two additional functions of the preliminary hearing. One is that of *discovery*—the pretrial procedure in which both parties receive information about evidence (witnesses, records, etc.) that will be used in the case. The preliminary hearing may give the defense some idea of the strength of the state's case, although the prosecutor does not have to show his or her entire hand. The second function involves testimony. The defense may want to obtain exact testimony from the state's witnesses (the entire preliminary hearing is usually recorded). In Los Angeles, for instance, the state tends to bring forth a fairly complete case, for most cases are ultimately settled in a "trial on the transcript" in which a judge makes a final disposition based on the transcript from the preliminary hearing.[49] The defendant has the right to waive the preliminary hearing, which most defendants do, often pleading guilty merely to shorten their stay in jail. Indeed, for many defendants, jail itself is a strong inducement to plead guilty.

The Grand Jury

The *grand jury* is a group of citizens (from twelve to twenty-three) who have the duty of hearing complaints in criminal cases and deciding whether the evidence presented by the prosecutor warrants handing down an *indictment* (or a *true bill*) charging a defendant with a crime. Grand juries are also authorized to carry out investigations of various problems existing (or alleged to exist) in a community, such as the conditions of public facilities (e.g., jails and hospitals) and alleged misconduct of public officials. The grand jury can only make recommendations to the prosecuting attorney; it is not authorized to determine guilt or innocence. (In reality, some of the findings of a grand jury may be so stacked against a defendant that, for all intents and purposes, the defendant has been proved guilty.) Grand jury sessions are not open to the public. Only the prosecutor, prosecution witnesses, court reporters, and other officials are allowed to be present. Lawyers representing defendants and defense witnesses are not allowed

Grand juries can examine criminal-law violations *prior* to an arrest. If they find probable cause, then a warrant is issued, and the criminal justice process begins. This often happens in drug cases and in government corruption and white-collar offenses. In most areas prosecutors use the grand jury only in important felony cases. Grand juries are always used in federal cases because they are guaranteed under the Fifth Amendment. Some states require that the grand jury

review all felonies. Defendants may (and usually do) waive a grand jury review.

More often than not, a felony case proceeds through the system via an information filed by the prosecutor's office rather than a grand jury indictment. After the preliminary hearing the defendant is brought into the trial court for the arraignment.

The Arraignment

The stage of the court process at which the defendant enters a plea is the *arraignment*. Usually all participants are present for the arraignment. The state is represented by one or two deputy district attorneys who sit at a table with large stacks of files in front of them, each file representing a case on the court docket. As the judge calls out the case number and the defendant's name, the defense counsel approaches a table opposite that of the state. In the district court of Las Vegas, Nevada, the following typically takes place (much of what the judge says is taken from a colloquy form that all judges use).[50]

The judge asks whether the defendant wants the information or indictment read in open court by the clerk. The defendant answers (or the attorney answers for the defendant), "no." The judge then asks the following questions: "What is your age?" "What is the extent of your formal education?" "Do you understand, read, and write the English language?" After these questions are answered, the judge then asks "Is the defendant ready to enter a plea?" followed by "What is your plea to the information?" If the defendant pleads not guilty, the judge sets a date for the trial. Most of the time, however, the defendant enters a guilty plea. After this is done, the judge then asks the following questions: "Is your plea of guilty freely and voluntarily made? Without threat or fear to yourself or anyone closely related to or associated with you?" After the defendant (or the defense attorney) answers those questions, the judge then asks the defense attorney: "Did you advise the defendant of the elements of the crime with which he (she) is charged, the burden of proof required by the state in the prosecution of this matter, and the defense, if any, available to him (her)?"

The defense attorney answers yes. The judge then asks the defendant the following series of questions:

You heard these questions Mr. (Ms.) (defendant's name)?

Did you understand them?

Did you have discussions with (defense attorney or deputy defender's office) on these matters?

Did you understand what you and he (she) were talking about?

All of these questions are answered yes. The judge then asks the defense attorney: "Was he (she) also advised of the penalty?" ("Yes, your honor.") "What was he (she) advised?" (The defense attorney states the penalties for the crime.) Turning to the defendant, the judge then asks the following questions:

Do you understand that the court could impose such a sentence by reason of your plea of guilty?

Do you understand also that you have the right to a speedy and public trial by an impartial jury, free of prejudicial publicity?

Do you understand you have the right to be confronted with the witnesses against you and to have an opportunity to cross-examine them?

Do you understand that you have the right to have compulsory process for obtaining witnesses in your favor?

Do you understand that you may refuse to testify or make any statement on your own behalf and the prosecution may not comment on your failure to testify at the trial?

Do you understand that you have the right to the assistance of counsel at all stages of these proceedings?

Knowing these rights are available to you, do you ask this court to accept your plea of guilty?

Is this a negotiated plea?

All of these questions are answered yes by the defendant, after which the judge asks: "What is the extent of these negotiations?" The defense attorney then explains what the nego-

tiations were. The judge also asks the representative from the district attorney's office if this is what the agreement was, to which the representative replies yes. After this, the judge once again turns to the defendant and asks the following series of questions:

Mr. (Ms.) (defendant's name), you heard the representations of counsel. Is that your understanding of the negotiations undertaken on your behalf by the public defender with the district attorney?

Aside from this, has anyone made any promise of lesser sentence, probation, reward, immunity, or anything else in order to induce you to plead guilty? (The defendant answers no even though plea bargaining, as we discuss later in this chapter, almost always implies the promise of a lesser sentence or some other kind of reward.)

Do you understand that the matter of probation and sentence is to be determined solely by this court and no one else?

Are you pleading guilty because in truth and in fact you are guilty, and for no other reason? (Again, the defendant answers yes when in fact he (she) should be saying no.)

What happened on (gives the date of the crime) that causes you to enter a plea of guilty? (Defendant briefly describes the crime.)

Do you have a copy of the information before you?

Are all the statements in that information true?

And you admit your guilt to this offense?

After the defendant answers yes to the final questions, the judge then states: "The court accepts the defendant's plea of guilty. This matter is referred to the Department of Parole and Probation for presentence investigation and report. Entry of judgment and imposition of sentence is set over to (day, month, and time)." And the ritual of the arraignment comes to a close.

All of the preceding takes no more than about ten minutes. Each year, all around the country, this scene (or something very similar to it) is repeated for thousands of cases. Members of the district attorney's office play a small role in the proceedings. At times it appears they are performing routine clerical duties that someone with very little legal training could perform. However, every once in a while—about 5 to 10% of the cases—the defendant pleads not guilty, and a date is set for trial. We discuss the criminal trial shortly, but first we need to consider what took place behind the scenes.

The bargaining and exchange that takes place out of public view is the rule rather than the exception. In the next section we explore this facet of the court system. Plea bargaining is the reality of criminal justice today. Instead of being handed down by judges and juries, sentences are negotiated in restaurants, bars, courtroom hallways, on the phone, and through other means *outside the courtroom.*

PLEA BARGAINING: MAINTAINING BUREAUCRATIC EFFICIENCY

At the end of each episode of *Rawhide* (a television series that aired 1959–1965 and starred, among others, Clint Eastwood), the trail boss always called out, "Head 'em up, move 'em out." This command, in our view, is an appropriate summary of the modern court system. It often resembles a cattle drive on the open range where the goal is to move cattle as quickly as possible toward their destination in order to make a quick sale and large profit. Justice often takes a back seat to the goals of the bureaucracy where cases need to be moved along as swiftly as possible so the system does not collapse. In many state court systems judges are evaluated or "graded" on how speedily they process their cases and how they manage their caseload rather than on the quality of justice produced. Approximately 95% of all convictions are the result of a guilty plea, including 83% of felony convictions.[51] The outcome of the case is negotiated (in a manner not unlike ordinary business deals or transactions) between the prosecuting attorney and the defense attorney. This negotiation is what is commonly referred to as *plea bargaining*.

The public and many in law enforcement do not like plea bargaining because it seems

that the offender "gets off easy." Most defendants, by the time they get to this stage, are guilty of some offense—usually something less serious than the original charge. The reality is that if one goes to trial and is convicted, the sentence is almost always more severe. But if the defendant "strikes a deal," he or she receives a benefit.[52] A guilty plea saves the state—and taxpayers—a lot of money.

In the plea-bargaining process the defendant, the defense attorney, and the prosecutor engage in negotiations during which the defendant pleads guilty in return for certain concessions. This procedure is used mainly to expedite cases, even though many within the system might deny this reality. In *Brady v. United States*, the Supreme Court ruled in 1970 that the state can constitutionally "extend a benefit to a defendant who in turn extends a substantial benefit to the state" (397 U.S. 742, 90 S. Ct. 1463, 1471, 25 L. Ed. 2d 747, 1970). Thus, plea bargaining is the classic quid pro quo—"You scratch my back and I'll scratch yours."

There are three types of bargains.[53] In *charge bargaining,* the defendant can plead guilty to a less serious charge (e.g. a guilty plea to petty larceny instead of the original charge of grand larceny), reducing the *level* of the offense. With this type of bargaining, a felony might be reduced to a misdemeanor. In *count bargaining,* the defendant pleads guilty to the most serious of several charges, and the remainder of the charges are dropped (pleading guilty to burglary in exchange for dropping possession of burglary tools, trespassing, etc.). *Sentence bargaining* exchanges a guilty plea for leniency. A defendant can plead guilty in return for a sentence to probation instead of prison. Another bargain in sentencing is a guilty plea to several charges in exchange for serving one *concurrent sentence* for all charges.

Historical Development of Plea Bargaining

Plea bargaining, as we know it today, did not become a dominant method of disposing of cases until the early part of the twentieth century. Prior to this time, courts in both

Europe and the United States either did not allow plea bargaining or strongly discouraged it. Most defendants pleaded not guilty and appeared before a judge or a judge and jury.[54] In 1824 only 11% of all defendants in Boston pleaded guilty. In 1839 in New York only 25% of all felony convictions were from guilty pleas. Compare these rates with those of today and you get an idea of how plea bargaining has changed.

Trials before the nineteenth century were conducted at a swift pace (about ten or twenty per day), mainly because there were so few cases, defendants had no lawyers, cases were not very complex, and the victims usually served as the prosecutors (or hired private counsel to prosecute the cases). There were few motions, no long speeches, no *voir dire* of jurors, and no other delaying tactics. There were also few rules of evidence or other procedural rules that could prolong trials. Because there was no professional police force to screen cases early, judges and juries dominated the judicial system.[55]

The appellate courts, when they heard such cases (which was rarely), were very unfavorable toward plea bargaining. There were several cases in the nineteenth century in which the courts reversed the lower-court decisions because there were guilty pleas. The first case in which the Supreme Court approved a guilty plea was in 1892 (*Hallinger v. Davis,* 146 U.S. 314), but there was no apparent "bargain," only a plea of guilty.[56]

Guilty pleas in return for certain concessions began to appear with more and more regularity after the turn of the twentieth century. Most of the bargaining that began to take place was part of the more widespread corruption within the criminal justice system. Both lawyers and the police, for instance, engaged in plea negotiations in return for specific fees from defendants. In one case a New York attorney made financial arrangements with a judge that enabled the attorney to "stand out on the street of the Night Court and dicker away sentences in this form: $300 for ten days, $200 for twenty days, $150 for thirty days."[57]

By the 1920s, as several state crime surveys around the country found, the majority

of all felony cases were disposed of by pleas of guilty. According to these surveys, the most noteworthy increase in guilty pleas came between 1910 and 1920. The majority involved rewards in the form of reduced charges, the most common of which was from a felony to a misdemeanor. Another common reward was that a guilty plea reduced one's chances of a prison sentence by about one-half.[58]

One of the principal reasons why plea bargaining was so common by the turn of the twentieth century was the last half of the nineteenth century was marked by the professionalization of criminal justice. There was also a growing belief that guilty pleas in combination with methods such as probation could "cure" the "deviants" of society. This belief was part of a change in perspective on punishment—a shift toward "treatment" in penological circles. Lawrence Friedman argues that there was a widespread assumption that the defendant had already been "tried," in effect, by the police and prosecutors. With the rise of professional police and public prosecutors, it was assumed that screening of cases had become more efficient.[59]

Another factor (as noted above) was the corrupt nature of the criminal justice system—not surprising given the widespread influence of political machines. In fact, many positions within the criminal justice system were given to people for service to these machines.[60] Offenders viewed the system as a place where bargaining and manipulation could take place, and so began the practice of bribery and the "fix."[61]

Albert Alschuler cites the increase in the volume of cases, in part because of the increase in the number of laws passed during the late nineteenth and early twentieth centuries, as a major cause of the growth of plea bargaining. Roscoe Pound noted that over half of those arrested in Chicago in 1912 violated laws that had not existed twenty-five years earlier. As a result of this increase there was tremendous pressure to expedite cases.[62]

Widespread changes in the political economy also affected plea bargaining. As Barak notes, it emerged as part of a much larger regulative movement within the criminal justice system.[63] In order to regulate social stability, the criminal justice system began to function more and more as a repressive state apparatus (for example, the repression of workers' movements and the Palmer Raids during and after World War I).[64] It is not coincidence that the majority of cases during this period involved poor people or immigrants. Typically, these people had no counsel, and plea bargaining became an efficient method of convicting and hence controlling them.[65]

Another related factor was the movement among business leaders to make social institutions (e.g., education, city government), including the criminal justice and juvenile justice systems, more efficient. Plea bargaining reflected such business practices as cooperation (which is the hallmark of the negotiation between prosecutor and defense counsel), coordination, and centralization. Indeed, "expediency, efficiency, and economy" became the watchwords of criminal justice and other reforms of the period.[66] An article in 1912 article advised: "the duties of the judicial office . . . can be directed toward increased *efficiency in the administration of justice* [emphasis in the original] and this, after all, is the only justifiable reform, change, modification or revolution which we ought to take with the courts."[67] In short, plea bargaining meant disposing of criminal cases efficiently, expediently, and economically.

Plea bargaining became standard practice within the criminal justice system in the early part of the twentieth century. It continues to be condemned by the appellate courts, but very few case ever reach the appeal stage. In *Santobello v. New York* the Supreme Court ruled in 1971 that plea bargaining is:

> an essential component of the administration of justice. Properly administered, it is to be encouraged. If every criminal charge were subjected to a full-scale trial, the States and the Federal Government would need to multiply by many times the number of judges and court facilities.[68]

The Plea-Bargaining Process

The plea-bargaining process may begin at the arresting stage. The police, fully aware of the reality of plea bargaining, often overcharge (if they don't, then the prosecutor does). The police also may overcharge in order to develop informants. For instance, they might apprehend a known addict and tell him that they will charge him with possession of drugs, attempting to sell drugs, or other offenses unless he helps them locate big-time drug dealers. Moreover, in their attempts to clear a number of unsolved crimes, the police may agree not to charge the offender with all the crimes if he confesses.[69]

Obtaining guilty pleas saves the prosecutors time and money, and it increases the prosecutor's "batting average" of convictions. The prosecutor, as well as other actors in the court system, knows full well that the system would break down completely if more than 10 or 15% of the cases went to trial. Prosecutors often deliberately overcharge as a "lever" to get a guilty decision.[70] Bureaucratic efficiency rather than justice seems to be the basic goal here. Moreover, seeking guilty pleas in order to increase the conviction rates of prosecutors is consistent with a capitalist ethic of producing "commodities"; in this case, the commodity is humans who are prosecuted.

Ironically, in most cases it is the defense attorney, not the prosecutor, who puts pressure on defendants to plead guilty. Multiple studies have found that defense attorneys seek guilty pleas from their clients instead of trying to have their cases dismissed.[71] Abraham Blumberg suggests that defense attorneys play the role of "double agents": they appear to be seeking acquittals for their clients but in reality are cooperating with the prosecutors to obtain guilty pleas. Blumberg further suggests that lawyers have a vested interest in maintaining good relations with the court if they want to have a steady caseload and a successful career. The client becomes a "secondary figure in the court system," and the defense attorney "has far greater professional, economic, intellectual and other ties to the various elements of the court system than he does to his client."[72] By the time the defendant arrives at this stage there is usually sufficient evidence to convict on *some* charge, so it is possible the defense attorney is acting in the defendant's best interest by avoiding a trial. However, this reasoning assumes that the defendant will be found guilty at trial, which may not be the case.

It is common knowledge among experienced court personnel that most plea-bargaining sessions are routine. There is a great deal of agreement among the participants, and often there are unspoken assumptions about what everyone expects. As in many other bureaucratic settings, court lawyers (after becoming enmeshed in the subculture norms of the court) develop a sense of typical cases, which David Sudnow has called **normal crimes.** For each crime, they believe that there are typical (i.e., normally occurring) offender characteristics, situations, or circumstances and certain types of sentences that are usually handed down. The novice lawyer learns from more experienced personnel that, for instance, "in cases such as this one, the defendant is usually an amateur, so we go easy the first time around. And the judge is usually willing to grant probation or a suspended sentence."[73] Comments made more than thirty years ago still ring true today:

> The P.D. [public defender] refers to offenses in terms of their social reality rather than their legal definition. That is, *legally* the case may be a burglary, but "really" it is just a petty theft. Likewise, Grand Theft Auto may be a serious crime according to the Penal Code, but because of the circumstances which typically surround it, everyone knows it's usually "nothing serious."[74]

Judges, too, go along with this procedure and deal with typical cases in rather routine ways. Often they engage in "pre-plea bargains" in their chambers with the district attorney and the defense attorney. One judge made the following comment:

> On a three count forgery case, the defense attorney asks the D.A., "Can I have one count?" The D.A. says, "Yes, which one?" The defense attorney says, "Count 2." And that's it. No bargain has been made. No promise that counts 1 and 3 will be dismissed in exchange for the plea to count 2. *It's simply that everyone knows what the standard practice is.* Or here's another example. The defense attorney comes into court and asks the D.A., "What does Judge Hall give on bookmaking cases?" The D.A. says, "He usually gives $150 fine on the first offense." The attorney says, "Fine. We'll enter a plea to count 1." Again no promise was made by anybody. *It's just that everyone knows what customarily will happen.*[75]

As implied in the scenario above, plea bargaining is typically done behind closed doors.

It is often suggested that plea bargaining takes place because the courts simply have too many cases, yet plea bargaining is just as likely to take place in courts with small caseloads. In addition, the extent of plea bargaining does not correlate with the overall crime rate of a jurisdiction or with the extent of court resources.[76] Plea bargaining can better be explained by the fact that by the time the case gets to this stage it may be what is commonly known as a "dead bang case"—one in which there is overwhelming evidence that the defendant is in fact guilty. Another factor is the fact that trials are expensive and time-consuming. If every offender (not to mention every victim) demanded "justice" or a "day in court," the system would completely break down.

Plea bargaining resembles a "supermarket with set prices and a high volume of business."[77] Once the courtroom workgroup decides the "going rate" for different crimes, not much actual bargaining takes place. Studies show that there is a high degree of regularity and predictability in how cases are disposed of in the court system. You can usually predict the outcome if you know the seriousness of the top charge in addition to the defendant's prior record. As a result, defendants who have been arrested and charged on several occasions "learn the ropes" and are thus able to take advantage of the bargaining system.

The Consequences of Plea Bargaining

One of the most common results of plea bargaining is that those who insist on a trial by jury typically receive harsher sentences than those who plead guilty. The negative consequences of going to trial are readily acknowledged by members of the court system.

> What often happens, though, is that by going to trial he [the defendant] gets convicted of a lot more serious charge than if he had taken a disposition to a lesser charge. . . . In (non-trial) dispositions, the judge is saying the defendant will get something less for pleading guilty. But if the case goes to trial, then the judge is no longer bound by any earlier conditions. . . . A plea bargain may involve a different charge than the charge at the trial, that's why the sentence would be different.[78]

Research shows that the seriousness of the offense plays a key role in determining whether a case will go to trial. Violent crimes (murder, rape, and manslaughter) are the most likely to go before a jury; most property crimes and especially drug offenses are settled by a guilty plea. However, even when controlling for the seriousness of the crime and even for the severity of the charge (e.g., first degree versus second degree, etc.), those who plead guilty and those who choose a bench trial are less likely to go to jail than those who go before a jury. Factors such as age, sex, race, jail status (at liberty or in jail), and type of counsel (public defender versus retained) did not affect the results. In other words, the key factor was whether a person went before a jury.[79]

Race affects plea bargaining. An analysis of almost 700,000 cases in California from 1981 to 1990 discovered that plea bargaining favored whites over minorities. Regardless of other factors (e.g., offense charged), whites did better than minorities at "getting charges dropped, getting cases dismissed, avoiding harsher punishment, avoiding extra charges, and having their criminal records wiped clean."[80] Of the 71,668 defendants with no prior record who were charged with a felony, one-third of whites, compared to one-fourth of minorities, received a charge reduction; minorities were much more likely than whites

to receive prison or jail sentences; for the sale of drugs, minorities were twice as likely to go to prison as whites. A public defender and a judge both admitted that such treatment stemmed from a combination of "unconscious stereotyping and deliberate discrimination."

If a white person can put together a half-way plausible excuse, people will bend over backward to accommodate that person. It's a feeling, "You've got a nice person screwing up," as opposed to the feeling that "This minority person is on a track and eventually they're going to end up in state prison."[81]

If the defendant is perceived as basically a good person who "made a mistake," then the final disposition is likely to be lenient; but if the defendant is perceived as a "criminal," then the final disposition is likely to be more severe. A close look at sentencing practices and the composition of today's prison system is solid proof of a systematic class and racial bias (see chapter 10).

The case of a black honor-roll student illustrates many of the issues of plea bargaining and race (as well as other aspects of the criminal justice system) In a hotel room on New Year's Eve, six male juveniles and two female juveniles engaged in consensual, videotaped sex. Genarlow Wilson of Douglasville, GA, then 17 years old, engaged in consensual oral sex with a 15-year-old girl. The mother of the girl originally said Wilson should not have been criminally charged but changed her statement after a visit from prosecutors. At the time, Wilson would have faced one year in prison had he had sexual intercourse with the girl rather than oral sex and would not have been required to register as a sex offender. (In 2006, lawmakers ended the difference in punishment for oral and vaginal sex.) The others accepted a plea bargain, but Wilson refused. Most had been in trouble before, but Wilson was a homecoming king with a 3.2 grade-point average and no criminal record; colleges were offering football scholarships. Wilson opted for a trial to avoid having a record as a child molester and sex offender. Instead, he was found guilty and received a sentence of 10 years because of mandatory sentencing guidelines. During Wilson's trial, a 27-year-old white teacher was found guilty of having sex with a 17-year-old student—exactly the type of crime for which child molestation statutes were written. She was sentenced to 90 days in jail and 3 years of probation.[82]

After he had served 28 months of his sentence, a judge ordered him released, saying:

> The fact that Genarlow Wilson has spent two years in prison for what is now classified as a misdemeanor, and without assistance from this court, will spend eight more years in prison, is a grave miscarriage of justice. If this court or any court cannot recognize the injustice of what has occurred here, then our court system has lost sight of the goal our judicial system has always strived to accomplish . . . justice being served in a fair and equal manner.[83]

The prosecutor filed a notice of appeal, arguing that Georgia law does not grant a judge the authority to reduce a sentence imposed by the trial court. The governor of Georgia agreed and said it would be unfair to treat Wilson differently from the others who took the plea deals.[84] On June 25, another judge ruled that Wilson's conviction made him ineligible for bail. On October 26, 2007, the Georgia Supreme Court overturned the conviction, finding the sentence "cruel and unusual punishment."[85] One commentator used the case as an example of why it is essential that prosecutors choose cases

> where the crime caused real harm to another person and where the potential punishment is proportional to the crime. The ability to secure a conviction isn't enough. . . . The point here is that the prosecutors should have shown the good judgment never to have brought the molestation charge in the first place. Prosecutors need to be more than inveterate slaves to the (often poorly written) law. And more broadly, we need to stop gauging our criminal justice system's effectiveness by how many people it puts in jail. We need to measure it by how well it metes out justice.[86]

THE CRIMINAL TRIAL

Most criminal cases are settled through a guilty plea. A few cases, however, do end up before a jury. The jury trial is supposed to be one of the cornerstones of the criminal justice system. Indeed, the right to a trial by a jury of one's peers is written in several parts of the U.S. Constitution, especially in the Sixth Amendment, which states that "in all criminal prosecutions, the accused shall enjoy the right to a speedy and public trial, by an impartial jury."

Trial Juries

For either state or federal charges, an accused person has the right to a trial if the offense is punishable by more than six months in prison. States and localities may, at their discretion, extend this guarantee to those accused of lesser offenses (*Baldwin v. New York,* 399 U.S. 66, 1970). The size of the trial jury has traditionally been twelve people, but the Supreme Court ruled in 1970 that a jury of six was constitutional.[87] Another traditional practice has been that a jury verdict must be unanimous. In 1972, however, the Supreme Court ruled in two decisions that unanimity is not always required.[88] In federal trials, however, jury verdicts must be unanimous.

Jury Selection

Ideally, the demographics of the jury match those of the community or a cross section of the community. This is not often the case, especially when we consider the methods by which juries have been selected. Until recently, the *master jury list* in most jurisdictions was compiled from voter registration lists, which left out large numbers of people, especially the poor and nonwhites, in addition to young people.

When a trial is scheduled, a jury pool, or **venire,** is selected. This is a list of people from whom a trial jury will be chosen; those on the list will be summoned to appear for jury duty. Not all of those on the list will actually serve. Several kinds of people are automatically disqualified: ex-felons, individuals below a certain age, those who are not residents of the United States, those unable to understand English, those who have personal connections with the case (e.g., relatives of the defendant), and those connected with the legal system (judges, lawyers, police officers, etc.).

The U.S. Supreme Court has ruled that a jury is "an inestimable safeguard against the corrupt or overzealous prosecutor and against the compliant, biased, or eccentric judge."[89] The first law the Supreme Court ever struck down as racially discriminatory was one that restricted jury service to white men only.[90] Despite such rulings, racial discrimination in the jury selection process is a problem. Several studies have found that black defendants, especially in the South, often face an almost all-white jury because most blacks were excluded for one reason or another.[91]

Because jury lists are commonly based on voter registration and because many African Americans (approximately 13%) have been deprived of the right to vote because they have been convicted of a felony (primarily drug offenses), the potential jury pool does not represent the community. Southern states have the highest percentage of blacks ineligible to vote because of felony convictions. Florida and Alabama lead the way with 30%.[92] Moreover, many jury lists are based on motor vehicle registration records and driver's license lists, where poor and racial minorities also are underrepresented. Because minorities and the poor change residences more frequently than do individuals who can afford to purchase homes, they are less likely to receive a jury summons. Another problem is that (for many different reasons, not the least of which is a general distrust of the criminal justice system) minorities are less likely to respond to a summons.[93] The important issue here is that poor people and racial minorities bring a much different perspective into the courtroom than do whites and the well-to-do. The Rodney King case provides an excellent illustration. The original trial, which resulted in acquittals of the white officers, was held in an almost all-white community—suburban Simi Valley, northwest of Los Angeles—rather than in South Central Los Angeles, where composition of the community would have been very different.

Perhaps the most critical point in the selection of the jury is the *voir dire* ("to see to

speak" in French), the examination of a potential juror in order to decide whether he or she is suitable for a particular case. Defense attorneys and prosecutors question prospective jurors about their biases and preconceived notions about the case. If the attorney for either side believes that a prospective juror would not decide the case in a fair manner, the attorney can issue a *challenge for cause* and prevent that person from serving on the jury. A more important type of challenge (and one more often used) is the **peremptory challenge**, which both the prosecutor and the defense may use to dismiss a potential juror without giving a reason. A limited number of challenges can be made. Attorneys' reasons for dismissing jurors may be based on hunches or on scientific criteria. The use of social scientists and jury consultants to create juror profiles has increased in recent years.

Racial bias often plays a key role during the peremptory challenge. In 1965, the Supreme Court ruled that a prosecutor who used peremptory challenges to eliminate all of the African Americans (6) in a jury pool did not violate the equal protection clause of the Constitution. *Swain v. Alabama* did state that if a defendant could establish that there was a *pattern* of discrimination in the jurisdiction, that would be a violation. However, the test was too stringent for defense lawyers to meet, so defendants had little chance of proving discriminatory jury selection.[94] In 1986, the Supreme Court rejected the necessity to show a pattern of discrimination. In *Batson v. Kentucky*, the Court ruled a defendant may establish a "case of purposeful discrimination solely on evidence concerning the prosecutor's exercise of peremptory challenges at the defendant's trial." The prosecutor must then "come forward with a neutral explanation for challenging black jurors."[95]

A review of published decisions between 1986 and 1992 involving *Batson* challenges found that "in almost any situation a prosecutor can readily craft an acceptable neutral explanation to justify striking black jurors because of their race."[96] The explanations include: too old, too young, employed as a teacher, did not make eye contact, made too much eye contact, lived or worked in the same neighborhood as the defendant, or had previously been involved in the criminal justice system. These neutral excuses are generally accepted by judges and fellow prosecutors and even some defense attorneys. As discussed in chapter 8, all the court officials are part of the same courtroom workgroup. They "travel in the same social circles, may well have contributed to the judge's election campaign, and may be personal friends with the judge," so the judge accepts such excuses as "genuine and rarely overturns them."[97]

Jury Decisions

Researchers who study the criminal court system often fiercely debate whether juries can render impartial verdicts. Since less than 10% of all criminal cases ever reach a jury, the potential answers affect only a very small percentage of defendants.

A trial by jury mostly serves a legitimating function. The existence of the jury system (even if most cases never go this far) legitimates the entire criminal justice system and reinforces the ideology of "equal justice for all." As Chambliss and Seidman remark: "The existence of the jury makes it possible for the judge and the whole judicial system to appear to be above the [class] struggle, making judgments fairly in the event of conflicts between the State and its subjects."[98]

The perception is that the trial system gives both the prosecutor and the defense attorney equal opportunity to present a case, and rules of evidence regulate the adversarial process so that the defendant receives fair trial. This further legitimates the criminal justice system and reinforces the idea that this is a society run by the "rule of law" rather than the rule of powerful men.

In a criminal trial, as in other courtroom procedures, there are many rituals, some of which are symbolic and reinforce dominant U.S. values (e.g., respect for the law, equal justice for all, the rule of law). Whether justice is really administered is open to question. The criminal trial, perhaps more than anything else, may simply be an attempt to legitimate the judicial system and the politi-

cal economy that surrounds and supports it. The trial, moreover, is supposed to be above politics and neutral. But during the late 1960s and early 1970s, this perspective on the trial (and the entire judicial system) was called into question. Jury verdicts of not guilty (especially in the Chicago 7 case), resulted in claims that the "system works" or "there *is* justice" in the United States. However, the length and cost of these trials were usually enough to break up or otherwise thwart a radical movement, and injustices continued to exist both inside and outside the judicial system. In 2007, there were a number of stories about partisan political activities in the Department of Justice.

> Justice requires that criminal prosecutions be subject to the rule of law, not to the whims of politicians. The government brings awesome power to bear against an individual in a criminal case. That power is legitimate only if exercised in an apolitical manner, based solely on the facts and neutral legal principles. . . . Indictments, jury verdicts, the arguments of prosecutors—none of these is worthy of respect if prosecution is perceived to be simply an exercise of raw political power. If the wall between politics and prosecution breaks down, the criminal law is stripped of its moral authority, and our very notion of what "justice" means is compromised.[99]

Stages in the Criminal Trial

The criminal trial, though a rare event, is clearly one of the most visible aspects of the entire criminal justice system. Celebrity trials, like that of O. J. Simpson, have a national following. They are important events involving a jury of rather ordinary men and women and can have far-reaching effects on the administration of justice, at least in terms of public perceptions of how the system works. Unfortunately, those public perceptions can be skewed. As discussed, the criminal trial is a rare event rather than a barometer of the entire criminal justice system.

There are several stages in a typical trial: (1) *voir dire* and jury selection, (2) opening statements by prosecutor and defense, (3) prosecutor's presentation of evidence, (4) defense motions and hearings on motions, which are of a constitutional nature or specifically reserved for the time of trial, (5) presentation of defense evidence, (6) rebuttal by the state, (7) prosecutor's closing arguments, (8) defense's closing arguments, (9) prosecutor's reply arguments, (10) judge's instructions to the jury, (11) jury deliberation and verdict.[100]

Pretrial Motions

Pretrial motions are written requests to the court by either the prosecutor or the defense attorney seeking certain objectives prior to trial; typically evidence on each motion is presented at separate hearings There are eight major types of pretrial motions.[101]

1. *Motion to dismiss.* Most commonly filed by the defense, this motion generally claims that there is not sufficient evidence to bring this case to court in the first place.

2. *Motion to determine the competency of the accused to stand trial.* The defense claims that the defendant is incompetent to stand trial, because of some form of "mental illness."

3. *Motion to suppress evidence obtained through unlawful search or seizure.* This is a very common motion for the defense. The court is asked to suppress evidence obtained in violation of the Fourth Amendment. If the hearing determines the evidence is inadmissible, the prosecution may not have sufficient evidence to pursue the case.

4. *Motion to suppress confessions, admissions, or other statements made to the police.* Like the previous example, this motion seeks to suppress various statements made to the police that may be in violation of the *Miranda* rule.

5. *Motion to suppress pretrial identification of the accused.* This relates to eyewitness identification that may violate due process standards.

6. *Motion to require the prosecution to disclose the identity of a confidential informant.* Unless the informant was an "active participant" in the offense, the prosecution is not usu- ally required to release such information (common in drug cases).

7. *Motion for change of venue.* Either the defendant or the prosecutor may request that the trial be moved to another location. This is most often done in cases where there has been extensive media coverage.[102]

8. *Motion for a continuance.* On a variety of grounds, either the prosecutor or the defense may request either a continuance or a postponement of the trial. Sometimes more time is needed to locate important witnesses or evidence. Often, additional time is needed by the defense if a new attorney is assigned to the case and needs more time to prepare. The request can also be because of personal reasons such as illness. This is probably one of the most common motions.

In many jurisdictions, most pretrial motions are disposed of in an "omnibus" procedure. The prosecutor and defense attorneys check off standard pretrial motions on an omnibus application form; the court reviews the requests and makes rulings at the end of the standard discovery period for that court. Figure 9.1 depicts a typical defense omnibus application.

The omnibus application form highlights the major issues for the upcoming trial or settlement negotiations. The twenty-three items are not exhaustive, but they represent the most common motions. Obviously if the defense can raise some doubt in the prosecutor's mind about the strength of the state's case, the prospects for resolution improve.

In a criminal trial, the accused has raised an "issue of fact"—that is, the accused has challenged the allegations made by the state. The basic issue is whether the defendant committed the alleged offense. Larger moral or social-political issues are usually ignored. Motives are rarely explored (except in rare instances of insanity defenses). The question becomes a rather simple one: Is the defendant guilty or innocent?[103]

Figure 9.1   A Typical Defense Application

THE SUPERIOR COURT OF _____ COUNTY IN AND FOR THE STATE OF _____

STATE OF _____,

Plaintiff

vs.

_____,

Defendant

_____   Case No.: 06-6-06666-0

                                        DEFENDANT'S OMNIBUS
                                        APPLICATION

_____

COMES NOW (Defense Attorney), and hereby makes the following applications and motions checked below:

	GRANTED	DENIED
1. To dismiss for lack of probable cause	_____	_____
2. To dismiss for failure of the citation, information, or indictment to state an offense.	_____	_____
3. To sever counts and for a separate trial.	_____	_____
4. To sever defendant's case and for a separate trial.	_____	_____
5. For discovery of all oral, written, or recorded statements made by defendant to investigating officers or third parties in the possession of plaintiff.	_____	_____
6. For discovery of the names, addresses, and a short summary of proposed testimony of plaintiff's witnesses (includes actual statements of witnesses).	_____	_____
7. To make more definite and certain (a bill of particulars).	_____	_____
8. To inspect physical and documentary evidence in plaintiff's possession.	_____	_____
9. For a hearing to suppress statements.	_____	_____
10. To suppress evidence in plaintiff's possession because of (1) illegal search, (2) illegal arrest and/or (3) illegal electronic surveillance.	_____	_____
11. To suppress evidence of the identification of the defendant.	_____	_____
12. To take the deposition of witnesses. OR, interview witnesses.	_____	_____
13. To secure the appearance of a witness at trial.	_____	_____
14. To inquire into the conditions of pretrial release.	_____	_____

(continued)

TO REQUIRE THE PROSECUTION:

15. To state:

    (a) If there was an informer involved;   _____   _____

    (b) Whether the informant will be a witness;   _____   _____

    (c) To state the name and address of the
        informant or claim the privilege.   _____   _____

16. To disclose evidence in plaintiff's possession
favorable to the defendant on the issue of guilt.   _____   _____

17. To disclose whether plaintiff will rely on prior acts
or convictions for proof of knowledge or intent.   _____   _____

18. To advise whether any expert witness will be called,
and if so to supply: names, qualifications, subject matter
of testimony, and report.   _____   _____

19. To supply any reports of tests of physical or mental
examinations known to the prosecution.   _____   _____

20. To supply any reports of scientific tests, experiments, or
comparisons and/or other reports to or from experts in the
control of the prosecution.   _____   _____

21. To permit inspection and copying of any books, papers,
documents, photographs, tangible objects, and real evidence
which the prosecution ostensibly obtained from the defendant
or which may be used at hearings or trial.   _____   _____

22. To supply any information known concerning prior convictions
of persons whom the prosecution intends to call as witnesses
at hearings or trial.   _____   _____

23. To inform the defense of any information known to the
prosecution which may indicate entrapment of the defendant.   _____   _____

DATED _____

_____

ATTORNEY FOR DEFENDANT

IT IS SO ORDERED:

DATED _____

_____

JUDGE

Defense Attorney_____

The Trial and The Judge

Television and movie portrayals of trials have provided a glimpse into the procedures at this stage. We will not review the specifics; instead we will highlight some of the images and realities in the final stage of the criminal trial. In the typical trial of a criminal case there are a number of roles, each with its own behavior expectations. We can conceive of the trial as analogous to a theater production. The major roles are those of judge, prosecutor, defense attorney, bailiff, marshal, defendant, members of the jury, spectators, and members of the press.

The judge's role is that of a neutral arbitrator. The defense attorney's role is that of a person speaking out on behalf of the client. The prosecutor represents the people or the state (which are supposed to be synonymous). The defendant is supposed to be passive and is not expected to want (or have the ability) to defend him- or herself. Spectators are supposed to be passive, sit quietly, and observe (as do all others) proper courtroom demeanor. Adherence to these formalities and the power relations within the courtroom process legitimate (as well as mystify) the existing judicial system and the law. Failure to adhere to these symbols can result in a "contempt of court" citation or removal from the courtroom.

Perceptive observers will note that there is a discrepancy between the public's notion of what a judge does and the reality. Judges and other legal actors at all levels perpetuate this myth. Chief Justice John Roberts Jr. opened his Senate confirmation hearing testimony on September 12, 2005 with "a brief but powerful pledge of judicial humility, fair-mindedness and respect for precedent." Likening the job of justice to that of baseball umpires, Roberts said, "They make sure everybody plays by the rules, but it is a limited role."[104] Continuing his sports analogy, Justice Roberts went on to say the role of the judge is just to call "balls and strikes." Assertions such as this perpetuate the public's belief that judges never look beyond the technical legal issue before them, and that "activist judges" who do look at the larger context are bad judges.

The fact is that all judges are activist judges and play a broad role in the judicial process. Judges constantly engage in a game of rhetorical justification; they apply the law based on their own political perspectives. Allan Hutchinson thinks a better analogy is a soccer referee, rather than a baseball umpire.[105] A soccer referee is not just trying to resolve factual disputes such as was the ball thrown over the plate or was a hit in or out of play. The referee also determines if the action of the player on the field was dangerous or if it significantly and unfairly altered the course of the game. If not, the referee simply calls "play on." Judges, like soccer referees, do not call every foul. Instead, they call only those that, from the judge's perspective, will unfairly or improperly affect the outcome of the proceeding. "As in soccer, an important aspect of legal play is that its course or unfolding cannot be predicted or controlled with any degree of confidence because there is always space both for innovation by individual players and for the intervention of luck, chance, or fate."[106]

The ideological influences on judges are far less determinant and far more developmental than customarily acknowledged. Although many decisions can be predicted and patterns in reasoning detected, there are also many instances where predictions fail.

> Every application of a rule is a remaking of the rule. Rule application is an occasion on which judges acknowledge, consciously or unconsciously, the values that hold certain social practices in place. As such, adjudication . . . is through and through about values, not facts and about persuasion, not demonstration. Applying rules is a political matter of taking sides: the only questions are *which* and *when*.[107]

As one studies criminal procedure and the role of judges, it is evident that all judges engage in the game of rhetorical politics.

ALTERNATIVE CASE PROCESSING AND NEW CRIMINAL COURT PROCEDURES

The traditional court system is extremely slow. It is procedural. It is difficult to negotiate, even for educated people without disabilities. Courts have operated in relative isolation from other societal institutions. They have not been very good about adapting to community needs and have generally failed to interact constructively with the communities they serve. The National Center for State Courts has recognized the need for the court system in the United States to change its focus. It has identified and articulated five broad performance areas that make up the basis for trial court performance standards.[108] The five categories specified in the performance standards include access to justice; expeditiousness and timeliness; equality, fairness, and integrity; independence and accountability; and public trust and confidence.[109]

Problem solving courts include, for example, drug courts, domestic violence courts, and mental health courts (problem solving courts are distinct from specialized dockets, which are dockets designed for improved case processing, not improved outcomes). They improve access to justice for victims; eliminate unnecessary and sometimes dangerous (in terms of victim safety) delays; increase court accountability; and restore public confidence in the courts. In addition to combining new judicial paradigms with court performance goals, judges who understand the specific dynamics of certain types of crime (such as domestic violence) can improve victim safety and offender accountability.

This section describes case processing methods that differ significantly from the traditional trial process described above. The traditional court system processes cases and makes legally justifiable decisions but never addresses the underlying social problems fueling the court's caseload. The current approach not only fails society but also fails to accomplish what it touts as its strength—the protection of individual rights. Alternative methods are the best hope of preserving respect for the legal system in the United States today.

Drug Courts

Astonishingly for a society that is theoretically based on the "rule of law," people frequently do not see the courts as very relevant. In response to perceptions of inadequacy, the court system began to experiment with collaborative, therapeutic specialized courts in the 1990s. The first of these courts to gain widespread acceptance was the "drug court." Most drug courts are a type of problem-solving court in which defendants must obtain treatment or face sanctions. The National Association of Drug Court Professionals and the National Drug Court Institute proclaim: "Drug courts represent the coordinated efforts of the judiciary, prosecution, defense bar, probation, law enforcement, mental health, social service, and treatment communities to actively and forcefully intervene and break the cycle of substance abuse, addiction, and crime. As an alternative to less effective interventions, drug courts quickly identify substance abusing offenders and place them under strict court monitoring and community supervision, coupled with effective, long-term treatment services.[110]

Drug courts are the future. They have grown from a grassroots movement for specialized courts to an "institutionalized way of doing business."[111] In 2006, there were 1,665 drug courts in operation and 386 additional planned.[112] There are drug courts in all 50 states and in 39% of all the counties in the United States. Drug courts may be the specialized court that succeeded in breaking the punitive and adversarial case processing mold, but they are not the only successful nontraditional court. Other courts using somewhat different models have also made significant inroads in changing criminal procedure.

Domestic Violence Court

Until the late 1970s and early 1980s when the feminist movement began to focus attention on the problem of violence against women, the U.S. legal system failed to offer effective legal protection to victims of domestic violence.[113] In the past, few batterers were arrested or prosecuted,[114] and women were often denied protective or restraining orders by the courts.

The situation in Clark County, Washington illustrates the problem. From 1979 through 1985, only a handful of misdemeanor domestic violence cases were assigned to indigent defense attorneys in the county.[115] In spite of increased legislative and public awareness, as well as an increase in domestic violence filings over the years, the courts in the county did not change their traditional approach. Prior to 1998,[116] the Clark County judiciary had been slow to accommodate the changes in case filings and was unresponsive to community needs. Operating entirely independently, some courts, victim advocacy groups, social services, and the medical treatment community tried to address the domestic violence problem. After a well publicized spousal abuse case, in which a husband had beaten and imprisoned his brain-damaged wife on his rotting sailboat, an editorial described the system for addressing domestic abuse as "a hasty compilation of bad habits, like a haphazard patch job on a roof not built for rain."[117]

The fragmented system plagued by overlapping jurisdictions had not developed from a theory of judicial administration or sound judicial principles; rather, it had developed on an ad hoc basis.[118] Domestic violence cases, especially low injury or noninjury domestic violence, failed to receive high priority, often squeezed out in the competition for judicial system resources. As a result, domestic violence victims were reluctant to seek relief from the court system.[119] Community members and individuals both within and outside the state's courts repeatedly voiced dissatisfaction with the legal system's response to domestic violence.[120] Whether unable or unwilling, the traditional court system did not respond to a clearly perceived, well documented, public safety and criminal justice issue in the community. In addition, response from the criminal justice system, when it happens, is usually quantitative—increased numbers, whether prosecutions or convictions.

Citizens in many communities began to demand a qualitative—meaning reforms that improve effectiveness—response. Merely increasing the number of perpetrators arrested and prosecuted has not been shown to reduce the incidence of domestic violence or its destructive impact on the community. Changing the nature of the judicial response qualitatively produces greater safety and reduced recidivism. The Washington State legislature acknowledged that public perceptions about the serious consequences of domestic violence, to society and victims alike, fueled its recognition of the necessity for early intervention.[121]

Therapeutic Jurisprudence

Therapeutic jurisprudence focuses on the outcome of the actions of legal actors and attempts to maximize positive therapeutic effects. The trial court performance standards represent a similar shift in thinking about the work of the court—from structures and processes to performance and outcomes.[122] "Therapeutic jurisprudence is an important and influential approach to legal analysis that investigates the law's impact on the emotional lives of participants in the legal system by encouraging sensitivity to therapeutic consequences that may result from the legal rules, procedures, and the roles of legal actors."[123] Therapeutic jurisprudence can serve as a model to criticize and modify "legal justice."[124] It can enhance the successful outcomes obtained in drug and mental health court settings. While creating the domestic violence court in Washington, the founders attempted to answer the question, "How can therapeutic jurisprudence function in a traditionally highly adversarial domestic violence court setting where punishment, deterrence, and traditional criminal objectives must remain a high priority?"[125]

Based on experiences with specialized problem-solving courts, we believe that therapeutic jurisprudence can coexist with most of the traditional values of our legal system and that the courtroom can serve as a venue where therapeutic, preventive, and restorative justice are dispensed rather than merely farmed out to others. Accomplishing this goal, however, can be tricky. Under the conventional adversarial approach, the judge would impose a punitive sentence and then wash his or her hands of the case. The case would not return before the judge unless a probation officer filed a violation, or the offender was arrested for a subsequent offense and appeared before the same judicial officer.[126] Under the new approach, all court personnel—judges, attorneys, and others who interact with the court system—must be willing to take on duties and provide services that go beyond the traditional roles. This task is complicated by the interrelated nature and complexity of our system of justice and the traditional lack of coordination of supporting services. The need to take these steps is critical, however, because past failures to apply therapeutic goals and practices to domestic violence cases has perpetrated a second assault on victims.[127] This occurs because the traditional system is generally insensitive to the collateral effects of the system's actions.

In addition to drug and domestic violence courts, mental health courts have become the third most popular specialized criminal problem-solving court in the United States. They are another excellent example of the court system attempting to respond to society's needs. Now let us see what the new therapeutic jurisprudence approach can do for the least fortunate in our society—the homeless, the disabled, and the mentally ill—citizens in every family and every community.

Mental Health Courts

No one in the U.S. court system sought an expanded role for the courts in dealing with mentally ill and homeless individuals, but the role was thrust on the criminal justice system by the actions of Congress and the state legislatures who closed many of the mental hospitals and other institutions for the disabled in the 1980s. After years of these displaced mentally ill individuals being recycled through our criminal justice system, we recognize that the courts themselves have become an important part of our mental health system.

One example of this widespread recognition is the Partners in Crisis movement. The movement began in Florida and consisted of a state-wide diverse group of stakeholders, including judges, law enforcement and correctional administrators, prosecutors, public defenders, behavioral health-care administrators, hospital administrators, and people recovering from mental illnesses who work together to advocate for police training, jail diversion programs, access to treatment services, and community collaborations for sharing resources and solving problems together.[128] This organization was replicated in a number of states and has been effective in mobilizing communities to address the problems of mentally ill individuals who find themselves in the clutches of the criminal justice system. Perhaps one of the reasons for the success of Partners in Criss is that it has resources and has been funded, in part, by a major pharmaceutical company.

In spite of some attempts to create a more humane response, there is no doubt that the nation's jails have become *de facto* the mental health institutions of this decade. In 2005, more than half the inmates in the country's prisons and jails reported mental health problems. One in three state prisoners, one in four federal prisoners and one in six jail prisoners had received some form of mental health treatment, often medication, during their current incarceration.[129] According to Fred Osher, director of health systems at the Council on State Governments, the findings "underscore what every prison administrator knows—that large numbers of individuals with mental health problems are cycling through their facilities."[130] The costs are astronomical. One study conducted by the Muskie School of Public Service at the University of Southern Maine showed that in Cumberland County, Maine, alone, "Annual jail health expenses have grown almost $2 million—or nearly 400%—since 1996."[131]

In order to address the needs of seriously mentally ill individuals in the legal system, a rapidly increasing number of jurisdictions have begun to develop mental health courts. These courts are designed to divert the mentally ill from jails and prisons into community-based programs that provide a range of services that may include housing, substance abuse treatment, traditional medical services, and psychological counseling. It is important to understand that while these unique courts have much in common with other courts designed to divert individuals from the criminal justice system, mental health courts are really a different model. They must take into account the diverse special needs of people with significant disabilities.

Particularly in jurisdictions where coordination between courts and mental health providers is poor, many mentally ill inmates may be done a disservice by clumsy attempts to implement such a court. At the time of publication of this book, there was no universally accepted standard model for mental health courts. While well intentioned, they often lack uniform principles, standardized procedures, and basic due process protections for their clients. While it is easy to see a critical need for mental health courts, it is harder to perceive the need for clear standards and a nationally disseminated model. While it is true that most justice is local, there are also many pitfalls and possible abuses, and a standardized model mental health court based on the principles of therapeutic jurisprudence can help communities avoid problems and insure the protection of rights, while also protecting the public.

One of the authors of this book (RBF) was a state trial court judge for seventeen years and established a community mental health court with procedural safeguards designed to protect the rights of court clients. Based on the author's experience, the key components of such a court include:

- Changing the court process. The traditional process should be changed so that it is collaborative, not adversarial, and suitable for court customers who may have a wide variety of disabilities. This may include providing nonattorney advocates for clients and dissemination of information to court clients graphically and orally. Technical rules should either not apply or should be limited.

- No stigmatizing labels. The court should take steps to make sure that persons passing through the court shall not be branded or stigmatized.

- The use of diversion, stays and other deferred sentencing processes. A mental health court may utilize a preplea diversion process, stays of prosecution, or a postplea deferred sentence process, but it is important that the client have the incentive of being able to avoid a criminal conviction.

- Least restrictive alternatives. In fashioning remedies and imposing sentences the court should use the least restrictive means consistent with public safety, sound treatment considerations, and the general welfare of the client. One of the purposes of the court is to get clients out of custody and into supportive programs that maximize therapeutic results.

- Enhancement of basic treatment. The court should not promote any specific mode of treatment for mental illness but should act to promote, wherever possible, the welfare of the individuals who come before it. This involves the court being a neutral clearinghouse for local treatment options. Evidence exists that recidivist offenders often exhibit skills deficits in the areas of interpersonal problem solving, self-management, and social interaction. Basic mental health treatment should be enhanced, where appropriate, with programs designed to teach interpersonal problem-solving skills and other cognitive behavioral approaches. The court must also consider the availability of funding for any alternative sentences imposed. Since resources are always scarce, the court should serve as an advocate for increasing resources for treatment and client support.

- Interdependent decision making. The court should support clients accepting responsibility for and affirmatively addressing their own mental health issues. A mental health court team should consider utilizing several models of supported decision making for the clients of the court.

- Unified court team. Every mental health court needs a unified court team dedicated to a collaborative, outcome focused, rather than adversarial approach.

- Court manual. Each court will need to create a manual so that everyone will have the same performance expectations. The manual should include additional specific procedures to be adopted by local court rule and new forms or documents specifically for mental health court operations.

- Coordination of treatment. As in the case of other courts utilizing therapeutic techniques, it is important to seize the opportunity provided by the trauma of the arrest to intervene in the perpetrator's life while he or she is still receptive. Dual diagnosis (drug usage and mental illness) is a common issue for mental health court clients and therefore court coordination of community resources and coordination of multiple treatment providers is a key court responsibility.

- Dynamic risk management. The court team must continually reassess the clients' adjustment and response to changing conditions and life's challenges. Reaction to aberrant behavior need not be severe, but must be immediate. This process is referred to as "dynamic risk management." The court rewards positive adjustment and sanctions willful noncompliance or behavior that endangers others. Judicial demeanor toward defendants and victims also can increase compliance with court orders as well as have therapeutic effects.[132]

The court should also have an effective complaint resolution mechanism. This author's response, implemented in the Vancouver, Washington Mental Health Court, was to modify the local court rules to provide for an immediate grievance hearing before another judge from the same jurisdiction, which could be private or public at the petitioner's request, to challenge the mental health court judge's perceived abuse of discretion. If abuse of discretion was found, a panoply of remedies is available for the aggrieved party.

The description above provides a limited view of one approach to address criminal justice system problems and abuses. The focus of these courts is to break the cycle of recidivism and secure favorable therapeutic outcomes at a lower financial cost than pre-

viously experienced. When one attempts to change criminal procedure and implement these new problem-solving courts, one has to deal with accusations that these courts are too expensive, too time consuming, and too burdensome on the judiciary. Nothing could be further from the truth. If these courts cost more and use more judicial manpower, it is only because the parties attempting to implement them have not made the necessary changes to the process and are implementing the courts incorrectly. Sometimes courts merely schedule similar cases for the same docket and proudly proclaim they have created an innovative domestic violence court or mental health court without really changing the way the court does business. Others are making a genuine attempt to address the substantive and procedural defects and deficiencies of the traditional criminal legal process. More money is not necessarily needed. In our experience with the Clark County, Washington court system, we were able to implement three such courts without any increase in the court budget and without outside grants (except for outside independent evaluation). As this book goes to press, many promising new approaches and techniques for case processing are being explored. Students may wish to explore the subject further.[133]

SUMMARY

We reviewed traditional criminal case processing and concluded with a brief introduction to new judicial paradigms. As cases proceed through the traditional court system, there are several distinct stages where cases are sifted and sorted, with some disappearing and others moving forward. The most important decision is made by the prosecutor, who makes the critical decision of whether to press charges after a police arrest. Typically, about 75% of cases are dismissed or reduced down to a misdemeanor. If processing continues, bail and pretrial detention become critical issues. At this stage, we see quite easily the effects of both class and race on decision making; minorities and the poor suffer decided disadvantages.

Once the prosecutor accepts a case, several stages follow. The first is the initial appearance. The defendant comes before a judge of a lower court and is given his or her rights; the charges are read; bail is set. If the defendant has no attorney, one is usually appointed or the public defender's office is notified. In the next stage, the preliminary hearing, the defendant comes before the same judge (usually), along with his or her lawyer, and hears some (or all) of the evidence that the state has. The prosecutor has to establish that there is probable cause that the defendant committed the crime. On some occasions a grand jury is used.

The next stage is the arraignment, which is normally a rather formal procedure. If the defendant's attorney has engaged in plea negotiations with the prosecutor, the judge asks some routine questions and sets a sentencing date. If not, then a trial date is set.

Plea bargaining is now the most common form of judicial disposition in the modern criminal court system, but it did not dominate the process until the end of the nineteenth century. Such negotiations take place mostly outside of the courtroom between the defense and prosecuting attorneys. Individuals who plead guilty (regardless of the offense) tend to receive lighter sentences than those who go to trial. Individuals who choose to exercise their rights and demand a jury trial are more likely to receive harsher penalties in the event they are found guilty. Trial juries are rarely used.

The newly emerging problem solving courts offer alternative approaches to the traditional adversarial adjudication of cases. They combine case processing with an explicit ethic of care. In the past dozen or so years, a remarkable transformation has occurred in the role of the courts. Courts traditionally functioned as governmental mechanisms to find facts; traditional courts limited their attention to the dispute named in the charges. Newer courts, however, attempt to understand and address the underlying problem that is responsible for the dispute and to help individuals deal effectively with the problem in ways that will prevent recurring court involvement. Problem-solving courts are specialized tribunals utilizing principles of therapeutic jurisprudence to deal with specific problems, often involving individuals who need social, mental health, or substance abuse treatment services. These include criminal cases involving drug or alcoholism, mental health problems, or domestic violence.

Key Terms

- arraignment
- bail
- discovery
- initial appearance
- *Mallory v. United States*
- nolle prosequi
- normal crimes
- peremptory challenge
- plea bargaining
- preliminary hearing
- pretrial motions
- pretrial preventive detention
- pretrial release
- problem solving courts
- therapeutic jurisprudence
- venire
- voir dire

Notes

[1] From a 1990 interview by coauthor Brown with a Midwestern trial judge that focused on pretrial detention.

[2] Robinson, P. H. and M. T. Cahill. *Law without Justice: Why Criminal Law Doesn't Give People What They Deserve.* New York: Oxford University Press, 2006, p. 3.

[3] Ibid., p. 4.

[4] Balko, Radley. "Blinded by the Law: Teen Sex Case Shows That Focusing on the Letter of the Law Doesn't Always Spell Justice." *Chicago Tribune* (June 24, 2007) sec. 2, p. 1.

[5] Filing multiple charges often has the effect of increasing the likelihood of a defendant's being unable to make bail, because for each charge an additional monetary amount is needed to secure bail, which in turn contributes to jail overcrowding because too many defendants cannot pay the additional fees. See Shelden, R. G. and W. B. Brown. "Correlates of Jail Overcrowding: A Case Study of a County Detention Center." *Crime and Delinquency* 37(3) (1991).

[6] Donziger, S. R. (ed.) *The Real War on Crime: The Report of the National Criminal Justice Commission.*

New York: HarperPerennial, 1996, p. 110; Myers, M. A. and J. Hagan. "Private and Public Trouble: Prosecutors and the Allocation of Court Resources." *Social Problems* 26(4): 439–451 (April 1979).

[7] Walker, S., C. Spohn, and M. DeLone. *The Color of Justice: Race, Ethnicity, and Crime in America* (3rd ed.). Belmont, CA: Wadsworth, 2007, pp. 185–188.

[8] Reiman, J. *The Rich Get Richer and the Poor Get Prison: Ideology, Class, and Criminal Justice* (8th ed.). Boston: Allyn & Bacon, 2007, pp. 122–123.

[9] *Mallory v. United States,* 354 U.S. 455, 1957.

[10] With most minor misdemeanor offenses, especially traffic cases, there is only one appearance in court. Typically, no lawyers are involved; the defendant pleads guilty and pays a fine. In cases of a simple citation, the accused sends a check and there is no court appearance. This chapter discusses the stages that generally occur with serious misdemeanors or felonies.

[11] Monks, G. P. *History of Bail.* 1982. [Online] http://www.cbaa.com/images/history.pdf

[12] *Bell v. Wolfish,* 441 U.S. 520, 533–534, 1979.

[13] United States Code, Title 18, Sections 3141–3150.

[14] *United States v. Salerno,* 481 U.S. 739, 1987; Rudolph Giuliani indicted Anthony Salerno, an alleged organized crime boss, for violating 29 federal laws. Giuliani requested that bail be denied because Salerno was a danger to the community (see Neubauer, D. W. *America's Courts and the Criminal Justice System* (5th ed.). Belmont, Ca: Wadsworth, 1996, pp. 241, 256–258).

[15] *United States v. Torres,* 929 E 2d 291–292 (7th Cir. 1991).

[16] *United States v. Winsor,* 785 F. 2d 755, 757 (9th Cir. 1986).

[17] 18 U.S.C. 3142 (g).

[18] S. Rep. No. 225, 98th Congress, 1st Session 23 (1983), reprinted 1984, U.S.C.C.A.N. 3182, 3206.

[19] Robinson and Cahill, *Law without Justice,* p. 5.

[20] *United States v. Himler,* 797 F. 2d 156, 160 (3rd Cir. 1986).

[21] *United States v. Friedman,* 837 E 2d 48, 49 (2nd Cir 1988).

[22] *United States v. Reynolds,* 956 E 2d 192 (9th Cir. 1992).

[23] 18 U.S.C. 3142(e).

[24] *United States v. Forma,* 769 F. 2d 243, 249 (5th Cir. 1985); *United States v. Ramirez,* 843 F. 2d 256, 257 (7th Cir. 1988).

[25] 18 U.S.C. 3142(e).

[26] *United States v. Orta,* 760 E 2d 887-92 (8th Cir. 1985).

[27] Among the most important of these studies are Foote, C. "Compelling Appearance in Court: Administration of Bail in Philadelphia." *University of Pennsylvania Law Review* 102: 1031–1079 (1954); Rankin, A. "The Effect of Pretrial Detention." *New York University Law Review* 39: 641–655 (June 1964); Suffet, F. "Bail Setting: A Study of Courtroom Interaction." *Crime and Delinquency* 12: 318–331 (October 1966); Single, E. "The Unconstitutional Administration of Bail: *Bellamy v. The Judges of New York City.*" *Criminal Law Bulletin* 8(6): 459–513 (July–August 1972); Farrell, R. and V. L. Swigert. "Prior Offense Record as a Self-Fulfilling Prophecy." *Law and Society Review* 12: 437–

453 (1978); Bynum, T. "Release on Recognizance: Substantive or Superficial Reform?" *Criminology* 20: 67–82 (1982); Patterson, E. B. and M J. Lynch. "Biases in Formalized Bail Procedures." In M. J. Lynch and E. B. Patterson (eds.), *Race and Criminal Justice.* New York: Harrow and Heston, 1991; Shelden and Brown, "Correlates of Jail Overcrowding."

[28] Walker, Spohn, and De Lone, *The Color of Justice,* p. 180.

[29] Patterson and Lynch, "Biases in Formalized Bail Procedures"; Stith, K. "Disparity in Sentencing—Race and Gender." *Federal Sentencing Reporter* 15(3): 160–146 (February 2003).

[30] Chiricos, T. G. and W. Bales. "Unemployment and Punishment: An Empirical Analysis." *Criminology* 29 (November 1991).

[31] Albonetti, C. A., R. M. Hauser, J. Hagan, and I. H. Nagel. "Criminal Justice Decision Making as a Stratification Process: The Role of Race and Stratification Resources in Pretrial Release." *Journal of Quantitative Criminology* 5: 57–82 (1989).

[32] Finder, A. "Jailed Until Found Not Guilty." *New York Times* (June 6, 1999) pp. 33–34.

[33] Neubauer, *America's Courts and the Criminal Justice System,* p. 249.

[34] Ibid. See also Wice, *Chaos in the Courthouse.*

[35] Pringle, P. "It's Brutal in the Bail Business." *Los Angeles Times* (March 25, 2005).

[36] Robinson, P. H. "Punishing Dangerousness: Cloaking Preventive Detention as Criminal Justice." *Harvard Law Review* 114(5): 1445 (March 2001).

[37] American Friends Service Committee. *Struggle for Justice.* New York: Hill & Wang, 1971, pp. 77–78.

[38] Walker, Spohn, and De Lone, *The Color of Justice,* p. 135.

[39] Shelden, R. G. *Criminal Justice in America: A Sociological Approach.* Boston: Little, Brown, 1982, p. 192.

[40] Shelden and Brown, "Correlates of Jail Overcrowding."

[41] Irwin, J. *The Jail.* Berkeley: University of California Press, 1985, p. 19.

[42] Miller, J. *Search and Destroy: African-American Males in the Criminal Justice System.* New York: Cambridge University Press, 1996, pp. 17–18.

[43] Cohen, T. H. and B. A. Reaves. *Felony Defendants in Large Urban Counties, 2002* (NCJ 210818). Washington, DC: Bureau of Justice Statistics, February 2006, p. 3.

[44] Ibid., pp. 21–22.

[45] Skolnick, J. "Social Control in the Adversary System." *Journal of Conflict Resolution* 11: 263 (1967).

[46] For a review of earlier studies see Shelden, *Criminal Justice in America,* chapter 7.

[47] Cohen and Reaves, *Felony Defendants in Large Urban Counties 2002,* p. 24.

[48] Scheb, J. M. and J. M. Scheb II. *Criminal Law and Procedure.* St. Paul, MN: West, 1989, p. 439.

[49] Ibid.

[50] Based on observations of the senior author (RGS).

[51] Cohen and Reaves, *Felony Defendants in Large Urban Counties 2002,* p. iv.

[52] Fuller, J. R. *Criminal Justice: A Peacemaking Perspective.* Boston: Allyn & Bacon, 1998, pp. 109, 114–115.

53 Neubauer, *America's Courts and the Criminal Justice System*, pp. 286–287.

54 Alschuler, A. W. "Plea Bargaining and Its History." *Law and Society Review* 13(2): 211–245 (Winter 1979).

55 Langbein, J. H. "Understanding the Short History of Plea Bargaining." *Law and Society Review* 13: 261–272 (Winter 1979).

56 Alschuler, "Plea Bargaining and Its History."

57 Ibid., p. 228.

58 Ibid., pp. 229–231.

59 Friedman, L. M. "Plea Bargaining in Historical Perspective." *Law & Society Review* 13(2): 247–259 (Winter 1979); Mather, L. M. "Comments on the History of Plea Bargaining." *Law and Society Review* 13: 281–285 (Winter 1979).

60 Haller, M. H. "Plea Bargaining: The 19th Century Context." *Law and Society Review* 13: 273–279 (Winter 1979).

61 For a good historical account of machine politics and other forms of government corruption around the turn of the twentieth century, see Steffens, L. *The Shame of the Cities*. New York: McClure, Phillips, 1904.

62 Alschuler, "Plea Bargaining and Its History," p. 234.

63 Barak, G. "In Defense of the Rich; The Emergence of the Public Defender." *Crime and Social Justice* 3: 2 (Summer 1975).

64 Wolfe, A. *The Seamy Side of Democracy*. New York: McKay, 1973, chapter 2.

65 Barak, "In Defense of the Rich"; Harring, S. "Class Conflict and the Suppression of Tramps in Buffalo, 1892–1894." *Law and Society Review* 11(5): 873–911 (Summer 1977).

66 Barak, "In Defense of the Rich," p. 6. The reader is encouraged to consult several excellent books covering the Progressive era that document the adaptation of the social order to the needs of American business. Some historians give specific examples of how certain business practices were copied in nonbusiness areas, such as in the public school system. For a review of this literature see Shelden, *Controlling the Dangerous Classes*. One of the excellent books is Kolko, G. *The Triumph of Conservatism: A Reinterpretation of American History, 1900–1916*. New York: Free Press, 1963.

67 Quoted in Barak, "In Defense of the Rich," p. 7.

68 *Santobello v. New York*, 404 U.S. 257, 1971.

69 Chambliss, W. J. and R. Seidman. *Law, Order and Power* (2nd ed.). Reading, MA: Addison-Wesley, 1982, pp. 404–405.

70 Neubauer, *America's Courts and the Criminal Justice System*, p. 291.

71 Newman, D. J. "Pleading Guilty for Considerations: A Study of Bargain Justice." *Journal of Criminal Law, Criminology and Police Science* 46: 780–790 (1954); Neubauer, D. W. *Criminal Justice in Middle America*. Morristown, NJ: General Learning Press, 1974; Blumberg, A. "The Practice of Law as a Confidence Game: Organization Co-optation of a Profession." In W. J. Chambliss (ed.), *Criminal Law in Action*. New York: Wiley, 1975. This discussion is further confirmed by recent studies, as summarized by Neu-

bauer, *America's Courts and the Criminal Justice System*, chapter 13.

72 Blumberg, "The Practice of Law as a Confidence Game," p. 264.

73 Sudnow, D. "Normal Crimes: Sociological Features of the Penal Code in a Public Defender's Office." *Social Problems* 12: 255–276 (Winter 1965).

74 Mather, L. M. "Some Determinants of the Method of Case Disposition: Decision-making by Public Defenders in Los Angeles." *Law and Society Review* 8: 200 (Winter 1973).

75 Ibid., p. 199.

76 Neubauer, *America's Courts and the Criminal Justice System* p. 287–288; see also Boland, B. and B. Forst. "Prosecutors Don't Always Aim to Please." *Federal Probation* 49: 10–15 (1985); Holmes, M., H. Daudistel, and W. Taggart. "Plea Bargaining and State District Court Caseloads: An Interrupted Time Series Analysis." *Law and Society Review* 26: 139–160 (1992).

77 Walker, S. *Sense and Nonsense about Crime and Drugs* (5th ed.). Belmont, CA: Wadsworth, 2001, p. 59.

78 Mather, "Some Determinants of the Method of Case Disposition," p. 206.

79 Eisenstein, J. and H. Jacob. *Felony Justice*. Boston: Little, Brown, 1977; Nardulli, P. E, R. B. Fleming, and J. Eisenstein. *The Tenor of Justice*. Urbana: University of Illinois Press, 1988; Ulmer, J. T. *Social Worlds of Sentencing*. Albany: State University of New York Press, 1997.

80 Donziger, *The Real War on Crime*, p. 112.

81 Ibid., p. 113.

82 Pitts, Leonard. "Waiting for Georgia to Come to Its Senses." *Chicago Tribune* (April 3, 2007) p. 17.

83 Shannon McCaffrey. "Judge Tosses Sentence in Consensual Teen Sex Case." *Chicago Tribune* (June 12, 2007) p. 3.

84 Shannon McCaffrey. "Official: Teen Case May Affect Molesters." *Chicago Tribune* (June 15, 2007) p. 11.

85 Tribune News Services. "Judge Denies Bail During Appeal in Teen Sex Case." *Chicago Tribune* (June 28, 2007) p. 8; Fausset, R. and J. Jarvie. "Court Overturns Sex Conviction." *Chicago Tribune* (October 27, 2007) p. 3.

86 Balko, "Blinded by the Law," p. 4.

87 *Williams v. Florida*, 399 U.S. 78, 1970.

88 *Johnson v. Louisiana*, 406 U.S. 356, 1972; *Apodaca v. Oregon*, 406 U.S. 404, 1972.

89 *Duncan v. Louisiana*, 391 U.S. 145, 1968.

90 Cole, D. *No Equal Justice: Race and Class in the American Criminal Justice System*. New York: New Press, 1999, p. 101.

91 Stevenson, B. A. and R. E. Friedman. "Deliberate Indifference: Judicial Tolerance of Racial Bias in Criminal Justice." *Washington and Lee Law Review* 51: 519–524 (1994).

92 Fellner, J. and M. Mauer. "Nearly 4 Million Americans Denied Vote Because of Felony Convictions." *Overcrowded Times* 9(5) (October 1998).

93 Cole, *No Equal Justice*, p. 104.

94 Walker, Spohn, and DeLone, *The Color of Justice*, p. 210.

95 *Batson v. Kentucky*, 476 U.S. 79, 1986.

96 Raphael, M. J. and E. J. Ungvarsky. "Excuses, Excuses: Neutral Explanations under *Batson v. Kentucky.*" *University of Michigan Judicial Law Reform* 229 (1993), cited in Cole, *No Equal Justice,* p. 120.

97 Cole, *No Equal Justice,* pp. 122–123.

98 Chambliss and Seidman, *Law, Order and Power,* p. 443.

99 Eliason, R. D. "Justice Suffers When It's Political. *Chicago Tribune* (May 24, 2007) p. 29.

100 Neubauer, *America's Criminal Courts,* pp. 311–324.

101 Scheb and Scheb, *Criminal Law and Procedure,* pp. 444–446.

102 One of the most famous cases involving pretrial publicity was that of Sam Shepherd, the Cleveland doctor convicted of killing his wife (both the television series and the movie, *The Fugitive,* were based on this case). Shepherd filed a number of appeals, and the Supreme Court eventually ordered a new trial because of the negative publicity; Shepherd had served 13 years of his sentence. F. Lee Bailey represented Shepherd at the new trial, and he was acquitted. The O. J. Simpson murder trial was moved from Santa Monica to downtown Los Angeles because it was questioned whether Simpson could get a fair trial in the location where the crime was committed. Timothy McVeigh was tried and convicted in Denver, Colorado, for the bombing of the Alfred P. Murrah Federal Building in Oklahoma City.

103 Chambliss and Seidman, *Law Order and Power.*

104 Mauro, T. and T. R. Goldman. "Roberts Pledges Judicial Humility in Opening Remarks." *Legal Times* (September 13, 2005).

105 See the nonfoundationalist analysis of law and adjudication in Hutchinson, A.C. *It's All In the Game.* Durham, NC: Duke University Press, 2000.

106 Hutchinson, p. 14.

107 Hutchinson, p. 80.

108 Casey, P. "Defining Optimal Court Performance: The Trial Court Performance Standards." *36 Court Review* 35(4): 24–29 (1998).

109 Ibid., p. 25.

110 The National Drug Court Institute. [Online] http://www.ndci.org/courtfacts.htm

111 Ibid.; see also Casey, P. M. and D. B. Rottman. *Problem Solving Courts: Models and Trends.* Williamsburg, VA: National Center for State Courts, 2003.

112 Summary of Drug Court Activity by State and County. November 22, 2006. [Online] http://spa.american.edu/justice/documents/2045.pdf

113 Gordon, L. *Heroes in Their Own Lives.* New York: Viking, 1988; Ford, D. A. "Wife Battery and Criminal Justice: A Study of Victim Decision-Making." *Family Relations* 32: 463, 472 (1983); Simon, L. "A Therapeutic Jurisprudence Approach to the Legal Processing of Domestic Violence Cases." *Psychology, Public Policy and Law* 1: 43–44 (1995).

114 Fenstermaker-Berk, S. and D. R. Loseke, "'Handling' Family Violence: Situational Determinants of Police Arrest in Domestic Disturbances." *Law and Society Review* 15: 317–319 (1980–1981); Hathaway, C. R. "Case Comment: Gender Based Discrimination in Police Reluctance to Respond to Domestic Assault Complaints." *Georgetown Law Journal* 75: 667–672 (1986). Virtually all proposals to reform societal responses to domestic violence center heavily on police as gatekeepers, yet police departments tend to devalue the handling of domestic violence calls. Buzawa, E. S., T. L. Austin, and C. G. Buzawa. "The Role of Arrest in Domestic versus Stranger Assault: Is There a Difference?" In E. S. Buzawa and C. G. Buzawa (eds.), *Do Arrests and Restraining Orders Work?* Thousand Oaks, CA: Sage, 1996 (finding that as the level of intimacy between the parties increases, the probability of an arrest for assault decreases).

115 Records of the law firm of Eling, Fritzler, and Lewis from 1979 to 1985. One of the authors (RLF) supervised indigent defense attorneys for the county.

116 This is the date that the Clark County Domestic Violence Court project first began operation as a pilot project under direction of the authors. The newly created Domestic Violence Court handled misdemeanor domestic violence prosecutions as well as civil protection orders that had previously been issued only by the Superior Court. The full-featured specialized court was awaiting approval from the District Court bench and officially began on June 30, 1998.

117 Editorial. "Local Police Can Help Future Victims the Most."

118 Fritzler, R. B. and L. M. J. Simon. "Creating a Domestic Violence Court: Combat in the Trenches." *Court Review* 37: 28–39 (Spring 2000).

119 Interview with Terri Lufkin, Director of SafeChoice Domestic Violence Program, YWCA of Clark County, in Vancouver, Washington (January 29 1998).

120 Ibid.

121 Ibid.

122 See Bureau of Justice Assistance. *Trial Court Performance Standards with Commentary* 1–2. Washington, DC: U.S. Department of Justice, 1997 and Casey, *Defining Optimal Court Performance,* p. 28 (indicating that the standards represent a shift in thinking about the work of the court—from structures and processes to performance and outcomes, the same shift that occurs when you apply principles of therapeutic jurisprudence).

123 Fritzler and Simon, "Creating a Domestic Violence Court," pp. 34–35.

124 Town, M. A. "Therapeutic Jurisprudence Forum: Court as Convener and Provider of Therapeutic Jurisprudence." *Review Jurisprudence U.P.R.*: 671–691 (1998).

125 This approach may raise concerns about the possible subordination of due process and other traditional justice values. This apparent conflict between innovative approaches and our traditional justice system must be carefully considered.

126 Interview with Robert Winsor, Acting Court Administrator, Clark County District Court, in Vancouver, Washington (April 10 2000). (Clark County District Court practice prior to January 1998 was that all new cases, regardless of type, would be assigned to judges rotationally according to the order received. The judges would then manage their respective caseloads independently.)

127 Simon, "A Therapeutic Jurisprudence Approach to the Legal Processing of Domestic Violence Cases."

128 Florida Partners in Crisis, Inc. [Online] http://www.floridapartnersincrisis.org

129 James, D. J. and L. E. Glaze. *Mental Health Problems of Prison and Jail Inmates* (NCJ 213600). Washington, DC: Bureau of Justice Statistics, September 2006, p. 1.

130 Eckholm, E. "Inmates Report Mental Illness at High Levels." *New York Times*, September 7, 2006.

131 Hench, D. "With Sicker Inmates, Costs for County Spiral." *Maine Sunday Telegram,* October 8, 2006, p. A6.

132 The above "key components" are derived from the author's experience presiding over a mental health court and are supported by a study of that court conducted by Portland State University funded by a federal GAINS grant. Regional Research Institute for Human Services. "The Clark County Mentally Ill Re-arrest Prevention (MIRAP) Program." Portland, OR: Portland State University, September 30, 2003. The Criminal Justice Mental Health Consensus Project provides links to several other mental health court evaluations as well as other articles on mental health courts.

133 A good starting point for further inquiry would be the International Network on Therapeutic Jurisprudence, [Online] http://www.law.arizona.edu/depts/upr-intj/; another is the Center for Court Innovation, [Online] http://www.courtinnovation.org/

ten

Sentencing

How often do you read about a case in the newspapers or learn about one on television in which the defendant receives a sentence that seems to make no sense whatsoever? Perhaps you have followed the details of the case. The sentence may seem too lenient or too harsh given the particulars of the case. Or perhaps you recall a similar case where the defendant received a sentence of life in prison for the identical crime, and the sentence in the recent case is five to ten years. Most of us have also learned about defendants being released because of "loopholes" in the law or "technicalities." You may have concluded that there is little rhyme or reason to the sentencing practices in the courts today.

In reality, such a conclusion is incorrect—largely because the only cases likely to be reported by the media are the "celebrated" cases in the wedding cake model of criminal justice (see chapter 1). The thousands of cases that are routinely processed daily in the nation's courts rarely come to our attention. There are actually many consistent patterns in the sentencing practices of the court system, and it is possible to predict what an actual sentence will be in the vast majority of cases.

In this chapter, we will review the various justifications or rationales for punishment. We then examine the different types of sentences for felony convictions, ranging from probation to the ultimate punishment—the death penalty. We will explore the various factors that influence the actual sentence, including race, gender, and social class. Finally, we will consider some alternatives to traditional sentences.

JUSTIFICATIONS FOR PUNISHMENT

Formal punishment of individuals as an organized reaction to lawbreaking raises many moral and ethical concerns.[1] There are four primary justifications to explain why we punish those who violate the law: (1) retribution, (2) isolation/incapacitation, (3) deterrence, (4) rehabilitation.

Retribution

Retribution is one of the oldest (and still popular) justifications for punishment. It is based on *lex talionis* (the law of retaliation), the "eye-for-an-eye and tooth-for-a-tooth" principle. In some societies, this principle was adhered to literally. In tribal societies where the basis of social solidarity was blood ties (of a family or clan), offenses were settled by either a feud or clan punishment. For instance, if a member of clan A injured a member of clan B, clan B felt justified (or duty bound) to retaliate against clan A, rather than just against the individual member who committed the offense. In more advanced tribal societies (and other types of societies) retaliation meant *restitution*—to return *in kind* (through fines or payments in kind). In this form of punishment, known as *wergeld* (literally, "man-money"), the victim was compensated either with money or with something else deemed valuable. In earlier societies the amount of compensation varied according to the crime and with the victim's social rank (the higher the rank, the greater the compensation). Today, retribution exists in some form, but when the basis for punishment is restitution (e.g., fines), the state rather than the victim is compensated.[2]

Isolation/Incapacitation

Isolation/incapacitation means that an offender should be isolated from society or otherwise prevented from committing additional crimes. According to this view, isolating offenders is the only purpose of punishment.[3] At a minimum, the offender cannot further victimize society *while incarcerated.* The practice of isolating offenders dates back many centuries and includes such forms of punishment as banishment, exile, transportation, and the castration of rapists. Imprisonment is the modern version of isolation.

Deterrence

Many believe that the purpose of punishment is *deterrence*—preventing or discouraging the commission of crimes. There are two versions of the deterrence argument. *Specific deterrence* is directed at an individual. The theory is that by punishing an offender for committing a crime, we deter him or her from committing crimes in the future. *General deterrence* rests on the assumption that punishing individual offenders sets an example for others and deters them from committing crimes in order to avoid punishment.

Rehabilitation

Rehabilitation is based on the belief that someone who commits a crime does so because of a problem. The individual's values, attitudes, work skills, education, or other characteristics are in some way deficient and should be improved upon through the use of various kinds of punishments to correct the problem. For example, the judge may sentence an individual to a period of probation with the stipulation of a drug treatment program for an addiction.

Keep in mind that all theories of punishment are rationalizations for administering punishment. They do not explain why certain forms of punishment are chosen or why forms of punishment that dominated certain periods of history disappeared and were replaced by other forms.[4]

THE SENTENCING PROCESS

The ultimate authority on sentencing lies with state legislatures, although the *sentencing structure* lies within all three branches of government. The legislative branch, however, has been largely responsible for the passage of laws and the establishment of sentences for each law. For most offenses, the legislatures give the courts several alternatives and a wide amount of discretion. For instance, first-degree burglary may call for a term of one to five years in state prison, or two years of probation, or a fine of $10,000.

The Sentencing Authority

Traditionally, the judicial branch (not only judges but the probation department as well) has had primary authority over who actually ends up in prison. An executive agency—the parole board—has had control over the actual length of time a person remains in prison. More recently the legislative branch has increased its control over sentencing.[5] Some recent legislative decisions have resulted in very drastic changes in the other two branches, especially mandatory sentencing structures, such as "three strikes and you're out" legislation in California and other states.

Given that judges and juries have a wide variation of penalties to impose on an offender, how do we account for the patterns of sentencing we observe? There are a number of different inputs that enter into the sentencing process.[6] These include the offender's status and race, gender, the offense, outside pressures (public, police, and prosecutors), the relative ability and status of the defense attorney, and personal relationships between defense counsel and the court. One of the keys to understanding the different types of sentences meted out in court is the presentence investigation report.

The Presentence Investigation Report

The *presentence investigation (PSI) report* is prepared by the probation department. The report is usually completed after the offender is convicted (through a plea or a jury trial) and focuses on both the legal and the social aspects of the case. The report contains information about the offender's prior record and the circumstances surrounding the crime for which the offender was convicted. The offender's past employment record, age, marital status, education, and many other nonlegal variables are discussed in some detail. The report closes with a specific sentence recommendation.[7] Several studies show that around 90% of the time judges go along with what probation departments recommend. Thus, a sentence is determined by the probation department, although its recommendation is likely to conform to whatever it believes a particular judge is likely to do.[8]

In theory, one of the most important facts considered about an offender is amenability to rehabilitation. If the presentence investigation reports that a defendant is "sorry" or "repentant," he or she may be sentenced to probation. The defense counsel tries to persuade the judge that the defendant is a "respectable" person, one who is not really a "criminal," and one whose reputation, family, and friends will suffer if a harsh (or any) sentence is imposed. It is important to note that if, in fact, the accused is perceived as a respectable member of the community, the sentence will probably be light. Judges normally consider the prior record of the offender as a major determining factor, so a white-collar offender or an upper-middle-class person who committed a felony will often have the advantage of no prior criminal record.

The PSI report is supposed to be purely objective. However, the "investigation" is often perfunctory, routine, and filled with numerous inaccuracies, hearsay, and rumors. Probation officers sometimes have a gut feeling about a certain defendant and the kind of sentence he or she "deserves." This prejudgment colors the information reported. For instance, most jurisdictions have a point system. Factors such as prior record, employment and educational history, and family background receive an assigned number of points, and the total score has a corresponding sentence recommendation. There is

enough ambiguity among the variables considered that weighting any or all of the factors will adjust the scores.

One of the authors (WBB) conducted a study in which several case scenarios were given to randomly selected presentence investigators. There was very little sentence-recommendation consistency. In fact, the participants (all veteran presentence investigators), using the same guidelines prescribed by their agency, rarely agreed on an appropriate recommendation. In fact, the only consistency found by the study was inconsistency in the decision-making process of recommending sentences.[9]

Some jurisdictions have discontinued presentence investigation reports for budgetary reasons. In Oregon, Pacific Policy and Research Institute and Pacific Sentencing Institute (private organizations) provide presentence reports for convicted persons. The reports are generated by defense attorneys and provide sentencing options and rationales for judges to depart from standard sentencing guidelines. Judges have found the alternatives useful and handed down reduced sentences.[10]

Increasingly, defendants with deep pockets hire experts on federal sentencing guidelines to make a presentation at the sentencing hearing. Conrad Black was convicted of fraud and obstruction of justice in a high-profile trial in Chicago. His defense team hired a former defense attorney, Jeffrey Steinback, for the sentencing hearing. A former prosecutor remarked: "I don't know if there is anyone better than Jeff in portraying the human side of a defendant. Jeff is a good voice and strikes the right chord with the court."[11] Presentations are designed to stir feelings of compassion and include information about age, health, charitable contributions, remorse, etc.

SENTENCES IN FELONY CASES

There are four major types of sentences in felony cases—imprisonment, probation, fines, and capital punishment—plus several variations.

Types of Sentences

If a defendant is sentenced to a term of imprisonment, there are several alternatives.[12]

Concurrent and consecutive sentences are handed down in cases in which the defendant is convicted of more than one crime or more than one count of the same crime (e.g., three separate burglaries, or five burglaries and two drug possession charges). A *concurrent sentence* combines the charges in one sentence. For instance, a defendant who is convicted of three counts of burglary, each carrying a maximum of five years, might be sentenced to a single five-year term. A defendant who received a *consecutive sentence* would serve the sentence for each of the three charges, for a total of fifteen years in prison.

The court can decide to sentence an offender to a prison term but then issue a *suspended sentence*, placing an individual on probation with the expectation of good behavior. If the individual does not violate any of the various conditions of probation, then he or she will be released from the sentence without serving any time in prison. However, if any of the conditions are violated or if a new crime is committed, the offender may be placed in prison to serve the original sentence.

An *indefinite sentence* specifies a minimum and maximum penalty for certain offenders, such as one to five years or ten to twenty years. In most states an inmate is eligible for *good-time credit* on the original sentence because of favorable behavior while in prison. This can reduce the actual time served on a sentence.

A *definite sentence* is a specific sentence set by the legislature, which allows the sentencing judge or corrections officials no discretion. In some states there is *determinate sentencing*, which allows the judge to set a fixed term within certain statutory parameters. The offender is required to serve a particular sentence with the possibility of early release. Another variation is a sentence of life *with* the possibility of parole and life *without* the possibility of parole. In Nevada, for instance, a person who is sentenced to life *with* the possibility of parole is eligible for parole consideration after five years (good-time credit is not counted). A person who is sentenced to life *without* the possibility of parole is eligible to go before a pardons board (similar to a parole board) after serving ten years. The pardons board can recommend that the inmate become eligible for consideration of parole. Thus, "life *without* the possibility of parole" does not completely eliminate the possibility of release. However, in most jurisdictions, release through the actions of the pardons board is extremely rare.

Mandatory sentences require offenders who commit certain types of crimes to be sentenced to a term in prison for a set minimum amount of time. The laws are almost always the result of a particularly heinous local crime or public outcries—often during an election year—that laws should be written to prevent such assaults. Legislators, eager to be perceived as "tough on crime" respond by passing mandatory sentence laws. In some states (Arizona is one), "use a gun, go to prison" laws give neither judges nor prosecutors any discretion. Similarly, *habitual offender laws* stipulate that after an offender is convicted of a set number of serious crimes (usually two or three major felony convictions), the individual is to be sentenced to a very lengthy term in prison, often for life (sometimes without the possibility of parole). Oregon's Measure 11 is one example.

Perhaps the most easily recognizable habitual criminal statute is California's *"Three Strikes and You're Out"*. The state statute (Section 667) was enacted March 7, 1994. Supporters wanted to ensure that legislators would not alter the law in the future. Both the California Correctional Peace Officer's Association and the National Rifle Association spearheaded the drive to place the proposition on the ballot. Proposition 184 was approved November 9, 1994, by 70% of the voters.[13] One of the main events triggering the law was the kidnapping and murder of 12-year-old Polly Klaas by a man who had been convicted of kidnapping twice before. Had Richard Allen Davis not been released early from his most recent sentence, he would have been imprisoned on October

1, 1993, when he kidnapped Polly Klaas.[14] He was convicted of murder and sentenced to death in 1996.

The law imposed a mandatory 25-year-to-life prison sentence for a third felony conviction. The California law was the second (Washington passed a law in 1993), and the most punitive of the habitual offender laws. Similar laws were legislated in 37 states by 1995. A product of political posturing and the cynical desire among politicians to get votes by playing on public fears of crime, legislators in California and elsewhere used the popular, catchy baseball phrase to obtain needed support. The most controversial portion of the California law was that after two prior felony convictions, any offense (violent or nonviolent) could be charged as a felony and trigger the "third strike."[15] This was the ultimate get-tough stance on crime, showing little regard for the consequences. In theory, the law was aimed at repeat, serious, violent offenders. Unfortunately, it was based on the erroneous assumption that the criminal justice system is "too lenient" on criminals (when in fact the opposite is true).

The principal issues associated with three-strikes policies are judicial discretion and the proportionality of punishment (linked to the Eighth Amendment's prohibition of cruel and unusual punishment). The U.S. Supreme Court paved the way for three-strikes legislation with its decision in *Rummel v. Estelle*. In 1973, William Rummel was convicted of a third felony in Texas. Under the state's recidivist laws, he received a mandatory life sentence. Rummel had been convicted of three property offenses; the total monetary value of all three crimes was less than $230. The Court distanced itself from the precedent of proportionality established in 1910 in *Weems v. United States*.[16]

> Texas' interest here is not simply that of making criminal the unlawful acquisition of another person's property, but is in addition the interest, expressed in all recidivist statutes, in dealing in a harsher manner with those who by repeated criminal acts have shown that they are incapable of conforming to the norms of society as established by its criminal law. The Texas recidivist statute

> thus is nothing more than a societal decision that when a person, such as petitioner, commits yet another felony, he should be subjected to the serious penalty of life imprisonment, subject only to the State's judgment as to whether to grant him parole. . . . Texas is entitled to make its own judgment as to the line dividing felony theft from petty larceny, subject only to those strictures of the Eighth Amendment that can be informed by objective factors.[17]

The Court took the position that Texas was not in violation for imposing a mandatory life in prison for three nonviolent offenses committed over a nine-year period and totaling less than $230. The Court cited the fact that both the District Court and the Court of Appeals had attached "particular importance to the probability that petitioner would be eligible for parole within 12 years," so that there was a possibility that he would not be serving a life sentence.

There have been hundreds of examples of relatively minor offenders sentenced to long prison terms under habitual criminal statutes. For instance, a Kansas mother of two was sentenced to life for possessing $40 worth of cocaine; a man in Southern California was sentenced to twenty-five years for stealing a couple slices of pizza. Leandro Andrade stole videotapes worth less then $85 on November 4, 1995, and he stole videotapes worth less than $69 from another store on November 18, 1995. Because he had three previous convictions, the judge sentenced him to two consecutive sentences of 25 years to life; each of the two misdemeanors triggered a third strike. The Ninth Circuit Court granted his appeal, but the Supreme Court dismissed the decision in *Lockyer v. Andrade* in 1993.[18]

What have been the results of the numerous "three-strikes" laws? To extend the baseball metaphor, habitual criminal statutes have *"struck out looking"* in terms of impact on the crime problem. In essence, there has been little if any impact on the overall crime picture. Supporters claimed that this law was responsible for a drop in crime in California. However, virtually all states experienced a drop in crime during the 1990s, including those with no three-strikes laws. Franklin

Zimring notes that California was already locking up the targets of the "three-strikes" legislation, but "the complaint was that it was failing to throw away the key."[19] The initial justification for the statute was to incapacitate dangerous offenders (specific deterrence). The rate at which California convicted offenders did not increase faster after the law took effect, yet the crime rate declined. The new justification for the laws became general deterrence.

As several studies have noted, most of the defendants sentenced under the three-strikes law have been nonviolent offenders and older offenders (who tend to have lower recidivism rates). The law has been responsible for more jury trials, as defendants try to avoid a third conviction. This costs taxpayers more and clogs the system. It has also been used as a plea-bargaining tool.[20] Because the law allows for "wobbler" cases—cases that can be punished as either misdemeanors or felonies at the discretion of the prosecutor—the prosecution has leverage for plea bargains so defendants can avoid the third strike.

Research on the impact of habitual offender laws shows that they target racial minorities. Data collected in Los Angeles County found that black offenders were targeted in 57% of the cases and were charged with three-strike offenses at a rate 13 to 17 times greater than white offenders. Blacks constituted about 7% of the total population, but they accounted for 20% of all felony arrests, 37% of those convicted of a "second strike," and 44% of those convicted of a "third strike."[21]

Sentencing Guidelines

There is a tendency within any capitalist society to try to make things efficient, streamlined, and systematized in an attempt to make outcomes more predictable. Around the turn of the twentieth century, Frederick Taylor advocated *scientific management,* a system to increase factory production by getting the most work out of each worker. The general aim was to increase profit systematically. The quest for efficiency and predictability spilled over into many other areas of social life, including the criminal justice system.[22]

Sentencing guidelines can be viewed as a result of the impulse toward efficiency and predictability. Dissatisfaction with the sentencing practices of certain judges in certain parts of the country prompted the move to develop guidelines. There was a general feeling, especially among the public, that the court system was too lenient (despite the fact that our system metes out the most severe sentences of any democratic society in the world). Another complaint was that there were too many disparities in sentencing (overlooking the unique context of each crime, which means no two cases are identical). Critics wanted to take some of the discretion away from judges, ostensibly to eliminate these discrepancies. Scientific management was applied to the court system; however, politics played a key role in the crafting of sentencing guidelines as well.

Guidelines started to be developed within the federal system and within some state court systems during the 1980s. In theory, each sentence would be based on a certain *score* reflecting the seriousness of the crime, the offender's prior criminal history, and the offender's "social stability" (education, employment history, marital history, etc.). Certain *points* would be assigned to each factor that went into the total "equation," so in the end there would be *uniformity* in sentencing. The guidelines developed in the state of Minnesota served as a model for other states. A judge needed only to look at a chart in order to determine what the sentence would be for an offender convicted in court. The chart showed a specific range for each offense (e.g., 30–36 months).[23]

The problem with this approach is clear: the courts are sentencing human beings to punishment that involves a loss of liberty. Efficiency under those circumstances differs starkly from, say, the efficiency of creating automobiles. Moreover, as some research has shown, the various factors that determined the length of a sentence tended to produce an increase in discrepancies based on race. Many have criticized the use of special "sentencing commissions" within some states, because they result in the kinds of discrepancies such guidelines were supposed to reduce. One report noted that in New York there were so many different political philosophies on the state commission that there was little agreement on the guidelines. Another report compared sentencing guidelines in Minnesota and Pennsylvania and found that sentences in Minnesota were much less punitive than sentences in Pennsylvania, in part because so many commission members in Pennsylvania had close ties to the political establishment.[24]

We have served on various state and local "commissions," "task forces," and the like, and it has been our experience that they are largely an exercise in futility. Most members act in their own self-interest (e.g., to please their employers or to pad their résumés) and to present the image that something is being done to solve a particular problem. At best, sentencing guidelines serve a symbolic purpose with little actual effect; at worst, disparities based on race and class have increased, especially when we consider the results of the "war on drugs."

The Sentencing Reform Act

There has always been a profound distrust between legislators and the judiciary. Lawmakers in Congress and state legislatures have not been satisfied with merely making the laws; they have repeatedly tried to take discretion away from judges in sentencing. Legislators like their constituents to believe that they are tough on crime and that they alone can save the American people from "soft" judges who will coddle the criminal.

The United States Sentencing Commission was created by the Sentencing Reform Act provisions of the Comprehensive Crime Control Act of 1984. It is an independent agency in the judicial branch of government, established to provide guidelines for sentencing policies and practices for the federal courts and to serve as an information resource for crime policy, including evaluating the effects of sentencing guidelines on the criminal justice system. The commission describes the sentencing guidelines as designed to:

- incorporate the purposes of sentencing (i.e., just punishment, deterrence, incapacitation, and rehabilitation);

- provide certainty and fairness in meeting the purposes of sentencing by avoiding unwarranted disparity among offenders with similar characteristics convicted of similar criminal conduct, while permitting sufficient judicial flexibility to take into account relevant aggravating and mitigating factors;

- reflect, to the extent practicable, advancement in the knowledge of human behavior as it relates to the criminal justice process.[25]

The guidelines take into account both the seriousness of the criminal conduct and the defendant's criminal record. Based on the severity of the offense, the guidelines assign most federal crimes to one of 43 offense levels. Each offender is also assigned to one of six criminal-history categories based on the extent and recency of his or her past misconduct.

The Sentencing Reform Act abolished parole for offenders sentenced under the guidelines. Under the law, inmates may earn up to 54 days of credit a year for good behavior. Sentencing guidelines went into effect November 1, 1987. In 1989, The Supreme Court in *Mistretta v. United States* rejected challenges by defendants that the Sentencing Reform Act was unconstitutional because it violated the separation of powers doctrine. It upheld the constitutionality of the Sentencing Commission as a judicial branch agency. Federal judges have sentenced more than 700,000 defendants under the guidelines.[26]

The Sentencing Reform Act had a substantial impact, but it was merely one of many mandatory sentencing schemes mandated by lawmakers in the 1980s and 1990s. Many state legislatures followed the federal guidelines in creating their state statutes. The Supreme Court decision in 2005 in *United States v. Booker*[27] sent shock waves through the U.S. criminal justice system. At trial, a jury convicted Booker of possessing at least 50 grams of crack cocaine with the intent to distribute. The judge, using evidence not presented at trial, found that he had distributed six times the amount of drugs and had also obstructed justice. Those enhancements raised his sentencing under the guidelines from a range of 210 to 262 months in prison to a range of 360 months to life. The judge sentenced Booker to 30 years. The Court ruled that judges could not use facts not proven before a jury to enhance a sentence beyond the maximum warranted for the convicted offense. The Federal Sentencing Guidelines were unconstitutional because they exposed defendants to sentences based on findings not presented to a jury and therefore violated the Sixth Amendment's guarantee of a trial by jury. The solution was to make the guideline system advisory rather than mandatory, which left many questions unanswered.

In 2007, the Court decided *Rita v. United States*.[28] Rita posed the question of whether a sentence within the guideline range should be considered presumptively reasonable.[29] Victor Rita was convicted of perjury (lying to a grand jury), and the sentencing guidelines specified a sentence of 33–41 months. His attorney sought a shorter sentence, arguing that the sentence range was unreasonable because it did not adequately address the defendant's history and characteristics and was longer than necessary for the crime committed. The appellate court disagreed and said a sentence within the guideline range is presumptively reasonable. The Supreme Court ruled that the appellate court can view a range in the federal guidelines as presumptively reasonable, although "the presumption is not binding." Although *Booker* established that the guideline ranges set by the U.S. Sentencing Commission were no longer mandatory, the justices ruled in *Rita* (eight justices ruled in favor, one dissented) that judges who follow the guidelines may be presumed to have acted reasonably. Douglas Berman, an expert on sentencing law, noted the ruling "doesn't tell us anything about what happens when a district court decides not to follow the general rules."[30]

The court agreed to hear two other cases involving sentencing guidelines in 2007: *Gall v. United States* and *Kimbrough v. United States*. *Gall* involves an Iowa college student who pleaded guilty to conspiracy to distribute a controlled substance (ecstasy). He was sentenced to three years probation rather than three years in prison, as the guidelines suggest. The Eighth Circuit Court of Appeals ordered resentencing, finding that such a departure from the guidelines required extraordinary justification.[31] The Court will determine whether it is appropriate to require district courts to justify a deviation from the sentencing guidelines with a finding of extraordinary circumstances. In *Kimbrough*, the Court will consider whether a sentencing judge can take into account the impact of the 100-to-1 crack/powder disparity in the sentencing guidelines (see discussion later in this chapter).

Sentencing in a Post *Booker* World

The court is no longer required to impose a sentence within the guideline range except in narrow circumstances. The overriding sentencing principle is parsimony after considering the complete range of relevant factors as directed by Congress, including the defendant's history and characteristics, the relative seriousness of the offense, the needs of the public, and the needs of the defendant.

While the Supreme Court attempted to address an obvious problem with sentencing practice, what we have both before and after the *Booker* decision is a sentencing process that is not based on evidence of what really works and also does not support the purposes and theory of our legal system. Reasonable mitigating circumstances, while given short shrift or forbidden by the pre-*Booker* guidelines, are essential to making an informed decision about an equitable sentence. But courts were provided with an "easy out" if they use the right language to stay within a standard sentencing range. The court must merely recite on the record that it considered all statutory sentencing factors and concluded that the sentence was just and proper.[32] Prosecutors still have the upper hand in determining what the judge will do. It remains to be seen what effect additional cases will have on mandatory sentencing. Despite *Booker*, the movement to restrict judicial discretion and make sentencing more ideological and less evidence based continues. The power in the process still favors the prosecutor, and the fundamental problems with sentencing schemes remain.

Friends in High Places

I. Lewis Libby, also known as "Scooter" Libby, (former corporate lawyer, policy advisor, and assistant to the president) served as chief of staff to Dick Cheney, Vice President of the United States, and as assistant to the vice president for national security affairs from 2001 to 2005 until he resigned after his indictment by a federal grand jury on five felony counts related to the disclosure of the then-classified identity of covert CIA operative, Valerie Plame. Unlike the ordinary criminal defendant, Libby was not fired. He resigned his government positions after his indictment and was named a senior advisor to the Hudson Institute.[33]

On March 6, 2007, the jury convicted Libby of lying to FBI agents and grand jurors (as did Victor Rita in the case discussed above) on four of the five counts, specifically: one count of obstruction of justice; two counts of perjury; and one count of making false statements to federal investigators. Judge Reggie Walton sentenced Libby to 30 months in federal prison, a fine of $250,000, and two years of supervised release, including 400 hours of community service.[34] Judge Walton ordered Libby to begin his sentence immediately, Libby's appeal of that order failed (July 2, 2007), and within hours President Bush commuted Libby's prison sentence, while leaving the other parts of his sentence intact.[35] Calling the sentence excessive, Mr. Bush did not rule out a full pardon at a later date.[36]

Knowledgeable commentators were disturbed by the apparent arbitrariness and hypocrisy involved in the commutation of the sentence. According to the *New York Times*, Libby's sentence was consistent with sentences imposed in other similar cases. In commuting Libby's prison sentence, "President Bush drew on the same array of arguments about the federal sentencing system often made by defense lawyers—and routinely and strenuously opposed by his own Justice Department."[37] Prior to this case, President Bush viewed the clemency power as limited to cases of demonstrable actual innocence. As he explained in his 1999 memoir, in every case, "I would ask: Is there

any doubt about this individual's guilt or innocence? And, have the courts had ample opportunity to review all the legal issues in this case?"[38] In commuting Libby's sentence, the president expressed no doubts about his guilt. He said he respected the jury's verdict.[39]

Another cause for concern was the president's use of the legal system to justify the commutation. As noted above, the president used the language of the criminal justice system to explain his decision. He termed the prison time "excessive" and stated that the felony conviction, a $250,000 fine, and a damaged reputation were sufficiently "harsh" punishments for his crimes.[40]

> Fairness and uniformity need to be coins of the sentencing realm. Is prison time "excessive" punishment for a defendant such as Libby? There are ways to answer that question: Lawyers are trained to analogize or distinguish other cases to suit their clients' interests, and to argue that judges should depart from sentencing guidelines. But that's not what happened here. The president pointed to no other arguably similar case where the defendant received a lesser (or no) prison term. Nor did he explain why those guidelines shouldn't apply to Libby. . . .
>
> Bush, by commuting Judge Walton's prison sentence of Scooter Libby with a legal (not political) justification, damaged the perception of fairness and uniformity we need in order to inspire confidence in our criminal justice system. And that is a shame. If the Department of Justice is to conform to the ideals to which it owes its name, there must be more than the mouthing of the language of justice. There must be strict adherence to universal principles that apply to all, irrespective of their particular lot in life.

The commutation of the sentence was unique in that it occurred before Libby had served even one day of his sentence and before he had exhausted his appeal remedies. The presiding judge "questioned whether it is legally possible to execute Mr. Bush's call for a commutation of the sentence but continue the two-year probation that was to follow." The judge commented that the law "does not appear to contemplate a situation in which a defendant may be placed under supervised release without first completing a term of incarceration."[41]

Libby was treated differently than other similarly situated felons because of his connections with the Bush administration. The commutation illustrates how class, position, and power affect the criminal process and outcomes. In spite of their "tough on crime" stance, conservative public officials looked the other way when the president took care of one of their own. Libby's legal fees were paid in large part by the "Libby Legal Defense Trust."[42] He paid his $250,000 fine by a cashier's check on July 2, 2007.[43] At the time this book went to press, Libby continued his lucrative, politically connected employment at the Hudson Institute.

"Typical" Sentences

In the final stage of the criminal court process—the actual sentencing of the guilty defendant—what sorts of sentences are "typical"? More than forty years ago sociologist David Sudnow observed that courtroom workgroups have a tendency to develop norms for "typical" crimes that carry "typical" sentences.[44] The norms are a form of stereotype. They describe the "typical" defendant, the "typical" circumstances surrounding the offense, and the "typical" sentence to be imposed. Over the years, defense attorneys, prosecutors, and judges develop shared ideas about what is an "appropriate" sentence for a particular offense and offender. The appropriate sentence usually takes into consideration the seriousness of the crime, the prior record of the defendant, and any aggravating or mitigating circumstances (which can vary considerably). However, lurking in the background of these cases are the various prejudices of the individual actors within the court system. The vast majority of those sentenced to prison are minorities and/or from very poor backgrounds.

Margaret Farnworth and her colleagues examined a sample of cases in which defendants were sentenced for possession of marijuana with the intent to sell.[45] They first examined the data on these sentences using only two categories. They operationalized

"race" as "white" and "nonwhite" and found no significant differences between the two groups as far as the sentence was concerned: whites were just as severely treated as nonwhites. However, Hispanics "disappear" in this method of analysis (the annual FBI crime report also groups Hispanics with whites). When Farnworth and her colleagues separated out Hispanics and controlled for a number of other factors, they found that whites received the least severe sentences, Hispanics received the most severe sentences, and blacks fell somewhere in between. Thus, bias is often obscured by the methods used in studies that claim no bias is present.

Sentences do, in fact, vary considerably. In 2002 state courts sentenced 41% of offenders to prison, 28% to jail, and 31% to probation.[46] There were also variations depending on the offense. For example, 91% of those convicted of murder were sent to prison, but only 42% of those convicted of aggravated assault were sent to prison (29% of them were granted probation). Property offenses varied considerably, with 46% of the burglary convictions receiving a prison sentence, compared to only 31% of the fraud cases. This particular example is noteworthy, because fraud is typically associated with offenders of higher socioeconomic status and is usually treated as a white-collar offense. For all property offenses, 38% received a prison sentence, 28% a jail sentence, and 34% probation. For all drug offenses, 39% received a prison sentence, 27% a jail sentence, and 34% probation. Thus, drug offenders and property offenders received almost identical sentences.

Both class and racial biases appear very early in the criminal justice process: when laws are written; during arrest and police processing; and during the setting of bail. Thus, by the sentencing stage, the majority of those left are racial minorities and the poor.[47] A Florida study found that the poor were no more likely to receive harsher sentences than the nonpoor for property crimes; however, they were sentenced more harshly for violent crimes and drug violations. A study of drunk-driving convictions found that those with the highest level of education (a measure of social class) received the most favorable treatment from charging through sentencing.[48] Another study found that among members of a group convicted of similar crimes who had similar prior records, unemployed people were more likely than those who were employed to be awaiting trial in jail (and for longer periods of time) and were twice as likely to be sent to prison.[49] In addition, several studies have found that those with public defenders (an indication of lower status because they must be indigent to be assigned a court-appointed attorney) are treated more harshly than those with private attorneys.

Most research reveals a racial bias at all stages of court processing, including sentencing. For instance, in the state of New York, minorities were more likely to be incarcerated even when other factors (like offense and prior record) were taken into consideration.[50] A study in Florida found that black defendants were far more likely to be sentenced under habitual offender laws—and thus receive a stiffer penalty—than their white counterparts, especially for drug and property crimes.[51] Racial and class bias is most flagrant when it comes to drug offenses (more about this later in the chapter).

It should be noted that some studies indicate that "prior record" and "seriousness of the offense" predict actual sentence better than race does. What these studies ignore, however, is the fact that in most instances race is closely related to the offense charged and also to prior record. As has been noted by many researchers, blacks and other minorities living in inner-city ghettos (especially in housing projects and "gang" territories) are practically guaranteed to have some contact with the police (if for no other reason than "driving while black" or "standing while black") and hence have a "prior record" (mostly minor offenses).[52] Some studies report more lenient treatment of blacks. Much of this "leniency" stems from the relationship between the victim and the offender. Generally speaking, when both the victim and the offender are black, the sentence will be much less severe than in cases where the victim is white and the offender is black. This is especially true for capital crimes.

CAPITAL PUNISHMENT: LEGALIZED HOMICIDE

Capital punishment is one of the oldest forms of punishment, dating back several thousands of years. It has had a long and turbulent history in the United States—ebbing and flowing through periods of disuse or abolishment through periods of more frequent application.

A Brief History

The first American execution was in 1608. Since then, there have been 15,575 recorded executions.[53] Early colonists brought the English tradition of execution to America. Since the laws tended to have their roots in religious practice, a variety of offenses were punishable by death. For example, some of the earliest executions were for bestiality, sodomy, piracy, concealing a birth, and witchcraft.[54] Executions became more frequent in the late 1800s and peaked in the 1930s when the United States averaged 167 executions per year. State sanctioned executions began to decline in the 1940s until reaching an all-time low between 1960 and 1976. There was 1 execution in 1977, none in 1978 and 1980, with a total of 11 through 1983. From 1984 through 1994 there were 246 executions, slightly more than 22 per year. From 1995 through 2006, there were 800 executions, an average of more than 66 per year. The peak year was 1999 with 98 executions.[55]

From 1976 to 2005, 6,940 people have been sentenced to death, with the largest number of death sentences (317) in 1996 and the lowest (128) in 2005.[56] There have been 1,086 executions from 1976 to July 2007: 620 of those executed were white (57%); 367 were black (34%), 75 were Hispanic (7%), and the remaining 24 were other races.[57] As of January 1, 2007, there were 3,350 people on death row. California had the largest number of death row inmates (660); Florida was second (397) and Texas was third (393).

Texas leads the country in executions since 1976 with 397; Virginia was a distant second with 98.[58]

After a de facto abolition of the death penalty, it was reactivated in 1977 with the execution of Gary Gilmore by a firing squad in Utah (this state is the only one that allows the prisoner a choice between a firing squad or hanging). As of July 2007, 38 states plus the federal government had the death penalty, although New York declared the death penalty unconstitutional in 2004 (one person remains on death row). Five of these states have not carried out an execution since 1976 (Kansas, New Hampshire, New Jersey, New York, and South Dakota).

The retention of capital punishment in the United States has not been without difficulty. From time to time Americans have expressed concerns over an issue involved in capital sentencing and/or executions, but the system responded in ways that appeased the public. Even the means of execution changed when it was viewed as cruel. For example, when members of society began to view electrocution as cruel and unusual punishment, states began using lethal injections.[59] In essence, an exploration of the history of capital punishment is actually an examination of evolving standards of decency. As the public becomes concerned over an issue related to death sentencing or executions, the laws evolve.

Legal History

Throughout recent U.S. history, the capital punishment system has faced a series of legitimacy crises.[60] A legitimacy crisis is a situation where the public recognizes the fallibility of the system. The first major crisis occurred in the early 1970s. Following the civil rights movement, racial disparity in sentencing was of great concern. Researchers began documenting extreme disparities in capital sentencing. This concern culminated in the Supreme Court's **Furman v. Georgia** ruling in 1972, a case so important that it resulted in nine separate opinions, one from each justice. In 1969, William Furman accidentally shot and killed an occupant of a home he was burglarizing. He was tried and convicted. The jury took only an hour and a

half to sentence him to death. According to Justice Brennan's opinion, "the jury knew only that he was black and that, according to his statement at trial, he was 26 years old and worked at Superior Upholstery."[61] The primary issue in the *Furman* ruling was a lack of consistency in capital sentencing due to a lack of guidelines for jurors. Essentially, the ruling found that existing statutes were unconstitutional due to their arbitrary and capricious application and their great potential for racial discrimination. Importantly, the Court did not rule that the death penalty *in and of itself* constituted cruel and unusual punishment in violation of the Eighth and Fourteenth Amendments of the Constitution.

Following the *Furman* ruling, 37 states reformulated their death penalty statutes in an attempt to reduce arbitrariness by providing guidelines for judges and jurors. These new laws were upheld in a series of Supreme Court decisions in 1976.[62] The most widely cited is the case of **Gregg v. Georgia**. The primary issue in the *Gregg* decision was not whether capital punishment was cruel and unusual, but whether or not the process of death sentencing was rational and objectively reviewable. The Court outlined two principles to guide legislatures in crafting their statutes. First, the statutes were required to provide objective criteria designed to limit sentencing discretion, and second, the Court required that judges or juries consider the character of the defendant. The Court ruled: "A punishment must not be excessive, but this does not mean that the states must seek the minimal standards available. The imposition of the death penalty for the crime of murder does not violate the Constitution." In two other decisions the Court ruled similarly (*Proffit v. Florida,* 1976 and *Jurek v. Texas,* 1976). However, in *Coker v. Georgia* (1977) the Court ruled that the death penalty for rape constituted cruel and unusual punishment.

Prior to *Furman*, appeals were not mandatory and many death row inmates did not pursue them. In fact, Robert Bohm reports that one-quarter of the prisoners executed in the 1960s had no appeals at all, and two-thirds never had their cases reviewed by a federal court.[63] The Supreme Court, in an attempt to achieve fairness in the process, ordered a mandatory review. Presently, most retentionist states automatically review both the conviction and sentence. The appeals process has been streamlined in recent years.[64] One important change in the appeals process since the *Gregg* ruling is that the Supreme Court will no longer consider issues raised for the first time pursuant to last-minute pleas for stays of execution, particularly when the claims could have been raised in prior petitions.

By 2007, 38 states had revised their death penalty statutes in an attempt to reduce arbitrariness. Typically, these statutes require a bifurcated trial. Phase one includes the presentation of evidence and aggravating factors for the purpose of a finding of guilt or nonguilt. When the jury convicts, the penalty phase begins. During this phase the prosecution urges the jury to return a death verdict, and the defense presents mitigating evidence. The primary difference between the new and old statutes is the required presentation of aggravating and mitigating evidence. To be death eligible, a homicide must be accompanied by one or more aggravating factors, as defined by state statutes. For example, some state statutes list armed robbery and rape as aggravating factors. Mitigators are also statutory and vary by state. For example, some statutes list diminished capacity due to drugs or alcohol as a mitigating factor.

Since the Court reinstated capital punishment in 1976, new issues emerged that have caused courts and legislatures to continue the reconstruction and reformulation of death penalty law. Two recent evolutions involved the execution of mentally retarded defendants and juvenile defendants. *Mental retardation* is described as substantial limitations in functioning that are characterized by significantly subaverage intelligence and limitations in skills related to self-care, communication, social skills, and work. The Court first addressed the issue of mental retardation and execution in 1989 in the case of *Penry v. Lynaugh* when it cited a "lack of national consensus" on executing the men-

tally ill and upheld the constitutionality of the practice.[65] In 2002, however, the Court changed its position.

By 2002, most death penalty states banned the practice of executing mentally retarded defendants. Public opinion polls revealed that a majority of Americans were opposed to the practice, and the American Bar Association established a policy opposing executions of those deemed to have an IQ of 70 or below. Clearly, a national consensus had formed. Thus, the Supreme Court declared in *Atkins v. Virginia* that executing an individual who meets all of the three criteria outlined by the American Association on Mental Retardation violates the Eighth Amendment. The criteria include:

1. Substantial intellectual impairment.

2. Impact of that impairment on everyday life of the individual.

3. Appearance of the disability at birth or during the person's childhood.

In a similar fashion, the Supreme Court changed its position on executing juvenile offenders. When polls indicated that the public opposed the execution of juvenile offenders, the Supreme Court banned the practice in *Roper v. Simmons*. The Court's 2005 ruling came despite a history of allowing juvenile executions in its *Stanford v. Kentucky* and *Thompson v. Oklahoma* rulings. In short, the courts and legislators respond to public outcries of cruel and unusual punishment. In listening and responding to these concerns, they legitimize capital punishment, which allows the practice to continue.

Wrongful Convictions

One issue that is often overlooked (but fortunately not forgotten by critics of the death penalty) is that of those wrongly convicted. One detailed study found evidence that some 400 defendants who had been sentenced to death were actually innocent of the crimes. An estimated two dozen had already been executed, and many more spent years in prison. Not surprisingly, a disproportionate number were African Americans.[66] During the past two decades more attention has been focused on the possibility that people could be sentenced to death when there may be some question about their guilt. A Columbia University study of 4,578 cases between 1973 and 1995 found that there were serious "reversible errors" in almost 70% of capital cases that were reviewed. Death sentences were overturned in two-thirds of the appeals, and ninety-five death row prisoners were exonerated. The use of DNA testing has resulted in 107 persons being released between 1989 and 2002, twelve of whom were on death row. Total error rates have reached as high as 70% in some courts.[67] From 1973 to July 2007, 124 people have been released from death row and declared innocent.[68]

Research reveals that numerous system factors can combine to result in wrongful convictions. For example, one study revealed that perjury, prosecutorial misconduct, and lack of evidence were the most common factors that led to wrongful convictions in death penalty cases.[69] These types of procedural problems have typically been the grounds on which the cases were reversed. In fact, in *Herrera v. Collins* the Supreme Court ruled that a claim of factual innocence based on new evidence is not grounds for granting an evidentiary hearing or a stay of execution. In short, the justices ruled that it is not the Court's place to "correct errors of fact," even if the errors could lead to the execution of an innocent person. Instead, the claim had to be accompanied by a procedural error.

The high-profile nature of death row exonerations led to another legitimacy crisis for the system of capital punishment. Public opinion polls revealed that recent reductions in Americans' support for capital punishment are tied to questions of fairness and the possibility of wrongful convictions.[70] Again, the system has responded in an attempt to alleviate these concerns.

In 2004, Congress passed the *Justice for All Act*. Title IV of the act is the *Innocence Protection Act*, which outlined procedures for DNA testing in possible innocence cases, implemented a program to improve the quality of defense in capital cases, and increased the compensation available to wrongfully convicted federal defendants. Importantly, this law is aimed at federal cases, which are a small portion of all capital prosecutions. Some states are, however, attempting to pass similar legislation. New laws are necessary because the resources needed to prove innocence are often unavailable to typical death row inmates.

The conviction of innocent people is a major problem with the criminal justice system in general, but with the death penalty, the consequences are amplified to the ultimate injustice. The finality of executions is the primary reason this issue is of such importance. No one is served when the wrong person is convicted and sent to death row. The system fails not only the condemned but also the victim and society. Some argue that releases of the wrongfully convicted are proof that the system and the appeals process work. Unfortunately, this is not always the case. Most of the releases have not been prompted by state sanctioned investigations. They resulted from undergraduate journalism students, private investigators, and family members uncovering perjured testimony and/or new evidence. Those released due to DNA evidence usually had to fight prosecutors for years before the state would allow the tests to be performed. Proving one's innocence from death row is not an easy undertaking. Often, it requires battles with state representatives who are willing to overlook evidence of wrongful conviction rather than admit that a mistake was made.

Meanwhile, the use of the death penalty has increased as appeals have declined, and the process from conviction to execution has accelerated. A few states, such as Texas, have turned executions into a "sideshow" (to use Senator Hatch's terminology) with crowds of people outside applauding as soon as a defendant is executed. African Americans and other minorities continue to receive the death penalty in numbers far greater than their proportion in the general population. Almost without exception, the executed are drawn from the ranks of the "dangerous classes."[71]

When asked about factors most effective in reducing violent offenses, police chiefs across the United States placed the death penalty in last place. The number one factor mentioned was reducing drug abuse (31%), followed by better economy and more jobs (17%), simplifying court rules (16%), longer prison sentences (15%), more police officers (10%), reducing the availability of guns (3%), and expansion of the death penalty (1%).[72]

The Race Factor

Death penalty proponents argue that the legal evolution of capital punishment has made the practice free of error, fair, and unbiased. The research in this area, however, indicates that the death penalty continues to be implemented in an arbitrary manner. Race figures prominently in the imposition of the death penalty. For instance, of the 4,172 prisoners executed between 1930 and 1995, over half (52%) were African Americans. Between 1930 and 1972, a total of 455 people were executed for rape, 89% of them African Americans.[73] When researchers consider the race of the victims, race once again enters into the picture. For instance, between 1976 and 2007, 79% of the victims of those executed were white, even though the homicide victimization rate for African Americans is six times as high as that of whites.[74] Tables 10.1 and 10.2 on the following pages illustrate the importance of race in every state.

Several studies have noted that there are vast discrepancies in the application of the death penalty according to the race of the victim and the race of the offender. When the victim is white and the offender is African American, the death penalty is given about 35% of the time, compared to only 14% when the relationship is reversed (i.e., African-American victim and white offender); the death penalty is given in 22% of the cases in which whites kill whites and in only 6% of the cases where African Americans kill African Americans. The race of the victim plays a key role in the prosecutor's decision to seek the death penalty and a jury's decision to impose it. Importantly, these patterns have been observed in all retentionist states that have been examined.[75]

An Amnesty International study found that since 1977, "Even though blacks and whites are murder victims in nearly equal numbers of crimes, 80% of people executed since the death penalty was reinstated have been executed for murders involving white victims." The study also found that more than one-fifth of blacks who were executed were convicted by all-white juries.[76]

Studies from specific states further document the role of race in the imposition of the death penalty. For instance, a study by Raymond Paternoster and Robert Brame found that Maryland's death penalty system is tainted with racial bias at every stage of the process, including whether or not the prosecutor seeks the death penalty in a murder case.[77] As in so many other studies, the researchers found that the race of the victim is a crucial factor. After publication of the study, the executive director of the Death Penalty Information Center remarked: "when it comes to the death penalty, white lives are considered more valuable than black lives in the state of Maryland."[78] Additionally, a recent Kentucky study revealed that prosecutors are more likely to seek the death penalty in cases where black offenders killed white victims.[79] Studies in such states as Indiana, Virginia, North Carolina, New Jersey, and also the federal system, found strong evidence of racial bias in the death penalty process.[80]

There have been consistent findings that African Americans are more likely than whites to be charged with capital crimes and to be sentenced to death.[81] Evidence of racial discrimination in the imposition of the death penalty has been documented in several studies, dating back more than seventy years.

- Guy B. Johnson studied homicide cases in Richmond, Virginia, and in five counties in North Carolina during the 1930s. He found that the death penalty was most often applied when the victim was white and the offender was black and least likely when both the offender and the victim were black.[82]

- Wolfgang, Kelly, and Nolde studied 439 cases of men sentenced to death in Pennsylvania for murder between 1914 and 1958. They found that 20% of whites had their sentences commuted to life imprisonment versus only 11% of blacks (a statistically significant relationship).[83]

Table 10.1   Current Death Row Prisoners by Jurisdiction and Race (January 1, 2007)

State	Total	Black	White	Latino	Asian	Native American
Alabama	195	93	100	2	0	0
Arizona	124	13	88	20	0	3
Arkansas	37	23	14	0	0	0
California	660	235	254	136	22	13
Colorado	2	1	0	1	0	0
Connecticut	8	3	3	2	0	0
Delaware	18	7	8	3	0	0
Florida	397	139	221	35	1	1
Georgia	107	50	53	3	1	0
Idaho	20	0	20	0	0	0
Illinois	11	3	5	3	0	0
Indiana	23	7	16	0	0	0
Kansas	9	4	5	0	0	0
Kentucky	41	9	31	1	0	0
Louisiana	88	55	30	2	1	0
Maryland	8	5	3	0	0	0
Mississippi	66	35	30	0	1	0
Missouri	51	21	30	0	0	0
Montana	2	0	2	0	0	0
Nebraska	9	1	5	3	0	0
Nevada	80	29	42	8	1	0
New Hampshire	0	0	0	0	0	0
New Jersey	11	6	5	0	0	0
New Mexico	2	0	2	0	0	0
New York	1	1	0	0	0	0
North Carolina	185	98	72	4	1	10
Ohio	191	96	88	3	2	2
Oklahoma	88	33	48	3	0	4
Oregon*	33	3	26	2	0	1
Pennsylvania	226	137	68	19	2	0
South Carolina	67	38	29	0	0	0
South Dakota	4	0	4	0	0	0
Tennessee	107	43	59	1	2	2
Texas	393	161	121	107	4	0
Utah	9	1	6	1	0	1
Virginia	20	12	8	0	0	0
Washington	9	4	5	0	0	0
Wyoming	2	0	2	0	0	0
U.S. Government	44	25	18	0	0	1
U.S. Military	9	6	2	0	1	0
Totals	3,357	1,397	1,523	359	39	38

*One person on death row in Oregon is of unknown ethnicity.
Source: NAACP. Death Row U.S.A. Winter 2007. [Online] http://www.naacpldf.org/content/pdf/pubs/drusa/DRUSA_Winter_2007.pdf

Studies of rape have also found a strong relationship between the race of the victim and the imposition of the death penalty.

• Elmer Johnson, in a study of rape cases resulting in the imposition of the death penalty in North Carolina between 1909 and 1954, found that blacks were more likely than whites to be executed. A study of Florida cases found that blacks who raped whites were much more likely to receive the death penalty than whites who raped blacks.[84]

Table 10.2   Executions by Jurisdiction and Race, 1976–2006

State	Total	Black	White	Latino	Asian	Native American
Alabama	35	16	19	0	0	0
Arizona	22	0	17	4	0	0
Arkansas	27	7	19	1	0	0
California	13	2	8	0	1	2
Colorado	1	0	1	0	0	0
Connecticut	1	0	1	0	0	0
Delaware	14	6	7	0	0	0
Florida	64	20	39	4	0	1
Georgia	39	13	26	0	0	0
Idaho	1	0	1	0	0	0
Illinois	12	5	7	0	0	0
Indiana	17	3	14	0	0	0
Kansas	0	0	0	0	0	0
Kentucky	2	0	2	0	0	0
Louisiana	27	13	14	0	0	0
Maryland	5	3	2	0	0	0
Mississippi	8	3	5	0	0	0
Missouri	66	26	39	0	0	1
Montana	3	0	3	0	0	0
Nebraska	3	2	1	0	0	0
Nevada	12	1	9	1	1	0
New Hampshire	0	0	0	0	0	0
New Jersey	0	0	0	0	0	0
New Mexico	1	0	1	0	0	0
New York	0	0	0	0	0	0
North Carolina	43	13	29	0	0	1
Ohio	24	9	15	0	0	0
Oklahoma	83	23	52	0	2	6
Oregon	2	0	2	0	0	0
Pennsylvania	3	0	3	0	0	0
South Carolina	36	12	24	0	0	0
South Dakota	0	0	0	0	0	0
Tennessee	2	0	2	0	0	0
Texas	379	135	183	57	2	2
Utah	6	2	4	0	0	0
Virginia	98	44	51	2	1	0
Washington	4	0	4	0	0	0
Wyoming	1	0	1	0	0	0
U.S. Government	3	1	1	1	0	0
U.S. Military	0	0	0	0	0	0
Totals	1,057	359	608	70	7	13

Source: Death Penalty Information Center. [Online] http://www.deathpenaltyinfo.org/article.php?scid=5&did=184#inmaterace

- Wolfgang and Riedel studied 3,000 rape convictions in eleven southern states between 1945 and 1965. They found that "among 1,265 cases in which the race of the defendant and the sentence are known, nearly seven times as many Blacks were sentenced to death as whites." They also found that 36% of blacks who raped whites were sentenced to death, while all other racial combinations resulted in only 2% being sentenced to death.[85]

More recent studies have found evidence that juries are often prejudiced against minorities and are more likely to convict (in capital cases) than they are to convict whites.[86] Finally, research has found that of the more than 15,000 executions between 1608 and 1986, a mere 30 cases were found (about 0.2%) in which a white person was executed for killing a black.[87]

The Controversy Continues:
McCleskey v. Kemp

One of the most significant Supreme Court cases concerning the death penalty was **McCleskey v. Kemp** in 1987.[88] The case originated in Georgia, as did *Furman* and *Gregg*. The defendant, Warren McCleskey, an African American, was convicted of killing a white police officer. The defense strategy for the appeal included research by David Baldus and his colleagues (referenced as the Baldus study in the court case) that revealed a disparity in Georgia's death sentencing based on the race of the victim. The study was a complex statistical analysis of capital convictions in Georgia. It found that blacks charged with killing white victims were 4.3 times more likely to receive death verdicts than others.[89] The Court assumed the validity of the Baldus study but found the statistics insufficient to demonstrate unconstitutional discrimination under the Eighth (irrationality, arbitrariness, and capriciousness) or Fourteenth (equal protection) Amendments.

> At most, the Baldus study indicates a discrepancy that appears to correlate with race, but this discrepancy does not constitute a major systemic defect. Any mode for determining guilt or punishment has its

weaknesses and the potential for misuse. Despite such imperfections, constitutional guarantees are met when the mode for determining guilt or punishment has been surrounded with safeguards to make it as fair as possible.

The Court ruled that "the Baldus study is insufficient to support an inference that any of the decision makers in his [McCleskey] case acted with discriminatory purpose."

What is perhaps most interesting about this ruling is that the Court appeared to be afraid of what the "logical conclusions" of such evidence might be. Justice Lewis Powell, writing for the majority, noted that such evidence "throws into serious question the principles that underlie our entire criminal justice system. . . . [I]f we accepted McCleskey's claim that racial bias impermissibly tainted the capital sentencing decision, we would soon be faced with similar claims as to other types of penalty." Not surprisingly, the ruling came in for immediate attack, including four dissenting justices (Blackmun, Marshall, Brennan, and Stevens). Heaven forbid, they suggested, that others might challenge such obvious biases, "even women" (wrote one justice). One scholar noted sarcastically that concluding that "at most" there appears to be a "discrepancy" is like saying that "at most" the many studies on lung cancer "indicate a discrepancy that appears to correlate with smoking."[90] Most of the critics voiced the opinion that this ruling sent a message that racial bias is perfectly constitutional. McCleskey was eventually executed in the electric chair on September 26, 1991. Justice Thurgood Marshall, who joined two other justices in a dissent for a stay of execution, stated that it appears that "the court values expediency over human life."[91]

David Cole has argued that it would be nearly impossible to prove that a prosecutor and a jury have imposed the death penalty in a particular case because of the defendant's race. "Defendants are precluded from discovering evidence of intent from the two actors whose discriminatory intent the *McCleskey* Court required them to establish."[92] For example, during the trial of a black man charged with the murder of a white man, both the judge and the defense attorney referred to the defendant, William Dobbs, as a "colored boy." The defense attorney also expressed his opinion that "blacks are uneducated and would not make good teachers, but do make good basketball players."[93] Several jurors referred to African Americans as "coloreds," and two admitted using "nigger" in their conversations.[94] Despite these indications of bias, Dobbs was sentenced to death, and his conviction was upheld by the Georgia courts.

The Supreme Court concluded that "discrimination is inevitable," a "natural by-product of discretion," and hence "constitutionally acceptable."[95] The highest court in the country failed to acknowledge racial bias. Some members of Congress responded to the *McCleskey* decision by adding a "Racial Justice Act" to the Omnibus Crime Bill of 1994. By a slim majority, the House voted for this provision, which would have allowed those on death row to challenge their sentence based on statistical evidence of race discrimination in capital cases, as had McCleskey. But it was defeated in the Senate and dropped from the 1994 bill. Senator Orin Hatch (R-Utah) remarked that this "so-called Racial Justice Act has nothing to do with racial justice and everything to do with abolishing the death penalty. . . . It would convert every death penalty case into a massive sideshow of statistical squabbles and quota quarrels."[96]

The Class Factor

Capital punishment also discriminates on the basis of social class. Indigent defendants are not merely disproportionately represented on death row—they *are* the death row population. As discussed in chapter 8, indigent status means public defenders or court-appointed attorneys, who are often the least capable of handling a capital case. As a result, compelling evidentiary and procedural issues are not raised at trial. If the issues are not raised at trial, it is virtually impossible to raise them on appeal. Poor defendants are not provided adequate resources for investigation, which impacts the ability to locate and interview witnesses,

gather evidence, and question scientific evidence offered by the state.[97]

The pervasive problem of inadequate counsel for poor defendants results from three primary issues. First, inadequate funding leads to court-appointed attorneys being poorly compensated. This offers little incentive to devote time to cases. Second, judges often fail to respond to incompetence at the trial level. Despite the fact that they recognize the problem, judges allow trials to continue and let appellate courts respond rather than delaying the case. Finally, the system tolerates a minimal standard of representation, not an "effective" standard.[98]

The American Bar Association (ABA) voiced its concern with the lack of adequate representation in capital cases when it called for a moratorium on capital cases until the issue of competent counsel can be rectified. The ABA concluded that the lack of quality representation among poor capital defendants is one of the principal failings of capital punishment. Inadequate counsel for the poor is not a new issue, and it has not been rectified in the post-*Furman* era. The problems that plague indigent defendants at trial continue throughout the legal process.[99]

The Gender Factor

The death penalty also discriminates on the basis of gender. Women are treated more benevolently in homicide cases and are less likely to receive death verdicts. Historically, executions of females have been rare. At the end of 2006, there were 59 women on death row (1.76% of the death row population). Eleven women have been executed since 1976.[100] Females account for only 2.8% of all confirmed executions since 1608.[101]

Females commit far fewer homicides than males and are far less likely to receive a death sentence when they are convicted of capital offenses. Victor Streib argues that gender bias in capital sentencing finds its roots in two areas. First, "the express provisions of the law," which refers to the idea that some statutory considerations may be applied differently on the basis of gender. For example, prior criminal history is a factor in charging decisions, and females are less likely to have prior violent offenses, which decreases the likelihood of a death penalty trial. Second, "the implicit attitudes, either conscious or subconscious, of key actors involved in the criminal justice process" contribute to gender bias.[102] Prosecutors, judges, and juries are less likely to view women as dangerous. This view of women impacts the charging and sentencing decisions of system functionaries in cases involving female defendants.

Deterrence and Brutalization

Much of the confidence Americans have in the death penalty revolves around the perception that punishment alters behavior. It is commonsensical to believe that offenders will not want to die and that the threat of capital punishment will have a general deterrent effect. Unfortunately, there is no credible evidence that the death penalty deters homicide or any other felony offenses. The simplest test of deterrence relates to the idea that states or countries with the death penalty should have lower homicide rates than those without capital punishment. There is no evidence to indicate that this is true. The United States is the only Western democracy that retains capital punishment; it is also the country with the highest homicide rate in the industrialized world. Comparative analyses of regions within the United States reveal the same pattern. Southern states, which are the most active death penalty states, have consistently had the highest homicide rates.[103] While the South accounts for about 80% of all executions, it is the only region with a homicide rate above the national average. Similarly, comparisons of states with the death penalty to those without reveal that the homicide rate for retentionist states is 6.6, while the rate for non-death penalty states is 3.5.[104]

Numerous studies of the deterrent effect of the death penalty have been conducted using diverse methodologies. There have been comparisons between contiguous states; studies of jurisdictions that abolished and reinstated capital punishment; research on homicides committed by prisoners and parolees; and studies of the murders of police officers. None of the studies found that capi-

tal punishment reduced homicides. Police officers and prison inmates are no safer in death penalty states than in non-death penalty states. Individually and collectively these studies reveal that the death penalty has no general deterrent effect on homicides or other felonies.

Specific deterrence is commonly cited as a reason to retain capital punishment. While it is certainly true that an executed offender will not recidivate, research reveals that recidivism is unlikely without executions. When the *Furman* decision declared existing death penalty statutes unconstitutional in 1972, the death sentences of 457 people were commuted. James Marquart and Jon Sorensen tracked and compared the behavior of the 47 Texas inmates to 156 inmates serving life sentences for similar crimes.[105] The study revealed that 75% of the *Furman*-commuted inmates and 70% of the comparison group did not commit a serious violation of prison rules and none in either group was implicated in a prison homicide. Marquart and Sorensen concluded that the former death row inmates were "not unusually disruptive or rebellious, nor did they pose a disproportionate threat to society."

Gennaro Vito and his colleagues tracked the behavior of all *Furman*-commuted inmates in the country.[106] Of the 177 who were paroled, eight committed another violent crime, including three homicides. The research revealed that the homicide recidivism rate for the entire group was 1.6%. The authors concluded that capital punishment does not offer society greater protection from homicide. In fact, some research has revealed that executions may have the opposite effect.

Since a 1935 study of Philadelphia, researchers have explored the possibility that executions have a *brutalization effect*. Some researchers have determined that the number of homicides increases during the period immediately before and after an execution. For example, William Bailey revealed a significant increase in stranger homicides following Oklahoma's resumption of executions in 1990.[107] In Arizona, Ernie Thomson found an increase in gun-related and spontaneous stranger homicides following executions.[108] Similarly, a California study found that more murders occurred in the days before, on the day of, and in the weeks following an execution.[109] This research suggests that not only does the death penalty fail to deter homicide but that the opposite may be true.

As this book went to press, the Supreme Court had scheduled *Baze v. Rees* to be heard in January. Two Kentucky death-row inmates argued that the three-drug cocktail used to kill death-row inmates in Kentucky should be considered cruel and unusual punishment. The Court allowed only one lethal injection to proceed after agreeing to consider the issue.[110] The Court has not considered the constitutionality of a method of execution since 1879 when the use of firing squads was upheld. Thirty-seven states administer lethal injections; 19 use it as the only method of execution.

The three injections perform different functions. The first stops pain; the second paralyzes the inmate; the third stops the heart. There have been significant problems with pancuronium bromide in the second shot.

> Medical experts testified at trial that there has been a high level of error in this shot, leaving the individual conscious and possibly able to feel the excruciating pain of the third shot. But because the second drug also paralyzes the individual, observers cannot necessarily tell if the person is experiencing any extreme sensation.[111]

Veterinarians in Tennessee and Texas are prohibited from using the drug in the second shot on animals.

Some legal scholars viewed the Supreme Court's decision to consider the method of administering the ultimate punishment to be a tacit endorsement of capital punishment. Others looked at the questioning of the mechanics as an indication of the public's ambivalence about state-sanctioned killing and noted that in Europe the public began questioning the method prior to the abolition of the death penalty.

THE IMPACT OF THE "WAR ON DRUGS"

More than any other public policy in the past hundred years, the war on drugs has had a huge impact on the criminal justice system. With the emphasis placed almost totally on a legalistic response to illegal drugs, the police have responded with literally millions of arrests for drug possession and sales during the past two decades. Not surprisingly there has been a predictable impact on the criminal courts and the rest of the criminal justice system. Table 10.3 illustrates startling changes in sentencing in the federal system for drug offenses. The number of convictions and the length of the average sentence have increased exponentially. Commitments to state prisons for drug offenses also increased dramatically. In 2004, there were 362,850 felony convictions to state prisons with an average sentence of 51 months versus 274,245 convictions in 1994 with an average sentence of 48 months. The increase in the number of convictions was about 21%, compared to an increase of 53% in the number of convictions from 1988 to 1992.[112]

A common view is that the drug war is necessary to save people—especially young people—from addiction to dangerous, illegal drugs. The two most dangerous drugs in terms of the number of deaths resulting from their use are tobacco and alcohol, but those drugs are legal. In addition, the people targeted in the drug war are not the drug dealers

Table 10.3 Sentences in Federal Courts for Drug Law Violations, 1950–2005

Year	Convictions	Average Sentence (in months)
1950	1,654	22
1960	1,232	73
1970	1,283	65
1980	3,479	55
1990	13,838	79
2005	24,786	86
% increase (1950–2005)	291%	

Source: Sourcebook of Criminal Justice Statistics. [Online] http://www.albany.edu/sourcebook/pdf/t5382005.pdf

who sell the most drugs or everyone who uses illegal drugs. The discrepancies based on race in the drug war are pervasive and extensive.

Numerous studies have shown that there are few racial differences in actual illegal drug use. The National Survey on Drug Use and Health (NSDUH) is conducted annually.[113] In 2006, the survey reported the following current illicit drug use by ethnicity for people aged 12 or older: Asians 3.6%, Hispanics 6.9%, whites 8.5%, blacks 9.8%, and Native Americans 13.7%.[114]

Despite similarities in the use of illicit drugs, there are disparities in convictions and sentences. Blacks are overrepresented in prisons relative to their proportion of the population and to their rates of drug offending; whites are underrepresented.[115] Between 1985 (when the drug war began in earnest) and 1995, the number of African American inmates sentenced for drug crimes increased by 700%.[116] Drug convictions constitute 24% of the admissions to state prisons for whites, but 38% for blacks.[117]

In June 1986 the country was shocked by the death of University of Maryland basketball star Len Bias three days after being drafted by the Boston Celtics. Bias, who was African American, died of a drug and alcohol overdose. Many in the media and public assumed that Bias died of a crack overdose (incorrectly, it was powder cocaine).[118] The death of Bias coincided with a "cyclone of press coverage about crack."[119] The media and politicians proclaimed an epidemic of instant addiction and lifetime damage to babies born to mothers addicted to crack. Fears fueled by the exaggerations and misinformation prompted Congress to pass The Anti-Drug Abuse Act of 1986 in late October 1986.

The Act established mandatory minimum sentences for federal drug trafficking crimes. The penalty for crack (most commonly used in poorer neighborhoods because it is less expensive than cocaine) was 100 times greater than the penalty for cocaine (same drug, different form). Individuals convicted of trafficking in 500 grams of powder cocaine or 5 grams of crack (the weight of two pennies) would be sentenced to at least 5 years imprisonment, without regard to any mitigating factors.

Congress continued passing mandatory-minimum legislation. The Omnibus Anti-Drug Abuse Act of 1988 created a 5-year mandatory minimum and 20-year maximum sentence for simple possession of 5 grams or more of crack cocaine. The maximum penalty for simple possession of any amount of powder cocaine or any other drug remained at no more than 1 year in prison.[120]

The U.S. Sentencing Commission has repeatedly requested that Congress change the different penalties. Congress did enact a provision in 1994 permitting relief from mandatory minimums for certain nonviolent, first-time drug offenders. Prior to that time, a judge was not allowed to impose a sentence below the minimum, with one exception. The Justice Department could request a reduction if a drug offender gave "substantial assistance" to the government in the prosecution of another drug offender. In a five-year period, nearly a third of the people sentenced in drug trafficking cases in the federal system had their sentences reduced under the substantial assistance provisions because they informed on other people.[121] In 2007, the Sentencing Commission again recommended that Congress change the 100-to-1 crack-to-powder ratio.[122] It reported that all defense lawyers and almost half of the prosecutors questioned had serious problems with mandatory minimum sentences, and most judges found the sentences unjust. The report criticized the transfer of power in courts from judges, who are supposed to be impartial, to prosecutors, who are not. Some federal judges have experimented with lesser sentences. As noted above, the Supreme Court will hear *Gall v. United States,* in which the defendant received probation. The Court will also consider the cocaine disparity when it hears the case of Derrick Kimbrough.

The difference in sentencing for crack vs. powder cocaine was responsible for significant racial disparities in the prison population. "Whites are disproportionately less likely to be prosecuted for drug offenses in the first place; when prosecuted, are more likely to be acquitted; and even if convicted, are much less likely to be sent to prison."[123] African Americans make up 15% of the country's drug users, yet they comprise 37% of those arrested for drug violations, 59% of those convicted, and 74% of those sentenced to prison for a drug offense.

> African Americans comprise the vast majority of those convicted of crack cocaine offenses, while the majority of those convicted for powder cocaine offenses are white. . . . African Americans constituted more than 80% of the defendants sentenced under the harsh federal crack cocaine laws, while more than 66% of crack cocaine users in the United States are white or Hispanic. . . . African Americans serve substantially more time in prison for drug offenses than do whites. The average sentence for a crack cocaine offense in 2003, which was 123 months, was 3.5 years longer than the average sentence of 81 months for an offense involving the powder form of the drug. . . . From 1994 to 2003, the difference between the average time African American offenders served in prison increased by 77%, compared to an increase of 28% for white drug offenders. African Americans now serve virtually as much time in prison for a drug offense at 58.7 months, as whites do for a violent offense at 61.7 months. The fact that African American defendants received the mandatory sentences more often than white defendants who were eligible for a mandatory minimum sentence, further supports the racially discriminatory impact of mandatory minimum penalties. . . .
>
> In 1986, before the enactment of federal mandatory minimum sentencing for crack cocaine offenses, the average federal drug sentence for African Americans was 11% higher than for whites. Four years later, the average federal drug sentence for African Americans was 49% higher. As law enforcement focused its efforts on crack offenses, especially those committed by African Americans, a dramatic shift occurred in the overall incarceration trends for African Americans, relative to the rest of the nation, transforming federal prisons into institutions increasingly dedicated to the African American community.[124]

Studies of individual states reveal similar results (see figure 10.1 on the next page). A study by the Justice Policy Institute found that while 28% of the population of Maryland is black, 68% of all those arrested for drug violations and an astounding 90% of those convicted of a drug charge were black. In Illinois, blacks constituted 90% of all drug admissions, and a black man was 57 times more likely to be sent to prison on drug charges than a white man.[125] The rate of drug offender admissions for black men in individual states ranges from 60 to 1,146 per 100,000 black men; in contrast, the rates for whites range from 6 to 139 per 100,000 white men. Nationwide, the rate of drug admissions to state prison for black men is thirteen times greater than the rate for white men. In ten states black men are sent to state prison on drug charges at rates that are 26 to 57 times greater than those of white men in the same state. "But for the war on drugs, the extent of black incarceration would be significantly lower."[126]

Not only were more African Americans sentenced for drug crimes, but the *severity* of their sentences increased compared to whites. In 2003 the average sentence to federal prison for whites for drug offenses was 67.6 months, compared to 110.5 for blacks.[127] When comparing powder and crack cocaine sentences in the federal system, the discrepancies are enormous. In 2003, African Americans constituted a phenomenal 81% of those sentenced for crack cocaine, compared to 31% of those sentenced for powder cocaine. Hispanics fared even worse for powder cocaine, constituting half of all those sentenced.[128]

Drug offenses accounted for 34% of all felony convictions in state courts in 2004. Males constituted 82% of those convicted of drug charges and females 18%.[129]

> Over the last 20 years, federal and state drug laws and policies have also had a devastating impact on women. In 2003, 58% of all women in federal prison were convicted of drug offenses, compared to 48% of men. The growing number of women who are incarcerated disproportionately impacts African American and Hispanic women. African American women's incarceration rates for all crimes, largely driven by drug convictions, increased by 800% from 1986,

Figure 10.1   Rate of Male Drug Offender Admissions to State Prison by Race

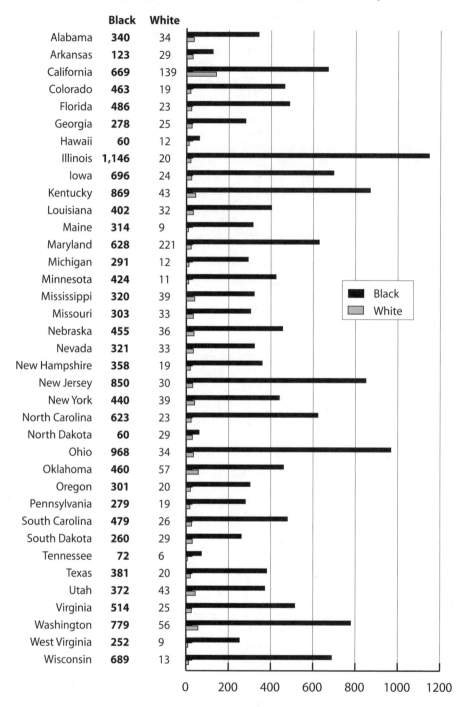

	Black	White
Alabama	340	34
Arkansas	123	29
California	669	139
Colorado	463	19
Florida	486	23
Georgia	278	25
Hawaii	60	12
Illinois	1,146	20
Iowa	696	24
Kentucky	869	43
Louisiana	402	32
Maine	314	9
Maryland	628	221
Michigan	291	12
Minnesota	424	11
Mississippi	320	39
Missouri	303	33
Nebraska	455	36
Nevada	321	33
New Hampshire	358	19
New Jersey	850	30
New York	440	39
North Carolina	623	23
North Dakota	60	29
Ohio	968	34
Oklahoma	460	57
Oregon	301	20
Pennsylvania	279	19
South Carolina	479	26
South Dakota	260	29
Tennessee	72	6
Texas	381	20
Utah	372	43
Virginia	514	25
Washington	779	56
West Virginia	252	9
Wisconsin	689	13

Source: Human Rights Watch. "Incarcerated America." April, 2003. [Online] http://www.hrw.org/backgrounder/usa/incarceration/

compared to an increase of 400% for women of all races for the same period. Sentencing policies, particularly the mandatory minimum for low-level crack offenses, subject women who are low-level participants to the same or harsher sentences as the major dealers in a drug organization.[130]

Social class and race play important roles at the sentencing stage of the criminal justice process (as they do at all stages). The remainder of the chapter considers alternatives to a prison or jail sentence.

ALTERNATIVES TO INCARCERATION

There are a number of alternatives to incarceration that are available to the courts. Keep in mind the fact that the purpose of these alternatives is diversion. *Diversion* is "a planned intervention with a treatment component and the goal of getting offenders out of the criminal justice system as early as possible.[131] This strategy is based on the belief that justice system processing often does more harm than good. The basis of the argument is that courts may inadvertently stigmatize some offenders (especially young offenders) for relatively petty acts that are best handled outside the court system or ignored entirely. Diversion programs are designed, in part, to deal with the problem of overcrowded juvenile detention centers, jails, and prisons, so that greater attention can be devoted to more serious offenders.

Diversion has been practiced since the beginning of the criminal justice system, in that most of the cases processed never make it to jail or prison. Some alternative sentence is usually imposed. The most common alternative has always been probation.

Probation

A sentence of probation suspends an offender's sentence to prison or jail and permits the offender to spend a certain amount of time in the community "under supervision" of the department of probation. If probation is granted, the defendant must meet certain conditions, such as keeping a job and reporting periodically to a probation officer.

The term of probation varies and depends on several factors. After the probationary term ends, the defendant is discharged and the sentence fulfilled. If at any time during the probationary period the defendant violates a law or the conditions of probation, the defendant can be sentenced to the original term in prison.

Suppose the original sentence is one to five years in prison, but the sentence is suspended pending the completion of two years on probation. If the offender successfully completes the two years without committing new crimes and without violating any of the conditions of probation, then the overall sentence is completed and the person is free.

Among the most controversial conditions of probation is urine testing. A national survey found that 27% of the motions to revoke probation were the result of an offender failing a drug test; 20% were for not participating in a required treatment program; 18.5% were for "absconding" (leaving the state or county without permission); 12% for committing a new felony and another 4% for committing a misdemeanor; 10% for "failure to report"; and 8.5% for other technical violations.[132] It should be noted that probation officers have a great deal of discretion about reporting violations. Probation officers range from relatively lenient individuals who view themselves as "social workers" and go out of their way to help offenders to "law and order" types who see themselves as cops and like to brag about the weapons they carry and the number of probation violators they have "nabbed."

Probation has its origins in English common law and is related to the practice known as *benefit of clergy,* which originated in the twelfth century (see chapter 9). Originally, only clergymen could be released under the supervision of the church. Later, the practice was extended to anyone who could prove literacy by reciting from the Bible.

In the United States, the origins of probation can be traced to the efforts of John Augustus, a Boston shoemaker. During the 1840s he volunteered to take on the responsibility of supervising offenders in the community as an alternative to sending them to prison or jail. In 1878, Massachusetts passed a law authorizing the use of probation. By 1917 the probation system was used in twenty-one states. Although probation for juvenile offenders was available in every state by 1925, it was not available to all adults until 1956.

The practice of placing offenders on probation originally was the result of humanitarian concerns. In recent years, however, the growth of the use of probation is often due to monetary concerns. It costs far less to supervise an offender on probation than while incarcerated. For instance, the average cost of probation is around $850 per year per offender, versus between $20,000 and $40,000 to house someone in prison for one year.[133]

The number of offenders placed on probation has increased dramatically since 1980 when the number totaled 1.1 million. In 1998 there were about 3.4 million probationers, and in 2005, there were 4.1 million. The percentage of white probationers was 53% versus 31% black. Of those on probation, 50% had felony convictions; 49% had been convicted of a misdemeanor.[134] No state allows probation as an alternative sentence for first-degree murder, but most states allow probation for almost all other crimes. Several states, however, have a list of crimes for which probation cannot be granted (e.g., Illinois, New York, and California have such lists for several crimes).

Probation officers are often seen as performing the duties of a social worker—they become a "broker" of services. An officer might help an offender get a job, find housing, and obtain various treatment services (e.g., drug treatment). It is common to use a "risk classification" analysis to assess the needs of the probationer and to determine the degree of risk he or she poses to the community. In communities wracked by violence, gangs, drugs, and general urban decay, the probation officer is tempted to remain in his or her office instead of making "house calls." This reluctance may be understandable given the sometimes dangerous conditions, but very often the probation officer is the only person standing between an offender and the temptations to return to crime.

Probation has become highly bureaucratized. Nearly every court system—both adult and juvenile—has a probation department connected to it in some way. Caseloads are large. The average probation officer supervises between 50 and 100 offenders, but sometimes the number reaches 300 or more.[135] Many who engage in this line of work are overwhelmed by the responsibilities and care little about the people they supervise. In fact, the "supervision" is often little more than surveillance consisting of a few phone calls. This approach leads to a high rate of *revocation* of the suspended sentence and incarceration for the original term. Given that there are so many conditions of probation, this outcome is not surprising.

One of the most popular variations of probation is *intensive supervision probation.* During traditional probation, an offender reports to the probation officer once a month or more, depending on the conditions of probation. Intensive supervision probation places many more restrictions on the offender, such as curfews, "house arrest" (staying at home unless going to work or school), electronic monitoring, frequent drug testing, and frequent visits by the probation officer.[136] The higher rate of failure among offenders placed on intensive supervision is rarely because these offenders are more dangerous or more prone to commit crime. The primary reason for the higher rate is that more frequent contact, more frequent drug testing, and more rules and regulations increase the likelihood of "detecting" a violation.[137]

Fines

Fines have been one of the most common forms of punishment throughout history. Fines are usually levied in misdemeanor cases (especially traffic cases) and for white-collar and corporate crimes. Rarely are fines used in felony cases, although the statutes often allow for it as an alternative. Crimes committed by individuals from class backgrounds similar to those who legislate the laws or to the judges who impose sentences are more likely to receive a sentence of a fine. The felonies committed by individuals of other class backgrounds usually result in the incarceration of the offender.[138]

Fines generate well over $1 billion for local governments. A substantial portion is from traffic violations, but fines are also used in combination with other sanctions. About 86% of the cases in lower courts involve fines, compared to 45% of the cases in the upper courts.[139] Fines are used in virtually every country as the preferred sentence. Scandinavian countries and Germany levy fines in about 90% of all cases.[140] Given the punitive nature of the United States, it is not surprising that fines here are often accompanied by a prison or jail sentence.

Restitution and Community Service

Restitution and community service are among the oldest sentences in the history of the criminal justice system. They date as far back as the Code of Hammurabi (around 1760 BC) and are mentioned in the Roman law of the Twelve Tables.[141] The sentences require the offender to do something *for the community*—in many cases this includes for the victims—rather than the community or state doing something *to the offender.* Restitution could be in the form of direct payment to persons victimized by the crime (e.g., the theft of money) or direct service to the community. Community service usually involves some type of work, such as cutting and pruning trees, painting park benches, removing graffiti, and picking up trash. Sometimes offenders with special skills—carpentry, electrical, and so on—work on special projects. Evaluations of this type of sentence generally claim a great deal of success and a high rate of compliance among offenders.[142]

Community service is related to *restorative justice*—an attempt to *restore* what was taken away by the criminal act. The goal is to restore the well-being of the victim and of the larger community while simultaneously seeing that the offender takes responsibility for his or her actions. Sometimes this is done through face-to-face meetings between offenders and their victims. Such a meeting, even in cases involving the murder of a loved one, often brings closure.

Home Confinement/House Arrest

Another alternative to incarceration that shows much promise is *home confinement;* more popularly known as *house arrest* (the popularity of this term reflects the punitive nature of U.S. society). An offender sentenced to a certain period of probation under home confinement must remain at home unless he or she is going to work or school or somewhere very specific. Usually, *electronic surveillance* verifies the conditions are being met. For example, an ankle bracelet may be attached to the offender, which will send a signal if the offender leaves the premises. In other instances, the probation officer activates a special telephone that automatically dials the offender's number at certain times, and the offender must answer within a specified number of rings. Some serious problems are associated with the monitoring devices themselves; some report that an offender is at home when he or she really is away, and vice versa.

Some question the constitutionality of home confinement, saying that it may violate the Fourth Amendment's protection against unreasonable searches and seizures. At the very least, it is at odds with the expectation that a person's home is private. Some critics wonder whether we are moving toward a "maximum-security society."[143] If the goal is to keep offenders away from harmful influences, the program may fail because there are no stipulations that acquaintances (including other offenders) are prohibited from visiting the person's home. If the goal of home confinement is to deter commission of additional crimes, the sentence will do nothing to prevent the offender from committing a crime while in the home (e.g., spouse and child abuse or assaults on visitors). The failure rate has been high for this program.[144]

Drug and Alcohol Treatment

Because so many offenders have serious drug or alcohol problems that bring them into contact with the criminal justice system, one popular alternative sentence is ordering the offender to get treatment. As a condition of probation, for instance, an offender may be ordered to attend AA or NA meetings, in addition to enrollment in special drug or alcohol treatment programs within the community.

A recent trend involves *drug courts,* which oversee court-ordered treatment in a community drug treatment program. The offender is assigned a primary counselor, a specific treatment plan is developed, and frequent appearances in drug court are required to help monitor the offender's progress. Whether this will be successful remains to be seen, especially in light of some research that questions claims of success.

Initial reports about the much-heralded Dade County Circuit Court (Miami) claimed success. Offenders sentenced by the drug court were less likely to be rearrested (or, if rearrested, had longer times between court appearances and rearrest) and were less likely to be incarcerated. Similar findings were reported for the Broward County (Florida) drug court.[145] However, more sophisticated analyses produced different results. Actual participation in drug courts has been rather poor. For instance, only 41% of those eligible for a Washington, DC, program attended. Completion of the program takes much longer than originally anticipated (cases were left open for eleven months, rather than the original goal of six). Further, many people drop out of the program.[146]

The jury is still out on drug courts. Any type of program that keeps offenders with drug problems out of prison is a necessary step, given the almost total lack of drug treatment programs in prison. California voters passed Proposition 36 in 2000; it mandated that in certain instances drug offenders should be sentenced to drug treatment rather than prison. A comprehensive study by the Justice Policy Institute found the following dramatic results:

- The rate of incarceration for adult drug-possession offenses has gone from 89 per 100,000 in December 2000 to 58 per 100,000 in December 2005—a 34.3% decrease.

- While opponents of the initiative warned that Proposition 36 might lead to an increase in violent crime, California's violent crime rate has declined since 2000 at a rate higher than the national average.

- Spending on drug treatment in California doubled since 2000.

- California has experienced a larger increase in drug treatment clients than the rest of the country.

- Proposition 36 and drug court completion rates are comparable.

- The effectiveness of using incarceration to prevent drug use and treatment relapse is not conclusive.

- Proposition 36 is saving the state hundreds of millions of dollars.[147]

Boot Camps

Given the punitive nature of U.S. society and its affinity for military-style discipline, it is not surprising that *boot camps* were seen as an attractive alternative to incarceration in prison or jail. Both law enforcement officials and politicians jumped on the bandwagon in the 1980s, viewing the boot camp as a "magic bullet" that would "shape up" young offenders. By 2000, there were 95 boot camps.[148]

Boot camps were designed for short periods of incarceration (about six months) in a facility separate from a regular prison. The inmates were relatively young, inexperienced, minor offenders. They participated in intense physical, educational, and drug abuse programs, followed by a period of intense supervision within the community. Most of these programs included military drills.[149] The rigor of the camps was popular with the public. Inmates rose early in the morning and adhered to a rigid training regimen led by a drill instructor who instilled discipline and respect for authority. The image reflected society's need to inflict some degree of pain while at the same time developing character and discipline.[150]

The reality had a dark side. Some drill instructors went overboard in their treatment of inmates. Excessive machismo and a population of juveniles who often had committed only misdemeanors was a disastrous combination. There were numerous incidents of verbal and physical abuse in boot camps; the physical abuse sometimes resulted in deaths.[151] One case in Arizona involved a boot camp director who was arrested on murder and child abuse charges following the death of a 14-year-old who collapsed and died in 116-degree heat. Two other boot camp workers were arrested, and one was charged with "spanking, stomping, beating and whipping more than 14 children."[152]

In January 2006, 14-year-old Martin Lee Anderson died one day after guards at a juvenile boot camp in Panama City, Florida, forced him to inhale ammonia. They were videotaped kicking, kneeing, and dragging him around for twenty minutes because he had been uncooperative during an exercise program.[153] Martin, a good student, was sent to boot camp for trespassing at school, a violation of his probation for taking his grandmother's car from a church parking lot. In May 2006 the legislature passed the Martin Lee Anderson Act, which eliminated the five boot camps in Florida.[154]

The Government Accountability Office (GAO) investigated boot camps and wilderness programs and released a report in 2007. Gregory Kutz told the House Committee on Education and Labor, "We found thousands of allegations of abuse, some of which involved death, at public and private residential treatment programs across the country between the years 1990 and 2007."[155] In 2005 alone, 33 states reported 1,619 staff members involved in incidents of abuse in residential programs.

The research on boot camps is clear: they are almost total failures when it comes to reducing crime. There is evidence that offenders do make some improvements *while in the program* (more favorable attitudes compared to those in prisons).[156] The research, however, concludes "Boot camps do not reduce crime."[157] Among the reasons for this lack of success is the fact that up to one-third of offenders never complete the program. Another reason is the tendency of judges to engage in *net widening*—putting extremely low-risk offenders in the program who could just as easily benefit from less rigid sentences.

Another reason why this type of program fails is that it ignores one of the leading principles behind real military boot camps: the promise of a reward at the end. Military boot camps hold out the promise of a career in the military, opportunities to advance in rank, education and training, and other benefits. In contrast, most boot camp graduates are simply released back into the community with few or no employment or educational prospects.

CASE DISPOSITION AND SENTENCING IN PROBLEM-SOLVING COURTS

One of the most critical aspects of problem-solving courts is to develop viable alternatives to incarceration. Risk management is an essential component. In the traditional criminal court context, alternatives to incarceration are usually narrowly defined, punitive sanctions. Even restorative tools such as work crews, restitution payments, or community service are regarded in a punitive context.

Problem-solving courts take a new, holistic approach to the issue of alternatives to incarceration. Judicial demeanor and philosophy are essential to the therapeutic, problem-solving court process. Praise and rewards are to be favored over punishment and partial confinement. One surprise of the problem-solving court experience is the way in which clients respond to the care and concern demonstrated by members of the court team. The assumption that clients wish to please appears accurate and seems, at least in this context, to be a very positive aspect—especially when compared to the common assumption in criminal courts that clients wish to reoffend. Most often, compliance issues can be resolved with an informal discussion, and penalties need not be imposed. When additional requirements are imposed on the client, it is usually in the context of adding structure or support to make it easier for the client to avoid inappropriate behavior. The additional requirements are not issued as punishment.

The idea of taking responsibility can put a positive spin on reasonable restitution requirements, again avoiding a punitive con-notation. Every effort is made to build on a feeling of accomplishment and sense of self-worth, not to destroy it. A telephone call to discuss the client's adjustments may help the client stay on track. Occasionally, a visit to the client's home by several members of the team, including the judge, can make a signif-icant impression.

Special processes are needed for many of the court's clients. Dual diagnosis clients (those with both substance abuse and mental health issues) make up a significant portion of the court's caseload. For these individu-als, it may be necessary to use supervised release processes with random drug or alco-hol testing or, in the alternative, electronic home monitoring with special equipment to detect alcohol use. In addition to encourage-ment and rewards, intermediate sanctions are the tools of the court. In this context, procedures such as alcohol and drug detoxi-fication programs (detox), etc. are not wholly punitive but applied to address a spe-cific transitory issue.

Conceivably, sentences to incarceration and/or involuntary commitment could be used. However, they are so restrictive and costly that they are reserved and imposed only as a last resort, and when safety is an issue. Serious sanctions are employed only in the case of new felonies or an indication that the integrity of the court would be threat-ened by allowing an individual to remain out of custody. When there is poor performance, the court is much more likely to use some of the following sanctions and tools in place of jail or even partial confinement.

- Require more frequent reporting (some-times on a daily basis).

- Impose mandatory activities to eliminate free time, increasing structure and reduc-ing the client's options for poor choices. Stress that freedom of choice comes with responsibility.

- "House calls" by court staff to check up on clients.

- Increased drug and alcohol screening.

- Telephone monitoring or electronic home confinement.

- Active probation—requiring the client to report to the probation officer as well as to the bench.

- Increased restitution payments or restor-ative justice projects.

- Work crew or alternative community ser-vice. (Work projects enhance self-esteem and a feeling of accomplishment, whether part of regular employment or work crew assignments.)

Employment and housing programs are of particular value in offender rehabilitation. The court team focuses on the causes of crim-inal activity and utilizes risk management and sanctions such as those listed above. The spe-cialized court allows a more rapid response and improved application of resources.

SUMMARY

In this chapter we considered the final act in the formal criminal justice process—sentencing. We described various justifica-tions for punishment (retribution, incapacita-tion, deterrence, and rehabilitation) and explained several sentencing options. The ultimate sentence is the death penalty, which, like all other aspects of the criminal justice system, is tinged with racism. The impact of race on sentencing is seen most clearly in the "war on drugs," which most often targets African Americans and other minorities. Various alternatives were ex-plored, including probation, the use of fines, house arrest, drug treatment and the contro-versial boot camps.

Key Terms

- boot camps
- concurrent sentence
- consecutive sentence
- definite sentence
- determinate sentencing
- deterrence
- diversion
- *Furman v. Georgia*
- general deterrence
- *Gregg v. Georgia*

- home confinement
- indefinite sentence
- isolation/incapacitation
- lex talionis
- *McCleskey v. Kemp*
- net widening
- presentence investigation (PSI) report
- rehabilitation
- restitution
- specific deterrence
- wergeld

Notes

1. Shichor, D. *The Meaning and Nature of Punishment.* Long Grove, IL: Waveland Press, 2006.

2. Barnes, H. E. *The Story of Punishment.* Montclair, NJ: Patterson Smith, 1972 [1930], chapter 2; Barnes, H. E. and N. K. Teeters. *New Horizons in Criminology.* Englewood Cliffs, NJ: Prentice-Hall, 1951, pp. 287–288.

3. Wilson, J. Q. *Thinking about Crime.* New York: Vintage Books, 1975; van Den Haag, E. *Punishing Criminals.* New York: Basic Books, 1975; Bennett, W. J., J. J. DiIulio Jr., and J. P. Walters. *Body Count.* New York: Simon & Schuster, 1996.

4. For a discussion of this and related questions, see Shelden, R. G. *Controlling the Dangerous Classes: A Critical Introduction to the History of Criminal Justice.* Boston: Allyn & Bacon, 2001.

5. Neubauer, D. W. *America's Courts and the Criminal Justice System* (8th ed.). Belmont, CA: Wadsworth, 2005, pp. 382–386.

6. Chambliss, W. J. and R. Seidman. *Law, Order and Power* (2nd ed.). Reading, MA: Addison-Wesley, 1982, pp. 447–472.

7. Neubauer, *America's Courts and the Criminal Justice System,* pp. 365–367.

8. These studies cover more than thirty years. See, for instance, Carter, R. M. and L. T. Wilkins. "Some Factors in Sentencing Policy." In R. M. Carter and L. T. Wilkins (eds.), *Probation, Parole and Community Corrections* (2nd ed.). New York: Wiley, 1976; Campbell, C., C. McCoy, and C. Osigweh. "The Influence of Probation Recommendations on Sentencing Decisions and Their Predictive Accuracy." *Federal Probation* 54: 13–21(1990).

9. Brown, W. B. "The Subjective Nature of Decision Makers in the Domain of Objective Sentence Processing." Unpublished doctoral dissertation, University of Nevada–Las Vegas, 1992; see also Rosencrance, J. "Maintaining the Myth of Individualized Justice: Probation Presentence Reports." *Justice Quarterly* 5: 235 (1988).

10. See the Pacific Policy and Research Institute Web site. [Online] http://www.pacpri.com

11. Sachdev, A. "Conrad Black Adds Sentencing Expert to Team." *Chicago Tribune* (July 24, 2007) sec. 3, p. 3.

12. Scheb, J. M. and J. M. Scheb II. *Criminal Law and Procedure.* St. Paul, MN: West, 1989, pp. 544–545.

13. Shichor, *The Meaning and Nature of Punishment.*

14. Walker, S. *Sense and Nonsense about Crime and Drugs* (6th ed.). Belmont, CA: Wadsworth, 2006. The father of Polly Klaas, Marc Klaas, publicly criticized this type of legislation. He formed the nonprofit KlaasKids Foundation, which, among other goals, seeks means of prevention rather than merely harsh reaction. He wrote the foreword to Peter Elikann's critique of the current "demonization" of children as "superpredators" (Elikann, P. *Superpredators: The Demonization of Our Children by the Law.* Reading, MA: Perseus, 1999).

15. Ibid.

16. *Weems v. United States,* 217 U.S. 349 (1910).

17. *Rummel v. Estelle,* 445 U.S. 263 (1980).

18. *Lockyer v. Andrade* (01-1127) 538 U.S. 63 (2003). The case was decided on March 3, 2003. The Court upheld another California third-strike case on the same date, *Ewing v. California,* (01-6978) 538 U.S. 11 (2003).

19. Zimring, F. E. *The Great American Crime Decline.* New York: Oxford University Press, 2007, p. 38.

20. Stolzenberg, L. and S. J. D'Alessio. "Three Strikes and You're Out: The Impact of California's New Mandatory Sentencing Law on Serious Crime Rates." *Crime and Delinquency* 43: 4 (1997); Turner, M. G., J. L. Sundt, B. K. Applegate, and F. T. Cullen. "Three Strikes and You're Out Legislation: A National Assessment." *Federal Probation* 59: 16–35 (1995); Dickey, W. "The Impact of 'Three Strikes and You're Out' Laws: What Have We Learned." *Overcrowded Times* 7(5) (October 1996).

21. Schiraldi, V. and T. Ambrosio. "Striking Out: The Crime Control Impact of Three Strikes Laws." *Justice Policy Institute* (March 1997); Dickey, W. and P. S. Hollenhorst. "Three-Strikes Laws: Massive Impact in California and Georgia, Little Elsewhere." *Overcrowded Times* 9(6) (December 1998); Males, M., D. Macallair, and K. Taqi-Eddin. "California's Three-Strikes Law Ineffective." *Overcrowded Times* 10(4) (August 1999).

22. One example is in the field of education. See Spring, J. *Education and the Rise of the Corporate State.* Boston: Beacon Press, 1972, pp. 95–96. As this relates to the modern police, see Shelden, *Controlling the Dangerous Classes,* chapter 2.

23. Wilkins, L. T., J. M. Kress, D. M. Gottfredson, J. C. Calpin, and A. M. Gelman. *Sentencing Guidelines: Structuring Judicial Discretion.* Washington, DC: U.S. Government Printing Office, 1978; Bureau of Justice Assistance. *National Assessment of Structured Sentencing.* Washington, DC: U.S. Department of Justice, 1996.

24. Petersilia, J. and S. Turner. "Guideline-Based Justice Prediction and Racial Minorities." In N. Morris and M. Tonry (eds.), *Crime and Justice* (vol. 15). Chicago: University of Chicago Press, 1987; Kramer, J. H. and L. Lubitz. "Pennsylvania's Sentencing Reforms: The Impact of Commission-Established Guidelines." *Crime and Delinquency* 31: 481–500 (1985); Tonry, M. "Sen-

tencing Commissions and Their Guidelines." In M. Tonry (ed.), *Crime and Justice: A Review of Research* (vol. 17). Chicago: University of Chicago Press, 1993; Martin, S. E. "The Politics of Sentencing Reform: Sentencing Guidelines in Pennsylvania and Minnesota." In A. Blumstein, J. Cohen, S. Martin, and M. Tonry (eds.), *Research and Sentencing: The Search for Reform* (vol. 2). Washington, DC: National Academy Press, 1983.

[25] United States Sentencing Commission. [Online] http://www.ussc.gov/general/USSCoverview_2005.pdf

[26] Ibid.

[27] 543 U.S. 220, 125 S. Ct. 738 (2005).

[28] *Rita v. United States* (06-5754) June 21, 2007.

[29] [Online] http://www.sentencingproject.org/NewsDetails.aspx?NewsID=440

[30] Lane, C. "Sentencing Guidelines 'Reasonable,' Justices Rule." *Washington Post* (June 22, 2007) p. A02.

[31] Drug War Chronicle. "Sentencing: Supreme Court to Decide Crack Sentencing Case." June 15, 2007. [Online] http://stopthedrugwar.org/chronicle/490/supreme_court_to_decide_crack_sentencing_case

[32] 18 U.S.C.A. § 3553. *U.S. v. Calvillo-Alvarez*, 166 Fed. Appx. 983 (9th Cir. 2006).

[33] Hudson Institute Communications. "Lewis Libby Joins Hudson Institute." Official press release, January 6, 2006.

[34] See history of *United States v. Libby*, Not Reported in F.3d, 2006 WL 3827534 C.A.DC, December 27, 2006.

[35] Statement by the President on Executive Clemency for Lewis Libby. [Online] http://www.whitehouse.gov/news/releases/2007/07/20070702-4.html

[36] Rutenberg, J. and S. Shane. "Libby Pays Fine; Judge Poses Probation Query." *New York Times* (July 6, 2007).

[37] Liptak, A. "Bush Rationale on Libby Stirs Legal Debate." *New York Times* (July 4, 2007).

[38] Liptak, A. "For Libby, Bush Seemed to Alter His Texas Policy." *New York Times* (July 8, 2007). Quotation from Bush, G. W. and K. Hughes, *A Charge to Keep.* New York: William Morrow cited in article.

[39] Ibid.

[40] Collins, P. "Libby Commutation Undermines Sentencing Process." *Chicago Tribune* (July 19, 2007) p. 21.

[41] Rutenberg and Shane "Libby Pays Fine."

[42] [Online] http://www.scooterlibby.com/about/

[43] Rutenberg and Shane, "Libby Pays Fine."

[44] Sudnow, D. "Normal Crimes: Sociological Features of the Penal Code in a Public Defender's Office." *Social Problems* 12 (Winter 1965): 255–276.

[45] Farnworth, M., R. Teske, and G. Thurman. "Ethnic, Racial and Minority Disparity in Felony Court Processing." In M. J. Lynch and E. B. Patterson (eds.), *Race and Criminal Justice.* Albany, NY: Harrow and Heston, 1991.

[46] Durose, M. R. and P. A. Langan. *State Court Sentencing of Convicted Felons, 2002* (NCJ 208910). Washington, DC: Bureau of Justice Statistics, 2005, table 1.2.

[47] Among the sources used here include: Hawkins, D. F. "Which Way toward Equality? Dilemmas and Paradoxes in Public Policies Affecting Crime and Punishment." In C. Herring (ed.), *African Americans and the*

Public Agenda. Thousand Oaks, CA: Sage, 1997; Radelet, M. and G. Pierce. "Race and Prosecutorial Discretion in Homicide Cases." *Law and Society Review* 19: 587–621 (1985); La Free, G. *Rape and Criminal Justice: The Social Construction of Sexual Assault.* Belmont, CA: Wadsworth, 1989; Spohn, C., J. Gruhl, and S. Welch. "The Impact of Ethnicity and Gender of Defendant on the Decision to Reject or Dismiss Felony Charges." *Criminology* 25: 175–191 (1987); D'Alessio, S. J. and L. Stolzenberg. "Socioeconomic Status and Sentencing of the Traditional Offender." *Journal of Criminal Justice* 21: 71–74 (1993); Lauritsen, J. L. and R. J. Sampson. "Minorities, Crime and Criminal Justice." In M. Tonry (ed.), *The Handbook of Crime and Punishment.* New York: Oxford University Press, 1998; Peterson, R. D. and J. Hagan. "Changing Conceptions of Race: Towards an Account of Anomalous Findings of Sentencing Research." *American Sociological Review* 49: 56–70 (1984).

[48] Nienstedt, B. C., M. Zatz, and T. Epperlein. "Court Processing and Sentencing of Drunk Drivers." *Journal of Quantitative Criminology* 4: 39–59 (1988).

[49] Chiricos, T. G. and W. D. Bales. "Unemployment and Punishment: An Empirical Assessment." *Criminology* 29: 701–724 (1991).

[50] Nelson, J. F. "Hidden Disparities in Case Processing: New York State, 1985–1986." *Journal of Criminal Justice* 20: 181–200 (1992).

[51] Crawford, C., T. Chiricos, and G. Kleck. "Race, Racial Threat, and Sentencing of Habitual Offenders." *Criminology* 36: 481–511(1998).

[52] See Chambliss, W. J. "Crime Control and Ethnic Minorities: Legitimizing Racial Oppression by Creating Moral Panics." In D. F. Hawkins (ed.), *Ethnicity, Race, and Crime.* Albany: State University of New York Press, 1995; and *Power, Politics and Crime.* Boulder, CO: Westview Press, 1999, for discussion of this problem.

[53] Death Penalty Information Center. *Executions in the United States 1608–1976.* [Online] http://www.deathpenaltyinfo.org/article.php?scid=8&did=1110

[54] Espy, M. W. and J. O. Smykla. (2004). *Executions in the U.S. 1608–1987: The Espy File.* [Computer file]. 4th ICPSR ed. University of Michigan. Ann Arbor, MI: Inter-university Consortium for Political and Social Research [producer and distributor].

[55] Death Penalty Information Center. *Executions by Year.* [Online] http://www.deathpenaltyinfo.org/article.php?scid=8&did=146

[56] Snell, T. L. *Capital Punishment, 2005.* Washington, DC: Bureau of Justice Statistics, December 2006.

[57] Death Penalty Information Center. *Fact Sheet.* [Online] http://www.deathpenaltyinfo.org/FactSheet.pdf

[58] Death Penalty Information Center. *Death Row Inmates by State.* [Online] http://www.deathpenaltyinfo.org/article.php?scid=9&did=188#state

[59] Bedau, H. A. *The Death Penalty in America: Current Controversies.* New York: Oxford University Press.

[60] Miller, K. *Wrongful Capital Convictions and the Legitimacy of the Death Penalty.* New York: LFB Scholarly Publishing, 2005.

[61] *Furman v. Georgia,* 408 U.S. 238 (1972).

[62] See *Proffit v. Florida*, 428 U.S. 242 (1976); *Jurek v. Texas*, 428 U.S. 262 (1976); *Gregg v. Georgia*, 96 Sup. Ct. 2902 (1976).

[63] Bohm, R. *Deathquest II: An Introduction to the Theory and Practice of Capital Punishment in the United States* (2nd ed.). Cincinnati, OH: Anderson, 2003.

[64] Dieter, R. C. *Innocence and the Death Penalty: The Increasing Danger of Executing the Innocent*. Washington, DC: Death Penalty Information Center, 1997.

[65] *Penry v. Lynaugh*, 492 U.S. 302 (1989).

[66] Radelet, M. L., H. A. Bedau, and C. E. Putnam. *In Spite of Innocence*. Boston: Northeastern University Press, 1992.

[67] Liebman, J. S., J. Fagan, S. Rifkind, and V. West. "A Broken System: Error Rates in Capital Cases, 1973–1995." *The Justice Project*. New York: Columbia University. [Online] www.thejusticeproject.org; Weinstein, H. "Inmate Seeks to Halt Execution for DNA Tests." *Los Angeles Times* (April 28, 2002); and "Md. Governor Calls Halt to Executions." *Los Angeles Times* (May 10, 2002).

[68] Death Penalty Information Center. *Exonerations by State*. [Online] http://www.deathpenaltyinfo.org/article.php?did=412&scid=6#inn-st. For a fascinating story of a man who spent 17 years on death row before being exonerated, see: "The Story of Harold Wilson: Convicted of Triple Murder, Sentenced to Die, Exonerated After 17 Years in Prison." *Democracy Now* (December 20th, 2005). [Online] http://www.democracynow.org/article.pl?sid=05/12/20/1434244.

[69] Miller-Potter, K. S. "Death by Innocence: Wrongful Convictions in Capital Cases." *The Advocate: A Journal of Criminal Justice Education and Research*. 24(6): 21–29 (September 2002).

[70] Unnever, J. D. and F. T. Cullen. "Executing the Innocent and Support for Capital Punishment: Implications for Public Policy." *Criminology and Public Policy*. 4(1) 3–38 (2005).

[71] Frazier, C. E. and E. W. Bock. "Effects of Court Officials on Sentence Severity." *Criminology* 20: 257–272 (1982).

[72] This information was taken from the 1995 Hart Research Poll of police chiefs. Death Penalty Information Center. "Public Opinion about the Death Penalty." [Online] http://www.deathpenaltyinfo.org/article.php?did=209&scid=23

[73] Wolfgang, M. E. and M. Riedel. "Race, Judicial Discretion, and the Death Penalty." *Annals of the American Academy of Political and Social Science*. (May 1973): 119–133.

[74] Death Penalty Information Center. July 2007. "Race of Death Row Inmates Executed Since 1976." [Online] http://www.deathpenaltyinfo.org/article.php?scid=5&did=184

[75] Baldus, D. C., G. Woodworth, and C. A. Pulaski. *Equal Justice and the Death Penalty: A Legal and Empirical Analysis*. Boston: Northeastern University Press, 1990; Gross, S. R. and R. Mauro. *Death and Discrimination: Racial Disparities in Capital Sentencing*. Boston: Northeastern University Press, 1989.

[76] Amnesty International. "Death by Discrimination—The Continuing Role of Race in Capital Cases." April, 2003. [Online] http://web.amnesty.org/library/index/engamr510462003

[77] Paternoster, R. and R. Brame. (2003) *An Empirical Analysis of Maryland's Death Sentencing System with Respect to the Influence of Race and Legal Jurisdiction*. University of Maryland: Department of Criminology.

[78] Death Penalty Information Center. *Maryland Study Finds That Race and Geography Play Key Roles in Death Penalty*. [Online] http://www.deathpenaltyinfo.org/PR-DPICMarylandStudy.pdf

[79] Keil, T. J. and G. F. Vito. "Capriciousness or Fairness? Race and Prosecutorial Decisions to Seek the Death Penalty in Kentucky." *Journal of Ethnicity in Criminal Justice* 4(3): 27–49 (2006).

[80] Death Penalty Information Center. *Race and the Death Penalty*. [Online] http://www.deathpenaltyinfo.org/article.php?did=105&scid=5

[81] Harries, K. and D. Cheatwood. *The Geography of Execution: The Capital Punishment Quagmire in America*. Lanham, MD: Rowman and Littlefield, 1997; International Commission of Jurists. "Administration of the Death Penalty in the United States." *Human Rights Quarterly* 19: 165–213 (1997).

[82] Johnson, G. B. "The Negro and Crime." *The Annals* 217: 93–104 (1941); see also Garfinkel, H. "Research Note on Inter- and Intra-Racial Homicides." *Social Forces* 27: 369–381 (1949).

[83] Wolfgang, M. E., A. Kelly, and H. C. Nolde. "Comparisons of the Executed and the Commuted among Admissions to Death Row." In M. E. Wolfgang, L. Savitz, and N. Johnston (eds.), *The Sociology of Punishment and Correction*. New York: Wiley, 1962.

[84] Johnson, E. H. "Selective Factors in Capital Punishment." *Social Forces* 36: 165–169 (1957).

[85] Wolfgang, M. and M. Riedel. "Race, Judicial Discretion, and the Death Penalty." In W. J. Chambliss (ed.), *Criminal Law in Action*. New York: Wiley, 1975, pp. 371–372.

[86] Barkan, S. B. and S. F. Cohen. "Racial Prejudice and Support for the Death Penalty by Whites." *Journal of Research in Crime and Delinquency* 31: 202–209 (1994).

[87] Radelet, M. L. "Executions of Whites for Crimes against Blacks: Exceptions to the Rule?" *The Sociological Quarterly* 30: 529–544 (1989).

[88] *McCleskey v. Kemp*, 481 U.S. 279 (1987).

[89] Baldus et al., *Equal Justice and the Death Penalty*.

[90] Kennedy, R. *Race, Crime and the Law*. New York: Vintage, 1998, p. 336.

[91] Walker, S., C. Spohn, and M. DeLone. *The Color of Justice: Race, Ethnicity, and Crime in America* (4th ed.). Belmont, CA: Wadsworth, 2007, p. 323.

[92] Cole, D. *No Equal Justice: Race and Class in the American Criminal Justice System*. New York: New Press, 1999, p. 135.

[93] Dieter, R. C. *The Death Penalty in Black and White: Who Lives, Who Dies, Who Decides*. June 1998. [Online] http://www.deathpenaltyinfo.org/article.php?did=539&scid=45

[94] Cole, *No Equal Justice*, p. 135.

95 Ibid., p. 137.

96 Quoted in Kennedy, *Race, Crime and the Law,* p. 346.

97 Bright, S. B. "Counsel for the Poor: The Death Sentence Not for the Worst Crime but for the Worst Lawyer."In H. A. Bedau (ed.), *The Death Penalty in America: Current Controversies.* New York: Oxford University Press, 1997, pp. 275–318; Coyle, M., F. Strasser, and M. Lavelle. "Fatal Defense: Trial and Error in the Nation's Death Belt." *The National Law Journal* 12(40): 30–44 (1990).

98 Bright, "Counsel for the Poor," pp. 275–318.

99 Ibid.

100 NAACP. *Death Row U. S. A.* Winter 2007. [Online] http://www.naacpldf.org/content/pdf/pubs/drusa/DRUSA_Winter_2007.pdf

101 Streib, V. L. "Death Penalty for Female Offenders." *University of Cincinnati Law Review.* 58(3): 874 (April 3, 2007). [Online] http://www.deathpenaltyinfo.org/FemDeathMar2007.pdf

102 Streib, "Death Penalty for Female Offenders," pp. 845–880.

103 Death Penalty Information Center. *Executions by Region.* [Online] http://www.deathpenaltyinfo.org/article.php?scid=8&did=186.

104 Potter, G. W. "Cost, Deterrence, Incapacitation, Brutalization and the Death Penalty: the Scientific Evidence." *The Advocate: A Journal of Criminal Justice Education and Research.* 22(1):24–29 (2000).

105 Marquart, J. W. and J. R. Sorensen. "Institutional and Post-Release Behavior of *Furman*-Commuted Inmates in Texas." *Criminology* 26: 677–693 (1988).

106 Vito, G. F., P. Koester, and D. G. Wilson. "Return of the Dead: An Update on the Status of *Furman*-Commuted Death Row Inmates." In R. M. Bohm (ed.), *The Death Penalty in America: Current Research.* Cincinnati, OH: Anderson, 1991, pp. 89–99.

107 Bailey, W. C. "Disaggregation in Deterrence and Death Penalty Research: The Case of Murder in Chicago." *Journal of Criminal Law and Criminology* 74(3): 827–859 (1983).

108 Thomson, E. "Deterrence versus Brutalization: The Case of Arizona." *Homicide Studies* 1: 110–128 (1997).

109 Bowers, W., G. L. Pierce, and J. F. McDevitt. *Legal Homicide: Death as Punishment in America, 1864–1982.* Boston: Northeastern University Press, 1984.

110 Kingsbury, A. "The Court Puts Death on Hold." *U.S. News & World Report* 143(17): 31 (November 12, 2007).

111 Ibid., p. 32.

112 Durose, M. R. and P. A. Langan. *Felony Sentences in State Courts, 2004* (NCJ 215646). Washington, DC: Bureau of Justice Statistics, July 2007, pp. 2–3; Langan, P. A. and J. M. Brown. *Felony Sentences in State Courts, 1994* (NCJ 163391). Washington, DC: Bureau of Justice Statistics, January 1997, pp. 2, 3.

113 Substance Abuse and Mental Health Services Administration. The survey was called the National Household Survey on Drug Abuse (NHSDA) prior to 2002.

114 Substance Abuse and Mental Health Services Administration. *Results from the 2006 National Survey on Drug Use and Health: National Findings.* (Office of Applied Studies, NSDUH Series H-32, DHHS Publication No. SMA 07-4293). Rockville, MD: Office of Applied Studies, 2006.

115 Cole, D. *No Equal Justice*; Parenti, C. *Lockdown America: Police and Prisons in the Age of Crisis.* New York: Verso, 1999; Miller, J. G. *Search and Destroy: African-American Males in the Criminal Justice System.* Cambridge: Cambridge University Press, 1996.

116 Currie, E. *Crime and Punishment in America.* New York: Metropolitan Books, 1998, pp. 12–13.

117 Source: Human Rights Watch Backgrounder. *Incarcerated America.* April 2003. [Online] http://www.hrw.org/backgrounder/usa/incarceration/

118 McCurdy, J. *Testimony at a United States Sentencing Commission Hearing on Cocaine and Sentencing Policy.* November 2006. [Online] http://www.aclu.org/crimjustice/gen/27357leg20061114.html

119 Gaines, L. K. and P. B. Kraska (eds.). *Drugs, Crime, & Justice* (2nd ed.) Long Grove, IL: Waveland Press, 2003, p. 7.

120 Ibid., p. 8; Congress allowed changes recommended by the sentencing commission to take effect November 1, 2007. Although the mandatory minimums remained, additional penalties were reduced. The changes are expected to lower the average prison term for crack offenders (82% of the offenders are black) to two months short of nine years. The sentence is still almost two years longer than the average sentence for powder cocaine (72% of those offenders are white or Hispanic). The commission was scheduled to meet to decide whether the new guidelines would be retroactive; if decided in the affirmative, about 19,500 inmates could be eligible for release. Rawe, J. "Congress's Bad Drug Habit." *Time* 170(21): 60 (November 19, 2007).

121 Sterling, E. E. *Drug Laws and Snitching: A Primer.* [Online] http://www.pbs.org/wgbh/pages/frontline/shows/snitch/primer/

122 U.S. Sentencing Commission. "Report to Congress—Federal Cocaine Sentencing Policy." [Online] http://www.ussc.gov/r_congress/cocaine2007.pdf

123 Vagins, D. J. and J. McCurdy. *Cracks in the System: Twenty Years of the Unjust Federal Crack Cocaine Law.* New York: American Civil Liberties Union, 2006, p. i. [Online] http://www.aclu.org/pdfs/drugpolicy/cracksinsystem_20061025.pdf

124 McCurdy, *Testimony.*

125 Schiraldi, V. and J. Ziedenberg. *Race and Incarceration in Maryland.* Washington, DC: Justice Policy Institute, 2003, p. 12; Human Rights Watch. *Punishment and Prejudice: Racial Disparities in the War on Drugs.* Part VI: Racially Disproportionate Incarceration of Drug Offenders. 2000. [Online] http://www.hrw.org/reports/2000/usa/

126 Ibid.

127 *Sourcebook on Criminal Justice Statistics, 2003,* Table 5.21.[Online] http://www.albany.edu/sourcebook/pdf/t5212003.pdf

128 *Sourcebook of Criminal Justice Statistics, 2003,* Table 5.39. [Online] http://www.albany.edu/sourcebook/pdf/t539.pdf

[129] Durose and Langan, *Felony Sentences in State Courts, 2004*, pp. 1, 2.

[130] Vagins and McCurdy, *Cracks in the System*, p. 3.

[131] Walker, *Sense and Nonsense about Crime and Drugs*, p. 221.

[132] Burke, P. *Policy-Driven Responses to Probation and Parole Violations*. Washington, DC: National Institute of Corrections, 1997.

[133] Donziger, S. R. *The Real War on Crime: The Report of the National Criminal Justice Commission*. New York: Harper Collins, 1996, p. 190; Austin, J. and J. Irwin. *It's about Time: America's Imprisonment Binge* (3rd ed.). Belmont, CA: Wadsworth, 2001, p. 223.

[134] Glaze, L. E. and T. P. Bonczar. *Probation and Parole in the United States, 2005* (NCJ 215091). Washington, DC: Bureau of Justice Statistics. November 2006.

[135] Petersilia, J. "Probation and Parole." In M. Tonry (ed.), *Handbook of Crime and Punishment*. New York: Oxford University Press.

[136] Gendreau, P., F. T. Cullen, and J. Bonta. "Intensive Rehabilitation Supervision: The Next Generation in Community Corrections?" *Federal Probation* 58: 72–78 (1994).

[137] Petersilia, J. and S. Turner. *Intensive Supervision for High Risk Probationers: Findings from Three California Experiments*. Santa Monica, CA: Rand Corporation, 1990.

[138] For documentation, see Shelden, *Controlling the Dangerous Classes*.

[139] Neubauer, *America's Courts*, pp. 351–352.

[140] Tonry, M. "Intermediate Sanctions." In M. Tonry (ed.), *Crime and Justice* (vol. 20). Chicago: University of Chicago Press, 1996.

[141] Shelden, *Controlling the Dangerous Classes*, chapter 1.

[142] Tonry, M. *Sentencing Matters*. New York: Oxford University Press, 1996.

[143] Marx, G. "*Surveillance and Society.*" In G. Ritzer (ed.), *Encyclopedia of Social Theory*. Thousand Oaks, CA: Sage, 2004. [Online] http://web.mit.edu/gtmarx/www/surandsoc.html

[144] Clear, T. and A. Braga. "Community Corrections." In J. Q. Wilson and J. Petersilia (eds.), *Crime: Public Policies for Crime Control*. San Francisco: ICS Press, 1995, pp. 421–444. For a more general critique of surveillance see Staples, W. G. *The Culture of Surveillance: Discipline and Social Control in the United States*. New York: St. Martin's Press, 1997.

[145] Goldkamp, J. and D. Weiland. "Assessing the Impact of Dade County's Felony Drug Court." *National Institute of Justice Research in Brief*. Washington, DC: U.S.

Department of Justice, December 1993; Terry, W. C. "Felony and Misdemeanor Rearrests of the First Year Cohort of the Drug Court in Broward County, Florida." Paper presented at the American Academy of Criminal Justice Sciences, Las Vegas, 1996.

[146] Harrell, A., S. Cavanagh, and J. Roman. "Evaluation of the DC Superior Court Drug Intervention Program." Washington, DC: National Institute of Justice, 2000.

[147] Ziedenberg, J. and S. Ehlers. "Proposition 36: Five Years Later." Washington, DC: Justice Policy Institute, April 13, 2006. [Online] http://www.justicepolicy.org/downloads/JPI007_Prop_36_LoRes.pdf

[148] Stephan, J. and J. Karberg. *Census of State and Federal Correctional Facilities, 2000* (NCJ 198272). August 2003, p. 12.

[149] Walker, *Sense and Nonsense about Crime and Drugs*, p. 233.

[150] Austin and Irwin, *It's about Time*, p. 167.

[151] St. John, K. "Governor's Costly Boot Camp for Teens: $12 million, 10 Graduates." *San Francisco Chronicle* (June 7, 2002); Parent, D. G. *Correctional Boot Camps: Lessons from a Decade of Research*. Washington, DC: National Institute of Justice, 2003.

[152] "Boot Camp Chief Held in Boy's Death." *Los Angeles Times* (February 16, 2002); see also the following stories: Thompson, D. "Three Disciplined in Suicide of 18-Year-Old at Youth Prison." *San Jose Mercury News* (July 21, 2006); Joyce, B. "A Shocking Form of Therapy." *Boston Globe* (June 19, 2006); Allen, S. "N.Y. Report Denounces Shock Use at School; Says Students Are Living in Fear." *Boston Globe* (June 15, 2006).

[153] Garcia, J. "Eight Indicted in Boot Camp Death." *Chicago Tribune* (November 29, 2006), p. 4.

[154] "Florida Boots Harsh Tactics." *U.S. News and World Report* 140(17): 6 (May 8, 2006).

[155] Government Accountability Office (October 10, 2007). "Residential Treatment Programs: Concerns Regarding Abuse and Death in Certain Programs for Troubled Youth." Statement of Gregory D. Kutz, Managing Director Forensic Audits and Special Investigations, and Andy O'Connell, Assistant Director Forensic Audits and Special Investigations.

[156] Mackenzie, D. L. and J. W Shaw. "Inmate Adjustment and Change during Shock Incarceration: The Impact of Correctional Boot Camp Programs." *Justice Quarterly* 7: 125–150 (1990).

[157] Walker, *Sense and Nonsense about Crime and Drugs*, p. 233.

eleven

Jails
Temporary Housing for the Poor

During the course of a year, around 18 million people are arrested and taken to jail. The U.S. culture has a strong belief in using "edifices," such as jails, to enforce the law through coercion. The vast majority of those who end up in a local jail do not receive a "get out of jail free card" as in game of Monopoly. Most have little or no capital with which to secure their release, matching the saying "those without capital get punishment."

Virtually every large city and small town has at least one jail. Many old jails—dating back to colonial times—have become tourist attractions. The modern jail is a purely local institution (mostly city or county operated). Usually you will find four types of prisoners in jails: (1) those serving short sentences for misdemeanor convictions (normally "public order" crimes like disturbing the peace, drunkenness, vagrancy, loitering, petty theft, or "contempt of court"—often failure to pay traffic fines), (2) those who have been convicted of a felony and are awaiting transfer to a prison, (3) those who are being held temporarily for other jurisdictions (including federal offenders), and (4) those awaiting their final court disposition. The last category accounts for the largest number of jail prisoners. They have not yet been convicted of a crime (although most will eventually plead guilty). They are usually in jail because they cannot afford bail, which is normally a relatively small amount ($500 or so). Jails are the modern-day equivalent of eighteenth and nineteenth century poorhouses, or as one writer has suggested, "the ultimate ghetto of the criminal justice system."[1]

THE HISTORICAL CONTEXT

The modern jail originated in England with the Norman Conquest in the eleventh century. Under Henry II, the jail (the English term is *gaol*) began to take on the characteristics and functions recognizable today. He worked to establish at least one jail under the control of a local sheriff in each county. By the thirteenth century, all but five counties had a jail. It should be noted that the county sheriff was a royal appointment, "a functionary who upheld his master's interests against local powers."[2] The illusion was that localities exerted control, but the power remained with the king. Masking the source of the power was a sophisticated method of social control.

Jails were almost exclusively used to house the poor. In fact, a term often used interchangeably with jail was that of *debtor's prison*. Ironically, the financing of local jails depended on user fees paid to jailers, yet the majority of prisoners were from the poorest classes—the fees adding to their misery.[3]

Corruption was rampant with little effort to correct the problem. Then as now, profit was available because of the existence of crime. The jails of London functioned as "brothels, taps, criminal clubs, and asylums for thieves, robbers, and fraudsmen, and when their raw material—prisoners—threatened to run out, minions would bring false charges to replenish the supply."[4] The well-being of the prisoners was virtually ignored. As a result of their poverty, many either starved to death or died from some disease.[5]

By the middle of the fourteenth century London jails were used as a threat to extract payment from those in debt. Those who had the means paid their debts to avoid being jailed, but those who were unable to pay were imprisoned. Some elected to remain in jail until their death to save their families from harassment, since creditors could not collect while the debtor was in jail.[6] Although the practice of jailing people because of their debts technically ended by the nineteenth century, many still went to jail on the charge of "contempt of court" failure to pay a fine. The charge differed, but the result was the same.

Jails in the American colonies served similar functions. Eventually, they became temporary holding facilities for those awaiting court appearances or those serving short sentences. People who could afford to do so secured their release pending their day in court through the system of bail (see chapter 9). The use of bail dates back to early English society (at least as early as AD 1000) and was originally established to insure that an accused appeared for trial. It was an outgrowth of mutual responsibilities of the collective where groups of ten families (under the control of the "tythingman") worked together to insure obedience to the law.[7] The families, in effect, pledged to ensure that the defendant would appear in court. Crime prevention was a collective responsibility, which was very practical in small, agrarian communities. Such a concept no longer applies in modern societies, characterized by mobility and anonymity. Bail is now a monetary or property pledge, often provided by the defendant's family, relatives, or friends.

Since the earliest history of jails, most of the people confined in them come from the poorest sectors of society.[8]

> No other public institution so well embodies the contradictions among which we live. Certainly symbols and instruments of order and law—to hold a prisoner implies deliberation and process rather than summary disposal—jails have equally been identified with grand and petty tyranny, sadism, corruption, extortion, debauchery, contamination, ruin, and despair. Refuges of last resort, the door from which the mad, sick, destitute, and unwanted could not be turned away, jails have also been, and are, places of terror, degradation, and suffering.[9]

WHO IS IN JAIL?

As of June 30, 2006 there were 766,010 prisoners held in local jails, with an incarceration rate of 256 per 100,000 population, up from 265,010 in 1985, with a rate of 108.[10] The jail incarceration rate for blacks in 2006 was 815, compared to 283 for Hispanics and 170 for whites. This translates to 1 of every 123 blacks in jail; 1 in every 353 Hispanics; and 1 in every 588 whites. The incarceration rate for males (457 per 100,000) was about 7 times the rate for females (66 per 100,000). The percentage of female jail inmates reached 12.9% in 2006. Almost 38% of the people held in jail had been convicted of a crime (32.9% of the men and 5% of the women). That means 62.1% of the people in custody had not been convicted (54.3% of the men and 7.8% of the women.)

Considering that over 14 million persons were arrested in 2005, it is reasonable to assume that the majority of these individuals spent at least a few hours inside a jail. Although about half were released within 24 hours, the number of people who spend at least some time in jail is staggering. Close to 10% of the adult population will spend some time in jail during the course of a year—and an astounding one-third or more of all African-American males will spend some time in jail during the course of a year.[11]

CONDITIONS IN JAILS

The adjectives used to describe contemporary American jails are decidedly unpleasant: degrading, filthy, inhumane, human jungles, to mention only a few. Many commissions have documented appalling conditions over the years, and the media have published journalistic exposés dating back as far as the 1930s.[12] Jails in other countries do not fare much better.[13]

Conditions have improved very little, as evidenced by the number of lawsuits filed on behalf of jail inmates for various unconstitutional conditions and the number of suicides that occur in local jails. In 2002 the suicide rate in local jails was 47 per 100,000 inmates (over 3 times the rate in State prisons). The suicide rate in the 50 largest jail systems (29 per 100,000 inmates) was half the rate in smaller jails (57 per 100,000).[14] In 1999, 412 jurisdictions in 46 states plus the District of Columbia were under some form of court order or consent decree to either limit the population or to improve specific conditions of confinement.[15] Suits have been filed charging overcrowding, inadequate medical and mental health care, inadequate recreational facilities and visitation policies, and sexual harassment and abuse.[16] Other conditions prompting suits involve food services, library services, grievance policies, fire hazards, disciplinary policies, religious policies, search policies, and education, training, and counseling programs.[17]

Conditions have been so bad that jails contracted to house prisoners for other states have been sued and ordered to return the prisoners to their original states. A Human Rights Watch report reveals widespread problems with jail conditions.

> A fourteen-month long Department of Justice investigation of conditions at Nassau County Jail resulted in a scathing report released in September 2000. The report said the jail had an "institutional culture that supports and promotes abuses." The documented abuses included brutal beatings by officers and officers paying inmates to beat other inmates, especially targeting sex offenders.[18]

In Pennsylvania "many local jails are struggling to meet even minimum standards for safety, housing, food quality and medical care."[19]

Gang rapes, suicide, and many other forms of violence are common in many large urban jails. The jail system in Los Angeles, for example, houses 21,000 inmates on any given day.[20] Adequate medical facilities are almost nonexistent, the food is poor, and the living conditions are generally unsanitary. Studies of the effects of jail overcrowding document adverse effects and horrible living conditions in many jails. Physiological effects include increased blood pressure and coronary problems; assaults by inmates and other behavioral problems are numerous. More general problems include lack of recreational and educational opportunities, poor food service, and lack of treatment programs (especially for drugs and alcohol). Problems with the jail staff include disciplinary practices and abuse from officers.[21]

The Los Angeles County jail system has a history of violence. In fact, the state's history was used as an argument before the Supreme Court in *Johnson v. California*. "Prison officials, citing the state's history of bloody race riots in prisons, say the temporary segregation is needed to assess whether a prisoner is a gang member or otherwise dangerous to members of another race."[22] The court ruled in 2005 that California cannot segregate inmates by race except under extraordinary circumstances in which segregation is the only way to maintain inmate safety.[23] In 2006, the state reverted to segregating jail prisoners temporarily.

Two thousand prisoners rioted at the North County Correctional Facility on February 3, 2006, triggering more than two weeks of riots at several facilities that left two inmates dead and more than 100 injured. Reporters remarked that the outbreaks were remarkably similar to violence in the county jails in 1971, 1985, 1996, and 2000.[24] The initial riot was attributed to the stabbing of a Latino prisoner at the main jail in downtown Los Angeles two days earlier. Wayne Tiznor, a black, 45-year-old convicted rapist in jail charged with a parole violation for failing to register as a sex offender, was killed during the riot at North County, during which metal bunks that were not bolted down were hurled and used as weapons. The next day, rioting broke out at Pitchess Detention Center, the building adjacent to North County. The system was placed on full lockdown February 5, which meant no phone privileges, visits, newspapers, televisions, radios, or court appearances.[25]

Prior to the riots, county jail system officials had resorted to using dorm-like living conditions, with "violent inmates living in large, open rooms despite wide agreement nationally that such offenders should be held in cells." As many as 100 prisoners are crowded into these dorms.[26] On February 9, the chief of custody ordered more than 100 prisoners in three dorms at the North Facility to strip naked, and their mattresses were removed for a day. Jail officials claimed the tactics were necessary to stop the fighting, but others viewed the actions as dehumanizing. The independent overseer of the Sheriff's Department commented that he understood privileges being taken away, but "it comes to a different level of basic human rights if you take away clothing and dignity."[27]

On February 13, Sean Anthony Thompson, who had been arrested one week earlier on suspicion of drug possession after he ran a stop sign, died after a fight in his cell at Men's Central Jail. The black, 38-year-old father of 3 was classified as a moderate security risk because he had previous convictions for non-violent felonies. He was attacked and killed while trying to help his 63-year-old black cellmate who was being threatened by 3 younger Latino cellmates who wanted his bunk bed because it had the best light for reading.[28]

Officials cited lack of adequate staff and overcrowding in the jail complex as the primary reasons for the riots.[29] The sheriff remarked that the more you crowd a facility, the more difficult it is to prevent violence. "Overall, Los Angeles County has fewer than 3,000 deputies and civilian assistants to police a jail system with 21,000 inmates a day. Cook County has 2,900 correctional officers for 10,000 inmates. New York has 9,300 officers guarding 14,000 inmates."[30] It is likely to get worse in California; there are predictions of an additional 23,000 prisoners in the next five years.[31] Crimes will continue to be committed, arrests made, and prisoners locked up in county and city jails.

Jail conditions have not changed much over the years. More than 30 years ago Jessica Mitford reported on an experiment involving judges, prosecutors, policemen and women, lawyers, and others who volunteered to spend a day and a night in Washington, DC's Lorton Jail.[32] She found that the usual procedure at entry into the

Women's Detention Center ("reception") included vaginal checks (to look for contraband drugs), heads examined for lice, spraying with Lysol, and other degrading ceremonies. There were many petty rules and regulations (including one against talking too loud), and there were bed checks at odd hours. Infractions of rules resulted in the violator being sent to "adjustment" (a euphemism for "the hole" or "solitary").

Mitford concluded that jails such as Lorton are a

> life of planned, unrelieved inactivity and boredom . . . no overt brutality but plenty of random, largely unintentional cruelty . . . a pervasive sense of helplessness and frustration engulfing not only the inmates but their keepers, themselves trapped in the weird complex of paradoxes that is the prison world.[33]

Mitford discovered that few of the women at Lorton had been charged with serious crimes; the majority having been accused of prostitution and drug offenses. She writes: "Is this not the essence of women's prisons, the punishment of unchaste, unwomanly behavior, a grotesque bow to long-outmoded nineteenth century notions of feminine morality?"[34] One of the judges who participated in the experiment declared: "We wouldn't stand for having the bears in the zoo treated as we treat the men in Lorton."[35]

THE CRIMINALIZATION OF THE MENTALLY ILL

In 2005, 64% of all jail inmates suffered from a mental health problem.[36] The human side of this grim statistic is illustrated all too frequently by the realities of street life in virtually every U.S. city. In one unusually violent incident, a Johns Hopkins professor was assaulted by a homeless man in San Francisco.[37] Ironically, the victim was attending the annual meeting of the American Psychiatric Association (APA), a group involved in the treatment of serious mental illnesses suffered by people like the homeless man who attacked the female professor. He was arrested and held in the county jail on two felony counts of assault and battery. The president-elect of the APA noted, "It seems to be tragically representative of what's happening these days. Those who need psychiatric care don't have it readily available."

The violence exhibited by the homeless man illustrates a trend that began back in the 1970s, at the start of a movement to deinstitutionalize mental patients. Proponents of deinstitutionalization wanted to end what they viewed as the warehousing of mental patients in facilities they believed were essentially dungeons and snake pits. The end result of this movement was the closing of many institutions and the release of mental patients into communities. While many were helped by this move, others have suffered. The dollars that had formerly supported the institutions were to have been diverted to outpatient services, but that happened all too rarely.

Local jails and state prisons now bear the responsibility of managing the problem of the mentally ill, even though they do not have the facilities, training, or resources to do so. The criminal justice system doesn't have a choice; more than half of all jail or prison inmates suffer from mental illness.[38] The homeless man who assaulted the professor had a history of being in the criminal justice system for psychiatric evaluations. During his first court appearance after the assault, it was determined that he could not understand what was going on.

Fiscal crises in virtually every state (brought about in part by increased expenditures on homeland security, the war on terrorism, and the invasion of Iraq) have resulted in severe cutbacks in services for the mentally ill. Communities will eventually pay even higher costs.

> Untreated and lacking access to long-term care, people with mental illnesses often end up with symptoms and behaviors that result in jail time. Cuts in state Medicaid budgets promise to exacerbate these problems. Not only is this shift in funding a blight on our society, it also costs money—a lot of money. Corrections officials, mental health workers, medication, amortization of build-

ings and time spent by police in court all cost more than treating patients appropriately in their community. This doesn't make financial sense, much less humanitarian sense.[39]

One of the few programs in San Francisco, a residential treatment facility, faces a $1.9 million cut, which would result in the loss of 20 of its 36 beds and its entire day treatment program serving 80 people.

In effect, deinstitutionalization has been replaced by the *criminalization of mental illness*, and those who are jailed receive little or no treatment. Reports from virtually every part of the country confirm the seriousness of the problems. For instance, in Lawrence, Kansas, the local jail has been feeling a huge drain on its resources. Undersheriff Kenny Massey stated: "We've become the mental health unit of Douglas County. We deal with a lot of people here who really ought to be dealt with somewhere else. We're not set up for this."[40] When people with mental health problems are released, many have no place to go and end up back in jail. The same situation faces South Bend, Indiana,[41] Mason, Georgia,[42] the jails of the state of Maine,[43] Los Angeles County,[44] and the state of Florida.[45]

THE FUNCTIONS OF JAILS: MANAGING THE "RABBLE" CLASS

The typical jail population has been described variously as "social refuse," "social junk," "riffraff," "social trash," "dregs," and many other, often more degrading, descriptions. After a detailed study of the San Francisco City Jail, John Irwin concluded that most jail prisoners have two essential characteristics: "detachment" and "disrepute." He uses "detachment" in the sense that the prisoners are not very well integrated into mainstream society, with few ties to conventional social networks, perhaps because they have rather unconventional values and beliefs (what comes first—few ties or unconventional values and beliefs—is an interesting debate beyond the scope of the current discussion). Irwin uses the term "disrepute" to mean that prisoners are offensive, irksome, often threatening, and perhaps dirty, smelly, and lacking social graces. Irwin uses the term "*rabble*" to designate the disorganized, disorderly, "lowest class of people."[46]

Irwin concludes that the characteristics of detachment and disrepute are larger factors in decisions by the police to arrest than are the crimes committed. The jail functions as a means of managing this rabble class. In this sense, the jail is a subsidiary of a much larger welfare system that regulates the poor.[47] The most serious offenders of this class—those who commit serious violent and property crimes—are eventually sent to prison. Although not all of the people in jail are *only* detached and disreputable, the jail still serves the overall purpose of managing people characterized by such traits.

Irwin's study parallels a study by Miller in Jacksonville, Florida.[48] In both locations, the majority of the offenses committed by jail prisoners were rather petty in nature. Irwin conducted extensive interviews with many of the prisoners and classified them according to the degree of seriousness of the charges against them and the degree of offensiveness they displayed. In general, using a seriousness scale devised by several prominent criminologists,[49] Irwin determined that only a very small percentage of crimes could be categorized as serious (around 4%), while the vast majority he classified as petty (scoring from 0 to 5 on a seriousness scale that goes as high as 35.7). Three was the average seriousness score from Irwin's sample.[50]

Irwin then classified the prisoners according to one of several types, the most common of which were what he termed "petty hustlers" (29% of his sample). This type was followed in frequency by "derelicts" and "corner boys" (each at 14%, for a total of 28%); followed by "aliens" (9%), "junkies," "gays," and "square johns" (each constituting 6%); and "outlaws" (really serious types, 4%), "lowriders" (4%), and "crazies" (4%). Most of these individuals (57%) represented a mild degree of offensiveness and committed mostly petty crimes.[51]

Clearly, most jail prisoners do not fit the popular image of the dangerous felon so often portrayed in both the media and by politicians. The authors have observed local campaigns to expand jail capacities and even build more jails based on such misconceptions, advanced by those with vested interests in building new jails. Research by two of the authors (RGS and WBB) on the county jail in Las Vegas clearly dispels these myths.[52] Moreover, data supplied by local jail officials reveal that most people jailed will be released within two to three days. This suggests that they were not that dangerous to begin with.

MANAGING FAMILIES, MENTALLY ILL, AND METHAMPHETAMINE USERS IN JAIL[53]

Participant action research guided the gathering of the information presented in this section. The story below is one of many that surfaced during one-on-one interviews and focus groups conducted at the Marion County Jail (Oregon). Each story is unique, but common threads connect many of the stories. Identifying those common threads is crucial to developing an understanding of the *methamphetamine* abuse problem and its effect on jails. Surveys, which are snapshots of time, can provide us with clues to a puzzle. One-on-one interviews and focus groups corroborate those clues and sometimes open previously concealed doors that contain solutions to the problems we want to solve.

She lives in a tree house overlooking a cemetery in Woodburn, Oregon. She is in her late 30s—although she looks much older—and admits that she likes and uses methamphetamine. She built the tree house from scrap material that she scavenged from nearby construction sites. "Somebody tears it down every time I get arrested," she said. "Then I got to build it all over again when I get out." She was one of more than 200 inmates who participated in the interview-focus group segment of the research project conducted at the Marion County Jail. She was in jail for theft and drug violations, has previously spent over 2 years in prison, and revealed that her mother and father had both spent time in prison. She has two children—somewhere, but has not seen them for several years—one might be with the father, she just does not know. She does not want to talk about her children—"it hurts too much." "I've been clean for over three weeks now," she said, referring to her most recent time in jail. "I'm getting my meds, but I won't get any more when I get out." Previously diagnosed with mental illness, she does not receive any assistance from the state—including medication. "The Sheriff gives me my meds, but first I have to get arrested for him to do that," she said. This inmate states that she has been in jail more than 50 times in her life. Outside of jail, she self-medicates with methamphetamine.[54]

Identifying the Problem of Methamphetamine Abuse

Although methamphetamine abuse has many common features, its principal attribute rests in its *complexity*. People, as a rule, do not wake up one morning, reject their productive lifestyles, and proclaim their commitment to methamphetamine abuse. People turn to methamphetamine for many reasons that are often interrelated. The effect of methamphetamine abuse on the community is contingent on multiple factors, including the number of users and the amount of methamphetamine available. The effects of methamphetamine abuse on jails also depend on a number of factors. How many methamphetamine "tweakers" (individuals who have been constantly high on methamphetamine for several days or more) are processed through the jail each week? If the daily count increases along with the number of methamphetamine users in the community, the jail will feel the crunch of methamphetamine abuse. There are no easy solutions to the methamphetamine abuse problem, but one thing is certain—we cannot arrest our way out of this problem. County law enforcement officials in 44 states say methamphetamine abuse is their number one drug problem.[55]

Methamphetamine: Yesterday and Today

The media has published a number of stories about manufacturing, distribution, sales, and use of methamphetamine over the past few years. In fact, the *New York Times* has published over 300 articles related to methamphetamine since 2001.[56] Some articles portray methamphetamine as a national catastrophe;[57] others allege that it is a regional problem.[58] These articles rarely, if ever, address the true legacy of methamphetamine.

Methamphetamine's legacy does not begin with the mom-and-pop illicit drug labs of the 1990s. The legacy began in Europe, in 1887, when Germany first synthesized amphetamine. By the mid 1920s amphetamine became a substitute for ephedrine, a popular drug for weight loss. It increased energy, enhanced athletic performance, and was useful for the treatment of asthma.[59] In 1932, Benzedrine (amphetamine) became a principal ingredient for nose inhalers, and by 1935, it was available in pill form through prescriptions. Amphetamine was popular on both sides of the battlefield during World War II. By 1951, federal law required prescriptions for all products containing amphetamine. The first over-the-counter methamphetamine inhaler hit the market in 1960, and doctors wrote 31 million prescriptions for amphetamine products (mostly for women) in 1967. Pharmaceutical companies produced over 10 billion legal amphetamine and/or methamphetamine tablets in 1970. Ice, a very addictive and potent form of methamphetamine, appeared in the 1980s. Clandestine methamphetamine labs surfaced in many rural communities in the 1990s.

In recent years, much of the methamphetamine in the United States is imported. "Oregon is a transshipment point for controlled substances smuggled to Washington and Canada."[60] Mexican methamphetamine and local producers are the two primary varieties of methamphetamine in Oregon, and methamphetamine is the most abused controlled substance in the state.

PUBLIC EXPECTATIONS: DO MORE WITH LESS

Local jail populations throughout the United States increased 3.8% annually from 1995 to 2006; the number of persons held in local jails increased from 507,044 in 1995 to 766,101 in 2006.[61] The budgets of communities need to increase to accommodate the increased numbers, or policies must be changed (i.e., more people released because facilities are overcrowded). Increased numbers mean increased administrative duties and more operating costs, often when there have been significant reductions in available resources. As a very basic example, people confined in jail cannot work. Less money earned means less taxes paid, plus the expense of housing, feeding, and monitoring the person in jail.

Public expectations about safety rarely change with the needs of the budget. One possible solution to the impasse of public expectations and limited resources is to prioritize and channel available resources to target multiple problems simultaneously. Many problems have similar contributing factors; strategies can be designed to address multiple issues. The Marion County Sheriff's Office recently targeted the combined problems of methamphetamine abuse and parents who are in jail.

THE MARION COUNTY JAIL IN SALEM, OREGON

The Marion County Jail in Salem, Oregon,[62] processes about 20,000 prisoners per year, of which 11,000–12,000 are new prisoners and 8,000–9,000 prisoners are repeaters or recidivists.[63] Survey data found that more than 73% of all participating prisoners were parents, and 75% of those parents used methamphetamine. Over the course of one year, parents incarcerated in the Marion County Jail will affect approximately 16,000–18,000 children. Thousands of children with parents in a county jail require some form of placement. The cost of keeping someone in jail plus the cost of keeping his or her children in foster care is significant,

and without examining and responding to the causes of methamphetamine abuse, that costs will continue increasing. Figure 11.1 illustrates the causal factors associated with methamphetamine abuse.

Figure 11.1 Factors Contributing to Methamphetamine Abuse

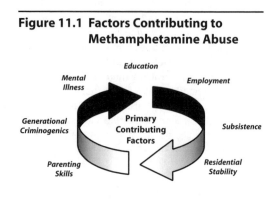

Jail Inmates

> "The first time I tried meth, I think I was about ten," a 22-year-old male inmate said. "My mom had been tweaking for a while, and I ran across some of her stash in a bedroom dresser. I had smoked some weed and drank a few beers by that time—so I wasn't worried about the outcome.... Since the first time I tried meth I have been in and out of jail so many times I wouldn't know how to guess. Once I start tweaking I just keep going till I crash. Crashing is the only way I know how to stop for a while—crashing and getting locked up. Right now, I'm cool. I been clean for several weeks now, but when I get out I am going back—I don't know how to stop cold. Treatment might help, but there is not treatment around here for me."[64]

Of the 442 jail inmates who participated in the study, 358 were male and 84 were female. The ethnicities of the participants were: African American (6.1%), American Indian (7.9%), Latino/Hispanic (26.9%), White (56.6%), and other ethnic groups (2.5%). The percentage of most ethnic/racial minorities incarcerated in Marion County Jail is disproportionate to their representation in the general population (see table 11.1).

Table 11.1 Racial Distribution of Jail Inmates in Marion County and the US[65]

Race/ Ethnicity	Marion Co. Jail	Marion County	United States
African American	6.1%	0.4%	12.8%
Native American	7.9%	0.6%	0.1%
Latino/Hispanic	26.9%	22.9%	14.5%
White (Not Hispanic)	56.6%	72.6%	66.8%
Other	2.5%	3.5%	5.8%

Table 11.2 Inmate Race/Ethnicity and Employment/Unemployment Prior to Their Current Incarceration

Race/ Ethnicity	Employed Prior to Incarceration %	Unemployed Prior to Incarceration %
African American	62.9	37.1
American Indian	57.1	42.9
Latino/Hispanic	73.9	26.1
White	64.8	35.2
Other	63.6	36.4

Inmate participant ages range from 16 to over 58 years, with a median age of 29 years. Over 22% of the participating inmates are married, 52% are single, and 26% are either divorced or separated. More than 80% of the general population over 25 years of age in Marion County have high school diplomas,[66] but only 34.9% of the inmates surveyed 25 years and older have high school diplomas. Only 37% of the male and 20% of the female inmates have high school diplomas. Many female participants who did not complete high school said they quit school because of early pregnancies. Most male participants who did not have high school diplomas said they quit school out of boredom, lack of interest, getting into trouble, or because their parents moved so frequently.

Most inmates (66.5%) had legitimate jobs immediately before their recent arrest; 38.1% of those inmates earned $1,000 or less per month, and 76.3% earned $1,500 or less per month. Most participants (64.7%) said they never had a job with employer-paid benefits. Native American inmates had the highest prearrest unemployment rates, and Latino/Hispanic inmates had the lowest prearrest unemployment rates (see table 11.2). Latino/Hispanic inmates were least likely among all racial/ethnic groups to have ever had employer paid benefits.

More than 25% of inmate participants indicated they had been in jail 10 or more times, and over 40% said they had been in prison. More than 25% did not have a place to live after their release from jail. Almost 60% of the participants said they had been homeless at some time in their lives. About 35% of

the respondents indicated they had previously received a diagnosis of a mental health problem. Nearly 10% of the participants indicated they had served in the military; over 85% had received an honorable discharge.

Over 74% of the inmates answered yes when asked if they had ever used methamphetamines: more than 70% of the males and 89% of the females. Of the parents in jail, 72% of the fathers and 94% of the mothers had used methamphetamines. Research suggests methamphetamine abuse is on the increase by females of childbearing age.[67] Nearly 40% of the participants indicated they were in jail because of their involvement with methamphetamines (36% of the males and 55% of the females). For inmates under 55 years of age, the percentages of methamphetamine users ranged from 65% of the males in the 23–30 age bracket to 100% of females in the 39–46 age bracket. Female use of methamphetamines, and the relationship of their current offense to methamphetamines, was equal to or greater than males in all age groups except for those in the 47–54 category (63% men; 50% women).

Over 86% of white inmates report using methamphetamines compared to 80% of Native Americans, 70.3% of African Americans, 52% of Latinos, and 60% of all other ethnic/racial group inmates. More than 45% of white and 45.7% of Native American inmate participants are currently in jail because of their involvement with methamphetamines, compared to 29.6% of African

Americans, 26.1% of Latinos, and 40% of other ethnic/racial groups.

Five Interrelated Factors

Education, employment, subsistence, residential stability, and mental illness are the five interrelated factors that have the strongest effect on individual behavior and life outcomes for the largest number of people.

> "I was arrested on my way home from work. I was supposed to see my Probation Officer on a Wednesday," explained the male inmate who was in his late 30s. "I had a choice. I could go see my P.O. and lose my job, or go to work and keep my job. I thought the P.O. would be happy with my choice." Elaborating on the events leading up to his recent arrest during a focus group session, the inmate said, "I have been around meth for quite a while. I have managed to stay off meth for over a year now after I got out of the joint. It is hard getting a job when you have a bunch of meth-related arrests hanging in the closet. I finally managed to get a job cutting Christmas trees. It paid good money and I thought I was going to have extra money to spend on my kids for Christmas. If I had told my boss that I had to go and report to my P.O., he would have told me good-bye and replaced me. Well, I have no money now for Christmas, and all I have to give my kids now is a court date. Even if they do not send me back to prison, it is going to be very hard to find a job in the winter to help support my kids. I don't even have a place to live now."[68]

Education and Employment

Over 65% of the jail inmate participants did not have a high school diploma, and more than 21% had a 9th grade or less level of education. The survey of the Marion County Jail inmates found that although education is a critical key to success, employment had a greater influence on methamphetamine use. Employed participants were less likely to use methamphetamines.

Subsistence

Subsistence is the umbrella term for the amount of money required for a person to survive; it includes food, clothing, and shelter. Most of the jail participants were at or beneath the poverty line established by the U.S. Department of Health and Human Services.[69] When we direct our attention to participants who were working mothers or fathers prior to their incarceration, 41% of the fathers and 52% of the mothers earned $1,000 or less per month, and 75% of the working fathers and 82% of the working mothers earned $1,500 or less per month.

Residential Stability

About 50% of the jail participants indicated they lived at their residence one year or less before their current incarceration. Females appear to have less residential stability than males. For instance, 31% of females, compared to 24% males lived at their residence less than six months before their most recent arrest. For mothers and fathers, the data show that 34% of mothers and 27% of the fathers lived at their residence less than six months before their current incarceration. One hundred and thirty-one (30%) participants report living at a residence between one to five years prior to the arrest that resulted in their current incarceration. More than 70% reported living in Oregon for ten or more years. Nearly 80% are residents of Marion County, and more than 90% of the respondents have other family members who live in Oregon.

Mental Illness

One hundred and twenty (27%) jail participants indicated they had applied for mental health services, 153 (35%) had been diagnosed with a mental illness condition, and 130 (29%) had received mental health services (although 37% had applied for social services).

More than 30% of male inmates and nearly 54% of females have had a formal mental illness diagnosis. Almost 40% of those who used methamphetamines and less than 20% of those who did not said they

> "I am a victim of chronic depression. The state diagnosed me with chronic depression years ago. My sister drowned—I was supposed to be watching her. I failed. I have no family. Well I do have a family but they have long since distanced themselves from me . . . I used to be on Oregon Health Plan. Now I am on the Marion Street Bridge Plan—methamphetamine at bargain basement prices."[70]

have had a diagnosis of mental illness. Of the male methamphetamine users, 34% had received a mental illness diagnosis, compared to 59% of the female users. Over 28% of participants who are fathers and nearly 57% of participants who are mothers indicate they have a mental illness diagnosis.

Incarcerated Parents in Jail and Methamphetamine Abuse

> "I love my children, but I am a horrible parent," cried the mother who is waiting for a court appearance that is likely to result in a prison sentence. "I got pregnant when I was 15 years old. I should have gotten an abortion but my mom and dad told me I couldn't. I knew I was not ready to be a parent. Now I have three kids. I will probably never see them again. I am going to prison and that is that. All my boyfriends—my babies' fathers—did meth. I was using meth when I first got pregnant. I didn't know how to stop. I don't know how to stop now. Prison will slow me down, but I will probably be looking for meth the day I get out." After several minutes of crying, the mother wiped away her tears and said, "At night, when I am trying to go to sleep I think about my kids. When I wake up I have the taste of meth in my mouth."[71]

There were 257 fathers and 67 mothers in the Marion County Jail. About 25% of these *incarcerated parents* were married, 30% were divorced or separated, and 44% were single. On average, each incarcerated parent had 2.38 children. Children of incarcerated parents are five times more likely to enter the criminal justice system compared to children without incarcerated parents, and 10% of children with incarcerated parents are more likely to experience incarceration before they reach adulthood.[72] We know that parental and family stability are essential for successful life-outcomes for children. Children who live in families with stable parental relationships, where the family has residential stability and gainful employment opportunities, are less likely to become statistics in the juvenile or criminal justice system.[73] Most parents in this study demonstrate behavioral patterns characteristic of fragile parental and family relationships, residential instability, employment histories that place them in or near poverty status, mental illness, and/or chronic episodes of recidivism.

Nearly one-half of the parents, including 49% of fathers and 51% of mothers, lived at their residence less than 12 months preceding their most recent arrest. When asked if they had a place to live following release from jail, 25% of the parents said no (22% of the fathers and 35% of the mothers). During interviews and focus groups, many fathers and mothers indicate they have experienced evictions due to job loss or inability to secure employment. Many indicate that their criminal records, particularly if that record includes involvement with methamphetamine, prohibit them from getting a job and/or a place to live. As one parent pointed out, "A misdemeanor that involves methamphetamines can be a life sentence."[74]

Twenty-five percent of the fathers in jail and nearly 60% of the mothers were unemployed immediately preceding their current arrest. Of those who had jobs, 38% earned less than $1,000 per month, and 77% earned less than $1,500 per month. Only 35% of the participating parents report having ever had a job with employer-paid benefits, which includes 40% of fathers and 18% of mothers.

Throughout the interviews conducted during this study, participants consistently stated that the lack of housing, limited or no access to prescribed medications, and inadequate mental illness assistance contributed to their problems of staying out of jail. The alternative of self-medicating, through the use of illegal substances, contributed to a sense of hopelessness—and the demonstrated risk of being jailed. Parents who use methamphetamines (58% of fathers and 50% of mothers) are more likely to have been in jail six or more times compared to parents who have not used methamphetamines (30.5% of fathers and 25% of mothers).

Generational Criminogenics

One-half of all jail participants stated that their fathers had been in jail; 18% of mothers had also been in jail. The percentage of fathers of the jail participants who had spent time in prison was 27% compared to 5% for their mothers. Parental criminal histories were fairly similar for male participants and for female participants, except for the category of mothers of the participants who had served time in jail. Of the female participants in jail, 30% had mothers who had also been in jail, versus 15% of the male participants. The rates reported for sibling incarceration were similar to those for parents. An average of 40% of those incarcerated in jail reported people in their father and mother's family who had been incarcerated.

Responding to Methamphetamine Abuse

The Marion County Sheriff, Raul Ramirez, has declared "We cannot arrest our way out of the methamphetamine problem. The survey of the prisoners in Marion County jail contributed to an experimental project. The vast majority of programs (when they exist) designed to help the children of incarcerated parents focus on prisons. The Marion County Children of Incarcerated Parents Initiative (CIPI) focuses on the jail.

Jail management and staff personnel are *first responders* in the world of corrections. Immediately following an arrest, the suspect is processed into the jail. The character, behavior, and history of the suspect are often not very well known. However, after conviction and transport to prison, those characteristics are more transparent. This transparency accommodates a more informed classification and needs assessment. State prisons receive most of their operating funds from the state budget. County jails receive most of

their funding from county budgets. The state disperses prisoners throughout its jurisdiction. Counties tend to keep their prisoners within local jurisdictional boundaries. Prison officials know that prisoners will have sentences of at least one year. Jail officials *know* they *do not know* how long they will be responsible for most of their prisoners. Confinement in jail can range from hours to months. Therefore, information becomes a crucial ingredient for both management of the people in custody and for program development for county jails. The information collected at intake facilitates the supervision of prisoners, the development of programs to prepare prisoners for re-entry into society, and the promotion of public safety and fiscal responsibility. Any community where parents are confined in jail, the mentally ill do not have access to services, affordable housing is in short supply, and employment opportunities are limited can benefit from designing a strategy to identify common problems and to seek solutions.

Outcomes

Research data provide a starting point. It is very difficult to determine how far you have driven if you had no knowledge what the odometer reading was before you started. A few of the Marion County Sheriff's Office outcomes include:

- Public awareness of the problems associated with methamphetamine abuse and incarcerated parents

- Strong community collaboration networks with much support for the Marion County Sheriff's Office

- New child-friendly visitation accommodations implemented at the Marion County Jail

- The continuation of parenting classes at the Marion County Jail

- Development of Project Backpack—sponsored by the Center on Juvenile and Criminal Justice at Western Oregon University, with a goal to provide backpacks with basic provisions to all indigent prisoners released from Marion County Jail

• A \$400,000+ grant for Methamphetamine Treatment awarded to the Marion County Sheriff's Office.

> "I am so happy that I was able to have a parent mentor to assist me as I went through the parent training classes at the work center," said one inmate who had just graduated from the parent training classes offered at the Marion County Jail. Continuing, she added, "I was so surprised that anyone would take an interest in me and my future and not want to take advantage of my vulnerability."[75]

After reviewing the Marion County Children of Incarcerated Parents Program and the Methamphetamine Initiative (see chapter 7), Darlene Hooley, a member of the House of Representatives, remarked, "What you have done in the sheriff's department is a huge paradigm shift. . . . Your willingness to rely on research and science so we can duplicate this is tremendous. . . . We need to find some additional money for this program because it works."[76]

Strategy Development

Complex causes of crises in criminal justice require complex systems solutions. Interrupting the revolving door between jails/prisons and communities is the key starting point. Justice investments that focus on repairing the root causes and resulting harms of the many civil and institutional failures that make young people and adults vulnerable to unlawful activity, criminalization, and incarceration will produce the most favorable outcomes. Methamphetamine abuse and incarcerated parents in jail are two examples that exhaust huge amounts of resources from public safety agencies and other local community institutions in many jurisdictions. Framing and prioritizing these problems is a community responsibility.

The jail survey was a viable starting point in Marion County. The data helped articulate the problems to be addressed. An inventory of problems and causal factors associated with them is a critical tool to educate the public. The next step is to convince organizations to work together. Many institutions are reluctant to commit scarce resources for issues or problems they view as outside their own domain. Community collaboration is crucial to the development of bipartisan agreement among elected officials and justice professionals. In many instances, it is the sheriff who must demonstrate the relationships of problems to various institutions and persuade them to assist in a fundamental restructuring of priorities to address crises in criminal justice. Growth in justice system spending has outstripped community investment in education, healthcare, and other community infrastructures. Community partnerships must emerge to identify and target common goals that further the interests of the entire community.

Summary

Perhaps the most telling characteristic of jails is that 62% of the people in custody are convicted of a crime. Throughout history, most of the people confined in jails have been poor. If people cannot afford bail, they lose their liberty before having been tried for the crimes of which they are accused. Historically, one of the major functions of jails has been the containment of what are often called the "rabble" class. Jails have become, in effect, a subsidiary of a much larger welfare system that regulates the poor. Jails represent the "ultimate ghetto of the criminal justice system."

The conditions of most jails are so bad that in dozens of jurisdictions across the country there are court orders to address the problem. In some instances, for example the Marion County Jail example in this chapter, officials (e.g. sheriffs) take it upon themselves to initiate changes.

Today, jails often function to manage the mentally ill and drug addicts, especially those engaged in heavy use of meth. As a case study of this issue, we took an extended look at the Marion County Jail. The characteristics of the population in that jail illustrate the populations in jails across the country. Alarmingly, racial overrepresentation of minorities in jail is common in jail populations. There is an urgency to develop programs to stop the revolving door in and out of the criminal justice system. Failure to do so will insure that the numbers of people in custody will continue to increase at a huge cost to taxpayers. We urge the use of scientific research coupled with community collaboration and participation to monitor and institute needed philosophical and policy changes in U.S. jails.

Key Terms

- criminalization of mental illness
- debtor's prison
- gaol
- incarcerated parents
- *Johnson v. California*
- methamphetamine
- rabble

Notes

[1] Goldfarb, R. *Jails: The Ultimate Ghetto of the Criminal Justice System.* New York: Doubleday, 1975; see also his book called *Ransom: A Critique of the American Bail System.* New York: Harper & Row, 1965.

[2] McConville, S. "Local Justice: The Jail." In N. Morris and D. J. Rothman (eds.), *The Oxford History of the Prison: The Practice of Punishment in Western Society.* New York: Oxford University Press, p. 299.

[3] Ibid., p. 300.

[4] Ibid., p. 301.

[5] Ibid., pp. 269–270.

[6] Ibid., pp. 302–303.

[7] Ibid., p. 311.

[8] See Shelden, R. G. *Controlling the Dangerous Classes: A Critical Introduction to the History of Criminal Justice.* Boston: Allyn & Bacon, 2001.

[9] McConville, "Local Justice," p. 297.

[10] Sabol, W. J., T. D. Minton, and P. M. Harrison. *Prison and Jail Inmates at Midyear 2006.* Washington, DC: Bureau of Justice Statistics, June 2007, p. 6; Gilliard, D. K. and A. J. Beck. *Prison and Jail Inmates at Midyear 1997.* Washington, DC: Bureau of Justice Statistics, January 1998, p. 6.

[11] Miller, J. G. *Search and Destroy: African American Males in the Criminal Justice System.* Cambridge University Press, 1996; Mauer, M. *Race to Incarcerate* (2nd ed.). New York: The New Press, 2006.

[12] President's Commission on Law and Administration of Justice. *Task Force Report: Corrections.* Washington, DC: U.S. Government Printing Office, 1967; U.S. National Commission on Law Observance and Enforcement (Wickersham Commission). *Reports.* Washington, DC: U.S. Government Printing Office, 1931. More recent reports/articles include: Joint Legislative Audit Review

Committee. "Oversight of Health and Safety Conditions in Local Jails." Richmond, VA. October 1994. [Online] http://leg1.state.va.us/cgi-bin/legp504.exe? 011+ful+SJ440E; "Prisons: Conditions Severe Even for Jails." *The Oregonian* (December 10, 2000). [Online] http://www.oregonlive.com/ins/index.ssf?/special/ current/ins/in_12sside10.frame

[13] Prison Reform Trust. *Prison Factfile.* London. [Online] http://news.bbc.co.uk/1/shared/bsp/hi/pdfs/03_ 04_06_prisons.pdf; National Union of Public and General Employees. "Ontario Judge Opens Hearing Into Inhuman Ottawa Jail." [Online] http://www. nupge.ca/news_2004/n04no04a.htm

[14] Mumola, C. J. *Suicide and Homicide in State Prisons and Local Jails* (NCJ 210036). Washington, DC: Bureau of Justice Statistics, August 2005, p. 1.

[15] Stephan, J. J. *Census of Jails, 1999.* Washington, DC: Bureau of Justice Statistics, August 2001, p. 16.

[16] Bronstein, A. J. and J. Gainsborough. "Prison Litigation: Past, Present, and Future." *Overcrowded Times* 7:3 (June 1996); Stojkovic, S. and J. Klofas. "Crowding and Correctional Change." In T. Alleman and R. L. Gido (eds.), *Turnstile Justice: Issues in American Corrections.* Englewood Cliffs, NJ: Prentice-Hall, 1998.

[17] The following are a sampling of the local jails under court order or consent decrees. [Online] State of Alabama, http://www.schr.org/news/docs/lloyd_v._ aladoc.pdf; Decatur, Illinois, http://www.schr.org/ prisonsjails/news/Morgan/news_morgan. decatur.02.htm; State of Texas, http://www.law. cornell.edu/supct/html/02-628.ZO.html; Baltimore, http://www.publicjustice.org/pdf/040826DUVDR.pdf; State of Ohio, http://www.drc.state.oh.us/web/2003% 20THF%20Guidelines.pdf

[18] Human Rights Watch. "U.S. Prisons." [Online] http://www.hrw.org/prisons/united_states.html

[19] Scolforo, M. "PA County Prisons Struggle To Meet Standards." *Associated Press* (December 20, 2005). [Online] http://realcostofprisons.org/blog/archives/ 2005/12/pa_68_county_ja.html

[20] Guccione, J., S. Pfeifer, and R. Connell. "1 Killed, 50 Hurt in County Jail Race Riot." *Los Angeles Times* (February 5, 2006).

[21] Mays, G. L. and L. T. Winfree, Jr. *Contemporary Corrections.* Belmont, CA: Wadsworth, 1998, p. 358; Stojkovic and Klofas, "Crowding and Correctional Change," pp. 98–99.

[22] Lane, C. "Justices Rule against Prisoner Segregation." *Washington Post* (February 24, 2005) p. A4.

[23] *Johnson v. California,* No. 03-636 (2005).

[24] Garvey, M. and S. Bernstein. "Cycle of Jail Woes Generates Few Fixes." *Los Angeles Times* (February 21, 2006).

[25] Garvey, M. and R. Winton. "Critics of Jails Voice Alarm. *Los Angeles Times* (February 14, 2006).

[26] Pierson, D. and M. Garvey. "Unrest Flares Up Again at L.A. County Jail." *Los Angeles Times* (February 8, 2006); Pfeifer, S. and J. Garrison. "L.A. County Jails Quiet after Flare-Up of Violence." *Los Angeles Times* (February 6, 2006); Bernstein and Garvey, "Dorms Fuel Jail Unrest."

27 Garvey, M. and S. Pfeifer, "Jail Inmates Were Stripped to Deter Riots. *Los Angeles Times* (February 18, 2006).

28 Garvey, M. and J. Leonard. "Urgent Appeal for Jail Safety." *Los Angeles Times* (February 15, 2006).

29 Pfeifer, S. and J. Garrison. "Sheriff Blames Lack of Staff for Jail Riot." *Los Angeles Times* (February 6, 2006).

30 Bernstein, S. and M. Garvey. "Dorms Fuel Jail Unrest." *Los Angeles Times* (February 12, 2006).

31 Warren, J. "Packed Prisons Brace for New Crush." *Los Angeles Times* (April 22, 2006).

32 Mitford, J. *Kind and Usual Punishment*. New York: Vintage, 1974.

33 Ibid., p. 30.

34 Ibid., p. 30.

35 Ibid., p. 31.

36 James, D. J. and L. E. Glaze. *Mental Health Problems of Prison and Jail Inmates*. Washington, DC: Bureau of Justice Statistics, September 2006, p. 1.

37 Seligman, K. "Street Attack Stuns Visiting Doctors." *San Francisco Chronicle* (May 23, 2003); see also Shelden, R. G. "Mentally Ill? Just Throw 'em in Jail." *Las Vegas Mercury* (July 24, 2003). [Online] http://www.lasvegasmercury.com/2003/MERC-Jul-24-Thu-2003/21496146.html

38 James and Glaze, *Mental Health Problems of Prison and Jail Inmates*, p. 1.

39 The quotation is from Marcia Goin, who was the APA president-elect when the professor was attacked in San Francisco. Goin, M. K. "The Wrong Place to Treat Mental Illness." *Washington Post* (July 8, 2007), p. B7. [Online] http://www.washingtonpost.com/wp-dyn/content/article/2007/07/06/AR2007070601930.html

40 Ranney, D. "Mentally Ill Strain Resources at Jail." *Lawrence Journal-World* (April 10, 2006). [Online] http://www2.ljworld.com/news/2006/apr/10/mentally_ill_strain_resources_jail/?city_local

41 Gallegos, A. "Local Jails See Far More Suicides than Prisons." *South Bend Tribune* (February 23, 2006). [Online] http://www.southbendtribune.com/apps/pbcs.dll/article?AID=/20060223/News01/602230403

42 "Making Mental Illness a Crime: For More Georgians, Disorders Mean Time in Jail, Not Treatment Centers." *The Mason Telegraph* (January 27, 2002). [Online] http://www.psychlaws.org/stateactivity/Georgia.htm

43 Citizens Committee on Mental Illness, Substance Abuse and Criminal Justice. "Report on the Current Status of Services for Persons with Mental Illness." September 2002. [Online] http://www.prisonsucks.com/scans/maine/maine_mental_illness_2002.pdf.

44 Shabo, H. E. "Social Costs: Criminal Justice and Mental Health System Gaps Which Contribute to the Criminalization of Mentally Disordered Persons." Superior Court of Los Angeles County. [Online] http://mentalhealthpolicy.berkeley.edu/papers/shabo.pdf

45 National Mental Health Association. "Mental Health: Pay for Services or Pay a Higher Price." This reported noted that in Florida "local jails in the state have become the largest public psychiatric hospitals, housing over 10,000 offenders with mental illnesses, many of whom are incarcerated for minor offenses." [Online] http://www1.nmha.org/shcr/community_based/costoffset.pdf

46 Irwin, J. *The Jail: Managing the Underclass in American Society*. Berkeley: University of California Press, 1985, pp. 1–2.

47 Piven, F. F. and R. Cloward. *Regulating the Poor: The Functions of Social Welfare*. New York: Vintage Books, 1972.

48 Miller, *Search and Destroy*.

49 Wolfgang, R. E., R. Figlio, and P. Tracy. "The Seriousness of Crime: The Results of a National Survey." Final Report to the Bureau of Justice Statistics, Washington, DC, 1981.

50 Irwin, *The Jail*, pp. 20–22.

51 Austin and Irwin, in their study of the prison system, discovered a similar distribution of offenders as Irwin did in his jail study. Austin, J. and J. Irwin. *It's about Time: America's Incarceration Binge* (3rd ed.). Belmont, CA: Wadsworth, 2001.

52 Shelden, R. G. and W. B. Brown. "Correlates of Jail Overcrowding: Case Study of a County Detention Center." *Crime and Delinquency* 37(3) (1991).

53 The remainder of the chapter is based on a series of articles coauthored by William B. Brown and Raul Ramirez (Marion County Sheriff). The first article appeared in *Sheriff* 58(6) 2006. Additional data can be found on the Web site. [Online] www.pacpri.org

54 Interview data collected (source name protected).

[55] National Association of Counties. *The Meth Epidemic in America: The Criminal Effect of Meth on Communities.* Washington, DC: Author, July 18, 2006. [Online] http://www.naco.org/Template.cfm?Section= Library&template=/ContentManagement/ ContentDisplay.cfm&ContentID=20709

[56] Google search of *New York Times* archives conducted on July 14, 2006.

[57] Jefferson, D. J. "America's Most Dangerous Drug." *Newsweek* (August 8, 2005).

[58] King, R. S. "The Next Big Thing? Methamphetamine in the United States." Washington, DC: The Sentencing Project, 2006.

[59] This drug is currently available for purchase on the Internet, with a six bottle (48 capsules per bottle) per month/per customer limit. Manufactured by Mega Pro International and offered under the brand name "Vasopro" by netnutri.com.

[60] Drug Enforcement Association. Drugs and Drug Abuse, States. Oregon, 2007. [Online] http:// www.dea.gov/pubs/states/oregonp.html

[61] Sabol, Minton, and Harrison, *Prison and Jail Inmates at Midyear 2006*, p. 8.

[62] Salem is the State Capital of Oregon and has a population of approximately 300,000 citizens and a geographic jurisdiction of nearly 1,200 square miles.

[63] One of the authors (WBB) surveyed 442 prisoners (76% of the total jail population) at the Marion County Jail in July 2005. Participation was voluntary. Later that year (October–December), more than 200 prisoners volunteered to participate in extensive one-on-one interviews and focus groups. The research identified and examined causal factors associated with methamphetamine abuse, which include the lack of education, limited parenting skills, a cycle of mental illness and homelessness, a lack of resources

such as medical and substance abuse treatment, and other contributing factors that include subsistence, residential stability, and generational criminogenics.

[64] Interview data collected (source name protected).

[65] July 9, 2005 jail survey data in Marion County, Oregon, and 2005 U.S. Census Bureau data used to develop Table 1.

[66] U.S. Census Bureau. State/County Quick Facts: Marion County, Oregon. [Online] http://quickfacts.census.gov/qfd/states/41/41047.html

[67] Hohman, M., Oliver, R., and Wright, W. *Methamphetamine Abuse and Manufacture: The Child Welfare Response*. National Association of Social Workers, 2004, 373–381.

[68] Interview data collected (source name protected).

[69] *The 2005 HHS Poverty Guidelines*. United States Department of Health and Human Services.

[70] Interview data collected (source name protected).

[71] Interview data collected (source name protected).

[72] Johnston, D. "Effects of Parental Incarceration." In K. Gabriel and D. Johnston (eds.), *Children of Incarcerated Parents*. New York: Lexington Books, 1995, p 5.

[73] Eddy, J. M. and J.B. Reed (2002) "The Antisocial Behavior of Adolescent Children of Incarcerated Parents: A Developmental Perspective." Oregon Social Learning Center; Johnson, E. I. and J. Waldfogel. "Children of Incarcerated Parents: Cumulative Risk and Children's Living Arrangement." 2002 (unpublished paper).

[74] Interview data collected (source name protected).

[75] Interview data collected (source name protected).

[76] "Hooley Applauds Efforts at County Jail to Fight Meth: The Program Relies on Research and Science," *Statesman Journal* (August 8, 2006).

twelve

The Modern Prison System

Prisons dot the American landscape. Because we become accustomed to seeing or reading about these institutions, we often take for granted that they are inevitable, a natural by-product of the existence of crime in society. However, the prison is a relatively recent phenomenon, taking root after the American Revolution and developing slowly until late in the twentieth century. Before we explore the modern U.S. prison system, we will look briefly at its history. We trace the development of the prison system through six periods: (1) 1790–1830: early American prisons; (2) 1830–1870: the Pennsylvania and Auburn systems; (3) 1870–1900: reformatories; (4) 1900–1946: the "Big House"; (5) 1946–1980: the "correctional institution"; (6) 1980 to the present: "warehousing."[1]

EARLY AMERICAN PRISONS, 1790–1830

The use of imprisonment as punishment did not occur until the late eighteenth century in the United States. Throughout colonial America, the most common form of punishment was a combination of banishment and various forms of public punishments, such as the stocks, the pillory, and branding. The primary method of social control was informal, with local families, the community, and the church providing most forms of punishment.

Shortly after the end of the American Revolution, a group of prominent citizens (including Benjamin Franklin, Benjamin Rush, and William Bradford) gathered to update the criminal code of 1718. The new law, passed in 1786, authorized a penalty of "hard labor, publicly and disgracefully imposed" for certain crimes.[2] Prisoners were sentenced to perform hard labor in the city streets, but the spectacle drew crowds of people sympathetic to the plight of the prisoners. A group called the Philadelphia Society for Alleviating the Miseries of Public Prisons worked to amend the law. In 1788, they suggested that sentences be more private—to the extent that they called for *solitary confinement* within the confines of the old Walnut Street Jail.[3]

The **Walnut Street Jail** became the first *state* prison in the United States, and it was part of a much larger effort to create a powerful and centralized state apparatus. This state apparatus helped perpetuate the existing class divisions. "The success of the Revolution at home was brought about by the creation of a class-divided society based upon private property, and the ratification of the new Constitution was to guarantee the privileges and power of the bourgeoisie."[4] James Madison stated quite clearly in *The Federalist* that "The diversity in the faculties of men, from which the rights of property flow, is not less an insuperable obstacle to a uniformity of interests. The protection of these faculties is the first object of government." Madison further argued that one of the duties of a government is to regulate various interests, including "a landed interest, a manufacturing interest, a mercantile interest, a moneyed interest, with many lesser interests."[5]

At the end of the eighteenth century, there was a great deal of disorder stemming from economic crises and general uncertainty over the future of American society. Shay's Rebellion was one of several revolts against the existing form of government and economy.[6] It also marked the beginning of the newly emerging ruling class of businesspeople who would eventually become the "tools and tyrants" of the government, "overwhelming it with their force and benefiting from its gifts."[7]

Prominent Americans were concerned about maintaining social order. As David Rothman writes: "What in their day was to prevent society from bursting apart? From where would the elements of cohesion come?" The major worry was whether the poor would "corrupt society" and criminals would "roam out of control." Thus, comprehension and control of deviance "promised to be the first step in establishing a new system for stabilizing the community, for binding citizens together. . . . And here one also finds the crucial elements that led to the discovery of the asylum."[8] Imprisonment slowly became a dominant method of punishing offenders. The prison system would become one of several methods of reforming and controlling the "dangerous classes." Two contrasting methods eventually structured most of the early attempts to punish offenders within the confines of large institutions.

THE PENNSYLVANIA AND AUBURN SYSTEMS OF PENAL DISCIPLINE, 1830–1870

Many reformers believed that criminals lacked respect for authority and proper work habits. They believed that a strict regimen of discipline and hard labor would correct those faults. Other reformers believed that criminals were "sinners" and needed to "repent" for their crimes. The idea of penance originated in the medieval monasteries of Europe, where monks who had broken their vows would demonstrate their sorrow for their sins and seek redemption through penitent behavior (the term *penitentiary* is derived from this concept).[9] Repentance could be accomplished only through solitary confinement and no contact with other prisoners or

the outside world. The two views of punishment—discipline through hard labor and solitary confinement to elicit repentance—came to be known respectively as the Auburn and Pennsylvania plans.

Two prisons were constructed following the *Pennsylvania plan* during the early nineteenth century. Western Penitentiary opened in 1826 in Pittsburgh; Eastern State Penitentiary opened in 1829 on Cherry Hill in Philadelphia. It was the largest public building in the country, and cost $800,000 to construct.[10] Silence, solitude, surveillance, and anonymity were the guiding features of the architecture. More than 300 prisons throughout the world were modeled after Eastern State. The cells were arranged like spokes on a wheel, all radiating from a common central area, which allowed for constant surveillance. Originally, the only activity allowed was reading the Bible. However, most of the inmates were poor and uneducated. Eventually, small exercise yards were added to the cells. Each prisoner was allowed short periods in the yard for daily exercise but spent most of the time inside the cell working at some menial task or individual craft. Each prisoner was blindfolded as he entered the prison to begin his sentence and was prohibited from contact with other prisoners. Only approved visitors from the outside were allowed to visit the prisoner.[11]

The *Auburn plan,* which emphasized work in association with other prisoners, began in New York and was supported by prominent citizens of the state, including political leader and former governor De Witt Clinton and former governor and former U.S. Supreme Court Chief Justice John Jay. The first prison modeled after this plan was called the Newgate Prison, which opened in New York in 1797. The second prison opened in Auburn in 1816.[12] In August 1890, Auburn was the site of the first death sentence carried out by electrocution.[13]

The Pennsylvania plan soon came into disfavor. The misery of complete isolation and near idleness drove many prisoners insane, and there was a significant rise in the number of suicides. The English novelist, Charles Dickens, visited Eastern State Penitentiary and called the conditions hopeless and denounced the psychological effects of isolation as secret punishment.[14] It should be noted that isolation continues today. Supermax prisons were designed to house the most incorrigible prisoners. Pelican Bay State Prison, located in remote Crescent City, California (just south of the Oregon border) has a security housing unit (SHU) in which prisoners are not allowed to congregate with one another or to work at any time during the day or night. They are locked up in windowless cells for twenty-three hours a day. Many prisoners reportedly go insane, and suicide is a constant problem.[15]

Prison administrators following the Auburn plan developed the *congregate system* and the *silent system.* Prisoners worked together during the day but were not allowed to speak to one another, and they were kept in solitary confinement at night. The Auburn plan was used by prisons throughout the nation during the nineteenth century. It became the dominant form because it was so profitable.

Prison administrators at Auburn called their system "humanitarian," but the system they created was almost as repressive as methods used in previous years. Elan Lynds, the first warden at Auburn, introduced the "lockstep" (prisoners marched single file, shuffling their feet and keeping their eyes right). He was a strong advocate of whipping, including the use of the cat-o'-nine-tails. Two Frenchmen, Gustave de Beaumont and Alexis de Tocqueville, who toured American prisons in 1831, noted that the Pennsylvania system produced "more honest men" and the Auburn system produced "more obedient citizens."[16] They also could have added that the Auburn system attempted to produce an ideal worker for the factory system, a worker who was obedient, passive, and silent and who would not complain about the grueling working conditions.[17]

The Auburn system fit nicely within the larger structure of capitalism, which thrives on cheap labor. As a method of punishment, the Auburn system was ideally suited for an emerging capitalist society. It attempted to inculcate habits of hard work, punctuality, and

obedience. In fact, early prison factories resembled factories; for a time, prisoners produced goods that were sold on the free market.

One of the most accepted architectural designs for prisons was the *panopticon.* Jeremy Bentham, an eighteenth century philosopher, based the plans on a military school his brother, Samuel, had designed in Paris to facilitate supervision. Both men were looking for a solution to the problem of supervising large numbers of men. The panopticon allowed the staff in the center tower to have constant surveillance over the inmates. An additional feature was to allow an observer to survey the prisoners without the prisoners being able to tell if they were being observed or not. Bentham described the panopticon as "a new mode of obtaining power of mind over mind, in a quantity hitherto without example." He also referred to "the *apparent omnipresence* of the inspector . . . combined with the extreme facility of his *real presence.*"[18]

Michel Foucault has argued that not only prisons but all hierarchical structures like the army, the school, the hospital, and the factory have evolved through history to resemble the panopticon.[19] He viewed it as the symbol of a paradigm shift in punishment reflecting increased governmental power and control—and a surveillance-oriented society.[20] Another modern example is the use of closed-circuit television surveillance cameras in cities everywhere.

REFORMATORIES, 1870–1900

By mid-century reformers and observers of the prison system noted with dismay the brutality that existed within these institutions. Beaumont and Tocqueville commented that while American society provided the most extended liberty, its prisons offered the spectacle of the most complete despotism.[21] As crime and disorder continued to rise in the United States, reformers searched for alternatives to the Pennsylvania and Auburn systems of discipline and custody.

In 1867 the governor of New York appointed two penologists, Enoch Cobb Wines and Theodore Dwight, to inspect the prisons, juvenile reformatories, county penitentiaries, and local jails in the state. As part of their investigation, they also visited correctional institutions in seventeen other states and Canada.[22] Their *Report on the Prisons and Reformatories of the United States and Canada* was published in 1867 and called for a new science of punishment.[23] They urged that the goal of these institutions should be rehabilitation rather than punishment. Among their suggestions were: reductions in the disparity in sentences; less emphasis on making a profit from the labor of prisoners; and more emphasis on industrial education, academic education, religion, and post-release supervision. Wines and Dwight promoted a new type of institution to separate hardened offenders from novice offenders, which they called an adult reformatory. The new institution would "teach and train the prisoner in such a manner that, on his discharge, he may be able to resist temptation and be inclined to lead an upright, worthy life."[24]

The *reformatory* idea received its impetus from Captain Alexander Maconochie, who headed the penal colony on Norfolk Island in Australia in the 1840s. Maconochie introduced the *mark system* whereby a prisoner's sentence would be reduced if he obeyed prison rules (the modern version is known as *good time*).[25] At about the same time in England, Sir Walter Crofton introduced the *Irish system,* which used indeterminate sentences and parole. If a prisoner proved he was "reformed" (a term that has never been precisely defined), he was given a pardon, or *ticket-of-leave.* The prisoner remained under supervision by the state until the expiration of his sentence. In the reformatory system in the United States, the ideas of Crofton and Maconochie were combined with innovations such as classification of inmates according to offense, personality, and other characteristics. The ticket-of-leave was eventually known as *parole.*[26]

The development of the reformatory came at a time of new hope among penologists. Wines convinced colleagues at the New York Prison Association to organize an international conference, which included 250 delegates from 24 states and a number of foreign countries. The gathering took place in Cin-

cinnati in 1870 and was called the National Congress of Penitentiary and Reformatory Discipline (this organization was later known as the American Prison Association and eventually became the American Correctional Association). Zebulon Brockway, a well-known penologist, presented "The Ideal of a True Prison for a State" to the appreciative gathering.[27] Brockway had worked at four institutions in New York, and was superintendent at two of them. In 1861, he left New York to become the first superintendent of the Detroit House of Correction.

The National Congress formulated a Declaration of Principles suggesting substantial prison reforms. The suggestions included an end to political appointments of prison administrators, greater participation of women in prison management, indeterminate sentences that could be adjusted depending on an individual's efforts and progress, classification of prisoners based on character, rewards for good conduct and hard work, expanded opportunities for education while in prison, an end to physical punishments, and improved sanitation.

The recommendations were incorporated by New York in an 1870 law that created the Elmira Reformatory. The purpose was to house "male first-time offenders between the ages of sixteen and thirty" and to provide "agricultural labor" and "mechanical industry." Following recommendations in the Declaration of Principles Elmira would: provide treatment based on a new medical model; use the indeterminate sentence, along with a very carefully calculated system of classification; provide "intensive academic and vocational instruction, constructive labor, and humane disciplinary methods." An intensive period of parole would follow, intended to extend treatment into the community.[28]

The Elmira Reformatory opened in 1876 (and still stands today); Brockway became the first superintendent, serving from 1876 to 1900. He introduced a wide variety of programs, including industrial and academic education, religious services, library facilities, an institutional newspaper, and a gymnasium. He called his new institution a "reformatory hospital" and the "college on the hill." However, the Elmira Reformatory under Brockway was a militarylike fortress that emphasized "coercion and restraint" and ushered in a new era of "treatment." Brockway defined "reformation" as the "socialization of the antisocial by scientific training while under complete governmental control." The Elmira Reformatory "became like a garrison of a thousand prisoner soldiers. . . . By means mainly of the military organization . . . [t]he general tone . . . gradually changed from that of a convict prison to the tone of a conscript fortress."[29] In reality, it became "benevolent repression" under a strict military form of discipline, rather than reform.[30]

The reformatories were designed to transform the "dangerous criminal classes" into "Christian gentlemen and prepare them to assume their 'proper place' in society as hardworking, law-abiding, lower class citizens." These institutions would also teach good old-fashioned "American values" such as "habits of order, discipline, self-control, cheerful submission to authority, as well as respect for God, law, country, and the principles of capitalism and democracy."[31]

Elmira and other reformatories failed to live up to the promise of reforming criminals, and "failed signally to provide the right sort of psychological surroundings to expedite this process [of reformation]. The whole system of discipline was repressive, and varied from benevolent despotism, in the best instances, to tyrannical cruelty in the worst."[32] Elmira was originally built to house five hundred inmates, but by 1899 it housed around fifteen hundred. This prompted one writer to comment: "What had begun as a bold experiment lost the inspiring impulse of its first promoters, and became routine work and mass treatment."[33] Beatings were routine, often done in the bathroom (called the "slaughterhouse" by inmates). Brockway himself administered some of the punishment. He was described by inmates as a "different man" at these times, as if he enjoyed the beatings. Brockway rationalized this by calling it part of his "scientific criminology" and renamed corporal punishment as "positive extraneous assistance." The

solitary confinement block was euphemistically called "rest cure cells."[34]

Elmira and many other "asylums," however, were never specifically designed for any purpose other than custody and control. More than this, it was a system of *class* control, for the prisons (then and now) were populated by the poor, the powerless, and (especially during the nineteenth century) immigrants.

During the nineteenth century, U.S. prisons gradually became huge, forbidding, granite and stone fortresses. These edifices were eventually called the "Big House," popularized in gangster movies in the 1930s and 1940s starring such famous actors as James Cagney and Humphrey Bogart.

THE "BIG HOUSE," 1900–1946

The *Big House* became the dominant type of prison until the late 1940s and early 1950s. Typically it was an enormous granite structure capable of housing two thousand or more prisoners, with some housing more than four thousand. Theoretically, the institutions were supposed to eliminate the most abusive forms of punitiveness and prison labor associated with prisons.[35] Most had large cell blocks with three or more tiers of cells, usually housing one or two men in each cell. Many were built in the late nineteenth century, such as Jackson (Michigan), San Quentin (California), Joliet (Illinois), and Sing Sing (New York), but most were built in the twentieth century, such as Stateville (Illinois) and Attica (New York).[36] Although the "Big House" was in some ways an "industrial" prison capable of producing various goods, most prisoners spent their time in relative idleness toward the end of the 1930s. Most businesses lobbied strongly to prevent what they perceived as unfair competition from prison labor. Eventually prisons produced products only for the state, such as license plates.

The reform agenda as practiced within reformatories during the late nineteenth and early part of the twentieth century ran up against the hard realities of life in "the Big House." The reality of the prison "is not one of the inmates exercising in the yard or attending classes or taking psychometric tests, but of the physical presence of the walls."[37] It was these high walls (some as high as 30 feet above the ground) that helped wardens and guards keep their jobs. Legislatures and the general public wanted the security symbolized by the walls. The prison administration was charged with: maintaining a "quiet joint" (i.e., no riots, no escapes, a smooth running institution). The high walls gave the public the illusion that "hardened criminals" were separated from society so they could no longer prey on innocent citizens.

Until 1895 prisoners convicted of federal crimes were housed in state prisons. The number of prisoners housed in state prisons more than doubled from 1,027 in 1885 to 2,516 in 1895. During this period federal prisoners were used as contract labor. But in 1897 Congress outlawed this practice, and state prisons began refusing federal prisoners.[38] Federal prisoners were first housed at Fort Leavenworth, an old military prison in the eastern part of Kansas, until the new prison opened in 1928. In the meantime two federal prisons had been built by the federal government, one in Atlanta (1899) and the other on McNeil Island, Washington (1907).[39]

From 1910 to 1919, Congress passed a number of federal laws. The Mann Act in 1910 (also known as the White-Slave Traffic Act) prohibited the transportation of females for immoral purposes across state lines. The Harrison Narcotics Tax Act in 1914 regulated and taxed the production and distribution of opiates. The Volstead Act (the National Prohibition Act) prohibited the sale or distribution of alcohol. The Dyer Act (National Motor Vehicle Theft Act prohibited the transportation of stolen motor vehicles across state lines. The increase in the number of federal violations resulted in a significant increase in federal prisoners. The Volstead Act, in particular, had a number of unintended consequences including the rise in organized crime. The sale and distribution of alcohol, a substance in demand by the general population, was prohibited. What had been a legitimate business became the province of criminal gangs—with the violence associated with confrontations over who would control the illegal market.

In 1925 Congress authorized the construction of a federal reformatory at Chillicothe, Ohio, and the construction of the first federal prison for women, which was opened in 1927 at Alderson, West Virginia.[40] The most famous federal prison was Alcatraz, which opened in 1934 on an island in San Francisco Bay, directly across from Fisherman's Wharf.

THE "CORRECTIONAL INSTITUTION," 1946–1980

The Federal Bureau of Prisons helped develop a new system of classification, new prison industries, a federal system of probation and parole, and new educational and vocational training programs. Perhaps most important was the new system of classification. First, there was a classification system according to types of prisons. Five types of facilities were developed: penitentiaries, reformatories, prison camps, hospitals, and drug treatment facilities. Second, within each facility, classification was done according to age, offense, sex, and other criteria. In the 1970s, the federal system established a classification system based on security level. Five levels were identified:

1. *Minimum:* mostly federal prison "camps." Many are next to military bases, and inmates provide additional labor for the base.

2. *Low:* double-fenced perimeters and mostly dormitory-style living arrangements.

3. *Medium:* cell-type living arrangements and double-fenced perimeters with electronic detection systems.

4. *High:* most commonly known as U.S. penitentiaries, with high-security perimeter double fences or walls, along with very close supervision of inmates in cell-type housing.

5. *Administrative:* special-needs institutions housing pretrial defendants, noncitizen detainees, and "extremely dangerous, violent, or escape-prone inmates."[41]

With the federal government leading the way, a new era of penology began to emerge, especially after World War II, with a new type of prison system and new terminology. Thus began the age of the "correctional system" and a host of new prison workers, whom Irwin has called *correctionalists,* a "growing body of college-educated employees and administrators of prisons, parole, and probation and a few academic penologists." They "were convinced and were able to convince many state governments and interested segments of the general population that they could reduce crime by curing criminals of their criminality."[42] Instead of a prison there was to be a "correctional system"; instead of prisoners or convicts, there would be "inmates"; and guards would be "correctional officers."[43] The prison system remained a system to house the "dangerous classes," but the new terminology masked the true functions and created the false impression that something positive was being accomplished within the walls.

Many of the "Big Houses" were replaced with "correctional centers." In line with a new era of "treatment," there also emerged a new three-level security classification: *maximum, medium,* and *minimum.* Examples of minimum-security prisons (most have no walls) include the California Institution for Men at Chino (a state institution), a federal institution at Seagoville, Texas, and another at Wallkill, New York.

Part of the corrections system included the emergence of the "rehabilitative ideal." The emphasis was on treatment (a term that was changed to "rehabilitation"). During the 1940s and 1950s, correctionalists implemented this new penology through three essential procedures: the indeterminate sentence, classification, and specific treatment programs.[44] Classification was to be done by a team of psychologists, social workers, counselors, and other professionals who formed a special "classification committee" to determine the proper course of treatment for the inmate. Advocates of this new penology pushed for changing the name of the American Prison Association to the American Correctional Association in 1954. New names were invented to replace old, punitive practices. The "hole" (locus of solitary confinement) was renamed the "adjustment center."

Soledad Prison in California was renamed the "California Treatment Facility." Fences (today reinforced with razor wire, some charged with electricity) and guard towers replaced granite walls.[45] The internal structure featured cell blocks with dayrooms and windows, pastel colors, libraries, gyms and educational facilities. Nevertheless, for all practical purposes, they remained essentially *prisons.*

The indeterminate sentence was implemented in most states. While some reformers advocated a sentence of zero to life for all offenders (in other words, literally a sentence of indeterminate length), most state legislatures implemented a modified version, such as one to ten years for larceny (in California, for example). More power was granted to parole boards as a result of indeterminate sentencing laws. Ideally, parole boards would release an offender only when they felt he or she was "rehabilitated." But this assumed that those in charge of the prisons "had procedures for identifying and changing criminal characteristics, which they did not, and that parole boards had procedures for determining when these changes had occurred, which they did not."[46]

The belief in rehabilitation was based on the *medical model* of treatment for criminals. Based largely on psychological theories of crime (see chapter 4), this model believed that criminals were sick and needed to be diagnosed and treated accordingly. Although classification was supposed to facilitate changing criminal behavior the procedures adopted never attained this ideal. Theories of criminal behavior were never developed sufficiently to suggest a reasonable "cure" for criminality, and treatment programs were never fully implemented in most prisons. Classification (and most other prison procedures) continued to be determined by concerns over custody and security.

For the most part, prisons in the post–World War II era differed little from their predecessors. Edgardo Rotman's assessment captures the basic problems of rehabilitation within these prisons:

> Despite the rhetoric of rehabilitation, this new wave of treatment euphoria shared

with previous efforts the same paucity of practical realizations. Because of the limited professional possibilities offered by the penitentiary setting, the treatment staff was still generally composed of less qualified individuals. In addition, there was a permanent conflict, ideological and professional, between the custody and the treatment staffs regarding issues of discipline and security.[47]

Irwin's comments echo those of Rotman:

The public and most government policy makers continued to demand that prisons first accomplish their other assigned tasks: punishment, control, and restraint of prisoners. In addition, the new correctional institutions were not created in a vacuum but planned in ongoing prison systems which had long traditions, administrative hierarchies, divisions, informal social worlds, and special subcultures among the old staff. The new correctionalists were never able to rid the prison systems of the old regime, though often they tried; and the old timers, many of whom were highly antagonistic to the new routine, resisted change, struggled to maintain as much control as possible, and were always successful in forcing an accommodation between old and new patterns. So correctional institutions were never totally, or even mainly, organized to rehabilitate prisoners.[48]

WAREHOUSING, 1980 INTO THE TWENTY-FIRST CENTURY

From the perspective of the business and political interests connected to prisons, business is booming. The incarceration rate is higher than in any other country in the world. In this section, we will look at the increased numbers of prisoners warehoused in prisons in the United States.

Prisons as a Growth Industry

In 1970, the state and federal prison population was less than 190,000; by 2005 it had soared to almost 1.5 million. Adding the jail populations to the figures results in a total incarcerated population of almost 2.2 million. Another 4.3 million people have been released but carry the status of ex-convict. The United States incarcerates more people than any other nation in the world. China, with a much larger population, ranks second, imprisoning 1.5 million.[49]

When we look at incarceration rates, the United States also leads the world—approximately 737 per 100,000 population (see table 12.1). Rephrased, 7 of every 1,000 U.S. residents are in prison or jail. The rate in the Russian federation is 624 per 100,000.[50] Western European countries have incarceration rates that range from 40 per 100,000 in Iceland to 149 in England and Wales.

The Norwegian criminologist, Nils Christie, in the third edition of his groundbreaking book on the crime control industry, noted that there is a huge difference between the United States and our northern neighbor Canada. Canada's incarceration rate of 107 is almost one-seventh the rate in the United States. He also notes that the two countries are very similar (in terms of the economic and political systems) except for one important exception: Canada has more of a "social safety net" (various welfare benefits) than the United States.[51]

Comparisons with other countries reveal the extent of the discrepancy in rates.

Table 12.1   Adults on Probation, in Jail or Prison, and on Parole, 1980–2005

Year	Total	Probation	Jail	Prison	Parole
1980	1,840,400	1,118,097	182,288	319,598	220,438
1985	3,011,500	1,968,712	254,986	487,593	300,203
1990	4,350,300	2,670,234	405,320	743,382	531,407
1995	5,342,900	3,077,861	507,044	1,078,542	679,421
2005	7,056,000	4,162,536	747,529	1,446,269	784,488
% increase (1980–2005)	283	272	310	353	256

Source: Sourcebook of Criminal Justice Statistics. [Online] http://www.albany.edu/sourcebook/pdf/t612005.pdf

Although the rate of property crime in the United States is similar to that of most Western European countries and Australia, the contrast in incarceration rates is stark. The Netherlands has a rate of 128; Australia 125, Portugal 121, Austria 105, Germany 93, Greece 90, Switzerland 90, Finland 68, and Italy 67;[52] The European Union, with 370 million people, has a total of 300,000 prisoners, which translates into an incarceration rate of 81.[53] Unlike the United States, many of these countries include people housed in various community facilities in their incarceration rates. While exact figures of offenders housed in community-based facilities in the United States is not known, there are more than 4.9 million under some form of supervision (see table 12.2), which makes the discrepancy between the United States and other countries even greater.

Between 1980 and 2005, the number of people confined in prisons or jails or supervised by the criminal justice system while on probation or parole grew by over 283%. Prisons had the largest increase (353%). During this time, the adult population increased by just 18%, thus contributing minimally to the increased numbers under supervision. In addition, the number of arrests went up by

only 41%, compared to an overall *decrease* in reported index crimes. The accelerating numbers of people imprisoned has been the result of a significant increase in the number of less serious offenders being convicted and sent to prison.

Prison building has been increasing. As of 2000, there were a total of 1,668 state, federal, and privately operated prisons, 204 more than in 1995 (a 14% increase). The largest growth has been for private prisons, from 110 in 1995 to 264 (a 140% increase) in 2000.[54] Researchers estimate that prison operating costs will increase by at least $2.5 billion per year to as much as $5 billion per year by 2011. The price of building new prison beds could reach $12.5 billion. The cost of each prison bed ranges between $25,000 and $100,000, depending on the security level.[55]

Drug Convictions

As mentioned previously, one of the primary causes of the surge in imprisonment is the "war on drugs." Table 12.3 shows the change in most serious offenses from 1985 to 2003. There were 8 times the number of drug offenses in 2003 compared to 1985. The drug offense category far outstripped any other category of offense in 2007. Drug offenses accounted for 53.6% of all those in federal prison. The next largest percentage of federal offenders (14.4%) had committed an offense in the weapons, explosives, and arson category. Robbery accounted for 5.2% of federal prisoners; burglary and property offenses 3.8%; and homicide, aggravated assault, and kidnapping was the offense category for 3.1% of the federal population.[56]

When analyzing drug populations from 1985 to 2003 within state prisons, we can clearly see a rapid growth for drug convictions. While in 1985 the drug offender population numbered almost 39,000, the numbers increased to almost 251,000 in 2003. In less than two decades, the number of drug offenders in state prisons increased 545% (see table 12.4).

The drug war dominates the attention of the criminal justice system and has had a profound impact on the prison system (see chapter 15 for further discussion).

Table 12.2 The Growing Prison Population, 1925–2005 (rates per 100,000 in state and federal prison)

Year	Number	Rate
1925	91,669	79
1935	144,180	113
1945	133,649	98
1955	185,780	112
1965	210,895	108
1975	240,593	111
1985	480,568	202
1995	1,085,363	411
2005	1,556,518	497

Sources: Maguire, K. and A. L. Pastore (eds.). *Sourcebook on Criminal Justice statistics—1996*. Washington, DC: Department of Justice, Bureau of Justice Statistics, 1997, p. 518; Sabol, W. J., T. D. Minton, and P. M. Harrison. *Prison and Jail Inmates at Midyear 2006*. Washington, DC: Bureau of Justice Statistics, June 2007, p. 6.

Table 12.3   Number of Sentenced Inmates in Federal Prison by Offense

Most serious offense	Number of Inmates[a]			% Change
	1985	1995	2003	1985–2003
Total	27,607	88,658	158,426	474%
Violent offenses[b]	7,768	11,409	16,688	115%
(Homicide, Assault, Robbery, Other Violent)				
Property offenses	5,289	7,842	11,283	113%
(Burglary, Fraud, Other Property)				
Drug Offenses	9,482	52,782	86,972	817%
Public-order offenses	2,514	15,655	42,325	1583%
(Immigration, Weapons, Escape/court, Other Public-order)				
Other/Unknown[c]	2,554	970	1,158	−54.7%

[a]Includes prisoners of any sentence length.
[b]Includes murder, nonnegligent manslaughter, and negligent manslaughter.
[c]Includes offenses not classifiable or not a violation of the United States Code.

Sources: Beck, A. J. and D. K. Gilliard. *Prisoners in 1994*. Washington, DC: Bureau of Justice Statistics, 1995, p. 10; Harrison, P. M. and A. J. Beck. *Prisoners in 2005*. Washington, DC: Bureau of Justice Statistics, 2006, p. 10.

Table 12.4   Offenders Sentenced to State Prisons by Offense, 1985–2003

Offense	1985	1995	2003	% Change
				1980–2000
Total	451,812	989,007	1,256,400	178%
Violent	246,200	457,600	650,400	164%
Property	140,100	237,400	262,000	87%
Drugs	38,900	224,900	250,900	545%
Public Order	23,000	66,100	86,400	276%

Source: Mumola, C. J. and A. J. Beck. *Prisoners in 1996*. Washington, DC: Bureau of Justice Statistics (1997), p. 10; Harrison, P. M. and A. J. Beck. *Prisoners in 2005*. Washington, DC: Bureau of Justice Statistics (2006), p. 9.

- In 2005 there were almost 1.85 million arrests for drug abuse violations (82% for possession, of which 38% were for possession of marijuana).[57]

- In 2004, blacks constituted about one-third of arrests for drugs, about 3 times their percent in the general population.[58]

- Women were more likely than men to be in state prison for a drug offense in 2005 (29% versus 19%).[59]

- State prisons held 250,900 people convicted of drug offenses in 2003—20.2% of all those in state prison.[60] In 1986, 9% of the state prison population had committed a drug offense. States spend a total of approximately 6.2 billion each year to house drug offenders.[61]

- Federal prisons held 96,972 people convicted of drug offenses in 2003, 55% of those incarcerated.[62] More than 80% of the growth in the federal prison population from 1985 to 1995 was because of drug convictions. In the decade from 1990 to 2000, the percentage of federal inmates convicted of violent felonies *decreased* from 17 to 10%, while the largest percentage increase (59%) in total growth of the federal prison population was for drug offenders. Federal spending to incarcerate drug offenders totals almost $3 billion per year.[63]

- The average sentence for a federal drug conviction in 2004 was 83.6 months versus an average of 61.3 months for all felonies.[64] Increased prosecutions and longer time served created an average annual increase in the number of drug offenders in federal prisons of more than 12% from 1986 through 1999.[65]

Modern prisons (along with local jails) constitute a type of *ghetto* or *poorhouse*[66] reserved primarily for the unskilled, the uneducated, the powerless—and, in increasing numbers, racial minorities, especially African Americans. That is why we attach the label, the **new American apartheid** to the system that warehouses poor minorities. This segment of U.S. society has seen a dramatic reduction in income and has become more involved in drugs and the violence associated with the drug trade—collateral consequences from the lack of legitimate means of goal attainment.[67]

THE NEW AMERICAN APARTHEID

Apartheid is a policy that produces systematic racial segregation or discrimination. The word *apartheid* was introduced to the world by South Africa in 1948.[68] The roots of the term are the Dutch *apart* (which means the same as the English word) and *heid* (a suffix that means "hood"). The new term was adopted to soften the image of the harsh racial segregation policies practiced by the South African government and to divert world attention from its discriminatory practices. Very soon, however, the world realized that the treatment of blacks in South Africa had not changed. South Africa made one more rhetorical attempt and introduced the concept of *autogenous development* (meaning produced independently of external influence). But the world quickly recognized this second exercise in semantics. It made no difference whether the extreme discriminatory practices were called *segregation, apartheid,* or *autogenous development;* the result was still racial isolation.

Prisonization of Urban Central Cities

Racial segregation is now a characteristic of many inner cities in the United States. Central cities contain 80% of the urban non-white population. One-third of the African-American urban population resides in the nation's ten largest central cities.[69] There have been symbolic attempts to reduce racial segregation in the cities. We use the term *symbolic* because these attempts have often been politicized and skewed to serve the interests of the elite, or they have been grossly underfunded to ensure their failure.[70] To illustrate, the Housing Acts of 1949, 1954, and 1965 provided federal funding to local authorities to acquire slum property and begin redevelopment of that property. In order to qualify for federal funds, local governments had to ensure that affordable living accommodations would be provided for displaced families living in the redevelopment zones. The process was commonly known as urban renewal, but its primary by-product was the displacement of the economically disadvantaged—most frequently minorities. The solution was high-density public housing.

Today, these public housing projects are often referred to as the "projects." Razing slum areas and constructing public housing often resulted in an overall reduction in living accommodations.[71] A study of African-American youth gangs in Detroit noted a net loss of 31,500 homes between 1980 and 1987. Today, many African Americans are once again involved in a removal program—but instead of being removed from one inner-city slum area to a more high-density slum area, they find themselves removed from the inner cities entirely and compartmentalized in the U.S. prison industry.[72]

Loic Wacquant argues that in the post-Civil Rights era the entire penal system (including all the components of the criminal justice system) took the place of the ghetto and previous methods of controlling the black population (e.g., slavery, the Jim Crow south, the northern ghettoes). The result is that the ghetto is *more like a prison*, while the prison, because of the breakdown of the old "inmate society," is *more like a ghetto.*[73] Moreover, he argues that "the increasing use of imprisonment" aims to "shore up" the caste divisions in society by "upsizing" the penal sector while "downsizing" the social welfare sector. Wacquant argues that this trend represents a merging of the "invisible hand" of the market with an "iron fist" so that a *carceral-assistential complex* engages in various methods to control this population.[74] The new "hyperghetto" now appears more like a prison than ever before, as the economic basis of the ghetto has shifted from directly servicing the black community (as was done by black professionals within the traditional ghetto) to servicing the state (with growing jobs within *public* bureaucracies). "At best," he argues, "the hyperghetto now serves the *negative economic function of storage of a surplus population* devoid of market utility, in which respect it also increasingly resembles the prison system."[75] The emerging social control bureaucracies are "largely staffed by the new black middle class whose expansion hinges, not on its capacity to service its community, but on its willingness to assume the vexing role of *custodian* of the black urban sub-proletariat on behalf of white society,"[76] via "on-the-ground extensions of the penal system" (e.g., probation and parole officers, along with "snitches" hired by the police).[77]

Further evidence that the ghetto resembles a prison is illustrated by a "prisonization" of public housing, retirement homes, homeless shelters, etc.—all of which have methods of surveillance that are borrowed from the penal system. Security guards, ID card checks, electronic monitoring, random searches, and resident "counts" operate similarly to the routine in prisons. Bentham's panopticon design for prisons has been replicated in many public schools in the inner city, which serve more to control than to educate. Such elaborate control mechanisms habituate "the children of the hyperghetto to the demeanor, tactics, and interactive style of the correctional officers many of them are bound to encounter shortly after their school days are over."[78]

Internal Exile

A study by Bruce Western and his colleagues examined the relationship between imprisonment in jail or prison and education and employment.[79] They found that between 1980 and 1999, the percentage of white males from 18 to 65 going to prison or jail increased from 0.4% to 1%. For black men, the percentage increased from 3.1% to 7.5%. The percentage of young adult males (ages 22–30) in jail or prison increased from .7% to 1.6% for white males, while the percentage for black males increased from 5.5% to 11.7%. When considering young adult males who dropped out of high school, the percentage going to prison or jail went from 3.1 to 10.3 for whites but went from 14 to 41.2 for blacks. Phrased differently, more than four out of every ten black high school dropouts ended up in jail or prison.

Among men born between 1965 and 1969, 22.3% of all black men but only 3.2% of all white men had prison records by 1999. Among high school dropouts, these percentages increased to 12.6 and 32.1 respectively. Among those with either a high school diploma or a GED, only 4.3% of white men and 23.5% of black men ended up in prison. For those who had at least some college, these percentages dropped substantially: only 1.1% of white males and 8.6% of black males had prison records by 1999. While education has an obvious impact, the black-white differences remain high.[80]

When tabulating the official unemployment figures, the government fails to include prisoners. The census bureau, however, adds the numbers of prisoners to the population of the small towns in which the prisons are located. The larger number for the population, with no corresponding income, raises the poverty rate for the towns, qualifying them for federal funding.[81] When researchers included the imprisoned population, the numbers changed dramatically for black males: one-third of the black male population was unemployed in 1999 compared to 16% of white males. Among high school dropouts between 22 and 30, the percentages were astounding: 70% of black males (counting those in prison or jail) were unemployed, compared to 27% of white males.[82]

Having a criminal record, especially a prison record, has always been a barrier to seeking reentry into society, but recently the invisible punishments have accelerated. Laws passed in the last decade have denied public housing, welfare benefits, and education loans to convicted felons. Such laws impact millions; about 13 million Americans are either serving time for a felony conviction or have been convicted of a felony sometime in the past. Moreover, a total of about 47 million (one-fourth of the adult population) have some kind of criminal record on file with a federal or state criminal justice agency.[83]

Jeremy Travis likens this to a form of "internal exile," the domestic equivalent to those convicts exiled to the American colonies (and Australia too) during the seventeenth and eighteenth centuries. However, prisoners at that time faced few barriers to participating in colonial life once they had served their sentence.[84] The barriers put distance between "them" and "us."

> The principal new form of social exclusion has been to deny offenders the benefits of the welfare state. And the principal new player in this new drama has been the United States Congress. In an era of welfare reform, when Congress dismantled the six-decades-old entitlement to a safety net for the poor, the poor with criminal histories were thought less deserving than others . . . there was little hesitation in using federal benefits to enhance punishments or federal funds to encourage new criminal sanctions by the states.[85]

The group of offenders that bears the heaviest burden of this exclusion are racial minorities. Todd Clear has pointed out that in many urban, poverty-stricken neighborhoods as many as one-fourth of the adult male residents are either in prison or in jail at some time during the year.[86] On January 1, 2006, 40% of all state or federal inmates serving a sentence of more than 1 year were black; 20% were Hispanic, and 35% were white.[87] Black females (156 per 100,000) were more than three times as likely to be in prison as white females (45 per 100,000). Hispanic females (76 per 100,000) were 1.7 times as likely to be in state or federal prison than white females. The incarceration rates for males in state and federal prisons were: 3,145 per 100,000 for blacks, 1,244 for Hispanics, and 471 for whites.

The Incarceration of African Americans

The lifetime chances of anyone living in the United States going to prison reached 6.6% in 2001, up from 1.9% in 1974.[88] As shown in table 12.5, each new cohort over the 30-year span faced increased risks of going to prison. The figures can be subdivided into age categories. The percentage of black males between the ages of 18 and 24 "ever incarcerated" in a prison as of 2001 was 8.5%, compared to only 1.1% for white males in that age group. For black males 25–34 the percentage was 20.4, compared to 2.8% for white males; for ages 35–44 the percentage of black males was 22 compared to 3.5 for white males. The percentages for Hispanic males fell between those for whites and blacks (4%, 9% and 10% for the 3 age categories).[89] The differences for females based on ethnicity reflected similar disparities.

In 2001 about 2.7% of all adults had been to prison (5.6 million); by the year 2010 it is estimated that this will rise to 3.4% (7.7 million).[90] Given that blacks are four or five times more likely than whites to ever experience incarceration, this suggests that by 2010 between 12 and 15% of all blacks will be in prison, if recent incarceration trends continue.

Table 12.6 illustrates the dramatic racial differences among incarcerated inmates. Note that at every age and for each gender, the highest rates of incarceration are for blacks, followed by Hispanics, and the lowest rates

Table 12.5 Lifetime Chances of Going to State of Federal Prison for the First Time

Race	1974	1991	2001
White male	2.2%	4.4%	5.9%
White female	0.2%	0.5%	0.9%
Black male	13.4%	29.4%	32.2%
Black female	1.1%	3.6%	5.6%
Hispanic male	4.0%	16.3%	17.2%
Hispanic female	0.4%	1.5%	2.2%

Source: Bonczar, T. P. *Prevalence of Imprisonment in the U.S. Population, 1974–2001*. Washington, DC: Bureau of Justice Statistics, August 2003, p. 8.

Table 12.6   Inmates in State or Federal Prisons and Local Jails, June 30, 2006 (rate per 100,000)

Age	Male				Female			
	Total	**White**	**Black**	**Hispanic**	**Total**	**White**	**Black**	**Hispanic**
Total	1,384	736	4,789	1,862	134	94	358	152
18–19	1,766	935	5,336	2,112	120	81	262	175
20–24	3,352	1,675	10,698	4,168	290	221	637	346
25–29	3,395	1,685	11,695	3,912	300	226	716	305
30–34	3,289	1,874	11,211	3,652	370	292	924	333
35–39	2,805	1,641	9,804	3,094	378	282	999	337
40–44	2,344	1,419	7,976	2,630	284	200	798	279
45–54	1,209	677	4,421	1,813	112	75	326	141
55+	256	170	869	543	12	9	28	26

Source: Sabol, W. J., T. D. Minton, and P. M. Harrison. *Prison and Jail Inmates at Midyear 2006*. Washington, DC: Bureau of Justice Statistics, June 2007, p. 9.

are for whites. The 1960s had a phrase: "If you're white, you're alright; if you're brown, stick around; if you're black, stay back." Little has changed in almost five decades.

The national trends are disheartening. Looking at individual states confirms the huge gaps in imprisonment rates along racial lines. In 2003 the incarceration rate for blacks in North Carolina was 1,121 compared to a rate of 184 for whites (2003 figures).[91] In Texas, blacks were incarcerated at a rate more than 5 times that of whites (3,734 vs. 694); the rate for Latinos (1,152) was more than 3 times the rate for whites. Blacks and Latinos constituted about 70% of the total prison population.[92] The incarceration rate of blacks for drug possession in Illinois is the highest in the country; 66% of inmates in prisons for drug offenses were black.[93] Chicago accounts for two-thirds of all drug offender arrests in Illinois. Assistant Public Defender Kristina Yi described the ethnicity of people passing through the Cook County Criminal Courts building: "Rarely did we get a case that involved someone that's not a minority. Usually they were young male blacks."

As noted in chapter 7, part of the explanation for the increased number of arrests and convictions of blacks for a drug offense is the difference in the markets. Drug sales in urban neighborhoods are much more likely to take place in the open. Laws designed to target drug sales, as with the cocaine laws discussed in chapter 10, often adversely affect blacks and minorities. The Illinois Controlled Substances Act prescribes mandatory prison terms for selling drugs within 1,000 feet of schools, churches, public housing, and parks. Ninety percent of Illinois inmates charged with violating "safe zone" laws are African American. The *Chicago Tribune* found that almost 70% of Chicago is located within 1,000 feet of such structures.[94]

> Twenty-five years after President Ronald Reagan declared a war on drugs, many law-enforcement officials and criminologists say drugs are now cheaper and more potent, and as easily available as ever. What the war did do was help drive the nation's prison population to more than quadruple its size from 1980 to 2005, with urban blacks and Latinos hardest hit—a dramatically disproportionate result of the different networks that developed to distribute drugs.

In the next chapter we take a look at life inside a prison through a detailed profile of the typical prisoner. Prisons bear no resemblance to the "country clubs" alluded to by uninformed politicians trying to get elected on a "get tough on crime" platform. Sadly, those repressive sentiments—and the legislation that follows—contribute to the problem of crime.

Summary

Prisons are a relatively recent invention in the United States. Of the two contrasting models of prisons, the Auburn plan eventually became the dominant one after the Pennsylvania plan's optimistic hopes for repentance proved even more repressive than regimented discipline. Mirroring the growth in federal prison populations in the early 1900s due to new legislation, the prison population skyrocketed in the last quarter century with the legislation intended to combat the "war on drugs." More prisoners require more prisons, and building accelerated to match the growth in prisoners.

The effects of the drug war and the prison-building frenzy have been most negatively felt in minority communities. The ethnic composition of the general population is 12.5% black, 14.5% Hispanic, and almost 75% white. Yet in 2005, 60% of all inmates with a prison sentence of more than one year were black or Hispanic. Most of the growth in the prison population has come from convictions for drug-related offenses—not from convictions for traditional crimes such as murder, robbery, and burglary. The prison system exemplifies a "new American apartheid," similar to residential segregation but even more devastating in its consequences.

Key Terms

- Auburn plan
- Big House
- congregate system
- correctionalists
- Irish system
- mark system
- new American apartheid
- parole
- Pennsylvania plan
- reformatory
- silent system
- statutes of labourers
- ticket-of-leave
- Walnut Street Jail

Notes

[1] The first five periods were suggested by John Irwin in his *Prisons in Turmoil*. Boston: Little, Brown, 1980. The last period (covering the years since Irwin's book) was suggested by Robert Weiss (personal communication).

[2] Takagi, P. "The Walnut Street Jail: A Penal Reform to Centralize the Powers of the State." *Federal Probation* (December 1975); see also Barnes, H. E. *The Story of Punishment*. Montclair, NJ: Patterson Smith, 1972 [1930], p. 81.

[3] Ibid., p. 23.

[4] Ibid., pp. 22–23.

[5] Madison, J. "No. 10: Madison." In A. Hamilton, J. Madison, and J. Jay (eds.), *The Federalist Papers*. New York: Mentor, 1961, pp. 78–79.

[6] Zinn, H. *A People's History of the United States* (2nd ed.). New York: HarperCollins, 1995, pp. 90–96.

[7] Chomsky, N. *Powers and Prospects*. Boston: South End Press, 1996, pp. 123–125, 154.

[8] Rothman, D. J. *The Discovery of the Asylum*. Boston: Little, Brown, 1971, pp. 58–59. Rothman (using a consensus argument) suggests that Americans wanted social order, although those with the most influence were a relatively small ruling elite that wanted a *certain kind of order,* one that would primarily benefit members of their own class. See Chomsky, *Powers and Prospects* for further elaboration.

[9] Mellosi, D. and M. Lettiere. "Punishment in the American Democracy: The Paradoxes of Good Intentions." In R. P. Weiss and N. South (eds.), *Comparing Prison Systems: Toward a Comparative and International Penology*. Australia: Gordon and Breach, 1998, p. 22.

[10] Shichor, D. *The Meaning and Nature of Punishment*. Long Grove, IL: Waveland Press, 2006, p. 97.

[11] Barnes, H. E. and N. Teeters. *New Horizons in Criminology*. Englewood Cliffs, NJ: Prentice-Hall, 1959, pp. 338–339.

[12] Barnes, *The Story of Punishment*, p. 132.

[13] The History of the Electric Chair. [Online] http://www.ccadp.org/electricchair.htm

[14] Shichor, *The Meaning and Nature of Punishment*, p. 98.

[15] Austin, J. and J. Irwin. *It's about Time: America's Incarceration Binge* (3rd ed.). Belmont, CA: Wadsworth, 2001, pp. 127–128; Hallinan, J. *Going Up the River: Travels in a Prison Nation*. New York: Random House, 2001, pp. 117–118.

[16] de Beaumont, G. and A. de Tocqueville. *On the Penitentiary System in the United States and Its Application in France*. Carbondale, IL: Southern Illinois University Press, 1964 [1833].

[17] Mellosi and Lettiere, "Punishment in the American Democracy."

[18] Bentham, J. *The Panopticon Writings*, ed. Miran Bozovic. London: Verso, 1995, p. 29–95. [Online] http://cartome.org/panopticon2.htm

[19] Foucault, M. *Discipline and Punish: The Birth of the Prison*. New York: Vintage Books, 1979.

[20] Shichor, *The Meaning and Nature of Punishment*, p. 94.

[21] de Beaumont and de Tocqueville, *On the Penitentiary System.*

[22] Pisciotta, A. *Benevolent Repression: Social Control and the American Reformatory-Prison Movement*. New York: New York University Press, 1994, p. 11.

[23] Wines, E. C. and T. Dwight. *Report on the Prisons and Reformatories of the United States and Canada*. New York: AMS Press, 1973 [1867]; ibid., p. 12.

[24] Quotation cited in Pisciotta, *Benevolent Repression,* p. 11.

[25] Morris, N. *Maconochie's Gentlemen: The Story of Norfolk Island and the Roots of Modern Prison Reform.* New York: Oxford University Press, 2002; For a short biography see the following Web site: http://www.cs.act.gov.au/amc/home/ambiography

[26] Simon, J. *Poor Discipline: Parole and the Social Control of the Underclass, 1890–1990.* Chicago: University of Chicago Press, 1993.

[27] Walker, S. *Popular Justice: A History of American Criminal Justice* (2nd ed.). New York: Oxford University Press, 1998, p. 95.

[28] Pisciotta, *Benevolent Repression,* pp. 12–13.

[29] Platt, A. *The Child Savers.* Chicago: University of Chicago Press, 1977, pp. 67–68.

[30] Pisciotta, *Benevolent Repression,* p. 22.

[31] Ibid., p. 4.

[32] Barnes, *The Story of Punishment,* p. 147.

[33] Platt, *The Child Savers,* p. 68.

[34] Walker, *Popular Justice,* pp. 97–98.

[35] Rotman, E. "The Failure of Reform: United States, 1865–1965." In N. Morris and D. Rothman (eds.), *The Oxford History of the Prison: The Practice of Punishment in Western Society.* New York: Oxford University Press, 1995, p. 165.

[36] Irwin, *Prisons in Turmoil,* p. 3; Killinger, G. F. and P. Cromwell (eds.). *Penology.* St. Paul, MN: West, 1973, p. 47.

[37] Rothman, D. *Conscience and Convenience: The Asylum and Its Alternatives in Progressive America.* Boston: Little, Brown, 1980, pp. 157–158.

[38] Rotman, "The Failure of Reform," p. 186.

[39] Allen, H. E., E. S. Latessa, B. S. Ponder, and C. E. Simonsen. *Corrections in America: An Introduction* (11th ed.). Upper Saddle River, NJ: Prentice-Hall, 2007, p. 207.

[40] Rotman, "The Failure of Reform," p. 187.

[41] Allen et al., *Corrections in America,* pp. 213–214.

[42] Irwin, *Prisons in Turmoil,* pp. 38–39; Rotman, "The Failure of Reform," pp. 169–171.

[43] Barnes and Teeters, *New Horizons in Criminology,* p. 440.

[44] Irwin, *Prisons in Turmoil,* p. 40; Rotman, "The Failure of Reform," pp. 169–170.

[45] Rotman, "The Failure of Reform," p. 190.

[46] Irwin, *Prisons in Turmoil,* pp. 41–42.

[47] Rotman, "The Failure of Reform," p. 190.

[48] Irwin, *Prisons in Turmoil,* pp. 46–47.

[49] Public Safety Performance. *Public Safety Spending: Forecasting America's Prison Population 2007–2011.* [Online] http://www.pewpublicsafety.org/pdfs/PCT%20Public%20Safety%20Public%20Spending.pdf

[50] International Centre for Prison Studies. July 2007. [Online] http://www.kcl.ac.uk//depsta/rel/icps/worldbrief/highest_to_lowest_rates.php

[51] Christie, N. *Crime Control as Industry* (3rd ed.). New York: Routledge, 2000, p. 31; see also Christie, N. *A Suitable Amount of Crime.* New York: Routledge, 2004, p. 59.

[52] International Centre for Prison Studies.

[53] Welch, M. "Force and Fraud: A Radically Coherent Criticism of Corrections as Industry." *Contemporary Justice Review* 6: 231 (2003).

[54] Stephan, J. J. *Census of State and Federal Correctional Facilities, 2000.* Washington, DC: Bureau of Justice Statistics, August 2003.

[55] Public Safety Performance, p. 18–19.

[56] Bureau of Prisons. *Quick Facts, 2007.* [Online] http://www.bop.gov/about/facts.jsp#4

[57] FBI, *Uniform Crime Reports, 2005.* Table 29, Arrest Table. [Online] http://www.fbi.gov/ucr/05cius/arrests/index.html

[58] Mauer, M. *Race to Incarcerate* (2nd ed.) New York: The New Press, 2006, pp. 35–36.

[59] Harrison, P. M. and A. J. Beck. *Prisoners in 2005.* Washington, DC: Bureau of Justice Statistics, 2006, p. 9.

[60] Harrison and Beck, *Prisoners in 2005,* p. 9.

[61] *Drug War Facts.* [Online] http://www.drugwarfacts.org/prisdrug.htm

[62] Ibid., p. 10.

[63] *Drug War Facts.*

[64] Bureau of Justice Statistics. *Compendium Federal Justice Statistics, 2004* (NCJ 213476). December 2006, p. 2.

[65] Scalia, J. *Federal Drug Offenders, 1999 with Trends 1984–99.* Washington, DC: Bureau of Justice Statistics, p. 7.

[66] For a more detailed treatment of the notion of jails and prisons as poorhouses see Morris and Rothman, *The Oxford History of the Prison.*

[67] Fowles, R. and M. Merva. "Wage Inequality and Criminal Activity: An Extreme Bounds Analysis for the United States." *Criminology* 34: 163–182 (1996).

[68] In 1948, the year the Nationalist Party came to power in South Africa and instituted apartheid, the Mississippi Supreme Court, in *Murray v. State,* decided that segregated seating in courtrooms was not a constitutional violation. The court argued that such seating arrangements were grounded firmly in community custom. It was not until 1963, in *Johnson v. Virginia,* that the U.S. Supreme Court ruled that segregated seating in a courtroom constituted a denial of equal protection (Higginbotham Jr., A. L. *Shades of Freedom: Racial Politics and Presumptions of the American Legal Process.* New York: Oxford University Press, 1996).

[69] Piven, F. F. and R. A. Cloward. *The Breaking of the American Social Compact.* New York: New Press, 1997.

[70] Handler, J. F. and Y. Hasenfeld. *We the Poor People: Work, Poverty, and Welfare.* New Haven: Yale University Press, 1997; Wilson, W. J. *When Work Disappears: The World of the New Urban Poor.* New York: Vintage Books, 1997; Massey, D. and N. Denton. *The American Apartheid: Segregation and the Making of the Underclass.* Cambridge, MA: Harvard University Press, 1993; Harrington, M. *The Other America.* New York: Macmillan, 1962, and *The New American Poverty.* New York: Penguin Books, 1984.

[71] Massey and Denton, *The American Apartheid.*

[72] Brown, W. B. "The Fight for Survival: African American Gang Members and Their Families in a Segregated Society." *Juvenile and Family Court Journal* 49(2): 1–14 (1998).

[73] Wacquant, L. "Deadly Symbiosis: When Ghetto and Prison Meet and Mesh." *Punishment and Society* 3:97 (2001).

[74] Ibid.

[75] Ibid., p. 105, emphasis in the original.

[76] Ibid., p. 106, emphasis in the original.

[77] Ibid., p. 107.

[78] Ibid., p. 108. The idea that schools are sort of "day prisons" has long been noted by critics. See Shelden, R. G. *Delinquency and Juvenile Justice in American Society.* Long Grove, IL: Waveland Press, 2006, chapter 10. See also Giroux, H. "The Politics/Color of Punishment." *Z Magazine* (February 2001). [Online] http://www.zmag.org/ZMag/articles/feb01giroux.htm

[79] Cited in Western, B., B. Pettit, and J. Guetzkow. "Black Economic Progress in the Era of Mass Imprisonment." In M. Mauer and M. Chesney-Lind (eds.), *Invisible Punishment: The Collateral Consequences of Mass Imprisonment.* New York: New Press, 2002, p. 169.

[80] Ibid.

[81] Shelden, R. G. "The Imprisonment Crisis in America: Introduction." *Review of Policy Research* 21: 5–12 (January 2004).

[82] Western et al., "Black Economic Progress in the Era of Mass Imprisonment," p. 172.

[83] Travis, J. "Invisible Punishment: An Instrument of Social Exclusion." In Mauer and Chesney-Lind, *Invisible Punishment*, p. 18.

[84] Ibid., pp. 19, 295.

[85] Ibid., p. 19.

[86] Clear, T. "The Problem with 'Addition by Subtraction': The Prison-Crime Relationship in Low-Income Communities." In Mauer and Chesney-Lind, *Invisible Punishment*, p. 202.

[87] Harrison and Beck, *Prisoners in 2005,* p. 9.

[88] Bonczar, T. P. *Prevalence of Imprisonment in the U.S. Population, 1974–2001.* Washington, DC: Bureau of Justice Statistics, August 2003, p. 7.

[89] Ibid., p. 6.

[90] Ibid., pp. 1–7.

[91] Prison Policy Initiative. [Online] http://www.prisonpolicy.org/articles/northcarolina.shtml

[92] Ziedenberg, J. and V. Schiraldi. "Race and Imprisonment in Texas." Washington, DC: Justice Policy Institute, 2005. [Online] http://www.justicepolicy.org/downloads/JPISTUDYRACEPRISONTEXAS05.pdf

[93] Little, D. "Drug War Enforcement Hits Minorities Hardest: Drug Arrests Reveal Racial Gap." *Chicago Tribune* (July 22, 2007) p. 1.

[94] Ibid.

thirteen

Doing Time in American Prisons

THE PRISON WORLD

A survey conducted by John Irwin and James Austin found that the typical prisoner incarcerated in the state prison system (where most prisoners are found) was an African-American male between the ages of 18 and 29 with less than a high school diploma convicted for either a property or a drug offense. The majority of prisoners had been sentenced as a result of a new court conviction (67%); about one-fourth had no prior felony convictions. More than one-fourth were on parole at the time they were arrested (29%); about 16% of the parole violators were sent back to prison for failing to meet parole specifications (mostly for flunking urine tests).[1]

Who Goes to Prison and for What Crimes?

At the beginning of 2004, 21% of state prisoners had been convicted for a property offense, 20% for a drug offense, and slightly over half for a violent offense (14% for robbery, 12% for murder, 9% for assault, 5% for rape, 11% for other violent offenses).[2] Of inmates released from prison in 1994, 77.5% had been sentenced for a nonviolent crime (two-thirds for either property or drug offenses) and about 84% had prior convictions. It would be misleading to say that all of the inmates released were nonviolent; approximately 10% had a prior conviction for a violent crime, and 31% had been arrested for a violent crime. Within 3 years, about 70% had been rearrested for a new crime, with almost 27% sent back to prison.[3]

The percentage of all admissions to state or federal prisons for parole violations has remained at more than one-third each year since 2000. In 2005, there were almost 677,000 new court commitments to state prison; of those, 232,229 were parole violators. The majority of people in prison today had prior convictions; often they were on parole or probation at the time of their latest crime.[4]

Prisoners generally have very little education. Among state prisoners, 40% never finished high school, while just under than 30% (28.5%) received a GED, and 23% received a regular high school diploma. Most of those who have a GED earned the degree while incarcerated. The proportion without a high school diploma increased by one-third between 1991 and 1997.[5]

Austin and Irwin focused on the lives of people sentenced to prison (going where raw statistics never go) in their examination of a sample of prisoners in three states: Nevada, Illinois, and Washington. They first examined the crimes for which prisoners had been convicted and sent to prison and the level of seriousness of the crimes.[6] They assigned four general categories, ranging from most serious to least serious. The most common category (52.6% of all inmates) was "petty crimes," defined as "crimes with no aggravating features"—that is, no large amount of money was involved, no one was injured, and so on. The category included shoplifting and smoking a marijuana cigarette (possession of marijuana is a felony in Nevada). The following is one example.

> Edmond is a 50-year-old white carpenter who works in Florida in the winter and

Seattle in the summer. He had been arrested once 22 years ago for receiving stolen property. He was passing through Las Vegas on his way to Seattle and says he found a billfold with $100 on a bar where he was drinking and gambling. The owner, who suspected him of taking it, turned him in. He was charged with grand larceny and received three years.[7]

The next largest category (29.4%) was "moderate crimes." Acts that resulted in minor injury, use of heroin, selling marijuana, use of a weapon, and theft of more than $1,000 are examples of crimes in the moderate category. The third category was "serious crimes" (13.2% of the inmates). These crimes included theft of more than $10,000, attempted murder, and the sale of heroin. The fourth category, "very serious crimes" (4.8%), included rape, manslaughter, homicide, and kidnapping.

Austin and Irwin also examined the "criminal careers" of these offenders, taking into account not only the current offense but also offenses committed in the past. They emphasize that the stereotype of the "career criminal" as a crazed person who commits one felony after another is not accurate; in fact, they found quite the opposite. They identified five distinct patterns of crime for the offenders studied: (1) "into crime" (43%), (2) "crime episode" (19%), (3) "being around crime" (18%), (4) "one-shot crime" (14%), and (5) "derelicts" (6%). These patterns are remarkably similar to those identified by Irwin and others in studies conducted around thirty years ago.[8]

Individuals in the "into crime" category were heavily involved in a wide variety of criminal behaviors, almost on a daily basis. They are described and describe themselves as "dope fiends," "hustlers," "gang bangers," and the like. More than half of these individuals were in prison before, and about a third of them served time as juvenile offenders. Most of these very active criminals, however, were convicted of "petty crimes" and did not fit the popular image of the "vicious predator." Rather, they were "disorganized, unskilled, undisciplined petty criminals who very seldom engaged in violence or made

any significant amounts of money from their criminal acts."[9]

Individuals in the "crime episode" category were much less involved in a criminal lifestyle than were members of the "into crime" group. Most had lived a relatively conventional life free of crime—although many were not exactly strangers to the world of crime. Most had been arrested a few times, and a few had served time. They got involved in some sort of "crime spree" (a drinking "binge," a party where things got "out of hand," etc.) and landed in prison.

Individuals in the "being around crime" category were what some researchers have called "corner boys."[10] These were mostly young males from lower-class neighborhoods where crime is a fact of life. The individuals within this category generally were not regular members of gangs or other groups involved in crime, but they were acquaintances. Occasionally they were confronted by the police, perhaps while "hanging out" with their friends, and exhibited some form of macho behavior in order to conform to the "code of the streets." That behavior could lead to an arrest. They might have been witnesses to a crime or were drawn into a crime because they saw an opportunity to make some easy money (without any careful planning).[11]

Individuals in the "one-shot crime" category had no prior serious involvement in crime. The seriousness of the offense or the fact that the crime was associated with some mandatory sentencing law landed them in prison. Austin and Irwin describe, for example, a middle-aged man who was out of work and was lured into buying some cocaine from an undercover drug agent.

Individuals in the "derelicts" category had, in Austin and Irwin's words, "lost the capacity to live in organized society." Most had extensive records, mostly for petty crimes. Thus, they had the highest rate of imprisonment (91% had a prior prison record), including doing time as a juvenile (71%). Most used drugs and alcohol rather extensively.

A Look Inside the Prison World

What happens inside a prison? How do people survive such confinement? Austin and Irwin provide a vivid description of the current "warehousing" of prisoners:

> Convicted primarily of property and drug crimes, hundreds of thousands of prisoners are being crowded into human (or inhuman) warehouses where they are increasingly deprived, restricted, isolated, and consequently embittered and alienated from conventional worlds and where less and less is being done to prepare them for their eventual release. As a result, most of them are rendered incapable of returning to even a meager conventional life after prison. Because most will be released within two years, we should be deeply concerned about what happens to them during their incarceration.[12]

If you spend any time examining the daily activities of a prison (whether as a prisoner, a member of the staff, or an outside observer), you are confronted with the fact that the emphasis at all times is on custody. At various times during a 24-hour period, all activities cease, and "counts" are made (at least four times daily and sometimes as often as every two hours). There are also periodic searches of cells, special passes permitting movement about the institution, and myriad rules and regulations governing just about every behavior imaginable. The "count" is the most important task for which the custody staff is responsible. It is a reflection of what is called the *lock psychosis*—"Prison inmates were feared as the *convict bogey*, which could be dealt with only by locking and relocking, counting, and recounting."[13] This exaggerated fear of inmates or ex-inmates is usually far out of proportion to any actual danger.

Prison Security Levels

Three types of prisons are found in nearly every state and in the federal prison system. A *maximum-security prison* is typically large and built like a fortress. Old maximum-security prisons (the "Big Houses," described in Chapter 12) have high, concrete walls. Newer models have chain-link fences topped with razor wire, along with strategically placed towers where guards with an assortment of firearms stand watch. A maximum-security prison for the most difficult offenders is the *supermax prison*. Examples

are the Federal Penitentiary at Marion, Illinois, the Federal Correctional Complex in Florence, Colorado, and Pelican Bay State Prison in Crescent City, California.

Opened in 1989 and reserved for the "most disruptive offenders" (all male), Pelican Bay was built at an estimated cost of $278 million. It was designed to hold 2,280 prisoners but in 2007 held 3,481 prisoners. Half of the inmates at Pelican Bay are in the Security Housing Unit (SHU) "designed for inmates presenting serious management concerns," including prison gang members and violent maximum security inmates.[14] This unit is completely segregated from the main prison. SHU prisoners spend almost 23 hours per day in their cells. They are permitted only an hour and a half for exercise in small, concrete yards with 20-foot-high cement walls. They eat all their meals in their cells. The SHU has its own infirmary, law library, and room for parole hearings.[15]

A similar unit is the Inmate Management Unit at the Oregon State Prison. Chuck Terry, a product of both the California and the Oregon prison systems, provides this description:

> Most of the people in here are dings, cell warriors, shit slingers, and PC [protective custody] cases. They call this the Thunderdome because of the way sound is intensified and echoes. The cell warriors and dings never seem to sleep. They make noise constantly; hollering, whistling, kicking the doors, jumping on the metal bunks, arguing, etc. IT'S LOUD. . . . We're trapped in a little cell 24 hours a day (or 23 1/2 hours 5 days, and 24 hours two days) and subjected to this psychotic noise and sleep deprivation. Then there's the design of the place. We're watched 24 hours a day. Try to take a shit and wipe your ass with a female cop watching you. Degradation![16]

Medium-security prisons are somewhat less restrictive and are often called "correctional institutions" or "correctional facilities." However, most have guard towers and chain-link fences topped with razor wire. Many have *congregate housing,* or dormitory-style living arrangements. One of the first prisons to use this design was the Norfolk Prison Colony in Massachusetts (later renamed Massachusetts Correctional Institution at Norfolk), which opened in 1931.[17] Some medium-security prisons have a podular design. Each pod has a congregate living area, common toilet and shower areas, and separate cells for each inmate. Each cell has a solid-core door with a lock controlled by the prisoner. Entry to the pod is controlled from the outside. These pods resemble college dormitories. There are fewer rules, and inmates in some areas may be allowed to wear civilian clothes when not working. Movement about the prison is not as restricted as in maximum-security prisons.[18]

Minimum-security prisons somewhat resemble college campuses (or in popular jargon, "country clubs"). Some are called "ranches" or "farms." Most prisoners housed in these kinds of institutions pose little security threat, and most are nonviolent offenders (many are white-collar offenders). Although movement around the campus is usually not restricted, inmates *are* confined and cannot leave the premises.

The Daily Routine

Most of the work in a prison is arranged to keep the institution running smoothly. Many prisoners are idle or work only a few hours each day. If the inmates work, the jobs generally consist of sweeping, cooking and serving meals, washing clothes and other prison articles, filing and typing and other administrative duties, library work, or running errands.

The jobs performed by the staff help maintain the prison and also reflect the overwhelming concern with custody. In 2005 there were 381,000 custody/security staff in U.S. prisons (state, federal and private).[19] Of those, 23% were women, and 33% were nonwhite. In 2002, there was an average of 5.8 inmates per correctional officer. On average, mental health staff represented only 2.9% of prison staff (counselors 1.8%; caseworkers, 1.7%; social workers, .7%; psychologists, .6%; psychiatrists, .2%; other, .8%).[20] With such minimal numbers, it is clear that rehabilitation is far less a priority than is custody.

What is a typical day like in a prison? Although the daily routine may vary from one institution to another, several accounts from different sources at different periods of time give a fairly accurate picture of this routine. We begin by quoting a former inmate's description of what occurred during his first few weeks in the Nevada State Prison in Carson City in 1978:

> For the first thirty days, all new inmates are held in the "fish tank." This is a portion of the prison where the incoming are initially diagnosed. Each inmate is given a cell, which is actually like a small room with a heavy metal door, and for most of the day that is where he stays. It is a time for prison officials to observe the inmates (like in a fish bowl), to administer medical and psychological tests, to have the inmate speak with the chaplain, and with the counselor, and to ascertain if there are any enemies in the general population who might cause the inmate harm (or find out if the inmate might have the idea of harming someone else). Haircuts are given (boot camp style), and showers are allowed once a day, and three meals are delivered to each cell by cart. Advice is given as to how to behave on the yard, and everyone is drilled on the rules and regulations and how the administration and guard staff operate. Inmate programs are explained, and the inmates are cautioned as to what type of activities to avoid (especially the "gang" related type).
>
> A good portion of my days were spent in isolation and I thought a great deal about "doing" my time. I wasn't exactly sure what to expect out there "on the yard," but I realized I would have to be very careful with whom I associated, with what I said and what I did. I would have to be very cautious with all aspects of my behavior, staying alert to both the inmates and the guards around me. I would have to pace myself as I got integrated into this community, a community where I would be spending a great deal of monotonous time; day to day, week to week, month to month, year to year.[21]

The following description details the routine in a maximum-security prison in Massachusetts:[22]

> 7:00 AM. Rise for the count. Wash and clean cell, making sure your bed is made. Also, stand at the door for the count.
>
> 7:20 AM. Breakfast.

8:00 AM. Work call. If you are unassigned, you go to the TV block or stay in your room.

11:35 AM. Work for the morning is complete and the men come in from the shop, returning to their rooms to wash up for dinner and to stand at the door for the count. This is the time to let the guard know if you do not want to go to the meal.

1:00 PM. Dinner over and this is the time for any announcements to be called, so listen for your name. You may be wanted to go to a hospital visit or the dentist. After any announcements, work call is again called and if and when you are assigned to a job you are to go to it.

3:45 PM. The men return from the shops at this time. This begins your free time. On clear days, the yard is open and you can go out until yard time is called. At this time the library is open to take books out and return them.

4:20 PM. Count time is called again, this time for supper. When count is called, return to your room and stand at the door.

5:45 PM. Another count is called at this time, and this is when the mail is given out, plus any receipts for money, etc.

6:00 PM. Count is called complete and the evening activities are announced: gym, avocation and discussion groups, etc.

10:00 PM. Count is again called to return to your room for the night, so stand at your door until the guard passes it.

11:00 PM. Lights out.

Bernadette Olson, who was an academic before she was incarcerated in a federal facility, kept a journal during her six months of incarceration. The entry below describes the hopelessness and repetitiveness of the daily routine.

> Staring across the compound I am overcome with feelings of sadness at the day that awaits me. Convict living is disconsolate, painful and ominous. Most of society will counter by saying "that is the point of prison." Everyday I look at rows and rows of razor wire, angry faces yelling at the masses, cubicles as empty as the women who live there, walls that seemed to close in around me, crowded with women society doesn't want—grown women fighting and acting out as they struggle to have some

small amount of control. There is repetition in everything we do—work, conversation, interactions—it all seems so meaningless. It reeks of hopelessness and shame. This *is* as painful as it is supposed to be, but what of restoration and healing? We are caged and warehoused, discarded as human waste.[23]

In the early 1980s, the senior author (RGS) spent two years observing life at the Southern Nevada Correctional Center in Jean, Nevada (a medium-security prison forty miles south of Las Vegas). At that time, most of the inmates had job assignments; at least this is what was indicated on the daily roster. In reality, most work lasted no more than two or three hours, if that much. Observations of this prison revealed a great deal of idleness. Men spent most of the day (in warm months) in the yard getting a tan, listening to the radio, playing cards, or engaging in other activities. Others spent the bulk of their time in the housing units either playing cards or watching television. There were televisions in each dormitory-type unit, and they were turned on during most of the day. One of the major complaints was boredom.

All of these activities take place within what Goffman calls a *total institution*. Everything that a prisoner does (eat, sleep, work, play, etc.) takes place within the confines of one physical space, whereas in the free world these activities take place in separate locations. In the ideal total institution,

> all phases of the day's activities are tightly scheduled, with one activity leading at a prearranged time into the next, the whole sequence of activities being imposed from above by a system of explicit formal rulings and a body of officials.[24]

Even in such an institution, however, the people confined do have some choices about the kinds of activities in which they will engage. The total institution in the sense that Goffman describes probably does not exist. Nevertheless, prisoners can (and many do) become totally dependent on those in charge. It is almost as if the prisoners return to a status of childhood. The prison provides all their basic needs, and they do not have to assume any responsibility for obtaining those needs. Watterson, in her study of women's prisons, describes this situation as analogous to a "concrete womb" (we revisit her study in chapter 17).[25]

The fact that prisoners do not have to make any important decisions about their lives is a crucial point. Most of us make many decisions throughout the course of our lives—constant decisions about meeting our most basic needs. We also are responsible for taking care of personal matters, some of which we do almost without thinking. For instance, we get up in the morning and drive to work, we shop for our food and decide what will be on the menu each night, we pay our monthly bills, and we make hundreds of other decisions that are part of everyday living. In a prison (or in other total institutions such as mental hospitals, army boot camps, and boarding schools), most of these decisions are made by those in command. The longer a person spends within such an institution, the greater the chance of becoming totally dependent and not learning how to meet these normal responsibilities. Little wonder that many prisoners find it so difficult to readjust to outside life, where they must be solely responsible for making decisions and meeting their own needs. In some cases, dependency becomes almost total.

What is it like to be locked up and shut away from the outside world? For most of us, it is impossible to imagine. Try to picture what life would be like if you were confined to the physical space of your campus. No matter how many things you could do, no matter how comfortable your housing, and no matter how many of your basic physical needs were met (food, shelter, clothing, etc.), you would soon long to escape because a critical basic need would be missing—freedom. The ability to move about and go where you want to go and to associate with whomever you want is a freedom we take for granted.

Some readers may believe that offenders deserve to suffer. Losing one's liberty is a jarring punishment. Subjecting prisoners to additional deprivations, degradations, and humiliation often produces anger and resentment. The desire to "get even" adds to recidivism rates.

The Pains of Imprisonment

Chuck Terry is an ex-convict who spent many years behind bars before becoming a college professor; he has written extensively about prison life from the point of view of those who "do time." He observes that the entire process, starting with an arrest and ending with a prison sentence, has a profound affect on the individual. He notes that the "forces" of these "correctional systems" have a tendency to "belittle and control individuals caught within their grasp." Fifty years ago, Harold Garfinkel described routine procedures (e.g., strip searches) as "status degradation ceremonies."[26] From the point of view of prisoners, "the social conditions of prison are usually seen as dehumanizing and in drastic need of change."[27]

Olson described her feelings when she entered the federal correctional facility.

> When I first arrived, everything was so foreign. The hard part for me was trying to reconcile the dissonance in my head of where I'd come from and how far I had fallen. Even now, when I close my eyes, I can still see, and smell, and hear the inside of the prison. Some days it feels so heavy and tangible. As a first time inmate, I found myself in an extremely confusing and chaotic world where nothing seemed to make sense, and time seemed to stand still. The constant struggle to take in everything and everyone around me left me sick and exhausted. There were so many rules and expectations, some were written, most were not. It doesn't take an inmate long to realize there are prison guidelines and there are convict guidelines; strict adherence to both is crucial. Coming to grips with the actuality of my criminal status and the constant reminders of my failed life filled me with dread. The lack of hope I felt when I thought about what life would hold for me upon release consumed me. I was one of "them" now, and only recently have I been able to fully appreciate how deeply I would be changed.[28]

More than forty years ago, Gresham Sykes conducted a study of the New Jersey State Prison in which he noted several different effects of incarceration on those confined.

He termed these effects **pains of imprisonment,** and they are equally relevant today.[29]

The *deprivation of liberty* is the most obvious and immediate deprivation. Individuals can, in fact, be subject to double deprivation if they are placed in segregation, or solitary confinement. Imprisonment is a "moral rejection" by society, often resulting in what Goffman called the *mortification of the self.*[30] The prisoner is stripped (both literally and figuratively) of his or her "self"—most personal possessions are taken away, and a number is assigned to replace one's name. The new prisoner, or "fish" (prison argot for an arriving prisoner), learns quickly that he or she occupies the lowest status. Many experience the equivalent of a "time out from personal identity."[31]

Second, the prisoner suffers the *deprivation of goods and services.* The things to which a person would have access in the outside world are prohibited in prison—a car, money, clothes, adequate medical services, and so on. Since the majority of prisoners are poor, the lack of access to goods may be less of a hardship because they had nothing on the outside. Some, in fact, may find survival easier in prison (especially if they have been there before) because they will receive "three squares a day."

Third, there is the *deprivation of heterosexual relationships.* While a few prisons allow conjugal visits, the privilege is usually restricted to married couples and to only a few hours at a time, frequently with some form of supervision by officials. Homosexuality is common; some of the relationships are voluntary, others are not. The most common form of homosexuality takes place between aggressive males (known variously as "wolves" or "jockers") and passive males (often called "punks"). An experienced "wolf" entices a young "fish" into a relationship by offering friendship and "protection" from other "wolves" and by showing affection with the presentation of various gifts (cigarettes, a "cushy" job, etc.). After a while, the wolf demands sex (usually threatening the "punk" with being "turned loose" as prey for other "wolves").

Deprivation of autonomy is the fourth loss. One's freedom of movement and opportunity to be creative and independent are severely thwarted in prison. Also, one's privacy is reduced considerably, especially in prisons that are overcrowded and where there are two or more prisoners to a room.

Finally, there is the *deprivation of security.* In the outside world a person is relatively free from personal victimization; in prison it is a constant threat. As Sykes suggests: "Rubbed raw by the irritants of custodial life, and frequently marked by long histories of aggressive behavior, inmates are likely to explode into violence or take what they want from other inmates with the threat of force." The prison world is a violent world, rife with many of the same kinds of aggression and exploitation found in the outside world, only more directly visible.[32]

More recent studies suggest that doing time in today's prisons has even more negative consequences. Austin and Irwin's study documents that more and more prisoners are becoming withdrawn, and many have become what Austin and Irwin term "crippled." Prisons are often built in remote areas of society, limiting the number of contacts with the outside because family and friends often do not have the resources to arrange transportation. "These practices, along with greatly diminished rehabilitative resources, are producing prisoners who have deteriorated in prison and return to the outside much less well equipped to live a conventional life than they were when they entered."[33] Many prisoners become alienated from the rest of the world. The alienation has five dimensions: (1) *powerlessness*— prisoners feel they cannot effect changes; (2) *meaninglessness*—prisoners do not know what to believe; (3) *normlessness*—deviant behaviors are the only means for achieving success; (4) *detachment*—disassociation from core beliefs and values of society; (5) *self-estrangement*—experiencing oneself as "alien and unworthy."[34]

The prison world is a society with relatively scarce goods and resources. Those who inhabit it create their own culture, rules, and statuses. As prisoners compete for a share of the available goods and services, a power structure often emerges.

The Inmate Social System

Like any other organization or institution, the prison is a cultural system with norms and corresponding social roles. Olson describes the social system: "Prison reality is indeed harsh and unrelenting, with a hidden culture of norms, values, and social roles not seen on the outside; a milieu that seemed to force us to think only about surviving day to day."[35]

Both the "keepers" and the "kept" learn to adapt to the highly unusual situation. The prison is an enclosed structure where a large number of people live under extreme conditions. The *inmate social system* provides "a way of life which enables the inmate to avoid the devastating psychological effects of internalizing and converting social rejection into self-rejection. In effect, it permits the inmate to reject his rejecters rather than himself."[36]

There is a set of social roles and cultural norms that existed long before the prisoner arrived, and it will exist long after the prisoner's departure. It is a subculture that experienced inmates learn to adapt to, so much so that even if transferred from one prison to another, from one jail to another, an inmate immediately is able to make adjustments and often feel "at home." (Because of the large number of interinstitutional transfers and the general mobility of people in society today, it is not unusual for a prisoner recently released from, say, Attica, to commit a crime in California and meet up with old friends in San Quentin, or vice versa.)

The Inmate Code

The *inmate code* is a set of norms that describes how prisoners should behave. This code "provides a philosophy of doing time, includes ways of implementing the maxims of the code, includes rationalizations for criminal behavior, and satisfactory solutions for obtaining illegal goods and services to mitigate the prison poverty imposed upon the inmates."[37] The code is similar to the "code of the streets" and is imported into the prison environment.[38] The following five rules are the most important:[39]

1. Don't interfere with inmate interests. This rule includes more specific injunctions, such as never rat on a con (to "rat" is to "snitch" or to be a "stool pigeon").

2. Don't lose your head. Do your own time.

3. Don't exploit inmates. Don't steal from fellow prisoners; share goods and services with others.

4. Don't weaken. Inmates should be able to "take it," to "be tough," and, above all else, "be a man."

5. Don't be a sucker. Don't trust guards or other staff, and don't work too hard.

Argot Roles

Another important part of the inmate social system is the assumption of distinct roles or social types. *Argot roles* include the following:[40]

1. *Rat,* otherwise known as the "squealer." This individual betrays others and is one of the most despised of all inmates in the prison world.

2. *Center man,* also known as the "square John." This individual tends to take on the perspectives and values of persons in charge of the institution, rather than those of the inmate culture; he usually comes from a relatively stable working-class background and does not have a long history of criminal offenses.

3. *Gorilla.* This individual uses violence as a means to gain specific ends; he often preys on weaker inmates to get what he wants. A variation is characterized as "tough."

4. *Weaklings,* the opposite of "gorillas" and "toughs." These individuals find it difficult to adapt to prison life. A variation is the "rapo," the inmate who continually maintains his innocence, which is a constant irritation to other inmates (who say "stop complaining" and "do your own time").

5. *Merchant,* also known as the "peddler" and "entrepreneur." This individual engages in a wide variety of economic activities (cigarettes, drugs, alcohol, etc.); also known as the "racketeer."

6. *Wolves, punks, fags.* These are homosexual roles. "Wolves" play the aggressive male role, "punks" are those who are "made" (victimized), and "fags" were homosexual prior to coming to prison.

7. *Ball buster.* This person is always giving prison staff a hard time and, from the inmate culture's view, makes things worse for others by always "fouling things up" and acting the "fool."

8. *Right guy.* In contrast to the "ball buster," the "right guy" can "take it" and "dish it out." He is the most loyal of inmates. He never "rats" and "does his own time."

9. *Tough guy and hipster.* The "tough guy," in contrast to the "ball buster," "is regarded by other inmates with a curious mixture of fear and respect"; this person "represents the deference of terror" and does not act "wild" but rather is cold and calculating and "won't take anything from anybody." The "hipster" puts up a false front, acts tough but really isn't, and tries too hard to belong.[41]

A former prisoner described the role of "right guy."

> Being "one of the boys" carried with it a certain set of responsibilities. These responsibilities centered on being a "right guy" and this meant that one would not walk away from confrontation, nor "let out" any information on what others might be doing. It also meant, at times, knowing about and even participating in behavior that could lead to serious problems.
>
> With these kinds of responsibilities one is forced to stay keenly aware of the surrounding circumstances, to stay on top of their game in order that the "right guy" reputation stays intact. It's a difficult and wearing activity, and you have little room to escape its pressures. And I could not forget that I had an additional sentence hanging over my head should I get into trouble. Despite my outward "coolness" and my being in with the right crowd, I recognized that I was in a precarious situation. I hoped, and sometimes prayed, that I could manage to keep everything going as smoothly as it had.[42]

These roles are not rigid, and they are not found in every prison. There are many variations, and not every prisoner fits into a particular category.

Doing Time and Prisonization

Donald Clemmer first used the term "*prisonization*" to refer to the process in which a person takes on "the folkways, mores, customs, and general culture of the penitentiary."[43] The extent to which one becomes enmeshed in the prison culture—that is, becomes prisonized—depends on factors such as age, previous prison experiences, length of sentence, relations with people on the outside, and type of crime committed. All prisoners, to some extent, become prisonized. Perhaps the ultimate indication of prisonization is the belief that life inside prison is better (or at least no worse) than life outside, which leads a released prisoner to commit new crimes and hope for apprehension and a return to prison.

Other studies have found that the extent of prisonization (measured in terms of prisoners' lack of commitment to staff role expectations and degree of commitment to the inmate social system) varied according to the length of time served. The percentage of prisoners exhibiting a high degree of conformity to staff role expectations *decreased* with the length of time served. The degree of prisonization corresponded to three phases of the prisoner's institutional career. During the early and late stages (the first and last six months of the sentence), there was a high degree of conformity. During the middle phase, there was a low degree of conformity. It should be noted, however, that less than half of the prisoners exhibited a high degree of conformity at any time. Many prisoners adhere to staff expectations only to the extent necessary to present a favorable image to increase the likelihood of being released. No doubt many are simply playing a "con" (or game) in order to present a favorable image.[44]

Researchers have found that adherence to prison norms is partly the result of adherence to similar norms on the streets. In fact, certain norms and values included within the inmate code are also found in certain segments of the population on the outside, especially in the lower-class world where most offenders reside. Irwin's study of inmates in the 1960s found that the degree of prisonization depends mainly on the type of criminal experiences a person has had and the degree to which one develops a criminal identity.[45]

Irwin identified three modes of adaptation to imprisonment: jailing, doing one's own time, and gleaning. *Jailing* is full participation in the prison world. Inmates who adopt this mode become highly prisonized. For those with a lot of prior experience in jails and prisons, the prison may become "reality" and the world outside an "illusion."[46] Prisoners who *do their own time* either plan to "go straight" and commit no more crimes or plan to return to a life of crime after release; they undergo no significant change of attitude or worldview while in prison. Inmates who engage in what Irwin calls *gleaning* look ahead to the time when they will be released and try to change their life patterns and self-concepts in a significant way, such as by returning to school or changing work careers.[47]

In Irwin's sample of 116 felons, 15% were *jailers* who "tend to make a world out of prison."[48] This role is especially characteristic of *state-raised youth*, offenders who "grew up" within various institutions (foster care, group homes, juvenile detention centers, or correctional facilities), spending very little time in free society. Irwin describes their worldview as distorted, stunted, and incoherent; the prison world is the only meaningful world.

Most of the prisoners who "do their own time" (they are often "right guys") are part of the "thief subculture." They stay out of trouble, they don't "rat," and they participate in a wide variety of officially supported programs. This type of participation is known as *programming*. It is a method used by many inmates (not just thieves) to get out as soon as possible. They participate, superficially, in many different "treatment" programs to "look good" to the parole board. Many prison administrators and various vocational and psychological staff members actively encourage inmates to "program."

Gleaning, according to Irwin, is becoming more common. Many prisoners become self-educated, learn a new trade, and in general attempt to "improve their minds" or "find themselves."[49] The experiences of one prisoner, Jim Palombo, demonstrate the importance of seeking self-improvement through the educational process. Completing his undergraduate degree while still in prison

was Palombo's method of turning his life around. Even while still in jail waiting for his prison sentence to begin, Palombo was formulating his plan:

> But I knew that I was fortunate. I still had possession of the abilities I had, until now, abused; abilities given to me by another source that I had wrongly credited to my own being. I was now hoping—no, I was making a pact with myself—that I would make my "time" pay off. I would put my abilities to proper use. I would somehow get a college education, and I would redeem myself with it. It was time to move on, and, as the ironies of life often are, it was in this kind of place, in jail, that I felt the spirit to make it happen.[50]

After arriving at the main prison (Nevada State Prison in Carson City), Palombo kept thinking about his plan:

> I was trying to numb myself to the surroundings, and at the same time I kept thinking about my parents and my family and myself. Education kept popping into my head. . . . I'll get into it, I'll learn, I'll get my degree, I'll not waste the years in here, I'll turn this all around and become something . . . something more than what this place was suggesting . . . I must do it.[51]

The Sub-Rosa Economy

The relative poverty of prison inmates is partially offset by the *sub-rosa economy* (secret or private transactions, an underground economy), often controlled by gangs inside the prison. The economic transactions often involve cigarettes, food, clothing, and drugs.

More than thirty years ago three researchers documented the existence of a *sub-rosa economy* within the prison system. Vergil Williams and Mary Fish studied Menard State Prison in Illinois, and R. Theodore Davidson studied San Quentin in California.[52] At Menard, there were several systematic "routes" of highly organized theft of food from the kitchen and cigarettes. At San Quentin, the smuggling of drugs was a lucrative activity, with potential profit in excess of $100,000 per year.

Prison inmates can be very resourceful, primarily because of the need to improve the deprivations of living within a system of forced poverty. Prisoners utilize waste materials that might seem useless to more advantaged observers. Williams and Fish described how inmates used potato peels to make beer. The production and distribution of homemade beer (often called "pruno") was a lucrative activity.

Many goods and services that are forbidden inside prison (but are taken for granted in the outside world) become symbols of prestige and status within the prison world.

> If a free world citizen pays a laundry worker to place an extra crease in his shirt, it is an act hardly worthy of note, as it is assumed to be a small matter of personal preference. When the convict pays a laundry worker [payment usually comes in the form of a pack of cigarettes or some other medium of exchange] to place a crease in his shirt it is significant, for he may be demonstrating to the convict world his power and economic acumen. He is expressing a modest version of the Veblenian "conspicuous consumption." In the free world, the inmate would attempt to excel in the standard American way of acquiring material goods coveted by others, especially material goods easily displayed to strangers as well as to friends. On the streets the inmate might drive the flashiest automobile on the block and wear dapper clothes. In prison, since he is required to be uniformly drab and poverty stricken, small adjustments to his uniform are his way of displaying success to friends and strangers alike—his mode of conspicuous consumption. Small uniform adjustments, a crease here and a tuck there, are no less significant on the inside than big automobiles on the outside.[53]

In many ways, the prison world is a microcosm of the outside society, especially when it comes to economic activities and "conspicuous consumption." Examples that we have seen within the Nevada prison system include personal coffee cups (in the chow hall prisoners have to drink coffee out of plastic drinking glasses); personal televisions, radios, and stereos in one's cell (which inmates call their "house"); personally decorated "houses"; and personalized clothing (especially shirts and shoes, for all prisoners are required to wear blue jeans) sent in from friends and family on the streets. In short, inmates do just about anything to make prison life more bearable. Perhaps these activities, including the making of pruno and the various sub-rosa economic activities, are a positive sign of mental health, indicating that at least prisoners are active and creative rather than dull and robotic.

Prison life is not at all like what most of the public imagines—a country-club existence where inmates loaf and watch their own televisions, work out with weights, enroll in education programs, eat good food, and generally have a great time at public expense. If prisons are so comfortable, why aren't there long lines of people waiting to get inside? With few exceptions, prisons are dangerous places. Although there are few deaths, the threat of injury through some type of attack is constant.

PRISON VIOLENCE

In the modern prison, a new inmate often faces some difficult decisions. In the words of an inmate at the maximum-security prison at Leavenworth, Kansas: "Every convict has three choices. He can fight [kill someone], he can hit the fence [escape], or he can fuck [submit]."[54] The inmate may be exaggerating the need to kill someone, but he highlights the need to be constantly vigilant to protect oneself from attacks.

Data collected by Austin and Irwin on violence in California's prisons demonstrate the extent of the problem. The total number of violent incidents grew from 365 in 1970 to 9,769 in 1998 and the *rate* (per 100 prisoners) increased from 1.4 to 6.6. Generally, the most common type of violent incident was an assault without a weapon; a close second for most of those years was an assault *with* a weapon. In 1998, about 43% of the violent incidents did not involve a weapon, while 23% did.[55]

Austin and Irwin explored some of the reasons for the increase in violence inside prisons. One reason is the reduction of resources—educational, recreational, vocational—available to prisoners. The get-tough policies of the past decades have resulted in more money being spent on security. Another reason is that there are fewer contacts with loved ones, because more and more prisons are built in remote rural areas (e.g., the prisons in extreme northern Michigan are at least a full day's drive for inmates' relatives living in Detroit, which most of the inmates call home). This remoteness has also contributed to an overall decline in local services and support (e.g., churches).[56]

> The ties with family and community that former prisoners depend on after release also promote safety during incarceration. Unfortunately, the distance between home and the correctional facility—and a culture in some facilities that does not welcome visitors—makes it hard to maintain those ties.[57]

Other reasons for the increase in violence noted by Austin and Irwin include the often arbitrary forms of punishment meted out by the prison staff and a growing number of what inmates refer to as "chickenshit rules." Increasingly, a "gulag mentality" has developed as the privileges extended to earlier generations of prisoners (such as the freedom to decorate their walls with pictures, to alter prison clothing, to keep birds and other small pets in their cells, etc.) have been slowly taken away. The warden at the federal prison at Lompoc, California, destroyed a row of beautiful old eucalyptus trees that had surrounded the prison for fifty years and then poisoned the squirrels that had lived in those trees and had provided enjoyment for the inmates (feeding them, watching them play, etc.). He then "mounted a genocidal war against the cats and raccoons that roamed the prison grounds." The inmates referred to him as "Defoliating Bob."[58] These small freedoms make a world of difference to prisoners, and their removal generates anger and resentment toward those in authority.

> If you put poor, underprivileged young men together in a large institution without anything meaningful to do all day, there will be violence. If that institution is overcrowded, there will be more violence. If that institution is badly managed . . . [including] poor mental health care, there will be more vio-

lence. And if there is inadequate supervision of the staff, if there is ineffective discipline, if there is a code of silence, if there are inadequate investigations, there will be even more violence. . . .

> Crowding, and the tremendous increase in the prisoner population that underlies it, fuels violence. Crowding severely limits or eliminates the ability of prisoners to be productive, which can leave them feeling hopeless; pushes officers to rely on forceful means of control rather than communication; and makes it harder to classify and assign prisoners safely and to identify the dangerously mentally ill. Services ranging from nutrition to dental and medical care are affected by crowding. Every vital service is diluted or made operationally impossible. And then there is simply the excessive noise, heat, and tension. This is fertile ground for violence.[59]

Prison Riots

In February 1980, a riot at the New Mexico State Prison left thirty-three inmates dead and more than eighty people injured. Most of the inmates who were killed were prison "snitches" or "rats." This was one of the most brutal prison riots in history. Ironically, several of the snitches who were killed had warned officials about a possible riot. The prison was severely overcrowded—at 150% over its capacity. Prior to the rioting, a group of inmates had filed a lawsuit citing, among other things, corruption and nepotism. Officials failed to act. After the riot, a federal district court was empowered to oversee the operation of the prison.[60]

Early Prison Riots

Prior to the 1960s, most riots were a protest about prison conditions. Rather than challenging the prison system itself or various social issues outside the prison system, prisoners rioted over bad food, abusive treatment by the guards, lack of job training, and so on.[61] Riots of this kind have been termed *frustration riots* because they result from inmates venting frustration over the lack of decent conditions and successful treatment programs. Between 1950 and 1953 alone there were more than fifty such riots.[62] One of the most famous, the Battle of Alcatraz, occurred in 1946. A group of inmates tried to take over the prison and escape. Similar to the events portrayed in the movie, *The Rock,* prison guards, Marines, the Coast Guard, the harbor police, and the Army all participated in protecting "the rock."

One reason why the riots were so narrowly focused was that those in power within the inmate social system (e.g., "gorillas" and "racketeers") had a vested interest in maintaining the status quo. Another reason was that few inmates had developed any kind of political or social consciousness.

Another form of rioting—*race riots*—emerged in the 1960s as more and more racial minorities were sentenced to prison. Ninety-eight such riots were reported from 1969 to 1970.[63] These disturbances were just a hint of what was to come.

The Politicalization of Prison Riots: 1960s and 1970s

As the civil rights movement grew during the early 1960s, a number of factions developed within it. One faction was the Black Muslims, a movement that found its way into the prison system (with the help of Malcolm X, an ex-con himself). The Black Muslims' insistence that African Americans were victims of white racism rather than personal inadequacies was especially relevant to African-American inmates, who for so many years had accepted the notion that they were "sick" or just plain "criminals." The Muslims "introduced the notion of collective oppression to black prisoners, which counteracted the prison ideology of individual pathology."[64] Their advocacy of organization, self-discipline, and collective unity presented definite threats to prison authority. Two tactics advocated by the Muslims were strikes and lawsuits. Inmates used these tactics to protest prison conditions and to extend their constitutional rights inside the prison walls. The Muslims influenced African-American prisoners to see themselves as part of a larger oppressed class that consisted of prisoners both inside and outside the prison walls.

During the 1960s, the prison became less isolated from the outside world; it became a center for radical activity. Qualitative changes in prison populations, specifically the influx of relatively more educated and politically sophisticated young whites and African Americans convicted for drug-law violations and protest activities, facilitated the change. The number of books and articles written by inmates and ex-inmates had a significant impact on militant inmates, fostering their belief that they were part of an oppressed class.[65]

As growing numbers of prisoners were "politicized," they extended protests beyond prison conditions to a broader political protest. The prison was viewed as more than a building filled with "criminals." Critics said that it was just one aspect of a much larger network of economic and political oppression in U.S. society.

One result was *political riots*, or rebellions. A number of these incidents occurred during the late 1960s, culminating in the rebellion in 1971 at Attica, one of the most violent in prison history. In California prisons there were strikes and revolts at San Quentin in 1967, 1968, and 1970, and at Soledad and Folsom prisons in 1970. Each of these revolts showed evidence of tremendous unity and a breakdown of racial animosities.[66] In 1970, inmates at the Tombs jail in Manhattan revolted and presented a list of demands that went beyond the jail itself; many of these demands were identical to those that would be made at Attica a year later.[67] The revolt at Attica was marked by even more unity and lack of racial animosities. Tragically, ten hostages and twenty-nine inmates were killed in the unprecedented attack by the New York State Police, ordered by the governor of New York. An additional eighty-five inmates, three hostages, and one state police officer were wounded.[68]

Recent Prison Riots: The Rage Riot

Following the 1970s rebellions, prison populations settled into a more routine existence. Prisoners lacked the solidarity that had been the hallmark of the political riots. One of the primary reasons for the fragmentation was the transfer of several thousand "troublemakers" to other institutions. Another reason was the end of the Vietnam War and the end of antiwar protests. Still another reason was the growing conservative backlash against the social protests and reforms of the 1960s. By the middle of the 1970s, the conservative view of crime became much more dominant. Some theorists speculate that a classic divide-and-rule strategy was used to control popular protests. Stereotypes about crime and criminals were perpetuated and manipulated to play on fears and insecurities.[69] The 1980s were marked by extensive greed and selfishness, which no doubt spilled over into prisons where it almost literally became "every man for himself."

In the late 1970s and beyond, spontaneous and expressive riots, known as *rage riots,* emerged.[70] Most of the violence was directed at fellow inmates rather than prison officials or the system itself, often the result of racial conflicts between rival gangs. Payback against specific inmates, as occurred in the New Mexico riots in 1980, escalated the confrontations. This behavior is typical in the prison world filled with hopelessness and alienation, where ideas about rehabilitation have been thrown in the trash basket of history.

One of the bloodiest riots took place in April 1993 at the Southern Ohio Correctional Facility in Lucasville, Ohio. Nine prisoners and one guard died. The riot was the culmination of tensions from severe overcrowding and an attempt to "integrate" prisoners. The ostensible attempt to satisfy a court order prohibiting segregation placed known white supremacists in cells with minority inmates. The inmates put aside their differences and demonstrated a unity between white and African-American prisoners reminiscent of Attica. They issued a list of 21 demands and held hostages for a total of 11 days.[71]

It remains to be seen what sorts of disturbances are on the horizon. Given the explosive mixture of severe overcrowding, budget cutbacks on prison rehabilitation programs, gangs, and deteriorating social conditions on the outside, we may see newer forms of prison rioting—perhaps even a return to the political riots of the late 1960s and early 1970s.

One cannot discuss prison violence without reference to the growing problem of gangs in the prison system. As many researchers have noted, the gang problem has emerged as one of the key issues confronting our society. Yet, the emergence of gangs cannot be understood apart from the deteriorating social conditions facing millions of inner-city people, especially African Americans and Hispanics.[72] With the growth of these urban gangs, it is not surprising that the criminal justice system has responded in its typical get-tough fashion, resulting in a phenomenal increase in the number of gang members receiving prison sentences—some excessively long.[73]

Prison Gangs

Gang activity in prisons has increased in recent years. Many *prison gangs* are extensions of the street gangs found in most large cities. Street-gang members sent to prison are generally offered immediate protection and membership in the prison version of their gang. Their arrival is something of a homecoming—they meet old friends from the streets. Aside from protection, gangs provide many services to their members. Gang members often have less trouble adapting to life in prison.

Most of the research and field studies on gangs has focused on street gangs. There have few systematic studies about prison gangs. Much of the research on prison gangs is based on responses to surveys that attempt to measure the extensiveness of gangs, problems in prisons caused by gang members, and strategies for monitoring and suppressing gang activity.[74] A few studies have included the political, administrative, and social contexts in which prison gangs developed.

The Extent and Nature of the Gang Problem in the Prison System

Gangs exist in virtually every adult and juvenile correctional institution. One survey found eight gangs with a total membership of 1,174 in the Texas prison system.[75] Another study found nine gangs with almost 2,500 members (including 1,000 members in the Mexican Mafia).[76] In 2005, the California Department of Corrections reported that of the more than 160,000 inmates in California prisons, 803 were prison gang members, 900 were associates, 325 were inactive members, and 1,050 were gang-member dropouts.[77]

The Florida Department of Corrections lists six major national prison gangs: NETA, Aryan Brotherhood, Black Guerilla Family; Mexican Mafia, La Nuestra, and Texas Syndicate.[78] NETA is a Puerto Rican prison gang formed in the 1970s to combat injustices at the hands of prison officials and other gang members in a Puerto Rican prison. By the 1980s it had spread to New York, New Jersey, and Connecticut. Today it is found in most inner-city neighborhoods and prison systems on the East Coast. Members see themselves as oppressed and unwilling to be governed by the United States. The Aryan Brotherhood is a white prison gang formed in 1967 at San Quentin to protect whites against blacks in prison. It later extended its reach to gambling, drug sales, and trafficking in "punks" in prison. Its motto is "In for life and out by death." The Black Guerilla Family is an African-American prison gang started in 1966 at San Quentin by George Jackson, a Black Panther. It is the most politically oriented prison gang. The Mexican Mafia was one of the first prison gangs and started in 1957 in California; the Texas chapter began in Huntsville in 1984. La Nuestra is another Mexican-American/Hispanic gang formed at Folsom State Prison in 1968 to combat the Mexican Mafia. It provides commissary goods at face value to its members and gets goods to members in administrative segregation. It emphasizes the psychological and physical protection of its members. The Texas Syndicate is also a Mexican-American/Hispanic gang, which originated in Folsom prison in the early 1970s. It is the oldest prison gang in Texas.

Survey research found that just over one-fourth (27.7%) of prison administrators said that gangs "significantly affected their correctional environment," while almost half (45.4%) said that their staff had had some training in dealing with the gang problem. Also, about 70% said that the gang problem had existed for less than five years, while about one-third said that the problem had existed for more than five years. When gangs control much of the illicit drug importation into prisons, there is a significantly higher threat of violence to staff.[79]

The varying results of the survey above highlight one of the problems with prison gang research. What definition is used to determine the existence of a prison gang, its activities, and who is a member? One study reports that the Bureau of Prisons (BOP) defines gangs based on their perceived threat to the orderly management of the prison. Specific gang membership is determined based on identifying signs, symbols, correspondence, prior official records, associations, or self-description by inmates. There is no requirement that a prison gang member be involved in prison misconduct. BOP differentiates the depth of affiliation with the prison gang. Those viewed as full-fledged, core people in the gang are designated as "members." Those who are thought to be members but whose credentials aren't fully established are called "suspects." Those who do business with or look out for the interests of the gang but have not yet joined are called "associates." The three designations are usually applied only to the most organized prison gangs whose conduct is believed to be menacing.[80]

Whatever definition is applied, errors in classification—and the methods chosen for control—can have long-term effects on inmates.

> Inmates self-report gang affiliation. We count gang members. We have catalogues of gang tattoos. However, no one thoroughly understands what "membership" means. No statistical data exist to disprove the adage "blood in, blood out" [gang membership ends only if a member dies]. No proofs exist that prison gang membership actually accelerates violent acts in frequency and magnitude beyond an expected level of offenses committed by a matched group of high-risk inmates.[81]

What are labeled prison gangs could also be identified as families, nations, and/or organizations.[82]

> Researchers have historically focused on the structure and nature of gangs in male prisons while ignoring the fact that "gangs" are more than just stereotypical predatory groups for exploiting others. They serve the

needs of their members, often providing safe harbors within the dangerous prison world. Thus, they can provide an extended psychological and emotional support system and also serve an economic function.[83]

The term prison gang originally included gangs formed in prison, such as the Mexican Mafia and Nuestra Familia and prison counterparts of street gangs, such as Gangster Disciples. Today prisons hold a number of criminally oriented groups, including terrorists and hate groups. "Security Threat Groups" and "Inmate Disruptive Groups" are new designations for affiliations in prison—with the same attendant problems of labeling.[84]

The Relationship between
Street Gangs and Prison Gangs

There are three perspectives that attempt to explain the development of prison gangs. One argues that prison gangs are imported street gangs. The second argues that prison gangs are indigenous, arising within the prison itself as a means of belonging and protection. The third perspective explains prison gangs as an attempt to imitate gangs in other prisons or gangs on the outside.[85]

The first perspective is the most common explanation for the emergence of prison gangs. We do know that there is a close relationship between youth street gangs and the prison system. Most of the gangs within any given urban area have direct counterparts within the state prison system. James Jacobs studied Stateville (one of the major prisons in Illinois) and found that the inmate system was organized in ways almost identical with the gangs on the streets of Chicago.[86] A nationwide survey found that twenty-one out of thirty-three state prison officials who indicated the presence of prison gangs said that the gangs had counterparts in the cities of their states.[87]

Information from the streets is relayed to prison gang members by visits from friends and relatives and by new prison inmates. As Jacobs notes: "the influx of gang members has been so great that a communication link between street and prison has been established merely through the steady commitment of members."[88]

According to Jacobs, prison gangs first emerged in the state of Washington in 1950 and in California in 1957. Prison gangs began in Illinois twelve years later. During the 1970s, states adjacent to California and bordering Mexico, as well as two states to the north of Illinois, found that gangs had developed inside their prison systems. In the 1980s, development continued in Missouri and Kentucky. Prison gangs spread by transfers or rearrests of gang members in other jurisdictions.

In most cases, an inmate in a new prison setting tried to reproduce the organization that had given him an identity in the prior prison setting. In other cases, charismatic leaders imitated what they had heard about other gangs. Many even adopted the name of a gang from another jurisdiction but had no affiliation or communication with it. Contributing to the growth of gangs has been the problem of racism within prison walls, with gangs usually being organized along racial lines.

Salvador Buentello, Robert Fong, and Ronald Vogel attribute the recent growth of prison gangs to judicial intervention in the area of prisoner's rights. They argue that the intervention weakened the authority of prison officials, especially in the area of providing protection for inmates. As a result, many inmates began to organize themselves for self-protection, but prison violence increased. In Texas, for example, homicides increased from twelve in 1982 to twenty-seven in 1985. Gangs are reportedly responsible for half of all prison management problems in the nation.[89]

Prison gangs, like those on the streets, adhere to a code of secrecy. They recruit based on "homeboy" preprison experiences and emphasize commitment to the gang. This loyalty is reflected in the expression "Blood in, blood out."[90] Gangs emphasize power and prestige, which is measured in terms of the ability to control other inmates and specific activities within the institution. Money and drugs, in particular, represent tangible symbols of a gang's ability to control and dominate others and to provide essential protection, goods, and services for its members. The gang's ability to bring status and prestige to its members reinforces gang commitment and solidarity.[91] Prison gangs are organized along racial and ethnic lines and have a well-defined hierarchical structure.

Hagedorn found most of the gang members he interviewed believed that "prison strengthens gang involvement," which is exactly the opposite of the intended effect of incarcerating gang members.[92] Irving Spergel notes that the prison "may be regarded both as facilitating and responding to gang problems."[93] Incarceration increases gang cohesion and membership recruitment in many institutions, and it can indirectly create more problems in the streets rather than less.

Some gangs were formed in prison and later transferred to the streets when members were released. Some gangs inside the prison system have unique histories and distinct origins. Therefore, we need to be cautious about accepting the common view that gangs are "mere extensions" of street gangs.[94]

Joan Moore argued that the prison system is only one of several institutions with which Chicanos in the Los Angeles area come into contact; other institutions include the welfare system and the police. She observed that there exists among many Chicano youth a sort of "anticipatory socialization" to prison. She also notes that "prison is an omnipresent reality in barrio life, and contact with it is continuous and drastic, affecting nearly everybody in the barrio. . . . Prison adaptations are seen by convicts themselves as variants of adaptations to street life."[95] Further, the prison

> is experienced as a climax institution of the Anglo world as it impinges upon the barrio. Prison exaggerates many of the familiar features of outside Anglo institutions. Even more important, social relationships in prison are familiar because the Chicano's fellows in prison are the same people he sees on the streets of Los Angeles. . . . [I]n exaggerated form, the prison is a climax institution representing the same forces that the Chicanos of Los Angeles have felt all their lives.[96]

Moore found that prison gangs provide many things to Chicano convicts. There is a strong emphasis on familylike relationships. One routine among Chicano prisoners is to watch the bus bring in new prisoners and look for "homeboys." They offer them immediate assistance and welcome them to the prison. These gangs are also very active participants in the sub-rosa prison economy of drug smuggling. Moore notes that within the prison system of California during the 1970s the so-called Mexican Mafia reportedly began to get involved in an illegal drug market outside the prison. In 1977, there was an indictment of thirty men who were involved in a $50 million a year heroin operation that was run from inside the prison.[97]

In contrast to the recruitment pressures experienced by the unaffiliated convict, the gang member from the street has no trouble adjusting to the new environment. Besides offering physical security, the gang in the prison, as on the street, serves important material and psychological functions for its members. The gang functions as a communication network, as well as a convenient distribution network for contraband goods. It also provides a source of identification and a feeling of belonging. Other gang members become one's family and are often referred to as "my homies" or just "homies" (short for "homeboy"). Gang members remain oriented toward the same membership group and leadership hierarchy as they did before coming to prison. Rather than experiencing a collapse upon passing through the gates, they maintain the same self-identity they held on the streets. The prison gang helps them in their transition to prison life.

Some valuable insights about prisons and gangs were provided by the popular rapper Ice T in an interview in *Playboy* magazine. He began by stating that "most gang members aren't afraid of getting thrown into jail. What do they have to lose? To most of them, jail is no different from home. They ain't going to do nothing but kick it with the homies in jail." Continuing, he said that the "gang mentality is pounded into your head in prison."

> There is drama in jail. By the time you come home, you're really banging. When the police take a gangster off the street and put him in jail, his criminal side is totally

reemphasized. . . . My hope is that the gang truce can reach into the prisons, because the prisons really run the streets. In the joint you get favors by seeing what you can do for somebody on the outside. . . . A lot of the guys who are getting killed on the streets are being reached by people in the joint. . . . All these shots are being called by people in the joint, and if they decide the war is over in there, then it will be over outside, too.[98]

A somewhat different perspective on prison gangs is provided by Ira Reiner, former district attorney in Los Angeles. He states that prison gangs

> are more akin to organized crime networks than to street gangs. . . . [F]ears of a prison/ street gang nexus seem to be overblown. No law enforcement authority interviewed for this report saw any trend toward prison gang control over street gangs. Individuals often belong to both types of gangs, and may move back and forth between them. . . . But apart from producing a pool of recruits for the business, street gangs rarely play any direct role in such [prison gang operated] enterprises.[99]

In their study of Texas prison gangs, Buentello, Fong, and Vogel state that eight prison gangs developed in the 1980s *within* the Texas prison system; they were not extensions of street gangs.[100] The prison gang develops in five stages. The first stage begins with the new inmate entering the prison system with feelings of isolation, fear, and loneliness. The inmate begins the *prisonization* process, described earlier in this chapter. To overcome his fears and sense of isolation, the inmate moves into the second stage when he begins to get involved in a small, informal "clique" of inmates with whom he feels comfortable and shares some common interests. Some of these informal groups disbanded when group members were transferred or released.

The third stage involves the development of "self-protection" groups. In a process similar to group formation on the outside, some members perceive hostility from other groups in the prison. The authors cite the examples of the Black Muslims and the

Texas Syndicate (formed by Texas-born inmates in the California prison system during the 1970s). Both provided protection. There is not yet a formal code of conduct, and leaders are usually selected based on individual charisma. The group does not generally participate in criminal activities and does not engage in violent behavior unless provoked. Eventually some of the members of these kinds of groups move on to the fourth stage.[101]

The fourth stage is reached when some members begin to exert stronger influence over others and over group activities. Eventually these individuals become leaders and begin to transform the group into a "predator group."[102] At this stage, members begin to discuss formal rules. They also begin to organize certain criminal activities, such as extortion, prostitution, gambling, and violence against other inmates, as they begin to enjoy more power over other inmates. In time, some of these groups evolve to the fifth stage, where they become prison gangs.

During this final stage, the group members begin to see themselves as "part of an established organized crime syndicate. Involvement in contract murder, drug trafficking, extortion, gambling, and homosexual prostitution is required of gang members."[103] The group has formal rules and a constitution; there is a hierarchy of leadership; and inmates are members for life, which means that they continue their criminal activities for the gang after they are released.

At first, gang members wore gang tattoos. Recently gangs changed the rule and no longer require members to do so. This makes it more difficult for officials to identify individuals as gang members. Gangs also now use "associates/sympathizers" and "wannabes" to help them in some of their criminal activities.

The connection between street gangs and the prison system is revealed by a recent indictment in Los Angeles. Ruben "Nite Owl" Castro, 46, a leader of the Mexican Mafia doing a life sentence at the "supermax" federal prison in Florence, Colorado, allegedly controlled a drug business for two branches of the Latino 18th Street gang (the

Shatto Park Locos and the Hoover Locos). Amazingly, he conducted the business inside the walls of the highest level security prison in the country. It houses the "Unabomber" (Theodore Kaczynski), the "shoe-bomber" (Richard Reid) and one of the 9/11 plotters (Zacarias Moussaoui).

PRISONERS' RIGHTS

As a result of the prison revolts of the 1960s and the civil rights movement, the courts abandoned their traditional *hands-off doctrine* toward prisons. This policy had been affirmed in an 1871 case (*Ruffin v. Commonwealth*) in which the Supreme Court ruled that, in effect, a person convicted of a crime and sent to prison becomes a "slave of the state" and forfeits all rights. This view changed dramatically, beginning in the mid-1960s. Since then there has been a tremendous increase in prison-related litigation. Between 1966 and 1994 the number of *habeas corpus* lawsuits filed by inmates in state prisons went from 5,830 to 11,918 (an increase of 104%), while the number of civil rights lawsuits went from a mere trickle of 281 to an astounding 37,925 during the same period (a 135-fold increase).[105] The most important Supreme Court decisions have centered on four fundamental constitutional rights: (1) First Amendment rights concerning free speech and religious practice, (2) Fourth Amendment rights concerning unreasonable searches and seizures, (3) Eighth Amendment rights concerning cruel and unusual punishment, and (4) Fourteenth Amendment rights concerning due process.

One of the first cases to impact prisons was *Cooper v. Pate*.[106] The Court ruled that prisoners were entitled to protection under the 1871 Civil Rights Act and thus could challenge the conditions of their confinement in the courts. In other words, prisoners could sue for such things as inadequate medical care, brutality by guards, theft of personal property, and other civil rights violations.

Among the most important First Amendment cases was a decision that arose from a suit filed by prisoners practicing the Black Muslim religion. In *Fulwood v. Clem-mer* the Court ruled that the Black Muslim religion was a bona fide religion, and prison administrators could not deny inmates the right to practice it.[107]

The Fourth Amendment prohibition of unreasonable searches and seizures has not resulted in many noteworthy cases. In *Bell v. Wolfish* the Supreme Court ruled in favor of traditional "strip searches" (including searches of body cavities following a visit from someone from the outside), as long as the reasons for the search "outweigh" the inmate's personal rights.[108] In *Hudson v. Palmer* the Court upheld the right of prison officials to search inmate cells and to take any personal property found.[109] However, the courts also ruled that such searches cannot be done merely to "harass or humiliate" inmates and that inmates do in fact have some degree of privacy.[110]

Bell v. Wolfish is also an important Eighth Amendment case. Some consider it one of the most important cases the Supreme Court has ever decided because it represented a "return to the hands-off approach to prisoners' rights."[111] This case determined that "double-bunking" did not constitute "cruel and unusual punishment." This was further reinforced in *Rhodes v. Chapman*, an Ohio case involving a prison designed to hold one inmate per 8 × 8 foot cell, in which fourteen hundred inmates were double-bunked.[112] The Supreme Court ruled that overcrowding is not necessarily dangerous if prison services are available and that living conditions may be "restrictive and harsh" because such conditions are part of the punishment prisoners receive as a result of being convicted. In order to be unconstitutional, the conditions must demonstrate deliberate attempts to inflict "wanton and unnecessary infliction of pain." It is interesting to note that the suit was supported by the American Medical Association and the American Public Health Association.

Many other cases have centered on Eighth Amendment rights. Perhaps the most famous grew out of the Cummins Farm Unit of the Arkansas State Penitentiary, where Warden Tom Murton discovered the bodies of inmates who had been killed and buried on prison grounds. It was also discovered that prison administrators used a number of cruel methods of punishment, including the "Tucker telephone" (attaching electrical wires to an inmate's testicles and administering a shock), whippings, beatings, and even killings.[113] A federal court ruled in *Holt v. Sarver* that such punishment constituted cruel and unusual punishment.[114] (This case was popularized in the film *Brubaker,* starring Robert Redford.) In a related case, *Pugh v. Locke*, federal judge Frank Johnson ruled that the Alabama prison system itself constituted cruel and unusual punishment and ordered prison officials to bring the prisons up to minimal standards or close down the entire system.[115]

One of the most controversial issues has been due process rights and prison disciplinary procedures. Certain disciplinary measures deprive inmates of certain liberties and privileges, such as good-time credits and access to the general population. One of the first issues addressed by the courts was solitary confinement (the "hole"). Although the courts have not ruled that solitary confinement in and of itself constitutes cruel and unusual punishment, it has been ruled that in some instances it does and that procedures culminating in a sentence to solitary confinement require certain due process safeguards. In a 1966 case, a federal district court ruled that confinement to a "strip" cell at the California Correctional Training Center at Soledad constituted cruel and unusual punishment.[116]

The key to this issue is the *disciplinary hearing.* Whenever an inmate is charged with an infraction of prison rules, he or she is granted a hearing before a disciplinary committee. It should be noted that within the prison system an inmate can be written up for the violation of some of the most petty and vague rules, such as being "disrespectful toward an officer," the definition of which is left entirely in the hands of prison guards. In *Wolff v. McDonnell,* the Supreme Court ruled that minimal due process safeguards should be observed because such procedures could result in the loss of good-time credit.[117] The Court specifically ruled that a written notice of all charges must be given at least twenty-four hours before the hearing, that the

inmate must be given a hearing before an "impartial tribunal or fact finder," and that a written statement noting the evidence relied on and the reasons for the disciplinary action must be given. The Court also said that the inmate does not have the right to counsel but left the door open concerning the issue of the right to counsel, saying that the decision "is not graven in stone." The inmate, however, may act in his or her own defense.

In a later decision, *Meachum v. Fano*, the Court ruled on a case involving the transfer of inmates to a more secure facility (from a medium- to a maximum-security prison). The Court noted that the Fourteenth Amendment applies when the extant liberty interest of a prisoner is threatened by the action of prison officials.[118] This principle involves the prisoner's remaining in the general prison population. In other words, once a prisoner has been granted something that has a significant liberty value (e.g., probation, parole, good-time credit, placement in the general population), the liberty cannot be taken away without due process.

Most of the Eighth Amendment cases have centered on the *conditions of confinement* within prisons. In several cases spanning around sixteen years (1976–1991) the Supreme Court ruled that those in charge of prisons must end brutality, unsanitary conditions, and inadequate food. Administrators must follow specific guidelines. In *Ruiz v. Estelle*, a federal judge in eastern Texas issued a far-reaching decree against the Texas Department of Corrections.[119] The judge ordered the department to change what were unconstitutional conditions, such as overcrowding, unnecessary use of force by guards, poor health-care practices, and the so-called building-tender system, which allowed some inmates to control others. Building-tenders (BTs) were "snitches" bribed by the prison (with special privileges) to report "troublemakers" (both inmates and guards) to prison authorities. Some have argued that one outcome of *Ruiz v. Estelle* was the disruption of the traditional social system (an informal system of control based on "divide and rule") and the creation of a new bureaucratic order. Since *Ruiz v. Estelle,* levels of violence have risen as inmate gangs have emerged to provide security and stability.[120]

Unfortunately, there is a "fly in the ointment" concerning the few rights that prisoners have been granted. Because of the many vague rules and regulations, the tremendous discretionary power exercised by prison officials, and the fact that months or even years may pass before the courts hear about abuses, prison inmates' constitutional rights may still be violated. One common method of violating these rights (and a very convenient method of control) is *administrative segregation.* In most prisons, prison officials can place an inmate in "close custody" or in solitary confinement in order to protect the inmate either from himself or herself or from others. The phrase "for his own protection," however, is open to abuse. Obviously, there is little argument in cases involving physical threats to inmates (e.g., rape) and the threat of suicide or escape. But in some cases, "for his own protection" can mean anything.

Recent Supreme Court rulings have signaled a return to the hands-off doctrine. In ***Wilson v. Seiter*** the Court ruled that, even though the inmates (in Ohio) experienced a number of horrible conditions (overcrowding, excessive noise, inadequate heating and cooling, improper ventilation, unsanitary dining facilities and food, etc.), these conditions were not the result of "deliberate indifference" by administrators.[121] The Court had ruled in an earlier case involving poor medical treatment that future cases concerning the Eighth Amendment must demonstrate "deliberate indifference."[122] What constitutes "deliberate indifference" and how one proves it is unclear. In the *Wilson* case, Justices White, Marshall, Blackmun, and Stevens, though concurring with the ruling, warned that this decision may result in "serious deprivations of basic human needs" and would not be rectified because of "an unnecessary and meaningless search for 'deliberate indifference.'"

Some have suggested that the modern era is a period of "one-hand-on, one-hand off" or "hands semi-off." One interpretation of recent Supreme Court rulings is that "prisoners have constitutional rights but that those rights are not unrestricted."[123] Olson puts the issue of prisoner's rights in perspective.

> Prisons today are indeed far less cruel than when they were first invented, but that does not mean that incarceration is an experience without pain. . . . The loss of freedom is indeed fundamental, as is the loss of social status, and the lifetime of labeling that come with being a convict. . . . The problem is not simply being locked up with hundreds of strangers but also with the difficulty of having one's self-esteem and identity inundated with the evidence of an unsuccessful life and the view that you are somehow less human and less worthy. Few see prison as an intricate social and psychological world, where the individual is extraordinarily overwhelmed and hampered with challenges so profound that one's very own identity is at stake. There is a self-loathing that develops among convicts (myself included), a personal feeling of diminished self-worth perpetuated by a system more concerned with effectiveness and efficiency than with human life.[124]

SUMMARY

Prison populations are at an all-time high and have increased in recent years in unprecedented numbers, largely as a result of the "war on drugs." Most of those currently incarcerated are drawn from the ranks of the unskilled and uneducated. The majority are nonwhite, especially African Americans.

One of the most important features of the prison system is the inmate social system, which has probably existed in some form since prisons were first built. Although many of the norms and values of the inmate social systems were brought into the prison from the culture of the streets, they nevertheless take on exaggerated importance inside the walls. One indication of this is the existence of a sub-rosa economy in which just about everything becomes a commodity to be bartered and exchanged. This economy and the inmate social system as a whole help mitigate the pains of imprisonment.

We discussed extreme responses to imprisonment—prison violence in general, and prison riots as a particular form of violence. Special attention was paid to the emerging importance of the existence of gangs within prisons. Gangs are a reflection of conditions existing on the outside and account for much of the violence inside prisons today.

We also discussed the issue of prisoners' rights. While prisoners have been granted a number of rights denied to them in the past, the rights secure only minimal relief from the most draconian pains of imprisonment.

Key Terms

- *Bell v. Wolfish*
- conditions of confinement
- *Cooper v. Pate*
- disciplinary hearing
- frustration riot
- *Fulwood v. Clemmer*
- gleaning
- hands-off doctrine
- *Holt v. Sarver*
- *Hudson v. Palmer*
- inmate code
- inmate social system
- lock psychosis
- minimum, medium, and maximum security prisons
- *Meachum v. Fano*
- pains of imprisonment
- political riot
- prison gang
- prisonization
- *Pugh v. Locke*
- race riot
- rage riot
- *Rhodes v. Chapman*
- *Ruiz v. Estelle*
- sub-rosa economy
- supermax prisons
- total institution
- *Wilson v. Seiter*
- *Wolff v. McDonnell*

Notes

[1] Austin, J. and J. Irwin. *It's about Time: America's Incarceration Binge* (3rd ed.). Belmont, CA: Wadsworth, 2001.

[2] Harrison, P. M. and A. J. Beck. "Prisoners in 2005." Washington, DC: Bureau of Justice Statistics, November 2006. [Online] http://www.ojp.usdoj.gov/bjs/pub/pdf/p05.pdf

[3] Durose, M. R. and C. J. Mumola. *Profile of Nonviolent Offenders Exiting State Prisons*. Washington, DC: Bureau of Justice Statistics, October 2004. [Online] http://www.ojp.usdoj.gov/bjs/pub/pdf/pnoesp.pdf

[4] Sabol, W. J., T. D. Minton, and P. M. Harrison. *Prison and Jail Inmates at Midyear 2006*. Washington, DC: Bureau of Justice Statistics, June 2007, p. 4.

[5] Harlow, C. W. *Education and Correctional Populations*. Washington, DC: Bureau of Justice Statistics, January 2003.

[6] Austin and Irwin based the "seriousness" of crime on what the general public thinks is serious, as measured by the Center for Studies in Criminology and Criminal Law at the University of Pennsylvania.

[7] Austin and Irwin, *It's about Time*, p. 27. In this specific example, it is important to note that this incident occurred in Nevada, where just about any offense committed within a gaming establishment is treated much more harshly than would otherwise be the case. One reason is that the state of Nevada wants to maintain an image suggesting that it is not only "tough on crime" but, more importantly, casinos are legitimate enterprises where people can come and have fun while feeling safe (see Farrell, R. and C. Case. *The Black Book and the Mob*. Madison: University of Wisconsin Press, 1995).

[8] Irwin, in research on a sample of offenders in California, found eight criminal identities: (1) the *thief* (8% of his sample); (2) the *hustler* (7%); (3) the *dope fiend* (13%); (4) the *head,* user of psychedelic drugs, such as marijuana and LSD (8%); (5) the *disorganized criminal,* who pursues "a chaotic, purposeless life, filled with unskilled, careless, and variegated criminal activity"—the bulk of convicted felons (27%); (6) the *state-raised youth,* young offenders who spent formative years in various kinds of state institutions (15%); (7) the *lower-class man,* from a lower-class background without a long criminal career but who happened to have committed a felony (6%); (8) the *square John,* conventional person from a stable working-class background who simply made a mistake (16%). See Irwin, J. *The Felon*. Englewood Cliffs, NJ: Prentice-Hall, 1970.

[9] Austin and Irwin, *It's about Time*, p. 41.

[10] For a classic case study see Whyte, W. F. *Street Corner Society*. Chicago: University of Chicago Press, 1943; see also Hagedorn, J. *People and Folks* (2nd ed.). Chicago: Lakeview Press, 1998.

[11] Shelden, R. G., S. Tracy, and W. B. Brown. *Youth Gangs in American Society* (3rd ed.). Belmont, CA: Wadsworth, 2004, pp. 86–90.

[12] Austin and Irwin, *It's about Time*, p. 90.

13 Allen, H. E., E. J. Latessa, B. S. Ponder, and C. E. Simonsen. *Corrections in America: An Introduction* (11th ed.). Upper Saddle River, NJ: Prentice-Hall, 2007, pp. 37, 247.

14 California Department of Corrections and Rehabilitation. [Online] http://www.cdcr.ca.gov/Visitors/fac_prison_PBSP.html

15 Austin and Irwin, *It's about Time,* pp. 117–129; Rush, G. *Inside American Prisons and Jails.* Incline Village, NV: Copperhouse, 1997, pp. 44–45; Mays, G. L. and L. T. Winfree Jr. *Contemporary Corrections.* Belmont, CA: Wadsworth, 1998, p. 155; Tracy, C. "Beyond the Veil: The Changing Nature of the Prison Experience from a Convict Perspective." Paper presented at the Annual Meeting of the Justice Studies Association, Norton, MA, May 30–June 1, 2001. An Associated Press story ("Death Toll in California's Prisons Highest in More Than a Decade." *Las Vegas Review Journal* (February 22, 1998) noted that a record number of 16 prisoners died in 1997 as a result of fights between prisoners, the highest since 1987, when 19 died. A total of 13 of these deaths occurred within the highest-security prisons housing the "most dangerous." The most deaths occurred at Pelican Bay, all resulting from clashes between inmates. The story also noted that there were almost 156,000 prisoners in California, severely crowding prisons at 193% of designed capacity.

16 Terry, C. "Beyond Punishment: Perpetuating Difference from the Prison Experience." *Humanity and Society* 24: 105–135 (May 2000).

17 Larson, C. and G. Garrett. *Crime, Justice and Society* (2nd ed.). Dix Hills, NY: General Hall, 1996, p. 338.

18 Mays and Winfree, *Contemporary Corrections,* pp. 156–157.

19 Allen et al., *Corrections in America,* p. 241.

20 Camp, C. G. (ed.). *The 2002 Corrections Yearbook.* Middletown, CT: Criminal Justice Institute, pp. 177, 181.

21 Palombo, J. *From Heroin to Heresy.* Binghamton, NY: William Neil, 2000, p. 30.

22 Larson and Garrett, *Crime, Justice and Society,* pp. 336–337.

23 Olson, B. *Degradation, Apathy, and Acceptable Casualties: A Woman's Journey through the Criminal Justice System.* Long Grove, IL: Waveland Press, forthcoming.

24 Goffman, E. *Asylums.* New York: Doubleday, 1961, p. 6.

25 Watterson, K. *Women in Prison: Inside the Concrete Womb.* Boston: Northeastern University Press, 1996.

26 Garfinkel, H. "Conditions of Successful Degradation Ceremonies." *American Journal of Sociology* 61: 420–424 (1956).

27 Terry, "Beyond Punishment."

28 Olson, B. *Degradation, Apathy, and Acceptable Casualties.*

29 Sykes, G. *Society of Captives.* Princeton, NJ: Princeton University Press, 1958.

30 Goffman, *Asylums,* p. 14.

31 Silberman, M. *A World of Violence: Corrections in America.* Belmont, CA: Wadsworth, 1995.

32 Sykes, G. *Criminology.* New York: Harcourt Brace Jovanovich, 1978, p. 525.

33 Austin and Irwin, *It's about Time,* p. 110.

34 Ibid., p. 112.

35 Olson, *Degradation, Apathy, and Acceptable Casualties.*

36 McCorkle, L. and R. Korn. "Resocialization within Walls." In N. Johnston, L. Savitz, and M. E. Wolfgang (eds.), *The Sociology of Punishment and Corrections.* New York: Wiley, 1962, p. 99.

37 Williams, V. and M. Fish. *Convicts, Codes and Contraband.* Cambridge, MA: Ballinger, 1974, p. 41.

38 Irwin, J. and D. Cressey. "Thieves, Convicts, and the Inmate Culture." *Social Problems* 10: 142–155 (Fall 1962).

39 Sykes, G. and S. L. Messinger. "The Inmate Social Code and Its Functions." In M. E. Wolfgang, L. Savitz, and N. Johnston (eds.), *The Sociology of Crime and Delinquency.* New York: Wiley, 1962, pp. 92–94. Although this article is quite dated, more recent research suggests that inmate codes are still very much part of the prison social system. See Mays and Winfree, *Contemporary Corrections,* pp. 199–200.

40 Sykes, *Society of Captives;* Irwin and Cressey, "Thieves, Convicts, and the Inmate Culture"; Schrag, C. "Some Foundations for a Theory of Corrections." In D. R. Cressey (ed.), *The Prison.* New York: Holt, Rinehart and Winston, 1966; Irwin, *The Felon;* Austin and Irwin, *It's about Time;* Terry, "Beyond Punishment."

41 Sykes, *Society of Captives,* p. 103.

42 Palombo, *From Heroin to Heresy,* p. 37.

43 Clemmer, D. *The Prison Community.* New York: Holt, Rinehart and Winston, 1958, p. 299.

44 Wheeler, S. "A Study of Prisonization." In Johnston, Savitz, and Wolfgang, *Sociology of Punishment and Corrections.* A cross-cultural study on prisons in five countries confirmed Wheeler's findings. Akers, R. L., N. S. Hayner, and W. Grunninger. "Time Served, Career Phase and Prisonization: Findings from Five Countries." In R. C. Leger and J. R. Stratton (eds.), *The Sociology of Corrections.* New York: Wiley, 1977; Austin and Irwin, *It's about Time,* p. 110.

45 Irwin, *The Felon;* Irwin, J. and D. Cressey. "Thieves, Convicts, and the Inmate Culture." *Social Problems* 10: 142–155 (Fall 1962).

46 Silberman, *A World of Violence,* p. 15.

47 Irwin, *The Felon,* p. 68.

48 Ibid., p. 74.

49 Ibid., pp. 76–78.

50 Palombo, *From Heroin to Heresy,* p. 20.

51 Ibid., p. 23.

52 Williams and Fish, *Convicts, Codes and Contraband;* Davidson, R. T. *Chicano Prisoners: The Key to San Quentin.* New York: Holt, Rinehart and Winston, 1974.

53 Williams and Fish, *Convicts, Codes and Contraband,* p. 51.

54 Quoted in Silberman, *A World of Violence,* p. 15.

55 Austin and Irwin, *It's about Time,* pp. 101–102.

56 Speaking of remoteness, journalist Joseph Hallinan visited one such remote prison in the extreme northwest part of Virginia, in a small area known as Wallens Ridge (in Wise County). He noted that visits by family and friends were rare. There were no accessible airports, train stations, or buses. He says this inac-

cessibility is intentional; the designers wanted the prison to be a place of exile. At the grand opening in April 1999, a large banner hung over the entrance read: "Future Destination of Virginia Exile." See Hallinan, J. *Going Up the River: Travels in a Prison Nation.* New York: Random House, 2001, pp. 206–208.

57 Gibbons, J. and N. Katzenbach. *Confronting Confinement: A Report of the Commission on Safety and Abuse in America's Prisons.* Vera Institute of Justice, June 2006, p. 12. [Online] http://www.prisoncommission.org/pdfs/Confronting_Confinement.pdf

58 Austin and Irwin, *It's about Time,* p. 107.

59 Gibbons and Katzenbach, *Confronting Confinement,* p. 23.

60 Colvin, M. "The 1980 New Mexico Prison Riot." *Social Problems* 29: 449–463 (1982).

61 Fox, V. *Violence behind Bars.* Westport, CT: Greenwood Press, 1974 (1956); Pallas, J. and R. Barber. "From Riot to Revolution." In R. Quinney (ed.), *Criminal Justice in America: A Critical Understanding.* Boston: Little, Brown, 1974.

62 Mays and Winfree, *Contemporary Corrections,* pp. 210–211.

63 Ibid.; Jacobs, J. B. *Stateville.* Chicago: University of Chicago Press, 1977.

64 Pallas and Barber, "From Riot to Revolution," p. 345.

65 See Fanon, F. *The Wretched of the Earth.* New York: Grove Press, 1963; Malcolm X. *The Autobiography of Malcolm X.* New York: Grove Press, 1966; Cleaver, E. *Soul on Ice.* New York: Dell, 1968; Jackson, G. *Soledad Brother.* New York: Bantam, 1970; Berrigan, D. *America Is Hard to Find.* Garden City, NY: Doubleday, 1972.

66 Pallas and Barber, "From Riot to Revolution"; Atkins, B. M. and H. R. Glick (eds.). *Prisons, Protest and Politics.* Englewood Cliffs, NJ: Prentice-Hall, 1972, pp. 99–140; Pell, E. *Maximum Security.* New York: Dutton, 1972, pp. 141–210; Mattick, H. "The Prosaic Sources of Prison Violence." *Society* (November–December, 1973); Yee, M. S. *The Melancholy History of Soledad Prison.* New York: Harper & Row, 1973.

67 Badillo, H. and M. Haynes. *A Bill of No Rights: Attica and the American Prison System.* New York: Outbridge and Lazard, 1972, pp. 13–34; Pallas and Barber, "From Riot to Revolution," pp. 349–350.

68 Wicker, T. *A Time to Die.* New York: Quadrangle/New York Times, 1975; Badillo and Haynes, *A Bill of No Rights.*

69 The use of fear and various racial stereotypes have been documented by Mann, C. R. *Unequal Justice: A Question of Color.* Bloomington: Indiana University Press, 1995; Baum, D. *Smoke and Mirrors: The War on Drugs and the Politics of Failure.* Boston: Little, Brown, 1996; and Chambliss, W. J. "Crime Control and Ethnic Minorities: Legitimizing Racial Oppression by Creating Moral Panics." In D. F. Hawkins (ed.), *Ethnicity, Race, and Crime.* Albany: State University of New York Press, 1995.

70 Mays and Winfree, *Contemporary Corrections,* pp. 211–212.

71 Goldstone, J. A. and B. Useem. "Prison Riots as Microrevolutions: An Extension of State-Centered Theories of Revolution." *American Journal of Sociology* 104 (4): 985–1029 (January 1999); Horn, D. "Lucasville Prison Riot: 10 Years Later." *The Cincinnati Enquirer* (April 6, 2003).

72 Shelden et al., *Youth Gangs in American Society.*

73 For a review of these policies, see ibid., ch. 9.

74 Gaes, G., S. Wallace, E. Gilman, J. Klein-Saffran, and S. Suppa. "The Influence of Prison Gang Affiliation on Violence and Other Prison Misconduct." Federal Bureau of Prisons, March 9, 2001. [Online] http://www.bop.gov/news/research_projects/published_reports/cond_envir/oreprcrim_2br.pdf

75 Buentello, S. R., S. Fong, and R. E. Vogel. "Prison Gang Development: A Theoretical Model." *The Prison Journal* 121: 3–14 (1991).

76 Ralph, P. H. and J. W. Marquart. "Gang Violence in Texas Prisons." *The Prison Journal* 121: 38–49 (1991).

77 Wallace, B. "Five Inmate Gangs Dominate California's Prison System." *San Francisco Chronicle* (February 24, 2005). The following Web site includes a list of prison gang profiles with information about location of operation, formation year, objectives, structure, organization, and known leaders: http://www.insideprison.com/prison_gang_profiles.asp

78 Florida Department of Corrections. [Online] http://www.dc.state.fl.us/pub/gangs/prison.html

79 Knox, G. W. and E. D. Tromanhauser. "Gangs and Their Control in Adult Correctional Institutions." *The Prison Journal* 121: 15–22 (1991).

80 Gaes et al., "The Influence of Prison Gang Affiliation."

81 Fleisher, M. S. "Societal and Correctional Context of Prison Gangs." [Online] http://www.prisoncommission.org/statements/fleisher_mark_s.pdf

82 [Online] http://www.insideprison.com/prison_gang_profiles.asp

83 Forsyth, C. J. and R. D. Evans. "Reconsidering the Pseudo-Family/Gang Gender Distinction in Prison Research." *Journal of Police and Criminal Psychology* 18(1): 16 (2003).

84 Fleisher, M. S. (2005). "Gang Management in Corrections." In P. M. Carlson and J. S. Garrett (eds.), *Prison and Jail Administration: Practice and Theory* (2nd ed.). Gaithersburg, MD: Aspen.

85 Knox and Tromanhauser, "Gangs and Their Control," p. 16.

86 Jacobs, J. B. "Street Gangs behind Bars." *Social Problems* 21: 395–408 (1974); Moore, J. W. *Homeboys: Gangs, Drugs, and Prisons in the Barrio of Los Angeles.* Philadelphia: Temple University Press, 1978; Hagedorn, *People and Folks.*

87 Camp, G. and C. Camp. *Prison Gangs: Their Extent, Nature, and Impact on Prisons.* Washington, DC: U.S. Department of Justice, 1985.

88 Jacobs, "Street Gangs behind Bars," p. 398.

89 Buentello et al., "Prison Gang Development."

90 Ibid., p. 3.

91 Jacobs, *Stateville.*

92 Hagedorn, *People and Folks,* p. 161.

93 Spergel, I. *Youth Gangs: Problems and Response.* Chicago: School of Social Work Administration, University of Chicago, 1990, p. 6.

94 Hagedorn, J. "Back in the Field Again: Gang Research in the Nineties." In C. R. Huff (ed.), *Gangs in America.* Newbury Park, CA: Sage, 1990, p. 248.

95 Moore, *Homeboys,* pp. 40, 98.

96 Ibid., pp. 94–95, 102.

97 Ibid., pp. 99–102, 218.

98 "On Prison, Bloods and the Hood." *Playboy Magazine* (November 1994) pp. 64–65.

99 Reiner, I. *Gangs, Crime and Violence in Los Angeles: Findings and Proposals from the District Attorney's Office.* Arlington, VA: National Youth Gang Information Center, 1992, pp. 50–51.

100 Buentello et al., "Prison Gang Development."

101 Ibid., p. 5.

102 Ibid., p. 8.

103 Ibid.

104 Mozingo, J. and R. Winton. "Federal Inmate Accused of Directing L.A. Drug Sales." *Los Angeles Times* (September 13, 2006).

105 Mays and Winfree, *Contemporary Corrections,* p. 348.

106 *Cooper v. Pate,* 378 U.S. 546, 1964.

107 *Fulwood v. Clemmer,* 206 F. Supp. 370, 1962. A similar case involved a Buddhist prisoner: *Cruz v. Beto,* 92 S. Ct. 1079, 1972.

108 *Bell v. Wolfish,* 441 U.S. 520, 1979.

109 *Hudson v. Palmer,* 468 U.S. 517, 1984.

110 *United States v. Lilly,* 576 F. 2d 1240, 5th Cir., 1978; *Block v. Rutherford,* 104 S. Ct. 3227, 1984.

111 Mays and Winfree, *Contemporary Corrections,* p. 356.

112 *Rhodes v. Chapman,* 452 U.S. 337, 1981.

113 Murton, T. and J. Hyams. *Accomplices to the Crime: The Arkansas Prison Scandal.* New York: Grove Press, 1969.

114 *Holt v. Sarver,* 300 F. Supp. 825, 1969.

115 *Pugh v. Locke,* 406 F. Supp. 318, 1976.

116 *Jordan v. Fitzharris,* 257 F. Supp. 674.

117 *Wolff v. McDonnell,* 418 U.S. 539, 1974.

118 *Meachum v. Fano,* 965 S. Ct. 2532, 1976.

119 *Ruiz v. Estelle,* 679 F. 2d 1115, 5th Cir., 1982.

120 Marquart, J. W. and B. M. Crouch. "Judicial Reform and Prison Control: The Impact of *Ruiz v. Estelle* on a Texas Penitentiary." *Law and Society Review* 19: 557–586 (1985).

121 *Wilson v. Seiter,* 501 U.S. 294, 1991.

122 *Estelle v. Gamble,* 429 U.S. 97, 106, 1976.

123 Mays and Winfree, *Contemporary Corrections,* p. 368.

124 Olson, B. "Degradation, Apathy, and Acceptable Casualties: Serving Time in a Women's Federal Correctional Institute." *Justice Policy Journal* 3(2): (Fall 2006). [Online] http://www.cjcj.org/pdf/degradation_apathy.pdf

fourteen

Getting Out of Prison
Problems with Reentry and Parole

Almost 650,000 people are released from state and federal prison yearly and return to their communities.[1] During the past couple of decades, these numbers have risen dramatically. As shown in figure 14.1, between 1980 and 2000 parole populations nationwide more than tripled. Studies of individual states reveal this change. For instance, in Ohio the number leaving prisons tripled between 1982 and 2002. In Illinois the number released between 1983 and 2001 increased by 157%.[2] Half (52%) of those released from prison in Illinois return to Chicago, and 34% return to six disadvantaged neighborhoods. Most of the prisoners lived in the same neighborhoods before their incarceration, reflecting a growing trend of what some have called the *recycling of prisoners* or the **perpetual prisoner machine**.[3] Two-thirds of those released in Illinois were black, and 40% had served time for drug offenses. Just over half had previously done time in an Illinois prison at least once; more than one-fourth (27%) had been readmitted to prison because of "technical" parole violations. Almost half (46%) left children behind.[4]

Figure 14.1 Parole populations, 1980–2000

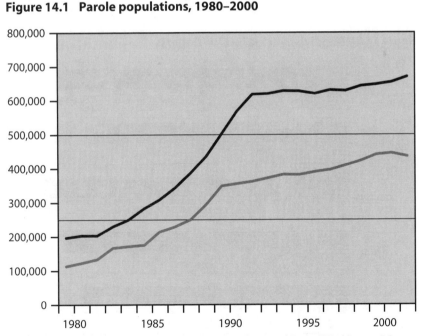

Source: Hughes, T. and D. J. Wilson. "Reentry Trends in the United States." Washington, DC: Bureau of Justice Statistics. [Online] http://www.ojp.usdoj.gov/bjs/reentry/reentry.htm

Several decades of research on *recidivism* show a consistent pattern, namely that about 65% of those released from prison will be arrested within three years for either a felony or "serious misdemeanor." More importantly, about two-thirds of them will be arrested within the first 12 months following their release.[5] Figure 14.2 shows the results for two cohorts, one released in 1983 and the other in 1994. About two-thirds were rearrested within three years of their release; just over half (51.8%) were returned to prison within three years. Most arrests were for property crimes (74%), drug offenses (67%), or public-order offenses (62%).[6] Interestingly, the percentage of rearrests in the most recent survey was exactly the same (65%) as one cited more than forty years ago.[7]

Released prisoners have a number of health issues. For example, prisoners are four times more likely to have tuberculosis, 9 to 10 times more likely to have Hepatitis C, five times more likely to have AIDS, and 8 to 9 times more likely to have HIV infection. As for mental illness, they are three to five times more likely to have schizophrenia or some other form of psychotic disorder, and

they are between 1.5 and three times more likely to suffer from a bipolar disorder. One-quarter suffer from alcohol dependence, and 83% used illegal drugs prior to their last offense, with one-third using at the time of the offense.[8]

After release from prison the individual faces a number of problems. He or she most likely continues to be under some type of supervision. With a criminal record, very few skills, and limited resources, the barriers to success on the outside are substantial. The limited opportunities increase the possibility of getting into trouble again.

INMATE VIEWS OF THE "OUTSIDE"

Life in prison can sometimes be dangerous, but an almost constant deleterious effect is the relentless boredom, which can negatively affect one's personality and worldview. Imprisonment produces a very disjointed and often unrealistic view of the outside world. A good deal of a prisoner's waking hours is spent visualizing and talking about what will happen after release. In one survey, 84% of the prisoners who expected to be

Figure 14.2   Recidivism Rates for Two Cohorts

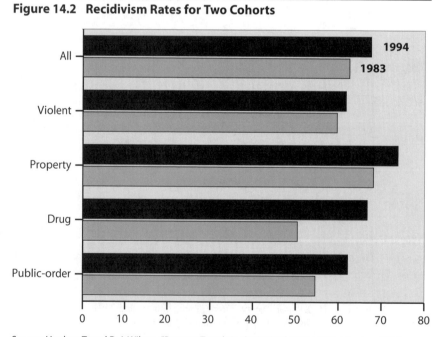

Source: Hughes, T. and D. J. Wilson. "Reentry Trends in the United States." Washington, DC: Bureau of Justice Statistics. [Online] http://www.ojp.usdoj.gov/bjs/reentry/reentry.htm

released on parole believed it would be easy to stay out of prison after release; 81% thought they would be able to avoid a parole violation. Most (87%) indicated that it would be *unlikely* or *very unlikely* for them to commit a crime or use drugs (81%) after release, even if they could do so without being caught. About two-thirds of the sample thought they would need help in dealing with challenges after release. Many (73%) wanted help obtaining more education and job training (72%); substantial numbers (73%) wanted help obtaining financial assistance, transportation, or health care after release; 51% wanted help getting counseling and mental health treatment (32%).[9]

Prisoners learn from others what is likely to happen after parole, a perspective that plays an important role in shaping their behavior when they are released.[10] Often they hear stories (some true, some false, but most of them exaggerated) about a particular individual and what he did when he got out, or they learn directly from those who return to prison on new charges. Irwin suggests that prisoners develop three perspectives on the degree of success following release: "making it," avoiding the "old bag," and "doing all right."

"Making It" and Avoiding the "Old Bag"

"*Making it*" refers to staying out of prison: keeping financially viable, coping with the parole system (e.g., avoiding being harassed by the parole agent and getting sent back for technical violations, or "some chickenshit beef," as some cons refer to it), and avoiding the "old bag"—that is, the deviant ways that resulted in the prison sentence the first place. Avoiding the "*old bag*" does not always mean staying perfectly "clean," for some do commit crimes. Staying out of the "old bag" more often means avoiding certain types of crimes or simply avoiding getting apprehended.

"Doing All Right"

"*Doing all right*" means making up for pleasures missed while in prison. Irwin identifies three styles of "doing all right" (remem-

ber, this is from a perspective shaped while the person is still in prison).

Conventional Styles

The *settling down* style means getting a job, getting married, and so on. The *transformation* style means seeking a new career, enrolling in college, and altering one's former lifestyle and work habits considerably. The *swinger* style means involvement in action-seeking activities such as nights on the town, parties, sports, picking up women, and trips to Las Vegas or other resort towns. The *playboy* style entails making plenty of money, leading the "good" life, driving fancy cars, and wearing good clothes. What prisoners see as the "good" life is shaped by what they see on television (they spend many hours watching television) and what they read in magazines. Thus, it is an exaggerated vision that leads to many problems of adjustment following release. A variation is the *rich old lady* scheme, which means finding a wealthy woman and leading the playboy life or, more realistically, finding and marrying a woman with a steady job.

Marginal Styles

These styles include getting involved in what Irwin calls *kinky occupations*, those on the margin between legality and illegality. Some occupations present more opportunities for illegal activities—bellboys, cab drivers, bartenders, working at casinos in Las Vegas or Atlantic City, and so on. There are also *artist styles* (writers, painters, musicians, etc.) and *student intellectual* styles. A recently emerging style is that of the *revolutionary* or *radical*—where politically aware prisoners join organizations (e.g., Black Panthers, Muslims, Socialists) to attempt to change society or to adopt radically different lifestyles.

Criminal Styles

These styles include the *big score* (one more major crime that, it is hoped, will result in a large monetary gain), drug deals, "hustles" (e.g., numbers, bookmaking, pool playing, gambling), and, most common among state-raised youth, "escapades"—going on a rampage and committing several crimes.

The plans of many prisoners go awry because their perceptions of life on the outside (from inside the prison) are distorted and exaggerated. The outside world, they soon learn, is more complicated then it seems on television and in magazines.

GETTING OUT OF PRISON ON PAROLE

Parole is the release of an offender from prison prior to the expiration of the original sentence. The majority of those released from prison each year are paroled. The number of people on parole has risen rapidly in recent years. In 1980 there were 220,438 on parole; by 2005 this number had risen by 251% to 784,408.[11]

Parole originated at the Elmira Reformatory in 1876. Another kind of parole, known as *aftercare,* began with juveniles sentenced to houses of refuge during the early nineteenth century.[12] Some argue that parole was a politically expedient method of addressing resentment over unequal sentencing practices. Prior to the establishment of parole, the only way to get an early release was through a grant of executive clemency by the governor. Clemency was a time-consuming process and sometimes proved politically embarrassing (for example, if someone granted clemency committed a new crime).[13] The parole system has a number of critics and few supporters. Conservatives often argue that parole lets "dangerous offenders" loose in the community (a gross exaggeration). Liberals argue that the decisions to release are too often arbitrary and without scientific foundation.[14]

Granting Parole

There are several "release mechanisms" whereby a prisoner is let out of prison. A *parole board* can grant a **discretionary release,** where the prisoner is released prior to the expiration of his or her sentence. The offender is conditionally released to the supervision of a *parole agent* employed by the department of parole within a state. In 1980, discretionary parole accounted for 55% of released prisoners; in 2004, the percentage had declined to 22%.[15] About 24% of inmates receive discretionary releases each

year. Sixteen states have abolished discretionary parole for all offenders.[16]

The most common method of release is **mandatory release.** The prisoner has served his or her entire sentence, minus what is known as "good time." This form of release is also conditional, because the prisoner is still under the supervision of a parole department. In 1980, mandatory parole accounted for 19% of those released from prison; in 2004, the percentage increased to 39%.[17]

A third method is **expiration of sentence,** which is an *unconditional release.* The prisoner has served his or her entire sentence and will have no supervision. The prisoner has, in common parlance, "done his time." This type of release has remained fairly steady since 1980 and accounted for 19% of releases in 2004.[18]

Members of parole boards usually are appointed by the governor of a state. Many boards are autonomous units; others are located in the state's department of corrections. Parole boards work very closely with institutional officials in making their decisions. They rely on the information and recommendations of prison staff, and they place a heavy emphasis on an inmate's behavior while in prison. The power of parole boards has been substantially reduced with the growth in determinate sentencing. One research study referred to the realignment of relationships of the three branches of government that resulted from the changes in sentencing. Both the judiciary and the executive branches (parole boards) lost discretion, while legislatures gained the power to determine the length of sentences.[19]

There are substantial variations among states. Some have completely abandoned the parole board model and release prisoners solely through mandatory release; others continue to use parole boards to make release decisions. In six states (California, Illinois, Indiana, Minnesota, New Hampshire, and New Mexico), less than 1% of release decisions are made by parole boards. In contrast, 19 states (including Florida, Pennsylvania, and Washington) use parole boards for more than 95% of the decisions. Other states use a combination. For example,

Ohio releases about half of its prisoners mandatorily by statute and half by parole board decisions. The national average is one in four prisoners released due to a parole board decision. However, the level of parole supervision has increased; four out of five prisoners are now supervised.[20] In addition, the number of revocations has increased dramatically (see below). "Despite parole's long history as a key component of American correctional systems, relatively little is known about the effectiveness of parole board release, community supervision, and parole revocation in terms of improving prisoner reintegration and reducing recidivism."[21]

The decision to grant parole is made during a parole hearing. At the hearing are the offender, the parole board, and, in many cases, prison officials and interested citizens. (Most state laws stipulate that any citizen may attend a parole hearing. This law is not well known, however, which probably keeps the hearings hidden from the view of the average citizen.) During the hearing the parole board reviews the prisoner's case and asks a series of questions. What factors weigh most heavily in the decision to parole? A prisoner's behavior *prior* to going to prison looms large, meaning that the person is still being judged for his or her behaviors that contributed to the crime long after conviction and sentencing. The nature of offense, any history of prior violence, and prior felony convictions are significant. Other factors, in order of importance, are: possession of a firearm, previous incarceration, prior parole adjustment, prison disciplinary record, psychological reports, and victim input.[22] Notice that "rehabilitation" (however this is defined) does not appear among the factors.

Attempts to predict the probability of success after release on parole have been largely unsuccessful. Clinical judgments are rarely definitive. Certain statistical predictors of recidivism, such as the U.S. Parole Commission's Salient Factor Score (SFS), fare better. The score is the total of points assessed for various background variables. One study looked at parole outcome in Texas, California, and Michigan and found the following factors to be the best predictors of recidivism: prior criminality, committing first offense at a young age, drug abuse, and poor employment history. Yet even these factors failed to predict more than 10% of the variance. Other studies have arrived at similar conclusions.[23]

In recent years a good percentage of the increase in parole populations reflects the fact that prisons are perpetually overcrowded. Indeed, the number of persons arrested and convicted has been consistently on the increase over the years, and parole boards may be under intense pressure to release prisoners if for no other reason than to make room for more.[24]

Success on Parole

How successful is parole? Most research looks at the whether parolees commit additional crimes and whether they are reincarcerated. One of the problems with researching recidivism is how we define it and how we measure it. It is often said that prisons are "schools of crime." One study found that in a comparison of people of comparable circumstances (background, offense, etc.), the group placed on probation and never sent to prison had a much lower rate of recidivism.

The rate of offending by parolees is generally less than it had been prior to their going to prison. The impact of rearrests of offenders released in Illinois and California on the crime rates in those states was negligible: about 2% or less. Reduced arrest rates were primarily because of simple maturation: as prisoners got older, their crime rates dropped considerably. Most prisoners have peak ages of criminality between 15 and 24. The typical prisoner is 30 or older when released—well beyond his or her "prime" as far as crime is concerned.[25] Most offenders eventually "age out" of criminality. Longitudinal studies have found that the vast majority of offenders cease their offending by age 40.[26]

THE INCREASE OF PAROLE FAILURES: WHY?

The increased number of parole failures and rising recidivism rates is not accompanied by a rising trend in serious crime committed by parolees. Between 1980 and 1996, the number of parole violations increased by 508% (from 28,817 to 175,305). However, fully two-thirds (68.5%) of parole violations were "technical" violations—no new crime was committed.[27] Austin and Irwin, after an exhaustive investigation into the prison and parole system, arrived at the following conclusion:

> This trend is attributable in large part to dramatic changes in the nature of parole supervision and the imposition of increasingly more severe conditions of supervision on parolees. Instead of a system designed to help prisoners re-adjust to a rapidly changing and more competitive economic system, the current parole system has been designed to catch and punish inmates for petty and nuisance-type behaviors that do not in themselves draw a prison term.[28]

What are technical violations? Every parole department has a number of rules and regulations that parolees must follow. They range from the obvious (compliance with all federal, state, and local laws) to rather vague stipulations (meet family responsibilities and support dependents). They also relate to situations that may be largely out of the control of the parolee, such as maintaining gainful employment. The parolee is also generally required to report to the parole officer at specified intervals and to notify the parole officer of any change in residence.

Parole revocation is a serious matter, and the U.S. Supreme Court opened the door to granting due process rights to parolees in 1972 in *Morrissey v. Brewer*.[29] Prior to this case, the courts had taken a hands-off position, concluding that parole boards are "administrative" in function. Intervening could damage their role as *parens patriae* (substitute guardian or parent) and disturb rehabilitative efforts. It was commonly held that parole was a "privilege" rather than a "right" and that a "contract" existed between the parolee and the parole board. Violating a parole condition constituted a violation of the contract. Moreover, it was believed that parole was still a form of custody, albeit outside prison walls. Revocation was not thought to be part of normal criminal prose-

cution; hence, due process rights were not applicable. The Court ruled that

> Whether parole is a right or a privilege is not the crucial question. The issue is the extent to which an individual would be "condemned to suffer grievous loss." The liberty enjoyed by a parolee is important: if terminated, some elements of due process must be involved. The state's interest in protecting society does not preclude or hinder an informal hearing at parole revocation.

One year later, the Court ruled in *Gagnon v. Scarpelli* that a parolee was entitled to two hearings, one at the time of arrest and detention and another when the final decision was made.[30] Yet despite this ruling, parolees are still not given such rights as the right to counsel, the right to call witnesses, or the right to an impartial judge and jury. Furthermore, parole can be revoked "if the board feels there is a preponderance of evidence that the parolee was not meeting parole obligations."[31]

In 1980, 17% of prisoners admitted to state prisons were parole violators (includes both those sent to prison for committing a new crime and those who returned for technical violations). By 1999, parole violators accounted for 35% of prison admissions. Almost one-third of those returned to prison had been sentenced for a new crime, while two-thirds violated conditions of their parole. There are tremendous variations in the percentages depending on the individual state. Prison admissions of parole violators in some states are less than 10% (Florida, Mississippi, Indiana, West Virginia, and Alabama). In Montana, Louisiana, and Utah more than half of prison admissions are parole violators. In California, the percentage is 67%. The variations point to distinct policy choices.

> At one extreme, a state could hypothetically choose to release all its prisoners without supervision—that state would have no parole violators and its prison admissions would be only new court commitments. At the other extreme, a state could place all its prison releases on parole supervision, supervise them closely, and aggressively revoke parole for the violations it discovers. That

state would have many parole violators and a high percentage of its prison admissions would be inmates who had violated their parole conditions on a previous case.[32]

Violating conditions of parole can include "failure to maintain verifiable residence" and "failure to pay supervision fees" (yes, in some jurisdictions the parolee is required to pay to be "supervised" by a parole agent). Common violations include failure to participate in drug testing and outpatient drug abuse counseling. Drug testing has become a convenient management tool for the parole system. Many parolees had serious drug problems in the past, and the results of drug tests send thousands back to prison.[33]

What should be underscored here—and we cannot emphasize this too strongly—is that the vast majority of parolees are extremely poor, lack a high school degree, have few job skills, and very little employment history. They are, in short, members of the growing *underclass* in U.S. society, part of the "surplus population" eliminated from the primary labor market through changes in the economic system. In short, they are "superfluous" as far as profits are concerned. One of the goals of the parole system is to "manage" this class.[34]

> For far too many of those not in custody life consists of forced idleness, deprivation, and exposure to criminal violence (conditions experienced by many *in* custody as well). The resulting sense of despair leaves many vulnerable to the attraction of drugs, unsafe sex, and involvement in criminal lifestyles.[35]

Since most parolees had few advantages prior to their prison sentence, it is not surprising that they find it almost impossible to find legitimate means of survival after release.

BEING ON PAROLE

The problem of reentry into society—or, as many inmates express it, "hitting the streets"—is an acute one for the majority of people released from prison. The problem is not unlike the problems confronted by soldiers returning from war. John Irwin offers this description:

The impact of release is often dramatic. After months of anticipation, planning, and dreaming, the felon leaves the confined, routinized, slow-paced setting of the prison and steps into the "streets" as an adult citizen. The problems of the first weeks are usually staggering and sometimes insurmountable. Becoming accustomed to the outside world, coping with parole, finding a good job—perhaps finding any job—and getting started toward a gratifying life style are at least difficult and for many impossible.

When released, the convict can be seen to be proceeding along a narrow and precarious route, beset with difficult obstacles. If the obstacles are too difficult, if satisfaction and fulfillment are not forthcoming, and/or his commitment to straightening up his hand is too weak, he will be diverted from the straight path toward systematic deviance. He himself believes in the route's precariousness and the high probability of his failure, and this intensifies its precariousness. Many of the obstacles are, however, both very real and very difficult.[36]

Parolees must immediately struggle to achieve some degree of financial support, affordable housing, clothes, and so on, just in order to apply for a job. They receive little in the form of financial assistance. In Nevada, for instance, they receive only $21 to help in the "transition" to normal life. Recent research indicates

> that a large share of ex-prisoners are concentrated in disadvantaged communities with high levels of poverty and unemployment. Recent research has also shown that prisoners who return to communities with higher concentrations of social and economic disadvantage have higher rates of recidivism.[37]

Irwin delineates three major obstacles the parolee faces: (1) "getting settled down" and "getting on your feet"; (2) "doing good"; and (3) coping with the parole system. The parole agent is often unable to empathize with the parolee and understand these problems. Part of this stems from the contradictory roles of the parole officer: he or she is both a police officer and a social worker. The average parole officer comes from a stable middle- or working-class background and usually fails to understand the client's lower-class background. The parole officer often does not have the time to help the parolee and has few resources for helping the parolee find work, a place to stay, clothes, money, and other necessities of life.

Getting Settled Down and Getting on Your Feet

Most parolees are very optimistic when they get out. For months they have been planning what they will do and how they will do it. Unfortunately, most of these plans are based on a highly idealized set of assumptions. The most immediate concern is to "get their feet on the ground" or "get into a groove of some kind." Their plans soon confront what Irwin calls "disorganizing events." First, they experience the impact of moving from one world (the prison) to another (the "streets"). Few are prepared for the demands they will face. The majority will be very lonely; their best friends may still be back in prison. Parolees immediately notice the dizzying pace of the outside world. Life in prison was slow and routinized, and the outside world seems too fast and chaotic by comparison. One inmate told Irwin: "I mean, I was shook, baby. Things were moving too fast, everybody rushing somewhere. And they all seemed so cold, they had this up tight look." Another inmate said: "The first thing I noticed was how fast everything moves outside. In prison everybody walks slow. Outside everyone's in a hurry."[38]

Doing Good

After "settling down" following the initial impact, those who have made it this far still face several obstacles to their goal of "doing good." These obstacles include becoming involved in what Irwin calls a "new meaning world." The parolee must find a group of people with whom he or she shares a "meaning of the world," or individuals with whom he or she has something in common. The parolee often runs into difficulty. Friends he or she knew and had something in common with prior to incarceration have had different experiences, and they may no longer have anything in common.

I feel lost . . . how crazy is that? I also feel guilty that I am out here, and they are still in there. I was in prison for 6 months, 6 months of hell, the lowest point in my life ever. I was down only a short time and I cannot even pretend that I know what it's like to serve a lengthy sentence. But even with my short sentence, there is a hole left in my soul and it feels like it can only be filled by those people who understand the damage that is done, the anger that creeps in, the idiosyncrasies that are acquired, and the dreams I cannot escape.[39]

Parolees may long for old prison buddies and old activities. Many end up spending a great deal of time around former "hangouts," such as bars and poolrooms.[40]

Many parolees do not "do good" when they get out. Many are unable to find work, few had any steady work experience prior to incarceration, and few acquired any marketable skills while in prison. If the parolee does find work, it may be seasonal. Some realize that the dreams they had in prison have vanished or were perhaps too unrealistic. When an ex-con fails to reach the level of what he considers "doing good," he is at a critical turning point. Another occurs after success in "making it" but little or no opportunity to go beyond this point.

Coping with the Parole System

The parolee also confronts problems with the parole system itself. He faces the conditions of parole—the set of rules that the parolee is supposed to follow. The parolee must deal with a parole system that is too often designed to "trail 'em, nail 'em, and jail 'em."[41] The director of the State of Nevada Department of Parole and Probation told us (RGS and WBB) in the late 1980s that "we train our agents to catch violators." Parole now consisted of law enforcement rather than a means of assisting reentry. One Las Vegas parole officer continually bragged about the absconders he had gone after and captured. In one case he traveled all the way to New Orleans to catch one of his parolees who had committed a couple of technical violations. He was, in common parlance, a gung ho type of agent who could not wait to catch someone violating a rule.

The parolee learns that the conditions of parole are a confusing combination of vague and comprehensive, so that it is almost impossible not to violate some of them. Indeed, in order to fulfill certain requirements of everyday living, some rules must be broken. For instance, in some jurisdictions one condition is that the parolee must obtain permission in order to drive a car and must also have a driver's license. To register a car, one must have insurance (which is not stated in the conditions). But before the parolee can afford insurance (and thus drive), the parolee must find a job, which usually requires driving to the place of employment. Another rule specifies that the parolee must not associate with ex-inmates or with people with "bad reputations." For most parolees, this is virtually impossible. In disadvantaged neighborhoods, it is common to know many people with an arrest record (even if the arrest was based only on "suspicion"). Also, the parolee must not drink alcoholic beverages "in excess." The definition is, once again, vague enough to catch almost every person in a violation. These two restrictions, especially the latter, are remnants of the puritanical and conservative elements of society that originally devised the rules. What this segment of society considers "proper" may be at odds with working- and lower-class lifestyles.

During the first few weeks on parole the parolee becomes aware that there is an important distinction between the formal expectations of the parole system itself and the informal expectations of the parole officer to whom the parolee is assigned. The parolee soon learns that the parole officer has a great deal of discretion. The nature of the officer's exercise of discretion will probably depend on whether the role of social worker or the role of parole officer is more dominant. While parole officers are assigned to "work with" the parolee, the details of that behavior are rarely made explicit. In addition, the parole officer is supposed to enforce the rules. The manner in which this is done, and the degree to which the rules and regulations are enforced, varies from one parole officer to another and from one parole office to another. Some spend much of their time

acting as vigilantes and go out of their way to catch their parolees committing infractions. Others (probably the majority) fall somewhere between the extremes of law enforcement officer and social worker.

The parole officer, it must be remembered, works within the parole system and is under constant pressure to be "on top" of a case. The parole officer must be constantly aware of what each parolee is doing. If there is a "blow up"—if the parolee commits a new crime—the parole officer must be prepared to answer to higher-ups. In order to do this, he or she must maintain a readiness to strictly enforce the rules. The parole officer has a strong incentive to please the parole board, and in many cases the parole board is reluctant to return a parolee to prison on one minor technical violation (although this does happen). Irwin found that parole officers tend to "bank" incidents of violations of parole rules (noting every minor violation committed by the parolee) to prepare for building a strong case if necessary.[42]

IS THE PAROLE SYSTEM SET UP TO FAIL?

The preceding discussion may lead the reader to believe that the entire parole system is set up and operated in such a way that failure is almost guaranteed for most ex-cons. A recent study in Kentucky provides some evidence of this.[43] Detailed interviews with a sample of men who had been returned to prison revealed several key components in the parole failures. One difficulty was the lack of programs within the prison itself that could help prepare prisoners for what to expect after their release. Massive cutbacks have resulted in virtually no college courses being offered. Although some vocational courses are offered, there is a severe shortage of space and available instructors. Most prisoners have to wait two or three years to get into a class.

Another problem they face is that they have so little money when they are released.

> The only interviewees who had money when they left the prison were those who had

money sent into them. The prisons do not provide "gate money," street clothes, or even a bus ticket home. Upon release, prisoners not picked up by family or friends at the front gate are forced to literally walk home.[44]

Perhaps the most significant problem is finding work. The available jobs paid minimum wage, which was insufficient to provide for the inmates themselves. Most had families to support, and the minimal wages were far too low to meet expenses. Many had to work more than one job.

Parole officers present problems as well, and most parolees distrusted them.

> One of the parole officers said "we ride them until they drop." This "blue grass" metaphor reflects the equestrian traditions of Kentucky. The parole officer was referring to the use of drug testing, surveillance, and investigation used to monitor the behavior of parolees.[45]

Given the limited funds available to most parolees, the mandatory requirement that they must pay to see their parole officers and to be tested for drugs seems a clear indication of a set-up for failure. The distrust of parolees for their parole officers complicates the almost insurmountable obstacles.

> The result is the parolees are unable to confide in or share their problems with the parole officers. Instead, they go through the monthly "report day" ceremony paying their fees (for supervision, drug tests, restitution, crime victims, programs) and pretending to "make it." They play a game of hide and seek, cops and robbers, or cops and dopers, and when they lose they are returned to prison.[46]

Another problem is coping with petty parole violations, which is one of the most common reasons for being returned to prison. One female parolee stated: "The last time I went to prison I went for possession of and use of alcohol. That was my two years. The time before that was curfew violation and absconding. The time before that it was curfew violation and dirty urine." She was not engaged in serious predatory criminal behavior. While "absconding" conjures up images of leaving the state or the country, it

refers simply to failing to appear on "report day" at the parole office.

A sixth problem was that many parolees did not get credit for the time served while in parole custody (awaiting a parole revocation hearing or waiting to be transferred back to prison). The concept of "time" is, understandably, of critical importance to prisoners, and anything that lengthens time in prison is painful. In many cases they end up serving more time than their original sentence, which is an obvious increase in the costs to taxpayers.

Finally, there is the ever-present problem of economics: most lived in poverty before their sentence and most returned to the same (or worse) conditions. The lack of economic resources, such as education and job skills, lead them back to committing crimes to survive. The authors of the study offer a sobering conclusion:

> The prison system is perpetuating growth on its own institutional failure to properly prepare prisoners for release. The parole system compounds the problem with the law enforcement style of supervision. The result is a revolving door that shuffles prisoners from one level of custody to another, from prison to parole, and from parole back to prison. The Kentucky state prison population will continue to grow because it is "recycling" the same individuals through the system.[47]

The lead author of this text (RGS) once presented a summary of the Kentucky study to his class, and one of the more conservative students posed the following question: "What are we supposed to do, feel sorry for them? They knew the rules and they broke them." His reaction summarizes a common view of crime and criminal behavior, which rarely considers the social context of the lives of offenders. It is perhaps best expressed by the phrase "If you can't do the time, don't do the crime." It is beyond the scope of this chapter (and in fact this book) to peel away the multiple layers under the snappy phrase. This common attitude, in our view, is symptomatic of many issues and helps contribute to our "perpetual prisoner machine." There seems to be very little recognition that not only does incarceration deeply impact the lives of prisoners, but it consumes vast amounts of our tax dollars. We have created a system that seems to guarantee failure, and we pay dearly for that failure.[48]

BARRIERS TO PAROLE SUCCESS: SOME "COLLATERAL CONSEQUENCES" OF MASS INCARCERATION

Being convicted of a crime has always had serious consequences. In recent years, however, the consequences have become more and more negative. Some scholars have argued that the overreliance on imprisonment as a form of social control has had "*collateral consequences*" (the term is borrowed, appropriately, from the military; the "war on crime" and the "war on drugs" have created numerous collateral casualties).[49]

Jeremy Travis distinguishes between "visible" and "invisible" punishments. The edifices of prisons are a visible reminder of society's desire to punish.[50] The numbers of people in prison are published in newspapers, and occasionally articles about the lengths of the sentences also appear. Invisible punishments are those the public rarely hears about or sees. Travis says invisible punishments are "accomplished through the diminution of the rights and privileges of citizenship and legal residency in the United States."[51] The laws that create these invisible punishments "operate largely beyond public view, yet have very serious, adverse consequences for the individuals affected."[52]

Travis also observes that these punishments take effect outside the formal court system since they are defined as "civil" and are treated as "disabilities" rather than "punishments." They are also invisible because they do not pass through the usual legislative committees; instead, they are often attached as riders to other pieces of legislation. Thus, there is little public debate about the fairness or efficacy of the sanction. Travis notes that the impulse to deny rights to offenders dates back to early Roman history, when an outlaw's wife was considered a widow and his children orphans.[53]

Today offenders can be denied public housing, welfare benefits, certain parental rights, and the ability to obtain an education through the denial of grants. Such indirect punishments impact a large proportion of the population—an estimated 47 million people have criminal records, while about 13 million are either serving time or have been convicted of a felony in the past. This amounts to what Travis calls a kind of "internal exile," like the "mark of Cain," where the offender becomes a "noncitizen."[54]

Among the changes in the law concerning ex-cons are the following:

1. 14 states permanently deny ex-felons the right to vote;
2. 19 states allow the termination of parental rights;
3. 29 states have made a felony conviction grounds for divorce;
4. 25 states place restrictions on the right to hold public office;
5. 33 states restrict firearm ownership.[55]

Disenfranchisement

The disenfranchisement of felons is not a new phenomenon. This course of action dates back to ancient Greece, a time when criminals were pronounced "infamous" and stripped of their right to attend public assemblies, hold office, make speeches, and serve in the army.[56] The rationale behind current disenfranchisement laws is that it is necessary to deny the right to vote to felons to maintain the "purity of the ballot box." It is believed that ex-offenders are impure because they chose to commit a crime and are incapable of voting for the "common good" of society. In 1978, the Fifth Circuit Court argued that "the state may exclude ex-offenders because they, like insane persons, have raised the questions about their ability to vote responsibly."[57]

In modern times felon disenfranchisement laws have had the greatest effect on African Americans due to the fact that this minority group is disproportionately represented in the criminal justice system. As of the end of 2002, all but two states had laws that deprived felons of the right to vote while serving a prison or jail sentence for a felony offense.[58] A mid-1990s study found that while 2% of *all* adults have been disenfranchised because of a felony conviction (mostly drug convictions), *about 13% of all black men* have lost the right to vote. In six states the percentage of black men disenfranchised is 25% or more, *and higher than 30% in Alabama and Florida*.[59] As of 2004, 2 million of the 5 million disenfranchised were African Americans.[60] The disenfranchisement rate for African American males is nearly twice that of whites. In some states that disenfranchise felons indefinitely, up to 40% of African American men may permanently lose their right to vote.[61] Disenfranchisement has no deterrent effect; it does, however, make the ex-offender feel less like a citizen and even more isolated.

One example of the impact of the high disenfranchisement rate for African Americans was the 2000 presidential election. More than 50,000 people were removed from the voting rolls in Florida. It was claimed that most had been convicted of a felony, but it turned out that 90% were innocent; over half were black or Hispanic voters, and mostly Democrats. Bush won Florida by 537 votes.[62]

An analysis of the 2000 presidential vote found that had ex-felons been allowed to vote, Al Gore would have won the presidency.[63] After controlling for other variables (including the fact that many ex-felons fail to vote) researchers found that "felon disenfranchisement has provided a small but clear advantage to Republican candidates in every presidential and senatorial election from 1972 to 2000."[64] The researchers commented on the implications of their study:

> Although we have specified the political consequences of felon disenfranchisement, we have only touched on the origins of these laws and the mass incarceration phenomenon that gives such force to them today. These questions are important for situating felon disenfranchisement within a broader model of social control of dispossessed groups. Proponents of the "new penology" argue that the focus of criminological interest has recently shifted from the rehabilitation of individual offenders to the social control of aggregate groups. The correctional population is subject to a number of

exclusions: They are often ineligible for federal grants (such as Pell Grants), they have restricted access to social programs, they face sharp disadvantages in the labor market, and they must live with the social stigma associated with a felony conviction. Restricted access to the ballot box is but a piece of a larger pattern of social exclusion for America's vast correctional population.[65]

It is important to emphasize here that the right to vote has been one of the central and most important features of democratic societies, as evidenced by the struggles of those to whom it was once denied: women, blacks, and others. For more than 100 years following the end of the Civil War, former slaves were prohibited from voting through various mechanisms, such as the "grandfather clause" (an ex-slave could only vote if his grandfather was once a registered voter—an obvious "catch-22") and various sorts of "tests" (e.g., reading ability, knowledge of the Constitution). Some of these methods have resurfaced in recent years for ex-felons. One recent study found that some states have instituted various "character tests" for ex-felons. In Florida, for example, ex-felons are asked if they drink alcohol, while in Kentucky an ex-felon has to provide letters of reference concerning his or her "good character" to be able to register to vote.[66]

The Impact on Informal Social Controls

Dina Rose and Todd Clear contend that one of the impacts of an overreliance on incarceration as a form of social control undermines a community's attempts to use informal methods of control.[67] This in turn leads to more, rather than less, social disorganization. This idea runs counter to "common sense" notions that tell us that removing "bad elements" from a community makes things safer. High incarceration rates contribute to problems such as inequality, family deterioration (e.g., when a father or a mother gets sent to prison), economic problems, etc. Human and social capital becomes weakened in communities with the highest incarceration rates.

The increasing tendency to house prisoners in faraway rural communities amounts to what Clear calls "coercive mobility." In many poor neighborhoods, up to 25% of the adult males are behind bars on any given day. This results in the removal of both *human capital* and *social capital* from these communities.[68] An estimated $25,000 per year leaves the community for every man who is incarcerated and goes directly to the communities that have the prisons.[69]

Incarceration affects three major disorganizing factors originally identified by Shaw and McKay.[70] First, incarceration results in an alteration of both the labor market and the marriage market.[71] Second, there is an increase in transience; as one person enters prison, someone else is released. The transience contributes to the third factor—the constant influx of new people affects cultural norms and values; the neighborhood becomes increasingly heterogeneous. Those released from prison bring the norms and values of the prison subculture to the neighborhoods.

Denial of Public Housing

One of the biggest challenges that a recently released offender faces after release is the inability to find and sustain adequate housing. Housing is essential to survival for everyone, ex-offender or not, yet 12% of U.S. prisoners are homeless after release from prison.[72] Upon release, ex-offenders have no resources, and many lack the skills necessary to apply for employment that would provide the income necessary to pay for adequate housing. Parolees must deal with the stigma attached to being an ex-offender, which may make finding employment—and therefore housing—impossible. Federally subsidized housing was designed to provide decent and affordable housing for low-income people and families, but federal housing is often denied to those convicted of a drug offense.

In order to reduce crime in public housing projects in urban areas, policies were designed that targeted those involved with drug trafficking, drug use, and violent crime. Housing authorities have the right to deny housing to:

1. Those who have been evicted from public housing because of drug-related criminal activity for a period of three years following eviction.

2. Those that have in the past engaged in a pattern of disruptive alcohol consumption or illegal drug use, regardless of how long ago such conduct occurred.

3. The catch-all category of those who have engaged in any drug-related criminal activity, any violent activity, or any other criminal activity if the public housing authority deems them a safety risk.[73]

Although housing authorities have been asked to consider the circumstances surrounding the crime and also to take into consideration whether or not the applicant has been rehabilitated, most fail to do so. There is no system of checks and balances, which allows most local housing authority agencies to be as stringent as they choose.

The harshness of this policy has damaging consequences for offenders, especially those convicted of a drug offense. Not only are ex-offenders unable to find housing, but they are also unable to live with family members who reside in public housing without putting the entire family at risk for eviction. Lack of housing is an issue that affects not only the offender, but the offender's family and community as well. Without adequate housing, many ex-offenders are forced to live on the streets. Fear of crime usually increases in communities where the homeless reside.

Many other studies have documented the importance of finding shelter. A study of a cohort of prisoners released from New York State prisons, who returned to New York City (where the majority of that state's prisoners live), found that 11.4% ended up in a homeless shelter and that of this group one-third were sent back to prison within a two-year period.[74]

A Human Rights Watch report concluded that "recidivism becomes a self fulfilling prophecy when offenders are released from incarceration with scant survival options."[75] With no income and no place to live, many are forced to go back to committing the crimes for which they were originally imprisoned.

Denial of Other Federal Benefits

In 1996 Congress passed the Personal Responsibility and Work Opportunity Reconciliation Act (also known as the Welfare Reform Act). The law replaced individual welfare with block grants known as TANF (Temporary Assistance for Needy Families).[76] Under TANF, welfare recipients must work in order to receive benefits and may only receive benefits for a five-year period. In addition, the act "requires that states permanently bar individuals with drug-related felony convictions from receiving federally funded public assistance and food stamps during their lifetime." Those who violate probation or parole conditions become "temporarily" ineligible for TANF, food stamps, Social Security benefits, and public housing. An interesting irony is that murderers and other violent felons may be eligible for some of these benefits, but not drug offenders.

When ex-offenders attempt to reenter society they have little or no money and may not have the skills necessary to gain employment. Public aid is a tool that could assist in providing some of the essentials for successful reentry but is readily denied. Without such support recidivism is highly likely to occur.[77] Denying an ex-offender benefits such as food stamps affects not only the ex-offender, but the entire household as well. Denial of access to aid compounds the stress of reentering society and increases the chance of reoffending, which in turn diverts taxpayer dollars into the criminal justice system.

In 1988, the Denial of Federal Benefits Program was established under section 5301 of the Anti-Drug Abuse Act (Public Law 100-690). This act provided federal and state courts "the ability to deny all or selected federal benefits to individuals convicted of drug trafficking or drug possession."[78] The rationale was that the threat of denial of these benefits would act as a deterrent to drug use and sales. Ironically, although the aim was also to save tax dollars, arrest, prosecution and imprisonment of parole violators creates even more expense. Another "collateral consequence" is the fact that under this program, students are ineligible for student financial aid if convicted of a drug offense. Unless the family has resources, an ex-offender who desires to pursue a college degree after release will find that his or her goals of self-improvement are blocked by the prohibition to borrow federal funds.[79]

SOME MODEL PROGRAMS

Many people have long recognized that successful reentry is essential for both ex-cons and the communities to which they return. There are several existing programs with proven track records and many new programs that have promise. In the final section of this chapter we will summarize a sample of these programs.

Delancey Street

The Delancey Street Foundation has achieved what many would have believed impossible: a program that helps some of the most intractable ex-offenders survive successfully in free society. Founded by Mimi Silbert (a clinical psychologist) and John Maher (former alcoholic, heroin addict, and criminal) in 1971, it consists of a "compound" in San Francisco near the bay. The area includes a variety of businesses operated by ex-cons, including an incredible restaurant (visited often by RGS), townhouses used as housing for the workers, a town hall, and even a park. Everything was built by the residents. Delancey Street "acts as a residential education center that assists former offenders and former substance abusers."

> At the core of the Foundation is the belief that behavior can be changed in a structured, supportive, market-driven environment in which individual responsibility and accountability are emphasized. Participants are required to stay in the program for two years, although the average stay is about four years. When participants arrive, they live in dorm-style rooms with as many as nine roommates and take on basic chores such as mopping and cleaning the parks. The system at the Foundation is based on an "each one teach one" principle, in which participants learn from each other and hand down skills so that others can move into new work positions. One of the first goals is to achieve a high school equivalency degree. Afterwards, participants learn skills at one of the Foundation's training schools: a moving and trucking school, a restaurant and catering services, a print and copy shop, retail and wholesale sales, paratransit services, advertising specialties sales, Christmas tree sales and deco-

rating, and an automotive service center, among others.

All the staff at the Delancey Street operations are former offenders or substance abusers or were homeless. Most of the funds generated by the Delancey businesses support the Delancey community; in return, the residents receive food, housing, and a small stipend. According to the program, more than 14,000 individuals have successfully graduated from the program and are leading independent lives. The Foundation has expanded over the years; about 1,000 residents live in five facilities across the nation.[80]

Although it has never been subjected to a thorough evaluation according to scientific research principles, we strongly believe in the concept and wonder why it has not been replicated throughout the country.

America Works, Inc.— Criminal Justice Program

This program started in New York in 1984 as a for-profit job placement agency, helping hard-to-serve welfare recipients obtain employment in the private sector. In 2001 it developed a criminal justice component that has focused on helping ex-cons through job readiness training (interviewing skills, etc.), job placement (receptionist, secretary, word processor, mailroom clerk, factory, security worker, etc.), supported work (providing four months of training), job retention services (through case management techniques where a case manager meets with both the client and the employer), and other supportive services.

This program was evaluated by the Manhattan Institute in 2002, which found that of 891 referrals during the first year of operation, over half (56%) completed the first day of orientation. Of that group, over three-fourths (77.6%) were placed into jobs. Out of those placed, just under half (44.5%) kept their job for at least 90 days. A total of 90 held their jobs for more than six months. The evaluators concluded:

> Even if America Works could not improve on the first year performance rate, the public saves $184,000 annually at the six-month final payment date. For every month

those 90 ex-offenders continue to work, up to another $225,000 is saved, or an additional $2.7 million a year. The cost-benefit ratio for this program to date is excellent. If employment can be sustained and retention rates improved, the savings to the taxpayer become enormous.[81]

Project RIO

The *Project RIO* (Re-Integration of Offenders) program began in 1985 in the state of Texas. Operated through the Texas Workforce Commission, it has more than 62 offices throughout the state and has a client load of about 16,000 parolees every year. The program starts within the prison and includes several different services, including skills testing, job readiness, and a "life skills" program (anger management, family relationships, and personal hygiene, among others). Job placement services are made available for all participants after release.

An independent evaluation of the program found that almost 70% of RIO participants found employment compared to 36% of a matched group of nonparticipants. Also, within one year after release, only 23% of RIO participants were returned to prison compared to 38% of a control group. The evaluation also found that the project saved more than $15 million in reincarceration costs.[82]

Pioneer Human Services

Beginning in 1962 in Seattle, Washington, *Pioneer Human Services* is one of the longest running programs in the country. The program provides a variety of services to ex-convicts and former substance abusers. "The program is a combination of correctional services, substance abuse services, behavioral health services, drug and alcohol-free housing, and employment in one of Pioneer's businesses." It is a large program, with about 1,000 staff and a budget of more than $55 million. They serve about 6,500 clients every year. They provide such services as housing, job training, and substance abuse treatment. The organization operates a number of different businesses (e.g., construction, printing, food services, etc.). A University of Washington study found that participants had a recidivism rate of about 6% after two years and that they had higher earnings than a control group.[83]

The Safer Foundation

Established in 1972 to provide vocational training to prisoners, *The Safer Foundation* assists offenders in gaining access to a union and finding employment. They operate programs in six locations in Illinois and Iowa and run two secure residential sites: PACE Institute (Programmed Activities for Correctional Education), a private school within Cook County Jail, and a work release center called Crossroads Community Correctional Center in Chicago.

The group provides walk-in postrelease services in Rock Island, Illinois and Davenport, Iowa. They provide such services as job referral and follow-up. It has "deliberately defined its target population broadly to include a wide range of former offenders: juvenile and adult probationers, parolees, community corrections residents, and people in the county jail." An evaluation of the program found that 59% of the clients placed in jobs remained in the job for 30 days and that these clients "were also more likely to remain employed and crime free up to a year after release."[84]

Independent Living and Supportive Living Programs

These are two promising programs operated by the Center on Juvenile and Criminal Justice (CJCJ) in San Francisco and Washington, DC.

The Independent Living Program (ILP) began in 1999 for youth diverted from or returning from residential detention who had no supportive home environment to which they could return. CJCJ houses 15 young adults aged 17 to 21 in furnished apartments. In addition to housing, clients receive a weekly stipend and around the clock monitoring and support. They work with ILP staff to develop an individualized and comprehensive "life plan" that involves accessing the particular support services that they need. ILP maintains a network of education services, substance abuse counseling, vocational training, mental health counseling, and other

community-based services. Case managers, who keep small caseloads, monitor the residents as they build their self-sufficiency. With this assistance, the youths can begin building all the necessary skills for independent living.

The Supportive Living Program began in 1992 in San Francisco; it is part of the Bay Area Parole Services Network, a project funded by the state Department of Corrections to reduce the number of state parolees returning to prison for parole violation. SLP provides drug and alcohol treatment services for sixteen participants, who are housed in two residential San Francisco neighborhoods for up to 180 days. When new clients enter the program, case managers work with them to develop individualized treatment plans to address their specific psychological and social needs. Case plans are culturally specific, and they typically include participation in education, employment, vocational training, family reunification, mental health, post-release housing, and life skills training.

Also distinct from traditional clinical approaches, SLP staff are selected not only on the basis of clinical training but also on experience-based knowledge of substance abuse and its dangers. An emphasis on commonality allows for closer identification between clients and staff and facilitates the development of trust and support. An addiction severity tool helps to assess clients' needs before deciding on treatment. SLP residents participate in weekly group and individual counseling sessions. SLP staff use Narcotics Anonymous and Alcoholics Anonymous methodology as well as spiritually based ideas to structure the rehabilitation process. Group sessions focus on relapse prevention, building support for ongoing recovery, anger management, life skills, employment readiness, and tools for completing parole successfully and staying out of criminal activity.

Although these two programs have not been formally evaluated, the authors have worked with this organization on several projects over the years and strongly believe that each program has great promise. Both programs address two major concerns for ex-convicts (both juveniles and adults): housing and work.[85]

SUMMARY

This chapter reviewed some of the important issues facing someone who has just been released from prison. For the ex-con there are a host of problems, which we characterize as barriers placed in the way of success, which in turn increases the possibility of getting into trouble again. With more than 650,000 prisoners released from prison each year, this becomes a national issue.

While in prison, inmates formulate a number of different plans about what they will do after they are released. Prisoners develop three perspectives on the degree of success following release: "making it," avoiding the "old bag," and "doing all right."

There are three mechanisms for release from prison: discretionary release, mandatory release, and expiration of sentence. The most common is mandatory release, where the prisoner has served his or her time, minus "good-time" credits. After release parolees face immediate problems, especially finding housing and employment. Among the barriers confronting some released offenders is denial of the opportunity to live in federally subsidized housing.

Recidivism rates are high; approximately two-thirds of those released from prison are rearrested within a three-year period. The parole systems in certain states contribute to high recidivism if the orientation is tilted toward "catching violators" rather than helping the ex-con go straight. Included in technical violations is testing positive for drugs, which accounts for a large number of those returned to prison. Other technical violations include failure to report, failure to find gainful employment, moving without permission, etc.

There are a number of promising programs designed to help ex-offenders adjust to life on the outside. These programs help participants develop the skills they lacked prior to incarceration and provide the essential foundations for success: housing and employment.

Key Terms

- collateral consequences
- Delancey Street
- discretionary release
- doing all right
- drug testing
- expiration of sentence
- Independent Living Program
- making it
- mandatory release
- old bag
- parole
- perpetual prisoner machine
- Pioneer Human Services
- project RIA
- recidivism
- safer foundation
- Supportive Living Program
- technical violations

Notes

[1] *Reentry.* Office of Justice Programs. [Online] http://www.reentry.gov/

[2] The Urban Institute. "Number of Prisoners Released in Ohio Triples in 2 Decades." November 20, 2003. [Online] http://www.urban.org/publications/900669.html; La Vigne, N. G., C. A. Mamalian, J. Travis, and C. Visher. *A Portrait of Prisoner Reentry in Illinois.* Chicago: The Urban Institute, 2003. [Online] http://www.urban.org/url.cfm?ID=410662

[3] See Dyer, J. *The Perpetual Prisoner Machine: How America Profits from Crime.* Boulder, CO: Westview Press, 2000.

[4] La Vigne et al., *A Portrait of Prisoner Reentry in Illinois.*

[5] Austin, J. and P. Hardyman. "The Risks and Needs of Returning Prisoner Population." *Review of Policy Research* 21: (January 2004). The two studies they cite were conducted by the Bureau of Justice Statistics, one in the early 1980s and the other in the early 1990s. These studies included all those arrested and sentenced to either jail or prison. Most were not sent to prison as they did not commit a felony and of those reincarcerated, about 85% were convicted of a nonviolent crime.

[6] Langan, P. A. and D. J. Levine. *Recidivism of Prisoners Released in 1994* (NCJ 193427). Washington, DC: Bureau of Justice Statistics, June 2002, p. 2.

[7] The figure was cited in Glaser, D. *The Effectiveness of a Prison and Parole System.* Indianapolis: Bobbs-Merrill, 1964.

[8] RAND Corporation. "Prisoner Reentry: What Are the Public Health Challenges?" Santa Monica: Author, June 24, 2003. [Online] http://www.rand.org/pubs/research_briefs/RB6013/index1.html

[9] La Vigne, N. G. and V. Kachnowski. *Texas Prisoners' Reflections on Coming Home.* The Urban Institute, October 2005, pp. 7–8.

[10] Irwin, J. *The Felon.* Englewood Cliffs, NJ: Prentice-Hall, 1970, ch. 4.

[11] Glaze, L. E. and T. P. Bonczar. *Probation and Parole in the United States, 2005* (NCJ 215091). Washington, DC: Bureau of Justice Statistics, November 2006. [Online] http://www.ojp.usdoj.gov/bjs/pub/pdf/ppus05.pdf; Beck, A., J. Brown, and D. Gilliard. *Probation and Parole in the United States, 1995* (BJS96143). Washington, DC: Bureau of Justice Statistics, June 1996. [Online] http://www.ojp.usdoj.gov/bjs/pub/pdf/pap95.pdf

[12] Pickett, R. *House of Refuge: Origins of Juvenile Reform in New York State, 1815–1857.* Syracuse, NY: Syracuse University Press, 1969.

[13] Simon, J. *Poor Discipline: Parole and the Social Control of the Underclass, 1890–1990.* Chicago: University of Chicago Press, 1993, p. 34.

[14] Walker, S. *Sense and Nonsense about Crime and Drugs* (6th ed.). Belmont, CA: Wadsworth, 2006, p. 228.

[15] Glaze and Bonczar, *Probation and Parole in the United States,* p. 8.

[16] Hughes, T. and D. J. Wilson, *Reentry Trends in State Parole.* Bureau of Justice Statistics. [Online] http://www.ojp.usdoj.gov/bjs/reentry/releases.htm#methodr

[17] Glaze and Bonczar, *Probation and Parole in the United States,* p. 8.

[18] Ibid.

[19] Travis, J. and S. Lawrence. *Beyond the Prison Gates: The State of Parole in America.* The Urban Institute, 2002, p. 7. [Online] http://www.urban.org/UploadedPDF/310583_Beyond_prison_gates.pdf

[20] Ibid., pp. 1, 4–7.

[21] Ibid., p. 2.

[22] Runda, J., E. Rhine, and R. Wetter. *The Practice of Parole Boards.* Lexington, KY: Association of Paroling Authorities, 1994.

[23] For summaries of these studies, see Petersilia, J. "Probation and Parole." In M. Tonry (ed.), *The Handbook of Crime and Punishment.* New York: Oxford University Press, 1998.

[24] Ibid.

[25] Austin, J. and J. Irwin. *It's about Time: America's Incarceration Binge* (3rd ed.). Belmont, CA: Wadsworth, 2001, pp. 142–143.

[26] Blokland, A., D. S. Nagin, and P. Nieuwbeerta. "Life Span Offending Trajectories of a Dutch Conviction Cohort." *Criminology* 43: 919–954; Laub, J. H. and R. J. Sampson. *Shared Beginnings, Divergent Lives: Delinquent Boys to Age 70.* Cambridge, MA: Harvard University Press, 2003; Kurlychek, M. C., R. Brame, and S. D. Bushway. "Scarlet Letters and Recidivism: Does an Old Criminal Record Predict Future Offending?" *Criminology and Public Policy* 5: 483–504.

[27] Austin and Irwin, *It's about Time.*

[28] Ibid., p. 144.

[29] *Morrissey v. Brewer,* 408 U.S. 471, 1972.

[30] *Gagnon v. Scarpelli,* 411 U.S. 778, 782, 1973.

[31] Austin and Irwin, *It's about Time,* p. 144.

[32] Travis and Lawrence, *Beyond the Prison Gates,* p. 22.

[33] Austin and Irwin, *It's about Time,* pp. 145–146, 162.

[34] For fuller treatment of this issue, see Shelden, R. G. *Controlling the Dangerous Classes: A Critical Introduction to the History of Criminal Justice.* Boston: Allyn & Bacon, 2001. More specific treatment of this subject as it applies to the parole system can be seen in Simon, *Poor Discipline,* especially chapter 5.

[35] Simon, *Poor Discipline,* pp. 141–142.

[36] Irwin, *The Felon,* p. 107.

[37] Vigne, N. G., C. Visher, and J. Castro. *Chicago Prisoners' Experiences Returning Home.* The Urban Institute, 2004. [Online] http://www.urban.org/UploadedPDF/311115_ChicagoPrisoners.pdf

[38] Irwin, *The Felon,* pp. 112–114.

[39] Olson, B. "Degradation, Apathy, and Acceptable Casualties: Serving Time in a Women's Federal Correctional Institute." *Justice Policy Journal* 3(2): (Fall 2006). [Online] http://www.cjcj.org/pdf/degradation_apathy.pdf

[40] Irwin, *The Felon,* pp. 131–134.

[41] Miller, J. G. *Search and Destroy: African-American Males in the Criminal Justice System.* Cambridge: Cambridge University Press, 1996, p. 131.

[42] Ibid., p. 162.

[43] Richards, S., J. Austin, and R. S. Jones. "Kentucky's Perpetual Prisoner Machine: It's About Money." *Review of Policy Research* 21(1): 93–106 (January 2004).

[44] Ibid., p. 99.

[45] Ibid., p. 100.

[46] Ibid., p. 101.

[47] Ibid., p. 102.

[48] Dyer, J. *The Perpetual Prisoner Machine;* Richards et al., "Kentucky's Perpetual Prisoner Machine; Austin and Hardyman, "The Risks and Needs of the Returning Prisoner Population; Petersilia, J. *When Prisoners Come Home: Parole and Prisoner Reentry.* New York: Oxford University Press, 2003.

[49] Mauer, M. and M. Chesney-Lind (eds.). *Invisible Punishment: The Collateral Consequences of Mass Imprisonment.* New York: New Press, 2002.

[50] Travis, J. "Invisible Punishment: An Instrument of Social Exclusion." In Mauer and Chesney-Lind, *Invisible Punishment,* pp. 15–36. Prisons occupy a clearly demarcated space within both the urban and rural landscape. Some are tucked away in very remote areas; others are visible to large numbers of people who drive past the formidable compounds. The structure of modern prisons reminds the general population that the nation's "outlaws" are housed behind formidable walls—a harsh reminder that "crime does not pay." The physical reminder of general deterrence as a social policy is hard to miss. Conversely, knowledge about high recidivism rates turns the edifice into a physical reminder of the failure of deterrence.

[51] Ibid., pp. 15–16.

[52] Ibid., p. 16.

[53] Ibid., p. 17.

[54] Ibid., pp. 18–19.

[55] Ibid., p. 22.

[56] Ibid., p. 17.

[57] "The Disenfranchisement of Ex-Felons: Citizenship, Criminality, and the Purity of the Ballot Box." *The Harvard Law Review* 102(6): 1300–1317 (April 1989).

[58] Petersilia, *When Prisoners Come Home.*

[59] Fellner, J. "Stark Racial Disparities Found in Georgia Drug Law Enforcement." *Overcrowded Times* 7(5)

(October 1996); Fellner, J. and M. Mauer. "Nearly 4 Million Americans Denied Vote Because of Felony Convictions." *Overcrowded Times* 9(5) (October 1998).

60 The "Felon Disenfranchisement Project." [Online] http://www.soc.umn.edu/%7Euggen/FD_summary.htm

61 Wheelock, D. "Collateral Consequences and Racial Inequality: Felon Status Restrictions as a System of Disadvantage." *Journal of Contemporary Criminal Justice* 21: 82–90 (2005).

62 Palast, G. *The Best Democracy Money Can Buy.* New York: Penguin Books, 2000.

63 Uggen, C. and J. Manza. "Democratic Contraction? Political Consequences of Felon Disenfranchisement in the United States." *American Sociological Review* 67: 777–803 (2002).

64 Ibid., p. 787.

65 Ibid., p. 796. See also the following: Feeley, M. M. and J. Simon. "The New Penology: Notes on the Emerging Strategy of Corrections and Its Implications." *Criminology* 30: 449–74 (1992); Wacquant, L. "Deadly Symbiosis: When Ghetto and Prison Meet and Mesh." *Punishment and Society* 3: 97; Western, B. and K. Beckett. "How Unregulated Is the U.S. Labor Market? The Penal System as a Labor Market." *American Journal of Sociology* 104: 1030–1060 (1999).

66 Mauer, M. and T. Kansal. *Barred for Life: Voting Rights Restoration in Permanent Disenfranchisement States.* Washington, DC: The Sentencing Project, 2005. [Online] http://www.sentencingproject.org/pdfs/barredforlife.pdf

67 Rose, D. and T. Clear. "Incarceration, Social Capital, and Crime: Implications for Social Disorganization Theory." *Criminology* 36(3): 441–479 (1998).

68 Clear, T. "The Problem with 'Addition by Subtraction'." In Mauer and Chesney-Lind, *Invisible Punishment,* 2002, pp. 181–193.

69 Clear, T. and D. R. Rose. *When Neighbors Go to Jail: Impact on Attitudes about Formal and Informal Social Control.* Washington, DC: National Institute of Justice, 1999.

70 Shaw, C. and H. McKay. *Juvenile Delinquency and Urban Areas.* Chicago: University of Chicago Press, 1972 [1942].

71 Wilson, W. J. *The Truly Disadvantaged.* Chicago: University of Chicago Press, 1987. Wilson discusses at length the decline in the "marriage market" for black women largely as a result of severe unemployment within the inner cities.

72 Petersilia, *When Prisoners Come Home.*

73 *No Second Chance: People with Criminal Records Denied Access to Public Housing.* New York: Human Rights Watch, November 2004. [Online] http://hrw.org/english/docs/2004/11/18/usdom9695_txt.htm

74 Metraux, S. and D. P. Culhane. "Homeless Shelter Use and Reincarceration Following Prison Release." *Criminology and Public Policy* 3: 139–160 (March, 2004). It appears that the growth in homelessness has paralleled the growth in prison populations. See Burt, M. R., L. Y. Aron, E. Lee, and J. Valente. *Helping America's Homeless: Emergency Shelter or Affordable Housing.* Washington, DC: Urban Institute, 2001; Gowan, T. "The Nexus: Homelessness and Incarceration in Two American Cities." *Ethnography* 3: 500–534.

75 Human Rights Watch, *No Second Chance.*

76 Travis, "Invisible Punishment," p. 23.

77 Rubinstein, G. and D. Mukamal. "Welfare and Housing—Denial of Benefits to Drug Offenders." In Mauer and Chesney-Lind, *Invisible Punishment,* pp. 37–49.

78 Bureau of Justice Assistance. *Denial of Federal Benefits Program and Clearinghouse.* July 2002. [Online] http://www.ncjrs.gov/pdffiles1/bja/193770.pdf.

79 The impact has been negative, to say the least. An estimated 189,065 college students have been denied student loans because of drug convictions, mostly for possession. Students convicted for violent crimes do not face this problem. Leinwand, D. "Drug Convictions Cost Students Their Financial Aid," *USA Today* (April 17, 2006); D. Saunders, "Drug-War Follies," *San Francisco Chronicle* (February 10, 2005).

80 Reentry National Media Outreach Campaign. "Delancey Street Foundation." [Online] http://www.reentrymediaoutreach.org/sp_education_dsf.htm.

81 The web site for the program is: http://www.americaworks.com/; see also http://www.reentrymedia outreach.org/sp_education_awi.htm; for the Manhattan Institute study see the following: Eimicke, W. B. and S. Cohen. "America Works' Criminal Justice Program: Providing Second Chances Through Work." November 29, 2002. [Online] http://www.manhattan-institute.org/html/cb_29.htm#07

82 Program Web site: http://www.twc.state.tx.us/svcs/rio.html; see also http://www.reentrymediaoutreach.org/sp_education_pr.htm; for an evaluation, see Finn, P. "Texas' Project RIO." Washington, DC: National Institute of Corrections, 1998. [Online] http://www.ncjrs.gov/pdffiles/168637.pdf

83 Program Web site http://www.pioneerhumanserv.com/; see also: http://www.reentrymediaoutreach.org/sp_education_phs.htm; for an evaluation see: Sommers, P., B. Mauldin, and S. Levin. "Pioneer Human Services: A Case Study." Seattle, WA: Northwest Policy Center, Institute for Public Policy and Management, Daniel J. Evans School of Public Affairs, University of Washington, 2000. [Online] http://depts.washington.edu/npc/npcpdfs/phsrep.pdf

84 Program Web site: http://www.saferfoundation.org; see also http://www.reentrymediaoutreach.org/sp_education_sf.htm; for an evaluation see: Finn, P. "Chicago's Safer Foundation: A Road Back for Ex-Offenders" (NCJ 167575). Washington, DC: National Institute of Justice, U.S. Department of Justice, 1998. [Online] http://www.ncjrs.org/pdffiles/167575.pdf

85 For more information about these and other programs operated by this organization go to their Web site: http://cjcj.org/

fifteen

The Prison Industrial Complex

Mass incarceration is extremely expensive. Think for a moment about the building and equipping of prisons—construction costs, electrical, plumbing fixtures, kitchen and laundry equipment, furniture, food, toilet paper, etc. The needs create opportunities for companies to profit by selling the myriad supplies necessary to operate a prison—or to design and build the prison, or to staff it. This phenomenon has been called the *prison industrial complex*. The interconnections among the criminal justice system, the political system, and the economic system are the subject of this chapter.

J. Robert Lilly and Paul Knepper used the phrase "correctional-commercial complex" to describe the alliance between government and private enterprise.[1] The patterns of interrelationships have been variously described as "policy networks," "subgovernment," or the "iron triangle." In comparing the correctional-commercial complex to the military-industrial complex, Lilly and Knepper described the "iron triangle" of the Pentagon, private defense contractors, and various members of congressional committees (e.g., armed services committees, defense appropriations committees). They argue that while such a system may not legally be a form of government, it nevertheless exerts greater influence than many of the more formal structures of the government. Decision making within any given policy arena often resides within a closed circle of government bureaucrats, agency heads, interest groups, and private interests—all of which gain from the allocation of public resources.

PRISONS AS A MARKET FOR CAPITALISM

Robert Heilbroner describes capitalism as:

a stratified society in which the accumulation of wealth fulfills two functions: the realization of prestige . . . and the expression of power. . . . Both aspects of capital can be seen in capitalist social formations, where the process of accumulating capital is pursued in part because it is the manner in which the dominant class expresses and renews its social control and in part because it is the typical means by which preeminence and distinction is achieved in the socioeconomic world. [One aspect of capitalism] is the insatiability that characterizes the process of capital, endlessly converting money into commodities and commodities into money. . . .

In turn this brings an implosive aspect to the expansion of capital, as daily life is scanned for possibilities that can be brought within the circuit of accumulation. The transformation of [routine] activities . . . into activities that also yield a profit to their organizers thus becomes an important "interior" reality into which capital expands. The steady movement of such tasks as laundering, cooking, cleaning, and simple health care—not to mention recreation and entertainment—from the exclusive concern of the private household into the world of business testifies to the internal expansion of capital within the interstices of social life. Much of what is called "growth" in capitalist societies consists in this commodification of life, rather than in the augmentation of unchanged, or even improved outputs.[2]

While Heilbroner was not delineating the intersection of capitalism and incarceration, he was describing how capitalism expands. Note the enthusiasm in the comments below about the expansion of potential profits to crime-related areas.

> "While arrests and convictions are steadily on the rise, profits are to be made—profits from crime. Get in on the ground floor of this booming industry now!"[3]

> "It's like a hotel with a guaranteed occupancy."[4]

> "In my mind there's no more recession-proof form of economic development. Nothing's going to stop crime."[5]

> "A business comes in and a year or two [later] it can't support itself . . . [a prison] is something you know is going to be there for a long time."[6]

> "The opportunities and options in the field are endless."[7]

> "There are no seasonal fluctuations, it is a non-polluting industry, and in many circumstances it is virtually invisible."[8]

> "If crime doesn't pay, punishment certainly does. . . ."[9]

The amount of money that flows into the coffers of the prison industrial complex from tax dollars alone is quite substantial. The expenditures for all correctional institutions came to $62 billion in 2004, which represents an increase of 97% over 1992 and an incredible 585% over 1982.[10] Expenditures by departments of probation and parole have also been increasing. In 1993 the average budget for probation and parole agencies was almost $70 million; in 2003 the average was almost $228 million, an increase of 226%.[11] The largest increase was for probation agencies, whose average budget increased to $165 million in 2002 from $40.5 million in 1993. The total expenditures for all probation and parole agencies in 2002 were $1.5 billion. The average cost per prisoner per day for food and medical costs was about $53 in 1994 and $62 in 2002.[12] The cost per year for one prisoner was about $22,600. The Federal Bureau of Prisons sought a budget of $5.15 billion in 2008, up from $330 million in 1980. In 1980 there were only 44 prisons housing 25,000 inmates; in 2007 there were 114 housing 193,600—36% above capacity.[13]

Literally thousands of companies, large and small, are seeking profits in this booming industry. Thousands of young men and women, many with college degrees from criminal justice programs at more than 3,000 colleges and universities, seek employment in the area. Most of these jobs offer not only good starting pay, but excellent benefits and a promise of future wage increases and job security. Many have formed unions, some of which wield a great deal of power.

Advertising Products

The amount of *advertising* in journals related to the industry is a clear indicator of how companies seek profits from the boom in corrections. Popular publications such as *Corrections Today*, *The American Jail*, and the annual *Directory* of the American Correctional Association (ACA) are replete with advertisements. There are also Web sites, such as "Corrections Connection" and its affiliated site "Correct Source—The Corrections Procurement Directory" that provide a search feature to find advertisers for the prison market.[14]

The ACA is one of the largest national organizations in the country. Their annual meetings draw hundreds of vendors, usually taking up an entire floor of a hotel or convention center. The Web site urges visitors to "Advertise with Us." Clicking on the link brings up the available vehicles for placing ads: *Corrections Today Magazine* (125,000 readers), *Corrections Compendium*, *Buyers' Guide of Correctional Products and Services*, banner advertising on the Web site, conference planning guide, conference program book, and three directories (juvenile and adult correctional departments; national jail and adult detention; and probation and parole agencies). One description of advertising opportunities states:

> *Corrections Today* also presents a first-hand look at the latest products, services and technologies available, thereby enabling

advertisers to reach their target market directly and maximizing their results in the corrections and criminal justice fields. Don't miss this wonderful opportunity for your advertisement to reach corrections professionals nationwide.

Also prominently displayed is a search feature called "Corrections Marketplace." If you enter, for example, "stainless steel," you will find 44 links to companies selling stainless steel products; entering "architect" summons 54 links, and "engineer" has 73 links. Anything connected to building, operating, and/or maintaining prisons and jails has a ready market. The corrections industry is a $50 billion a year industry.[15]

Reach Out and Touch Someone

Industry giants such as AT&T, Bell South, Sprint and MCI have found prisons to be an excellent market for long-distance business. Inmates all over the country spend countless hours on the telephone talking with relatives. Because inmates are not allowed to have personal phones, any calls are billed to the receiver. Collect calls are far more expensive than any other rate. AT&T has an advertisement that reads: "HOW HE GOT IN IS YOUR BUSINESS. HOW HE GETS OUT IS OURS." At their own expense, MCI installed pay phones throughout the California prison system. They levy a $3 surcharge for each phone call made, paid by the recipient. MCI offered the Department of Corrections 32% of the profits.[16] Perhaps the old advertisement that urged customers to "reach out and touch someone" should be updated to include "and be ready to pay exorbitant costs if that someone is in prison." Long-distance rates for the general population have fallen sharply in the last decade, but those lower fees do not apply to collect calls.

An investigative reporter found that the state of California received about $35 million a year through agreements with long-distance phone companies. Phone charges to relatives of those locked up in the California Youth Authority resulted in about $85 million in revenue for the state in 2001. After several years of protests over the fees, the state signed a three-year contract with

WorldCom and Verizon that cuts rates for adult prisoners by 25% and for juveniles by 78%. As a result of this agreement, the average 11-minute phone call to a family member outside the immediate area would be just over $5.[17]

Prison Construction

Not surprisingly, prison construction itself has become a booming business. During the 1990s a total of 371 new prisons opened. (About 92,000 new beds were added each year.) In 1999 alone, 24 new prisons opened at a total cost of just over $1 billion. In the mid-1970s there were about 600 state prisons;[18] the number is now more than 1,300. The average cost of building a new prison came to $105 million (about $57,000 per bed, which is more than the starting salary of public school teachers or newly hired assistant professors and even some full professors). Also, in 1999 a total of 146 prisons were adding or renovating beds at a cost of $470 million (about $30,000 per bed).[19] As of January 2002 a total of 28 new institutions were under construction and another 58 were being renovated or adding new beds. Most of the new beds were in either maximum- or medium-security institutions, where the costs are the highest. The total estimated costs of these new building projects were more than $1.5 billion.[20]

The construction of new prisons has become such a big business that there is a special newsletter called *Construction Report*, just to keep vendors up to date on new prison projects.[21] A Google search on the Internet turns up dozens of companies advertising for prison construction. One example is Kitchell which "has successfully delivered over 110,000 correctional beds, including over 130 criminal justice projects in 17 states."[22] These projects include 42 state prisons, 29 adult jails, and 30 juvenile facilities. Kitchell also builds police stations, court facilities, and camps.[23]

Corporate Interests: The Role of ALEC

The *American Legislative Exchange Council* (ALEC) illustrates the connections between politics, economics, and the criminal justice system. Council membership consists of state legislators (about 2,400 representing about one-third of all state lawmakers), private corporation executives (many from Fortune 500 companies) and criminal justice officials. The stated purpose is to promote free markets, small government, states' rights, and privatization. Corporate membership dues range from $5,000 to $50,000 annually.[24] Corrections Corporation of America is a member of this group; other members include Ameritech, AT&T, Bayer, Bell Atlantic, Bell South, DuPont, GlaxcoSmithKline, Merck & Co., Sprint, and Pfizer, to name just a few. Companies and foundations that have supported ALEC through various grants include: Ameritech, Exxon Mobil, Chevron, the Proctor and Gamble Fund, Exxon Educational Foundation, Bell Atlantic Foundation, and Ford Motor Company Fund.[25]

The organization compiles papers and policy statements on a wide variety of issues, including crime and punishment. They helped draft such legislation as mandatory minimum sentences, three strikes laws, and truth in sentencing. One of the nine categories of "model legislation" listed on the Web site is "Criminal Justice and Homeland Security."[26] The category is subdivided into bail (11 pieces of legislation), community theft (11), courts and sentencing (12), crimes against children (4), criminal acts (8), drugs (14), felons (5), firearms (11), juveniles (3), prisons (6), protecting personal information (2), vehicular misconduct/enforcement (6), victims' rights (4) and miscellaneous (7).

Tommy Thompson, former governor of Wisconsin and former secretary of the Department of Health and Human Services, was once a member of ALEC. He freely admitted, "I always loved going to these meetings because I always found new ideas. Then I'd take them back to Wisconsin, disguise them a little bit, and declare [them as] mine."[27] Edwin Bender of the National Institute on Money in State Politics discussed what happens at ALEC model legislation meetings.

Bayer Corporation or Bell South or GTE or Merck pharmaceutical company sitting at a table with elected representatives, actually hammering out a piece of legislation—behind closed doors, I mean, this isn't open to the public. And that then becomes the basis on which representatives are going to their state legislatures and debating issues.[28]

As noted in previous chapters, laws such as these greatly increased the prison population, which in turn increased the opportunities for profit.

RURAL PRISONS: UPLIFTING RURAL ECONOMIES?

Most prisons constructed during the past two decades have been built in rural areas, largely because of the promises of economic stimulus to these areas coupled with the cost savings to the states. There are more prisoners in the United States than there are farmers. Many rural towns have become "dependent on an industry that itself is dependent on the continuation of crime-producing conditions."[29] Between 1980 and 2000, "more than half of all rural counties added prison work to their available employment mix."[30] Prisons, casinos, and animal confinement units for raising or processing hogs and poultry have become the three leading industries in rural areas.

During the 1960s and 1970s an average of four new prisons per year were built in nonmetropolitan areas. During the 1980s, the numbers increased fourfold to about 16 per year. During the 1990s, the average increased to 24.5 per year—a new prison was opened about every 15 days. During this decade, 57% of all new prisons were in nonmetropolitan counties, which had only 19% of the total population.[31] By the end of the 1990s, there were about 235,000 prisoners and 75,000 workers in the new rural prisons built that decade.

The use of incarceration to attempt to solve crime and the welcoming of prison construction to offset severe economic downturns in rural areas has created a situation in which prisoners from primarily urban communities are incarcerated in tiny, rural towns. During the 1990s, a total of 245 prisons were built in 212 of the country's 2,290 rural counties. Many of these are in the rural Great Plains towns of Colorado, Oklahoma, and Texas. Because the Census Bureau counts prisoners, the population in these 212 counties increased 12% in the 1990s, compared to only 1.5% in the 1980s. In three Oklahoma cities with new prisons (Hinton, Sayre and Watonga), the population increased by more than 40%.

The population of Sayre, Oklahoma, is 4,144. It is home to the North Fork Correctional Facility (1,4440 inmates) operated by Corrections Corporation of America (CCA).[32] The prison employs 270 people (most earn between $17,000 and $19,000 per year) and "is responsible for lifting Sayre's spirits and reigniting its economy."[33] CCA is the largest taxpayer in Sayer; the prison pays $411,000 in property taxes, while spending $2.5 million for goods and services in Oklahoma. The prisoners are also cogs in Sayre's economic engine. "They pay the 3.5% sales tax levied by the city for the snacks and sodas they buy in the commissary. They also pay a 35% to 45% tax for the telephone calls, roughly 100 per day, all collect, all long distance."[34]

Many other businesses have opened to handle the population growth. Near Interstate 40, a Flying J Truck Stop was opened and now employs 117 people and pays around $150,000 year in sales taxes. The economic effects are not all positive. The turnover among prison employees is high (about 70% per year), and there has been a drain on demands for city services. Further, Wisconsin's prison growth has stopped and they will not be sending any more prisoners to other states within 10 years.[35]

There are many states that have several prisons built within a few miles of one another (described by one critic as "penal colonies"). Tracy Huling reports that in the town of Ionia, Michigan (population 10,569), there are six state prisons, which ties it with Huntsville, Texas (population 35,078), for the most prisons in any city in the country.[36] Ionia became one of Michigan's fastest growing communities with a much improved economy with penitentiaries employing 1,584 workers earning wages

totaling $102 million a year. Spillover effects included customers for stores and revenue for the city government—nearly $1.2 million of the city's $3.8 million budget came from the prisons.[37]

County and local leaders in these rural areas often engage in a vigorous campaign to get prisons built in their area. In Texas some towns "bombarded the [Texas Department of Criminal Justice] with incentives that range from country club memberships for wardens to longhorn cattle for the prison grounds."[38] In Rush City, Minnesota (population 2,102), civic leaders raised $700,000 in donations and another $40,000 from the city to buy the acreage for the site of the new prison. Tiny Shelby, Montana (population 3,216), used a $500,000 block grant and another $800,000 in federal grants to pay for the infrastructure so that CCA could build its prison, the Crossroads Correctional Facility.[39]

Michigan's Upper Peninsula illustrates the growth of prisons in rural areas and the overall impact on local economies. There are nine prisons and four minimum-security prison camps; all but two of these were opened during the past two decades. While only 2% of the state's population lives there, about 18% of its prisoners are housed there.[40]

In Newberry, in the Upper Peninsula of Michigan, a prison replaced a mental health center in 1996, which resulted in the county (Luce) having one of the highest ratios of prisoners to total population (13% of the population are in prison). One supporter, a local businessman, said that "the $12 million payroll coming into the community was just a big plus." In Chippewa County (population 38,543) there are five state prisons. In Kinross Township, a town of about 6,000, the prisons employ over 1,000 people, making it the second largest employer. Many in Kinross were looking forward to the possibility that McDonald's would open a restaurant, partly because prisoners are allowed to buy food once a month from local restaurants—an obvious "captive market."[41]

Pelican Bay State Prison in Crescent City, California (population 4,006), cost $277 million to build; it has become the largest employer in the county. Before the prison was built, Crescent City was a dying town, with most of its population living in poverty or near poverty (20% unemployment rate). Of the county's 17 sawmills, only four were operating, while the fishing industry was dead. During the 1980s a total of 164 businesses folded. The town essentially donated the land and utilities to land the prison, which now provides around 1,500 jobs, a payroll of over $50 million, and a budget of more than $90 million. The prison also indirectly created more business, such as a $130,000 contract to haul the garbage, a new hospital, a K-Mart, and a new Safeway market. Housing starts have doubled since then, as did the value of real estate, while collecting $142 million in real estate taxes, up from $73 million ten years earlier.[42]

Politicians often seek assistance from private enterprise when it comes to building prisons. Faced with severe overcrowding in the state prisons in the 1980s, New York Governor Mario Cuomo found that real estate prices were too expensive near the city of New York. A Republican state senator from the northern part of New York arranged for low prices on land for prisons. Twenty-five years ago, the area had only two prisons; today it has over 20.[43] One prison now occupies land formerly used for the Olympic Village at Lake Placid, while others have opened in abandoned factories and sanatoriums.[44] A total of 36 prisons have been built in New York since 1980.[45] These prisons bring in about $425 million in annual payroll and operating expenses—in effect, an annual "subsidy" of more than $1,000 for each person in the area.[46] The prison boom "has provided a huge infusion of state money to an economically depressed region."[47] The annual salary is around $36,000 for a correctional officer in this area, more than 50% higher than the average salary.

In Malone, New York (located about 15 miles south of the Canadian border), a $180 million maximum-security prison opened in 1999. The original plan called for holding prisoners in a 14 by 8.5 foot cell for 23 hours per day (reminiscent of the "Pennsylvania System.") The prison, scheduled to hold 1,500 prisoners, was projected to create about 500 jobs, which would offset the 750 jobs lost when a local shoe factory closed. Malone already had two medium-security institutions; the new prison brought the prison population in Malone to around 5,000. One writer noted that "prisons have become the North Country's largest growth industry." New businesses sometimes follow the building of new prisons; four new drugstores and eight new convenience stores opened in Malone.[48] "If crime doesn't pay, punishment certainly does, at least for isolated towns like Malone."[49]

There are five prisons in Franklin County (population 51,134), where the city of Malone is located.[50] New York houses 63,500 inmates in 17 maximum-security prisons, 37 medium-security prisons, 13 minimum-security prisons (4 are designated as "shock incarceration facilities"), 3 minimum-security camps, and one drug treatment center (in Willard, population 600 in western New York, on the shores of Seneca Lake). Less than 40% of the population of New York State lives in what is considered the "upstate" area. Over 70% of the prisoners are from the New York City area, while about 90% of the prisoners are incarcerated in upstate prisons.[51] Most of the boom in upstate New York stems from the "Rockefeller drug laws" passed in the 1970s, which set severe punishments for drug offenders. Prisons sentences have tripled since the passage of these laws, and almost two-thirds (62.5%) of those convicted were nonviolent drug offenders.[52]

One consequence of building so many prisons in upstate New York is that families of inmates have to make a very long trip to visit their relatives. This fact has created yet another business. In 1973 an ex-convict founded Operation Prison Gap, a bus service that transports families to the prison facilities. They now have 35 buses and vans traveling on weekends and holidays.[53]

Some Downsides to Prison Expansion

Not everyone is happy about locating prisons in small towns, and some recent studies have shown little or no economic and social benefits. For instance, in the town of Braham, Minnesota (population 1,276), citizens rejected putting a prison there, with one local critic saying they would have to change their motto from "Homemade pie capital of Minnesota" to "Prison capital of Minnesota." In the town of Clintwood, Virginia (population 1,549, located on the far western edge of the state), the largest employer in the area (250 jobs) had been Travelocity after the coal industry died. In 2004 when Travelocity moved its operations to India, the joke around Clintwood was "that the only secure jobs are at the new state prison, because they are not going to be shipping the convicts to India anytime soon." The director of the local Chamber of Commerce stated, "It's not quite as bad as being a nuclear waste dump site. But we're the dump site for human misery."[54] When a prison was proposed for Pembina County, North Dakota, local citizens protested. Opponents were concerned about the negative changes the prison would bring, such as impeding tourism. Proponents talked about the jobs that would be created if a 500-bed prison were built, claiming that the impact would be "tremendous" and "recession-proof."[55] Not all prisons, however, are immune from recession.

As virtually every state is undergoing a budget crisis, cutting back on prison expenses—including closing some facilities—has become one option. In Illinois, with a budget shortfall of about $1.3 billion for fiscal year 2002, Governor George Ryan closed the prison at Joliet. He also proposed closing Vienna Correctional Center and the Valley View Youth Center in St. Charles, but later substituted a prison in Sheridan (population 2,435) for Vienna.[56] Other states are finding that building and maintaining prisons is very expensive, and they have already taken steps to alleviate the problem:

- Several states have reformed "mandatory minimum" sentencing laws by returning sentencing discretion to judges, including Alabama, Mississippi, Michigan, Indiana, Connecticut, Louisiana, North Dakota, and Utah.[57]

- Several states (e.g., California and Arizona) have passed special referendums concerning alternative sentencing for drug offenders.[58]

- Some states have instituted parole reforms, including early release.[59]

- Many states are cutting other costs, such as food and health services.[60]

- Some states have closed down entire prisons to save money.[61]

- Some states have put new construction on hold to save money and to find alternatives.[62]

A $90 million jail was built in tiny (population 2,400) Cape Vincent (near the St. Lawrence River) in 1988. With downward trends in prison populations, residents are worried that what they thought was a recession-proof industry may come to an end. One prison worker said, "Who ever thought crime would go down? Who ever thought we would run out of inmates?"[63] Many who previously supported building prisons in Mississippi are now changing their minds. A former police chief in charge of the state's corrections department, who never had any qualms sending people to jail, now complains that for too many people the only reason to build prisons is to "make money off inmates," and he added that this has "gotten a little too skewed for my liking."[64]

Thomas Johnson, an economist at the University of Missouri, points to another downside to prison expansion. When communities attempt to weigh the impact of a prison on the economy of the community, there is a tendency to overestimate the economic advantages. Johnson notes that prisons, unlike other industries, do not generate further economic development through associated industries. For example, a manufacturing industry, such as an automobile assembly plant, requires parts produced by other industries, such as tires, radios, etc. Prisons, however, "generate very few linkages to the economy."[65] Despite the fact that Franklin County in New York has five prisons, a planned food-processing plant was never built.[66]

One link, as noted by a county prosecutor, is not one the community would endorse. The prison in his jurisdiction nearby doubled the number of felonies he had to handle, primarily from incidents occurring within the prison.[67] Bent County, Colorado (located in the far southeastern part of the state, with a population less than 6,000), reported a similar experience. Court filings jumped up by 99% after the opening of a private prison in Las Animas (population 2,758).[68]

Contrary to expectations, most prison jobs, as well as prison construction jobs, do not go to locals. Barriers to locals obtaining positions include the possession of job-specific skills and correctional guard union membership.[69] A study of rural prisons in California revealed that less than one-fifth of the jobs were filled by locals.[70] Many prison workers drive long commutes from large urban areas. In Missouri, 67% of the prison jobs were filled by people living outside the county where the prison was located.[71]

In many places where prisons have been built, most of the locally owned businesses have closed, giving way to Wal-Marts, McDonald's, and the like. This is what happened in Tehachapi, California, a small town of just under 11,000 between Mojave and Bakersfield along Route 58. Two prisons are located there and 741 local businesses went belly up during the past decade, while being replaced by chain stores.[72]

Smaller, economically depressed communities look for "salvation through incarceration,"[73] but the existing studies on the economic impacts of prisons on localities have not found significant improvements. The Sentencing Project looked at employment rates and per capita income over 25 years in rural counties in New York and found "no significant difference or discernible pattern of economic trends" between counties where a prison was located and those without a prison.[74] Iowa State University found that many towns that had made sizeable investments in prisons were not finding sufficient returns on their investments.[75] A study in Texas looked at consumer spending and found no impact in 75% of the areas studied.[76]

Exploiting Prisoners to Enhance Rural Populations

There may be some economic benefits from prisons, but the gains in one community represent a loss in another.

> The economic benefits of new prisons may come from the flow of additional state and federal dollars. In the decennial census, prisoners are counted where they are incarcerated, and many federal and state funding streams are tied to census population counts. . . . The federal government distributes over $140 billion in grant money to state and local governments through formula-based grants. Formula grant money is in part based on census data and covers programs such as Medicaid, Foster Care, Adoption Assistance, and Social Services Block Grant. Within a state, funding for community health services, road construction and repair, public housing, local law enforcement, and public libraries are all driven by population counts from the census. Every dollar transferred to a "prison community" is a dollar that is not given to the home community of a prisoner, which is often among the country's most disadvantaged urban areas. According to one account, Cook County Illinois will lose nearly $88 million in federal benefits over the next decade because residents were counted in the 2000 Census in their county of incarceration rather than their county of origin.[77]

Even though prisoners cannot vote in almost every state, they are counted, resulting in a "phantom" population of rural prisoners.[78] For example, the small Arizona town of Florence has a population of 17,054, according to the 2000 census.[79] The census figure, however, does not reveal that 11,830 of those residents are prisoners. On two occasions since 1980, the town has paid the Census Bureau for special recounts—because additional head counts mean additional dollars. For each dollar generated by local taxes and fees, Florence receives $1.76 more because of the prison population. Florence now has

> new town offices, a new park and a new senior center. . . . The rebuilt little-league facilities boasts a digital score board and dug-

outs. New police and fire facilities are under construction, and officials are planning a $1 million community center with a pool—all without a local income tax or any substantial increases in sales or property taxes.[80]

Arizona had the eighth highest incarceration rate (529) in the country in 2006.[81] After Corrections Corporation of America began housing prisoners from Washington, DC in its prison in Florence, the African-American population of the town more than doubled to over 1,500. Florence now has two state prisons, three private prisons, plus the U.S. Immigration and Naturalization Service detention center. This little town can now brag about having "the highest percentage of prison inmates of any U.S. town of more than 10,000."[82]

Florence is not the only small town to reap such benefits. Calipatria, California, has a population of 7,289, thanks to 4,095 prisoners; Ionia, Michigan has a population of 10,569 that includes 4,401 prisoners—they used some of the federal money to install laptop computers in the town automobiles and to turn a National Guard armory into a community center.[83] Sussex County, Virginia appears to be the fastest growing county in the country, thanks mostly to the fact that between 1998 and 1999 two new prisons increased its population by 23%. According to the 2000 census, there are now 12,504 residents. Two small Arizona towns, Gila Bend (population 1,980) and Buckeye (population 6,537) competed for adult and juvenile prisons to be built in their district. Buckeye won and stands to receive more than $10 million in federal subsidies.[84] One-third of the population of Malone, New York (mentioned above) consists of prisoners. The town receives more federal dollars because the population with prisoners is 15,000.[85]

Another benefit of adding prisoners to the census count is that their lack of income lowers the average incomes of the community to below the official poverty level, thereby qualifying the area for even more federal funds. Gatesville, Texas with 9,095 prisoners qualified for poverty status; the town received $4.2 million in state grants, which it used to upgrade water lines and to

build new roads. Another irony to all of this is the fact that while these prisoners help towns qualify for large sums of federal dollars, they are not included in the official unemployment figures. By including prisoners in the official unemployment figures, the unemployment rate for African Americans increases to almost 40%, and unemployment totals increase 2–3%.[86]

During the first decade of the twenty-first century, about $2 trillion in federal funds will be distributed based on the 2000 census count. When offenders from poor urban areas are sentenced to prisons located in small towns, those dollars follow the prisoners and leave the original communities. Minnesota's state demographer Tom Gillaspy estimates that the census "directs $2,000–$3,000 per person counted to any given community each decade, *not including additional census-based funding distributed to poor communities*" [emphasis added].[87]

Finally, mention should be made of the impact rural prisons have had on redistricting. One result of the "phantom" increase in rural populations is an increase in the voting power of rural districts, many of whom have added additional congressional seats. The Prison Policy Initiative has argued that by allowing mostly white rural districts "to claim urban black prisoners as residents for purposes of representation resembles the old three-fifths clause of the Constitution that allowed the South extra representation for its slaves. . . ." Such a policy also means that legislators in rural areas "can devote more attention to their 'real constituents,'" while at the same time those who support building new prisons in their rural areas have additional clout in state legislatures.[88] The state of Florida will soon have a significant redrawing of political boundaries, thanks to 90,411 prisoners (50.2% are African American).[89] Gulf County has two prisons that contribute to its population numbers (13,332). The attorney general of Florida issued opinions in 2001 that said county commissions and school boards "must include prisoners when redistricting." In Florida and in the other states where prisoners are denied a vote, the voting power of large numbers of mostly minority urban communities are transferred to rural, mostly white areas.[90] A statement from a former New York State legislator sums up the feelings of many politicians: "When legislators cry 'Lock 'em up!' they often mean 'Lock 'em up' in my district."[91]

THE AMERICAN "GULAG"

In *The Gulag Archipelago,* Alexander Solzhenitsyn exposed the deprivations of the network of prison labor camps of the former Soviet Union located primarily in isolated areas like Siberia.[92] Joseph Stalin instituted the forced-labor camps in the 1920s; the number of camps grew from around 350,000 in 1929 to more than 1.5 million by 1931.[93] While some dissenters were imprisoned in the camps, the gulags were primarily designed as production units and the majority of prisoners were males from the lower classes. The forced-labor camps were essential for Russian war efforts during World War II.[94] Gulags persist to the present day, not only in Russia, but in such countries as China, North Korea, and the Sudan.[95]

Gulags are often associated with third world or totalitarian societies. However, the United States had its own version during World War II.

> In February 1942, President Franklin D. Roosevelt signed an executive order that moved nearly 120,000 Japanese and Japanese Americans into 10 isolated relocation centers in Arizona, Arkansas, California, Colorado, Idaho, Utah, and Wyoming. The temporary, tar paper-covered barracks, the guard towers, and most of the barbed-wire fences are gone now, but the people who spent years of their lives in the centers will never forget them.[96]

Several authors have suggested similarities between the modern U.S. prison system and gulags. In the early 1990s Norwegian criminologist Nils Christie suggested that the "crime control industry" in the United States was beginning to look like the equivalent of the Russian gulag.[97] In 1996, Stephen Richards used the term *gulag* in an article to describe the modern prison system.[98] Syndicated columnist Alexander Cockburn also referred to the U.S. prison system as a gulag in one of his articles.[99]

The U.S. prison system bears a number of similarities to gulags. As noted previously, the bulk of prisons (especially those built during the past 20 years) are located in rural areas. There are a number of human rights abuses in U.S. prisons (and also jails and juvenile correctional facilities), including cruel and unusual punishment (e.g., long periods in solitary confinement) and extreme brutality and violence. In addition, the forced labor in prisons produces profit for the states in which they are housed.

Texas is a classic example. It has over 100 prisons; most have been built since 1980, and 80 have been built in the 1990s. It also has eight "parole confinement facilities" and five substance abuse felony punishment facilities.[100] In 2006, its prison population was 161,575, second in the country to California (173,453).[101] The prison incarceration rate in Texas (687) ranked number two in the nation; Louisiana (797) ranked first. By July, 2000, Texas had used all six-digit numbers and created prisoner number 1,000,000.[102]

An example of the rural nature of most of these facilities can be seen by sampling some of the towns where they are located (population according to the 2000 census): Iowa Park (6,431), Teague (4,557), Dilley (3,674), Brazoria (2,781), Marlin (6,628), Rusk (5,085), Woodville (2,415), Navasota (6,789), and Cuero (6,571). Several Texas prisons and other facilities are located in towns not even found on a map—places like Lovelady, Midway, Tennessee Colony (with three separate prisons each housing over 3,000 inmates), Rosharon (four prisons housing over 6,000 inmates) and Venus (housing a privately run prison with 1,000 inmates). There's also the town of Beeville, located between Corpus Christie and San Antonio, along U.S. Route 181. With a population of just over 13,000, Beeville has two prisons with about 7,200 prisoners. Joseph Hallinan described the town as a "prison hub," not unlike what Detroit was to cars—and they are trying to bring in more prisons.[103]

The Texas prison system budget in 2006 was $2.6 billion.[104] Farming is big business, with control over more than 134,000 acres (about 200 square miles), operating the largest horse and cattle herds in the entire state (more than 10,000 head of cattle and around 1,500 horses). Texas Correctional Industries operates 42 factories within 32 prisons, which provide

> garments and cloth products; janitorial supplies; laundry supplies; name plates and easels; park equipment; stainless steel security fixtures and food service equipment; school bus renovation services, tire recapping, repairs and retreading; first aid and safety equipment; cardboard boxes and file boxes; dump truck beds and accessories; Texas state flags and red safety flags; bedding; dorm furniture, lounge furniture, office furniture, and furniture refinishing services; general printing services; draperies and hardware; traffic control signs; metal security components; property identification stickers; and license plates.[105]

The Web site also notes: "State law defines to whom TCI may provide products and services: city, county, state, and federal agencies, public schools, public universities, private or independent institutions of higher education, public hospitals and political subdivisions are eligible to buy from TCI."

Turning to the state of Michigan, as of 2005, there were 45 prisons and 13 prison camps (including one boot camp); 18 were built in 1990 or later.[106] The rural nature of the prisons in this state is just like Texas. Some examples include: Munising (2,539), Baraga (1,785), Carson City (1,170), Grass Lake (1,082), New Haven (3,071), St. Louis (4,494), Newberry (2,686), Eastlake (441), Freeland (5,147), and Standish (1,581). There are nine prisons in the Upper Peninsula housing more than 5,000 inmates. There are four facilities in Kinchebe, one of which is located on an abandoned Air Force Base purchased by the state in 1978. The facility at Newberry was opened in 1996 on the site of a former state mental institution.[107] In 2005 there were 49,546 inmates and a prison incarceration rate of 489.[108]

As in the state of Texas, prisoners in Michigan make a variety of products for sale to nonprofit organizations. Michigan State Industries produces a number of products, including: MSI survey stakes (used for various construction products), boarding piers ("The perfect boarding dock to begin a day of sun and fun on the lake!"), a PCI Task Chair ("Introducing the latest in ergonomic luxury"), panel systems furniture (offering "a complete repertoire of office panel systems to our customers"), kitchen cabinets, building blocks, mattresses, linens ("sheets, blankets, towels, pillows, and more"), clothing ("everything you need from coveralls to rainwear"), and even refurbishing ("MSI can bring your furniture back to life!"), print shop, and optical lab.[109]

California provides a third example of the gulag mentality. As of 2006, there were 50 state prisons (in 1980 it had just 12 prisons) plus 38 forestry camps and a multitude of community facilities. As of October 2006 there were more than 172,000 prisoners, causing officials to decide to begin transferring as many as 22,000 out of state, at a cost of about $51 million.[110] Some examples of the rural nature of California's prisons include: Calipatria (7,289), Imperial (7,560), Ione (7,129), Crescent City (4,028), and Jamestown (3,017).

Additional examples can be found in any other state in the country. For instance, Tamms, Illinois has a population of 724. It is located in the extreme southern part of the state and is home to a "supermax" prison. Each cell cost $120,000 to build and $35,000 per year to operate. A sign outside of town proudly announces the prison: "Welcome to Tamms, the home of Supermax." A local fast-food restaurant, "Burger Shack 2," sells a "Supermax burger." There's a long waiting list for employment at the facility, which pays $25,000 per year to start—not bad in a poor area where good paying jobs are lacking.[111]

Finally, it should be noted that these rural prisons in some ways resemble a return to the days of slavery. Black men and women are segregated from their own communities and placed in remote areas. At Angola prison in Louisiana, one can see prisoners coming in from the fields at the end of each day.[112] Ironically, after years of struggle since the days of slavery, literally millions of the great-

great-grandchildren of former slaves find themselves in almost identical situations. As just one example, blacks are imprisoned at a rate almost eight times greater than whites, despite the fact that whites use illegal drugs at a rate five times greater than that of blacks.[113]

THE PRIVATIZATION OF PRISONS: MORE PROFITS FOR PRIVATE INDUSTRY

David Shichor notes that private enterprise has a long-standing relationship with imprisonment. However, the relationship has changed.

> Contemporary prison privatization differs from nineteenth-century private involvement. In the past, private entrepreneurs paid the government for the use of prison labor; today the government pays corporations for the management and operation of prisons. Previously, government agencies could expect some monetary return from private contracts. Today, government agencies hope to save money by "outsourcing" operations; all profits are made by corporate businesses.[114]

Although opposition from labor unions and severe unemployment during the Depression effectively ended the practice of private companies leasing prison labor, private contractors were involved in the management of many correctional programs during the twentieth century. Most of the programs were community-based and involved the diversion of offenders from the formal system. Incarceration, however, remained a governmental function. The enormous increase in prison sentences starting in the 1980s and the burden of correctional costs opened the door to private business becoming involved in the operation of prisons. More than three decades ago, researchers warned against "creeping capitalism" where "services and responsibilities that were once monopolized by the state" were transferred to "profit-making agencies and organizations."[115] *Privatization* of prisons involves a private corporation either constructing a facility and contracting with a state to house prisoners or taking over the operations of an existing jail or prison.

Privatization raises significant issues. The government generally has a monopoly on coercive power to enforce the law.

> In actuality, there is growing involvement of the private, for-profit sector in this process: private police, private security companies, private probation reports, private substance-abuse programs, private correction companies, etc. By contracting out some of these functions, the government gives away a portion of its authority and control over the criminal justice process to private companies, which may influence this process for profit-making purposes. . . .
>
> Private companies have a vested interest in keeping facilities full and expanding their business. They will, therefore, be active in creating and supporting increased demand for their services—using their influence and lobbying power to press for stricter laws that guarantee more and longer prison sentences. At the institutional level, the staff in private facilities could actively impact the conditions and even the length of confinement through disciplinary actions. Although government monitors of private facilities usually hold the disciplinary hearings for inmates who have violated the rules, the employees of the private companies write up and report the alleged violations.[116]

Through privatization, states can get around voter resistance to prison construction bonds by having private corporations build the prison. The private corporation then sends the bill for services to the state and thus taxpayers.[117] This represents a classic case of socializing the costs and privatizing the benefits. In 1983, there were fewer than 3,000 beds under contract to private corporations. By the end of 1999, that number had grown to more than 145,000 in the United States, the United Kingdom, and Australia.[118]

The largest private prison corporation is *Corrections Corporation of America (CCA)*. Founded in 1983, the company is headquartered in Nashville, Tennessee and employs more than 16,000 people. By 2007, it managed 65 facilities in the United States with a capacity of 72,500. During its 24-year existence, CCA encountered serious problems. Its stock went as high as $45 in 1998, sank to $0.18 per share but regrouped and was selling for $25.50 per share in September 2007. Its Web site includes the following information

- CCA specializes in the design, building, and management of prisons, jails and detention facilities and providing inmate residential and prisoner transportation services in partnership with government.
- The company is the fifth largest corrections system in the nation, behind only the federal government and three states.
- CCA is the founder of the private corrections industry and is the nation's largest provider of jail, detention, and corrections services to governmental agencies.
- CCA has approximately 72,500 beds in 65 facilities, including 40 owned facilities [the largest number are in Texas, followed by Tennessee], under contract for management in 19 states and the District of Columbia.
- The company manages more than 62,000 inmates including males, females, and juveniles at all security levels and does business with all three federal corrections agencies, almost half of all states, and more than a dozen local municipalities.
- CCA continues its market leadership position in the corrections industry managing over 50% of all beds under contract with private operators in the United States.
- CCA joined the NYSE in 1994 and now trades under the symbol CXW.[119]

Russell Clemens, an economist with the Department of Research for the American Federation of State, County, and Federal Employees, noted that "problems regarding security, staffing, and quality of services have plagued prison privatization from its inception." He pointed out that in addition to numerous escapes there have been problems pertaining to both health care and food service that characterize "the low quality of service in privately operated prisons."[120] Other problems include failure to control violence, substandard conditions that have resulted in prisoner protests and uprisings and criminal activity on the part of some CCA employees, including the sale of illegal drugs to prisoners.[121]

The following incidents received the most public attention, "but they were not anomalies. Countless instances of escapes, riots, brutality, and other sorts of operational problems" in private facilities have been discovered.

- In 1996 two convicted sex offenders from Oregon escaped from a CCA facility near Houston. Texas officials, who were unaware that out-of-state inmates were housed at the facility, realized that they had no authority to prosecute the convicts for the escape because there were no laws on the books in Texas about escaping from a private correctional facility. [Texas and other states now have legislation to address these circumstances.]
- In August 1997, videotape surfaced in a lawsuit brought by an inmate that captured abuses by guards at the Brazoria County Detention Center run by Capital Correctional Resources Inc. The video, originally shot as footage for a training film, showed guards kicking inmates, coaxing guard dogs to attack them, and shocking at least one prisoner with a stun gun. Inmates from Missouri were housed at Brazoria; when the videotape surfaced, Missouri removed its inmates.
- In 1998 six inmates escaped and a series of fatal inmate stabbings attracted national attention to a CCA prison in Youngstown, Ohio, that houses inmates from the District of Columbia. In March 1999, the company agreed to pay $1.6 million to settle a class action lawsuit brought by prisoners who had been abused, denied medical care, and not properly segregated from more dangerous inmates.
- In April 2000 the federal government pressured authorities in Louisiana to take control of the Jena Juvenile Justice Center away from the private company operating it. There had been widespread brutality at the facility, some of it carried out by guards or encouraged by them. Conditions at Jena were so severe that some youths mutilated themselves so they would be transferred to the medical unit, where they could more easily avoid beatings and rapes.[122]

- In April 2007 Indiana officials suspended plans to accept more inmates from Arizona at New Castle Correctional Facility. Operated by GEO group, the full-scale riot involved about 500 inmates, including newly arrived prisoners from Arizona who were upset about policies at the medium-security prison.[123]

- In September 2007 inmates rioted and set two buildings on fire at a private eastern Kentucky prison run by CCA after the population doubled and privileges, including visits from friends and family, were cut.[124]

In a detailed study of 60 private prisons (constituting half the total privatized prisons in the country), Good Jobs First found that the promised benefits to state and local governments have failed to materialize. More importantly, however, they found that at least 73% of the prisons had received a development subsidy from local, state, or federal government sources; over one-third (37%) received low-cost construction benefits via tax-free bonds or other government-issued debt securities; 38% received property tax abatements; and another 23% got subsidies for things like water, sewer or utility hook-ups, access roads, etc. The study could find no evidence of whether or not the privatization of prisons had the desired effects on local communities.[125]

SUMMARY

The prison industrial complex represents an interconnection among the criminal justice system, the political system, and the economic system. It is a vast, profit-oriented system that often places the protection of the public and the rehabilitation of offenders at a lower priority than profit. The system employs thousands of people. Companies spend millions of dollars to advertise their products to obtain a share of the market where expenditures to $60 billion each year.

Prison construction boomed during the last two decades of the twentieth century. The numbers of convictions for drug offenses plus mandatory-minimum sentencing created the need for more prisons to hold the offenders. Most of the prisons were constructed in rural areas, which hoped to improve their depressed economies. The transfer of prisoners from urban areas, where most had been convicted, to rural areas removes federal dollars from the original communities and increases payments to the host areas. The location of prisons in rural areas and the incarceration of so many people from less advantaged situations prompt comparisons to gulags.

We concluded the chapter with the ultimate example of the interplay of economics and the criminal justice system: prison privatization. The rationale that private corporations will relieve taxpayers of the enormous burden of expenditures on corrections has not been proven.

Key Terms

- advertising
- American Legislative Exchange Council (ALEC)
- commodities
- Corrections Corporation of America (CCA)
- *Corrections Today*
- free market
- gulags
- privatization

Notes

[1] Lilly, J. R. and P. Knepper. "The Correctional-Commercial Complex." *Crime and Delinquency* 39:152 (1993).

[2] Heilbroner, R. L. *The Nature and Logic of Capitalism.* New York: W. W. Norton, 1985, pp. 53–54, 60.

[3] From an advertising brochure from an investment firm called World Research Group, cited in Silverstein, K. "America's Private Gulag." In D. Burton-Rose, D. Pens, and P. Wright (eds.), *The Celling of America: An Inside Look at the U.S. Prison Industry.* Monroe, ME: Common Courage Press, 1998, p. 156.

[4] From Ron Garzini, private prison booster, quoted in Parenti, C. *Lockdown America: Police and Prisons in the Age of Crisis.* New York: Verso, 1999, p. 211.

[5] From the city manager of Sayre, Oklahoma, which had just opened a maximum-security prison. Kilborn, P. T. "Rural Towns Turn to Prisons to Reignite Their Economies." *New York Times* (August 1, 2001); Street, P. "Race, Place, and the Perils of Prisonomics." *Z Magazine* (July/August 2005). [Online] http://zmagsite.zmag.org/JulAug2005/street0705.html

6 From the town supervisor of Chesterfield, New York, quoted in Welch, M. *Punishment in America: Social Control and the Ironies of Imprisonment.* Thousand Oaks, CA: Sage, 1999, p. 24.

7 From an advertising brochure for the University of Phoenix, which claims that you can "earn your degree in 2 to 3 years, in most cases." It offers courses in many different locations, with classes starting almost every month. The brochure notes: "According to the Bureau of Labor Statistics, the field of criminal justice will expand faster than most other occupations through 2008." Courses are taught by "experienced lieutenants, police chiefs, and captains" and "covers the latest theories, techniques, and technologies being used in criminal justice today." A business reply card is included in this brochure.

8 From a California Department of Corrections official explaining some of the benefits of putting a prison in a rural area. Quoted in Huling, T. "Building a Prison Economy in Rural America." In M. Mauer and M. Chesney-Lind (eds.), *Invisible Punishment: The Collateral Consequences of Mass Imprisonment.* New York: New Press, 2002, p. 200.

9 Duke, L. "Building a Boom behind Bars: Prisons Revive Small Towns, but Costs Are Emerging." *The Washington Post* (September 8, 2000) p. A1.

10 Bureau of Justice Statistics. *Direct Expenditures by Criminal Justice Function, 1982–2004.* [Online] http://www.ojp.usdoj.gov/bjs/glance/tables/exptyptab.htm

11 Camp, C. G. and G. M. Camp. *The Corrections Yearbook: Adult Corrections 2002.* Middletown, CT: Criminal Justice Institute, 2003, p. 205.

12 Ibid., pp. 106–107.

13 *Prison System FY 2008 Performance Budget.* U.S. Department of Justice. [Online] http://www.usdoj.gov/jmd/2008justification/pdf/38_bop_se.pdf

14 The urls for the Web sites are http://www.corrections.com/vendor and http://www.corrections.com/

15 Biewen, J. *Corporate-Sponsored Crime Laws.* April 2002. [Online] http://americanradioworks.public radio.org/features/corrections/print1.html

16 Schlosser, E. "The Prison-Industrial Complex." *The Atlantic Monthly* (December 1998) p. 63.

17 Warren, J. "Inmates' Families Pay Heavy Price for Staying in Touch." *Los Angeles Times* (February 16, 2002).

18 Lawrence, S. and J. Travis. *The New Landscape of Imprisonment: Mapping America's Prison Expansion.* Washington, DC: The Urban Institute, 2004.

19 Schlosser, "The Prison-Industrial Complex."

20 Camp and Camp, *The Corrections Yearbook,* pp. 84–85.

21 Dyer, J. *The Perpetual Prisoner Machine: How America Profits from Crime.* Boulder, CO: Westview Press, 2000, p. 13.

22 [Online] http://www.kitchell.com/criminal.shtml

23 The State of North Carolina also appeared in the Google search. Between 1990 and January 2004 the North Carolina Department of Corrections opened a total of 21 correctional facilities (including a youth center and two work farms). [Online] http://www.prisonpolicy.org/articles/nc_ prison_

construction.html. To view the proliferation of prisons from 1900 to 2000, visit http://www.prisonpolicy.org/atlas/proliferation1900-2000.html

24 [Online] http://alecwatch.org/chaptertwo.html

25 [Online] http://alecwatch.org/chapterfour.html

26 [Online] http://www.alec.org/criminal-justice.html

27 Biewen, *Corporate-Sponsored Crime Laws.*

28 Ibid.

29 Huling, "Building a Prison Economy in Rural America," p. 198.

30 Ibid., p. 199.

31 Ibid.; see also Clement, D. "Big House on the Prairie." *Fedgazette* (January 2002). [Online] http://minneapolisfed.org/pubs/fedgaz/02-01/house.cfm

32 http://www.doc.state.ok.us/field/private_prisons/northfork.htm

33 Kilborn, T. "Rural Towns Turn to Prisons to Reignite Their Economies." *New York Times* (August 1, 2001).

34 Ibid.

35 Ibid.

36 Huling, pp. 206–207.

37 Street, "Race, Place, and the Perils of Prisonomics." There are plenty of other examples. In the Wisconsin town of Stanley (population 1,898) a "spec" prison was completed in the year 2000, built by a company called Dominion Venture Group. The state finally purchased the facility for $75 million in October 2001. The mayor of Stanley, David Jankoski, stated that "we needed something to bring back vitality to the community. . . . An article in the *Chicago Tribune* (March 2001) was titled: "Towns Put Dreams in Prisons," referring to many small towns in the southern part of Illinois, areas short on jobs. In the rural "heartland" of Michigan, Wisconsin, Minnesota, Montana, and North and South Dakota, spending on prisons skyrocketed during the past 20 years. Per capita spending in North Dakota, for instance, went from about $25 to about $75 between 1980 and 2000, while Michigan's per capita spending went from less than $50 to almost $200 during this time. The number of prisoners tripled in Montana and South Dakota and quadrupled in North Dakota and Wisconsin during these two decades. Incarceration rates for these states increased at about the same rate, with Michigan's rate going from about 150 to almost 500 and the rates in both Montana and South Dakota going from under 100 to more than 300 (Clement, "Big House on the Prairie").

38 Donziger, S. R. *The Real War on Crime: The Report of the National Criminal Justice Commission.* New York: HarperCollins, 1996, p. 94.

39 Clement, "Big House on the Prairie."

40 Ibid.

41 Ibid.

42 Parenti, *Lockdown America,* p. 212.

43 Dyer, *The Perpetual Prisoner Machine,* p. 17.

44 Schlosser, "Prison Industrial Complex," pp. 57–58.

45 Duke, "Building a Boom behind Bars."

46 Dyer, *The Perpetual Prisoner Machine,* p. 17.

47 Schlosser, "Prison Industrial Complex," pp. 57–58.

[48] Wray, L. R. "New Economic Reality: Penal Keynesianism." *Challenge* 43(5): 52 (2000).

[49] Duke, "Building a Boom behind Bars."

[50] [Online] http://www.docs.state.ny.us/faclist.html

[51] Prison Policy Initiative. "Diluting Democracy: Census Quirk Fuels Prison Expansion." [Online] http://www.prisonpolicy.org/articles/dilutingdemocracy.pdf

[52] Duke, "Building a Boom behind Bars."

[53] Schlosser, "Prison Industrial Complex," p. 58.

[54] Streitfeld, D. "A Town's Future is Leaving the Country." *Los Angeles Times* (March 28, 2004).

[55] Clement, "Big House on the Prairie."

[56] Landis, P. "Hard Time." [Online] http://illinoisissues.uis.edu/features/2002june/time.html

[57] Greene, J. and V. Schiraldi. "Cutting Correctly: New Prison Policies for Times of Fiscal Crisis." Washington, DC: Justice Policy Institute, February 2002. [Online] http://www.cjcj.org/pdf/cut_cor.pdf

[58] Ibid.

[59] Ibid. See also Marks, A. "Strapped for Cash, States Set Some Felons Free." *The Christian Science Monitor* (January 21, 2003); Butterfield, F. "Inmates Go Free to Reduce Deficits." *New York Times* (December 18, 2002).

[60] Greene, J. and T. Roche. "Cutting Correctly in Maryland." Washington, DC: Justice Policy Institute, February 2003.

[61] Ibid. These states include Florida, Illinois, Michigan, Ohio, Utah, and Virginia. Other states, like New York, Texas, and Nevada, have "downsized" unneeded prison space by closing prison housing units.

[62] Associated Press. "In Illinois, Pennsylvania and Wisconsin, Newly Built Prisons Remain Shut, as States Face Budget Crunch." January 8, 2003.

[63] Rhode, D. "A Growth Industry Cools as New York Prisons Thin." *New York Times* (August 21, 2001).

[64] Gruley, B. "Wanted: Criminals: Why Did Mississippi Agree to Pay for Cells for 'Ghost Inmates.'" *Wall Street Journal* (September 6, 2001).

[65] Clement, "Big House on the Prairie."

[66] Huling, p. 201.

[67] Clement, "Big House on the Prairie."

[68] Huling, p. 204.

[69] King, R., M. Mauer, and T. Huling. *Big Prisons, Small Towns: Prison Economics in Rural America.* Washington, DC: The Sentencing Project, 2003, pp. 2, 15–16.

[70] Huling, p. 206.

[71] King, R., M. Mauer, and T. Huling. *Big Prisons, Small Towns,* p. 14.

[72] Ibid., p. 202. The lead author (RGS) has been to Tehachapi on numerous occasions over the years and has seen this development firsthand.

[73] Duke, "Building a Boom behind Bars."

[74] King, Mauer, and Huling, *Big Prisons, Small Towns*, p. 2.

[75] Lawrence and Travis, *The New Landscape of Imprisonment*, p. 3.

[76] Chuang, S. C. "The Distribution of Texas State Prisons: Economic Impact Analysis of State Prison Sitting on Local Communities." PhD dissertation, University of Texas, Arlington, 1998.

[77] Lawrence and Travis, *The New Landscape of Imprisonment*, p. 3.

[78] Prison Policy Initiative, "Diluting Democracy."

[79] Kulish, N. "Annexing the Penitentiary." *The Wall Street Journal* (August 8, 2001).

[80] Ibid.

[81] Sabol, W. J., T. D. Minton, and P. M. Harrison. *Prison and Jail Inmates at Mid-Year 2006.* Washington, DC: Bureau of Justice Statistics, June 2007, p. 13.

[82] Kulish, "Annexing the Penitentiary."

[83] Ibid.

[84] Huling, "Building a Prison Economy in Rural America," p. 211.

[85] Duke, "Building a Boom behind Bars."

[86] Western, B. and K. Beckett. "How Unregulated Is the U.S. Labor Market? The Penal System as a Labor Market." *American Journal of Sociology* 104: 1030–1060 (1999).

[87] Maynard, M. "Prison Math." October 25, 2000. [Online] http://www.citypages.com/databank/21/1038/article9083.asp

[88] Prison Policy Initiative, "Diluting Democracy."

[89] *Florida Inmates in Prison on 12/31/06 by Sex, Race, & Age.* [Online] http://www.dc.state.fl.us/pub/statsbrief/inmates.html

[90] Huling, "Building a Prison Economy in Rural America," p. 212.

[91] Ibid., p. 213.

[92] Solzhenitsyn, A. *The Gulag Archipelago.* New York: Bantam Books, 1970.

[93] Conquest, R. "Playing Down the Gulag." *Times Literary Supplement* (February 24, 1995); Harris, J. R. "The Growth of the Gulag: Forced Labor in the Urals Region, 1929–1931." *The Russian Review* 56: 265–281 (1997).

[94] Christie, N. *A Suitable Amount of Crime.* New York: Routledge, 2004, p. 57.

[95] Collins, C. and J. L. Askin-Steve. "The Islamic Gulag: Slavery Makes a Comeback in Sudan." *Utne Reader* (March–April 1996); Lilly, J. "Great Leader's Gulag: Siberian Timber Camps are Relics of the Cold War." *Far Eastern Economic Review* 21–22 (September 9, 1993); Pasqualini, J. "Glimpses Inside China's Gulag." *The China Quarterly* 134: 352–358 (1993); Tracey, D. "Inside North Korea's Gulag." *Reader's Digest* 143: 149–155 (1993); Wu, H. "The Need to Restrain China." *Journal of International Affairs* 49: 355–360 (1996).

[96] *The War Relocation Camps of World War II: When Fear Was Stronger than Justice.* [Online] http://www.nps.gov/nr/twhp/wwwlps/lessons/89manzanar/89manzanar.htm. See also Robinson, G. *By Order of the President: FDR and the Internment of Japanese Americans.* Cambridge: Harvard University Press, 2001, and *Children of the Camps.* [Online] http://www.pbs.org/childofcamp/history/index.html

[97] Christie, N. *Crime Control as Industry: Towards Gulags, Western Style* (3rd ed.). New York: Routledge, 2000 [1993].

[98] Richards, S. "Commentary: Sociological Penetration of the American Gulag." *Wisconsin Sociologist* 27: 18–28 (1996).

[99] Cockburn, A. "With 'Gladiator Days,' Prisons Adopt the Gulag Paradigm." *Las Vegas Review-Journal* (November 12, 1999) p. 11B.

[100] [Online] http://www.tdcj.state.tx.us/stat/unitdirectory/all.htm

[101] Sabol, Minton, and Harrison, *Prison and Jail Inmates at Mid-Year 2006*, p. 13.

[102] Ziedenberg, J. and V. Schiraldi. *Texas Leads U.S. in Incarceration Growth.* Washington, DC: Justice Policy Institute, 2000, p. 3.

[103] Hallinan, J. *Going up the River: Travels in a Prison Nation.* New York: Random House, 2003, pp. 3–4.

[104] [Online] http://www.tdcj.state.tx.us/finance/budget/OperatingBdgtFY06.pdf

[105] Texas Department of Corrections: http://www.tdcj.state.tx.us/faq/faq-tci.htm

[106] Michigan Department of Corrections Web site. [Online] http://www.michigan.gov/corrections/0,1607,7-119-1381_1388---,00.html

[107] It is ironic that many state mental institutions were closed in the 1960s and 1970s as part of a "deinstitutionalization" movement, only to have many of the same buildings now housing prison inmates. It has been estimated that as many as 70% of prison inmates suffer severe mental problems (Schlosser, E. "The Prison Industrial Complex." *The Atlantic Monthly* (December, 1998).

[108] Sabol, Minton, and Harrison, *Prison and Jail Inmates at Mid-Year 2006*, p. 13.

[109] [Online] http://www.michigan.gov/msi/0,1607,7-174-23873---,00.html

[110] Thompson, D. "California to Transfer Inmates Out of State." *Los Angeles Times* (October 21, 2006).

[111] Hallinan, *Going Up the River*, pp. 101, 111, 126.

[112] Personal communication from Marianne Fisher-Giordano, Professor at Grambling State University.

[113] *International Herald Tribune* (June 6, 2000) cited in *Index on Censorship* 29: 114 (September/October, 2000).

[114] Shichor, D. *The Meaning and Nature of Punishment.* Long Grove, IL: Waveland Press, 2006, p. 119.

[115] Spitzer, S. and A. T. Scull. "Privatization and Capitalist Development: The Case of Private Police." *Social Problems* 25: 18–29 (1977).

[116] Shichor, *The Meaning and Nature of Punishment*, p. 120.

[117] Dyer, *The Perpetual Prisoner Machine*, p. 245.

[118] Tabarrok, A. (ed.) *Changing the Guard: Private Prisons and the Control of Crime.* Oakland, CA: Independent Institute, 2003, p. 22.

[119] [Online] http://www.correctionscorp.com/aboutcca.html

[120] Dyer, *The Perpetual Prisoner Machine*, p. 203.

[121] Mattera, P. and M. Khan. *Corrections Corporation of America: A Critical Look at Its First Twenty Years.* Corporate Research Project of Good Jobs First, 2003, pp. iv–v. [Online] http://www.goodjobsfirst.org/pdf/CCA%20Anniversary%20Report.pdf

[122] Mattera, P. and M. Khan. *Jail Breaks: Economic Development Subsidies Given to Private Prisons.* Washington, DC: Good Jobs First, October, 2001, pp. 5–6.

[123] Associated Press. "Indiana Halts Transfer of More Arizona Inmates." April 25, 2007. [Online] http://www.msnbc.msn.com/id/18294136/

[124] Yetter, D. and M. Pitsch. "Prison Riot Followed Increase in Inmates." *The Courier-Journal* (Louisville, KY) (September 17, 2004). [Online] http://www.prisonpolicy.org/news/courier09172004.html

[125] Mattera and M. Khan. *Jail Breaks*, p. v.

sixteen

The Juvenile Justice System

Juveniles commit a wide variety of offenses, ranging from the trivial (curfew violation and loitering) to deadly serious (murder and assault). Self-report studies indicate that practically every youth at some point during their teenage years engages in behavior that could theoretically result in an arrest. Most are never arrested, and only a very small percentage end up in the juvenile justice system. Attitudes about how to sanction the behavior of people under the age of 18 have varied dramatically since the country was founded.

A Brief History of the Juvenile Justice System[1]

The appearance of adolescence as a social category in the nineteenth century coincided with an increasing concern for the regulation of the "moral behavior" of young people.[2] Although entirely separate systems to monitor and control the behavior of young people began to appear during the early part of the nineteenth century, differential treatment based on age did not mushroom overnight. The roots of the juvenile justice system can be traced to much earlier legal and social perspectives on childhood and youth. One of the most important of these was a legal doctrine that originated in the chancery courts of medieval England.

Parens patriae established that the king, in his presumed role as the "father" of his country, had the legal authority to take care of the people, especially those who were unable, for various reasons (including age), to take care of themselves. For children, the king or his authorized agents could assume the role of guardian to be able to administer their property. By the nineteenth century this legal doctrine had evolved into the practice of the state assuming wardship over a minor child and, in effect, playing the role of parent if the child had no parents or if the existing parents were declared unfit.[3]

In the American colonies, for example, officials could "bind out" as apprentices "children of parents who were poor, not providing good breeding, neglecting their formal education, not teaching a trade, or were idle, dissolute, unchristian or incapable."[4] During the nineteenth century, *parens patriae* supplied (as it still does to some extent) the legal basis for court intervention into the relationship between children and their families.[5]

Interest in the state regulation of youth was directly tied to explosive immigration and population growth. Between 1750 and 1850 the population increased from 1.25 million to 23 million. The population of some states, like Massachusetts, doubled in numbers, and New York's population increased fivefold between 1790 and 1830.[6] Many of those coming into the United States during the middle of the nineteenth century were of Irish or German background; the fourfold increase in immigrants between 1830 and 1840 was in large part a product of the economic hardships faced by the Irish during the potato famine. The social controls in small communities were simply overwhelmed by the influx of newcomers, many of whom were either foreign born or of foreign parentage. Juvenile delinquency emerged as one among many social problems faced by urban dwellers.[7]

The term itself originated around the early 1800s and combined two very different connotations: (1) *delinquent,* meaning failure to do something that is required (as in a person being delinquent in paying taxes) and (2) *juvenile,* meaning someone who is subject to being molded (i.e., open to change—"redeemable").[8] In the early 1800s, formal systems emerged to control the behavior of working- and lower-class youths, including the juvenile justice system and uniformed police.[9]

Throughout the nineteenth century social reformers constantly called attention to the fact that young children, some as young as six or seven, were locked up with adult criminals in jails and prisons and were also appearing with increasing regularity in criminal courts. It was believed that such practices were not only inhumane but would also inevitably lead to the corruption of the young and the perpetuation of youthful deviance or perhaps a full-time career in more serious criminality.[10]

The history of juvenile justice policies in the United States can be viewed as cyclical—fluctuating from rehabilitation and the best interests of the child (based on the *parens patriae* doctrine) to an emphasis on rights/responsibilities that also apply to adults and the punishments for violating those responsibilities. In recent years the cycle has shifted toward the latter view, emphasizing due process rights and punishment.[11]

The cycle began with a Pennsylvania Supreme Court ruling in 1838.[12] That court ruled in **Ex Parte Crouse** that the Bill of Rights did not apply to juveniles. Based on the *parens patriae* doctrine, the court asked, "May not the natural parents, when unequal to the task of education, or unworthy of it, be superseded by the *parens patriae* or common guardian of the community?" Further, the Court observed that: "The infant has been snatched from a course which must have ended in confirmed depravity."[13]

The court found that the Philadelphia House of Refuge (and presumably all other **houses of refuge**) was "not a prison, but a school." Because of that classification, it was not subject to procedural constraints. Further, the aims of such an institution were to reform the youngsters within them "by training . . .

[them] to industry; by imbuing their minds with the principles of morality and religion; by furnishing them with means to earn a living; and above all, by separating them from the corrupting influences of improper associates."[14]

An Illinois Supreme Court ruling in 1870 challenged the findings in *Crouse.* Although the facts were almost identical to the *Crouse* case, the outcome was the exact opposite. Daniel O'Connell was incarcerated in the Chicago House of Refuge—not because of a criminal offense, but because he was "destitute of proper parental care, and growing up in mendicancy, ignorance, idleness or vice."[15] His parents, like Mary Crouse's father, filed a writ of *habeas corpus,* charging that his incarceration was illegal. The Illinois Supreme Court had jurisdiction over *habeas corpus* cases and had ordered the release of 16 boys from the reform school previously. However, they decided to use the O'Connell filing to review the constitutionality of imprisoning children who had not committed a crime. Robert Turner was the superintendent of the reform school. The Illinois Supreme Court based its decision in **People v. Turner** on three factors. First, Daniel was being *punished,* not treated or helped by being institutionalized. Second, the court considered the *realities* or *actual practices* of the institution, rather than any theoretical "good intentions." Third, the court concluded that Daniel was being imprisoned, basing their reasoning on traditional legal doctrines of the criminal law and emphasizing the importance of *due process* safeguards.

> In our solicitude to form youth for the duties of civil life, we should not forget the rights which inhere both in parents and children. The principle of absorption of the child in, and its complete subjection to the despotism of, the State, is wholly inadmissible in the modern civilized world.[16]

In short, while the court in the *Crouse* case viewed the houses of refuge in a very rosy light, the court in the *Turner* case viewed the refuge in a much more negative light, addressing its cruelty and harshness of treatment.[17]

Turner had implications beyond Illinois. Isaac Redfield, a former chief justice of the

Vermont Supreme Court, characterized *Turner* as a decision that would affect reformers who viewed the state as a worthy parent for delinquent children. He saw the United States as a patchwork of diverse nationalities, religions, and political opinions and believed that reformers were intent on molding "one homogeneous compound of purity and perfection, which these men greatly desire."[18] Redfield believed *Turner* would protect the liberty of those in the minority so that, for example, a Catholic "child cannot be torn from home and immured in a Protestant prison, for ten or more years, and trained in what he regards a heretical and deadly faith, to the destruction of his own soul."[19] He also believed that more cases would follow since "there is a wide field of debatable ground between the dominion of punishment for crime and that of mere improved culture."[20] The child-saving movement of the late nineteenth century emphasized that children were developmentally different from adults, and reformers believed the state should guarantee that all children had a childhood. These efforts resulted in an expansion of state powers to regulate the lives of children and their families.

Established in 1899, the juvenile court in Chicago was, in part, a method of circumventing the ruling in *Turner*.[21] In *Commonwealth v. Fisher* in 1905 (another Pennsylvania case), the court returned once again to the logic of the *Crouse* case, which remained the guiding force until the 1966, when the Supreme Court first ruled that certain Constitutional rights should be accorded to children.

JUVENILE LAWS

The juvenile court today has jurisdiction over youths under a certain age who (1) violate laws applicable to adults, (2) commit *status offenses,* and (3) are dependent or neglected. The upper age of juvenile court *jurisdiction* in most states is 17. In 10 states, the upper age limit is 16; in three states it is 15.[22]

One of the most controversial aspects of juvenile law involves **status offenses**. The distinguishing characteristic of juvenile law is that youths under a certain age may be arrested and processed for behavior in which

adults are free to engage. Most of the controversy stems from the vagueness of the statutes; some of it stems from the *parens patriae* justification for state intervention; and much of it stems from differential application. The double standard treatment of males and females will be discussed in more detail in the next chapter. After more than 150 years, these laws are still being applied more vigorously against the children of the poor, and they are just as vague as they have always been. The ambiguity of the statutes gives those in authority a tremendous amount of discretionary power and often leads to arbitrary decisions based on subjective value judgments colored by class, race, and sexual biases. These laws also tend to reinforce the dependent status of youth. One text on juvenile law noted that: "The relationship between the child, his parents, and society is fundamentally a property relationship. Most of the laws relating to children reflect the prevailing attitude that they are the possessions of their parents or the state and not very valuable possessions at that."[23]

During the past three decades there has been an increase in the use of attorneys in juvenile court cases and a greater emphasis on procedural rights, at least in the courts in major metropolitan areas. One reason for this change can be attributed to several important Supreme Court decisions in the late 1960s. **Kent v. United States** was decided in 1966.[24] The case presented important challenges to the procedures of the police and juvenile court officials in cases where juveniles commit an offense that would be a major felony if committed by an adult. Sixteen-year-old Morris Kent raped a woman and stole her wallet in September 1961. The juvenile court judge turned Kent over to the jurisdiction of an adult court—without a hearing, without having talked with Kent's lawyer, and without having released a copy of the information contained in Kent's social service file, which had contributed to the decision to try him as an adult. Kent was convicted and sentenced in adult court to a term of thirty to ninety years in prison.

The Supreme Court ruled that when a judge considers whether to transfer a case from the juvenile court to an adult court, a juvenile is entitled to a hearing and has the right to counsel. The court must provide a written statement giving the reasons for the waiver, and the defense counsel must be given access to all records and reports used in reaching the decision to waive. Justice Abe Fortas wrote the opinion and issued one of the strongest indictments of the juvenile court ever:

> There is no place in our system of law for reaching a result of such tremendous consequences without ceremony—without hearing, without effective assistance of counsel, without a statement of reasons. It is inconceivable that a court of justice dealing with adults, with respect to a similar issue, would proceed in this manner. . . . There is much evidence that some juvenile courts . . . [lack] the personnel, facilities and techniques to perform adequately as representatives of the State in a *parens patriae* capacity, at least with respect to children charged with law violation. There is evidence, in fact, that there may be grounds for concern that the child receives the worst of both worlds; that he gets neither the protection accorded to adults nor the solicitous care and regenerative treatment postulated for children.

The Court reversed the conviction.

Perhaps the most significant case regarding juvenile court procedures was *In re Gault*[25] decided in 1967. The sheriff took Gerald Gault, aged fifteen, into custody at a detention home without notifying his parents after a neighbor complained about receiving a lewd telephone call that she believed had been made by Gault. At the time, Gault was on six months probation after having been found delinquent for being in the company of a boy who had stolen a wallet. He was not given adequate notification of the charges; he was not advised that he could be represented by counsel; and his accuser did not appear in court. Gault was convicted of the offense and sentenced to the State Industrial School until the age of twenty-one. Gault's attorneys filed a writ of *habeas corpus* in the Superior Court of Arizona, which was denied.

On appeal to the U.S. Supreme Court, Gault's attorneys argued that the juvenile code of Arizona was unconstitutional. The justices found in favor of Gault and held that juvenile court procedures at the adjudicatory hearing stage must include (1) adequate written notice of charges, (2) the right to counsel, (3) privilege against self-incrimination, (4) the right to cross-examine accusers, (5) a transcript of the proceedings, and (6) the right to appellate review. Justice Fortas again wrote the decision.

> Ultimately, however, we confront the reality of that portion of the Juvenile Court process with which we deal in this case. A boy is charged with misconduct. The boy is committed to an institution where he may be restrained of liberty for years. It is of no constitutional consequence *and of limited practical meaning* that the institution to which he is committed is called an Industrial School. The fact of the matter is that, however euphemistic the title, a "receiving home" or an "industrial school" for juveniles is an institution of confinement in which the child is incarcerated for a greater or lesser time. His world becomes "a building with whitewashed walls, regimented routine and institutional hours." Instead of mother and father and sisters and brothers and friends and classmates, his world is peopled by guards, custodians, state employees, and "delinquents" confined with him for anything from waywardness to rape and homicide.
>
> In view of this, it would be extraordinary if our Constitution did not require the procedural regularity and the exercise of care implied in the phrase "due process." Under our Constitution, the condition of being a boy does not justify a kangaroo court. . . .
>
> The essential difference between Gerald's case and a normal criminal case is that safeguards available to adults were discarded in Gerald's case. The summary procedure as well as the long commitment was possible because Gerald was 15 years of age instead of over 18. . . . For the particular offense immediately involved, the maximum punishment would have been a fine of $5 to $50, or imprisonment in jail for not more than two months. Instead, he was committed to custody for a maximum of six years. If he had been over 18 and had com-

mitted an offense to which such a sentence might apply, he would have been entitled to substantial rights under the Constitution of the United States as well as under Arizona's laws and constitution. . . . So wide a gulf between the State's treatment of the adult and of the child requires a bridge sturdier than mere verbiage, and reasons more persuasive than cliché can provide.

The *Gault* decision began what many have referred to as a "revolution in juvenile court practices." (Unfortunately, neither *Gault* nor subsequent cases have considered a juvenile's rights prior to the adjudicatory hearing, such as during intake and detention decisions.)

Another significant case was **In re Winship.**[26] Justice Brennan wrote the decision, which addressed how much proof is necessary to support a finding of delinquency. In 1970 when the case was decided, the standard was "a preponderance of the evidence." Rejecting the idea that the juvenile justice system was a civil system, the Supreme Court held that the due process clause of the Fourteenth Amendment required that delinquency charges in the juvenile system have to meet the same standard of "beyond a reasonable doubt" required in the adult system.

In sum, the constitutional safeguard of proof beyond a reasonable doubt is as much required during the adjudicatory stage of a delinquency proceeding as are those constitutional safeguards applied in *Gault*—notice of charges, right to counsel, the rights of confrontation and examination, and the privilege against self-incrimination. . . . Where a 12-year-old child is charged with an act of stealing which renders him liable to confinement for as long as six years, then, as a matter of due process the case against him must be proved beyond a reasonable doubt.

In **McKeiver v. Pennsylvania** in 1971 the Court dealt with the right of trial by jury, normally guaranteed to adults but traditionally denied to juveniles.[27] The Court ruled that jury trials were admissible but not mandatory within the juvenile court.

> We must recognize, as the Court has recognized before, that the fond and idealistic hopes of the juvenile court proponents and early reformers of three generations ago

have not been realized. . . . Too often the juvenile court judge falls far short of that stalwart, protective, and communicating figure the system envisaged. The community's unwillingness to provide people and facilities and to be concerned, the insufficiency of time devoted, the scarcity of professional help, the inadequacy of dispositional alternatives, and our general lack of knowledge all contribute to dissatisfaction with the experiment. . . . Despite all these disappointments, all these failures, and all these shortcomings, we conclude that trial by jury in the juvenile court's adjudicative stage is not a constitutional requirement. . . . If the formalities of the criminal adjudicative process are to be superimposed upon the juvenile court system, there is little need for its separate existence. Perhaps that ultimate disillusionment will come one day, but for the moment we are disinclined to give impetus to it.

In this decision the Court reasoned that a number of problems might arise if jury trials were mandatory, among them publicity, which would be contrary to the confidentiality characteristic of juvenile justice. Ten states currently allow jury trials for juveniles.

Breed v. Jones[28] was decided nine years after *Kent* and involved essentially the same issue—waiver to the adult court. However, in this case, Jones' lawyer argued that his client had been subjected to "double jeopardy," since he was adjudicated in juvenile court and then was tried again in an adult court for the same crime. The Supreme Court agreed with this argument, saying that juvenile courts must hold transfer hearings prior to adjudication.

Courts have determined that juveniles adjudicated and committed to correctional facilities have a *right to treatment*. A case decided in 1954 ruled that juveniles could not be held in institutions that did not provide any form of rehabilitation.[29] In a 1972 case, *Inmates of the Boys' Training School v. Affleck*, a federal court ruled that since the purpose of the juvenile court is rehabilitation, youths have a right to treatment if committed to an institution.[30] The case established certain minimal, such as sufficient clothing to meet seasonal needs, proper bedding (sheets, pillow cases, etc.), daily showers, personal hygiene supplies, minimal writing materials, and access to books and other reading materials. It "shocks the conscience" that some jurisdictions did not follow such standards until this ruling.

The Violent Crime Control and Law Enforcement Act of 1994 gave the Attorney General the authority to investigate and to seek judicial remedies when the practices of administrators of juvenile justice systems violate the federal rights of incarcerated juveniles. The Special Litigation Section has investigated conditions of confinement in more than 100 juvenile facilities in sixteen states. It currently monitors conditions in more than 65 facilities that operate under settlement agreements with the United States. The cases involved both publicly and privately operated facilities, as well as conditions for youths being held prior to their juvenile court adjudication and those placed in facilities as a result of being adjudicated delinquent. The investigations and subsequent settlements focused on constitutional rights to reasonable safety, adequate medical and mental health care, rehabilitative treatment, and education. Several of the cases involved allegations of staff abuse, preventable youth-on-youth violence, excessive use of restraints and isolation, and the problems of overcrowding.[31]

JUVENILE COURT: THE STRUCTURE

The centerpiece of the juvenile justice system is the juvenile court. The size and functions of these courts vary from one jurisdiction to another. Some jurisdictions hear cases on special days in other courts. Other jurisdictions have facilities that range from a small courthouse with a skeleton staff to a large, bureaucratic complex with many separate divisions (often occupying different buildings over several acres of land) and employing over 1,000 personnel. Some juvenile courts (e.g., Honolulu, New York City, Las Vegas) are called *family courts* and handle a wide variety of family-related problems (e.g., child custody, child support, etc.).

Typically, juvenile courts are part of municipal courts, county courts, or other types of court systems, depending on an area's governmental structure. Most of the courts have the following divisions: (1) intake and detention, (2) probation, (3) records, (4) psychological services, (5) judges and personnel staff, (6) medical services (doctors and nurses), and (7) volunteer services.

Among the most important juvenile court personnel are the judges, referees, probation and parole officers, and the defense and prosecuting attorneys. Judges are usually elected officials and have a wide variety of duties, not unlike judges in the adult system. Referees (sometimes called "masters") are typically lawyers who perform some of the same functions as judges and supplement the roster of juvenile court judges.

Defense attorneys have become a regular fixture of juvenile court since *Gault;* frequently they are part of the public defender system. However, many youths who appear in juvenile court are still not represented by an attorney.

The prosecutor is generally a member of the local district attorney's office assigned to the juvenile court (other district attorneys may be assigned to areas like domestic violence, gang prosecution, appeals, etc.). Like their criminal court counterparts, they are involved in every stage of the process, including such important decisions as whether or not to charge, what to charge, whether or not to detain, and whether or not to certify a youth as an adult.

There are several other important personnel within a juvenile court, many of whom make some very important decisions. These include intake workers (who are generally the first personnel a youth actually sees when taken into custody and who also affect decisions about detention or release), detention workers (who supervise youths who are detained), and probation and parole officers (who supervise youth placed on probation and those released from institutional care, respectively).

One of the first decisions made at intake is whether a case should be processed in the criminal (adult) justice system rather than in the juvenile court. Most states have more than one mechanism for transferring cases to criminal court: prosecutors may have the authority to file certain juvenile cases directly in criminal court; state statute may order cases meeting certain age and offense criteria be excluded from juvenile court jurisdiction and filed directly in criminal court; and a juvenile court judge may waive juvenile court jurisdiction in certain juvenile cases.[32]

The number of cases (3.2%) waived to adult court peaked in 1991. In 2004, the number of cases waived was 1.9%. However, the decline in the number of judicial waivers was affected by state legislation that specifically excluded some offenses from juvenile court jurisdiction, as well as legislation permitting the prosecutor to file certain cases directly in criminal court.[33]

While the juvenile court differs in many significant ways from the adult system, there are also numerous similarities. For instance, cases proceed generally from arrest through pretrial hearings through the actual court process to disposition and finally to some form of punishment and/or treatment in a "correctional institution." The juvenile court, however, has different terminology for the stages in the process. For instance, *taking into custody* is the same as being arrested; *detention* is a form of jailing. In juvenile court, a *petition* is the equivalent to an indictment, a trial is called an *adjudicatory hearing*, a *dispositional hearing* is roughly the equivalent of a sentencing hearing in the adult system, and a sentence is called a *commitment*. Parole is known as *aftercare*.[34] Figure 16.1 on p. 356 illustrates the various stages within the typical juvenile court, along with standard definitions.

JUVENILE JUSTICE: THE PROCESS

Generally, the police decision to take a youth into custody for an alleged offense sets the juvenile justice process in motion.

The Initial Contact: The Police

The largest percentage of referrals to the juvenile court comes from the police (over 80%). In most jurisdictions the police have several options when contact with a juvenile is made (either because of a citizen complaint or an on-site observation of an alleged offense). First, they can, and often do, simply warn and release (for instance, telling a group of young people hanging around a street corner to "move along" or "go home"). Second, they can release after filling out an interview card ("field investigation card" or "field contact card"). Third, they can make a "station adjustment" where a youth is brought to the police station and then either (1) released to a parent or guardian or (2) released with a referral to some community agency. Fourth, they can issue a misdemeanor citation, which will require the youth and a parent or guardian to appear in juvenile court at some future date (not unlike a traffic ticket). Fifth, they can transport a youth to the juvenile court after making a formal arrest.

One of the most revealing statistics is the number of times the police use a particular option. In 2004, 70% of juveniles arrested were referred to juvenile court; 7% were referred directly to criminal court; and 21% were handled within law enforcement agencies and released (the other 2% were referred to welfare or other agencies).The proportion of juvenile arrests sent to juvenile court increased from 58% in 1980 to 70% in 2004.[35] This reflects the general trend toward increasing formality in our response to human problems. Schools used to handle minor conflicts such as fights; now, we have literally thousands of "assaults" processed through the juvenile courts. Parents and community groups (mental health workers, counselors, youth leaders, sports coaches, etc.) used to handle various other youth problems.

Does this mean that the offenses committed by youths are getting more serious and thus require more formal processing? No. The offenses for which the majority of youths are charged remain minor—as they have always been.

Police Discretion and Juveniles

The police, of course, have a great deal of *discretion* as to what courses of action to take when dealing with juveniles, or any other member of the public for that matter. As described above, the police have several alternatives available when they encounter

Figure 16.1   Processing Juveniles through the System

Arrest

Police generally follow one of three options after arresting a juvenile: they can release the youth with a simple warning, issue a misdemeanor citation (like a traffic ticket, ordering the youth to appear in court on a certain date), or physically take the youth to the juvenile court and the intake division, where he or she is booked.

Intake

If the police decide to take the youth to court, intake is the next step. The intake process is an initial screening of the case by staff members, who collect preliminary information (e.g., name, address, phone, names of the parents, the alleged offense, and other personal information about the youth). Probation officers (sometimes called "intake officers") review the forms filled out by the staff members. A decision is then made to drop the charges (e.g., for lack of evidence), to handle the case informally, or to file a *petition* to appear in court.

Diversion

If the intake decision is to handle the case informally, probation staff (usually in cooperation with the prosecutor's office) will either release the youth without any further action or propose a diversion alternative. Diversion entails having the youth and his or her parent or guardian agree to complete certain requirements instead of going to court. This may include supervision by the probation department and satisfying requirements, such as curfew, restitution, community service, substance-abuse treatment, etc. If the youth successfully completes the program, the charges are usually dropped; if not, the youth is brought back to court via a formal petition.

Detention

If the case is petitioned to court, the next major decision is whether to detain the youth or release him or her to a parent or guardian, pending a court appearance. The reasons for detaining a youth usually include: (1) safety (does the youth pose a danger to self or to others) or (2) flight risk (does the youth pose a risk to flee or not appear in court). If the youth is detained, then a hearing must be held (called a "detention hearing") within a certain period of time (normally 24 to 72 hours), in order for a judge to hear arguments as to whether the youth should be detained any longer. Bail is not generally guaranteed.

Transfer/Waiver

In rare cases, a youth may be transferred or "waived" to the adult system. This is usually (but not always) done only in the case of extremely serious crimes or when the youth is a "chronic" offender.

Adjudication

The juvenile court equivalent of a trial in the adult system is called an *adjudication hearing*. Rather than a jury hearing the case, the final decision rests with a judge or referee. Both defense and prosecuting attorneys present their cases if the youth denies the petition (i.e., pleads not guilty). If a youth admits to the charges (which happens in the majority of all cases), the case proceeds to the next stage.

Disposition

The *disposition hearing* is the equivalent of the sentencing stage in the adult system. Numerous alternatives are available at this stage, including outright dismissal, probation, placement in a community-based program (e.g., "boot camp," wilderness programs, group homes, substance abuse facility, etc.) or incarceration in a secure facility (e.g., "training school").

Aftercare

This stage occurs after a youth has served his or her sentence. It is the equivalent to "parole" in the adult system and, in fact, is often called "youth parole."

---

delinquent behavior. They can release with a warning, or they can release after filling out a report that does not constitute an arrest but nevertheless is an official record of deviant behavior. It is important to note that this information may be used against the youth at a later date. The youth does not have the opportunity to review or to contest the charges in the report, a problem that the courts have not yet addressed. After taking the youth to the police station, officers can decide to release him or her to a parent or guardian or to a community, mental health, or social welfare agency—or they can start the intake process.[36]

The police are provided with few guidelines about how to determine what action to take. In most states the police are empowered to arrest juveniles without a warrant if there is "reasonable grounds" to believe that the child (1) has committed a delinquent act, (2) is "unruly," (3) is "in immediate danger from his surroundings," or (4) has run away from home.

Decades ago Joseph Goldstein observed that police decision making represents "low visibility decisions in the administration of justice."[37] Police officers make decisions largely out of public view with little public scrutiny—discretion is inherent in the job. Full enforcement of the law is an impossibility, largely because of procedural restrictions governing the police (e.g., laws restricting search and seizure), the ambiguity of many laws, and limited police manpower.

Clemens Bartollas writes that the police officer is a "legal and social traffic director who can use his or her wide discretion to detour juveniles from the juvenile justice system or involve them with it."[38] The following factors seem to be the most influential in determining the course of action the police take when confronting a juvenile who may be in violation of the law.[39]

1. *The nature of the offense.* The more serious the offense, the more likely formal action will be taken.

2. *Citizen complainants.* If a citizen has made a complaint and remains on the scene demanding that an arrest be made, the police will comply.

3. *Gender.* Males are far more likely than females to be referred to court, since their offenses are typically more serious. There are some exceptions, such as when girls act contrary to role expectations and the complainant is a parent.[40]

4. *Race* (this is such an important issue that a separate section will be devoted to it later in this chapter). Studies have concluded that race is the most critical variable in determining how far into the system a youth is processed.[41]

5. *Social class.* In general, the lower the social class, the more likely a youth will be formally processed. Police often believe parents from wealthy neighborhoods have the resources to handle the problem.

6. *Individual factors of the offender.* Factors such as prior record, age, the context of the offense, the offender's family, etc. influence arrest decisions.

7. *The nature of police-youth encounters.* Much research has focused on the *demeanor* or attitude of the youth. If the youth appears cooperative and respectful, no formal action will be taken. All other things being equal, if the youth is hostile or, in police parlance, "flunks the attitude test," formal action generally follows. Race, class, and gender play a role here; lower class and minority males are far more likely than white males and females to flunk the attitude test.[42]

8. *Departmental policies.* Police departments vary with regard to policies about how to handle juveniles. Some emphasize formal handling, and others stress informal handling, with predictable results that some have much higher referral rates than others.[43]

9. *External pressures in the community.* The attitudes of the local media and the public, the social status of the complainant or victim, and the extent to which local resources are available to provide alternative services affect the decisions made.[44]

Demeanor seems to be a particularly important factor, especially when it comes to juveniles. Youths who "smart off" or otherwise do not display the "proper" deference are usually the most likely to be formally processed. This is especially the case with minor offenses and even when there is little or no evidence that a crime has been committed.[45] As with social class, race can affect this equation because many African-American youths are angry at the white establishment, resent being targeted for enforcement, and view the police as representatives of oppression. Many minority youths, especially gang members, display a defiance that is interpreted as a challenge to the police.[46] Departmental policies and external pressures are particularly important when the delinquent behavior involves drugs. Indeed, drug arrests and subsequent referrals to court for these charges have had an enormous impact on the juvenile justice system.

Juvenile Arrests

Who is arrested? What are they arrested for? What is the gender distribution of arrests? The statistics in tables 16.1 and 16.2 show that the majority of juveniles who are arrested are charged with property offenses (some serious, but mostly minor) along with drug offenses and a variety of rather petty crimes (disorderly conduct, liquor laws, etc.). More specifically, the majority of juvenile arrests are for Part II offenses, with the largest number of arrests falling in the category "all other offenses," followed by "other assaults," "disorderly conduct," and "drug offenses." Only "larceny/theft" is a Part I offense, and the majority of arrests in this category are for shoplifting.

From 1997 to 2007, the number of persons arrested who were under 18 years of age declined 24%. Juvenile arrests declined in almost every category—sometimes dramatically (i.e. 53% for motor vehicle theft). The only Part I category that increased in the 10-year period was "other assaults" (2.4%).[47] Other assaults are mostly minor personal crimes, resulting in few injuries. The bulk of these offenses occur near or around schools and in the home. Violent crime decreased 20% and property crime decreased by 44%. The only increases in Part II offenses were for embezzlement (2.7%), prostitution (14.5%); driving under the influence (1.2%), and disorderly conduct (which increased 7.5% and accounted for 9.3% of all juvenile arrests in 2006). Police all over the country have engaged in crackdowns on places where teenagers congregate, because of increased attention to both gangs and drugs. This has resulted in higher arrest rates for relatively minor offenses, but not much more.[48]

Table 16.2 compares the number of arrests in 1994 and 2006, in order of the most frequent offense. Note that in both years "all other offenses" and larceny-theft ranked either first or second. Other assaults appeared in the top five in both years, while disorderly conduct and drugs replaced runaways and vandalism in 2006.

Table 16.3 on p. 360 shows the number of arrests by gender. Contrary to popular opinion and media accounts, there has been no "wave of violence" among girls.[49] Juvenile arrests are higher for males (in general, substantially higher) in every category except

prostitution. The ten-year trend in juvenile arrests showed a decline in every category for males except embezzlement (0.1% of all arrests); the overall decrease was 26.4%; for females, the decline was 17.6%. Violent crime declined 21.6% for males and 11.7% for females. Arrests for property crime declined 47.6% for males and 34.6% for females. Drug arrests declined 13.7% for

Table 16.1   Total Arrests, Under 18, 2006

	Number	Percent
Total Arrests	1,268,950	100
Index Crimes		
Murder	710	0.1
Rape	2,104	0.2
Robbery	19,219	1.5
Aggravated Assault	34,434	2.7
Burglary	49,482	3.9
Larceny-Theft	165,840	13.1
Motor Vehicle Theft	17,342	1.4
Arson	4,794	0.4
Total Violent	56,467	4.4
Total Property	237,458	18.7
Total Index	293,925	23.2
Part II Offenses		
Other Assaults	141,986	11.2
Forgery/Counterfeiting	2,054	0.2
Fraud	4,447	0.4
Embezzlement	912	0.1
Stolen Property	12,680	1.0
Vandalism	68,868	5.4
Weapons	27,198	2.1
Prostitution	788	0.1
Other Sex Offenses	9,293	0.7
Drugs	108,087	8.5
Gambling	405	0.0
Offenses against the Family	2,978	0.2
DUI	11,074	0.9
Liquor Laws	78,530	6.2
Drunkenness	10,338	0.8
Disorderly Conduct	118,160	9.3
Vagrancy	1,284	0.1
Curfew and Loitering	80,440	6.3
Runaway	68,127	5.4
All Other Offenses (includes suspicion)	227,376	17.9

*Less than 0.1 percent.

Source: U.S. Department of Justice, Federal Bureau of Investigation, *Crime in the United States*, 2006, Table 32. [Online] http://www.fbi.gov/ucr/cius2006/data/table_32.html

Table 16.2   Rank Order of Juvenile Arrests, 1994 and 2006 (percent distribution)

1994		2006	
1. Larceny-theft	(19.6%)	1. All Other Offenses	(17.9%)
2. All Other Offenses	(14.5)	2. Larceny-Theft	(13.1)
3. Runaways	(8.2)	3. Other Assaults	(11.2)
4. Other assaults	(7.9)	4. Disorderly Conduct	(9.3)
5. Vandalism	(6.1)	5. Drugs	(8.5)
Subtotal	(56.3%)		(60.0%)
6. Disorderly conduct	(6.0)	6. Curfew & loitering	(6.3)
7. Drugs	(5.7)	7. Liquor Laws	(6.2)
8. Curfew & loitering	(5.6)	8. Vandalism	(5.4)
9. Liquor laws	(4.9)	9. Runaways	(5.4)
10. Motor Vehicle Theft	(3.3)	10. Burglary	(3.9)
Total	(82.8%)		(87.2%)

Source: Federal Bureau of Investigation, *Crime in the United States*, 2006, Table 32. [Online] http://www.fbi.gov/ucr/cius2006/data/table_32.html

males but increased 2.1% for females. There were increases in the other assaults (18.7%) and disorderly-conduct (33.3%) categories that suggest the increased number of arrests could be the result of where the police focus their attention rather than a significant change in the behavior of females.

The statistics above recount the number of arrests. What happens *after* an arrest by the police? How many cases are dismissed? How many are reduced to lesser offenses? How many result in a petition to juvenile court? How many result in some form of incarceration?

JUVENILE COURT PROCESSING

It is impossible to talk about juvenile court processing without reference to race and drug offenses. Race and socioeconomic status can affect both the offense and the *visibility* of the offense,

Race, the "War on Drugs," and Referrals to Juvenile Court

There is abundant evidence that the "war on drugs" has, in effect, resulted in a targeting of African Americans on a scale that is unprecedented in U.S. history. As research by Jerome Miller has shown, young African-American males have received the brunt of law enforcement efforts to "crack down on

drugs." He notes that in Baltimore, for example, African Americans were arrested at a rate six times that of whites—more than 90% of the arrests were for possession.[50]

The national rate of all drug arrests was about the same for black and white juveniles in 1980 (around 400). As the "war on drugs" expanded, the arrest rate for black youths went from 683 in 1985 to 1,200 in 1989 (five times the rate for whites) to 1,415 in 1991. Between 1987 and 1988 the number of whites brought into the juvenile court remained virtually the same (up 1%); the number of minorities referred to the court increased by 42%.[51]

A study by Edmund McGarrell found evidence of substantial increases in minority youths being referred to juvenile court, thus increasing the likelihood of being detained. The detention, petition, and placement of minorities, however, exceeded what would have been expected given the increases in referrals. The increase in formal handling of drug cases has been devastating to minorities. "Given the proactive nature of drug enforcement, these findings raise fundamental questions about the targets of investigation and apprehension under the recent war on drugs."[52] As noted in a study of Georgia's crackdown on drugs, the higher arrest rate for African Americans was attributed to one single factor.

Table 16.3   Arrests of Persons under 18, by Sex, 2006

	Male		Female	
	Number	**Percent**	**Number**	**Percent**
Total	899,669	100	369,281	100
Index Crimes				
Homicide	675	0.1	35	*
Forcible Rape	2,058	0.2	46	*
Robbery	17,425	1.9	1,794	0.5
Aggravated Assault	26,440	2.9	7,994	2.2
Burglary	43,638	4.9	5,844	1.6
Larceny-Theft	98,168	10.9	67,672	18.3
Motor Vehicle Theft	14,230	1.6	3,112	0.8
Arson	4,131	0.5	663	0.2
Total Violent	46,598	5.2	9,869	2.7
Total Property	160,167	17.8	77,291	20.9
Total Index	206,765	23.0	87,160	23.6
Part II Offenses				
Other Assaults	94,367	10.5	47,619	12.9
Forgery/Counterfeiting	1,360	0.2	694	0.2
Fraud	2,882	0.3	1,565	0.4
Embezzlement	502	0.1	410	0.1
Stolen Property	10,793	1.2	1,887	0.5
Vandalism	59,827	6.6	9,041	2.4
Weapons	24,471	2.7	2,727	0.7
Prostitution	201	*	587	0.2
Other Sex Offenses	8,418	0.9	875	0.2
Drugs	90,326	10.0	17,761	4.8
Gambling	382	*	23	*
Offenses against the Family	1,820	0.2	1,158	0.3
DUI	8,546	0.9	2,528	0.7
Liquor Laws	50,162	5.6	28,368	7.7
Drunkenness	7,877	0.9	2,461	0.7
Disorderly Conduct	78,637	8.7	39,523	10.7
Vagrancy	939	0.1	345	0.1
Curfew and Loitering	56,042	6.2	24,398	6.6
Runaway	29,666	3.3	38,461	10.4
All Other Offenses (includes suspicion)	165,686	18.4	61,690	16.7

*Less than 0.1%

Source: Federal Bureau of Investigation, *Uniform Crime Reports*, 2006, Table 33. [Online] http://www.fbi.gov/ucr/cius2006/data/table_33.html

It is easier to make drug arrests in low-income neighborhoods.... Most drug arrests in Georgia are of lower-level dealers and buyers and occur in low-income minority areas. Retail drug sales in these neighborhoods frequently occur on the streets and between sellers and buyers who do not know each other. Most of these sellers are black. In contrast, white drug sellers tend to sell indoors, in bars and clubs and within private homes, and to more affluent purchasers, also primarily white.[53]

The drug offense case rate for black juveniles increased dramatically from 1985 to 1988, remained stable for a time and then peaked in 1996 at 12.7—253% higher than the 1985 rate of 3.6. From that peak year, the drug offense case rate for black juveniles declined 35% by 2004. The rate for white juveniles increased 13% from 1996 to 2004, and the rate for Asian juveniles increased 19%. In 2004, age-specific drug offense case rates were comparable for white juveniles and black juveniles through age 13. By age 17 the black drug offense case rate was nearly 2 times the white rate and more than 7 times the rate of Asian juveniles. Between 1985 and 2004, on average, black youth were involved in 31% of all cases of drug offense violations and 47% of all detained cases.[54]

Regardless of whether race, class, or demeanor is statistically more relevant, one fact remains: growing numbers of African-American youths are finding themselves within the juvenile justice system. They are more likely to be detained, more likely to have their cases petitioned to go before a judge, more likely to be waived to the adult system, and more likely to be institutionalized than their white counterparts.[55] "At each stage of the process, there's a slight empirical bias. And the problem is that the slight empirical bias at every stage of the decision making accumulates. By the time you reach the end, you have all minorities in the deep end of the system."[56] African-American youths constitute only 15% of the total population, but they are 26% of those arrested, 44% of those detained, 46% of those sent to adult court, and 58% of those who end up in state prison.[57]

Quite often the discrepancies are even starker when we look at individual cities. In Columbia, South Carolina, African Americans make up less than 20% of the total juvenile population, yet they constitute 60% of all juvenile arrests.[58] In 1996 the arrest figures were almost split evenly between whites and blacks (50% black, 49% white), but in 2003 it was 60% black and only 39% white. The police have concentrated their patrols in increasing numbers in the city near Westside, a 12-square block of mostly black residents. As a result, the detention rate for black youth is far greater than for whites.

Racial bias is cumulative, starting long before the police ever come in contact with a youth. As will be discussed later in the chapter, black youths are found in detention centers and juvenile correctional facilities at a rate that is four times that of whites. Differences exist regardless of the offense charged.

Some believe that the overrepresentation of minority youth is a result of their committing more crimes than whites. However, self-report surveys and surveys on drug use contradict that belief.[59] The differential is more likely the result of police policies (e.g., targeting low-income, mostly minority neighborhoods) or the location of some offenses in more visible places (especially drug use).

The Impact of Social Class

Social class is another important factor. While juvenile court and arrest statistics do not give any indication of the class backgrounds of youths, studies over the years have documented class bias at each stage of the process. A massive longitudinal study of over 10,000 cases in Philadelphia determined that at every step, minorities and youths from the lowest socioeconomic backgrounds were processed further into the system than whites and those from higher-class backgrounds.[60] Some studies have suggested that social class, rather than race per se, best predicted police decisions. For instance, research by Robert Sampson found that the overall socioeconomic status of a *community* was more important than other variables, although race figured prominently. In general, the lower the socioeconomic standing of the community as a whole, the greater will be the tendency for the police to formally process youth they encounter.[61] Remember that minorities, especially African Americans, are far more likely than whites to be found within the lower class and living in poverty.[62]

William Chambliss conducted a study that took place over 30 years ago, which remains relevant today.[63] His findings reveal the subtle—and sometimes not so subtle—nuances of class bias in the definition and response to "delinquency." He underscores the importance of social definitions in what constitutes "delinquency." Definitions of what is considered to be "normal" youthful behavior, part of "growing up," "sowing wild oats," and "boys will be boys" are very much influenced by social class position. Over several years Chambliss observed two groups of teenagers, which he called the "Saints" and the "Roughnecks," and how the police, the school system, and the community in general responded to their deviant activities. The Saints were eight white boys from upper-middle-class backgrounds, and the Roughnecks were six white boys from lower-class backgrounds.

Both groups engaged in a wide variety of delinquent behavior. The Saints, for instance, developed a very ingenious scheme for cutting school and did so successfully almost every day. They had access to cars and traveled often to a nearby town where they were not known and would not be seen by members of their own community. On weekends, in particular, they would drive to the town about 25 miles away and "raise hell"—engaging in vandalism, drinking and driving, shouting obscenities to girls and police, and committing various "pranks" (such as removing warning signs from areas where the road was being repaired or where it was washed out). The Saints were viewed by teachers and local community members as "good kids" and "promising young men" with a "bright future." Teachers and police regarded their activities (when they were caught, which was rare) as "pranks" or "kid's stuff." In short, it was characterized as behavior that would not lead to more serious problems or criminal activity. Most of the boys were "A" and "B" students (despite their frequent absences from school).

The Roughnecks engaged in activities very similar to those of the Saints, but their activities were more visible to the local community.

> This differential visibility was a direct function of the economic standing of the families. The Saints had access to automobiles and were able to remove themselves from the sight of the community. In as routine a decision as where to go to have a milkshake after school, the Saints stayed away from the mainstream of community life. Lacking transportation, the Roughnecks could not make it to the edge of town. The center of town was the only practical place for them to meet since their homes were scattered throughout the town and any noncentral meeting place put an undue hardship on some members. Through necessity the Roughnecks congregated in a crowded area

where everyone in the community passed frequently, including teachers and law enforcement officers.[64]

Since the Roughnecks were from the lower class, they fit the stereotype of "criminal" or those "headed for trouble," and police and others acted accordingly. The police picked them up more frequently and harassed them, creating a strong dislike for the police by the Roughnecks, and vice versa. The demeanor of the two groups differed. The Saints were respectful and deferential toward those in authority, while the Roughnecks did not defer to authority. From the perspective of the police, teachers, and the local community, the Roughnecks were "bad kids," and their acts "proved" they were "headed for trouble." Local residents would say; "Too bad that these boys couldn't behave like the other kids in town; stay out of trouble, be polite to adults, and look to their future."[65] In school they were characterized as "poor students," although they did manage to keep a "C" average.

Not only did the Roughnecks have police records (while the Saints did not), but they also had rather predictable adult careers. One ended up serving a life sentence for murder; another was sentenced to a 30-year sentence for murder; and another became a small-time gambler. A fourth was last known to be a truck driver. Two were athletes while in school and received scholarships to college, from which they eventually graduated. Both became coaches at the high school level. In contrast, one of the Saints became a doctor; another became a lawyer; a third was working on a PhD; four held high-ranking positions in the business world; only one failed to finish college.

How can we explain the difference between these two groups? Chambliss observes:

> The answer lies in the class structure of American society and the control of legal institutions by those at the top of the class structure. Obviously, no representative of the upper class drew up the operational chart for the police which led them to look in the ghettoes and on street-corners—which led them to see the demeanor of lower-class youth as troublesome and that

of upper-middle-class youth as tolerable. Rather, the procedures simply developed from experience—experience with irate and influential upper-middle-class parents insisting that their son's vandalism was simply a prank and his drunkenness only a momentary "sowing of wild oats" and experience with cooperative or indifferent, powerless, lower-class parents who acquiesced to the law's definition of their son's behavior.[66]

The juvenile justice system and other control/processing institutions (e.g., schools) help maintain the class structure by channeling youth in directions perceived as appropriate to their class background. By defining certain acts as "delinquent," the juvenile justice system (at least in effect), helps prevent upward mobility for the majority of lower-class youths. It is noteworthy that the two Roughnecks who "made it" did so through their athletic abilities, one of the few mechanisms of upward mobility for lower-class youths.

Social class helps determine many, if not most, of the life chances of people in the United States.[67] When combined with race, the restrictions can be truly devastating. Take, for instance, decisions made by the police and courts. Members of racial minorities and the lower classes tend to have their behaviors defined as felonies, while whites and more privileged youths are far more likely to be charged with misdemeanors, if charged at all. In juvenile courts all over the country, minorities and lower-class youth will be processed further into the system than their more privileged and white counterparts. Even when out-of-home "placements" are ordered, the more privileged youth are sent to group homes or well-funded drug treatment programs paid for by insurance, while their lower class and minority counterparts are sent to public facilities.

The Intake Process and the Decision to Detain

Juveniles enter the juvenile court after having been referred to it by a law enforcement agency or a parent or guardian. Sometimes a young person may receive a misdemeanor citation (not unlike a traffic citation) that informs the individual that he or she must appear in court on or before a certain date.

After arrival, the juvenile is subjected to *intake screening*, another unique feature of the juvenile court. This division is staffed by full-time employees of the court, who are usually college graduates with majors such as social work, sociology, or criminal justice. One of the first decisions made is whether or not the case falls within the jurisdiction of the court. Then, it has to be determined whether the youth will be detained before the hearing and whether a petition requiring a formal court appearance before a judge will be filed. Customarily, the youth and a parent or guardian is interviewed at intake.

The options available to the court representative at this stage vary somewhat among jurisdictions but fall into four categories: (1) dismissal, (2) informal supervision, or "informal probation," (3) referral to another agency, and (4) formal petition to the court.

The decision about whether the youth needs to be placed in detention is usually based on written court policies. Detention after a court referral means that the juvenile will be placed in a secure facility until the disposition of the case has been determined. Juveniles can also be detained by the police prior to a referral and by the courts after disposition while awaiting placement. The three typical reasons for detention are (1) the youth may harm others or himself or herself or be subject to injury by others if not detained; (2) the youth has no parent, guardian, or other person able to provide adequate care and supervision, is homeless, or is a runaway; and (3) it is believed that if not detained the youth will leave the jurisdiction and not appear for court proceedings. The intake staff is usually instructed to consider the nature and severity of the current offense and previous offenses (if any), the youth's age, the youth's conduct within the home and at school, ability of the parents or guardians to supervise the youth, whether the current offense is a continuation of a pattern of delinquent behavior, and the willingness of the parents or guardian to cooperate with the court.

Intake staff use a *risk assessment instrument* to assign points depending on the type of offense committed, probation or warrant status, where the youth resides, and whether he or she was under the influence of drugs or alcohol at the time of the offense. The instruments are designed to make an "objective" determination of whether the youth should be released or detained. However, the theory behind the analysis is seriously flawed; it assumes that there is a valid method of predicting who is most likely to commit a crime if released. One study found that the risk assessment score assigned to youths placed in detention was a poor predictor of recidivism.[68] Another study found that probation officers often use risk assessment instruments to "certify" what they have already decided based on "gut feelings" and prejudices.[69] Moreover, the majority of those detained have not committed a serious crime.

It could be argued that detention should be reserved for youths who are charged with serious crimes. As shown in table 16.4, this is not the case. Only about one-fifth of those detained are charged with a serious violent crime (19%), while the largest percentage are charged with a "technical violation" (violation of a court order or violation of probation or parole, which does not include a new offense, as these are the "most serious offenses").

After the decision to detain has been made, the intake officer has several options. These include: (1) counsel, warn, and release, sometimes called *informal adjustment*; (2) *informal probation* (release under certain conditions, with supervision by a volunteer or a regular probation officer; after a certain period of time if no new offense is committed, the case is dismissed); (3) referral to another agency; (4) outright dismissal; (5) file a *consent decree* (somewhat more restrictive than informal probation); or (6) file a petition to have the youth appear in court for a formal *adjudicatory hearing.*[70]

As mentioned earlier, race figures prominently in the decision to detain. The rate of detention for African-American youths for all offenses by juveniles in 2004 was almost five times that of their white counterparts and twice that of Hispanics. The rate per 100,000 juveniles was 214 for blacks, 106 for Hispanics, and 47 for whites. The rate for personal crimes was 73 for blacks, 31 for Hispanics, and 13 for whites.[71] Between 1985 and 2004, black juveniles were involved in 29% of all delinquency cases but 37% of all detained cases. In 2004 black juveniles were twice as likely to be detained for cases involving drug offenses than white juveniles.[72]

In the wake of the Supreme Court decisions in the *Kent* and *Gault* cases, a movement began in the late 1960s to try to keep young offenders out of juvenile court. If they were processed, the goal was to *divert* them out of the system as quickly as possible. The research that was done in conjunction with the two court decisions (and a great deal of research immediately following them) demonstrated the need for some type of diver-

Table 16.4 Juveniles in Detention, by Offense, Sex, and Race (percent distribution), 2003

Most Serious Offense	Total	Sex		Race		
		Male	Female	White	Black	Hispanic
Violent Crime Index	19%	21%	12%	14%	23%	21%
Other person	11%	11%	15%	13%	11%	8%
Property Crime Index	19%	20%	15%	20%	19%	18%
Other property	4%	5%	3%	5%	4%	4%
Drug	8%	8%	6%	8%	8%	8%
Public Order	10%	10%	10%	9%	11%	11%
Technical Violation	23%	21%	29%	25%	20%	26%
Status Offense	5%	4%	10%	6%	4%	4%

Source: Sickmund, M., Sladky, T. J., and Kang, W. (2005) "Census of Juveniles in Residential Placement Databook."
[Online] http://ojjdp.ncjrs.org/ojstatbb/cjrp/asp/Offense_Detained.asp?state=0&topic=Offense_
Detained&year=2003&percent=column

sion.[73] If youths are not diverted from further processing, they move to the adjudication stage of the juvenile court process.

Adjudication

Adjudication is the juvenile court counterpart to trial in adult court, but it has some significant differences. Very often the hearings are informal (sometimes they are merely conversations between a judge, parents, and the child), and they are closed to the public and to reporters. In recent years the procedures have become more formal, especially in large metropolitan courts—almost as formal as an adult court.

There are two types of hearings. The *adjudicatory hearing* is the "fact-finding" stage of the juvenile court process. Following this stage is the *dispositional hearing*. These two stages are roughly the equivalent of the trial and sentencing stages of the adult system. In most urban courts both the defense and the prosecutor present the evidence of the case. Like the adult counterpart, hearsay evidence is inadmissible; the defendant has the right to cross-examine a witness; he or she is protected against self-incrimination; and a youth's guilt must be proven beyond a reasonable doubt.

In the majority of juvenile courts, the dispositional hearing is a separate hearing (a *bifurcated* system). During this hearing, the judge relies heavily on two important court documents, usually prepared by the probation department of the court. One document is the *legal* file that contains a complete referral history, including the nature of all the offenses that brought the youth into court prior to the current offense, along with prior dispositions. The other document is probably the most important, for it contains a wide range of personal information about the juvenile. This is known as the *social* file, which contains such information as family background, school records, psychological profile, and the like. Together these two documents aid the probation department in preparing what is known as the *presentence report*, roughly the equivalent of the one prepared in the adult system.

Perhaps the most important part of the presentence report is the recommendation. Typically some sort of a "treatment plan" is prepared for the case, along with the actual sentence. More often than not, the judge agrees to the recommendation.[74]

There are several alternative dispositions available to juvenile court judges. These alternatives can be grouped into four major categories: (1) dismissal, (2) probation, (3) commitment to an institution or "out-of-home placement" (with several different types, according to level of security, ranging from group homes to training schools), and (4) waiver to an adult court.

In 2004, 1,660,700 juvenile cases were processed; 57% were handled formally, and 43% were handled informally. Of the cases petitioned, 39% were dismissed at intake, often for lack of legal evidence; 67% resulted in the youth being adjudicated delinquent (of those, 63% received probation; 22% were placed in a residential facility), and 1% were waived to criminal court.[75]

The most severe disposition is commitment to an institution. Once again race appears to be a big factor. Regardless of the offense, both African-American and Hispanic youth have the highest rates of commitment. The rates of commitment for all offenses by juveniles in 2004 were 528 for blacks, 238 for Hispanic, and 140 for whites. The rates for person offenses were 200 for blacks, 85 for Hispanics, and 47 for whites.[76]

It is not being suggested that everyone connected with the juvenile justice system is racist and practices discrimination, although stereotypes about youth from certain race or class backgrounds definitely exist. Part of the problem is institutional in that such negative stereotypes are deeply imbedded in our culture. Juvenile courts and police departments are largely staffed by whites. The widespread poverty and joblessness affecting minority communities result in the lack of available resources (e.g., alternatives to formal court processing) to deal with crime-related issues and the general failure of schools.

Many studies have reported that prior record, current offense, and previous sentences are among the most important factors in determining the final disposition.[77] Other studies have noted the importance of race and other social factors.[78] Some data show that prior record is, statistically speaking, more important than race. However, these studies fail to consider that race can contribute to prior record because of cultural biases that affect police practices (especially drug cases) and the existence of various forms of racial profiling.[79]

JUVENILE COURT STATISTICS

Obtaining accurate data on juvenile court processing is difficult for several reasons. First, the most common source has been the Office of Juvenile Justice and Delinquency Prevention, which publishes surveys of juvenile court case processing based on the voluntary submission of data from both state and local agencies to the National Juvenile Court

Data Archive. The information submitted is not uniform and is not derived from any probability sampling procedure. Moreover, not all states are included. In the most recent report, only 1,785 juvenile court jurisdictions in 36 states (containing 68% of the juvenile population in the country) met the criteria for inclusion in the national estimates.[80]

Second, and perhaps most importantly, the statistics are grouped into FBI offense categories (Index and Part II crimes). As shown in table 16.5, the four major categories are: person, property, drug law violations, and public order offenses. Note that this categorization is based on the *most serious offense charged*, so that if a juvenile has multiple charges of a less serious nature, these

Table 16.5   Referrals to Juvenile Court, 2002

Most Serious Offense	Number of Cases	Percent Change	
		1985–02	1997–02
Total Delinquency	**1,615,400**	**41%**	**−11%**
Person Offenses	**387,500**	**113**	**−2**
Homicide	1,700	41	−25
Rape	4,700	8	−14
Robbery	21,500	−13	−36
Aggravated Assault	47,400	32	−26
Simple Assault	270,700	174	6
Other Violent Sex Offenses	16,400	150	31
Other Person Offenses	25,200	144	18
Property Offenses	**624,900**	**−10**	**−27**
Burglary	100,000	−29	−29
Larceny-Theft	284,400	−13	−29
Motor Vehicle Theft	38,500	0	−30
Arson	8,100	18	−10
Vandalism	94,800	11	−18
Trespassing	50,800	−5	−24
Stolen Property	22,100	−20	−32
Other Property	26,200	45	−16
Drug Law Violations	**193,200**	**159**	**1**
Public Order Offenses	**409,800**	**113**	**7**
Obstruction of justice	182,600	180	10
Disorderly conduct	108,500	145	18
Weapons offenses	35,900	85	−19
Liquor law violations	28,200	57	96
Nonviolent sex offenses	15,500	16	20
Other public order	39,000	23	−25
Violent Crime Index	**75,300**	**13**	**−29**
Property Crime Index	**431,000**	**−16**	**−29**

Source: Snyder, H N. and Sickmund, M. (2006). *Juvenile Offenders and Victims: 2006 National Report*. Washington, DC: Office of Juvenile Justice and Delinquency Prevention, p. 157.

offenses are not included in the totals. Thus, the data present a very incomplete picture.

In 2002 there were an estimated 1,615,000 delinquency cases processed in juvenile courts across the nation. The majority were either property offenses (39%) or public order offenses (25%). Relatively few were serious violent offenses (homicide, rape, robbery, and aggravated assault, constituting only 4.6% of all cases). The most common offense against the person was that of "simple assault" (totaling about 17% of all delinquency cases). Drugs accounted for almost 12% of the total. Note that drug referrals increased 159% from 1985 to 2002, more than any category except simple assault (174%) and obstruction of justice (180%).

The most obvious thing about these figures is the minor nature of the majority of the referrals. For instance, the category of public-order offenses includes "obstruction of justice"[81] (45% of all public order offenses and a referral particularly subject to the exercise of discretion). As mentioned above, this category had the greatest percentage change from 1985 to 2002. While "person offenses" comprised 24% of all referrals, the bulk of these were "simple assaults" (70% of all person offenses), the second highest percentage increase from 1985. Of property offenses, the most frequent offense (46%) was larceny-theft. Burglary ranked second among the property offenses, but decreased 29% since 1985. The numbers in table 16.4 represent only delinquency referrals and do not include several thousand cases classified as "status," "dependency" and "abuse and neglect." Simple assault, larceny-theft, obstruction of justice, disorderly conduct, vandalism, and trespassing account for 1,185,000 of the 1,625,400 total delinquency cases—74% of all referrals to juvenile court. These offenses vary substantially from the media image of juvenile predators running wild.

PRISONS OR "CORRECTIONAL" INSTITUTIONS: WHAT'S IN A NAME?

Within the formal juvenile justice system, the most severe disposition is commit-ment to a secure facility, most frequently called a "juvenile correctional institution." Over the past 180 years, terms have ranged from houses of refuge, to reform schools, to training schools. Notice that none of these names include the word "prison." However, when one cannot leave and there are walls or fences surrounding the area, one is, in fact, "imprisoned." Americans have a hard time admitting what we do with young offenders and hide the reality behind more pleasant terminology.[82] The plain and simple truth is that these are prisons.

Commitment to an Institution

Individual states vary a great deal in where they place the juvenile, the length of stay, and the conditions of release. The most common arrangement (27 states) is that the agency that administers a state's institutions makes decisions as to where juveniles will be committed. In 23 states, the juvenile court takes a significant role in the determination of where the juvenile will be placed, but more commonly the court's role ends after having ordered a commitment.[83] There are six variations in disposition that determine the actual time a juvenile will spend in an institution.[84]

1. *Indeterminate only:* This is the norm in 20 states. Regardless of the adjudicated offenses, the commitment is for an indefinite period of time, which could theoretically last until juveniles reach the age determined by the state to represent adult status. The exact length of stay is at the discretion of the releasing authority.

2. *Indeterminate with a minimum:* Four states add a minimum period of time that must be served to the indeterminate commitment.

3. *Indeterminate up to a maximum:* Five states specify that a youth cannot be confined for more than a certain period. An example would be California, where a juvenile cannot be confined longer than the maximum sentence that could have been imposed if the crime had been committed by an adult.

4. *Indeterminate with minimums and maximums:* This exists in just one state, Pennsylvania, where the court determines the

minimum period of the sentence "that is consistent with the protection of the public and the rehabilitative needs of the juvenile," but then "reviews the commitment periodically thereafter." Also, the maximum time served cannot exceed four years or the maximum time if convicted as an adult.

5. *Determinate and indeterminate:* A total of 13 states authorizes courts to fix an exact period of confinement but also permits them to order indeterminate commitments as well.

6. *Determinate only:* In six states the commitment is for a period of time set by the court.

The decision to release a youth from confinement is made by the institution where the youth is confined, the original court, a *youth parole board,* or some combination of these authorities. In 24 states the decision is with the institution; in 10 states it lies with the committing court; in 7 states a parole board makes this decision; and in ten states and the District of Columbia the decision is made by a combination of the agencies.[85]

Youths can be committed to several different types of custodial facilities: detention center (26%), shelter (10%, reception/diagnostic center (4%), group home/halfway house (38%), boot camp (2%), ranch/wilderness camp (5%), or *training school*/long-term secure facility (13%). Detention centers are generally local, while long-term secure facilities are usually operated by the state; group homes are frequently private facilities. In 2002, there were 2,964 custodial facilities; 69% were public—28% local and 40% state—and 31% were private.[86] More than half of all the facilities confined fewer than 20 juveniles, but almost half of all juvenile offenders were committed to large facilities (holding more than 100). The largest facilities (holding more than 200) accounted for 3% of all facilities but confined 27% of juvenile offenders. In 2002, 36% of the facilities housed more juveniles than they were designed to hold.

The amount of security varies depending on the type of confinement. "The use of fences, walls, and surveillance equipment is increasingly common in juvenile facilities."[87] In detention centers, 39% of the facilities had fences with razor wire, as did 37% of training schools and 32% of boot camps. Daytime locks confined 8 in 10 juveniles for at least part of the day. More than 90% of both committed and detained offenders in public facilities were in locked facilities.

In 2004, there were 2,821 allegations of sexual violence reported in juvenile facilities (an average of about 1 allegation per 50 beds in a facility). One-third of all reported incidents of sexual violence against juveniles occurred in state-operated facilities, and two-thirds occurred in local or privately operated facilities. Youth-on-youth incidents accounted for 59% of the incidents (67% nonconsensual); 41% were staff-on-youth incidents (75% nonconsensual). Staff-on-youth violence accounted for 56% of the incidents in state-operated facilities and 33% in local or privately operated facilities. Although females accounted for just 11% of the custody population, they were the victims in 34% of the substantiated incidents of sexual violence in state-operated facilities. In private facilities, where they were 17% of the population, they were victims in 37% of the sexual violence incidents.[88]

Racial Composition of Juvenile Institutions

The percentage of incarcerated youth who are racial minorities has risen steadily over the years. The national percentage of minorities in training schools was 23% in 1950, 32% in 1960, 40% in 1970, and 62% in 2003.[89] In contrast, the majority of youths confined in *private* facilities are white. This is no doubt because most of the costs are paid for by family members, usually through their insurance. The highest percentage of black juveniles in residential confinement is 81% in the District of Columbia, compared to a national average of 38%. The next highest totals are in Louisiana and Delaware (69%), New Jersey (67%), Georgia (65%), South Carolina (62%), and Virginia (61%). The highest percentage of Hispanic juveniles confined is 49% in California, compared to a national average of 19%. The next highest totals are in Arizona (45%), Texas (41%), Colorado (26%), Massachusetts (26%), Nevada (25%), and Connecticut (21%).

The national rate of commitment per 100,000 juveniles is 754 for blacks to 190 for whites; the rates in Nevada are 958 for blacks and for 289 for whites.[90] In 1999 Summit View Correctional Center opened in North Las Vegas to house offenders classified as "Level IV"—the highest classification in the state based on the alleged degree of "dangerousness." This new category was based on a point system—the youth's prior record determined the point total. The higher the points, the higher the classification. Careful investigation by the lead author (RGS) found no scientific rationale for the point system, and no research was cited to legitimate the system. Not surprisingly, the higher the level of classification, the greater the percentage of minorities. Summit View was built and operated by a private company called Correctional Services Corporation. Within one year of opening, the prison experienced a number of problems, including too many empty beds. The state could not find enough "dangerous" youth to qualify for Level IV (in fact, for a time the prison "borrowed" a few "Level III" youths from the detention center at the juvenile court in Las Vegas). They did, however, find a large number of minority youths to house in this prison; 80% of the youths were minorities.[91]

Some Effects of Incarceration

What is life like in secure training schools today? Sadly, it isn't much different than it was in the past. Several studies covering a period of around 30 years document the abuses within these institutions.[92]

The National Assessment of Juvenile Corrections surveyed 42 juvenile prisons in the 1970s.[93] The study focused on the effects on youths of being institutionalized. "Newcomers," those who had been at the facility two months or less, were distinguished from "veterans," those who had been incarcerated nine months or more. The survey found significant differences between programs having large proportions of veterans and those

having relatively few veterans. "Veterans" were significantly more likely than "newcomers" to: (1) commit more offenses and have friends who had committed offenses while incarcerated; (2) have learned more ways to break the law while incarcerated (46% of the veterans, compared to 20% of the newcomers); and (3) become "hardened" over time ("hardened" was measured in several ways, such as being critical of the staff, previous encounters with institutions, number and seriousness of offenses while incarcerated, and other indicators). It was also found that the longer a youth remained in the institution, the more the youth would: (1) fight with other youths, (2) use drugs, (3) steal something, (4) run away, and (5) hit a staff member. These problems became the most acute when there was a critical mass of veterans within a program. It was found that these problems were more apparent in the larger institutions (training schools).

The Inmate Social System

As mentioned in chapter 13, John Irwin found that *state-raised youth* (offenders whose formative years were spent in confinement in institutions) had distorted, stunted, and incoherent worldviews; their only meaningful world was the prison.[94] Juvenile institutions have a very potent *inmate subculture* (as do adult prisons).[95] In most of the larger institutions there is a hierarchy within a strongly defined peer subculture. The most commonly found social roles are those of the "toughs" or "dukes" and "punks"; the latter are the lowest in social status (victimized sexually or "punked out").

A very detailed study of an institution in Columbus, Ohio, by three criminologists in the 1970s focused on the extent of victimization in institutions. It described a brutal social system. Within the "jungle" (the term used by the inmates themselves) the powerful preyed on the weak.[96] Some youths assumed aggressive social roles. The "cottage leaders" were known variously as "wheel," "bruiser," "duke," and "heavy." "Lieutenants" worked for the leaders and were called "vice president," "tough boy," "thug," "bad dude," and even "wise guy" (borrowing organized crime terminology). "Sexual exploiters" were called such names as "daddy" and "booty bandits." Other youths were manipulators; they did what was necessary to survive and to make their stay easier—to "go their own time." They were known as "slick," "cool," and "con man." Those who engaged in various businesses were known as "peddlers" or "merchants."[97] Passive youth were not deeply involved in the inmate social system and were generally "pro-staff." They were referred to as "straight kid," "quiet type," and "bushboy." Some youths were put down as "messups," "weak-minded," and "lame." Those who were victimized sexually were called "punks," "sweet boy," "girl," and "fag."[98]

The authors of the study returned 15 years later for a follow-up. What they found was not encouraging. They discovered that the youth culture still existed and victimized the weak, although less for sex than for food, clothing, and toiletries. Consensual sexual behavior seemed to be more prevalent, violent juveniles were in the minority, and the majority were minor drug dealers, addicts, and users of drugs. Gangs did not dominate within the institution, as popularly believed. Most discouraging was the fact that treatment had "all but disappeared," with the lone exception of a drug abuse program. The authors quoted one social worker who said, "We don't do anything in here for kids." Another member of the staff added "This place is a warehouse for children."[99]

Juveniles as Victims

In 2006, there were 73.7 million children seventeen-years-old or younger in the United States; 58% were white, 20% Hispanic, 15% black, 4% Asian, and 4% other races. Of those children, 18% lived in poverty.[100] In 2005, 44% of people under the age of 19 were victims of violent crime.[101] Countless more suffer from child abuse and neglect. As discussed earlier in the chapter, juveniles account for 15% of all arrests—and arrests do not indicate guilt or the seriousness of the offense. Juveniles are far more frequently victims—whether victims of crime, poverty, or inadequate schooling—than they are the cause of serious crime.

During the 1980s, the public perceived that serious juvenile crime was increasing and that the system was too lenient with offenders. Although there was substantial misperception regarding increases in juvenile crime, many states responded by passing more punitive laws. Some laws removed certain classes of offenders from the juvenile justice system and handled them as adult criminals in criminal court. Others required the juvenile justice system to be more like the criminal justice system and to treat certain classes of juvenile offenders as criminals but in juvenile court. As a result, offenders charged with certain offenses now are excluded from juvenile court jurisdiction or face mandatory or automatic waiver to criminal court.[102]

Juvenile justice policies in the United States are again in the phase where rehabilitation and the best interests of the child have been replaced with an emphasis on punishments for violating accepted behavior. We need to change how we perceive youths and their potential and to work toward providing the services that youths in trouble desperately need.

Racial Injustice in the South

In 2006, an incident occurred in Jena High School in rural Louisiana that highlights all the issues discussed in this chapter. Jena is a former mill town with a population of about 3,000—12% black and 85% white. There was a large oak tree in the school courtyard where, by convention, whites would gather. During the first week of classes, a black student asked the vice principal if he could sit under the tree and was told he could sit wherever he liked. He and several black friends went over to the tree to visit some white friends. The next day, three nooses were hanging on the tree's branches. The three white boys who admitted hanging the nooses received three-day, in-school suspensions. The principal had recommended that the three be expelled, but the superintendent overruled, saying "Adolescents play pranks. I don't think it was a threat against anybody."[103]

The school held an assembly in early September and invited the district attorney,

Reed Walters, who appeared flanked by police officers and told the students, "I can be your best friend or your worst enemy. With the stroke of my pen, I can make your lives disappear."[104] During the Thanksgiving holiday weekend, one black student was beaten at a party primarily attended by whites; the white student who threw the first punch was charged with simple battery and given probation. A young white man pulled a shotgun on three black students; a black student wrestled the gun away. The white youth was not charged with anything; the black student was charged with theft of a firearm.[105] When school resumed, a black student punched a white student, Justin Barker, who was exiting the gym, knocking him unconscious; a group of five other black students allegedly joined the attack. The white student was treated for injuries at the hospital and released; he attended a class-ring ceremony that evening. Walters originally charged six black students with attempted murder. All six were expelled from school.[106]

Sixteen-year-old Mychal Bell was prosecuted as an adult; he was jailed in December because he was unable to post $90,000 bail. He refused the district attorney's plea-bargain offer, because he did not want to plead guilty to a felony. As jury selection began, Walters reduced the charges to aggravated second-degree battery and conspiracy.[107] On June 28, 2007, an all-white jury convicted Bell after a trial in which his court-appointed attorney (who had tried to convince him to accept a plea bargain) did not challenge the composition of the jury, excluded Bell's parents from the courtroom, and rested his case without calling any witnesses. The aggravated battery charge alleged the use of a dangerous weapon. The district attorney introduced no evidence of a gun, knife or other weapon; he argued that the tennis shoes Bell was wearing at the time of the attack qualified as a dangerous weapon—and the jury agreed.[108] A number of individuals and institutions protested the conviction. School officials cut down the tree in July, "hoping to eliminate it as a focus of protests."[109] The case continued to attract attention, and about 20,000 demonstrators arrived in Jena on September 20.

Earlier in September, a circuit court of appeal in Louisiana ruled that the district attorney had improperly tried Bell as an adult.[110] Walters first vowed to appeal that ruling (which he later decided not to pursue), and immediately initiated juvenile proceedings. He also said he would vigorously pursue his cases against the rest of the teenage defendants, insisting that the white victim had been forgotten amid the controversy. The ruling did not order Bell released, and he remained in jail unable to pay the bond.

Judge J. P. Mauffray Jr. (the presiding judge at the criminal trial) agreed to release Bell on $45,000 bond on September 27.[111] The Congressional Black Caucus asked the U.S. Department of Justice to investigate possible civil rights violations and prosecutorial misconduct. "This shocking case has focused national and international attention on what appears to be an unbelievable example of the separate and unequal justice that was once commonplace in the Deep South."[112]

Bell's taste of freedom was short-lived. On October 11, he went to juvenile court for a scheduled hearing. Mauffray revoked a prior probation and sentenced him to 18 months on previous charges of simple battery and criminal destruction of property.[113] The judge ordered all proceedings closed and directed all lawyers in the case not to speak publicly about it. David Utter, founder of the Juvenile Justice Project of Louisiana, commented: "I don't know the motivation for this judge and the district attorney, but what they did goes against the grain of our juvenile code, which holds that home and the community are the best place to treat juveniles."[114] On October 22, a coalition of major media companies filed a First Amendment petition to open the proceedings against Bell, charging that Mauffray's orders are contrary to Louisiana juvenile laws, precedents set by the Louisiana Supreme Court, and the state and U.S. Constitutions.[115]

The Jena 6 case is an example of unequal justice.

> Far harsher criminal charges were brought against the black youths for fighting than the white students for similar infractions. What's true also is that all of the students

equally have used poor judgment and all should be held accountable. But considering the circumstances, none of them should have to pay with their lives by possibly facing long prison terms. And that's what the black students are facing. As Richard Cohen from the Southern Poverty Law Center said, the data consistently show that black people are treated more harshly than white people in the criminal justice system. "Blacks aren't often given the benefit of the doubt. If discretion is exercised, it's more often exercised in an adverse way to blacks."[116]

SUMMARY

This chapter began with a brief history of the juvenile justice system, starting with the houses of refuge in the 1820s through the founding of the juvenile court in 1899. It was noted that the major justification for state intervention into the lives of children and families came from the early English doctrine of *parens patriae*. The chapter also reviewed the processing of cases through the various stages of the juvenile justice system, which really begins with juvenile laws. These laws describe the jurisdiction of the juvenile court for behavior which would also be criminal for adults as well as a variety of laws applicable to juveniles only because of their age ("status offenses").

Once they are in the court system itself, a process known as *intake screening* takes place. A critical decision is made at this stage that has significant consequences—the decision to detain. Race plays a key role; minorities are far more likely to be detained for any offense. Detention affects other stages within the court process, such as adjudication and the final disposition. It was noted that at each stage of the process there are several dispositional options. The final disposition following adjudication may involve commitment to a juvenile institution. Again, minorities are disproportionately represented.

The juvenile court, in spite of the promises of a century ago, has not had a very positive record of achievement. Dissatisfaction with the court (accusations of being too lenient being the most frequent) has resulted in a movement to certify youths as adults.

The results have been far from promising, and once again minority youth experience the brunt of the impact. Certification is not applied frequently. When applied, it has had little or no impact on youth crime.

This chapter also reviewed what are euphemistically called "correctional institutions," even though in reality they are *prisons.* Over the years there have been several reports of substandard care within many of these facilities. A high proportion of youths housed within these institutions suffer some serious mental disorders, and these facilities are ill-equipped to handle such problems. Most of these institutions are merely an extension of the nineteenth-century houses of refuge, where "treatment" is often an afterthought and recidivism rates continue to be high. Several of these institutions, such as the California Youth Authority, continue to be places of violence and warehousing. Within many of these institutions, physical abuse is often an everyday occurrence, both by the staff and by other youths. Again, minority youth are the most likely to be housed in such prisons.

Finally, the case of the "Jena 6" was summarized. Here we have a classic example of both "zero tolerance" and racial injustice that illustrates some of the issues explored in this chapter.

Key Terms

- adjudication hearing
- aftercare
- commitment
- detention
- dispositional hearing
- *Ex Parte Crouse*
- family courts
- house of refuge
- *In re Gault*
- *In re Winship*
- intake screening
- *Kent v. United States*
- *McKeiver v. Pennsylvania*
- parens patriae

- *People v. Turner*
- petition
- status offenses
- taking into custody
- training school

Notes

[1] This section is adapted from Shelden, R. G. *Controlling the Dangerous Classes: A Critical Introduction to the History of Criminal Justice.* Boston: Allyn & Bacon, 2001, chapter 5.

[2] Platt, A. *The Child Savers.* Chicago: University of Chicago Press, 1977; Empey, L. *American Delinquency.* Homewood, IL: Dorsey Press, 1982.

[3] Sutton, J. R. *Stubborn Children: Controlling Delinquency in the United States, 1640–1981.* Berkeley: University of California Press, 1988.

[4] Rendleman D. R. "Parent Patriae: From Chancery to the Juvenile Court." In F. L. Faust and P. J. Brantingham (eds.), *Juvenile Justice Philosophy.* St. Paul: West, 1974, p. 63.

[5] Rothman, D. J. *The Discovery of the Asylum.* Boston: Little, Brown, 1971; Krisberg, B. and J. Austin. *Reinventing Juvenile Justice.* Newbury Park, CA: Sage, 1993; Shelden, *Controlling the Dangerous Classes*, chapter 5.

[6] Empey, *American Delinquency*, p. 59.

[7] Brenzel, B. *Daughters of the State.* Cambridge: MIT Press, 1983, p. 11.

[8] Bernard, T. J. *The Cycle of Juvenile Justice.* Oxford: Oxford University Press, 1992, pp. 49–55.

[9] Informal systems of control have always been reserved for the more privileged youths, while the less privileged have been subjected to formal systems of control. In addition, with few exceptions, minority youth have been much more likely to be viewed as unredeemable criminals rather than juvenile delinquents (i.e., "malleable" and thus "redeemable"). As a result, the greatest numbers of youths waived to adult court in recent years have been minorities.

[10] Pickett, R. *House of Refuge.* Syracuse, NY: Syracuse University Press, 1969; Platt, *The Child Savers.*

[11] Bernard, *The Cycle of Juvenile Justice.*

[12] Shelden, R. G. "Confronting the Ghost of Mary Ann Crouse: Gender Bias within the Juvenile Justice System." *Juvenile and Family Court Journal* 49: 11–25 (1998).

[13] *Ex Parte Crouse*, 4 Wharton (Pa.) 9 (1838), pp. 9–11.

[14] Ibid., p. 11.

[15] *The People of the State of Illinois, Ex Rel. Michael O'Connell v. Robert Turner, Superintendent of the Reform School of the City of Chicago.* 55 Ill. 280; 1870 Ill. LEXIS 355. [Online] http://plaza.ufl.edu/edale/Illinois%20v.%20Turner.htm

[16] Ibid.

[17] Bernard, *The Cycle of Juvenile Justice*, pp. 70–72; "People v. Turner," in Faust and Brantingham, *Juvenile Justice Philosophy.*

[18] Tanenhaus, D. S. "Between Dependency and Liberty: The Conundrum of Children's Rights in the Gilded Age." *Law and History Review* 23(2): par. 38 (Summer 2005). [Online] http://www.historycooperative.org/journals/lhr/23.2/tanenhaus.html#REF83

[19] Ibid.

[20] Ibid., par. 39.

[21] Shelden, R. G. *Delinquency and Juvenile Justice in American Society.* Long Grove, IL: Waveland, p. 30.

[22] Kappeler, V. E. and G. W. Potter. *The Mythology of Crime and Criminal Justice* (4th ed.). Long Grove, IL: Waveland Press, 2005, p. 221.

[23] Mnookin, R. H. *Child, Family and State: Problems and Materials on Children and the Law.* Boston: Little, Brown, 1978, p. 546.

[24] *Kent v. United States* (383 U.S. 541, 1966). [Online] http://caselaw.lp.findlaw.com/cgi-bin/getcase.pl?court=US&vol=383&invol=541

[25] *In re Gault* (387 U.S. 1, 1967). [Online] http://caselaw.lp.findlaw.com/cgi-bin/getcase.pl?navby=volpage&court=us&vol=387&page=21

[26] *In re Winship* (397 U.S. 358, 1970). [Online] http://caselaw.lp.findlaw.com/cgi-bin/getcase.pl?court=US&vol=397&invol=358

[27] *McKeiver v. Pennsylvania* (403 U.S. 528, 1971). [Online] http://caselaw.lp.findlaw.com/cgi-bin/getcase.pl?court=US&vol=403&invol=528.
Two other cases were heard at the same time: *In re Terry* (438 Pa., 339, 265A.2d 350, 1970) and *In re Barbara Burris* (275 N.C. 517, 169 Sk. E. 2d 879, 1969k). The major decision for all three cases was issued in *McKeiver.*

[28] *Breed v. Jones* (421 U.S. 519, 1975). [Online] http://caselaw.lp.findlaw.com/scripts/ getcase.pl?court=us&vol=421&invol=519

[29] *White v. Reid*, 125 F. Supp. 647, D.D.C., 1954.

[30] 346 F. Supp. 1354 D.R.I., 1972. An identical conclusion was rendered in *Nelson v. Heyne* concerning an Indiana training school (355 F. Supp. 451 N.D. Ind. 1973). Finally, in *Morales v. Turman* (364 F. Supp. 166 E.D. Tex. 1973) the U. S. District Court for the Eastern District of Texas made this right more specific, saying a number of criteria had to be followed to insure that youths received proper treatment, such as establishing certain minimal standards.

[31] U.S. Department of Justice, Civil Rights Division, Special Litigation Section. "Juvenile Correctional Facilities." [Online] http://www.usdoj.gov/crt/split/juveniles.htm

[32] Stahl, A. L., C. Puzzanchera, A. Sladky, T. A. Finnegan, N. Tierney, and H. N. Snyder. *Juvenile Court Statistics 2001–2002.* Pittsburgh, PA: National Center for Juvenile Justice, 2005, p. 25.

[33] Ibid., p. 34.

[34] *Juvenile Justice Glossary.* [Online] http://www.juvenilejusticefyi.com/juvenile_justice_glossary.html

[35] Snyder, H. N. *Juvenile Arrests 2004.* Washington, DC: Office of Juvenile Justice and Delinquency Prevention, p. 5.

[36] Krisberg and Austin, *Reinventing Juvenile Justice*, pp. 86–87; Bartollas, C. *Juvenile Delinquency* (6th ed.). Boston, MA: Allyn & Bacon, 2003, p. 415.

[37] Goldstein, J. "Police Discretion Not to Invoke the Criminal Process: Low Visibility Decisions in the Administration of Justice." *Yale Law Journal* 69: 543–594 (1960).

[38] Bartollas, *Juvenile Delinquency*, p. 412.

[39] Ibid., pp. 412–414; Bartollas, C. and S. J. Miller. *Juvenile Justice in America* (3rd ed.). Upper Saddle River, NJ: Prentice-Hall, 2001, pp. 70–71.

[40] This is documented in Chesney-Lind, M. and R. G. Shelden. *Girls, Delinquency and Juvenile Justice* (3rd ed.). Belmont, CA: Wadsworth, 2004, chs. 7 and 8.

[41] Wolfgang, M. E., R. Figlio, and T. Sellin. *Delinquency in a Birth Cohort*. Chicago: Aldine, 1972; Bishop, D. and C. E. Frazier. "The Influence of Race in Juvenile Justice Processing." *Journal of Research in Crime and Delinquency* 25: 242–263 (1988).

[42] Piliavin, I. and S. Briar. "Police Encounters with Juveniles." *American Journal of Sociology* 70: 206–214 (1964); Werthman, C. and I. Piliavin. "Gang Members and the Police." In J. Skolnick and T. C. Gray (eds.), *Police in America*. Boston: Little, Brown, 1975; Klinger, D. A. "Demeanor or Crime? Why 'Hostile' Citizens Are More Likely To Be Arrested." *Criminology* 32: 475–493 (1994); Worden, R. E. and R. L. Shepard. "Demeanor, Crime and Police Behavior: A Reexamination of the Police Services Study Data." *Criminology* 34: 61–82 (1996).

[43] Goldman, N. *The Differential Selection of Juvenile Offenders for Court Appearance*. New York: National Council on Crime and Delinquency, 1967.

[44] Bazemore, G. and S. Senjo. "Police Encounters with Juveniles Revisited: An Exploratory Study of Themes and Styles in Community Policing." *Policing: An International Journal of Police Strategy and Management* 20: 60–82 (1997); see also Pope, C. and W. Feyerherm. "Minority Status and Juvenile Justice Processing: An Assessment of the Research Literature" (Parts I and II). *Criminal Justice Abstracts* 22 (2, 3) (1990).

[45] Bartollas and Miller, *Juvenile Justice in America*, p. 144.

[46] Jankowski, M. S. *Islands in the Street: Gangs and American Urban Society*. Berkeley: University of California Press, 1990.

[47] Federal Bureau of Investigation. *Crime in the United States*, 2006, table 33. [Online] http://www.fbi.gov/ucr/cius2006/data/table_32.html

[48] McCorkle, R. and T. Miethe. *Panic: Rhetoric and Reality in the War on Street Gangs*. Saddle River, NJ: Prentice-Hall, 2001.

[49] Ibid. See also Chesney-Lind and Shelden, *Girls, Delinquency and Juvenile Justice*.

[50] Miller, J. G. *Search and Destroy: African-American Males in the Criminal Justice System*. New York: Cambridge University Press, 1996, p. 8; similar documentation can be found in the following studies: Currie, E. *Reckoning: Drugs, the Cities, and the American Future*. New York: Hill and Wang, 1993; Tonry, M. *Malign Neglect: Race, Crime, and Punishment in America*. New York: Oxford University Press, 1995; Lockwood, D., A. E. Pottieger and J. A. Inciardi. "Crack Use, Crime by Crack Users, and Ethnicity." In D. F. Hawkins (ed.), *Ethnicity, Race, and Crime*. Albany: SUNY Press, 1995.

[51] Miller, *Search and Destroy*, pp. 84–86.

[52] McGarrell, E. "Trends in Racial Disproportionality in Juvenile Court Processing: 1985–1989." *Crime and Delinquency* 39: 29–48 (1993).

[53] Fellner, J. "Stark Racial Disparities Found in Georgia Drug Law Enforcement." *Overcrowded Times* 7(5): 11 (October 1996).

54 Stahl et al., *Juvenile Court Statistics 2001–2002*, pp. 20–21, 27.

55 Walker, S., C. Spohn, and M. DeLone. *The Color of Justice: Race, Ethnicity, and Crime in America* (4th ed). Belmont, CA: Wadsworth, 2007, pp. 392–395.

56 Center on Juvenile and Criminal Justice. "Race and Juvenile Justice." 2004. [Online] http://cjcj.org/jjic/race_jj.php, emphasis in the original.

57 Building Blocks for Youth. "And Justice for Some." April 2000. [Online] http://cjcj.org/jjic/race_jj.php

58 Moore, D. "As Some U.S. Cities Make Progress in Lowering the Number of Blacks in Juvenile Detention, Columbia's Numbers Rise." *Columbia Tribune* (February 8, 2004). [Online] http://archive.columbia tribune.com/2004/feb/20040208feat051.asp

59 Johnston, L. D., P. M. O'Malley, J. G. Bachman, & J. E. Schulenberg. (2007). *Monitoring the Future: National Results on Adolescent Drug Use: Overview of Key Findings, 2006* (NIH Publication No. 07-6202). Bethesda, MD: National Institute on Drug Abuse, p. 46.

60 Wolfgang, Riglio, and Sellin, *Delinquency in a Birth Cohort.*

61 Sampson, R. J. "SES and Official Reaction to Delinquency." *American Sociological Review* 51: 876–885 (1986).

62 See Reiman, J. *The Rich Get Richer and the Poor Get Prison* (8th ed.). Boston: Allyn & Bacon, 2007. Looking at case files in just about any juvenile court—from one end of the country to the next—will reveal that kids from privileged environments, with intact families and many resources available, will be far more likely to avoid a court appearance; their cases are usually settled at intake. The author has personally examined in detail more than 1,000 such cases in Las Vegas. Sitting in the waiting areas just outside courtrooms, he has observed that the only people dressed in clothing that would indicate higher social classes are court probation officers, judges, and lawyers.

63 Chambliss, W. "The Saints and the Roughnecks." In W. J. Chambliss (ed.), *Criminal Law in Action.* New York: John Wiley, 1975.

64 Ibid., p. 77.

65 Ibid., p. 74.

66 Ibid., p. 78.

67 For good summaries of this literature, see: Gilbert, D. *The American Class Structure* (5th ed.). Belmont, CA: Wadsworth, 1998; Marger, M. N. *Social Inequality: Patterns and Processes* (3rd ed.). New York: McGraw-Hill, 2005.

68 Shelden, R. G. "Detention Diversion Advocacy: An Evaluation." *OJJDP Juvenile Justice Bulletin* (September 1999).

69 Brown, W. B. "The Presentence Report and Risk Assessment." Unpublished doctoral dissertation, University of Nevada–Las Vegas, Department of Sociology, 1992.

70 Bartollas and Miller, *Juvenile Justice in America*, p. 110.

71 Sickmund, M., T. J. Sladky, and W. Kang. "Census of Juveniles in Residential Placement Databook." 2005. [Online] http://ojjdp.ncjrs.org/ojstatbb/cjrp/asp/Offense_Detained.asp?state=0&topic=Offense_Detained&year=2003&percent=rate

72 Stahl et al., *Juvenile Court Statistics 2001–2002*, pp. 27, 29.

73 One catalyst for the need for diversion came from: President's Commission on Law and Administration

of Justice. *Task Force Report: Juvenile Delinquency and Youth Crime*. Washington, DC: U.S. Government Printing Office, 1967.

[74] Bartollas and Miller, *Juvenile Justice in America*, pp. 122–123.

[75] OJJDP Statistical Briefing Book (March 19, 2007). [Online] http://www.ojjdp.ncjrs.org/ojstatbb/court/JCSCF_Display.asp?ID=qa06601&year=2004&group=1&type=1&text=#

[76] Sickmund et al., "Census of Juveniles in Residential Placement Databook." [Online] http://ojjdp.ncjrs.org/ojstatbb/cjrp/asp/Offense_Committed.asp?state=0&topic=Offense_Committed&year=2003&percent=rate

[77] Bortner, M. A. *Inside a Juvenile Court: The Tarnished Idea of Individualized Justice*. New York: New York University Press, 1982; Thornberry, T. P. "Race, Socioeconomic Status and Sentencing in the Juvenile Justice System." *Journal of Criminal Law and Criminology* 64: 90–98 (1973), and "Sentencing Disparities in the Juvenile Justice System." *Journal of Criminal Law and Criminology* 70 (Summer 1979); Cohen, L. E. *Delinquency Dispositions: An Empirical Analysis of Processing Decisions in Three Juvenile Courts.* Washington, DC: U.S. Department of Justice, 1975.

[78] Peterson, R. D. "Youthful Offender Designations and Sentencing in the New York Criminal Courts." *Social Problems* 35 (April 1988).

[79] Chambliss, W. J. (1995). "Crime Control and Ethnic Minorities: Legitimizing Racial Oppression by Creating Moral Panics." In Hawkins, *Ethnicity, Race, and Crime*; Chambliss, W. J. *Power, Politics, and Crime.* Boulder, CO: Westview 1999; Cole, D. *No Equal Justice: Race and Class in the American Criminal Justice System*. New York: The New Press, 1999.

[80] Stahl et al., *Juvenile Court Statistics 2001–2002*, p. 74.

[81] This term seems to be a catchall of several different offenses, including "intentionally obstructing court or law enforcement efforts in the administration of justice, acting in a way calculated to lessen the authority or dignity of the court, failing to obey the lawful order of a court, escaping from confinement, and violating probation or parole. This term includes contempt, perjury, bribery of witnesses, failure to report a crime, and nonviolent resistance of arrest." Ibid., appendix B, p. 82.

[82] War rhetoric is similar—killing innocent civilians is called "collateral damage."

[83] Griffin, P. and M. King. "National Overviews." *State Juvenile Justice Profiles*. Pittsburgh, PA: National Center for Juvenile Justice, 2006. [Online] http://www.ncjj.org/stateprofiles/overviews/faq12.asp

[84] Ibid. More detail and individual state procedures are available on the Web site.

[85] Ibid.

[86] Snyder, H. N. and M. Sickmund. *Juvenile Offenders and Victims: 2006 National Report.* Washington, DC: Office of Juvenile Justice and Delinquency Prevention, 2006, p. 218, 222.

[87] Ibid., p. 219–220.

[88] Ibid., pp. 230–231.

[89] *Statistical Abstracts of the U.S.* Washington, DC: U.S. Government Printing Office, 1975, p. 419; 2003 figures from Sickmund et al., "Census of Juveniles in Residential Placement Databook." [Online] http://ojjdp.ncjrs.org/ojstatbb/cjrp/asp/State_Race.asp?state=&topic=State_Race&year=2003&percent=row

[90] Sickmund et al., "Census of Juveniles in Residential Placement Databook." [Online] http://ojjdp.ncjrs.org/ojstatbb/cjrp/asp/State_Race.asp?state=&topic=State_Race&year=2003&percent=rate

91 Shelden, R. G. "If it Looks Like a Prison . . ." *Las Vegas City Life* (August 13, 1999). [Online] http://www.sheldensays.com/i_told_you_so.htm

92 For a particularly gruesome account of actions within one of these "correctional" institutions see the movie *Sleepers* (starring Brad Pitt, Robert DeNiro, and Dustin Hoffman).

93 Vinter, R. D., T. M. Newcomb, and R. Kish (eds.). *Time Out: A National Study of Juvenile Correctional Programs*. Ann Arbor: National Assessment of Juvenile Corrections, The University of Michigan, 1976.

94 Irwin, J. *The Felon*. Englewood Cliffs, NJ: Prentice-Hall, 1970, p. 74. These types still can be found in many prisons today. See Austin, J. and J. Irwin. *It's about Time: America's Incarceration Binge* (3rd ed.). Belmont, CA: Wadsworth, 2001.

95 Barker, G. E. and W. T. Adams. "The Social Structure of a Correctional Institution." *Journal of Criminal Law, Criminology and Police Science* 49: 417–499 (1959); Polsky, H. *Cottage Six*. New York: Russell Sage Foundation, 1962; Jesness, C. F. *The Fricot Ranch Study*. Sacramento: State of California, Department of the Youth Authority, 1965; Street, D., R. D. Vinter, and C. Perrow. *Organization for Treatment*. New York: Free Press, 1966.

96 Bartollas, C., S. H. Miller, and S. Dinitz. *Juvenile Victimization: The Institutional Paradox*. Beverly Hills: Sage, 1976.

97 Bartollas and Miller, *Juvenile Justice in America*, pp. 264–265.

98 Ibid.

99 Miller, J. H., C. Bartollas, and S. Dinitz, "Juvenile Victimization Revisited: A Study of TICO Fifteen Years Later" (unpublished manuscript), cited in Bartollas and Miller, *Juvenile Justice in America*, pp. 265–266.

100 Federal Interagency Forum on Child and Family Statistics. *America's Children: Key National Indicators of Well-Being*. Washington, DC: Author, July 2007, pp. x–xi. [Online] http://www.childstats.gov/pdf/ac2007/ac_07.pdf

101 *Violent Victimization Rates by Age, 1973–2005*. [Online] http://www.ojp.usdoj.gov/bjs/glance/tables/vagetab.htm

102 Snyder, H. N. and M. Sickmund. *Juvenile Offenders and Victims: 2006 National Report*. Washington, DC: Office of Juvenile Justice and Delinquency Prevention, 2006, p. 96.

103 Editorial. "Racism in a Small Town." *Chicago Tribune* (September 20, 2007) p. 20.

104 Kovach, G. C. and A. Campo-Flores. "A Town in Turmoil." *Newsweek* (August 27, 2007).

105 "Racism in a Small Town."

106 Witt, H. "Racial Demons Rear Heads." *Chicago Tribune* (May 20, 2007) p. 3.

107 Witt, H. "Charge Reduced in 'Jena 6' Case." *Chicago Tribune* (June 26, 2007) p. 4.

108 Witt, H. "Louisiana Teen Guilty in School Beating Case." *Chicago Tribune* (June 29, 2007) p. 7.

109 Witt, H. "Demonstrators Descend on Jena." *Chicago Tribune* (September 20, 2007) p. 14.

110 Black, L. "Jackson Takes Jena 6 Case to Top." *Chicago Tribune* (September 24, 2007) sec. 2, p. 3.

111 Witt, H. "Jena 6 Defendant Out of Jail." *Chicago Tribune* (September 28, 2007) p. 4.

112 Ibid.

113 Witt, H. "Jena 6 Teen's Return to Jail Draws Queries." *Chicago Tribune* (October 13, 2007) p. 3.

114 Ibid.

115 Witt, H. "Court Asked to End Jena Trial Secrecy." *Chicago Tribune* (October 23, 2007) p. 4.

116 Trice, D. T. "Jena 6 Case Isn't Perfect, But It's Clear." *Chicago Tribune* (September 24, 2007) Sec. 2, p. 1.

seventeen

Women and the Criminal Justice System

I did not know the daughter of Yvette War-rington, one of my nontraditional criminal jus-tice students. Shevonne Warrington was the older of Yvette's two children; she had changed after the suicide death of her father several years earlier.[1] She began using methamphetamine and eventually ended up in Oregon's prison system, where she gave birth to a boy. Yvette temporarily adopted her new grandson. Several months later, Yvette was sitting in my office and blaming her-self for the problems her daughter was experienc-ing. Later that evening I received an e-mail from Yvette saying that when she arrived home the police were waiting in her driveway. They told her that her daughter had died from a heroin overdose. Several weeks later Yvette found a poem written days before Shevonne's death.

Damn poison keeps pulling us down and spinning our heads all around until "fuck"!! we're all six feet underground. Then listen, no sound at last our souls are at ease for now we are truly free!

No more racing thoughts, no longer can we cause our loved ones worries or pain. All their questions and prayers have been answered, for now they know exactly where we are. I pray they can finally have a true night's sleep.

Shevonne Warrington
Former Oregon Prisoner
(Died drug overdose 11/22/06)

WOMEN AND THE LAW: A HISTORICAL OVERVIEW

Several stereotypical images of women have helped shape both the law and the defini-tions of what behaviors and what kinds of people are considered criminal: (1) woman as the pawn of biology (controlled by biological forces beyond her control); (2) woman as pas-sive and weak; (3) woman as impulsive and nonanalytical (needs the logical guidance of a man); (4) woman as impressionable and in need of protection (childlike and gullible); (5) the active woman as masculine (if traditional role abandoned, behavior deemed unnatural); (6) the criminal woman as purely evil (woman who "falls from grace" and the normally pure state of womanhood); and (7) the Madonna-whore duality (a woman is either a paragon of virtue or a seductress).[2] Stereotypes of female criminals have persisted since the nineteenth century. One observer noted that women pris-oners today are viewed as "tramps," "cheap women," "wild," "loose," "immoral," and "fallen"; they have broken not only social laws but also unwritten moral laws as well. In popular films they are often portrayed as "amazons" or "bull dikes," "crude nympho-maniacs," or even "psychopaths."[3]

These images have developed over the centuries, and there is a parallel tradition in law back to ancient Greece and Rome that views women as perpetual children. In ancient Greece, for instance, only men could be citizens in the political arena, and most of the slaves were women. In Rome the status of women and slaves improved somewhat under the rule of **patria potestas** ("power of the father"), although the term implied more a *property relationship* than a family relationship. The woman had to turn any income she received over to the head of the household; she had no rights outside of the family and no rights concerning her children or rights to divorce. Unlike slaves, women could not be emancipated under Roman law. A woman's relationship to her husband was designated by the concept of *manus* (hand)— the basis for the tradition of asking a woman's father for "her hand in marriage."[4]

Gerda Lerner defines **patriarchy** as

> the manifestation and institutionalization of male dominance over women and children in the family and the extension of male dominance over women in society in general. It implies that men hold power in all the important institutions of society and that women are deprived of access to such power.

The legal institution is one of various institutions controlled by men and used to control women. Lerner uses the analogy of a stage in a theater to illustrate the concept of patriarchy.

> Men and women live on a stage, on which they act out their assigned roles, equal in importance. The play cannot go on without both kinds of performers. Neither of them "contributes" more or less to the whole; neither is marginal or dispensable. But the stage set is conceived, painted, defined by men. Men have written the play, have directed the show, interpreted the meanings of the action. They have assigned themselves the most interesting, most heroic parts, giving women the supporting roles.[5]

Lerner notes that as women become more aware of this inequality, they begin to protest, asking for more roles, and more equality in determining what is assigned. At times they may "upstage the men," and at other times they may stand in for a male performer. Yet even when they win equal access to desired roles, they must first "qualify" according to terms set by the men, who are the judges of whether women measure up. Preference is given to women who are "docile," and those who act differently are punished—by ridicule, ostracism, and exclusion. In time, women realize that getting "equal" parts does not translate into "equality," as long as the script, stage setting, props, and so on are controlled by men.[6]

Recall the discussion of commodification from chapter 15. Parenti describes the concept as it applies to women: "the process of objectifying and transforming the female appearance and body to fit marketable (that is, marriageable) standards."[7] Women have gone through hundreds of different procedures over the years (stretching lips and necks, flattened breasts during certain times and expanded at other times, painted nails and lips, etc.) to attract the attention and/or the approval of men.

Much of Roman law was eventually incorporated into English common law, which in turn was copied (with few significant changes) in the United States. For several years, the only law book used was Blackstone's *Commentaries on the Laws in England,* originally published in 1765. American family law incorporated Blackstone's famous dictum that the husband and wife are as one and that one is the husband.[8]

Under the early U.S. legal system, a wife could not sue, execute a deed, or engage in any other similar practices without the consent of her husband. Women were denied the right to vote until 1921; in general, laws that were "designed to protect the interests of 'persons' simply did not apply to women." In fact, the Supreme Court ruled in 1867 that a woman who had completed law school and had passed the bar in Illinois nevertheless had no right to practice law. The Court stated that the "natural and proper timidity and delicacy which belongs to the female sex evidently unfits it for many of the occupations in civil life" and the "destiny and mission of women are to fulfill the noble and benign offices of wife and mother."[9]

Throughout colonial America a woman had no identity independent of her relationship with her father or her husband. The husband had rights over his wife that resembled in many ways the rights of masters over their slaves. Even if a man killed his wife, the law would treat him with far more leniency than his wife would receive if she killed him. In fact, a man who killed his wife was treated almost the same as if he had killed an animal or a servant. Colonial law was often very specific about women. Some crimes were designated as women's crimes, and they were severely punished. For instance, the crime of being a "common scold" was reserved for women who spoke too loudly in public or berated their husbands. Punishment for scolding consisted of public humiliation through the use of "ducking stools" and "branks." The former was a chair on which the female offender sat, which was then submerged in a pool of water several times. The latter was a metal cage that fit over the head with a metal tab inserted into the mouth (sometimes also fitted with a spike) over the tongue to prevent the "scold" from talking. The witch hunts in the late seventeenth century are chilling examples of the use of the legal system to punish women who dared challenge the male power structure. Most of the women labeled witches were those who were outspoken or had gained informal power either as healers or as community leaders.[10]

Although woman played an active role in efforts to pass the Thirteenth, Fourteenth, and Fifteenth Amendments that extended equal rights to all "persons," the amendments did not apply to women.[11] Not until 1971, in the case of *Reed v. Reed* did the Court extend the equal protection clause of the Fourteenth Amendment to women.[12] Before this time, the prevailing attitude was perhaps best reflected in an 1869 Illinois Supreme Court decision. The court stated that "God designed the sexes to occupy different spheres of action, and that it belonged to men to make, apply, and execute the laws."[13]

Even in cases where the law supposedly "protected" women as victims of rape, abduction, seduction, and carnal abuse, the "victim" had to "prove that she had, in fact, been a victim," that "she had led a chaste and virtuous life prior to the crime against her."[14] In fact, there was once a law, in Mississippi, that granted the right of husbands to beat their wives, a law upheld by that state's supreme court in 1824. The law was overturned by the U.S. Supreme Court in 1874.[15]

The feminist movement of the nineteenth century led to several significant changes in the legal status of women. The *Married Women's Property Acts* granted women certain property rights previously denied them. Some jurisdictions passed laws that recognized domestic violence as a crime. In the first part of the twentieth century, women made some progress in the workplace. These few gains were, however, scattered and localized. In general, the law and the legal system continued to treat women as second-class citizens.[16]

Recall from chapter 1 that the first stage in the criminalization process is legislation. The behavior that is considered a social harm is defined in laws written by legislators, who are influenced by public opinion and by interest groups who try to influence public policy. As Natalie Sokoloff, Barbara Price, and Jeanne Flavin caution:

> The Courts and the law, however, do not exist in a society that is neutral with regard to gender, race, nationality, class, age, sexual orientation, or physical ability. Consequently, the legal system frequently fails to acknowledge that legal rights are sometimes overshadowed by political realities.[17]

Because of the long tradition of treating women as property, for centuries men were not held accountable for their crimes against women. Their crimes were overlooked because of entrenched sexism in the male-dominated legal system.[18] Until 1976, men could not be charged with raping their wives. Nebraska was the first state to pass a law defining that behavior as a crime. Although all fifty states have now passed similar laws, thirty-two states allow for exceptions in their statutes. "Although today women are seen as equal before the law, socially entrenched biases continue to pose barriers to full recognition of women's rights as human beings."[19]

WOMEN AND CRIME

Women commit far less crime than men. Of the 10.5 million arrests in 2006, 24% (2.5 million) were women.[20] In addition, the crimes women commit are far less serious than those men commit (see table 17.1). There are very significant gender differences in the overall patterns of crime, and the "careers" of female offenders are of much shorter duration than those of male offenders. Although women are less likely than men to end up in prison, their rate of imprisonment has increased significantly in recent years.[21]

Table 17.1   Arrests by Sex, 2006

Offense	Male (%)	Female (%)
Total	76.3	23.7
Index Crimes		
Homicide	89.1	10.9
Rape	98.7	1.3
Robbery	88.7	11.3
Aggravated assault	79.3	20.7
Burglary	85.5	14.5
Larceny-theft	62.3	37.7
Motor-vehicle theft	82.3	17.7
Arson	83.0	17.0
Violent crime	82.2	17.8
Property crime	68.8	31.2
Part II Crimes		
Other assaults	75.0	25.0
Forgery and counterfeiting	60.9	39.1
Fraud	55.5	44.5
Embezzlement	47.3	52.7
Stolen property	81.1	18.9
Vandalism	83.2	16.8
Weapons	92.0	8.0
Prostitution	35.8	64.2
Sex offenses (except rape and prostitution)	91.3	8.7
Drug-abuse violations	81.1	18.9
Gambling	90.0	10.0
Offenses against family and children	75.5	24.5
Driving under the influence	80.0	20.0
Liquor laws	72.9	27.1
Drunkenness	84.5	15.5
Disorderly conduct	73.9	26.1
Vagrancy	77.8	22.2
All other (except traffic)	77.1	22.9
Suspicion	78.0	22.0
Curfew and loitering	68.9	31.1
Runaways	43.4	56.6

Source: Federal Bureau of Investigation. *Crime in the United States, 2006*. [Online] http://www.fbi.gov/ucr/cius2006/data/table_42.html

Patterns of Female Crime

For centuries, women have been arrested primarily for relatively minor offenses. This pattern can be traced as far back as fourteenth-century England. Most of the women transported to Australia on convict ships during the late eighteenth and early nineteenth centuries were poor women (servants, maids, and laundresses) who had been convicted of petty theft (mostly shoplifting) or prostitution. Most of them experienced sexual abuse aboard the ships, and about one-third died along the way. In the American colonies these offense patterns continued, with the addition of the offense of "unruly woman" to the list. Later in the nineteenth and well into the early twentieth century women—the vast majority of whom lived on the margins of society and were disproportionately immigrants and racial minorities—were arrested for public-order offenses and minor theft.[22]

The patterns continue today. Women generally have been arrested for such offenses as larceny–theft (which has consistently been ranked number one of all offenses committed by women, including juveniles; the most common offense within this category is shoplifting[23]), fraud (mostly what is known as "welfare fraud"—a reflection of the poverty of these women), drugs, disorderly conduct (which in many cases is actually prostitution), and a host of other minor offenses subsumed under the category "all other offenses."[24] There have been some changes in the patterns of arrest, however.

One new trend is the increase in arrests for assault—aggravated assault, "other assaults," offenses against the family and children—and arrests for drug offenses. The increased arrests for assaults can be attributed mostly to the increased attention given by law enforcement to domestic violence. It is ironic that women have historically been the victims of violence within the home (along with children), and the behavior wasn't even recognized as a crime. Now that laws have changed, police now arrest both partners in the majority of cases.[25]

Prior victimization is a significant background variable for women who commit certain crimes. Studies indicate that the majority of women who commit murder kill someone they knew intimately, such as a husband or boyfriend. Many of the women (40 to 78%, depending on the study), had experienced abuse; many of them fit the battered-woman syndrome. Over half of all women prisoners have experienced some form of abuse; more than one-third experienced sexual abuse. One of the pathways leading women into a life of crime and repeated contacts with the criminal justice system is victimization by the men in their lives.[26] Kathleen Daly describes a typical pattern that begins with an intolerable home situation, which leads to running away, which results in prostitution as a source of income to survive on the streets, which replicates the cycle of victimization either by male clients or intimate male friends.[27] Eleanor Miller found an almost identical scenario in her research on a group of women offenders in Milwaukee. The women she studied had abusive parents (often alcoholic), and their lives of crime typically began with running away, after which they became involved in the lives of a variety of abusive men.[28]

Class, Race, and Women Offenders

As with their male counterparts, any analysis of women, crime, and criminal justice must consider the interrelationship of class and race. Hundreds of studies covering more than a century confirm that class and race are strong predictors of crime and play significant roles in the processing of offenders through the criminal justice system.[29] Indeed, even a cursory review of the literature shows that the vast majority of female offenders, especially those who end up in prison, are drawn from the lower class and are racial minorities.[30]

Women's crime cannot be separated from the overall social context within which it occurs. In recent years the plight of women has not improved a great deal. Women have entered the labor force in increased numbers in recent years, but their employment is largely in traditional "female" occupations. Women constitute over 92% of all nurses,

74% of all teachers, 75% of all office and administrative support positions (clerical work, cashiers, etc.), and 78% of all personal care and service occupations.[31] While some gains have been made, women still earn less than men. As men lose higher paying jobs, women have seen increased percentages of employment. In 1960, 89% of all married men and 32% of married women were in the labor force; in 2005, the male percentage had decreased to 77%, and the female percentage had increased to 61%.[32]

Increasing numbers of households consist of a woman and her children, contributing to what is sometimes called the *feminization of poverty* (a somewhat misleading term in that it might be interpreted as suggesting that the problem is racially neutral). In 1960 only 6% of all families with one or more children were headed by a woman; by 2005 the percentage was 23.4 (versus 4.7% of households headed by the father). The mother was the head of the household in half of the African-American families compared to 16% for white families, 10% for Asian families, and 25% for Hispanic families.[33] In 2004, 29% of families with a black female head of household had incomes below the poverty level compared to 8.1% of families with a white female head of household, and 20.5% of families with a Hispanic female head of household.[34]

Daly provided a detailed example of the role of class and race in her study of women offenders in a court system in New Haven, Connecticut. From a larger sample of 397 cases, she focused on 40 men and 40 women who were sentenced to prison through all the stages of the criminal justice process. Of the 40 women, 60% were African American, 12% were Puerto Rican, and the remaining 28% were white. Half of the women were raised in single-parent families; only two grew up in middle-class households. Most of these women were described by Daly as having grown up in families "whose economic circumstances were precarious"; in about two-thirds of the cases the biological fathers were not present while they were growing up. Only one-third completed high school or earned a GED (General Education Diploma). Two-thirds "had either a sporadic or no paid employment record," and over 80% were unemployed at the time of their most recent arrest.[35]

Next, we discuss the history of women's prisons from the early nineteenth century to the present day, and then we examine the daily reality of life inside a women's prison.

WOMEN'S PRISONS

As discussed in chapter 11, the modern prison system did not emerge until the late eighteenth and early nineteenth centuries. Prior to the mid-nineteenth century, women offenders were housed in the same institutions as men, although in separate areas. Men, women, children, and the mentally ill—for both petty and serious offenses—suffered the deplorable conditions of early jails and workhouses. The first effort to separate women offenders from men took place in 1853.

Historical Origins

In colonial America few women (or men) offenders were incarcerated. Of the white women who were arrested, most were charged with violations of religious law (e.g., violation of the Sabbath, adultery). They were held in local jails for trial, and the usual punishment was a form of public reprimand and humiliation, such as whipping or the "stocks and the pillory."[36] For African-American women the situation was quite different, because the majority were either slaves or indentured servants.[37] Most violations of laws by these women were handled informally on the plantation, but occasionally the slave owners had to rely on the local criminal justice system. In such cases they often used what were called "Negro Courts," set up specifically for slaves who violated laws that were applicable to slaves but not whites—for example, "striking the master three times" (punishable by death). Sentences of death or even incarceration were rarely imposed on slaves because such action would have removed a worker from the fields. Not until after the Civil War did African Americans begin to appear in penal institutions in large numbers, usually because of "Jim Crow"

laws and "black codes." Many were subjected to the "convict lease" system.[38]

American jails were often extensions of the earlier workhouses and poorhouses. In 1797, the first institution for felons only, Newgate Prison, opened in New York. Women offenders were housed in an area separate from men.[39] Treatment of prisoners, both male and female, changed dramatically in the 1820s after the Auburn State Prison (also housing both men and women in separate quarters) opened. Overcrowding soon set in (a condition that continues to plague prisons).

There was little interest in the women offenders, who were viewed with particular distaste. Conditions were so bad that the prison chaplain once remarked that it was bad enough for male prisoners, "but to be a female convict, for any protracted period, would be worse than death."[40] When Newgate was closed in the 1820s, the men were all eventually transferred to Auburn prison, and the women were sent to Bellevue Penitentiary in New York City. However, conditions were so horrible at Bellevue that a women's prison was built at Mount Pleasant, New York, (on the grounds of Sing Sing Prison) and opened in 1839.[41] Around the same time a "women's annex" was built on the grounds of the Ohio Penitentiary and opened in 1837. At this time it was widely believed that women offenders should be treated more harshly than their male counterparts. This belief was justified by the argument that the female offender was more depraved than her male counterpart because, having been born pure, she had "fallen" farther from grace than he; in fact, she was often blamed for the crimes of men.[42]

Most of the activities female prisoners performed in these early prisons (activities still performed today) were designed to "fit them for the duties of domestic life." At first there was little or no separation of male and female prisoners. Several reformers, such as Elizabeth Fry (1780–1845), Dorothea Dix (1802–1887), Clara Barton (1821–1912), and Josephine Shaw Lowell (1843–1905), began to advocate for separate facilities and other changes. One of the first results of reform activities was the hiring of female matrons, beginning in Maryland after the Civil War. The majority of nineteenth and early twentieth-century prison reformers were women from the upper class.[43]

Separate facilities for women emerged following the 1870 meeting of the National Congress on Penitentiary and Reformatory Discipline in Cincinnati. One of the resolutions of this conference was that the goal of prisons should be *rehabilitation* rather than punishment. In 1873 the first prison for women was opened, the Indiana Women's Prison. Kathryn Watterson notes:

> It embraced the revolutionary notion that women criminals should be rehabilitated rather than punished. Young girls from the age of sixteen who "habitually associate with dissolute persons" and other uneducated and indigent women were ushered into the model prison apart from men and isolated from the "corruption and chaos" of the outside world. The essential ingredient of their rehabilitative treatment would be to bring discipline and regularity into their lives. Obedience and systematic religious education would, it was felt, help the women form orderly habits and moral values.[44]

Several other women's prisons were opened over the next forty years, including the Massachusetts Prison at Framington (1877), the New York Reformatory for Women at Westfield Farm (1901), the District of Columbia Reformatory for Women (1910), and the New Jersey Reformatory for Women at Clinton (1913). These institutions were intended to be "separate, home-like institutions" where women "would have an opportunity" to "mend their criminal ways" and "learn to be good housewives, helpmates and mothers."[45]

Estelle Freedman suggests that four factors contributed to the rise of the women's prison movement between 1870 and 1900: (1) an apparent increase in female crime after the war and an increase in women prisoners; (2) the women's Civil War social service movement; (3) the emergence of charity and prison reform movements in general, many of them emphasizing the problem of crime and the notion of rehabilitation; and (4) the beginnings of a feminist movement that emphasized a separatist approach and a rein-

terpretation of the notion of the "fallen woman." The alleged crime wave among women following the war primarily involved the wives and daughters of men who had died in the war. The large number of deaths during the war created a class of poor women who began to be arrested for mostly public-order offenses and offenses against morality, such as "lewd and lascivious carriage, stubbornness, idle and disorderly conduct, drunkenness, and vagrancy, as well as fornication and adultery." Several reformers placed the blame for the rise of female criminality on the attitudes and sexist practices of men. Josephine Shaw Lowell complained that many women "from early girlhood have been tossed from poorhouse to jail, and from jail to poorhouse, until the last trace of womanhood in them has been destroyed." She condemned law officers who regarded women "as objects of derision and sport" and who "wantonly assaulted and degraded numerous young women prisoners." Many specifically blamed the "double standard" whereby men condemned female sexual activity while condoning their own and, moreover, arrested and imprisoned prostitutes but not the men who enjoyed their services. Finally, reformers complained of male guards in prisons where women were confined. Investigators found that women "may be forced to minister to the lust of the officials or if they refused, submit to the inflection of the lash until they do."[46]

Reformers argued that women prisoners would be treated more fairly and would be more likely to amend their behavior if they were confined in separate institutions controlled by women. Reformers countered male resistance by arguing that "the shield of a pure woman's presence" would enable them "to govern the depraved and desperate of her own sex."[47] The first reformatories relied on "domestic routines." After release, women were placed in "suitable" private homes as housekeepers. These institutions, and most to follow, were designed according to the "cottage plan." Separate housing facilities were as similar as possible to an average family home in order to teach those who were confined to become good homemakers.

Although the women reformers often claimed to be staunch feminists, the organization of prison life they created was perfectly suited to keeping women in their traditional "place." In fact, the design won the approval of many skeptical men, one of whom commented, "Girls and women should be trained to adorn homes with the virtues which make their lives noble and ennobling. *It is only in this province, that they may most fittingly fill their mission.*"[48] The end result, of course, perpetuated women's traditional roles of dependency as housewives and maids. Even a cursory look at women's prisons today reveals that little has changed, especially the treatment of women as children and training them to continue their domestic roles.

Not surprisingly, the early prison system reflected the segregation practices of the general society. African-American women were housed in prisons where there was little or no hope of any sort of rehabilitation (i.e., "custodial" prisons); white women were placed in "reformatories" where there was at least a formal commitment to rehabilitation.[49] In 1880 African-American women constituted 86% of the female inmates in the South, compared to only 7% in the Northeast, 29% in the Midwest, and 20% in the West. In 1904 the percentages had increased to 90% in the South, followed by 48% in the Midwest.[50] In 1923 almost two-thirds (64.5%) of the women inmates in custodial prisons were African American, compared to only 11.9% in reformatory institutions. By 1978, African-American women constituted half of the total female prison population. The percentages declined somewhat beginning at the end of the 1980s, largely because more white and Hispanic women were also being sentenced on drug charges.

The federal prison system for women developed much later than the state prison system. Women convicted of federal crimes were generally sentenced to state prisons, but as the number of female inmates grew after the Civil War, efforts were made to open the federal system to women. The first of the federal prisons for women only was in Alderson, West Virginia. When it opened in 1927,

it housed 50 women in fourteen cottages. By 1929 there were more than 250 inmates, most of whom had violated various drug laws (the Harrison Act of 1914 outlawed several kinds of drugs) and the Volstead Act of 1919 (Prohibition).[51] Largely in response to the rise of organized crime (which was a direct result of Prohibition), legislation passed in 1930 created the federal Bureau of Prisons, which authorized the construction of several new prisons.[52]

Largely because of the war on drugs, the number of new women's prisons has dramatically increased in recent years. Between 1940 and the end of the 1960s, only twelve new women's prisons were built. In the 1970s, seventeen were built; in the 1980s, thirty-four.[53]

Increasing Rates of Incarceration

Women constitute around 24% of all those arrested and about 7% of those in prison, but their numbers and their rate of incarceration have been increasing dramatically during the past twenty years. In 2005 there were 98,602 women in federal and state prisons (compared to 8,675 in 1975). Women accounted for 6.7% of all prisoners (versus 3.6% in 1975).[54] The number of women incarcerated increased 1037% in thirty years, while the percentage of women prisoners increased 86%. The incarceration *rate* of women rose from 8 per 100,000 in 1965 (also the rate in 1975) to 65 per 100,000 in 2005, an increase of 713% (see table 17.2).

These increases do not match the increases in women's crime as measured by arrests, except if we consider the impact of the "war on drugs" along with greater attention to domestic violence. Between 1976 and 1999 there was a very dramatic change in the criminal justice system's response to female drug use—and to all illegal drug use—as well as to domestic violence. The increased attention to domestic violence led to an increase in arrests of women for both aggravated assault and "other assaults."[55]

The increase in the incarceration of women is not related to increases in criminality among women; instead, it is directly related to alterations of various criminal jus-

Table 17.2   Incarceration Rates of Men and Women in State and Federal Institutions, 1925–2005

Year	Total	Male	Female	Ratio
1925	79	149	6	24.8:1
1945	98	193	9	21.4:1
1965	108	213	8	26.6:1
1985	202	397	17	23.4:1
2005	491	929	65	14.3:1
Percentage Increase				
1965–1985	87%	86%	112.5%	
1985–2005	143%	134%	282%	
1965–2005	355%	336%	713%	

Source: Pastore, A. L. and K. Maguire, eds. Sourcebook of Criminal Justice Statistics. [Online] http://www.albany.edu/sourcebook/pdf/t6282005.pdf

tice policies. Specifically, more women are incarcerated now than twenty years ago due to changes in legislation related to sentencing and drug offenses and to the current guidelines for parole and probation violations.

The Drug War Connection

The war on drugs has been a major contributor to the change in women's incarceration rates. Official data indicates that 29% of female inmates are incarcerated for drug offenses.[56] Almost one-third of the women in state prisons reported committing theft and property crimes to support a drug habit.[57]

In 1984 a total of 28% of female offenders in federal prisons were drug offenders; by 1995 their percentage had more than doubled, to 66%.[58] During the last couple of decades of the twentieth century the proportion of women convicted of felonies in federal court who were given probation declined from about two-thirds to around one-fourth, and the average time served by women on drug offenses rose from 27 months in 1984 to 67 months in 1990.[59] Between 1986 when mandatory sentencing was enacted and 1996, the number of women sentenced to state prison for drug crimes increased from 2,370 to 23,700. During those same years, the arrests of women for a drug offense increased 95% (compared to 55% for men).[60] The number of convictions for simple possession between 1990 and 1996 increased 41%.[61]

A study of sentencing trends in three states (California, Minnesota, and New York) found that between 1986 and 1996 the number of women sentenced to prison increased tenfold, and drug crimes accounted for half of this increase (for men, drugs accounted for about one-third). These states differed significantly: in New York, a state that passed stringent drug legislation, drugs accounted for 91% of the increase in women incarcerated, compared to 55% in California and 26% in Minnesota. In New York, twice as many women were sent to prison for drugs in 1996 as in 1986, in 1986 one of every twenty women arrested for drugs was sent to prison, and in 1996 one out of every seven was. This trend paralleled drug arrests in New York: total arrests for women increased by only 15% during this time, but drug arrests jumped up by 61% (drug convictions accounted for 82% of the overall increase in convictions of women in state courts). As usual, race figured predominantly, as 77% of Hispanic women, 59% of African American women, but only 34% of white women were sentenced for drug crimes during this period.[62] Florida also enacted a super-tough stance on drugs. During the 1980s, admissions to prison for drugs increased by 1,825% for all offenders—and 3,103% for female offenders.[63]

Contrary to popular views, most drug offenders arrested and sent to prison are rarely drug "kingpins." The vast majority are low-level users and dealers. Most women become involved in the illegal drug business in association with a man with whom they are intimate. Much of the increase in women prisoners comes from the impact of mandatory sentencing laws. Under many of these laws, mitigating circumstances (e.g., having children, few or no prior offenses, nonviolent offenses, coercion by male associate) are rarely acknowledged. One survey found that just over half (51%) of women in state prisons had no prior offense or only one prior offense, compared to 39% of male prisoners.[64]

In addition to more arrests for drug law violations and mandatory minimums, the development of new technologies in drug use detection has impacted the increased incarceration of women. It is common for female parolees to be returned to prison for failing random drug tests.[65] For example, a study that examined female incarcerations in California, Oregon, and Hawaii found that a majority of new admissions of female inmates were actually women who violated parole conditions and that these violations were largely due to drug use.[66] The drug war has affected women's lives in numerous ways: more women are raising children alone because their partners are incarcerated; more women are incarcerated; and the state is policing women's bodies for evidence of drug use during pregnancy.[67] In short, it is not possible to remove the drug war from a discussion of increased incarceration of women since 1980.

Social Junk or Social Dynamite

The patriarchal structure of U.S. society affects attitudes about women's behavior and can affect police response to behavior, but the increase in women's incarceration rates is more likely related to issues of social class, racism, and the protection of existing power structures. In the 1960s, the second wave women's movement led to women being viewed as a dangerous class.[68] Historically, women were not threatening to the structure of society and were, on many levels, ignored. Even the suffrage movement and subsequent voting rights legislation did not threaten the power structure of society.

Steven Spitzer argued that surplus labor and the inherent class contradictions under capitalism produce a population of individuals who must be controlled. He categorized this problem population into two groups, "social junk" and "social dynamite." Both groups are marginal to the economy, and neither occupies positions of power sufficient to secure adequate distributions of resources for themselves.[69] When women began to demand equal rights, pay, and opportunity in the 1960s and 1970s the perception of women as social junk changed to one of social dynamite.

"Social junk" was a description coined to describe people who have fallen through the cracks of the social system and depend on others for basic needs. Members of this population lack secure employment, due either to a lack of skills, a lack of need for their skills, or some physical or psycho-social inability to function within the limits imposed by society. Social junk is a relatively harmless burden to society. Historically, women were social junk. In contemporary society, the demonization of drugs and drug users since the 1970s has contributed to the characterization of women who use drugs as social junk.

"Social dynamite" refers to people who have either fallen or jumped through the cracks of the social system, but who are rebellious and potentially violent over their perceived failure. People in this group may be dangerous to society and certainly threaten the status quo. Spitzer argued that the power elite safeguard themselves from social junk by creating agencies, such as social welfare for the poor and social security for the old. These agencies ease the plight of those in need and keep them from asking, "Why don't we have a more egalitarian economic system?" Social dynamite, however, does ask this question. This group, by definition, threatens the entire economic system, especially economic elites. Social dynamite, because of its dangerousness, is often dealt with by repressive agencies. Elites tend to use laws to label social dynamite as "criminals."[70]

Spitzer's characterizations update the thoughts of Marx and Engels on the ruling ideology to include repressive laws directed at an especially dangerous class.[71] He argued that when groups begin to ask questions about their collective status in society they become especially dangerous to the elite. This is the case with women and also with African Americans. The civil rights and women's movements led to both groups being viewed as threatening to the existing social order. During the 1950s, African Americans fought for equality through the court system. This legalistic approach was tedious and social change was slow. In the 1960s, however, the struggle for equality became high profile and was fought with peaceful resistance and violence. The gains from the various approaches could be perceived as threatening the status quo power structure.

Race, Class, and Gender

When it comes to the criminal justice system's response to female offenders, it is often difficult to separate class, race, and gender. The prevailing view, however, has been that the system acts in a "chivalrous" manner toward female offenders, consistently giving them more lenient treatment than male offenders. Many scholars have believed that criminal justice officials are lenient because they want to "protect" women offenders, perhaps because they remind them of their wives or mothers. However, as Merry Morash and Pamela Schram warn, "the inference that any leniency in their decisions can be attributed to their chivalry or paternalism is quite a stretch from the available data."[72]

The concept of *chivalry* emerged as a service institution during the Middle Ages, when knights protected women from dangers. While chivalrous attitudes contain an element of treating individuals as if they were in an elevated position (on a pedestal), there is also a trade-off. Men hold the more powerful status over women, who need protection. Chivalry is also a racist and classist concept. "Women of a certain social class and color are perceived as more worthy of chivalrous treatment than other women."[73] Field observations of police officers confirm the suspicion that "demeanor" also plays a significant role. A detailed analysis of field observations of over five thousand police–cit-

izen encounters in twenty-four cities found that although offense type is important, age, race, and demeanor all played important roles. Significantly, it was discovered that female offenders who were young, African American, or hostile did not receive any preferential treatment, while white women who displayed a calm and deferential attitude received lenient treatment by the police.[74]

Racial disparities in the incarceration of women have been consistently documented in the post-civil rights era. For example, a 1979 study revealed that African-American women received longer sentences than their white counterparts even when the same offense had been committed.[75] Candace Kruttschnitt found that black women convicted of disturbing the peace or of drug law violations in Minnesota were sentenced more severely than other women offenders.[76] Unfortunately, these patterns have continued. A 1995 study revealed disproportionate sentencing patterns in three states.[77] After comparing arrest and sentencing rates of female offenders, Mann concluded that women of color are discriminated against based on their gender, race, and socioeconomic status.

Perhaps the most outrageous form of judicial sexism was the unremitting targeting of pregnant women addicted to drugs, especially crack cocaine. Larry Siegel notes that there was a concerted effort to criminalize pregnancy in the case of women addicted to drugs, as if arresting them and putting them in prison would cure their drug problem. He notes the racial bias in the crackdowns. In 1989 in Florida, more than 700 pregnant women in public and private clinics were tested for drugs. There was virtually no difference by race in the percentage that tested positive (15.4% of white women tested positive versus 14.1% of the African-American women). African-American women, however, were almost ten times more likely to be reported to the authorities for drug abuse.[78]

Barbara Bloom and Meda Chesney-Lind state: "The incarceration of women of color, especially African Americans, is a key factor in the increase in the number of women in prison."[79] Impoverished African-American women are primary victims of the drug war in two ways. First, they are incarcerated for drug offenses at far higher rates than their white counterparts. Second, they are the partners, mothers, and daughters of those who are the focus of the drug war.

In 2006, African-American women (68,800) accounted for 34% of all women (203,100) in state or federal prisons and jails, while the percentage of Hispanic women (32,400) was 16%. The differences in *rates* were even more dramatic: African-American women had an incarceration rate of 358, while the rate for Hispanic women was 152, compared to 94 for whites.[80] In short, it is impossible to remove the issue of race from a discussion of women in prison. It is significant that the disproportionate imprisonment of blacks is reducing the voting rights of this population, as noted in chapter 14.

Women in Prison

Historically, female inmates were relatively rare. Few states had standalone female prisons, and the number of female inmates was small. The 1960s witnessed a modest increase in the number of women incarcerated, but since the 1980s the number of women in prison has increased drastically.[81] In 1996, there were 75,000 incarcerated women.[82] In 2006, there were approximately 203,000 women in federal and state prisons and local jails.[83] In 1970 women accounted for about 3% of inmates; in 2006 the percentage was 10%. From 1995 through 2005, the average increase in the rate of growth for female prisoners was 4.6%; the number of women in prison increased at almost twice the rate of men since 1985 (404% vs. 209%).[84] The U.S. incarcerates approximately ten times more women than western European countries, even though the combined female population there is about the same size as the number of women in the United States.[85]

More than a third of female inmates in state or federal prison were held in the three largest jurisdictions: Texas, the Federal Bureau of Prisons, and California. Black females were twice as likely (156 inmates per 100,000 people in the general population) to

be incarcerated in state or federal prisons as Hispanic females (76 per 100,000), and three times more likely to be incarcerated than white females (45 per 100,000). The rates for females were consistent across all age groups.[86] The three states with the highest rates of incarceration were Oklahoma (129), Idaho (110), and Mississippi (107). The lowest rates were Rhode Island (10), Massachusetts (12), and Maine (17).[87] If we include jail populations and look at the rates within each ethnicity, the disparity is even greater. There were 94 white female inmates per 100,000 white women in the general population; 152 Hispanic female inmates per 100,000 Hispanic women; and 358 black female inmates per 100,000 black women.[88]

Women prisoners share some of the same characteristics as the men who are sent to prison; the majority are young, single, poor, persons of color, substance abusers, with limited education, very few vocational skills, and almost no job experience.[89] Almost half (42%) of the women in state prison did not have a high school diploma or GED, versus 18% in the general population.[90] Only 20% of women in prison are enrolled in high school or GED classes. When arrested, 60% of the women (compared to 40% of men) incarcerated had not been employed full-time; half did not work in the month before their arrest. Incomes were under $600 a month for 37% of incarcerated women in the month leading up to their arrest (versus 28% of men). Less than one-third of the women are enrolled in a vocational program in prison. The combination of a lack of education, few skills, and a criminal record significantly hinders a woman's ability to find a job within a year after release from prison; only 40% are able to do so.[91]

Offenses Committed

Women are primarily arrested and incarcerated for property and drug offenses. Women accounted for 35% of all violent offenses in 2005. The percentages of violent female offenders were essentially the same across all races (about half of all white, black, and Hispanic women committed a violent offense).[92] When women do commit acts of violence, it is overwhelmingly directed at a partner or spouse, and their rates of partner homicide are less than half of that of men. The other primary difference between the violence of men and women is that violence by women is more likely to be in self-defense.[93] White females (26.5%) were more likely to be serving time for a property offense. Drug offenses showed the largest disparity in sentencing with 46.6% of all women serving sentences for a drug offense in state and federal institutions being black or Hispanic, versus 14% of white female inmates.[94]

Male prisons are much more likely to be characterized by violence, interpersonal conflict, interracial tension, and gang activity.[95] Perpetrators were male in 91.3% of inmate-on-inmate sexual violence incidents, and they were the victims in 88.4% of the incidents.[96] Violence directed at staff and other inmates is far less likely to occur in female institutions.[97] Homosexual activity is present in both types of facilities, but among women it is more likely to be a consensual activity.[98]

Using the common benchmark of five or more arrests, the majority of incarcerated women were not career criminals. Almost half (45.8%) had no prior prison sentences; they were "first timers." One of the effects of the "war on drugs" and women drug users is that it has criminalized those who in previous years would have been placed on probation rather than sentenced to prison.[99]

Motherhood

Two-thirds of women incarcerated in state prison are mothers; over 2.4 million children have a parent in prison.[100] A majority of parents are incarcerated more than 100 miles from their previous residence; in federal prisons, 43% of parents are more than 500 miles away from their home. Over half of female prisoners have never had a visit from their children. Recall the expense of phone calls from prison. One-third of the mothers in prison have never spoken with their children by phone.

> I want to tell other mothers that I know the pain they're feeling; the awfulness that comes because we don't know where our

children are, the anxiety that comes around certain dates like birthdays knowing we can't call to say "I love you." I know the loss of joy in those days, because they're not things to celebrate without our children. I know, because we're all facing the same problem of not being able to see our children due to the fact that we're convicted and it is more painful to not see our children, or have the chance to talk to them than the sentence we have to serve.[101]

Most children of incarcerated women live with a grandparent, other relative, or a friend. One-third of the mothers have never spoken with their children while incarcerated. Women in prison are five times more likely than men to report having children removed from their immediate families; 10% reported children living in a foster home. The Adoption and Safe Families Act of 1997 allows the state to terminate parental rights if children remain in foster care for 15 of the last 22 months. More than 60% of mothers in prison will serve more than 24 months of their current sentence.

> Incarcerated women experience physical, emotional, and psychological trauma in prison that haunts them throughout their lives. In recent years, an increasing number of studies and reports have also highlighted how a mother's incarceration affects the emotional and psychological well-being of her children, who are often placed in the care of friends or family—possibly leading to financial and emotional hardship on family members—or end up in an overburdened child welfare system. Less well documented, but no less significant, are the impacts of women's incarceration on family and community members dependent on them for support and care.[102]

Substance Abuse

More than half (60%) of the women in state prison have a history of drug dependence, yet only 1 in 5 women in state prisons and 1 in 8 in federal prisons receives treatment for substance abuse.[103] Even for non-drug offenses, drug use and addiction are contributing factors to incarceration; 40% of women in state prisons and 19% of women in federal prisons committed the offense for which they were sentenced to prison while under the influence of drugs; one-third committed the offense to obtain money to buy drugs.

Physical and Sexual Abuse

More than three-quarters (79%) of the women in state and federal prisons reported past physical abuse; 60% reported past sexual abuse.[104] Women's drug abuse is often related to the trauma of physical or sexual abuse. Studies have found a significant correlation between physical and/or sexual abuse and subsequent drug or alcohol addiction in women. As Neil Websdale and Meda Chesney-Lind note: "To make sense of male violence against women is to grasp the limited social, political, and economic opportunities available to women. . . . The constellation of disadvantaged situations women live out expose them to violence at the hands of men."[105] Women imprisoned for a drug offense are often suffering from extreme socioeconomic and psychological stress. Incarceration exacerbates the mental anguish of physical, psychological, and sexual abuse. Without adequate mental-health care, there can be serious health consequences for incarcerated women.

When incarceration is the primary response to all crime, some of the most vulnerable citizens, as illustrated by the background characteristics noted above, are caught in the "ever-widening net cast by current drug laws through provisions such as conspiracy, accomplice, liability, and constructive possession, which expand criminal liability to reach partners, relatives, and bystanders."[106] Male and female inmates share some of the same demographics, but they differ in terms of the types of offenses they commit, their prison culture, and the problems they face in prison.

Coping with Imprisonment

A primary difference in the culture in male and female institutions is strategies for coping with imprisonment. For example, male inmates tend to fit into two groups: those who identify with the outside world and try to maintain their former identities while attempting to make changes in their lives and those who become "jailers" and "make a world out of prison."[107]

Both males and females who go to prison suffer a number of pains of imprisonment. For women, however, there are some important qualitative differences. Watterson notes that the institutionalization process in women's prisons (and to a certain extent in men's prisons) is "synonymous with forced dependency. The controls of prison which attempt to regulate lives, attitudes, and behavior are synonymous with those used during infancy."[108] The role of the prison system over prisoners is like that of parent to child. The prison teaches you to be manipulative, to lie, to be dependent, not to love others, and not to trust others. You learn to take orders and with the inevitable acceptance of the custodial regime comes an erosion of self-determination, independence, and a sense of responsibility.

Men in prison form a number of informal groups, gangs, and cliques. These relationships are often short-lived, and close attachments are rare. For women, however, one of the most common adaptations to life in prison is the formation of "families," a fact that has been amply documented, in both adult and juvenile institutions.[109] Since the 1960s researchers have been aware that many female inmates adopt family roles—"father," "mother," and often a "brother" and/or "sister"—that help provide a sense of belonging. This dynamic has not been found in male institutions.

The majority of women in prison have husbands and children on the outside and do not generally receive much support from them. The influence of traditional roles is probably the most important factor contributing to the formation of prison families. Women have been socialized to believe the family is the center of life. One of the ways in which women have chosen to adapt to the prison world is modeled on traditional roles—recreating family life, even if their own family was highly dysfunctional and abusive.[110]

> In the context of prison society, it is not shocking to meet someone's institutional

wife or grandfather. On several occasions while visiting prisons, I met a woman's entire prison "family" and saw the interweaving of wife, grandmother, son, wife-in-law, daughter.[111]

For women in prison, the close bonds of a "family" help to alleviate the pains of imprisonment. Such relationships, though not without problems of their own, help to create the kind of ideal family many of them never had on the outside. Because of this, many women never want to leave. Some, upon release, do things that will automatically bring them back to prison. As one female prisoner stated: "It's that security. It's that instant gratification coming back and having everybody holler and say, 'Look, Pat's back,' all happy to see you."[112]

Craig Forsyth and Rhonda Evans note that comparisons between male and female prisoners and the groups they form are difficult because gender stereotypes affect perceptions. Because we are socialized to believe that women value attachments more than men, the discourse describing those attachments reflects that socialization. Forsyth and Evans point out that both male and female gangs in and out of prison use the term family to describe their affiliations. "Women and men continue to create temporary worlds in prison, and both gangs and pseudo-families are transient means of survival. Indeed, males and females endure the degradation, powerlessness, and deprivation of prison in much the same way."[113]

While it has been understood as the dominant coping strategy of female inmates for decades, recent research has revealed that the development of pseudofamilies is on the decline. As the prison industry has changed its rhetoric from that of rehabilitation to retribution, women have changed the way they view and cope with doing time.[114] As their numbers increase, female inmates are tending to adopt strategies more similar to males.

Special Problems Faced by Female Inmates

Women have different health care needs than men. These differences lead to special problems for female inmates. We discussed motherhood above. Two other categories are medical neglect and sexual abuse in prison.

Medical Neglect

The possibility of pregnancy, HIV/AIDS, histories of physical and/or sexual abuse, and the need for annual gynecological exams presents a costly dilemma for prison administrators. Often, prisons fail to meet the medical needs of female inmates. Medical neglect includes a variety of issues ranging from failure to provide health care to reproductive issues. It is not uncommon for female inmates to have little or no access to medical attention when suffering from diseases that are treatable.[115] Of particular concern is treatment for AIDS/HIV. The drugs that are available to treat AIDS/HIV symptoms are very expensive, which means that incarcerated patients do not receive treatment or are forced to pay out-of-pocket, although charging inmates for medical attention is a violation of international standards and a highly unlikely option given the socioeconomic circumstances of most women in prison. More women (2.4%) in state prison are HIV positive than men (1.8%).[116]

Incarcerated women frequently experience delays in receiving medication for heart conditions, depression, sickle cell anemia, and asthma. Ineffective medical treatment is frequently the result of a lack of medical staff in prisons. One report found that of the $21,000 annual cost per prisoner in California, more than half ($11,000) was spent on security; $3,125 (14%) for health care, and $900 (4.5%) for education and training.[117] There are insufficient qualified medical professionals available to inmates; nonmedical staff often screen inmate requests for treatment.[118] Michael Vaughn and Leo Carroll found that "Prison medical care sometimes is delivered by unlicensed physicians, doctors with substance abuse problems, doctors with criminal histories, and licensed and qualified doctors who treat ailments for which they lack training or experience."[119]

Correctional facilities that do attempt to maintain adequate health care facilities and personnel have very high turnover rates.

Often, the working conditions and low pay impede the ability of corrections departments to maintain adequate numbers of employees in the health field.

> As a result of poverty, substance abuse, and years of poor health care, prisoners as a group are much less healthy than average Americans. Every year, more than 1.5 million people are released from jail and prison carrying a life-threatening contagious disease.... Unfortunately, most correctional systems are set up to fail. They have to care for a sick population on shoestring budgets and with little support from community health-care providers and public health authorities. Around the country, some physicians are operating on a license that restricts their work to correctional facilities because they are deemed not qualified to provide care in the community.[120]

People with mental illness often end up in prison. State inmates with mental health problems were twice as likely to have been homeless before arrest as other inmates. They were on the economic and social margins of society. If untreated, people with mental illness may be unstable and break the law. They then confront punitive law enforcement and sentencing policies. Over half (51%) of state inmates with mental health problems were convicted of nonviolent offenses, primarily drug and property offenses. One in five had no prior criminal sentence; another one in three were nonviolent recidivists. Prison environments pose unique challenges to mentally ill inmates, who often cannot cope with the stress of prison life. They are likely to be victimized by other inmates and have difficulty following the rules. Correctional officers are not trained to work with this population.[121]

A much higher percentage of women (73%) in state prisons and federal prisons (61%) had mental health problems than men (55% state; 44% federal).[122] Female state prisoners who had a mental health problem were more likely than those who did not to: be substance dependent (74% compared to 54%); have used cocaine or crack in the month before arrest (34% vs. 24%); have been homeless in the year before arrest (17%

vs. 9%); have suffered past physical or sexual abuse (58% vs. 44%); have parents who abused alcohol or drugs (47% vs. 29%); have had a physical or verbal assault charge since admission (17% vs. 6%); had 3 or more prior sentences to probation or incarceration (36% vs. 29%).

One of the most neglected areas of inmate health is the treatment of mental health issues, including substance abuse. Between 1991 and 1997 the proportion of prisoners receiving drug treatment declined from 40% to 18%.[123] This reduction is due to the fact that prisons are ending their programs at increasing rates. Other mental health needs of inmates are also ignored. For example, very few corrections institutions provide counseling for women who experienced domestic and/or sexual victimization prior to incarceration. Additionally, attempts to access treatment for mental health issues often lead to the dispensing of psychiatric medication without psychotherapeutic exams.[124]

The area of reproductive health is a source of many medical problems facing incarcerated women. In the 1990s, 100% of prisons offered some obstetric and gynecological services, about half offered mammograms and pap smears, and very few provided access to abortion services.[125] Generally, inmates must request heath treatment for a specific problem. This is particularly problematic for cervical and breast cancers. Often, these illnesses are asymptomatic until the disease has progressed. Without pap smears and mammograms to detect them, incarcerated women face more serious outcomes than women who can readily seek medical attention.

Incarcerated pregnant women are a special population and require additional services. Due to the nature of their situations, they are at an advantage. As indicated previously, 100% of corrections facilities for women offer obstetric care. While the care they receive may not compare to that of pregnant women under the care of private OB-GYNs, they are not ignored. One problem often faced by these women relates to the use of restraint devices during labor and/or delivery. Currently, 33 states allow and/or require pregnant women to be shackled and/or handcuffed during transportation to a hospital to give birth and 18 allow the same during labor and delivery.[126] The decision to restrain these women is based on state law and prison policy rather than the woman's criminal history.

Sexual Abuse

Sexual abuse of inmates includes behaviors ranging from rape to voyeurism, inappropriate sexual relationships and sexual harassment to prostitution. It is virtually impossible to know the precise number of female inmates victimized by sexual abuse. In fact, as late as 1990, 40 states did not even have legislation that banned sexual misconduct between correctional officers and inmates.[127] Rates of sexual abuse of inmates are difficult to estimate. Anecdotal evidence indicates that it is common.[128] At the heart of this issue is the employment of males in female institutions. Utilizing male custodians opens the door to the sexual victimization of women. Female inmates are often required to shower, use the toilet in front of, and even endure strip searches by male guards. Not only does this situation present the opportunity for sexual assaults to occur, it is indicative of the power differential that impedes consensual sexual activity. Many sexual assaults of female inmates are done under the guise of official conduct. For example, inmates report being touched on the breasts and genitals while being searched, and having male staff watch them undress in their cells. The National Institute of Corrections investigated this issue in the Arizona prison system and concluded that there was no official purpose for male guards to frequently stare at women during dressing, showering, and use of toilet facilities.

Female inmates who are victimized through various forms of sexually abusive behaviors often have little recourse available to them. Retaliation for reporting abuse often impedes women's abilities to seek protection. For example, one woman who participated in a lawsuit against the District of Columbia testified to being beaten, raped, and sodomized by three male custodians who informed her that the attack was in response to her notification of authorities regarding a previous assault.[129] When women do formally complain, they are rarely offered protection, and their complaints are often ignored. The stereotype of women in prison as "bad girls" makes it difficult for incarcerated women to convince authorities that victimization actually occurred.[130]

In sum, female inmates face a multitude of special problems. Some are shared with male inmates and others are gender specific. The attention paid to the plight of female inmates has increased in recent years among academics and the court system. Allegations of abuse are leading to lawsuits, and women are winning. Correctional facilities are responding to court rulings and the research of academics.

Lack of Programs

Less than one in three women is enrolled in a vocational program while in prison.[131] Some modern women's prisons offer a few college courses and some training with computers, but prisons offering education and training programs are in the minority. Although the amount of time served had increased substantially because of determinate sentencing, participation in prison educational and vocational programs declined dramatically between 1991 and 1997. A national study in 2004 found that

> the numbers of prisoners receiving some postsecondary education had increased since the mid-1990s, when programming was at the height of political disfavor, but that only five percent of prisoners were enrolled in any form of post-secondary education. The bulk of those prisoners—89%—were incarcerated in just 15 state prison systems. . . . Education—particularly at the college level—also reduces rule-breaking and disorder in prison. Studies show that post-secondary education can cut recidivism rates by nearly half.[132]

Some of the "training" currently provided provides a form of cheap labor for corporations. In Arizona, for example, inmates help book reservations for the Best Western hotel/motel chain.[133] Few conditions compromise safety more than idleness. But because lawmakers have reduced funding for programming, prisoners today are largely inactive and unproductive.[134]

If prisoners are warehoused without any opportunity to improve their education or skills, they are less likely to find a job after release and are less likely to stay out of prison. Walter Dickey, former secretary of the Wisconsin Department of Corrections, notes: "If you don't have programs, whether they're schools, jobs, factories . . . that make up the naturally occurring forces that bring compliance with your rules, you are much more likely to be relying on force and handcuffs."[135] Corrections officers at Bedford Hills (a maximum-security prison for women in New York) reported that offering college classes in the facility reduced disciplinary problems, enhanced prisoners' self-esteem, improved their ability to communicate effectively, and helped them become more active in determining their future.[136] Cognitive-behavioral programs can help prisoners understand the motivations behind their behavior and the consequences. The programs can reduce misconduct in correctional facilities plus lower recidivism rates by at least 10%.[137]

The public has frequently been misinformed about postsecondary correctional education programs, as illustrated by the debates over Pell Grant eligibility in 1994. Prison education programs benefited from the creation of the Pell Grant program in 1972; many prisoners were eligible for the federal, need-based financial aid for education. In the early 1990s, there was considerable criticism of the use of Pell Grants to fund higher education for prisoners. The arguments said prisoners should not enjoy such benefits in an era of budget cuts for social programs and that money for prisoners took money away from law-abiding students. Despite the fact that less than 1% of the total $6 billion Pell Grant funding in the 1993–94 academic year went to prisoners—and that no students were ever denied a Pell Grant because of prisoner participation in the program—a provision in the Violent Crime Control and Law Enforcement Act of 1994 prohibited anyone incarcerated in a state or federal correctional facility from receiving a Pell Grant.[138]

Occasional headlines such as "Wife-killer learns his way out of prison"—about an Indiana man who reduced his sentence by using "good time" credits offered to prisoners who complete educational programs—create negative public perceptions. The public rarely reads that educational programs reduce recidivism and save tax dollars or that many states apply fairly stringent eligibility requirements about which prisoners are eligible for postsecondary educational opportunities.[139]

Despite lack of funding and public support, there have been efforts to establish prison programming to help inmates. Programs such as substance abuse treatment, life skills training, vocational training, and educational programs are integral to changing the patterns that led to incarceration and to successful re-entry into society after release from prison. "By improving the mental, physical, and social well-being of prisoners, as well as providing them with job training and other skills, these programs benefit society at large by reducing crime and strengthening communities."[140]

Martha Stewart, who served five months in a federal women's prison camp in Alderson, West Virginia for obstruction of justice in a justice department investigation of stock trading, eloquently summarizes the plight of many incarcerated women.

> When one is incarcerated with 1,200 other inmates, it is hard to be selfish. . . . So many of the women here . . . will never have the joy and well-being that you and I experience. Many of them have been here for years—devoid of care, devoid of love, devoid of family. I beseech you all to think about these women—to encourage the American people to ask for reforms, both in sentencing guidelines, in length of incarceration for nonviolent first-time offenders, and for those involved in drug-taking. They would be much better served in a true rehabilitation center than in prison where there is no real help, no real programs to rehabilitate, no programs to educate, no way to be prepared for life "out there" where each person will ultimately find herself, many with no skills and no preparation for living.[141]

Young Women and the Juvenile Justice System

As discussed in chapter 16, the deviant behavior of young people was handled largely on an informal basis prior to the nineteenth century.

The Development of Institutions for Girls

The idea of patriarchy reinforces the sanctity and privacy of the home and the power of the patriarch to discipline his wife and children. Further, the notion of *parens patriae* assumes that the state can legally act as a parent, exercising many of the implicit parental powers possessed by fathers. Therefore, government leaders eventually utilized *parens patriae* to justify extreme government intervention in the lives of young people. Arguing that such intervention was "for their own good," "for their own protection," or "in the best interests of the child," the state during the eighteenth century became increasingly involved in the regulation of adolescent behavior.

The *Ex Parte Crouse* Case

Without her father's knowledge, Mary Ann Crouse had been committed to the Philadelphia House of Refuge by her mother on the grounds that she was "incorrigible." Her father filed a habeas corpus petition, arguing that the incarceration was illegal because Mary Ann had not been given a jury trial.[142] As discussed in chapter 16, the justices of the Pennsylvania Supreme Court in 1838 rejected the appeal, saying that the Bill of Rights did not apply to juveniles, many parents were unfit, and the Philadelphia House of Refuge had a beneficial effect on its residents because it was a "school."[143]

The only testimony solicited by the justices to support their conclusion that the Philadelphia House of Refuge was a school rather than a prison was from those who managed the institution. The reality was that houses of refuge followed a strict military regimen, and there was an enormous amount of abuse within the institutions. Corporal punishment (girls in one institution were "ducked" under water), solitary confinement, and a "silent system" were part of the routine.[144] Work training was practically nonexistent, and outside companies contracted for cheap inmate labor. Religious instruction was often little more than Protestant indoctrination (many of the youngsters were Catholic). Education, in the conventional meaning of the word, was almost nonexistent.

The first reform school for girls was the State Industrial School for Girls in Lancaster, Massachusetts, established in 1856.[145] The Home of the Good Shepherd (established in 1875 in Memphis, Tennessee) was designed for the "reformation of fallen . . . women and a home or house of refuge for abandoned and vicious girls."[146] Because the girls had "fallen from grace," they needed to be saved. Lancaster's first superintendent, Bradford K. Peirce, stated: "It is sublime to work to save a woman, for in her bosom generations are embodied, and in her hands, if perverted, the fate of innumerable men is held."[147] Lancaster was a model for all juvenile training schools. What sorts of crimes had the girls confined there committed? Over two-thirds had been accused of moral rather than criminal offenses: vagrancy, beggary, stubbornness, deceitfulness, idle and vicious behavior, wanton and lewd conduct, and running away.[148] Of the first ninety-nine inmates at Lancaster, 47% were immigrants (many were Irish).

The Child-Saving Movement

The *child-saving movement,* along with the juvenile court, had a special meaning for girls. The child-saving movement made much rhetorical use of the value of such traditional institutions as the family and education: "The child savers elevated the nuclear family, especially women as stalwarts of the family, and defended the family's right to supervise the socialization of youth."[149] But while the child savers were exalting the family, they were also crafting a governmental system that would have the authority to intervene to an unprecedented extent in the lives of young people.

The concern of the child savers went far beyond removing the adolescent criminal from the adult justice system. Many of their reforms were actually aimed at "imposing sanctions on conduct unbecoming youth and disqualifying youth from the benefit of adult privileges."[150] Pervasive state intervention into the life of the family was grounded in colonial laws regarding "stubborn" and "neglected" children and perceptions that "parents were godly and children wicked."[151] Most child savers actually held an opposite opinion—that children were innocent and either the parents or the environment was morally suspect. Although the two views seem incompatible, they have coexisted in the juvenile court system since its inception. At various times one view or the other has predominated, but both bode ill for young women, because girls and their moral behavior were of specific concern to the child savers. Scientific and popular literature on female delinquency expanded enormously during this period, as did institutions specifically devoted to the reformation of girls.

The evolution of what might be called the "girl-saving" effort was the direct consequence of a coalition between some feminists and other Progressive-era movements. Concerned about female victimization and distrustful of male (and to some degree female) sexuality, prominent women leaders, including Susan B. Anthony, found common cause with the more conservative social purity movement around such issues as the regulation of prostitution and raising the age of consent. Eventually, in the face of stiff judicial and political resistance, the concern about male sexuality more or less disappeared from sight, and the delinquent girl herself became the problem. The solution: harsh "maternal justice" meted out by professional women.[152]

The Juvenile Court

The offenses that bring girls into the juvenile justice system reflect the system's dual concerns: adolescent criminality and moral conduct. Historically, they have also reflected a unique and intense preoccupation with girls' sexuality and their obedience to parental authority.

In Los Angeles in 1903, women reformers vigorously advocated the appointment of women court workers in juvenile court to deal with the "special" problems of girls. This court was the first in the country to appoint women "referees" who were invested with nearly all the powers of judges in girls' cases. Women were also hired to run the juvenile detention facility in 1911. Cora Lewis, chair of the probation committee asserted: "in view of the number of girls and the type of girls detained there . . . it is utterly unfeasible to have a man at the head of the institution." The civic leaders and newly hired female court workers "advocated special measures to contain sexual behavior among working-class girls, to bring them to safety by placing them in custody, and to attend to their distinctive needs as young, vulnerable females."[153]

Girls were the losers in the reform effort. Studies of early family court activity reveal that almost all of the girls who appeared in these courts were charged with immorality or waywardness. The sanctions for such misbehavior were extremely severe. For example, the Chicago family court sent half the girl delinquents (but only a fifth of the boy delinquents) to reformatories between 1899 and 1909. In Milwaukee, twice as many girls as boys were committed to training schools.[154] In Memphis, females were twice as likely as males to be committed to training schools.[155] In Honolulu in 1929–1930, over half the girls referred to juvenile court were charged with "immorality," which meant there was evidence of sexual intercourse; 30% were charged with "waywardness." Half of the juveniles committed to training schools in Honolulu well into the 1950s were girls.[156] Envisioned as a "benevolent" institution that would emphasize treatment rather than punishment, the juvenile court turned out to be a mixture of the two orientations.

Relatively early in the juvenile justice system's history, a few astute observers became concerned about the abandonment of minors' rights in the name of treatment, saving, and protection. An evaluation of several hundred cases in the Wayward Minor Court in New York City during the late 1930s and early 1940s found that there were serious problems with a statute that brought young women into court simply for disobedience of parental commands or because they were in "danger of becoming morally depraved." The study warned that the "need to interpret the 'danger of becoming morally depraved' imposes upon the court a legislative function of a moralizing character."[157]

Studies of the processing of cases between 1950 and the early 1970s documented the impact of such judicial attitudes. Girls charged with status offenses were often more harshly treated than their counterparts charged with crimes. They were far more likely to be incarcerated than boys charged with status offenses and sometimes even more likely than boys charged with serious crimes. Although girls were technically incarcerated in training schools for the "big five" offenses (running away from home, incorrigibility, sexual offenses, probation violation, and truancy), researchers found that "the underlying vein in many of these cases is sexual misconduct by the girl delinquent."[158] Another study, conducted in the early 1970s in a New Jersey training school, revealed large numbers of girls incarcerated "for their own protection."[159]

Studies of the juvenile courts during the past few decades suggest that court personnel participated directly in the judicial enforcement of the sexual double standard. Such activity was most pronounced in the system's early years, but there is evidence that the pattern continues. Elements of other crimes are described in statutes, but standards of evidence for status offenses are much more subjective. While this allows consideration of mitigating circumstances, it also opens the door to discriminatory application and disregard for civil rights, which are, at least to some extent, protected by the law.

The *double standard of juvenile justice* was indirectly challenged in the 1970s by passage of the *Juvenile Justice and Delinquency Prevention Act,* which encouraged states to divert and deinstitutionalize status offenders. Challenges quickly surfaced after the act's passage.[160] Juvenile justice officials were successful in narrowing the definition of status offender in the amended act so that any child who violated a "valid court order"

would not be covered under the deinstitutionalization provisions.[161] The change, never publicly debated in either the House or the Senate, effectively gutted the act by permitting judges to reclassify a status offender who violated a court order as a delinquent. This meant that a young woman who ran away from a court-ordered placement (a halfway house, foster home, or the like) was no longer eligible for diversion and deinstitutionalization. Another method to circumvent the act was "*bootstrapping*" status offenders into delinquents by issuing criminal contempt citations, referring or committing status offenders to secure mental health facilities, or referring them to "semisecure" facilities.[162]

The 1992 reauthorization of the JJDP Act addressed the double standard of juvenile justice and the lack of services for girls. Funds were authorized to analyze gender-specific services and to develop policies to prohibit gender bias in placement and treatment. The reauthorization also made bootstrapping more difficult and warned that all dispositions other than placement in secure detention should have been exhausted before such commitment. The reauthorization of the JDDPA Act in 2002 maintained the core protections from 1974. The 2002 law confirms the link between child maltreatment and juvenile delinquency but it did not revisit the girls' issues highlighted in 1992.[163]

SUMMARY

In this chapter we discussed how women have historically been given second-class treatment within both the adult and the juvenile justice systems. Women of color and poor women have felt the brunt of the criminal justice system. Recent data on women in prison show tremendous increases in their rate of imprisonment, due chiefly to the "war on drugs."

The history of the juvenile justice system in the United States demonstrates that sexism has pervaded the institution since its inception. The roots of this pattern can be traced to the *parens patriae* doctrine. Fittingly, the first and most significant legal challenge to the doctrine, *Ex Parte Crouse,* involved the incarceration of a girl on the grounds that she was "incorrigible." The evolution of the contemporary juvenile justice system was accelerated by the growth of institutions for delinquent and wayward youths, starting with houses of refuge and concluding with the establishment of training and reform schools. These schools were set up largely to save young people from the temptations of city life and precocious sexuality, and there they were taught domestic skills and moral precepts.

The establishment of the first juvenile court in 1899 capped years of effort by people described as child savers to extend state control over the lives of youth. Girls were the losers in the reform movement as vast numbers were referred to juvenile courts for immorality and waywardness and institutionalized for those offenses. By the middle of the twentieth century, status offenses like running away replaced charges of immorality. Court observers noted that status offences were buffer charges for sexual misconduct. After more than 100 years of existence, juvenile courts continue to dispense discriminatory forms of justice to the girls entering the system for noncriminal status offenses.

In 2006, 203,000 women were incarcerated in the nation's jails, state, and federal prisons. More than 423,000 girls were processed by the juvenile justice system in 2002. Congress and state legislatures pass laws that significantly increase the number of prisoners. Decisions about what to define as a crime and the punishment for it are affected by culture, class, and gender. Women caught in the net of those decisions lose their liberty and are confined in institutions that lack the funds necessary for minimum essentials. Communities targeted by drug laws lose mothers, caregivers, and breadwinners to incarceration, affecting the well-being of children and families.

The public knows very little about the criminal justice process and even less about the conditions of confinement. Society has focused only on punishment, but the consequences of that punishment have been devastating to the women sentenced to prison and to their communities. Education about these issues and debates about whether the punishment fits the crime or whether the punishment creates an environment that inevitably causes more social problems is a first step toward meaningful reform.

Key Terms

- bootstrapping
- child-saving movement
- chivalry
- double standard of juvenile justice
- feminization of poverty
- Juvenile Justice and Delinquency Prevention Act
- Married Women's Property Acts
- *patria potestas*
- patriarchy
- *Reed v. Reed*

Notes

[1] Yvette was a student of coauthor WBB.
[2] Rafter, N. H. and E. A. Stanko (eds.). *Judge, Lawyer, Victim, Thief: Women, Gender Roles and Criminal Justice.* Boston: Northeastern University Press, 1982, pp. 2–4; Pollock, J. M. "Gender, Justice, and Social Control: A Historical Perspective." In A. V. Merlo and J. M. Pollock (eds.), *Women, Law, and Social Control* (2nd ed.). New York: Allyn & Bacon, 2006, p. 4.
[3] Watterson, K. *Women in Prison: Inside the Concrete Womb.* Boston: Northeastern University Press, 1996, p. 33.
[4] Eisenstein, Z. R. *The Female Body and the Law.* Berkeley: University of California Press, 1988, pp. 58–59; Terkel, G. *Law and Society: Critical Approaches.* Boston: Allyn & Bacon, 1996, pp. 6–7.
[5] Lerner, G. *The Creation of Patriarchy.* New York: Oxford University Press, 1986, p. 239.
[6] Ibid., pp. 12–13.
[7] Parenti, M. *Land of Idols: Political Mythology in America.* New York: St. Martin's Press, 1994, p. 150.
[8] Eisenstein, *The Female Body and the Law*, pp. 58–59.
[9] Chambliss, W. J. and T. F. Courtless. *Criminal Law, Criminology, and Criminal Justice.* Belmont, CA: Wadsworth, 1992, p. 31.
[10] Pollock, "Gender, Justice, and Social Control," pp. 7–9.
[11] Terkel, *Law and Society*, pp. 177–178.
[12] *Reed v. Reed* (404, U.S. 71, 92 S. Ct. 251, 30 L.Ed.2nd 225, 1971).
[13] Feinman, C. *Women in the Criminal Justice System.* New York: Praeger, 1980, p. 58.
[14] Ibid., p. 60.
[15] Eitzen, D. S. and M. B. Zinn. *In Conflict and Order* (8th ed.). Boston: Allyn & Bacon, 1998, p. 335.

[16] Terkel, *Law and Society;* Faludi, S. *Backlash: The Undeclared War against American Women.* New York: Anchor Books, 1991; MacKinnon, C. *Toward a Feminist Theory of the State.* Cambridge, MA: Harvard University Press, 1989.

[17] Sokoloff, N. J., B. A. Price, and J. Flavin. "The Criminal Law and Women." In B. A. Price and N. J. Sokoloff (eds.), *The Criminal Justice System and Women: Offenders, Prisoners, Victims, and Workers.* New York: McGraw-Hill, 2004, p. 12.

[18] Karmen, A. "The Victimization of Girls and Women by Boys and Men: Competing Analytical Frameworks." In Price and Sokoloff, *The Criminal Justice System and Women,* p. 289.

[19] Ibid., p. 13.

[20] Federal Bureau of Investigation. *Crime in the United States, 2006.* [Online] http://www.fbi.gov/ucr/cius2006/data/table_42.html

[21] Donziger, S. *The Real War on Crime: The Report of the National Criminal Justice Commission.* New York: HarperCollins, 1996; Chesney-Lind, M. and L. Pasko. *The Female Offender: Girls, Women and Crime* (2nd ed.). Thousand Oaks, CA: Sage, 2004.

[22] Boritch, H. and J. Hagan. "A Century of Crime in Toronto: Gender, Class and Patterns of Social Control, 1859–1955." *Criminology* 28: 567–599 (1990); Chesney-Lind and Pasko, *The Female Offender,* ch. 5.

[23] Chesney-Lind, M. and R. G. Shelden. *Girls, Delinquency and Juvenile Justice* (3rd ed.). Belmont, CA: Wadsworth, 2004.

[24] Miller, E. *Street Woman.* Philadelphia: Temple University Press, 1986; Steffensmeier, D. "Trends in Female Crime: Is Crime Still a Man's World?" In B. R. Price and N. J. Sokoloff (eds.), *The Criminal Justice System and Women* (3rd ed.). New York: McGraw-Hill, 2004, pp. 95–112.

[25] Chesney-Lind and Pasko, *The Female Offender.*

[26] There are numerous studies of the abuse of women and the connection with subsequent criminality. See, for instance, Miller, *Street Woman*; Sheffield, C. J. "Sexual Terrorism: The Social Control of Women." In B. B. Hess and M. M. Ferree (eds.), *Analyzing Gender: A Handbook of Social Science Research.* Newbury Park, CA: Sage, 1987; Stout, K. "A Continuum of Male Controls and Violence against Women: A Teaching Model." *Journal of Social Work Education* 27: 305–319 (Fall 1991); Walker, L. E. *The Battered Woman.* New York: Harper/Perennial, 1980.

[27] Daly, K. "Women's Pathways to Felony Court: Feminist Theories of Lawbreaking and Problems of Representation." *Review of Law and Women's Studies* 2(1152): 14 (Fall 1992).

[28] Miller, *Street Woman;* see case summaries in Chesney-Lind and Shelden, *Girls, Delinquency and Juvenile Justice,* ch. 10.

[29] See, for example, Hawkins, D. F. (ed.). *Ethnicity, Race, and Crime.* Albany: State University of New York Press, 1995; Mann, C. R. *Unequal Justice: A Question of Color.* Bloomington: Indiana University Press, 1995; Walker, S., C. Spohn, and M. DeLone.

The Color of Justice (4th ed.). Belmont, CA: Wadsworth, 2007; Reiman, J. *The Rich Get Richer and the Poor Get Prison* (8th ed.). Boston: Allyn & Bacon, 2007; Chesney-Lind and Pasko, *The Female Offender.*

[30] Daly, "Women's Pathways to Felony Court"; Miller, *Street Woman.*

[31] U.S. Bureau of the Census. *Statistical Abstract of the United States.* Section 12: Labor Force, Employment, and Earnings, table 602 [Online] http://www.census.gov/prod/2006pubs/07statab/labor.pdf

[32] Ibid., table 582. [Online] http://www.census.gov/compendia/statab/tables/07s0582.xls

[33] U.S. Bureau of the Census. *Statistical Abstract of the United States.* Section 1: Population, table 64. [Online] http://www.census.gov/prod/2006pubs/07statab/pop.pdf

[34] Ibid., tables 41, 44.

[35] Daly, "Women's Pathways to Felony Court," pp. 23–24.

[36] Collins, C. F. *The Imprisonment of African-American Women.* Jefferson, NC: McFarland, 1997, p. 4–5.

[37] Sellin, J. T. *Slavery and the Penal System.* New York: Elsevier, 1976.

[38] Shelden, R. G. "From Slave to Caste Society: Penal Changes in Tennessee, 1840–1915." *Tennessee Historical Quarterly* 38: 462–478 (Winter 1979).

[39] Rafter, N. H. *Partial Justice: Women, Prisons, and Social Control* (2nd ed.). New Brunswick, NJ: Transaction Books, 1990, pp. 4–5.

[40] Freedman, E. B. *Their Sisters' Keepers: Women's Prison Reform in America, 1830–1930.* Ann Arbor: University of Michigan Press, 1981, p. 16.

[41] Rafter, *Partial Justice,* p. 6; Watterson, *Women in Prison,* p. 196.

[42] Freedman, *Their Sisters' Keepers,* pp. 17–18.

[43] Ibid; see also Platt, A. *The Child Savers* (rev. ed.). Chicago: University of Chicago Press, 1977.

[44] Watterson, *Women in Prison,* p. 198.

[45] Ibid.

[46] Freedman, *Their Sisters' Keepers,* pp. 14, 59–60.

[47] Ibid., p. 61.

[48] Ibid., p. 62, emphasis added by Freedman.

[49] Rafter, *Partial Justice,* pp. 142–146; Collins, *The Imprisonment of African-American Women.*

[50] Collins, *The Imprisonment of African-American Women,* p. 46.

[51] Prohibition is a perfect illustration of legislation defining what is criminal. People were imprisoned for selling alcohol because it was declared an illegal substance. Today alcohol, tobacco, and many prescription drugs are far more dangerous than marijuana and other illegal drugs—causing more than 500,000 deaths each year. Corporate producers of these dangerous substances have the money and power to keep such substances legal.

[52] Collins, p. 21.

[53] Donziger, *The Real War on Crime,* p. 152, p. 148.

[54] Pastore, A. L. and K. Maguire, eds. *Sourcebook of Criminal Justice Statistics.* Table 6.28. [Online] http://www.albany.edu/sourcebook/pdf/t6282005.pdf

[55] Chesney-Lind and Pasko, *The Female Offender.*

[56] Harrison, P. M. and A. J. Beck, *Prisoners in 2005.* Washington, DC: Bureau of Justice Statistics, November 2006, p. 9.

[57] Correctional Association of New York. *Women in Prison Fact Sheet.* [Online] http://www.correctionalassociation.org/WIPP/publications/Women%20in%20Prison%20Fact%20Sheet%202007.pdf; see also Inciardi, J., D. Lockwood, and A. Pottieger. *Women and Crack Cocaine.* New York: Macmillan, 1993; Anglin, M. D. and Y. Hser. "Addicted Women and Crime." *Criminology* 25: 359–307 (1987).

[58] Pollock, J. M. *Women, Prison, and Crime* (2nd ed.). Belmont, CA: Wadsworth, 2002, p. 7.

[59] Chesney-Lind and Pasko, *The Female Offender,* pp. 143–144.

[60] Drug War Facts: Women. [Online] http://www.drugwarfacts.org/women.htm

[61] Greenfield, L. A. and T. L. Snell. *Women Offenders.* Washington, DC: Bureau of Justice Statistics, December 1999.

[62] Mauer, M., C. Potler, and R. Wolf. "The Impact of the Drug War on Women: A Comparative Analysis in Three States." *Women, Girls and Criminal Justice* 1(2): 21–22, 30–31 (2000), cited in Pollock, *Women, Prison, and Crime,* pp. 5–6.

[63] Donziger, *The Real War on Crime.*

[64] Ibid., p. 152.

[65] Bloom, B. and Chesney-Lind, M. "Women in Prison: Vengeful Equity." In R. Muraskin (ed.), *It's a Crime: Women and Criminal Justice* (4th ed.). Upper Saddle River, NJ: Prentice Hall, 2007.

[66] Anderson, D. *Crime and the Politics of Hysteria.* New York: Times Books, 1995.

[67] Lyman, M. D. and G. W. Potter. *Drugs in Society: Causes, Concepts and Control* (5th ed) Cincinnati, OH: Anderson, 2007; Miller-Potter, K. S. "Protecting the Womb: The Myth of Privacy in Reproduction." *Free Inquiry in Creative Sociology* 30 (2): 135–147 (2002).

[68] Shelden, R. G. *Controlling the Dangerous Classes.* Boston: Allyn & Bacon, 2001.

[69] Spitzer, S. "Toward a Marxian Theory of Deviance." *Social Problems* 22: 638–651 (1975).

[70] Ibid.

[71] Marx, K. and F. Engels. *The German Ideology.* New York: International Publishers, 1968; for a good and brief summary of the term "ideology," see Bottomore, T., L. Harris, V. G. Kiernan, and R. Miliband (eds.). *A Dictionary of Marxist Thought.* Cambridge, MA: Harvard University Press, 1983.

[72] Morash, M. and P. J. Schram. *The Prison Experience: Special Issues of Women in Prison.* Long Grove, IL: Waveland Press, 2002, p. 56.

[73] Ibid., p. 6.

[74] Visher, C. A. "Gender, Police Arrest Decisions, and Notions of Chivalry." *Criminology* 21: 15–28 (1983).

[75] Foley, L. A. and C. E. Rasche. "The Effect of Race on Sentence, Actual Time Served, and Final Disposition of Female Offenders." *Journal of Experimental Social Psychology,* 15: 133–146 (1979).

[76] Kruttschnitt, C. "Social Status and the Sentences of Female Offenders." *Law and Society Review* 15: 247–265 (1980–1981).

[77] Mann, *Unequal Justice.*

[78] Siegel, L. "The Pregnancy Police Fight the War on Drugs." In C. Reinarman and H. G. Levine (eds.), *Crack in America: Demon Drugs and Social Justice.* Berkeley, CA: University of California Press, 1997, p. 251.

[79] Bloom and Chesney-Lind, "Women in Prison," p. 195.

[80] Sabol, W. J., T. D. Minton, and P. M. Harrison. *Prison and Jail Inmates at Midyear 2006* (NCJ 217675). Washington, DC: Bureau of Justice Statistics, June 2007, p. 9.

[81] Kerness, B. "Monitoring Women and Children in U.S. Prisons." *New Politics* 4(10): 32 (2006).

[82] Bureau of Justice Statistics. *Prisoners in 1996.* Washington, DC: U.S. Department of Justice, 1997.

[83] Sabol et al. *Prison and Jail Inmates at Midyear 2006,* p. 9.

[84] The Sentencing Project. *Women and the Criminal Justice System, Briefing Sheets.* Washington DC: Author. May 2007. [Online] http://www.sentencingproject.org/PublicationDetails.aspx?PublicationID=586

[85] Drug War Facts.

[86] Harrison and Beck, *Prisoners in 2005,* p. 8.

[87] Ibid., p. 5.

[88] Sabol et al. *Prison and Jail Inmates at Midyear 2006,* p. 9.

[89] Reynolds, M. "Educating Students about the War on Drugs: Crime and Civil Consequences of a Felony Drug Conviction." In L. M. Williams (ed.), *Women, Crime, and the Criminal Justice System. Women's Studies Quarterly* 32(3–4): 246–260 (2004).

[90] Harlow, C. W. *Education and Correctional Populations.* Washington, DC: Bureau of Justice Statistics, January 2003, p. 1.

[91] The Sentencing Project, *Women and the Criminal Justice System.*

[92] Harrison and Beck, *Prisoners in 2005,* p. 9.

[93] Browne, A. "Violence in Marriage: Until Death Do Us Part?" In A. Cardarelli (ed.), *Violence between Intimate Partners: Patterns Causes, and Effects.* Needham Heights, MA: Allyn & Bacon, 1997, pp 48–69; Ferraro, K. J. "Battered Women: Strategies for Survival." In Cardarelli, *Violence between Intimate Partners: Patterns Causes, and Effects,* 1997, pp. 124–140; Maguigan, H. "Battered Women and Self-defense: Myths and Misconceptions in Current Reform Proposals." *University of Pennsylvania Law Review* 140: 379–486 (1991).

[94] Harrison and Beck, *Prisoners in 2005,* p. 9.

[95] Eigenberg, H. M. (1990). "The National Crime Survey and Rape: The Case of the Missing Question." *Justice Quarterly.* 7:655–671.

[96] Beck, A. J. and P. M. Harrison. *Sexual Violence Reported by Correctional Authorities, 2005* (NCJ 214646). Washington, DC: Bureau of Justice Statistics, July 2006, p. 6.

[97] Struckman-Johnson, C. and D. Struckman-Johnson. "Sexual Coercion Reported by Women in Three Midwestern Prisons." *Journal of Sex Research* 39(3): 217–227 (2002); Greer, K. R. "The Changing Nature of Interpersonal Relationships in a Women's Prison." *Prison Journal* 80(4): 442–469 (2000).

98 Eigenberg, H. M. "Correctional Officers and Their Perceptions of Homosexuality, Rape, and Prostitution in Male Prisons." *Prison Journal* 80(4): 415–434 (2000).

99 Chesney-Lind and Pasko, *The Female Offender.*

100 American Civil Liberties Union (ACLU), Break the Chains: Communities of Color and the War on Drugs, and The Brennan Center at NYU School of Law. *Caught in the Net: The Impact of Drug Policies on Women and Families.* March 2005, p. 49. [Online] http://www.aclu.org/images/asset_upload_file393_23513.pdf

101 Ibid.

102 ACLU et al., *Caught in the Net,* p. 47.

103 The Sentencing Project, *Women and the Criminal Justice System.*

104 ACLU et al., *Caught in the Net,* pp. 18–19.

105 Websdale, N. and M. Chesney-Lind. "Doing Violence to Women: Research Synthesis on the Victimization of Women." In Price and Sokoloff, *The Criminal Justice System and Women,* p. 304.

106 ACLU et al., *Caught in the Net,* Executive Summary.

107 Irwin, J. "The Prison Experience: The Convict World." In G. S. Bridges, J. G. Weis, and R. D. Crutchfield (eds.), *Criminal Justice.* Thousand Oaks, CA: Pine Forge Press, 1996.

108 Watterson, *Women in Prison,* pp. 77–79.

109 Giallombardo, R. *Society of Women: A Study of Women's Prisons.* New York: Wiley, 1966, and *The Social Order of Imprisoned Girls.* New York: Wiley, 1974; Ward, D. H. and K. S. Kassebaum. *Women's Prisons.* Chicago: Aldine, 1965; Hefferman, E. *Making It in Prison: The Square, the Cool and the Life.* New York: Wiley, 1972; Hefferman, E. "Making It in a Woman's Prison: The Square, the Cool and the Life." In R. M. Carter, D. Glaser, and L. T. Wilkins (eds.), *Correctional Institutions* (2nd ed.). Philadelphia: Lippincott, 1977; Owen, B. *In the Mix: Struggle and Survival in a Women's Prison.* Albany: State University of New York Press, 1998.

110 Watterson, *Women in Prison,* pp. 285–308.

111 Ibid., p. 288.

112 Ibid., p. 63.

113 Forsyth, C. J. and R. D. Evans. "Reconsidering the Pseudo-Family/Gang Gender Distinction in Prison Research." *Journal of Police and Criminal Psychology,* 18 (1): 22 (2003).

114 Gartner, R. and C. Kruttschnitt. "A Brief History of Doing Time." *Law and Society Review* 38(2) (2004).

115 Anderson, T. "The Impact of Drug Use and Crime Involvement on Health Problems Among Female Drug Offenders." *Prison Journal* 82(1): 50–69 (2002); Berkman, A. "Prison Health: The Breaking Point." *American Journal of Public Health* 85(12): 1616–1619 (1995).

116 Maruschak, L. M. *HIV in Prisons, 2005.* Washington, DC: Bureau of Justice Statistics, September 2007, p. 1.

117 ACLU et al., *Caught in the Net,* pp. 48–49.

118 Dabney, D. A. and M. S. Vaughn. "Incompetent Jail and Prison Doctors." *Prison Journal* 80(2): 151–184 (2000).

119 Cited in: The Commission on Safety and Abuse in America's Prisons. *Confronting Confinement.* New York: Vera Institute, June 2006, p. 40. [Online] http://www.prisoncommission.org/pdfs/Confronting_Confinement.pdf

120 Ibid., p. 13.

121 Fellner, J. "Prevalence and Policy: New Data on the Prevalence of Mental Illness in U.S. Prisons." [Online] http://hrw.org/english/docs/2007/01/10/usdom15040.htm

122 James, D. J. and L. E. Glaze. *Mental Health Problems of Prison and Jail Inmates.* Washington, DC: Bureau of Justice Statistics, September 2006, pp. 4, 10.

123 Owen, B. "Women and Imprisonment in the United States: The Gendered Consequences of the U.S. Imprisonment Binge." In S. Cook and S. Davies (eds.), *Harsh Punishments: International Experiences of Women's Imprisonment.* Boston: Northeastern Press, 1999, pp. 81–98.

124 Dabney and Vaughn, "Incompetent Jail and Prison Doctors."

125 National Commission on Correctional Health Care Position Statement. "Women's Health in Correctional Settings." "Inmate Health Care, Part II." *Corrections Compendium* 23(11) (1997).

126 Amnesty International. *Abuse of Women in Custody: Sexual Misconduct and Shackling of Pregnant Women,* 2006. [Online] http://www.amnestyusa.org/women/custody/; National Institute of Corrections. *Current Issues in the Operation of Women's Prisons.* Washington, DC: U.S. Department of Justice, (1998).

127 Ibid.

128 See Henriques, Z. W. and E. Gilbert. "Sexual Abuse and Sexual Assault of Women in Prison." In R. Muraskin (ed.), *It's a Crime: Women and Justice* (2nd ed.). Upper Saddle River, NJ: Prentice Hall, 2000, pp. 253–268.

129 *Prisoners of the District of Columbia Department of Corrections v. District of Columbia.* 877F Supp 634 (1994).

130 Bloom and Chesney-Lind, "Women in Prison," pp. 183–204.

131 The Sentencing Project, *Women and the Criminal Justice System.*

132 The Commission on Safety and Abuse in America's Prisons. *Confronting Confinement,* p. 28.

133 Pollock, *Women, Prison, and Crime,* p. 93.

134 The Commission on Safety and Abuse in America's Prisons. *Confronting Confinement,* p. 12.

135 Ibid., p. 28.

136 Erisman, W. and J. Contardo. *Learning to Reduce Recidivism: A 50-State Analysis of Postsecondary Correctional Educational Policy.* The Institute for Higher Education Policy, 2005, pp. 7–8. [Online] http://www.ihep.org/pubs/PDF/Recidivism.pdf

137 The Commission on Safety and Abuse in America's Prisons. *Confronting Confinement,* p. 28.

138 Ibid., p. x.

139 Ibid., p. 43.

140 Ibid., p. ix.

141 ACLU et al., *Caught in the Net,* p. 4.

142 For a more detailed look at this case see Shelden, R. G. "Confronting the Ghost of Mary Ann Crouse: Gender Bias in the Juvenile Justice System." *Juvenile and Family Court Journal* 49: 11–25 (1998).

143 Pisciotta, A. "Saving the Children: The Promise and Practice of *Parens Patriae, 1838–98*." *Crime and Delinquency* 28: 411 (1982).

144 Shelden, *Controlling the Dangerous Classes*, ch. 5.

145 Brenzel, B. 1975. "Lancaster Industrial School for Girls: A Social Portrait of a 19th Century Reform School for Girls." *Feminist Studies* 3: 41 (1975). See also Brenzel, B. *Daughters of the State.* Cambridge, MA: MIT Press, 1983.

146 Shelden, "Sex Discrimination in the Juvenile Justice System," p. 58.

147 Brenzel, *Daughters of the State*, p. 4.

148 Ibid., p. 81.

149 Platt, *The Child Savers*, p. 98.

150 Ibid., p. 199.

151 Teitelbaum, L. E. and L. J. Harris. "Some Historical Perspectives on Governmental Regulation of Children and Parents." In L. E. Teitelbaum and A. R. Gough (eds.), *Beyond Control: Status Offenders in the Juvenile Court.* Cambridge, MA: Ballinger, 1977, p. 34; Schlossman, S. and S. Wallach. "The Crime of Precocious Sexuality: Female Delinquency in the Progressive Era." *Harvard Educational Review* 8: 65–94 (1978); Odem, M. *Delinquent Daughters: Protecting and Policing Adolescent Female Sexuality in the United States, 1885–1920.* Chapel Hill: University of North Carolina Press, 1995.

152 Odem, *Delinquent Daughters*, p. 128.

153 Odem, M. and S. Schlossman. "Guardians of Virtue: The Juvenile Court and Female Delinquency in

Early 20th Century Los Angeles." *Crime and Delinquency* 37: 190–192 (1991).

[154] Schlossman and Wallach, "The Crime of Precocious Sexuality," p. 72.

[155] Shelden, R. G. "Sex Discrimination in the Juvenile Justice System: Memphis, Tennessee, 1900–1917." In M. Q. Warren (ed.), *Comparing Male and Female Offenders.* Newbury Park, CA: Sage, 1981, p. 70.

[156] Chesney-Lind and Shelden, *Girls, Delinquency and Juvenile Justice*, ch. 7.

[157] Tappan, P. *Delinquent Girls in Court.* New York: Columbia University Press, 1947, p. 33.

[158] Vedder, C. B. and D. B. Somerville. *The Delinquent Girl.* Springfield, IL: Charles C. Thomas, 1970, p. 147.

[159] Chesney-Lind and Shelden, *Girls, Delinquency and Juvenile Justice.*

[160] Schwartz, I. M. *(In)Justice for Juveniles: Rethinking the Best Interests of the Child.* Lexington, MA: Lexington Books, 1989.

[161] U.S. Statutes at Large. Ninety-Sixth Congress, 2d session (1980). Public Law 96-509, December 8, 1980. Washington, DC: U.S. Government Printing Office.

[162] Costello, J. C. and N. L. Worthington. "Incarcerating Status Offenders: Attempts to Circumvent the Juvenile Justice and Delinquency Prevention Act." *Harvard Civil Rights–Civil Liberties Law Review* 16: 42 (1981–82).

[163] Shelden, R. G. *Delinquency and Juvenile Justice in American Society.* Long Grove, IL: Waveland, 2006.

eighteen

Making Changes
Reforming Criminal Justice and Seeking Social Justice

Over 150 years ago Karl Marx made an astute observation about society's response to crime, forewarning of what we have come to call the *crime control industry*:

> The criminal produces not only crime but also the criminal law; he produces the professor who delivers lectures on this criminal law; and even the inevitable textbook in which the professor presents his lectures as a commodity for sale in the market.... Further, the criminal produces the whole apparatus of the police and criminal justice, detectives, judges, executioners, juries, etc.... Crime takes off the labour market a portion of the excess population, diminishes competition among workers, and to a certain extent stops wages from falling below the minimum, while the war against crime absorbs another part of the same population. The criminal therefore appears as one of those natural "equilibrating forces" which establish a just balance and open up a whole perspective of "useful" occupations.[1]

Marx provides an interesting perspective on the business of criminal justice. He points to areas that are often ignored when analyzing how the criminal justice system works. If the public takes any interest in the system, it is usually to express a desire to make it work better—meaning to eliminate or significantly reduce crime. Ironically, the crime control industry has a vested interested in *not* reducing crime to any great extent. It may attempt to make the current system more efficient at capturing and convicting criminals, but that does not generally result in any significant reduction in the overall rate of crime. Despite huge increases in expenditures on the criminal justice system over the past thirty years, the overall rate of crime has changed little.

WHERE WE ARE

Chapters 3 and 4 discussed various perspectives on criminal justice and theories of crime. Here we will highlight some current views on crime and punishment. David Garland notes that the criminological frameworks used to support current practices are sometimes diametrically opposed.

> There is a *criminology of the self*, that characterizes offenders as normal, rational consumers, just like us; and there is a *criminology of the other*, of the threatening outcast, the fearsome stranger, the excluded and the embittered. One is invoked to routinize crime, to allay disproportionate fears and to promote preventative action. The other functions to demonize the criminal, to act out popular fears and resentments, and to promote support for state punishment.[2]

Between these two views was the dominant perspective that Garland calls "welfarist criminology," where the offender was perceived as disadvantaged or poorly socialized. Until the concept fell out of favor in the 1970s, it was the state's responsibility, "in social as well as penal policy, to take positive steps of a remedial kind."[3]

Garland also highlights the discrepancy between local criminal justice agencies that have attempted to reduce the criminal justice response to crime based on the belief that high rates of imprisonment are an ineffective waste of scarce resources versus legislatures that pass punitive laws and mandatory incarceration ("punitive segregation," in Garland's terminology) based on the attempt to satisfy public demand for protection.

> The limits of police and punishment are recognized in one policy only to be ignored in another. . . . Crime control exhibits two new and distinct patterns of action: an *adaptive strategy* stressing prevention and partnership and a *sovereign state strategy* stressing enhanced control and expressive punishment.[4]

In *Governing through Crime,* Jonathan Simon discusses how changes in social, economic, and political factors affected the response to crime.[5] As background, he quotes Michel Foucault's reference to the derivation of the word government, which historically referred to more than political structures and the management of states.

> Rather, it designated the way in which the conduct of individuals or of groups might be directed—the government of children, of souls, of communities, of families, of the sick. It covered not only the legitimately constituted forms of political or economic subjection but also modes of action, more or less considered and calculated, that were destined to act upon the possibilities of action of other people. To govern in this sense is to structure the possible field of action of others.[6]

Simon notes that this broader definition of government extends the focus from the state to the:

> array of actors operating in parallel fields of civil society, including academia, philanthropy, religious ministries, corporations, and the like. These actors have always played a role in the exercise of state power. . . . When we govern through crime, we make crime and the forms of knowledge historically associated with it—criminal law, popular crime narrative, and criminology—available outside their limited original subject domains as powerful tools with which to interpret and frame all forms of social action as a problem for governance.[7]

Simon also instructs that all governance, whether public or private, takes place within a structure of legal authority—whether the authority of public officers, parents, employers, or property owners, to name a few. Since all legal authority is backed by the possibility of punishment through the criminal law and enforcement by legalized force, all governance is "through the implied threat of making resistance at some stage a crime."[8]

After World War II, the United States experienced a period of affluence. The suburban lifestyle was created, marked by increasing numbers of college graduates. The late 1960s brought the Vietnam War, a social revolution, and increased population from the baby-boom cohort, all of which affected social standards and strained the economy. Politicians began framing "American anxieties about the decline of civility and the economy into volitional narratives about street crime."[9] As Simon notes, governing through crime is less a story

> of extending state power through crime than it is one in which the importance the state has assigned to crime nudges out other kinds of opportunities that a different hierarchy of public problems might produce— e.g., a government obsessed with governing by educating would produce all kinds of incentives to define various people as efficient or deficient in educating.[10]

Simon uses high school drug testing policy as an "example of how crime can interpret and frame even social action seemingly far away from any real examples of crime."[11] The Oklahoma district required all middle and high school students to consent to drug testing if they participated in any extracurricular activity, even though the district stated that it had discovered no evidence of serious drug use or problems in the schools. In 2002, the Supreme Court in *Board of Education of Independent School District No. 92 of Pottawatomie County v. Earls* upheld the policy, stating "the nationwide drug epidemic makes the war against drugs a pressing concern in every school." Simon comments:

> In a sense, the Court has it just right. A nationally constructed understanding of

drugs as a threat has made it incumbent on school officials who wish to be perceived as doing a competent job in governing their schools to implement strategies drawn from the war on crime.[12]

Simon also notes that the effect of governing through crime on schools, in addition to the costs of drug testing and maintaining such surveillance, was evident in how the *Earls* decision characterized schools as institutions of confinement. Justice Thomas referred to public school teachers as being tasked with the "difficult job of maintaining order and discipline." Simon points out that the opinion does not acknowledge the "mission of educating their students rather than simply maintaining custody against a range of risks colored above all by crime."[13]

The family is another symbol that has been altered by the focus of governing through crime.

> Once a space deemed too private for the intrusion of criminal justice, the family has become crisscrossed by tension resulting from crime, domestic violence, child abuse, school misconduct, and housing and insurance exclusions. The family is also where we most directly experience the arts of governance, both as subjects, and, for those of us who become parents, rulers of a most uncertain and frail sort. Perhaps no other set of relationships more powerfully anchors the constellation of meanings and practices we call governing through crime. In a very real sense, our ability to roll back the penal state and its mass imprisonment may depend most on our ability to talk ourselves down from the way we prioritize the avoidance of crime risk in shaping our family life.[14]

According to Simon, there are two faces of governing through crime: the penal state (mass imprisonment) and the security state (building gated communities; fortifying public and private spaces against crime). Fears about crime and children or the family as victims were, in part, a displacement of social unease with the new roles of women in the workplace and a result of longer commutes to work, separating parents from the communities in which their children were

alone for longer hours. As parents, "Americans from a whole range of economic and social positions have found themselves supporting the legal policies that lead to mass imprisonment. Families invest in high-priced security systems, which often increase insecurities rather than relieving fears and prompt them to embrace incarceration as a means of incapacitating potential threats.

> The centrality of fear of crime as a motivation and the centrality of security as a promise create a strong sense of entitlement. . . . One indication of this is the fearsome degree to which the phenomenon once known as NIMBY (Not in My Back Yard) has proliferated from local struggles against drug treatment centers or halfway houses to even sports fields and schools because these are perceived as linked to disorder and, ultimately, crime.[15]

The intractability of some problems is most poignantly displayed in the family. Creating protection against spousal or child abuse also created the potential for miscategorization of behavior and increased fears of the potential danger—and more conflicting images.

> This is not to say that a single monolithic trend is altering the family. The picture of the family as a governable space regarding domestic violence is much different than the one that emerges from the gated community. In one context, the family appears as a nest of potential conflicts and abuses with the possibility that surveillance, deterrence, and punishment must be carried down to the micro level. In another, the family appears as a "crime-free zone." In one frame, parents (father and mother) are potential offenders; in another, they are potential victims and, most important, the parents of potential victims. In one context, the state operates as a coercive agency ready to involve itself in intimate family decisions should violence and crime emerge either from or near their midst. But at the same time, in a different context, the state, so powerful for some, devolves into a distant and largely ineffectual force that cannot be relied upon to provide even minimal family security.[16]

The emergence of market-oriented, middle-class culture shaped society's relations of class, race, and gender. Economic, political, ideological, and cultural trends influence the punishment systems that emerge. "A punishment system is not only a cultural product of a society; it is also one of many mechanisms that helps reproduce a society's culture."[17]

WHAT DOESN'T WORK

In *Sense and Nonsense about Crime and Drugs*, Samuel Walker debunks commonly accepted ideas about how to solve criminal justice problems. The first proposition in his book is: "Most current crime control proposals are nonsense."[18] Below are some of the solutions he critiques.

1. *Increase the response time after a crime has been committed.* There is no evidence that this will alter the crime rate to any significant degree, mostly because the vast majority of crimes are "cold" by the time someone reports them.[19]

2. *Repeal or modify the exclusionary rule and the* Miranda *warning.* Far from "handcuffing" the police, these two rules have had a positive effect on the way police do business, adding a degree of professionalism to police work. In addition, the "exclusionary rule" applies to a small proportion of all cases.[20]

3. *Selectively incapacitate career criminals.* In general, the use of incarceration to reduce crime, whether selective incapacitation or gross incapacitation, does not produce any significant reduction in crime.[21]

4. *Make sentences mandatory.*[22] Three-strikes laws and other mandatory sentences have no impact on the crime problem. In fact, they make matters worse by locking up low-level offenders and causing severe overcrowding in most prisons, costing taxpayers billions of dollars.

5. *Concentrate on prosecuting career criminals.*[23] This proposal is based on the assumption that a few "career criminals" commit a disproportionate amount of crime and locking them up for long periods of time will cause the crime rate to go down. This is absolutely not true, according to many studies.

6. *Abolish the insanity defense and plea bargaining.*[24] Because the insanity defense is so rarely used, abolishing will have little impact on crime. Plea bargaining does not "let criminals off the hook," as the public sometimes believes. In fact, the danger of plea bargains is the discretionary power they give to prosecutors (see chapter 9). Abolishing plea bargains would have no impact on crime, but it would have a tremendous effect on criminal justice expenditures—fewer plea bargains would equal more trials, which would equal more judges, which would require more jail space.

7. *Limit the appeals criminals can file.*[25] This is another simplistic solution, with no basis in fact, because few criminals file appeals.

8. *Use diversion to reduce crime.*[26] Most diversion programs, as implemented, have little or no impact on crime because (a) they concentrate mostly on low-level offenders and (b) they tend to "widen the net" by bringing more offenders under the watchful eyes of the criminal justice system. (One of the exceptions is the Detention Diversion Advocacy Project, described later in this chapter.)

9. *Boot camps will reduce crime.*[27] This is another common myth; the concept appealed to the public and to politicians wanting to sound tough on crime. The fact is that these programs have practically no impact on crime.

10. *Add more prisons and/or send more people to prison.* A lot of research has been done on this issue, and the general conclusion is that building more prisons or sending more offenders to prison has had little impact.[28]

The beliefs listed above are based more on faith than on hard data. Declaring a "war on crime" or a "war on drugs" or a "war on gangs" (not to mention a "war on terrorism") are rhetorical descriptions to make people feel as though great efforts are being made, but the programs fail miserably.

ADDRESSING THE PROBLEM OF SOCIAL INEQUALITY

Before we can attempt to reduce crime and suffering in the United States, we must first consider the social context of crime. Any effort to achieve *social justice* will first require addressing the amount of social inequality in our society. It may be impossible to achieve equal justice in a society with so much inequality. Throughout this book, we have repeatedly pointed out the effects of inequality on the nature and extent of crime and also on the response by the criminal justice system. The effect is summarized nicely by the title of Reiman's book, *The Rich Get Richer and the Poor Get Prison*. When we speak of social inequality, we almost invariably include *racial* inequality. The twin issues of the income gap between the wealthy and the poor and the income discrepancy between minority racial or ethnic groups and the majority must be analyzed before we take on the more general issue of achieving justice.

In an analysis of all income reported in 2005, just over half (51.5%) was the total amount earned by 90% of Americans; the remaining 10% collected 48.5%—the largest amount collected by that group since 1928 (49.3%) and a 33% increase over the late 1970s. The people in the top 1% earned 440 times as much as the average person in the bottom half, nearly doubling the gap from 1980. Emmanuel Saez, an economist at Berkeley, noted that growing disparities are significant in terms of social and political stability. "If the economy is growing but only a few are enjoying the benefits, it goes to our sense of fairness. It can have important political consequences."[29] While the income gap grows, prisons and jails continue to overflow. Moreover, the federal budget swells with increased military spending, while funds for domestic programs decrease.

Before we continue, let's take a look at one of the most commonly overlooked effects of widespread imprisonment—namely, the effect it has on unemployment rates, especially for African Americans. As many critics have noted, the "official" unemployment rate always underestimates the extent of the problem by ignoring those who have part-time work but want full-time work and those who have given up looking. However, another large group is excluded from these figures: those in prison or jail. With an estimated 2 million prisoners, this is a sizable number. For African-American men, the unemployment rate becomes an astounding 40%.[30] Most of the rise in incarceration rates stems directly from the "war on drugs."

ENDING THE "WAR ON DRUGS"

The "war on drugs" has had a devastating toll on U.S. citizens, especially the poor and racial minorities. The negative consequences have been far-reaching: the exploding prison population, the targeting of racial minorities (and their disenfranchisement), the enormous costs to taxpayers, and little or no impact on drug use. Conversely, the drug war has benefited some groups, including law enforcement agencies being paid enormous sums of money. Fighting any "war" benefits a number of people, whether it be the "war on poverty," "war on gangs," or the "war on terrorism."

The drug war has helped create and perpetuate a prison-industrial complex. If legislatures create laws that prohibit behaviors or substances that people want, someone will take the risk of meeting that demand to make a profit. Illegal markets operate identically to legal markets. The production and distribution of commodities are based on the "law of supply and demand," which dictates that where there is a demand for a commodity, someone will engage in the act of supply. If the commodity has been considered a "vice" (such as prostitution, gambling, drugs, and alcohol depending on the laws at the time) and the criminal justice system attempts to limit access to it, the profits will be higher because the commodity has been defined as illegal. When society uses the law to attempt to reduce either the supply or the demand of something that is desired, it fails miserably and suffers drastic consequences.

Defining something that is highly desired by the general public as illegal opens the door for a number of opportunities—

both legal and illegal. Criminal syndicates may seize the opportunity to provide the outlawed commodity. Bribery—paying police officers to look the other way or judges to dismiss a case—is one illegal behavior that exists because of the inflated profits from an illegal commodity. Other effects include the violation of individual rights (sometimes in an effort to score a big arrest), and the violence of turf wars between rival street gangs over the lucrative markets. Individuals who want the product or service will ignore the law; other individuals may perceive that the laws are differentially enforced or that the law unfairly targets particular segments of the population. In either case, another consequence is widespread disrespect for the law.[31] There is also a great deal of money to be made legitimately by people working in the criminal justice system. Largely as a result of fighting the drug war, the "criminal justice industrial complex" has become a booming business. Taxpayers pay in excess of $200 billion per year for the police, the courts, and the correctional system—up $10 billion from the cost in 1970. Fighting the drug war is big business. The same can be said of the "war on gangs."

The fact is we do not seem to be winning the drug war. At least, we are not winning in the usual sense of the word: people are finding it easier and easier to obtain drugs, street prices of illegal drugs have dropped considerably, and hardly a dent has been made in the amount of drugs coming into the country. But in another sense many are in fact "winning"—if we define *winning* as making huge profits and the expansion of drug war bureaucracies. Jobs have been created and lucrative contracts awarded to build prisons, to provide police cars, and to supply various technologies such as drug testing.

Part of the problem is that drugs are a huge business enterprise. Consider these facts:[32]

- The global illicit drug market has an estimated value of $13 billion at the production level and $322 billion at the retail level, an amount that is higher than the GDP of 88% of the countries in the world. A kilogram of heroin sold for an average of $4,000 in Pakistan; in the United States, it sold for $66,250. There are about $7 billion in drug profits coming out of Colombia each year (legitimate exports are only slightly greater at $7.6 billion); Colombian cartels spend about $100 million on bribes to officials each year.

- The estimated economic cost of alcohol abuse is around $148 billion, compared to drug-abuse costs of around $97 billion. Concerning this $97 billion, 60% of the costs are related to law enforcement and imprisonment; only 3% were from the victims of drug-related crime. An estimated 85,000 die each year from alcohol abuse, plus an additional 16,000 from motor vehicle accidents where alcohol was involved.

- In 1969 the government spent $65 million on the drug war; in 1982 the amount totaled $1.65 billion; in 1998 the totals surpassed $17 billion; and in 2005 the combined total money spent at the state and federal levels was an astronomical $50 billion.

- The government continues to focus on the supply side rather than the demand side of the equation. Interdiction efforts intercept only 13% of the heroin and 28 to 40% of the cocaine shipments. Profits in illegal drugs are so inflated that 75% of all drug shipments would have to be intercepted to seriously reduce the profitability of the business.

Drugs, whether legal or illegal, are profitable commodities—profitable for the supplier, the seller, and the "drug warriors" trying to "win" the "war."[33] Consider the number of contractors needed to build a prison or jail (engineers, architects, builders, electricians) plus suppliers of all the equipment (locks, fences, furniture, computers, etc.) and daily maintenance (suppliers of linen, food, medical supplies, etc.). Billions of dollars are to be made in the "prison industry," not to mention salaries and benefits for those working in the system (police officers, court workers, judges, prison guards, etc.). The education and training of the next generation of "drug warriors" is also linked to the criminal justice industrial complex. Attempts to change the response of the criminal justice system to the demand for drugs will have to confront both the fact that some people want the commodity and that others support the use of punishment as a solution.

Disparity in Targets

Younk Ik Cho, a researcher at the University of Illinois, Chicago notes that one of the most significant misconceptions about drug use is that we "spontaneously assume that the majority of people who use illegal drugs would be minorities, which is not true."[34] The police are also affected by the perception. Paul Butler, law professor at George Washington University, comments that the police selectively enforce the drug laws in the black community because they believe blacks need more drug law enforcement.

> Police and prosecutors use the statistics about the number of African Americans who get arrested for drug use as a reason to look more closely at African Americans for that crime. And, of course, if you're especially looking among African Americans, then you'll find more African Americans. There's an important relationship between looking for something and finding it.[35]

Chapter 17 discussed the impact of the war on drugs on women of color, including selective testing of pregnant women of color for drug use.

> Numerous studies demonstrate that law enforcement officers improperly use race as a proxy for criminal propensity. A woman's first point of contact with the net cast by the war on drugs is often the result of a law enforcement officer's discretionary—and racially informed—decision regarding whom to stop and search.[36]

Black women are five times more likely to live in poverty and to receive welfare. As a result, poor women are more likely to be visible to various government institutions from public hospitals to welfare agencies. Their drug use is more likely to be detected and reported. "Poor black women have been selected for punishment as a result of an inseparable combination of their gender, race, and economic status."[37]

The war on drugs quadrupled the prison population from 1980 to 2005. The laws that were passed disproportionately affected urban minorities. "The more lawmakers try to fine-tune drug laws, the more pronounced the imbalance becomes."[38] As discussed in chapters 7 and 10, the sentencing laws that implemented a 100 to 1 disparity for crack versus powder cocaine have targeted minorities. In addition, "safe zone" laws increase penalties for drug sales near schools, churches, parks, and other public places. In densely populated minority neighborhoods, almost any location meets the criteria for increased penalties. For example, almost 70% of Chicago is within the safe zones. Selling drugs within those areas carries a mandatory prison term; 90% of Illinois inmates with a primary offense of violating a "safe-zone" law are African American. We have also discussed how differences in selling drugs in open-air markets in urban areas versus less visible sales in suburban areas make minorities more vulnerable to detection and imprisonment.

African Americans make up 13% of illicit drug users but 32% of those arrested for drug violations and 53% of those incarcerated in state prisons for drug crimes.[39] In Illinois, more than 70% of illicit drug users are white, but 66% of inmates in Illinois prisons for drug offenses are black; Illinois has the highest incarceration rate of blacks for drug possession in the country. A Cook County (the county in which Chicago is located) public defender commented on the homogeneity of the people in the Criminal Courts building.

> You can't miss once you walk into that building that the majority of civilians coming in for their own cases or a loved one's case are predominantly black people. There are some female blacks arrested for simple possession, some older blacks, very few and far between some Caucasian males brought in for simple possession. But rarely did we get a case that involved someone that's not a minority. Usually they were young male blacks.[40]

Myths and Realities about Drugs and Crime

Most experts on drug use have come to the conclusion that there are *two drug problems,* one related to the general population, the other related to those living in extreme poverty, including those caught up in the criminal justice system. In recent years, while the use of illegal drugs by the general population has declined, there has been a significant increase in drug use among the poorest segments of our society.[41]

The connection of drugs to crime is a complex issue, but generally we can say that there are three aspects of the drug–crime connection. First, there are *drug-defined crimes*—possession and sale of illegal drugs. Second, there are *drug-related crimes,* such as those (e.g., robbery) committed to support one's habit or violence associated with the pharmacology of the drug. Third, there are *crimes associated with drug usage,* meaning that the offender was using drugs around the time the crime was committed but the crime was not directly caused by drug use.

What is important to note is that while the majority of high-rate offenders use drugs, most started their criminal careers *before* the onset of drug use, and some started their criminal careers and their drug use about the same time. It must also be stressed that *the overwhelming majority of those who used an illegal drug sometime in their lives became neither drug addicts nor career criminals.* Thus, reducing illegal drug use will not guarantee a lowering of the crime rate.[42]

What about the dangerousness of illegal drugs? It is beyond the scope of this chapter to explore the harmfulness of the various drugs on the market—both legal and illegal. We know for a fact what alcohol and tobacco usage does to individuals, their families, and their communities. The extent of the harm done by substances that have been made illegal is not known with any degree of certainty, although some studies document the negative long-term consequences of the use of cocaine and especially heroin.[43] Nevertheless, one set of statistics underscores the dramatic differences between tobacco and alcohol on the one hand and illegal drugs like cocaine and heroin on the other. Every year, on average, there are between 400,000 and 450,000 tobacco-related deaths, between 80,000 and 100,000 alcohol-related deaths, roughly 32,000 deaths from prescription drugs, and 17,000 deaths related to the "hard drugs" (cocaine, heroin, etc.). How many deaths are attributed to marijuana? Zero.[44]

There is continuing controversy over marijuana use. Although marijuana is not a totally benign substance, the negative consequences of marijuana use are far less than most other drugs. To be sure, there are some harmful effects, such as the ingestion of carbon monoxide (one marijuana cigarette delivers three times more tar to the system than one tobacco cigarette).[45] However, most hard-core tobacco smokers go through a pack a day or more, whereas the typical marijuana user smokes significantly less. Contrary to popular myth, marijuana is not a "gateway" drug—leading to the use of more serious drugs.[46] Most of those who use marijuana do not progress to the harder drugs.

A Modest Proposal

What are the available alternatives? Do we legalize all drugs to remove the enormous profits available because they are illegal? Do we legalize them with some regulations and restrictions (e.g., minors prohibited from using)? Do we legalize only some drugs (e.g., marijuana)? Do we "decriminalize" some or all drugs? Do we involve the criminal justice system in only indirect ways, such as having drug courts or drug treatment sentences instead of jail or prison (as stipulated in a recent California referendum, known as Proposition 36)?

The average cost per day is $67.55 for each state prison inmate. It costs states approximately $16.9 million per day to imprison drug offenders—almost $6.2 billion per year.[47] Since legalizing all drugs is politically infeasible for the foreseeable future, we recommend two actions. First, legalize marijuana, with some restrictions for youth (as there are for alcohol). Law enforcement made more arrests in 2006 (1.9 million) for drug abuse violations than for any other offense. Of those, 39% (almost 739,000) were for possession of marijuana.[48] Even this modest proposal will receive considerable resistance, especially from those in charge of enforcing the drug laws and those profiting from the prison-industrial complex. The usual argument is that such a policy would mean that we condone the use of marijuana. But we condone the use of alcohol and tobacco, both of which are also drugs. We can discourage use of marijuana—and other drugs as well—by using the methods that were so successful in reducing the demand for tobacco. Further, because there is no evidence that marijuana use leads to any serious problems (with some exceptions, to be sure)—and no one dies from it—why criminalize it?[49]

Second, for those addicted to drugs, treatment options should be made available.[50] Reducing expenditures on enforcement and interdiction by 10% could shift almost 1 billion dollars to education and treatment, substantially increasing the budgets for those options and the opportunities for improved public health.[51] It is clear that providing treatment instead of jail or prison is much more cost-effective. One study noted that every dollar spent on drug treatment results in an overall $3 social benefit (less crime, more employment, etc.). One illustration is the *Treatment Alternatives to Street Crime (TASC) project.* Under this plan, instead of going to jail or prison, an offender is placed under community-based supervision in a drug treatment program.[52]

EXPANDING DIVERSION PROGRAMS, AVOIDING NET WIDENING

As noted in chapter 10, diversion has been in practice throughout the history of criminal justice. Diversionary programs have a strong theoretical background in labeling principles (see chapter 4) that evolved from Tannenbaum's "dramatization of evil" (shifts the focus from the act to the actor), Lemert's "secondary deviance" (internalizing labels of others) and Becker's "outsiders" (creation of deviance by social groups labeling acts as "deviant" and treating persons so labeled as "outsiders").[53] Legal interaction by the criminal justice system may actually perpetuate crime or delinquency by processing cases that might otherwise be ignored, normalized in their original settings, or better dealt with in more informal settings within the community.

One of the most immediate responses to the labeling perspective was the 1967 President's Commission on Law Enforcement and Administration of Justice report, which called for the creation of "youth services bureaus" to develop alternative programs for juvenile offenders in local communities and many different programs for adult offenders. The establishment of these youth services bureaus began a move toward diverting youths, especially status offenders and other nonserious delinquents, away from the juvenile court. These bureaus were quickly established in virtually every community regardless of size.[54]

There are concerns about prejudice, discrimination, civil rights violations, and *net widening* in the application of diversion programs. Net widening, in particular, has generated a substantial amount of attention. A true diversion program (and the original concept behind diversion) places those who would ordinarily be processed through the criminal justice system into an alternative program. So, for example, if 1,000 arrestees would normally be processed through the criminal justice system, *diversion* would occur if 300 of the arrestees were placed in alternative programs. *Net widening* would occur if the 300 assigned to alternative programs were *not* among the original 1,000, thus placing 1,300 people under some type of supervisory control.

Most of the research on diversion programs has centered on juvenile offenders. However, the same concepts apply to adults. The essential key is diverting as many offenders out of the criminal justice system as possible and providing the comprehensive services they need. One excellent example of such a program is the Detention Diversion Advocacy Project.

The Center on Juvenile and Criminal Justice (CJCJ) created the original *Detention Diversion Advocacy Project* (DDAP) in 1993 in San Francisco. The major goal was to reduce the number of youths in court-ordered detention and provide them with culturally relevant community-based services and supervision.

DDAP is designed to accomplish the following goals:

1. To provide multilevel interventions to divert youth from secure detention facilities;

2. To demonstrate that community-based interventions are an effective alternative to secure custody and that the needs of both the youths and the community can be met at a cost savings to the public;

3. To reduce disproportionate minority incarceration.

The DDAP program involves two primary components. *Detention Advocacy* involves identifying youth likely to be detained pending their adjudication. Once a potential client is identified, DDAP case managers present a release plan to the judge. The plan includes a list of appropriate community services that will be accessed on the youth's behalf. The plan also includes specific objectives for evaluating the youth's progress while in the program. Emphasis is placed on maintaining the youth at home. If the home is not a viable option, the project staff will identify and secure a suitable alternative. If the plan is deemed acceptable by a judge, the youth is released to DDAP's supervision. *Case Management* provides frequent, consistent support and supervision to youths and their families, linking them to community-based services and closely monitoring their progress. Case management services are field-oriented, requiring the case manager to have daily contact with the youth, his or her family, and significant others. Contact includes a minimum of three in-person meetings a week. Additional services are provided to the youth's family members, particularly parents and guardians, in areas such as securing employment, day care, drug treatment services, and income support.

Clients are primarily identified through referrals from the public defender's office, the probation department, community agencies, and parents. Admission to DDAP is restricted to youths currently held, or likely to be held, in secure detention. The individuals selected are those deemed to be at risk for engaging in subsequent criminal activity based on a risk assessment instrument developed by the National Council on Crime and Delinquency. The target population is persons whose risk assessment scores indicate that they would ordinarily be detained—or what Miller terms the "deep-end" approach.[55] By focusing on *detained* youth, the project ensures that it remains a true diversion alternative and does not engage in net widening.

Because the project deals only with youths who are awaiting adjudication or final disposition, their appropriateness for the project is based on their likelihood of attending their court hearings and whether they can reside in the community under supervision without unreasonable risk. This is similar in principle to someone in the adult system being released on bail pending court hearings. Client screening involves gathering background information from probation reports, psychological evaluations, police reports, school reports, and other pertinent documents. Interviews are conducted with youths, family members, and adult professionals to determine the types of services required. Once a potential client is evaluated, DDAP staff presents a comprehensive community service plan at the detention hearing and requests that the judge release the youth to DDAP custody.

The primary goal of DDAP is to design and implement individualized community service plans that address a wide range of personal and social needs, including linguistic and medical needs. The quality and level of services are monitored by DDAP staff, along with the youth's participation. Because youth services in San Francisco have been historically fragmented by ethnicity, race, and community, a more unified approach is being tried with DDAP to address the needs of the various communities in the most culturally appropriate manner. It has become a neutral site within the city, staffed by representatives from CJCJ and several other community-based service agencies.

The senior author (RGS) conducted an evaluation of this program, which consisted of comparing a group of youths referred to DDAP with a similarly matched control group that remained within the juvenile justice system.[56] The results showed that after a three-year follow-up, the recidivism rate for the DDAP group was 34%, compared to a 60% rate for the control group. Detailed comparisons holding several variables constant (e.g., prior record, race, age, gender) and examining several different measures of recidivism (e.g., subsequent commitments, referrals for violent offenses) showed that the DDAP youths still had a significantly lower recidivism rate. There are three key reasons for the success of the program.

First, the caseloads (an average of 10 cases per DDAP caseworker) are extremely low in comparison to the caseloads of probation officers (ranging from 50 to 150). Smaller caseloads typically result in more intensive supervision, allowing caseworkers to spend more quality time with their clients *in the field* (e.g., in their homes, on street corners, at school), rather than endless hours in an office making phone calls and doing paperwork and other bureaucratic chores.

Second, DDAP is a program that is out of the mainstream of the juvenile justice system—it is a true alternative rather than one of many bureaucratic extensions burdened by the usual bureaucratic restrictions. For instance, the qualifications for being a caseworker with DDAP are not as stringent as those in the juvenile justice system (i.e., age restrictions, educational requirements). From casual observations of some of these caseworkers, researchers have been impressed with their dedication and passion to helping youth. Moreover, the backgrounds of these workers were similar to the backgrounds of some of their clients (similar race, neighborhood of origins, language, arrest records, "street" experience, etc.).

Third, the physical location of DDAP seems user friendly and lacks the usual macho appearance of the formal system. There are no bars, no concrete buildings, no devices for screening for weapons, no "cells" for "lockdown," and so on. Further, the DDAP workers are not "officers of the court" with powers of arrest and the usual accouterments of such occupations (e.g., badges, guns).

There could also be a possible fourth explanation (speculation at this time since there are insufficient data to support the con-clusion). Perhaps the small caseloads and constant contact allow DDAP caseworkers to be "on top of the case" and thus able to "nip in the bud" potential problems. If police officers encounter a youth in a possible arrest situation and are aware of DDAP, they may decide to contact the caseworker, who might persuade the officers that the situation could be handled without a formal arrest. We have no way of knowing whether this occurs with any degree of regularity. If it does, such a procedure may be a positive sign, because youths from more privileged backgrounds are often treated this way by the police if they believe that someone in authority can "handle" the youth informally. Many youths have been saved the stigma of formal juvenile processing by such intervention by significant adults in their lives.

Since the evaluation was completed DDAP programs have been established in Baltimore, Washington, DC, and Philadelphia. An evaluation was conducted on the program in Philadelphia, also showing positive results.[57]

The most recent DDAP program in California started in 2002. *Pathways to Change* was part of a program called *Safe Passages*, a collaborative of city and county officials, community-based organizations, and community members organized to create programming for Oakland youth. The Pathways to Change case managers come from six partnering agencies, many of which have decades of experience providing services in Oakland, including individual and family counseling, job training, youth violence issues, substance abuse treatment, as well as services specific to different race and ethnic groups represented in Oakland. Pathways to Change is now one of two initiatives for youth offenders in Oakland under a program known as the *Mentoring Center*.[58]

Though certainly not a "magic bullet," DDAP has much promise. The basic principles behind this program (case management, etc.) can easily be applied to adults. It models the possibility of dealing with many criminal matters in the community rather than within the justice system. In terms of both human dignity and cost savings, it is a valuable alternative.

We would be remiss if we did not note that there are limitations to any proposals that are offered as an alternative to using the criminal justice system as a response to crime. If the focus is on the reaction to crime, there will be no attempt to address the root causes of crime. There is only so much tinkering with the justice system that can be done. As the criminalization model in chapter 1 shows, people are funneled (and sometimes refunneled) through the system. The numbers of people processed may increase or decrease, but there is a steady supply. Addressing some of the root causes of crime requires a different focus.

BROAD-BASED NATIONAL STRATEGIES TO REDUCE CRIME

The criminal justice system represents a *reactive* approach to the problem of crime. In other words, the system *responds,* after the fact, to crime. Certainly there are ways in which this response can be made more productive. But a better approach would be to make a serious attempt to be *proactive*—that is, to try to *prevent* the circumstances most likely to produce crime. Because there are numerous *social* causes of crime, it is necessary to find the causes and to act to alleviate them as much as possible.

Over the years, many researchers have offered versions of how such responses should be structured. One example is offered by the criminologist Elliot Currie.[59] He suggests five general categories for a national strategy to address the general problem of crime. First, he recommends early educational interventions (e.g., programs such as Head Start) based on the assumption that lack of preparedness for school, especially among lower-class minorities, leads to poor school performance and dropping out, which in turn are related to delinquency. Second, the United States should expand health and mental health services including prenatal and postnatal care. This is based on evidence that the most violent youths suffer from childhood traumas of the central nervous system, exhibit multiple psychotic symptoms, and

have experienced severe physical or sexual abuse.[60] Third, Currie suggests family support programs, especially for families dealing with child abuse and other forms of domestic violence. Abused children are far more likely than nonabused children to become abusers themselves. The majority of prison inmates, especially violent ones, experienced severe physical, emotional, or sexual abuse or some combination of all three. Fourth, Currie recommends doing something constructive with offenders after they have broken the law. In other words, do not merely warehouse them in a correctional setting. He notes that an ingredient found in virtually all successful rehabilitation programs is improving skills—work skills, reading and verbal skills, problem-solving skills, and so on. Fifth, there is a pressing need for drug and alcohol abuse treatment programs. The current focus on interdiction and punishment has not reduced the problem of drug abuse; it has burdened the correctional system with more prisoners than it can handle, reducing the very limited funds for drug rehabilitation.

On a more general level, Currie suggests that we as a society need to reduce racial inequality, poverty, and inadequate services; most importantly, we need to prepare the next generation for the labor market of the future. With this in mind, he outlines four goals for the decades ahead: (1) reduction of inequality and social impoverishment, (2) an active labor market policy that aims at upgrading job skills, (3) a national family policy (e.g., a family leave law), and (4) establishment of economic and social stability in local communities. The frequent moving of capital and employment opportunities has forced many families to relocate to seek better jobs, which has weakened the sense of community and the development of networks that would provide support. In addition, he suggests the need for a national research agenda to study the effectiveness of these policies in order to find what works.

Mark Colvin has also written about the need for national strategies; his focus is social reproduction—the process through which institutions, mostly families and schools, socialize children and prepare them for productive roles in society.[61] His main thesis is that these institutions have largely failed to foster the social bonds necessary for young people develop the skills and connections necessary for legitimate avenues to adulthood and employment. The result is that many are becoming marginal to the country's economic institutions. This failure to invest early in human development and human capital contributes to the growing crime rate and increasing expenditures for welfare and prisons. There is a need for a "national comprehensive program aimed at spurring economic growth, human development, and grass-roots, democratic participation in the major institutions affecting our lives and those of our children."[62]

Colvin argues that neither conservative deterrence approaches nor liberal approaches to rehabilitation have been very effective, mainly because they are reactive policies. We need to redirect our focus away from the question of "what to do about crime" to "what to do about our declining infrastructure and competitiveness in the world economy." Replacing the military-industrial complex with an educational-industrial complex is a necessary first step.[63]

As Colvin notes, education must be more than what the term has traditionally meant—formalized public schooling leading to a diploma. He says that education "must include families, schools, workplaces, and communities." He offers seven specific proposals:[64]

1. *Short-term emergency measures.* Programs such as the Civilian Employment Training Act (CETA) and income subsidies for poor families are needed to help alleviate joblessness and human suffering. Colvin stresses the importance of comprehensive programs that affect a broader spectrum of people.

2. *Nationwide parent-effectiveness programs.* These types of programs should be required in the senior year of high school and also offered in adult education programs along with counseling programs for new parents.[65]

3. *Universal Head Start preschool programs.* Certified preschool programs should be accompanied by free day care programs to increase the opportunities for participation.

4. *Expanded and enhanced public education.* This includes several interrelated proposals: (a) increase teachers' salaries; (b) change certification to open up the profession to noneducation majors; (c) increase the school year to 230 days (from the 180-day average) to compete with Germany and Japan (which average 240 days per year); (d) focus especially on problem-solving skills; (e) offer nontraditional courses such as "outward bound" and apprenticeships; (f) use peer counseling and student tutoring; (g) eliminate tracking; (h) award stipends for attending school and bonuses for good grades to eliminate the need for students to work; (i) establish nonviolent conflict resolution programs; and (j) get students more active in school policies to help prepare them for participating in democracy as adults.

5. *National service program.* After completing high school, a youth should have the opportunity to complete two years of national service (possibilities include health care, nursing, environmental cleanup, day care services, care for the elderly, and so on) and to earn educational and vocational stipends for the service. The participation would provide much-needed labor for public works projects and would allow young people to participate in the improvement of their communities. Communities would benefit from the energy of youths.

6. *Enhancement of workplace environments.* Young people must have hope that they are headed for a good-quality job. Labor laws that emphasize workplace democracy could create noncoercive work environments. This helps to attract and reward creative individuals who are needed to compete in a global economy.

7. *Programs for economic growth and expanded production.* Investments aimed at what is good for the general public rather than profit are needed, as well as more investment in research and industrial techniques.

A variation of the proposals offered by both Currie and Colvin comes from Margaret Phillips and is a good example of a theory-based intervention.[66] Phillips elaborates on the importance of unemployment as a key factor related to crime. Her goal is to show why there is a connection between these two variables. Her thesis is that the stress associated with poverty and feelings of powerlessness (which are correlated) result in the tendency to be present oriented—that is, unable to plan for the future because of a belief that your life is out of control. This is part of the irresponsibility typically associated with crime and delinquency.

Phillips notes that most theories fall somewhere within the old "nature versus nurture" debate and uses a strike at the Hormel Meatpacking Company in Austin, Minnesota, in the mid-1980s as an illustration. Hormel broke the strike by hiring workers from outside the town. Many local workers were left jobless, and the rates of crime—especially domestic violence—and alcohol and drug abuse rose noticeably. These increases were explained by a ripple effect common after plant closures, when crime in general—and domestic violence in particular—increases, along with suicides, stress-related illnesses, and drug and alcohol abuse. What is perhaps most interesting is that there is a corresponding decrease in citizen participation in civic activities, which decreases the amount of informal social control. Phillips concludes by noting that there is abundant evidence that poverty and economic dislocation play an important role in crime, as well as in the lack of self-control.[67]

Phillips's theory tries to combine the role of environmental (especially socioeconomic) factors with individual responsibility and powerlessness.

> The essence of powerlessness is the feeling that nothing one does matters; taking responsibility for one's acts assumes the understanding that one's acts have consequences. Taking control of one's life implies the understanding that one can have some control over the future. Thus empowerment is a prerequisite for taking responsibility, and the most basic kind of empowerment is economic, the ability to support oneself and a family.[68]

This would logically lead us to consider full employment as a solution to the crime problem. It even suggests a Works Progress Administration (WPA) project like what occurred in the 1930s.

Next, Phillips outlines the link between powerlessness and irresponsibility. She begins by noting that if there is such a thing as a criminal personality type, then such a person would tend to be present oriented and irresponsible. This kind of person sees himself or herself as having little or no control over the future and is therefore extremely tied to the present. This theme can be seen, at least implicitly, in the techniques of neutralization noted by Sykes and Matza (see chapter 4). Many delinquents see themselves as receivers of effects, rather than as active doers. This leads to irresponsibility, which in turn leads to what Matza called "drift," a condition that places one at risk of becoming a delinquent.[69]

Phillips then turns to an area seemingly unrelated (and usually considered off-limits) to sociologists—namely, medical evidence that links poverty and lack of security to fatalism and various physiological effects. Quoting studies by an epidemiologist and a biologist, she notes that there is a connection between the symptoms of stress and the lack of control over one's fate. Stress stems from such things as a lack of nurturing, not knowing what tomorrow will bring, seeing people suffering and dying on a regular basis, and being subjected to criminal victimization. These stressors are especially pronounced in a society of scarcity (which includes many inner-city ghettos). A person's psychological defenses become limited, and one is unable to develop a sense of autonomy and inner psychological strength to cope. When scarcity exists, a normal psychological defense mechanism is to view one's own situation as uncontrollable and oneself as helpless. This in turn leads to attempts to control others (via various sorts of crime, especially violence).[70] It is easy to understand why delinquents from these kinds of backgrounds would be so present oriented. Yet it is important to view such characteristics as a result of the stress produced by poverty, discrimination, and oppression—factors that point to political and economic solutions.

Phillips next focuses on some common causes of feelings of powerlessness (in addition to poverty itself and the corresponding lack of resources).

1. *Joblessness and underemployment.* There is a need for jobs with livable wages.

2. *Population size.* There is a need to develop small neighborhood units so that people will become more empowered (the "safety in numbers" idea).

3. *Alcohol and drug abuse.* Often a means to escape stress, such abuse results in a lack of control, leading to irresponsibility, crime, and perhaps addiction. There is a desperate need for more resources for both treatment and prevention of alcohol and drug abuse.

4. *Low IQ.* Hard-core offenders, especially those in prison, have lower than average IQs. Resources for special education programs early in life would help.

5. *Child abuse.* Families most at risk are those with low income, low educational levels, and significant stress. Abuse is strongly correlated with crime—a high percentage of inmates experienced severe abuse throughout childhood and adolescence.[71]

Phillips offers several interrelated proposals to address these problems. She begins by noting that programs are needed that empower people to become independent and to learn to be responsible. Incarceration of any type fails to do this. Some alternative sentencing programs may help (victim–offender reconciliation, probation programs that require substance-abuse treatment, etc.). On a national level, Phillips suggests that some of the following types of programs might well succeed:

1. *Full employment.* Examples include WPA-type programs and "reindustrialization from below" (i.e., the Tennessee Valley Authority of the 1930s).

2. *Welfare reform.* Reform should include programs that would provide transitional publicly funded jobs.

3. *Health care insurance for all.*

4. *Low-income housing for the homeless.*

For Phillips, the key to solving the problem is empowerment through education, which also includes having meaningful work at livable wages and developing tools that assist offenders in taking some control over their lives.

RESTORATIVE JUSTICE

Restorative justice aims to end the pain and suffering of the victims of crime—not just the victims of "normal" crimes but the victims of all crimes and all forms of human rights abuses. The usual response to crime—especially violent crime—is a desire to "get even" by seeking "just deserts" against offenders, but this response has always proved to be counterproductive. In fact, it goes against virtually every religious tenet.[72] As Gandhi and Martin Luther King Jr. taught and demonstrated, the only way to end violence is *not* to reciprocate in kind. In other words, to end the cycle, just stop the violence. King, in his acceptance speech for the Nobel Peace Prize in 1964, said: "The choice today is not between violence and nonviolence. It is either nonviolence or nonexistence."[73]

There is certainly some truth to the idea that the only way to rid oneself of hurt and anger is through forgiveness. Indeed, the English poet Alexander Pope (1688–1744) wrote, "To err is human, to forgive divine."[74] Unfortunately, forgiveness seems out of step in our current political/economic system. Forgiveness would be more in line with a political/economic system "that sees acknowledgment of a harm done, and apology for it, and forgiveness offered in return, as processes that are personally healing for all involved and simultaneously restorative of community."[75]

The underlying aim of restorative justice is to cease further objectification of those who have been involved in the violent act—the victim, the offender, the families connected to these two individuals, and the community at large. Restorative justice lets all of the individuals involved engage in a healing process through traditional mediation and conflict resolution techniques in order to "help those affected by the harm dissolve their fears, and hates, and resentments and thereby recover a sense of their former selves." Through this process the person most directly harmed "is able to achieve a greater sense of inner-healing and closure for any traumatic loss of trust, self-worth, and freedom . . . [while] the harmed person might also achieve a modicum of reparation for his or her losses as well as be able to reduce his or her fears of being harmed."[76]

Proponents of restorative justice know full well what a difficult sell it is within a capitalist society. As Dennis Sullivan and Larry Tifft observe, the change needed "transforms all of our conceptions of political economy, that is, how we view power and money, and how we assess human worth."[77] Embracing the principles of restorative justice allows us to move beyond power and control over others to a more healing resolution.

Some Concluding Thoughts

In this chapter we provided a brief outline of some specific recommendations that might help reduce the crime problem. Most of the suggestions are based on a change in focus. Before we can achieve equal justice, we must first look at ways of changing the unequal aspects of society. Making the existing justice system more "efficient" (as many recommend) would essentially mean making more arrests of the poor and racial minorities and sending more people to prison.

This is not to say that good people are not needed to work within the system; indeed, that is also a primary need. Many who work in the criminal justice system are conscientious and dedicated and fully understand the inequities within the larger society and within the justice system itself. One of the senior author's (RGS) former students who works in a juvenile court once said, "I hate the system, but I love my kids." We have heard from police officers who have reinforced the idea that the police institution is like an "army of occupation" within the ghettos. We have met many people who work inside jails or prisons and hate what

these institutions do to people—both those incarcerated and those who work there. As a prison guard observed, "We are all doing time here. But we [the guards] just do it in eight-hour shifts."

We have no "magic bullets" that would make the problem go away. No one does. But we are hopeful that you realize that this is the reality that faces you as you prepare for a career within the criminal justice system or for some other career. In either case you may be able to have some impact on the crime problem—a positive impact on specific individuals with whom you come in contact. This in itself can be rewarding. But you must also realize that for every individual that you help "go straight" there are hundreds, perhaps thousands, you will not be able to reach and millions more who are likely to come into the system in the future.

Because crime is still very much with us, perhaps in the new millennium we should be looking elsewhere for answers. In recent years many criminologists have been searching in other directions for answers. One direction has been in the area of philosophy, various Eastern religions, and some of the views of Native Americans. Many of us have begun to seriously examine some of the more recent writings of Richard Quinney, whose latest works point us in the direction of "peacemaking" by seeking peace within ourselves and various nonviolent and noncoercive alternatives to crime, which is consistent with the restorative justice idea.[78]

Although we do not claim to have all the answers, after about thirty years of studying and teaching about the subject of crime and delinquency, we are convinced that fundamental changes need to be made in the way we live and think before we will see any significant decrease in these problems. In discussing delinquency, for example, it is important to note that we are always talking about the "problem of delinquency" or the "problem of youth" or that youth in trouble need to change their attitudes, behaviors, lifestyles, methods of thinking, and so on. It seems that it is always *they* who have to change. What is invariably included in this line of thinking is the use of labels to describe these youths (and adult offenders too). The labels change in concert with the changing times.

As Jerome Miller noted, we began with "possessed" youths in the seventeenth century, then moved to the "rabble" or "dangerous classes" in the eighteenth and late nineteenth centuries, and to the "moral imbeciles" and the "constitutional psychopathic inferiors" in the early twentieth century.[79] We continued through the twentieth century and into the twenty-first with the "psychopaths" of the 1940s and the "sociopaths" of the 1950s and finally to recent labels such as "compulsive delinquent," the "learning disabled," the "unsocialized aggressive," the "socialized aggressive," and the "bored" delinquent. Miller observes that the growth of professionalism has increased the number of labels exponentially. He suggests that the problem with these labels is that it seems to be a way "whereby we bolster the maintenance of the existing order against threats which might arise from its own internal contradictions." And it reassures us

> that the fault lies in the warped offender and takes everyone else off the hook. Moreover, it enables the professional diagnostician to enter the scene or withdraw at will, wearing success like a halo and placing failure around the neck of the client like a noose.[80]

More important, we continue to believe that harsh punishment works, especially the kind of punishment that includes some form of incarceration, so that the offender is placed out of sight and—not coincidentally—out of mind.

Throughout the past two centuries we have continued to succumb to the "edifice complex." We love to build edifices, no matter what they are called (a new courthouse, a new prison, a new correctional center, a new police station, etc.). Perhaps it is because politicians like to have some kind of permanent structure to leave behind as a legacy so they can tell the people who voted for them to look at this or that building as proof that they have done something about crime. Or perhaps it is because the buildings house profitable processes and are part of the huge crime control industry.

We believe it is time for society to quit looking solely at "troubled youth" or "criminals," or even at their "troubled families" and "troubled communities," as the source of crime and all the fears it engenders. It is time that those of us among the more privileged sectors of society consider that we are also part of the problem, perhaps more so. In short, if anyone wants to know where the answers lie and where to begin to look for solutions, we think it prudent that all of us begin by looking in the mirror. We should begin by asking ourselves: Is there anything that I can do differently? Is there something wrong with *my* attitudes, *my* beliefs, or *my* actions that may contribute to the problem? If we want some answers, we should begin by searching *within ourselves.* This is the message from those who espouse Eastern philosophies. Vietnamese Zen master and poet Thich Nhat Hanh suggests:

> When you plant lettuce, if it does not grow well, you don't blame the lettuce. You look into the reasons it is not doing well. It may need fertilizer, or more water, or less sun. You never blame the lettuce. Yet if we have problems with our friends or our family we blame the other person. But if we know how to take care of them, they will grow well, like lettuce. Blaming has no positive effect at all, nor does trying to persuade using reason and arguments. That is my experience. No blame, no reasoning, no argument, just understanding. If you understand, and you show that you understand, you can love, and the situation will change.[81]

The thrust of Hanh's book is that before we can achieve peace on earth, which includes a world without crime and suffering, we have to develop peace within ourselves. How else can we make the world a better place, unless we make our own lives better? How can we tell the "criminals" in our midst how to live their lives if we do not set good examples? As Richard Quinney has written: "If human actions are not rooted in compassion, these actions will not contribute to a compassionate and peaceful world. If we ourselves cannot know peace, be peaceful, how will our acts disarm hatred and violence?"[82] Without such hatred and violence, there would be no need to even have, much less need to control, the "dangerous classes." There is a lot of work to do.

Key Terms

- crime control industry
- Detention Diversion Advocacy Project (DDAP)
- net widening
- restorative justice
- Treatment Alternatives to Street Crime (TASC) project

Notes

[1] Marx, K. "The Usefulness of Crime." In D. Greenberg (ed.), *Crime and Capitalism* (2nd ed.). Philadelphia: Temple University Press, 1993, pp. 52–53.

[2] Garland, D. *The Culture of Control: Crime and Social Order in Contemporary Society.* Chicago: University of Chicago Press, 2002, p. 137.

[3] Ibid.

[4] Ibid., pp. 138, 140.

[5] Simon, J. *Governing through Crime: How the War on Crime Transformed American Democracy and Created a Culture of Fear.* New York: Oxford University Press, 2007.

[6] Michel Foucault, quoted in ibid., pp. 16–17.

[7] Ibid., p. 16.

[8] Ibid., p. 14.

[9] Ibid., p. 22.

[10] Ibid., pp. 21–22.

[11] Ibid., p. 17.

[12] Ibid.

[13] Ibid., p. 18.

[14] Ibid., pp. 205–206.

[15] Ibid., p. 202.

[16] Ibid., pp. 204–205.

[17] Colvin, M. *Penitentiaries, Reformatories, and Chain Gangs: Social Theory and the History of Punishment in Nineteenth Century America.* New York: Palgrave Macmillan, 2000, p. 2.

[18] Walker, S. *Sense and Nonsense about Crime and Drugs* (6th ed.). Belmont, CA: Wadsworth, 2006, p. 11.

[19] Ibid., pp. 92–93.

[20] Walker, pp. 100–105.

[21] Ibid., p. 142. A recent study by the Center on Juvenile and Criminal Justice further documents the failure of the incapacitation model. Males, M., D. Macallair, and M. G. Corcoran. "Testing Incapacitation Theory: Youth Crime and Incarceration in California." San Francisco: Center on Juvenile and Criminal Justice, 2006. [Online] http://cjcj.org/pdf/testing_incapacitation.pdf

[22] Ibid., pp. 146–150.

[23] Ibid., pp. 158–161

[24] Ibid., pp. 161–171.

[25] Ibid., pp. 171–173.

[26] Ibid., pp. 221–224.

[27] Ibid., pp. 232–233.

[28] Ibid., pp. 144–145. For the latest research on this issue see Stemen, D. "Reconsidering Incarceration: New Directions for Reducing Crime." New York: The Vera Institute, 2007. [Online] http://www.vera.org/publications/publications_5.asp?publication_id=379

[29] Johnston, D. C. "Income Gap is Widening." *New York Times* (March 29, 2007). [Online] http://www.nytimes.com/2007/03/29/business/29tax.html?_r=1&ref=business&oref=slogin

[30] Western, B. and K. Beckett. "How Unregulated Is the U.S. Labor Market? The Penal System as a Labor Market." *American Journal of Sociology* 104: 1030–1060 (1999).

[31] Walker, *Sense and Nonsense about Crime and Drugs,* p. 272. See Shelden, R., S. Tracy, and W. B. Brown, *Youth Gangs in American Society* (3rd ed.). Belmont, CA: Wadsworth, 2004.

[32] A variety of sources have been consulted for this information, in particular the Web site for *Drug War Facts.* [Online] http://www.drugwarfacts.org/index2.htm. See especially [Online] http://www.drugwarfacts.org/economi.pdf; also see the following Web sites: http://www.drugpolicy.org/homepage.cfm; http://www.drugsense.org/html/; http://www.pbs.org/newshour/bb/latin_america/jan-june01/colombiadrug_03-02.html; http://www.pbs.org/wgbh/pages/frontline/shows/drugs/charts/

[33] Miller, R. L. *Drug Warriors and Their Prey: From Police Power to Police State.* Westport, CT: Praeger, 1996.

[34] Little, D. "Drug War Enforcement Hits Minorities Hardest." *Chicago Tribune* (July 22, 2007) p. 23.

[35] Ibid.

[36] American Civil Liberties Union (ACLU), Break the Chains: Communities of Color and the War on Drugs, and The Brennan Center at NYU School of Law. *Caught in the Net: The Impact of Drug Policies on Women and Families.* March 2005, p. 28. [Online] http://www.aclu.org/images/asset_upload_file393_23513.pdf

[37] Ibid., p. 30.

[38] Little, "Drug War Enforcement Hits Minorities Hardest," p. 23.

[39] Ibid.

[40] Ibid.

[41] Sources for the following discussion: Walker, *Sense and Nonsense about Crime and Drugs,* chapter 13; Inciardi, J. *The War on Drugs III.* Boston: Allyn & Bacon, 2002, chapter 10; Miron, J. *Drug War Crimes.* Oakland: The Independent Institute, 2004.

[42] Walker, *Sense and Nonsense about Crime and Drugs*, pp. 264–265.

[43] Inciardi, *The War on Drugs* III, pp. 283–285; see also Clark, T. "Heroin: The Problem with Pleasure." [Online] http://www.naturalism.org/heroin.htm and "Keep Marijuana Illegal—For Teens." [Online] http://www.naturalism.org/marijuan1.htm

[44] These data are taken from the following sources: "Governor Pushes Legalization of Drugs during U. of Mexico Speech." *Daily Lobo* (September 25, 2000); Duhigg, C. "Tokin' Reformer." *The New Republic* (April 3, 2000);

Pierce, N. "Prison Reform: A Moment to Seize?" *Nation's Cities Weekly* (March 6, 2000); see also the following Web sites: http://www.drugwarfacts.org/causes.htm#item1; http://drugpolicy.org/homepage.cfm

[45] Inciardi, *The War on Drugs III*, p. 282.

[46] *Drug War Facts.* [Online] http://www.drugwarfacts.org/gatewayt.pdf.

[47] Ibid., [Online] http://www.drugwarfacts.org/economi.pdf

[48] Federal Bureau of Investigation. *Crime in the United States.* Arrests. [Online] http://www.fbi.gov/ucr/cius2006/arrests/index.html

[49] One of the best books concerning the legalization of drugs is Miron, *Drug War Crimes.*

[50] Documented in Inciardi, *The War on Drugs III*, ch. 10 and pp. 305–308; and Walker, *Sense and Nonsense about Crime and Drugs,* ch. 13. See also Miron, *Drug War Crimes.*

[51] *Drug War Facts.* [Online] http://www.drugwarfacts.org/economi.pdf

[52] Inciardi, *The War on Drugs III*, pp. 306–307.

[53] Tannenbaum, F. *Crime and the Community.* New York: Columbia University Press, 1938; Lemert, E. *Social Pathology.* New York: McGraw-Hill, 1951; Becker, H. S. *Outsiders: Studies in the Sociology of Deviance.* New York: Free Press, 1963.

[54] President's Commission on Law Enforcement and Administration of Justice. *The Challenge of Crime in a Free Society.* Washington, DC: U.S. Government Printing Office, 1967.

[55] Miller, J. *The Last One over the Wall* (2nd ed.). Columbus: Ohio State University Press, 1998, and *Search and Destroy: African-American Males and the Criminal Justice System.* New York: Cambridge University Press, 1996.

[56] Shelden, R. G. "Detention Diversion Advocacy: an Evaluation." *OJJDP Juvenile Justice Bulletin* (September 1999). [Online] http://cjcj.org/pdf/ojjdp_ddap.pdf

[57] Feldman, L. B. and C. E. Kubrin. *Evaluation Findings: The Detention Diversion Advocacy Program Philadelphia, Pennsylvania.* Washington, DC: Center for Excellence in Municipal Management, George Washington University, 2002. [Online] http://cjcj.org/pdf/ddap_philly.pdf

[58] For more information see their Web site: http://www.mentor.org/program_services.html

[59] Currie, E. "Confronting Crime: Looking toward the Twenty-First Century." *Justice Quarterly* 6: 5–25 (1989). See also Currier, E. *Crime and Punishment in America.* New York: Metropolitan Books, 1998.

[60] See Dryfoos, J. *Adolescents at Risk.* New York: Oxford University Press, 1990.

[61] Colvin, M. "Crime and Social Reproduction: A Response to the Call for 'Outrageous' Proposals." *Crime and Delinquency* 37 (4): 436–448 (1991).

[62] Ibid., p. 437.

[63] Ibid., pp. 439–440.

[64] Ibid., p. 446.

[65] Patterson, G. R., P. Chamberlain, and J. B. Reid. "A Comparative Evaluation of a Parent-Training Program." *Behavior Therapy* 13: 636–650 (1982).

[66] Phillips, M. B. "A Hedgehog Proposal." *Crime and Delinquency* 37: 555–574 (1991).

[67] Ibid., p. 558.

[68] Ibid., pp. 558–559.

[69] Sykes, G. and D. Matza. "Techniques of Neutralization." *American Journal of Sociology* 22: 664–670 (1957); Matza, D. *Delinquency and Drift.* New York: Wiley, 1957.

[70] Sapolsky, R. M. "Lessons of the Serengeti: Why Some of Us Are More Susceptible to Stress." *The Sciences* (May/June 1988) 38–42; Sagan, L. A. *The Health of Nations.* New York: Basic Books, 1989.

[71] Currie, E. *Confronting Crime.* New York: Pantheon, 1985.

[72] Restorative justice is not practiced much, despite the fact that most religions preach this and similar principles. In fact, a multitude of horrors have been committed worldwide in the name of Christianity (see Ellerbe, H. *The Dark Side of Christian History.* San Rafael, CA: Morningstar Books, 1995.

[73] Quoted in Seldes, G. (ed.). *The Great Thoughts.* New York: Ballantine Books, 1996, p. 253.

[74] Ibid., p. 376.

[75] Sullivan, D. and L. Tifft. *Restorative Justice as a Transformative Process.* Voorheesville, NY: Mutual Aid Press, 2000, p. 6.

[76] Ibid., p. 9.

[77] Ibid., p. 34.

[78] Quinney, R. and J. Wildeman. *The Problem of Crime: A Peace and Social Justice Perspective* (3rd ed.). Mountain View, CA: Mayfield, 1991; Quinney, R. *For the Time Being.* Albany: State University of New York Press, 1999.

[79] Miller, *Last One over the Wall*, p. 234.

[80] Ibid., p. 234.

[81] Hanh, T. N. *Peace Is Every Step.* New York: Bantam Books, 1991, p. 78.

[82] Quinney, R. "Socialist Humanism and the Problem of Crime: Thinking about Erich Fromm in the Development of Critical/Peacemaking Criminology." In K. Anderson and R. Quinney (eds.), *Erich Fromm and Critical Criminology.* Chicago: University of Illinois Press, 2000, p. 26.

Index